Culinary Arts Institute®

1001 Great Recipes
from around the World

Culinary Arts Institute
A DIVISION OF DELAIR PUBLISHING COMPANY INC.

ISBN: 0-8326-0624-3

Contents

Note. In some recipes you will find a dot • before an ingredient or in the instructions. This indicates that an additional recipe is needed to complete the dish you are making. You will find the added recipe title, exactly as cited, in heavy type in the index.

Appetizers

1 *Fried Cheese (Saganaki)*

Kefalotyri or kasseri cheese,
  sliced lengthwise in
  ¼-inch-thick wedges (about
  1 pound for 4 people)
2 egg yolks mixed with 2
  tablespoons water
Flour
Olive oil
2 lemons, cut in quarters

1. Dip cheese slices into egg-yolk mixture, then into flour, coating each side evenly. Shake off excess flour.
2. In a 10-inch skillet, heat a ¼-inch layer of olive oil. When the oil begins to smoke, add the cheese. Fry first on one side, then on the other.
3. Remove from skillet and squeeze some lemon juice on each slice. Serve immediately. Allow 2 slices of Saganaki for each person.

2 *Crisp Cheese Crackers (Tyrobiskota)*

¼ cup sesame seed
2 cups all-purpose flour
Salt (optional)
½ teaspoon ground red pepper
1½ cups grated kefalotyri cheese
¾ cup butter, softened
¼ cup olive oil
2 egg yolks, beaten, for brushing
Sesame seed

1. Combine ¼ cup sesame seed, flour, salt, red pepper, and cheese. Work in butter and oil, using hands. Mix until dough holds together.
2. Roll dough out on lightly floured board. Cut into small diamond shapes. Transfer to cookie sheets. Brush with egg yolks and sprinkle with sesame seed.
3. Bake at 350°F about 12 minutes, or until golden.

About 3 dozen

3 *Marrow Canapés*

8 large marrow bones, cut in
  2-inch pieces
Salted water
½ cup butter
1 loaf cocktail-size black bread,
  cut in thick slices
¼ cup minced parsley
Ground red pepper

1. Using a thin sharp knife, loosen marrow from bones and remove. Soak marrow in salted water for 24 hours. Drain.
2. Cut marrow into ½-inch-thick rounds and poach in simmering water until tender (2 to 3 minutes). Remove with a slotted spoon. Drain on paper towels.
3. Melt butter in a skillet. Fry slices of bread on both sides.
4. Spread slices with marrow. Sprinkle with parsley and red pepper.
5. Place under broiler for a moment. Serve hot.

12 to 15 pieces

4 *Peppery Peanut Butter and Coconut Sandwiches*

8 slices white bread
6 tablespoons peanut butter
2 tablespoons butter, softened
1 teaspoon Tabasco
½ cup freshly grated or chopped
  flaked coconut

1. Remove crusts from bread. Flatten each slice with a rolling pin and cut into 3 strips.
2. Combine peanut butter, butter, and Tabasco.
3. Spread peanut butter mixture on bread; dip in coconut. Roll each bread strip to form a pinwheel.
4. Chill thoroughly before serving.

2 dozen appetizers

5 *Cocktail Meatballs* (Keftethes)

1 large onion, minced
2 tablespoons olive oil
1½ pounds freshly ground round steak (half each of lamb and veal)
3 tablespoons cracker meal
2 cups firm-type bread, crusts removed
2 eggs
6 tablespoons chopped parsley
2 teaspoons oregano, crushed
1½ teaspoons mint
2 tablespoons vinegar
    Salt and pepper to taste
    Flour
    Olive or corn oil for deep frying heated to 365°F

1. Brown half of onion in 2 tablespoons oil in a small frying pan. Mix with the uncooked onion and add to meat in a large bowl. Add the remaining ingredients except flour and oil. Toss lightly with two forks to mix thoroughly.
2. Dust hands with flour. Roll a small amount of meat at a time between palms, shaping into a ball.
3. To heated fat in deep fryer, add the meatballs a layer at a time. Fry until browned on all sides (about 12 minutes). Serve hot.

30 to 40 meatballs

6 *Eggplant Appetizer* (Salata Melitzana)

1 large eggplant
1 medium onion, minced
1 garlic clove, crushed in a garlic press
1 teaspoon chopped parsley
½ teaspoon freshly dried mint
½ cup olive oil
1 tablespoon wine vinegar (or more to taste)
    Juice of 1 large lemon
    Salt and pepper to taste

1. To prepare eggplant, place in a baking pan and prick top in four or five places with a fork.
2. Bake at 350°F about 45 minutes, or until skin is wrinkled and the surface is soft.
3. Cool eggplant slightly and cut in half. Scoop out the flesh and place in a blender. Add onion, garlic, parsley, and mint. Blend until well mixed.
4. Combine olive oil, vinegar, and lemon juice. Add to the eggplant mixture and blend well. Season with salt and pepper.
5. Chill. Serve with **toasted French** or **pita bread.** May also be used as a dip for fresh vegetables, or served separately as a first course.

About 4 cups

7 *Olive Canapés*

1 pound Greek olives, pitted
2 tablespoons olive oil
4 hard-cooked eggs, mashed
    Pinch dry mustard
1 clove garlic, crushed in a garlic press
    Pepper to taste
    Egg yolks, hard-cooked and chopped for garnish
    Scallions (green part), minced for garnish

1. Put olives and olive oil into a blender; purée. Blend in remaining ingredients except yolks and scallions.
2. Serve on **crackers,** or mound in a dish and serve crackers separately. Garnish with egg yolks and scallions.

1 cup

8 *Yogurt Dip*

2 cups plain yogurt
1 garlic clove, crushed in a garlic press
1 teaspoon dill
1 teaspoon mint
1 teaspoon wine vinegar

1. Combine all ingredients. Chill.
2. Serve with **toasted pita bread** or as a dip for **fresh vegetables.** May also be served as an accompaniment to roast meats or with pilaf.

2 cups

9 *Red Caviar Dip* (Taramosalata)

1 jar (4 ounces) tarama (fish roe)
10 slices firm-type whole wheat bread, crusts removed
Water
1 medium onion, minced
2 cups olive oil
Juice of 2 or 3 lemons

1. Beat tarama in a mixer for 5 minutes at medium speed.
2. Sprinkle bread lightly with water and squeeze very dry. Add bread, slice by slice, to tarama, beating after each addition. Add onion and beat. Slowly pour in olive oil, alternating with lemon juice to taste. Beat until fluffy. Refrigerate.
3. Serve with **crackers** or small pieces of crusty **Greek bread.**

5 cups

Note: Store in the refrigerator no longer than a week.

10 *Salami Cornucopias*

1 package (8 ounces) cream cheese
¼ cup grated kefalotyri cheese
¼ teaspoon pepper
Pinch dry mustard
½ pound salami, sliced very thin

1. Combine cheeses, pepper, and mustard. Beat well.
2. With a small knife or spoon, put a teaspoon of the mixture at the bottom of a salami slice.
3. Roll over to form a cornucopia. Secure with a wooden pick.

18 to 20 cornucopias

11 *Kalamata Olives*

2 pounds kalamata olives preserved in brine
¾ cup wine vinegar
¼ cup olive oil

1. Rinse olives in ½ cup wine vinegar. Drain.
2. Pour olive oil and remaining vinegar in a glass jar. Add the olives. Shake well. Store in refrigerator until ready to serve.

12 *Baked Clams Oregano*

12 clams
3 tablespoons minced onion
Salt and pepper to taste
1 teaspoon oregano
1 teaspoon minced parsley
5 tablespoons olive oil
Juice of 1 lemon

1. Open clams. Arrange side by side in a small baking dish.
2. Combine onion, salt, pepper, oregano, parsley, olive oil, and lemon juice. Spoon on clam meat.
3. Bake at 325°F about 7 minutes, or until clams curl slightly at the edges.

3 servings

13 *Yialandji Dolmathes*

1 jar (32 ounces) grapevine leaves
1 quart water
½ cup olive oil
3 medium onions, finely chopped
1½ cups long-grain rice
　　Juice of 2 lemons
2 tablespoons pine nuts
1 tablespoon dried black currants
2 teaspoons dill
2 teaspoons mint
¼ cup minced parsley
　　Salt and pepper to taste
　　Water (about 1 cup)
　　Olive oil (about 1 cup)

1. To prepare grapevine leaves, rinse leaves thoroughly in cold running water to remove brine.
2. Bring 1 quart water to a boil. Add leaves and parboil 3 minutes. Drain.
3. Select 4 or 5 heavy leaves and line bottom of a medium-size Dutch oven. Set aside.
4. To prepare filling, heat ½ cup olive oil in a medium skillet. Add onion and cook until translucent. Remove with a slotted spoon.
5. In a saucepan, parboil rice in 1 cup water until liquid is absorbed.
6. Combine rice, onion, lemon juice, pine nuts, currants, dill, mint, and parsley. Season with salt and pepper. Cool.
7. To fill grapevine leaves, place a leaf on a working surface, rough side up with stem pointing toward you. Place about a teaspoon of the rice mixture at the base of the leaf. Lift the bottom sides of the leaf up onto the filling. Fold both the right and left sides of the leaf over the filling. Roll up, tucking the edges in.
8. Place the stuffed grape leaves (dolmathes) side by side in the Dutch oven to cover the bottom. Put a second layer on top of the first one. Continue to do this until all the stuffed leaves have been put in.
9. Add water and olive oil to cover. Place an inverted plate on the dolmathes. Bring to boiling. Cover Dutch oven, lower heat, and simmer 1 hour. Taste a dolma to see if rice is tender. If necessary, continue cooking.
10. Cool dolmathes in liquid. Remove carefully with a spoon. Chill in refrigerator 24 hours before serving. Serve cold.

About 50 dolmathes

Note: Dolmathes will keep 10 days in the refrigerator.

14 *Sesame Seed Dip* (Tahi)

½ cup tahini (sesame seed paste)
2 tablespoons olive oil (or more to taste)
¾ cup water
　　Juice of 1 lemon
2 garlic cloves, crushed in a garlic press
½ cup walnuts
　　Salt and pepper to taste
¼ cup sesame seed, toasted

1. In a blender, combine all the ingredients except sesame seed until smooth and milky white in color. Refrigerate.
2. Garnish with sesame seed. Serve with **crackers** or as a vegetable dip.

About 1 ¾ cups

15 *Anchovy Fillets*

½ pound anchovy fillets
preserved in salt
Wine vinegar (2 or more cups)
2 tablespoons olive oil

1. Separate fillets. Scrape scales and as much of the salt as possible from each fillet.
2. Soak in wine vinegar 5 to 10 minutes, changing as often as necessary until the vinegar remains clear.
3. Drain fillets on paper towels.
4. Arrange fillets on a serving platter. Drizzle with 1 tablespoon fresh vinegar and the olive oil.
5. Serve as an hors d'oeuvre or in anchovy salad.

16 *Fried Calf, Lamb, or Chicken Livers (Sikotakia Tyganita)*

1 pound livers, cut in small
pieces (do not cut chicken
livers)
1½ cups flour, seasoned with
pepper for dredging
Olive oil for frying
2 lemons, quartered
Salt to taste

1. Rinse livers in cool water. Drain on absorbent paper.
2. Dip livers in flour. Shake off excess.
3. In a deep skillet, heat olive oil to smoking. Brown livers on both sides over medium heat.
4. Squeeze lemon juice on each piece. Season with salt. Serve at once.

4 servings

17 *Barbecued Lamb Innards (Splinandero Karsaniko)*

1 large intestine
Innards (heart, liver, kidneys,
lungs, and sweetbreads) from
a milk-fed calf
Salt to taste
1 tablespoon vinegar
¾ cup olive oil
Juice of 2 to 3 lemons
2 garlic cloves, crushed in a
garlic press
2 teaspoons pepper
2 teaspoons oregano
1 teaspoon thyme
2 lamb casings, washed and
drained
Pepper to taste

1. Rinse intestine in lukewarm water. Using a long spit, turn inside out. Rub salt over surface. Wash thoroughly in lots of lukewarm water.
2. Put innards in a large bowl. Cover with lukewarm water. Add salt and vinegar. Let stand ½ hour. Drain. Discard membranes and connective tissues. Cut into pieces.
3. Combine olive oil, lemon juice, garlic, 2 teaspoons pepper, oregano, and thyme. Add innards. Marinate in refrigerator 4 to 6 hours, turning occasionally.
4. Drain innards, reserving marinade. Knot one end of casing, then stuff with innards and knot other end.
5. Put a skewer beside the filled casing (splinandero). Tie the splinandero to the skewer with the empty casing by turning the casing around the length of the skewer.
6. Charcoal-broil over embers heated until they are white, turning about every 10 minutes and brushing frequently with the marinade. Cook until tender (about 2½ hours). Remove from spit. Cut into 2-inch pieces. Sprinkle with pepper. Serve hot.

10 to 20 pieces

18 *Pickled Mushrooms (Grzybki Marynowane)*

4 pounds small mushrooms
4 cups boiling water
1½ tablespoons salt
Marinade:
  1¾ cups water
 15 peppercorns
  2 bay leaves
 2½ tablespoons salt
  ¾ cup sugar
  ¾ cup vinegar

1. Cut the mushroom stems off even with the caps.
2. Cook over medium heat in boiling water with salt until they sink to the bottom, about 10 to 15 minutes.
3. Remove mushroom caps; place in small sterilized jars.
4. Make marinade. Boil water with peppercorns and bay leaves for 30 minutes. Add salt and sugar. Stir until dissolved. Add the vinegar, bring to boiling.
5. Pour hot marinade over mushroom caps. Close the jars. Keep refrigerated 2 or 3 days before serving.

4 pints

19 *Beet Relish (Ćwikła)*

1 can (16 ounces) whole beets, drained
¼ cup prepared horseradish
¼ cup sugar
¼ cup vinegar
¼ cup water
1 tablespoon grated onion
1 teaspoon salt
⅛ teaspoon pepper

1. Grate or mince beets.
2. In casserole or other container with a cover, mix beets with remaining ingredients. Cover.
3. Store in refrigerator for at least 1 day before serving.

About 2 cups

20 *Feet in Aspic (Galareta z Nóżek Wieprzowych)*

1½ pounds pigs' feet or calves' feet
½ pound lean pork or veal shanks
3 carrots, pared
1 onion, cut in quarters
2 stalks celery or 1 small celery root
2 bay leaves
5 peppercorns
3 whole allspice
2 cloves garlic, crushed (optional)
Water
1 tablespoon salt
½ cup chopped fresh parsley
⅓ cup vinegar
Lemon wedges
Parsley sprigs

1. Have the butcher skin and split pigs' feet.
2. Cook pigs' feet, pork, vegetables, bay leaves, peppercorns, allspice, garlic, and water to cover in a covered saucepot 2 hours on low heat. Skim off foam and add salt, parsley, and vinegar; cook 2 hours.
3. Strain off the stock; set aside. Take out pigs' feet and carrots. Discard onion and spices. Dice meat and slice carrots.
4. Arrange sliced carrots on bottom of an oiled 2-quart mold. Put meat on top of carrots in mold. Add parsley. Pour stock into mold.
5. Chill until set, at least 4 hours. Skim off fat.
6. Unmold onto platter. Garnish with lemon wedges and parsley sprigs.

8 servings

21 *Pickled Watermelon Rind*

3 pounds watermelon rind
Salted water (use 3 tablespoons
    salt for each quart of water)
2 pounds sugar
3 cups distilled white vinegar
6 pieces stick cinnamon (3 inches
    each)
2 tablespoons whole allspice
2 tablespoons whole cloves
2 tablespoons whole mustard seed

1. Cut rind into 1-inch cubes; trim off outer green skin and bright pink flesh.
2. Soak overnight in enough salted water to cover. Drain.
3. Heat sugar and vinegar to boiling.
4. Tie spices in cheesecloth bag.
5. Add spice bag and melon rind to vinegar mixture. Cook, uncovered, until melon is transparent, about 45 minutes.
6. Discard spice bag.
7. If desired, add a few drops red or green food coloring to the rind.
8. Pack watermelon rind tightly into hot, sterilized jars. Pour boiling syrup over watermelon to within ⅛ inch from top, making sure vinegar solution covers rind. Seal each jar at once.

3 pints

22 *Dill Pickles (Kiszenie Ogórków)*

3 pounds 4-inch cucumbers
2 cloves garlic, crushed
1 cup distilled white vinegar
5 cups water
½ cup salt
3 tablespoons dried dill weed

1. Scrub cucumbers.
2. Place a layer of dill on bottom of a large ceramic bowl or crock. Cover with half the cucumbers. Add another layer of dill, then the remaining cucumbers. Add garlic. Top with a final layer of dill.
3. Mix vinegar, water, and salt. Pour over dill and cucumbers. Add more water, if needed, to cover completely.
4. Cover bowl with a china plate to hold pickles under the brine. Let stand in a cool place 4 days.
5. Seal in sterilized jars.

4 pints pickles

23 *Fresh Mushrooms in Sour Cream*
(Grzyby ze Smietaną)

1 pound fresh mushrooms, sliced
⅔ cup sliced green onions with tops
2 tablespoons butter or margarine
1 tablespoon fresh lemon juice
1 tablespoon flour
1 cup dairy sour cream
2 tablespoons chopped fresh dill or
    1 tablespoon dill weed
¼ teaspoon salt
⅛ teaspoon pepper
    Small rounds of rye or Melba
    toast

1. Sauté mushrooms and onions in butter and lemon juice for 4 minutes. Stir in flour. Cook slowly, stirring 1 minute. Add sour cream, dill, salt, and pepper. Cook and stir 1 minute.
2. Serve warm on toast.

About 2 cups

24 *Pork Pâté (Pasztet Wieprzowy)*

1½ pounds ground fresh pork
½ pound salt pork, diced
5 medium onions, quartered
2 pounds sliced pork liver
3 eggs, beaten
1½ teaspoons salt
½ teaspoon black pepper
1 teaspoon marjoram
½ teaspoon nutmeg
¼ teaspoon allspice
1 tablespoon beef flavor base
½ pound sliced bacon

1. Combine fresh pork and salt pork in a roasting pan. Roast at 325°F 1 hour, stirring occasionally.
2. Remove pork from pan and set aside. Put onions and liver into the pan. Roast 20 minutes, or until liver is tender. Discard liquid in pan or use for soup.
3. Combine pork, liver, and onion. Grind twice.
4. Add eggs, dry seasonings, and beef flavor base to ground mixture; mix well.
5. Line a 9×5×3-inch loaf pan (crosswise) with bacon slices. Pack ground mixture into pan. Place remaining bacon (lengthwise) over top of ground mixture.
6. Bake at 325°F 1 hour. Cool in pan.
7. Remove paté from pan. Chill.
8. To serve, slice paté and serve cold with **dill pickles** and **horseradish.**

About 4 pounds

25 *Flybanes (Muchomorki)*

8 hard-cooked eggs
4 small tomatoes
    Salt and pepper
    Mayonnaise
    Lettuce

1. Peel the eggs. Cut off both ends so eggs will stand evenly. Stand the eggs on a small tray; they will serve for mushroom stems.
2. Cut the tomatoes in halves lengthwise. Remove cores. Sprinkle with salt and pepper. Put each tomato half over an egg as a mushroom cap. Dot the caps with mayonnaise. Garnish the tray with lettuce.

8 flybanes

26 *Ham Pudding (Budyń z Szynki)*

3 cups (about 1 pound) ground ham
2 cups warm unseasoned mashed
    potatoes
2 tablespoons melted butter
4 eggs, separated
1 teaspoon salt
½ teaspoon pepper
    Ham fat or drippings
    Fine bread crumbs
    Mustard Sauce (page 63) or
      Horseradish Sauce (page 88)

1. Mix ham and potatoes well.
2. Put butter and egg yolks into a small bowl of electric mixer; beat until thick and creamy.
3. Fold egg yolks into ham mixture; add salt and pepper.
4. With clean beaters, beat egg whites until stiff, but not dry.
5. Fold half of egg whites into the ham mixture; stir gently. Fold in the rest of the egg whites.
6. Grease a 1½-quart casserole with ham fat. Coat with bread crumbs. Spoon ham mixture into prepared casserole; cover.
7. Bake at 350°F 45 minutes.
8. Serve with sauce.

About 6 servings

27 *Ham and Egg Rolls (Jajka Zawijane w Szynce)*

6 hard-cooked eggs
12 thin slices cooked ham
    Lettuce leaves
    Mayonnaise
    Pickles

1. Peel the eggs; cut in halves.
2. Roll each half of egg in a slice of ham. Secure with wooden pick.
3. Arrange lettuce leaves around ham and egg rolls on serving plate. Decorate with mayonnaise and garnish with pickles.

12 rolls

28 *Mustard Butter (Masło Musztardowe)*

½ cup butter (at room temperature)
½ cup prepared mustard

1. Beat the butter with the mustard until creamy.
2. Spread on toast rounds to serve with **sardines** or **herring**.

1 cup

29 Onion-Chive Butter
(Masło Szczypiorkowe lub Koperkowe)

1 tablespoon sliced green onion
1 tablespoon snipped chives
½ cup butter (at room temperature)

1. Blend onion, chives, and butter.
2. Form into a roll about 1 inch in diameter. Chill.
3. Cut into small disks.

About ⅔ cup

30 Spring Cottage Cheese Spread
(Twarożek Wiosenny)

1 carton (12 to 14 ounces) cottage cheese
½ cup dairy sour cream
8 radishes, shredded
3 tablespoons sliced green onion
½ teaspoon salt
  Lettuce leaves
  Radish roses
  Rye or French bread

1. Mix cottage cheese with sour cream. Add radishes, onion, and salt; toss to mix well.
2. Mound on lettuce leaves. Garnish with radish roses. Surround with bread.

About 2⅓ cups

31 Chicken Liver Spread (Pasta z Kurzej Wątróbki)

½ pound chicken livers
1 cup milk
¼ cup rendered chicken fat or margarine
1 medium onion, cut in quarters
3 hard-cooked eggs, peeled and cut in half
½ pound cooked ham or cooked fresh pork, cut up
¼ teaspoon salt
¼ teaspoon pepper
⅛ teaspoon garlic powder (optional)

1. Soak livers in milk 2 hours. Drain livers and discard milk.
2. Melt fat in skillet. Add livers and onion and cook over medium heat until tender.
3. Combine livers, pan drippings, and all remaining ingredients. Grind or mince.
4. Add extra melted chicken fat or margarine, if desired, to make spread of desired spreading consistency.

About 4 cups

32 Purée of Anchovies (Purée Sardelowe)

1 can (2 ounces) flat anchovy fillets, drained
3 slices stale white bread
  Water
½ cup dairy sour cream or mayonnaise
1½ teaspoons vinegar

1. Mince or pound anchovy fillets.
2. Moisten bread with enough water to cover; then squeeze dry. Break into bits or mince with a fork. Blend in sour cream and vinegar to make a smooth purée. Serve as a spread with dark bread rounds.

About 1 cup

33 *Tangerine Yakatori*

This colorful Japanese-style appetizer is as pleasing to the eye as it is to the taste.

½ cup tangerine or orange juice
¼ cup dry white wine
3 tablespoons light soy sauce
½ bunch green onions, cut in
    1-inch pieces
2 large tangerines or oranges,
    peeled, sectioned, and seeded
2 large whole chicken breasts,
    skinned, boned, and cut in
    1x¼-inch strips

1. Combine all ingredients in a mixing bowl. Refrigerate covered 2 hours, stirring occasionally. Drain; reserve marinade.
2. Thread ingredients alternately on wooden skewers. Broil 4 inches from heat until chicken is done (about 3 minutes on each side).
3. Heat marinade until bubbly. Serve in individual cups as a dipping sauce.

4 servings

34 *Individual Chicken Terrines*

Crisp carrots and the delicate flavor of brandy enliven this appetizing dish.

½ cup thinly sliced small carrots
¼ cup brandy
2 pounds boned chicken, coarsely
    chopped
1 small onion
1 small carrot
1 teaspoon salt
¼ teaspoon nutmeg
1 egg, lightly beaten
2 teaspoons vegetable oil
2 tablespoons ice water
1½ tablespoons matzo meal or
    white cornmeal
    Vegetable oil
    Watercress
● Cucumber Sauce, if
    desired

1. Simmer carrot slices in brandy in a covered saucepan just until tender (about 3 minutes). Remove carrots with a slotted spoon; reserve. Mix a quarter of the chicken with brandy; remove from heat and let stand 45 minutes. Drain.
2. Mince remaining chicken, the onion, and carrot in a food processor or blender; remove to a mixing bowl. Stir in marinated chicken, salt, nutmeg, egg, oil, and ice water; mix well. Sprinkle matzo meal over mixture; mix well.
3. Layer the carrot slices in bottom of 8 lightly oiled 6-ounce custard cups. Spoon chicken mixture over carrots, smoothing top of mixture. Cover cups tightly with aluminum foil; place in a baking pan. Pour boiling water into baking pan, halfway up sides of custard cups.
4. Bake at 325°F 40 to 45 minutes, or until mixture is set. Remove cups from water. Remove foil. Let stand 5 minutes.
5. Terrines can be served hot, or refrigerated until chilled and served cold. To unmold, run knife around edge of cups and invert on individual plates. Garnish with watercress. Serve with Cucumber Sauce, if desired.

8 servings

Note: For a luncheon entrée, follow directions above, using six 10-ounce glass dishes. Bake until mixture is set.

35 Crab Meat and Bean Sprouts with Omelet Strips

2 eggs
3 tablespoons water
1 tablespoon dry sherry
1 tablespoon light soy sauce
1 tablespoon walnut or vegetable oil
4 green onions, chopped
¾ cup chopped green pepper
1 cup sliced fresh mushrooms
2 cups drained fresh or canned bean sprouts
1 tablespoon light soy sauce
8 ounces fresh or 1 can (7¾ ounces) crab meat, drained and flaked
1 teaspoon toasted sesame seed

1. Beat eggs with water, sherry, and 1 tablespoon soy sauce. Heat half the walnut oil in a small skillet. Cook egg mixture in skillet until set but still moist on top; remove to plate and cut egg into strips.
2. Heat remaining walnut oil in a wok or medium skillet. Cook and stir vegetables and 1 tablespoon soy sauce until vegetables are just tender (about 3 minutes). Add crab meat and omelet strips; cook and stir until thoroughly heated (about 1 minute). Sprinkle with toasted sesame seed. Serve immediately.

4 servings

36 Broiled Fish Quenelles

The traditional method of poaching is given along with our new, easy broiling method. The quenelles puff to a light texture when cooked.

2 pounds skinned fish fillets (all trout or a combination of trout, whitefish, or pike)
½ cup chopped onion
⅓ cup chopped carrot
1 egg, beaten
2 teaspoons vegetable oil
1½ teaspoons salt
1½ teaspoons matzo meal or white cornmeal
3 tablespoons ice water
Watercress

1. Place all ingredients except 1 tablespoon of the ice water and watercress in a blender or food processor; purée until the consistency of a paste. Add remaining ice water if necessary (mixture should hold together and be easy to handle).
2. Form fish mixture into oval patties, using ½ cup for each. Place on a lightly oiled cookie sheet.
3. Broil 4 inches from heat until patties are well browned and slightly puffed (8 to 10 minutes on each side). Serve immediately. Garnish with watercress.

8 servings

Note: Fish quenelles can be poached, if desired. Simmer covered in a large skillet in 1½ quarts Fish Stock (page 26) until puffed and cooked through the center (about 10 minutes). Remove from stock with slotted spoon. Serve hot or refrigerate until chilled. Garnish as above.

37 Oysters in Mushroom Purée

1 pound mushrooms, coarsely chopped
1 quart oysters, liquor reserved
¼ cup dry sherry
½ cup soft bread crumbs
2 garlic cloves, minced
1 teaspoon salt
¼ teaspoon freshly ground pepper
● Beef Stock
Watercress

1. Simmer mushrooms and 1 cup of the oysters in the sherry in a covered saucepan 8 to 10 minutes. Drain; press all moisture out of mushrooms.
2. Purée mushrooms and cooked oysters in a food processor or blender; pour into a shallow 1½-quart casserole. Stir in the bread crumbs, garlic, salt, and pepper. Stir in reserved oyster liquor. Stir in stock, if necessary, to make purée of a thick sauce consistency. Arrange remaining oysters in purée.
3. Bake covered at 350°F 20 minutes.
4. Serve in shallow bowls or ramekins. Garnish with watercress.

6 to 8 servings

38 *Seviche*

In this specialty of Mexico, the lemon juice actually "cooks" the fish.

1¼ pounds whitefish fillets,
    skinned and cut in 2x¼-inch
    strips
1 cup fresh lemon juice
2 green chilies, seeded and
    minced
1 teaspoon snipped fresh or ½
    teaspoon dried oregano
    leaves
1 tablespoon snipped fresh or
    1½ teaspoons dried coriander
    leaves
1 tablespoon olive oil
1 teaspoon salt
¼ teaspoon freshly ground
    pepper
2 large tomatoes, peeled, seeded,
    and chopped
1 medium green pepper, finely
    chopped
1 small yellow onion, finely
    chopped
¼ cup fresh lime juice
    Radish slices
    Ripe olives

1. Place fish in a shallow glass bowl; pour lemon juice over it. Refrigerate covered 6 hours, stirring occasionally. Drain; discard lemon juice.
2. Mix remaining ingredients except radish slices and olives with fish in a medium bowl. Refrigerate 30 minutes.
3. Serve on chilled plates; garnish with radish slices and olives. Or spoon into **fluted lemon shells.**

8 servings (½ cup each)

39 *Chilled Artichoke Plate*

Elegant in flavor and appearance. Serve with Individual Chicken Terrines (●) or Broiled Fish Quenelles (●) for an exquisite luncheon.

  4 medium artichokes
●   Chicken Stock
  ¼ cup lemon juice
  1 teaspoon salt
  ½ pint cherry tomatoes
●   ¾ cup Mock Béarnaise Sauce
  *1 pound fresh asparagus, cut in
    2-inch pieces

1. Snip tips from artichoke leaves with scissors. Simmer artichokes in 1 inch of the stock with lemon juice and salt in a large covered saucepan until tender (about 45 minutes). Lift from pan with tongs; let cool. Refrigerate until chilled.
2. Carefully scoop seeds from tomatoes, using small end of a melon-ball cutter. Fill tomatoes with ¼ cup of the sauce; refrigerate.
3. Scrape choke from artichoke bottoms. Place artichokes in center of individual plates and dollop each with 2 tablespoons sauce. Arrange raw asparagus pieces and tomatoes attractively on plates. Serve immediately.

4 servings

*The flavor and texture of raw young asparagus is delightful. If asparagus is tough, simmer in 1 inch of stock until just tender (about 8 minutes); drain and refrigerate until chilled.

  Frozen asparagus (10 ounces) can be used; cook according to package directions and refrigerate until chilled.

40 *Celery Appetizer*

This lovely first course can be expanded to a luncheon entrée with the addition of shrimp or chicken.

8 stalks celery, cut in julienne
    strips (about 3 cups)
● ½ cup Mock Mayonnaise
½ teaspoon celery seed, crushed
¼ teaspoon salt
2 teaspoons minced shallots
½ teaspoon wine vinegar
Lettuce cups
Pimento strips

Mix all ingredients, except lettuce and pimento, just until combined. Refrigerate covered until cold. Serve in lettuce cups; garnish with pimento.

6 servings

Note: If desired, mix in 1 cup cooked diced shrimp or chicken breast, increasing Mock Mayonnaise by 2 tablespoons. Season to taste with salt.

41 *Lombardy Green Tart*

1 package (10 ounces) frozen
    chopped spinach, thawed
2 cups low-fat cottage cheese
1 medium zucchini, minced
2 stalks celery, minced
1 bunch green onions, green part
    only, minced
2 tablespoons snipped parsley
2 teaspoons snipped fresh or 1
    teaspoon dried marjoram
    leaves
2 teaspoons snipped fresh or 1
    teaspoon dried thyme leaves
4 eggs, lightly beaten
½ teaspoon salt
⅛ teaspoon freshly ground
    pepper
Lettuce leaves

1. Press all liquid from spinach.
2. Combine all ingredients, except lettuce leaves, in a bowl. Mix thoroughly. Spoon mixture into a lightly oiled 9-inch pie plate.
3. Bake at 375°F 45 minutes. Cut into wedges to serve. Serve hot, or refrigerate until chilled and serve on lettuce.

6 servings

Lombardy Green Salad: Follow recipe for Lombardy Green Tart. Omit eggs, baking, and lettuce. Serve chilled on a bed of **fresh spinach leaves.**

42 *Vegetable Mélange with Mustard Sauce*

1 large yellow squash or
    zucchini, pared and minced
3 medium carrots, minced
¼ cup minced onion
¼ cup minced dill pickle
4 ounces Swiss cheese, minced
⅓ cup prepared mustard
⅓ cup dill pickle juice
1 teaspoon sugar
½ teaspoon curry powder
1 garlic clove, minced
Lettuce cups

Combine squash, carrot, onion, pickle, and cheese in a medium bowl. Mix remaining ingredients, except lettuce cups; pour over vegetables and stir to coat well. Refrigerate until well chilled. Serve in lettuce cups.

6 servings

43 *Tomato Toast (Crostini di Pomodori)*

¼ cup finely chopped onion
2 tablespoons butter or margarine
  Italian-style tomatoes (canned), drained
1 teaspoon sugar
⅛ teaspoon salt
1 egg yolk, fork beaten
¼ to ½ teaspoon Worcestershire sauce
¼ cup shredded Parmesan cheese
4 slices white bread, toasted, crusts removed, and toast cut in quarters
  Snipped fresh parsley or crushed dried basil or oregano

1. Add onion to heated butter in a heavy saucepan and cook until tender, stirring occasionally.
2. Force enough of the drained tomatoes through a sieve to yield 1½ cups. Add to onion with sugar and salt; cook, stirring occasionally, until liquid evaporates and mixture is thick (about 25 minutes).
3. Stir a small amount of tomato mixture into egg yolk; blend thoroughly and return to saucepan. Cook and stir 5 minutes.
4. Mix in Worcestershire sauce and half of cheese; spread generously on toast quarters. Sprinkle half of appetizers with the remaining cheese and half with the parsley.
5. Broil appetizers 3 to 4 inches from heat until bubbly. Serve hot.

16 appetizers

44 *Avocado Cocktail Dip*

1 large ripe avocado
2 teaspoons lemon juice
1 small slice onion
¼ cup mayonnaise
6 drops of Tabasco
  Salt to taste
  Potato chips

1. Halve and peel avocado, reserving 1 shell. Cube avocado and put into container of an electric blender. Add lemon juice, onion, mayonnaise, Tabasco, and salt. Process until puréed.
2. To serve, pile avocado mixture into reserved shell; place on a serving dish and surround with potato chips for dipping.

About 1 cup

45 *Savory Cheese Custards*

1 large yellow onion
¼ teaspoon salt
1½ teaspoons poppy seed
1 cup instant nonfat dry-milk solids
2 cups water
2 teaspoons Worcestershire sauce
2 teaspoons Dijon mustard
¼ teaspoon salt
2 eggs
2 ounces Jarlsberg or Parmesan cheese, finely shredded

1. Bake onion at 400°F until tender when pierced with a fork (about 1½ hours). Let cool. Peel onion and chop finely (about 1½ cups). Mix onion with ¼ teaspoon salt and the poppy seed; spoon mixture into the bottom of 4 ramekins or custard cups.
2. Process dry-milk solids, water, Worcestershire sauce, mustard, ¼ teaspoon salt, and eggs in a food processor or blender until very smooth.
3. Pour mixture into ramekins; sprinkle cheese over mixture. Place ramekins in a shallow baking pan; pour 1 inch boiling water into pan.
4. Bake at 325°F 30 to 40 minutes, or until custard is set and a knife inserted between center and edge comes out clean. Serve warm, or refrigerate and serve cold.

4 servings

46 *Eggs with Anchovies (Jajka ze Sardelkami)*

4 hard-cooked eggs
Lettuce leaves
16 anchovy fillets
2 tablespoons mayonnaise
1 dill pickle, sliced
1 tomato, sliced

1. Peel the eggs; cut in halves.
2. Arrange eggs, yolks up, on a dish covered with lettuce leaves.
3. Place 2 anchovy fillets over each egg to form an "X."
4. Garnish with mayonnaise, pickle, and tomato slices.

8 egg halves

47 *Veal Pâté (Pasztet z Cielęciny)*

1 pound pork liver, cut up
2 cups milk
6 dried mushrooms or 8 ounces fresh mushrooms
1 large onion, quartered
1 bay leaf
5 peppercorns
1 pound veal, cut up
1 pound sliced bacon
2 cups chicken bouillon
3 slices white bread
3 eggs
½ teaspoon nutmeg
Pinch allspice
Salt and pepper

1. Soak liver in milk 1 hour. Drain; discard milk.
2. Scrub mushrooms gently with a brush. Put dried mushrooms into a large saucepan. Add onion, bay leaf, peppercorns, veal, bacon, and bouillon; simmer 1 hour. Add the liver and fresh mushrooms (if used). Simmer 30 minutes longer.
3. Strain off the bouillon and soak bread in it.
4. Combine mushrooms, onion, veal, ¾ of the bacon, liver, and bread. Grind twice.
5. Combine eggs with ground mixture, season with nutmeg, allspice, and salt and pepper to taste. Mix very well.
6. Line a 9×5×3-inch pan with the remaining bacon. Pack with the meat mixture. Cover with foil.
7. Bake at 350°F 1 hour. Cool.
8. Serve with Horseradish Sauce (page 88), or Red Beets with Horseradish (page 79).

About 12 servings

Turkey Pâté: Follow recipe for Veal Pâté, using **turkey** or **chicken livers** instead of pork liver and **turkey meat** instead of veal. Omit allspice.

48 *Liver Pâté*

This is not baked, but made with gelatin and chilled. Calories can be cut by serving with vegetables rather than the usual crackers.

1½ cups chopped onion
1 cup chopped celery
● 1½ cups Chicken Stock
1 cup dry white wine
1 teaspoon paprika
⅛ teaspoon ground allspice or cloves
¼ teaspoon garlic powder
4 drops Tabasco
1¼ teaspoons salt
1½ pounds chicken livers, membranes removed
2 envelopes unflavored gelatin
½ cup cold water
Assorted vegetable relishes

1. Simmer onion and celery in stock and wine in an uncovered saucepan until liquid is reduced to 2 cups (about 15 minutes). Stir in paprika, allspice, garlic powder, Tabasco, and salt; simmer 2 minutes. Stir in livers; simmer covered until livers are tender (about 15 minutes). Drain; discard liquid.
2. Sprinkle gelatin over cold water; let stand 3 minutes. Set over low heat, stirring occasionally, until gelatin is dissolved (about 5 minutes).
3. Purée half the livers and vegetables along with half the gelatin mixture in a food processor or blender. Repeat with remaining ingredients; combine the two mixtures.
4. Pour mixture into a lightly oiled 1½-quart mold or bowl or ten 6-ounce custard cups. Chill until set (about 4 hours).
5. Serve from mold, or unmold onto platter and accompany with assorted vegetables.

10 to 12 servings

49 *Pickled Zucchini (Zucchini con Olio e Aceto)*

3 to 4 zucchini
5 tablespoons olive oil
2 cloves garlic, quartered
½ teaspoon oregano
¼ teaspoon salt
1 bay leaf
   Wine vinegar

1. Wash zucchini and trim off ends. Cut crosswise into ¼-inch slices.
2. Heat 3 tablespoons olive oil in a skillet. Add zucchini and cook slowly until browned. Drain on absorbent paper. Cool and put into a pint screw-top jar.
3. Combine 2 tablespoons oil, garlic, oregano, salt, and bay leaf. Pour into jar. Add enough wine vinegar to cover zucchini.
4. Store, covered, in refrigerator at least 24 hours. Serve cold.

1 pint pickle

50 *Pickled Mushrooms (Funghi con Olio e Aceto)*

1 pound fresh mushrooms (½-inch caps)
   White vinegar
   Hot water
¼ cup olive oil
2 teaspoons salt
2 teaspoons peppercorns
2 cloves garlic, quartered
1 teaspoon ground mace

1. Clean mushrooms and put into a saucepan. Pour in equal amounts of white vinegar and hot water to cover mushrooms. Bring to boiling; cook 6 minutes. Drain and cool.
2. Pack mushrooms into a pint screw-top jar and add a mixture of oil, salt, peppercorns, garlic, and mace. Add enough white vinegar to cover mushrooms.
3. Store, covered, in refrigerator 2 days. Drain and serve cold.

1 pint pickle

51 *Italian Shrimp (Scampi Italiano)*

½ cup olive or other cooking oil
¾ teaspoon salt
¼ teaspoon black pepper
½ teaspoon garlic powder
¼ cup minced parsley
1 whole pimento, mashed
2 pounds large fresh shrimp, shelled and deveined
3 tablespoons butter or margarine
3 tablespoons lemon juice

1. Mix oil, salt, pepper, garlic powder, parsley, and pimento. Dip shrimp in mixture and cook in a hot skillet over low heat about 2 minutes on each side. Spoon 2 or 3 tablespoons of the oil mixture over shrimp; cover and cook until tender (5 to 8 minutes), turning once.
2. Transfer shrimp to a serving dish. Add butter and lemon juice to the skillet; stir and heat until mixture begins to sizzle. Pour over shrimp and serve hot.

About 6 dozen shrimp

52 *Pickled Carrots (Carote con Olio e Aceto)*

6 to 8 medium carrots, pared and cut in strips
   Boiling salted water
2 tablespoons olive oil
1 clove garlic, cut in halves
1 hot green pepper
½ teaspoon salt
   Wine vinegar

1. Cook carrots in a small amount of boiling salted water in a covered saucepan until just tender. Drain and cool.
2. Pack carrots in a pint screw-top jar and add oil, garlic, hot pepper, and salt. Cover carrots with wine vinegar.
3. Store, covered, in refrigerator at least 24 hours. Drain and serve cold.

1 pint pickle

53 *Marinated Pimentos*

2 to 3 tablespoons red wine vinegar
2 cloves garlic, minced
1 bay leaf
½ teaspoon salt
½ teaspoon pepper
2 tablespoons olive or other
    cooking oil
2 tablespoons chili sauce
2 jars or cans (7 ounces each)
    whole pimentos, drained and
    torn in half or in large pieces
1 can anchovy fillets
¼ cup slivered ripe olives
1 tablespoon lemon juice

1. Put the vinegar, garlic, bay leaf, salt, and pepper into a saucepan; simmer 5 minutes.
2. Blend in oil and chili sauce; pour over pimentos. Let stand about 3 hours.
3. To serve, drain pimentos and garnish with anchovy fillets and ripe olives. Drizzle lemon juice over all.

About 6 servings

54 *Eggplant Appetizer-Relish (Caponata)*

¾ cup olive oil
2 cloves garlic, crushed or minced
1 large eggplant, sliced, pared, and
    cut in small cubes (about 3
    cups)
½ cup chopped green pepper
½ cup chopped onion
¼ cup finely chopped parsley
1 tablespoon sugar
½ teaspoon crushed oregano
¼ teaspoon crushed basil
1 teaspoon seasoned salt
    Few grains black pepper
1 cup canned tomato paste
¼ cup water
3 tablespoons red wine vinegar
1 can (4 ounces) mushroom stems
    and pieces (do not drain)
½ cup very small pimento-stuffed
    olives

1. Heat the oil and garlic in a large, heavy skillet. Add the eggplant, green pepper, onion, and parsley; toss to mix. Cover tightly and cook over low heat about 10 minutes.
2. Meanwhile, blend sugar, oregano, basil, salt, and pepper. Add tomato paste, water, and wine vinegar; mix well. Add to mixture in skillet and stir in remaining ingredients. Cover and cook gently until eggplant is just tender (not mushy).
3. Turn into a bowl and store, covered, in refrigerator overnight to allow flavors to blend.
4. Serve with **crackers.**

About 4 cups relish

55 *Pears with Roquefort*

This recipe can be served appropriately as a dessert as well as a first course.

4 small pears
2 tablespoons Roquefort or blue
    cheese, crumbled
½ cup low-fat cottage cheese
¼ cup Neufchatel cheese
2 teaspoons brandy
2 tablespoons water
    Watercress

1. Cut entire top off pears; reserve. Using melon-ball cutter, carefully scoop out pears, leaving a ¼-inch shell. Discard core and seeds. Finely chop pulp.
2. Purée pulp with cheeses, brandy, and water in a food processor or blender. Fill cavity of pears with cheese mixture. Replace tops on pears. Garnish with watercress. Serve with a knife and fork.

4 servings

56 George's Greek-Style Artichokes
(Carciofi alla Greca George's)

6 artichokes
4 ounces fresh mushrooms, sliced
⅔ cup coarsely chopped onion
½ cup olive oil
½ cup dry white wine
   Juice of 1 lemon
30 fennel seeds
¼ teaspoon coriander
   Salt and pepper to taste

1. Rinse artichokes and discard the hard outer leaves. Quarter artichokes, remove and discard "choke" or fuzzy part, and arrange the pieces in a large baking pan or shallow heat-resistant casserole having a cover. Allow plenty of space for the artichokes.
2. Cover artichoke pieces with the mushrooms and onion. Then pour over them a mixture of oil, wine, lemon juice, and dry seasonings.
3. Cover and place over medium heat. Bring to a rapid boil and cook about 1 minute.
4. Set in a 350°F oven about 30 minutes, or until artichokes are tender.
5. Remove from oven; cool at room temperature, then refrigerate to chill thoroughly. Serve cold.

About 8 servings

57 Deep-Fried Plantain

Green plantain
Ice water
Peanut oil for deep frying, heated
   to 365°F
Salt

1. Peel plantain; reserve the skin. Slice the plantain on the slant in 2½-inch pieces. Soak in water.
2. Without draining, drop a few pieces of plantain into the oil. Fry for 2 minutes. Remove, using a spoon with a long handle. Repeat until all pieces are fried.
3. Place a fried plantain piece inside the reserved skin. Press between the palms of the hands to flatten the fried plantain; the edges will be jagged. Remove from skin and deep-fry again until golden brown. Flatten and refry all pieces. Drain on absorbent paper. Sprinkle with salt and serve hot.

58 *Pasties* *(Pâtes Chauds)*

1 cup ice-cold water
1 teaspoon salt
3 cups all-purpose flour
1¼ cups vegetable shortening
   Cold milk (about ¼ cup)
   Beef Filling (½ recipe)
1 egg yolk, beaten

1. Combine water and salt. Place flour in a large mixing bowl and make a well in the center. Pour salted water into well and mix lightly with a spoon without kneading. Place dough in refrigerator 30 minutes.
2. Roll the dough into a rectangle ¼ inch thick. Spread half the shortening on the dough. Fold one side over the middle and spread this section with the remaining shortening. Fold over the remaining section and again roll out to ¼-inch thickness. Fold again into thirds and roll out. Repeat this rolling process a third time. Refrigerate dough overnight.
3. Roll the dough to about ½-inch thickness. Cut the dough into 2½-inch rounds. Roll out trimmings to cut more rounds.
4. Place a tablespoonful of filling in the center of half the dough rounds. Brush the edges with milk. Cover with remaining rounds, lightly pressing the edges down. Brush the tops with egg yolk. Place pasties on a baking sheet with sides. Place a pan of hot water on the bottom rack of the oven.
5. Bake at 400°F 30 minutes, then turn the oven control to 300°F and bake 20 minutes, or until golden brown.

1 dozen

59 *Beef Filling*

2 parsley sprigs
¼ small green hot pepper or
   6 dried Italian pepper pods
2 shallots, chopped
1 garlic clove
½ pound ground beef, cooked
● 1 cup Béchamel Sauce
   (use beef broth)

1. In a mortar, pound to paste the parsley, pepper, shallot, and garlic.
2. Add seasoning paste and cooked beef to Béchamel Sauce; mix well.

Note: Half of the filling is needed for Pasties; use remainder for hot sandwiches or as desired.
   Filling may also be made with leftover cooked chicken, fish, tongue, ham, or mushrooms. Follow above procedure, using chicken or fish broth in Béchamel Sauce.

60 *Pork Tidbits* *(Grio)*

2 pounds pork loin
½ orange
½ lime
   Salt, pepper, and garlic to taste
2 cups water
½ cup bacon drippings
● Ti-Malice Sauce
● Deep-Fried Plantain

1. Remove bones from pork loin and cut meat into small cubes, keeping all the fat on the meat. Rub meat first with the cut side of orange, then with cut side of lime. Season with salt, pepper, and garlic.
2. Put the meat and water into a Dutch oven and cook covered over high heat until all water has evaporated, leaving the fat only.
3. Add bacon drippings to meat in Dutch oven and fry meat over medium heat, stirring occasionally, until meat is brown and crisp.
4. Heap meat on a round platter, sprinkle generously with sauce, and surround with plantain pieces.

61 *Meatballs with Breadfruit*

1 breadfruit (about 1 pound)
1 garlic clove
1 teaspoon lime juice
1 tablespoon chopped chives
2 parsley sprigs
3 eggs
1 cup cooked ground meat
½ cup finely ground peanuts
  Oil for frying, heated to 365°F
● Tomato Sauce Creole

1. Peel breadfruit. Boil about 20 minutes in salted water, or until soft; drain. Mash as for potatoes.
2. In a mortar, pound to a paste the garlic, lime juice, chives, and parsley. Combine paste with mashed breadfruit, 2 eggs, and cooked ground meat; beat until fluffy. Roll into walnut-size balls; coat with beaten egg and then peanuts.
3. Fry in heated fat until golden. Drain on absorbent paper. Serve hot with the sauce as a dip.

Note: Breadfruit may also be combined with ham, poultry, game, salt cod, or salt herring.

62 *Meatballs à l'Haitienne*

4 white bread slices
1 cup milk
1 pound freshly ground lean beef
2 slices smoked ham or bacon, minced
  Salt and pepper to taste
1 garlic clove, crushed in garlic press
1 tablespoon tomato paste
½ cup flour
½ cup grated Parmesan cheese
  Fat for frying, heated to 365°F
● Tomato Sauce Creole

1. Soak bread in milk 5 minutes, then mash and mix with ground beef, minced ham, salt, pepper, garlic, and tomato paste. Roll into walnut-size balls; coat with flour and then with cheese.
2. Fry in heated fat until golden brown. Drain on absorbent paper. Serve hot with the sauce as a dip.

Note: These meatballs may be made larger for a main course and are usually served with Cornmeal (●) and a salad.

63 *Cocktail Puffs* (*Marinades*)

1 tablespoon coarse salt
2 peppercorns
1 scallion or green onion, cut in pieces
2 parsley sprigs
⅛ teaspoon ground mace
1 teaspoon lime juice
4 drops Tabasco
1 cup all-purpose flour
1 tablespoon baking powder
2½ cups water
1 egg yolk
1 cup chopped cooked calf's brains, chicken, turkey, smoked herring, shrimp, lobster, or fish
2 egg whites, stiffly beaten
  Peanut oil for frying, heated to 365°F

1. In a mortar, pound to a paste the salt, peppercorns, scallion, parsley, mace, lime juice, and Tabasco.
2. Sift flour with baking powder into a bowl. Mix in water, seasoning paste, egg yolk, and desired cooked ingredient. Fold in beaten egg white.
3. Pour the batter by tablespoonfuls into the heated fat; it will spread. Gather the batter with a circular motion as it floats on top of the fat and looks like a wafer. Fry until crisp, golden, and lacelike. Drain on absorbent paper. Serve hot.

64 Codfish Fritters

½ pound salt cod
3 dried Italian pepper pods or
    1 very small piece hot pepper
2 garlic cloves
2 green onions, cut in pieces
2 parsley sprigs
2½ cups all-purpose flour
1 teaspoon baking powder
1 cup light beer
    Peanut oil, heated to 365°F
● Dilled Avocado Sauce for Fish

1. Soak cod in cold water overnight. The next day, drain the cod, add fresh water, and bring to a boil. Drain, cool, and shred finely.
2. In a mortar, pound together to a paste the pepper pods, garlic, onion, and parsley.
3. Sift flour with baking powder into a bowl; stir in beer. Add the seasoning paste and shredded cod; mix well.
4. Drop batter by teaspoonfuls into heated oil. Fry until golden. Drain on absorbent paper. Serve hot with the sauce.

65 Haitian Rarebit

8 kaiser rolls
16 slices American or Cheddar cheese
½ cup sweet pickle relish
1 cup chopped cooked ham, chicken,
    beef, or tongue
8 tablespoons butter or margarine,
    melted

1. Split rolls. On bottom half of each roll, place in the following order: 1 slice cheese, 1 tablespoon sweet pickle relish, 2 tablespoons chopped meat, and another slice cheese. Replace top of roll.
2. Generously brush top and bottom of sandwiches with melted butter.
3. Place rolls in a large skillet over medium heat. Cover with a lid slightly smaller than the skillet and weight it down over the rolls. Brown both sides until cheese melts. Serve immediately.

8 servings

66 Shrimp Paste à la Creole

    Fresh shrimp
● Court Bouillon for Fish and
    Shellfish
¼ cup butter, melted
1 garlic clove, crushed in a
    garlic press
⅛ teaspoon ground mace
⅛ teaspoon pepper
    Tabasco to taste

1. Cook enough shrimp in bouillon to make 4 cups shelled shrimp.
2. Put shrimp, hot melted butter, garlic, mace, pepper, and Tabasco into container of an electric blender; process 10 seconds.
3. Serve on toasted cassava or Melba toast.

67 *Chicken Fritters Guadeloupe*

2 cups minced cooked chicken
3 tablespoons finely chopped parsley
2 tablespoons finely chopped chives
3 tablespoons fresh bread crumbs
1 tablespoon grated onion
1 tablespoon curry powder
  Salt to taste
¼ teaspoon cayenne or red pepper
¼ cup Dijon mustard
½ cup dry bread crumbs
1 egg, beaten with 1 teaspoon
  peanut oil
  Oil for frying, heated to 365°F

1. Mix chicken with parsley, chives, fresh bread crumbs, onion, and seasonings. Shape mixture into walnut-size balls, roll in dry bread crumbs, then in beaten egg, and again in bread crumbs. Chill in refrigerator.
2. Just before serving, fry in hot oil until golden brown. Drain on absorbent paper and serve hot.

68 *Eggplant Fritters*

3 long thin eggplants
1 tablespoon lime juice
  Salt, pepper, and cayenne or
    red pepper to taste
1½ cups all-purpose flour (about)
¾ cup beer (about)
  Oil for deep frying
    heated to 365°F
  Salt

1. Slice eggplants into eighteen ½-inch rounds. Season with lime juice, salt, and ground peppers. Marinate 15 minutes.
2. Make a batter the consistency of whipping cream by mixing flour with beer.
3. Dip and coat eggplant slices in batter. Fry in heated oil until golden brown. Drain on absorbent paper. Sprinkle lightly with salt. Serve hot.

Artichoke Fritters: Follow recipe for Eggplant Fritters. Substitute **artichoke hearts** or **bottoms** for eggplant rounds.

69 *Corn Fritters*

1 cup fresh corn kernels
½ cup butter
1 cup all-purpose flour
4 eggs
  Corn oil for frying,
    heated to 365°F

1. Cook corn until soft in boiling salted water in a saucepan; drain thoroughly, reserving 1 cup liquid. Melt butter with corn liquid in saucepan, add flour, and cook, stirring rapidly, until mixture is smooth and rolls away from the sides of pan.
2. Remove from heat and add the eggs, one at a time, beating well after each addition. Stir in cooked corn.
3. Drop batter by spoonfuls into heated oil and fry until golden and well puffed. Drain on absorbent paper. Serve hot.

70 *Acra*

5 dried Italian pepper pods or
    1 small piece hot pepper
1 tablespoon coarse salt
6 peppercorns
½ medium onion, chopped
2 garlic cloves
1 egg
1 cup finely grated malanga root*
  Peanut oil for frying,
    heated to 365°F

1. In a mortar, pound together to a paste the pepper pods, salt, peppercorns, onion, and garlic.
2. Add seasoning paste and egg to grated malanga root; beat until light.
3. Drop mixture by spoonfuls into heated oil and fry until golden. Drain on absorbent paper.

20 fritters

*Malanga root can be found in Puerto Rican markets.

71 Oysters Barquettes Gourmet Club Port-au-Prince

●   Pastry (see Turnovers Aquin,
1 jar pickled oysters, drained
● ¾ cup Béchamel Sauce
   (use fish broth)
1 cup coarsely chopped artichoke
   hearts
   Finely shredded Swiss cheese

1. Prepare pastry, roll out, and cut to fit barquette or other small molds. Press dough firmly into molds against bottom and sides. Prick with a fork. Fill with beans or lentils, if desired.
2. Bake at 375°F 12 minutes. Pour out beans, if used. Unmold and set aside.
3. Measure 1 cup oysters; reserve remainder for garnish.
4. Combine sauce, artichoke hearts, and 1 cup oysters. Spoon mixture into barquettes and sprinkle with cheese. Glaze under a broiler; top each with an oyster. Serve hot.

72 Turnovers Aquin

Aquin is a small town in the south of Haiti renowned for its mangrove oysters.

1½ cups all-purpose flour
¼ teaspoon salt
⅓ cup peanut oil
2 tablespoons ice-cold water
1 jar pickled oysters
   Milk for brushing
   Peanut oil for deep frying,
     heated to 365°F

1. For pastry, combine flour and salt in a bowl. Mix in oil and ice-cold water. Gather dough into a ball and roll out very thin between 2 sheets of waxed paper. Cut out 3-inch rounds with cookie cutter or inverted glass.
2. Slightly off center on round, place 3 oysters. Fold in half, coming to within ¼ inch of the opposite edge. Moisten rim with a pastry brush dipped in milk. Fold rim back over itself to seal.
3. Fry in heated fat until golden. Drain on absorbent paper.

73 Salt Cod Salad (Mor Marinée)

1 pound dried cod fillet
3 peppercorns, cracked
1 whole clove, cracked
⅛ teaspoon nutmeg
5 dried Italian pepper pods or
   1 small hot pepper
1 sweet pepper, cored, seeded, and
   julienned
4 shallots, chopped
2 garlic cloves, crushed in a
   garlic press
1 cup olive oil
¼ cup wine vinegar
¼ cup chopped mixed chives and
   parsley
●   Biscuits Port-au-Prince

1. Put cod into a sieve and slowly pour 2 quarts very hot water over it. Shred fish and remove all bones and skin. Add peppercorns, clove, nutmeg, pepper pods, julienne of pepper, shallots, and garlic; mix well. Add olive oil and vinegar; mix again. Marinate 3 days in refrigerator.
2. Mound marinated mixture on a serving platter. Sprinkle with mixture of chives and parsley. Serve on halved hot buttered biscuits.

74 Pickled Herring in Sour Cream
(Śledzie Marynowane w Śmietanie)

6 pickled herring, drained
1 large onion, peeled and chopped
6 hard-cooked eggs, peeled and
    chopped
1 apple, cored and chopped
1 teaspoon lemon juice
1 cup dairy sour cream
1 clove garlic, crushed (optional)
¼ teaspoon salt
⅛ teaspoon pepper
2 tablespoons chopped fresh dill or
    parsley

1. Cut herring into small cubes. Mix herring with onion, eggs, apple, and lemon juice.
2. Combine sour cream, garlic (if desired), salt, and pepper; add to herring mixture and mix well. Sprinkle with dill.
3. Serve with **dark bread**.

4 to 6 servings

75 Egg Crowns

6 hard-cooked eggs, peeled and
    sliced
30 small rounds of buttered bread
1 package (3 ounces) cream cheese
    (at room temperature)
2 tablespoons mayonnaise
1 teaspoon prepared mustard
½ teaspoon salt
½ teaspoon vinegar
1 jar (2 ounces) pimento strips,
    drained
    Watercress

1. Remove yolks from eggs; put into a sieve over a bowl. Place rings of white on buttered bread.
2. Sieve egg yolks and ends of whites.
3. Mix sieved eggs, cream cheese, mayonnaise, mustard, salt, and vinegar. Beat until smooth.
4. With 2 spoons or pastry tube and star tip, fill each egg white ring with yolk mixture. Garnish with pimento strips and watercress.

30 canapés

Chilled Artichoke Plate, page 20
Cucumber Sauce, page 39
Individual Chicken Terrines, page 18

Sauces

76 *Mayonnaise* (Mayoneza)

2 egg yolks
½ teaspoon salt
¼ teaspoon white pepper
½ teaspoon dry mustard
   Wine or tarragon vinegar
   (about 3 tablespoons)
1½ cups olive oil

Beat egg yolks until thick and lemon colored. Beat in salt, pepper, dry mustard, and half of the vinegar. Beating constantly, trickle in 1/3 cup olive oil, add ½ teaspoon vinegar, and trickle in remaining olive oil. Check for consistency. If the Mayonnaise is too thick, add vinegar drop by drop and mix by hand until the appropriate consistency is achieved. Adjust seasoning.

About 1½ cups

Note: If Mayonnaise curdles, wash beater. Beat an egg yolk until thick in a small bowl. Slowly add curdled mixture, beating constantly, to form a new emulsion. Another egg yolk may be necessary. If so, beat again until thick, add mixture slowly.

77 *Garlic Mayonnaise* (Mayoneza me Skortho)

4 garlic cloves, crushed in a
   garlic press
¼ teaspoon salt
2 egg yolks
   Olive oil (about 1 cup)
   Juice of ½ lemon, or more to
   taste
   Salt and white pepper

Combine garlic, salt, and egg yolks. Slowly add oil, a drop at a time, beating vigorously until 2 to 3 tablespoons have been added. Add remaining oil in a steady stream, beating constantly. Add lemon juice, beating well. Season with salt and pepper.

About 1½ cups

78 *Tomato Sauce* (Saltsa me Domates)

3 tablespoons butter
1 large onion, chopped
2 pounds fresh ripe tomatoes,
   peeled and chopped
2 teaspoons sugar
2 whole cloves
1 bay leaf
1 garlic clove, crushed in a garlic
   press
1 teaspoon vinegar
   Salt and pepper to taste

Melt butter in a saucepan; add onion and cook until translucent. Add tomatoes and remaining ingredients. Simmer uncovered 20 minutes.

3 cups

Note: A variation served during Lent is Anchovy Tomato Sauce. To prepare, use **olive oil** instead of butter, decrease sugar to 1 teaspoon, increase vinegar to 2 teaspoons; and add ½ **tube anchovy paste** or **1 can (2 ounces) anchovies**, drained and cut into small pieces.

79 *Mustard Sauce* (Sos Musztardowy)

¾ cup dairy sour cream
⅓ cup mayonnaise
2 tablespoons prepared mustard
¼ teaspoon salt
¼ teaspoon sugar

1. Mix all ingredients well.
2. Serve with cold pork, ham, or hard-cooked eggs.

About 1¼ cups

80 Sour Cream Sauce (Sos Śmietanowy)

2 hard-cooked eggs
1 cup dairy sour cream
1 teaspoon prepared mustard or dill
¼ teaspoon sugar
¼ teaspoon salt
⅛ teaspoon pepper

1. Press eggs through a sieve. Add sour cream and beat with a mixer at medium speed 3 minutes. Add mustard, sugar, salt, and pepper. Beat 1 minute at high speed.
2. Serve with ham or veal.

1½ cups

81 Mushroom Sauce (Sos Grzybowy)

1 pound mushrooms, sliced
1 large onion, chopped
1 cup chicken or meat broth or bouillon
3 tablespoons flour
2 tablespoons melted butter
½ cup dairy sour cream
1 teaspoon lemon juice
Salt and pepper

1. Simmer mushrooms with onion in bouillon 15 minutes.
2. Blend flour into butter. Stir into mushrooms. Bring to boiling, stirring.
3. Remove from heat. Stir in sour cream, lemon juice, and salt and pepper to taste.

3 cups

82 Green Onion Sauce (Sos Szczypiorkowy)

1 cup dairy sour cream
3 tablespoons sliced green onion
1 egg yolk, beaten
2 tablespoons prepared mustard
1 teaspoon lemon juice
½ teaspoon sugar
¼ teaspoon salt

1. Combine sour cream, green onion, egg yolk, prepared mustard, lemon juice, sugar, and salt.
2. Serve hot or cold.

About 1⅓ cups

83 Cold Horseradish Sauce (Sos Chrzanowy Zimny)

6 ounces prepared cream-style horseradish
1 large apple, pared and shredded
1½ cups dairy sour cream
½ teaspoon sugar
¼ teaspoon salt

1. Mix horseradish with apple. Add sour cream; stir in sugar and salt.
2. Serve with cold meat, hard-cooked eggs, and fish.

About 2½ cups

84 Tartar Sauce (Sos Tatarski)

2 hard-cooked eggs
2 tablespoons finely chopped mushrooms
2 tablespoons salad oil
2 teaspoons prepared mustard
2 teaspoons pickle liquid
¼ teaspoon salt
¼ teaspoon sugar
½ cup mayonnaise
½ cup dairy sour cream
¼ cup finely chopped dill pickles

1. Mash cooked egg yolks. Chop whites separately.
2. Sauté mushrooms in oil. Blend in mashed egg yolks, mustard, pickle liquid, salt, and sugar.
3. Blend mayonnaise into sour cream. Add chopped egg whites, egg yolk mixture, and pickles; mix well.

About 2 cups

85 *Mock Crème Fraîche*

Crème fraîche is a heavy cream which is fermented naturally. It is very thick and nutlike in flavor and is used in French cooking to give body to sauces. Unlike sour cream, it will not curdle when cooked. Crème fraîche has recently become available in this country; it is very high in calories and very expensive. Our version has half the calories and is simple and inexpensive to make.

1½ cups Neufchatel cheese
● 6 tablespoons Low-Fat Yogurt

1. Mix cheese and yogurt in a blender or food processor until smooth and fluffy. Place in small jars; cover tightly.
2. Set jars in a warm place (100° to 125°F) for 2 hours; see Note. Cool and refrigerate. Stir before using.

About 2 cups

Note: Use an oven thermometer in making Mock Crème Fraîche, as temperature is very important. A gas oven with a pilot light will be about 125°F. Turn electric oven to as warm a setting as necessary to maintain temperature. Mock Crème Fraîche can be refrigerated up to 3 weeks.

86 *Madeira Sauce*

¼ cup chopped celery
¼ cup chopped carrot
2 tablespoons chopped green onion
1 tablespoon cooking oil
1 quart water
2 beef bouillon cubes
1 chicken bouillon cube
½ bay leaf
Pinch ground thyme
Few grains freshly ground black pepper
1 tablespoon tomato sauce
¼ cup water
2 tablespoons flour
⅓ cup Madeira

1. Cook celery, carrot, and onion in hot oil in a large saucepot until dark brown, but not burned.
2. Stir in 1 quart water, bouillon cubes, bay leaf, thyme, and pepper. Bring to boiling, and simmer until liquid is reduced by half.
3. Strain the liquid. Stir in tomato sauce and bring to boiling.
4. Vigorously shake ¼ cup water and flour in a screw-top jar. While stirring the boiling mixture, slowly add the flour mixture. Cook 1 to 2 minutes, then simmer about 30 minutes, stirring occasionally.
5. Just before serving, stir Madeira into sauce and bring sauce to boiling.

About 2⅓ cups sauce

87 *Green Garlic Sauce* (Pesto Genovese)

3 cloves garlic, peeled
3 tablespoons minced sweet basil leaves or 2½ teaspoons dried basil leaves
3 tablespoons grated Parmesan or Romano cheese
1 tablespoon chopped pinenuts or walnuts
¼ teaspoon salt
4 to 6 tablespoons olive oil
1 tablespoon chopped fresh parsley

1. In a mortar, mix garlic, basil, cheese, nuts, and salt. Grind mixture with a pestle to a smooth paste.
2. Still grinding, add very gradually enough olive oil to make a smooth sauce. Stir in parsley.
3. To serve, add desired amount of sauce and a tablespoon of butter to hot pasta and mix well at the table. Accompany with grated cheese, if desired.

About ½ cup sauce

Note: Sauce may be stored in refrigerator with a little olive oil on top.

88 Low-Fat Yogurt

1 quart 2% milk
¼ cup instant nonfat dry-milk
    solids
2 tablespoons low-fat natural
    yogurt

1. Mix milk and dry-milk solids in a medium saucepan. Heat to scalding (150°F); cool to 110°F. Stir in yogurt.
2. Transfer mixture to a glass or crockery bowl. Cover with plastic wrap; wrap bowl securely in a heavy bath towel. Set in a warm place (100° to 125°F)* for 4 to 6 hours, until yogurt has formed.
3. Place several layers of paper toweling directly on yogurt; refrigerate covered until cold.

About 1 quart

*A gas oven with a pilot light will be about 125°F; however, use an oven thermometer, as temperature is very important. Turn an electric oven to as warm a setting as necessary to maintain temperature.

Excess liquid and a coarse texture will result if temperature is too high. Liquid can be drained with a nylon baster. Blend yogurt in a food processor or blender to restore texture.

Note: This recipe can be made using skim or reconstituted dry milk, although the product will not be as rich.

Purchased low-fat natural yogurt can be substituted in any recipe.

89 Avocado Sauce

Mexican guacamole was the idea behind this flavorful sauce.

2 medium avocados, peeled and
    chopped
1 small pared zucchini, chopped
1 tablespoon minced onion
2 teaspoons lemon juice
¼ teaspoon chili powder
1 small tomato, seeded and
    chopped
¼ teaspoon salt

1. Purée avocados, zucchini, onion, lemon juice, and chili powder in a food processor or blender; stir in tomato and salt. Refrigerate covered until chilled (about 1 hour).
2. Serve over pork, veal, poultry, fish, or vegetable salads.

About 3 cups

90 Cauliflower Sauce

This sauce has a rich, creamy texture and lends itself well to any recipe calling for a white sauce.

¾ pound cauliflower
● Chicken Stock
½ teaspoon salt
¼ teaspoon freshly ground white
    pepper
2 tablespoons dry white wine
1 teaspoon snipped fresh or ½
    teaspoon dried thyme leaves
2 ounces Swiss cheese, shredded
    Snipped parsley (optional)

1. Remove leaves and tough stalks from cauliflower; separate into flowerets. Simmer cauliflower, covered, in 1 inch of stock until tender (about 8 minutes); drain.
2. Purée cauliflower with remaining ingredients, except cheese and parsley, in a food processor or blender. Heat thoroughly over low heat. Stir in cheese; heat, stirring constantly, until cheese is melted (about 2 minutes).
3. Stir parsley into sauce, if desired, and serve immediately as a sauce or soup.

About 1⅓ cups

91 *Garlic-Parsley Sauce*

Garlic cloves lose their pungency and develop a delicate flavor when poached. Flavors of garlic, mushrooms, green onion, and parsley merge in this hearty sauce.

30 large garlic cloves, peeled
   Water
● ¾ cup Chicken Stock
1½ cups sliced fresh mushrooms
1 teaspoon minced green onion
1 tablespoon snipped parsley
¼ teaspoon salt
½ teaspoon bottled brown
   bouquet sauce

1. Cover garlic cloves with water in a saucepan; heat to boiling and drain. Repeat 2 more times. Add remaining ingredients, except brown bouquet sauce, to garlic in saucepan; simmer, covered, 15 minutes.
2. Purée all ingredients and brown bouquet sauce in a food processor or blender. Heat in a saucepan to serve hot, or refrigerate and serve cold.
3. Serve on roast beef, steak, or veal. Or fill **mushroom caps** with sauce; bake at 300°F 15 minutes.

About 2 cups

Note: Substitute ¼ cup stock for red wine, if desired.

92 *Seasoned Dark Green Sauce*

*1 pound spinach, washed and
   stems removed
1 teaspoon anchovy paste
1 large garlic clove, minced
1 drop Tabasco
1 tablespoon instant nonfat
   dry-milk solids
● ¾ to 1 cup Chicken Stock

1. Simmer spinach with water clinging to leaves in a covered saucepan until spinach is tender (about 7 minutes); drain.
2. Purée in a food processor or blender with remaining ingredients, adding amount of stock necessary for a medium sauce consistency. Heat in a saucepan to serve hot or refrigerate to serve cold.
3. Serve over poultry, fish, or cooked vegetables. Or serve as a vegetable in small bowls and top with yogurt.

About 2 cups

*1 package (10 ounces) frozen leaf spinach can be used. Cook according to package instructions; drain well.

93 *Green Peppercorn Sauce*

Green peppercorns are the whole unripe berries from the pepper vine. They are generally processed and packed in brine. Their pungent flavor makes this a distinctive sauce.

● 1 cup Chicken Stock
2 tablespoons brandy
1 tablespoon arrowroot
   Cold water
¼ pound fresh mushrooms,
   chopped
● ¼ cup Mock Crème Fraîche
½ teaspoon salt
¼ teaspoon freshly ground
   pepper
2 tablespoons drained green
   peppercorns

1. Heat stock and brandy.
2. Mix arrowroot with a little cold water; stir into stock. Simmer, stirring constantly, until stock has thickened (about 4 minutes). Stir in remaining ingredients. Heat thoroughly. Serve immediately.

About 2½ cups

94 *Light Green Sauce*

1 cup finely chopped lettuce
Peel of 1 large zucchini
¼ cup parsley sprigs, stems removed
1 tablespoon chopped green onion
⅔ cup low-fat ricotta cheese
¾ teaspoon salt
⅛ teaspoon freshly ground white pepper
2 teaspoons fresh lemon juice
● ⅓ to ½ cup Chicken Stock

1. Purée all ingredients in a food processor or blender, adding amount of stock necessary for a medium sauce consistency.
2. Serve over hot or cold vegetables, poached fish, or chicken.

About 1¼ cups

95 *Artichoke Sauce*

This sauce is so elegant in flavor that you would never guess it is so easy to make.

1 can (8 ounces) artichoke hearts, cut in quarters
¼ cup low-fat ricotta cheese
● ⅓ to ½ cup Chicken Stock
¼ teaspoon salt
⅛ teaspoon freshly ground white pepper

1. Purée all ingredients in a food processor or blender, adding more stock if necessary for a fairly thick consistency. Heat in a saucepan to serve hot, or refrigerate and serve cold.
2. Serve with veal, pork, fish, vegetables, or eggs.

About 1½ cups

Note: To serve as a soup, add more stock to sauce for desired consistency.

96 *Cucumber Sauce*

1 medium cucumber, pared, seeded, and finely chopped
● Chicken Stock
● 1½ cups Low-Fat Yogurt
1 tablespoon snipped fresh or 1½ teaspoons dried dill weed
¼ teaspoon salt
Dash freshly ground white pepper

1. Simmer cucumber in 1 inch of stock in a covered saucepan until tender (about 5 minutes); drain off and discard stock.
2. Mix cucumbers with remaining ingredients. Serve cold, or heat and serve warm.

About 2 cups

Note: Snipped coriander or mint can be used in place of dill in this recipe.

97 Cumberland Sauce

½ cup fresh cranberries
2 teaspoons grated orange peel
1 large navel orange, peeled and finely chopped
2 tablespoons brandy
½ cup port wine
¼ cup orange juice
● ¼ cup Beef Stock
1 teaspoon prepared mustard

1. Process cranberries, orange peel and chopped orange, and brandy in a food processor or blender until finely ground.
2. Transfer mixture to a saucepan; stir in remaining ingredients. Simmer uncovered until sauce is of medium thick consistency (about 15 minutes). Serve hot, or refrigerate and serve cold.
3. Serve over duck, pork, ham, or over cottage cheese or fruit salads.

About 1½ cups

98 Mock Hollandaise Sauce

Our recipe boasts one-third the calories of the traditional hollandaise sauce. It has an enjoyable, smooth texture and tart flavor with no butter or egg yolks added.

½ cup Neufchatel cheese
● 3 tablespoons Low-Fat Yogurt
Dash salt
Juice of ½ lemon

1. Mix all ingredients in a blender or food processor until smooth and fluffy.
2. Cook over simmering water until hot and thickened. Serve immediately or refrigerate and serve cold. Stir before using.

¾ cup

Mock Béarnaise Sauce: Stir **1½ teaspoons snipped fresh** or **½ teaspoon dried tarragon leaves** and **½ teaspoon minced shallots** into sauce before heating.

Mock Mayonnaise: Stir **1½ teaspoons Dijon mustard** and **½ teaspoon sugar** into sauce before heating. Refrigerate until cold.

Note: The above sauces can be refrigerated up to 3 weeks.

99 Herbed Mock Mayonnaise

Mock Mayonnaise given a new flavor twist can be used as a sauce, a salad dressing, or a dip for raw vegetables.

● 1 cup Mock Mayonnaise
2 teaspoons snipped fresh or 1 teaspoon dried crumbled tarragon leaves
2 teaspoons snipped fresh chervil or parsley
½ garlic clove, minced
½ teaspoon minced onion

Mix all ingredients. Refrigerate 3 hours or overnight. Stir before serving.

1 cup

100 *Citrus Mayonnaise*

- 1 cup Mock Mayonnaise
- 1 tablespoon fresh orange juice
- 1 tablespoon fresh lemon juice
- 1 teaspoon grated orange peel
  Dash ground white pepper

Mix all ingredients in a small bowl. Refrigerate covered ½ hour. Stir before serving.

About 1 cup

101 *Madeira Sauce*

- 1 cup Chicken Stock
  Juice of 1 lemon
- 1 teaspoon Worcestershire sauce
- ¼ teaspoon salt
- ⅓ cup Madeira wine
- 1 tablespoon arrowroot
  Cold water
- 1 tablespoon snipped parsley

1. Heat stock, lemon juice, Worcestershire sauce, salt, and Madeira in a small saucepan.
2. Mix arrowroot with a little cold water; stir into stock mixture. Simmer, stirring constantly, until thickened (about 3 minutes). Stir in parsley. Serve immediately.

About 1½ cups

102 *Savory Tomato Sauce*

- 5 large tomatoes, peeled, cored, and coarsely chopped
- ⅔ cup chopped green onions
- ⅔ cup chopped celery
- 1 large green pepper, cored and chopped
- 2 tablespoons snipped parsley
- ¾ cup tomato juice
- ½ teaspoon cumin
- ¼ teaspoon chili powder
- ¼ teaspoon garlic powder
- ⅛ teaspoon ground cloves
- 1½ teaspoons salt

Mix all ingredients in a 3-quart saucepan. Simmer uncovered until sauce is of medium, not thick, consistency (about 1 hour).

About 1 quart

103 *Green Onion Sauce*

- 2 bunches green onions, sliced
- 1 medium zucchini, cut in 1-inch pieces
- 1½ to 1⅔ cups Chicken Stock
- ½ teaspoon salt

1. Simmer onions and zucchini in 1½ cups stock in a covered saucepan until tender (about 10 minutes).
2. Purée vegetables, stock, and salt in a food processor or blender, adding more stock if necessary for a medium sauce consistency. Heat in a saucepan to serve hot, or refrigerate and serve cold.
3. Serve over cooked vegetables, roast beef, pork, or lamb, or . as a dip for raw vegetables.

About 2 cups

Note: To serve as a cold soup, thin with ½ cup stock and top with a **dollop of yogurt.**

104 *Middle Eastern Sauce*

1 cup raw soybeans
3 cups water
1 teaspoon salt
● ½ cup Low-Fat Yogurt
1 teaspoon cumin
½ teaspoon sesame or vegetable oil
¼ teaspoon curry powder
1 teaspoon minced garlic
¼ to ½ teaspoon salt

1. Simmer soybeans in water with 1 teaspoon salt in a covered saucepan 3 hours; drain, reserving ½ cup liquid.
2. Purée soybeans with remaining ingredients in a food processor or blender; add reserved liquid as necessary for a medium sauce consistency.
3. Serve warm over steamed vegetables, chicken, or lamb. Or refrigerate until chilled and serve as a dip for assorted vegetables.

About 2½ cups

105 *Vinaigrette Dressing*

Chicken stock replaces most of the oil in this recipe. Great as a sauce, salad dressing, or marinade.

1 tablespoon fresh lemon juice
1 tablespoon olive or vegetable oil
● ¼ cup Chicken Stock
2 teaspoons snipped parsley
1 teaspoon snipped fresh or ½ teaspoon dried basil leaves
2 teaspoons distilled white vinegar
1 teaspoon Dijon mustard
1 small garlic clove, minced
⅛ teaspoon salt
Freshly ground white pepper

Measure all ingredients into a jar with a tight cover; shake vigorously. Refrigerate dressing until chilled. Shake before serving.

About ½ cup

106 *White Vegetable Purée*

You will enjoy the rich texture of this hearty sauce—puréed turnips and potatoes form the base.

¾ pound white potatoes, pared and cut in 1-inch pieces
¾ pound turnips, pared and cut in 1-inch pieces
Water
¼ cup instant nonfat dry-milk solids
½ cup 2% milk
1 teaspoon salt
¼ teaspoon freshly ground white pepper
1 tablespoon clarified butter
● ¼ to ⅓ cup Mock Crème Fraîche if desired

1. Simmer potatoes and turnips in 1½ inches water in a large covered saucepan until tender (about 20 minutes). Drain vegetables; reserve cooking liquid.
2. Purée vegetables with milk solids, milk, salt, pepper, and butter in a food processor or blender. Add reserved cooking liquid and Mock Crème Fraîche, if used, for desired consistency. Return mixture to saucepan and heat thoroughly.

About 2 cups

Note: This recipe can be served as a soup if thinned with skim milk.

107 *Custard Sauce*

● 1 cup Low-Fat Yogurt
  1 egg yolk
  2 teaspoons honey or apple
    concentrate

Beat all ingredients until fluffy. Serve immediately or refrigerate until chilled.

About 1¼ cups

108 *Beef Stock*

1 pound lean beef stew cubes
1 pound lean veal stew cubes
½ pound beef soup bones
3 carrots, cut in 2-inch pieces
1 tomato, quartered and seeded
2 medium yellow onions,
    quartered
1 stalk celery,
    cut in 2-inch pieces
1 garlic clove, minced
1 teaspoon salt
  Bouquet garni:
  ½ teaspoon dried thyme
    leaves
  1 bay leaf
  2 sprigs parsley
Water

1. Place meats, vegetables, garlic, salt, and bouquet garni in an 8-quart Dutch oven. Pour in water to cover (about 3 quarts). Simmer covered 2 to 2½ hours. Cool slightly.
2. Strain stock through a double thickness of cheesecloth into a storage container. Taste for seasoning. If a more concentrated flavor is desired, return stock to saucepan and simmer 20 to 30 minutes, or dissolve **1 to 2 teaspoons instant beef bouillon** in the stock.
3. Store covered in refrigerator or freezer. Remove solidified fat from top of stock before using.

2 to 2½ quarts

Note: Refrigerated stock is perishable. If not used within several days, heat to boiling, cool, and refrigerate or freeze to prevent spoilage. Stock can be kept frozen up to 4 months.

109 *Chicken Stock*

5 pounds chicken backs and
    wings, or stewing chicken,
    cut up
3 carrots, cut in 2-inch pieces
2 medium yellow onions,
    quartered
1 stalk celery, cut in 2-inch
    pieces
2 teaspoons salt
  Bouquet garni:
  ¾ teaspoon dried thyme
    leaves
  ¾ teaspoon dried rosemary
    leaves
  1 bay leaf
  4 sprigs parsley
  2 whole cloves
Water

1. Place chicken, vegetables, salt, and bouquet garni in an 8-quart Dutch oven. Pour in water to cover (about 4 quarts). Simmer covered 2 to 2½ hours.
2. Strain stock through a double thickness of cheesecloth into a storage container. Taste for seasoning. If more concentrated flavor is desired, return stock to saucepan and simmer 20 to 30 minutes, or dissolve 1 to 2 teaspoons instant chicken bouillon in the stock.
3. Store covered in refrigerator or freezer. Remove solidified fat from top of stock before using.

3 to 3½ quarts

Note: Refrigerated stock is perishable. If not used within several days, heat to boiling, cool, and refrigerate or freeze to prevent spoilage. Stock can be kept frozen up to 4 months.

110 *Fish Stock*

2 pounds fresh lean fish with
    heads and bones, cut up
1 medium yellow onion,
    quartered
½ teaspoon salt
1 cup dry white wine
    Bouquet garni:
        4 sprigs parsley
        1 bay leaf
        ½ teaspoon dried thyme
          leaves
        1 sprig celery leaves
        2 peppercorns
    Water

1. Rinse fish under cold water. Place fish, onion, salt, wine, and bouquet garni in a 3-quart saucepan. Pour in water to cover (about 1½ quarts). Simmer covered 2 hours. Cool slightly.
2. Strain stock through a double thickness of cheesecloth into a storage container. Taste for seasoning. Add a small amount of salt and lemon juice, if desired. If a more concentrated flavor is desired, return stock to saucepan and simmer 30 to 45 minutes.
3. Store covered in refrigerator or freezer.

About 1 quart

Note: Use white firm-fleshed fish such as halibut, cod, flounder, or lemon sole. Frozen fish can be used if necessary.
    Refrigerated stock is highly perishable. If not used within 2 days, heat to boiling, cool, and refrigerate or freeze to prevent spoilage. Stock can be kept frozen up to 2 months.

111 *Canned Stock*

6 cups canned chicken or beef
    bouillon or clam juice
2 medium carrots, cut in 2-inch
    pieces
2 medium onions, peeled and
    quartered
¾ cup dry white wine, if desired
    Bouquet garni:
        4 sprigs parsley
        2 bay leaves
        1 teaspoon dried thyme
          leaves

1. Combine all ingredients in a 2-quart saucepan. Simmer covered 45 minutes.
2. Strain stock through a double thickness of cheesecloth into a storage container. Refrigerate.

About 1½ quarts

112 *White Clam Sauce (Salsa alla Vongole)*

¼ cup olive oil
1 clove garlic, thinly sliced
¼ cup water
½ teaspoon chopped parsley
½ teaspoon salt
¼ teaspoon oregano
¼ teaspoon pepper
1 cup (8-ounce can) whole
    littleneck clams with juice

1. Heat oil and garlic in a skillet until garlic is lightly browned.
2. Remove from heat. Add water, parsley, and dry seasonings; mix well. Stir in clams with juice. Heat thoroughly.
3. Serve hot on **cooked spaghetti** or **macaroni**.

About 1½ cups sauce

Red Clam Sauce: Follow recipe for White Clam Sauce. Sieve **3½ cups canned tomatoes,** stir in with water and seasonings, and simmer about 10 minutes. Add clams and heat.

About 5 cups sauce

113 *Tomato Sauce*

1 clove garlic
2 tablespoons olive oil
3 pounds fully ripe plum tomatoes, peeled, seeded, and diced; or use 9 cups canned peeled plum tomatoes, sieved
1 teaspoon salt
¼ teaspoon freshly ground black pepper
1 tablespoon dried basil

1. Peel garlic and cut in thirds. Put into a deep skillet with olive oil. Heat until garlic is browned. Flatten garlic and move it around in the oil. Discard garlic.
2. Add tomatoes all at one time to skillet. Mix in salt, pepper, and basil. Cook over low heat, stirring occasionally, about 10 minutes. Continue cooking, stirring occasionally, until sauce thickens (about 20 minutes).

About 6 cups sauce

114 *Rosy Sauce (Salsa Rosata)*

From Antico Martini, a famous restaurant on St. Mark's Square in Venice, comes this delightfully smooth and piquant dressing for seafood.

¾ cup ketchup
½ cup mayonnaise
½ cup whipping cream
2 tablespoons cognac
1½ teaspoons Worcestershire sauce
1 teaspoon prepared horseradish
4 drops Tabasco

1. Mix all ingredients; chill thoroughly.
2. Arrange chilled **cooked seafood** on **lettuce**, drizzle with **lemon juice** and spoon on sauce.

About 1½ cups sauce

115 *Italian Dressing*

6 tablespoons olive oil
3 tablespoons wine vinegar
1 clove garlic, crushed in a garlic press
¼ teaspoon salt
⅛ teaspoon pepper

1. Place all ingredients in a screw-top jar, shake well, and chill.
2. Just before serving, beat or shake thoroughly.

About ½ cup dressing

Anchovy Dressing: Follow recipe for Italian Dressing. Add **1 teaspoon prepared mustard** and **2 finely chopped anchovy fillets** to jar before shaking.

116 *Butter and Garlic Sauce (Salsa al Burro e Aglio)*

¾ cup butter
2 cloves garlic, peeled and thinly sliced
¼ cup water
½ teaspoon finely chopped parsley

1. Melt butter in skillet. Stir in garlic and cook slowly until slightly browned. Remove from heat and cool slightly.
2. Slowly add water and parsley. Cook about 10 minutes and serve over **cooked spaghetti**.

About 1 cup sauce

Butter and Cheese Sauce: Follow recipe for Butter and Garlic Sauce. Omit garlic. Mix butter sauce with spaghetti and sprinkle with **¼ cup grated Parmesan cheese**.

117 *Clam Sauce (Salsa di Vongole)*

¼ cup finely chopped onion
3 tablespoons butter
2 tablespoons flour
¼ teaspoon salt
⅛ teaspoon white pepper
1 can (12 ounces) clam juice
3 tablespoons finely chopped
    parsley
¼ to ½ teaspoon thyme
1 jar (7½ ounces) whole clams,
    drained and cut in pieces
1 can (2½ ounces) minced clams,
    drained

1. Add onion to hot butter in a saucepan and cook until soft. Blend in a mixture of flour, salt, and pepper. Heat until bubbly.
2. Remove from heat and add the clam juice gradually, stirring constantly. Mix in parsley and thyme. Bring to boiling; stir and cook 1 to 2 minutes. Stir in the clams; heat thoroughly.

About 2¼ cups sauce

118 *Tomato Sauce with Meat*

1 cup chopped onion
1 clove garlic, minced
3 tablespoons olive oil
½ pound ground beef
½ pound ground pork
1 can (28 ounces) Italian-style
    tomatoes, drained
3 cans (6 ounces each) tomato
    paste
2 cups water
2½ teaspoons salt
½ teaspoon pepper
1 teaspoon oregano

1. Add the onion and garlic to hot oil in a large, deep skillet and cook until onion is soft.
2. Add the ground meat, separate it into small pieces, and cook until lightly browned. Stir in tomatoes, tomato paste, water, and a mixture of salt, pepper, and oregano. Cook, uncovered, over low heat about 1 hour, stirring occasionally.

About 7½ cups sauce

119 *Marinara Sauce*

2 medium cloves garlic, sliced
½ cup olive oil
1 can (28 ounces) tomatoes,
    sieved
1¼ teaspoons salt
⅛ teaspoon pepper
1 teaspoon oregano
¼ teaspoon chopped parsley

1. Brown garlic in hot olive oil in a large, deep skillet. Add gradually, stirring constantly, a mixture of the tomatoes, salt, pepper, oregano, and parsley. Cook rapidly uncovered about 15 minutes, or until sauce is thickened; stir occasionally. If sauce becomes too thick, stir in ¼ to ½ **cup water.**
2. Serve sauce hot on **cooked spaghetti.**

4 cups sauce

120 *Medium White Sauce*

2 tablespoons butter
2 tablespoons flour
½ teaspoon salt
⅛ teaspoon pepper
1 cup milk (use light cream for a
    richer sauce)

1. Heat butter in a saucepan. Blend in flour, salt, and pepper; heat and stir until bubbly.
2. Gradually add the milk, stirring until smooth. Bring to boiling; cook and stir 1 to 2 minutes longer.

About 1 cup

Thick White Sauce: Follow recipe for Medium White Sauce. Use 3 to 4 tablespoons flour and 3 to 4 tablespoons butter.

Thin White Sauce: Follow recipe for Medium White Sauce. Use 1 tablespoon flour and 1 tablespoon butter.

Béchamel Sauce: Follow recipe for Medium White Sauce. Substitute ½ **cup chicken broth** for ½ cup milk; use ½ cup cream for remaining liquid needed. Stir in **1 tablespoon minced onion.**

121 *Quick Italian Tomato Sauce (Salsa di Pomodoro)*

1 cup chopped onion
¼ cup olive oil or cooking oil
1 clove garlic, minced
¼ cup grated carrot
1 tablespoon finely snipped parsley
¼ teaspoon basil, crushed
⅛ teaspoon thyme, crushed
2 cans (8 ounces each) tomato
    sauce
½ cup beef broth (dissolve ½ beef
    bouillon cube in ½ cup boiling
    water)

1. Add onion to hot oil in a saucepan and cook until tender. Stir in the garlic, carrot, and parsley; cook about 3 minutes, stirring frequently.
2. Blend in remaining ingredients. Simmer gently until flavors are blended (about 10 minutes).

About 3 cups sauce

122 *Green Sauce (Salsa Verde)*

1 tablespoon chopped parsley
1 tablespoon chopped watercress
1 tablespoon chopped capers
1 small clove garlic, peeled and
    chopped
¼ teaspoon salt
⅛ teaspoon pepper
6 tablespoons olive oil
3 tablespoons lemon juice

1. Place parsley, watercress, capers, garlic, salt, and pepper in a mortar. Crush with a pestle to make a smooth paste.
2. Add olive oil, 1 tablespoon at a time, beating vigorously with a fork or spoon after each addition. Slowly add lemon juice, beating constantly.
3. Serve with **artichokes, cooked spaghetti, shrimp,** or **any fried fish.**

About ½ cup sauce

123 *Tomato Meat Sauce (Ragù di Pomodoro)*

¼ cup olive oil
½ cup chopped onion
½ pound beef chuck
½ pound pork shoulder
7 cups canned tomatoes with
    liquid, sieved
1 tablespoon salt
1 bay leaf
1 can (6 ounces) tomato paste

1. Heat olive oil in a large saucepot. Add onion and cook until lightly browned. Add the meat and brown on all sides. Stir in tomatoes and salt. Add bay leaf. Cover and simmer about 2½ hours.
2. Stir tomato paste into sauce. Simmer, uncovered, stirring occasionally, about 2 hours, or until thickened. If sauce becomes too thick, add ½ **cup water.**
3. Remove meat and bay leaf from sauce (use meat as desired). Serve sauce over **cooked spaghetti.**

About 4 cups sauce

Tomato Sauce with Ground Meat: Follow recipe for Tomato Meat Sauce. Brown ½ **pound ground beef** in **3 tablespoons olive oil,** breaking beef into small pieces. After removing meat from sauce, add ground beef and simmer 10 minutes longer.

Tomato Sauce with Mushrooms: Follow recipe for Tomato Meat Sauce. Clean and slice ½ **pound mushrooms.** Cook slowly in 3 tablespoons melted butter until lightly browned. After removing meat from sauce, add mushrooms and simmer 10 minutes longer.

Tomato Sauce with Chicken Livers: Follow recipe for Tomato Meat Sauce. Rinse and pat dry ½ **pound chicken livers.** Slice livers and brown in **3 tablespoons olive oil.** After removing meat from sauce, add livers and simmer 10 minutes longer.

Tomato Sauce with Sausage: Follow recipe for Tomato Meat Sauce. Brown about ½ **pound Italian sausage,** cut in 2-inch pieces, in **1 tablespoon olive oil.** After removing meat from sauce, add sausage and simmer 10 minutes longer.

124 *Oil and Garlic Sauce (Salsa all' Olio e Aglio)*

½ cup olive oil
4 cloves garlic, thinly sliced
½ cup water
1 tablespoon chopped parsley
⅛ teaspoon pepper

1. Heat olive oil in a skillet. Stir in garlic and cook until browned. Remove skillet from heat and cool slightly.
2. Slowly stir in water. Add parsley and pepper. Simmer about 10 minutes. Serve over **cooked spaghetti.**

About 1 cup sauce

Garlic Sauce with Anchovies: Follow recipe for Oil and Garlic Sauce. Stir in **5 chopped anchovy fillets** with the parsley.

Garlic Sauce with Walnuts: Follow recipe for Oil and Garlic Sauce. Add **2 tablespoons chopped walnuts** with the parsley.

Garlic Sauce with Capers: Follow recipe for Oil and Garlic Sauce. Add **2 tablespoons capers** with the parsley.

Oil and Onion Sauce: Follow recipe for Oil and Garlic Sauce, substituting **1 medium onion**, thinly sliced, for the garlic.

125 *Bolognese Meat Sauce (Ragù Bolognese)*

2 tablespoons butter
1 medium onion, finely chopped
1 small carrot, finely chopped
1 small stalk celery, finely chopped
¾ pound ground beef
¼ pound ground lean pork
¼ cup tomato sauce or tomato paste
½ cup white wine
1 cup beef broth or stock
½ teaspoon salt
¼ teaspoon pepper

1. Melt butter in a skillet. Stir in onion, carrot, and celery. Cook until tender. Add meat and cook over low heat 10 to 15 minutes.
2. Add tomato sauce, wine, ¼ cup broth, salt, and pepper; mix well. Simmer about 1¼ hours. Stir in remaining broth, a small amount at a time, while the sauce is simmering. Sauce should be thick.

About 2½ cups sauce

126 *Fresh Tomato Sauce*

Following is a recipe for a simple uncooked table sauce which is ideal for topping tacos and tostadas. If preferred, one of the many bottled hot sauces of chilies and/or tomatoes may be used as well.

2 large ripe tomatoes, peeled and cored
¼ cup chopped onion
2 canned jalapeño chilies, finely chopped (more or less may be used, to taste)
1 tablespoon chopped cilantro (optional)
¼ teaspoon salt
Pepper (optional)

1. Chop tomatoes into small pieces. Add remaining ingredients and allow flavors to blend at least 30 minutes before using.
2. Store in refrigerator.

About 2 cups sauce

127 *Chicken Stock*

1 large stewing chicken, cut in serving pieces
4 quarts water
1 large onion, chopped
1 stalk celery, sliced
1 carrot, pared and sliced
1 clove garlic, minced
2 teaspoons salt
¼ teaspoon pepper

1. Rinse chicken and place in large kettle. Cover with the water. Bring to boiling. Add all remaining ingredients. Cover kettle, reduce heat, and simmer until chicken is tender (about 2 hours).
2. Cool; remove chicken and use in other recipes calling for cooked chicken. Strain broth, skim fat, and refrigerate broth until ready to use. (Or the broth, with or without vegetables, may be used as a simple soup.)

About 3 quarts stock

128 *Béchamel Sauce*

2 tablespoons butter
3 tablespoons flour
1½ cups hot milk, beef broth, or
 chicken broth
 Salt and pepper to taste
½ cup whipping cream

Melt butter over medium heat; stir in flour. Using a whisk, stir rapidly until smooth. Gradually add milk or other liquid, stirring constantly. Bring sauce to a rapid boil and boil 4 minutes, or until sauce is thick and reduced to half its original volume. Season with salt and pepper. Reduce heat and stir in cream. Heat thoroughly, but do not boil.

About 1⅔ cups

129 *Ti-Malice Sauce*

8 large shallots, sliced
 Juice of 3 limes
1 cup water
¼ cup bacon drippings
3 garlic cloves
1 fresh green hot pepper or
 2 preserved cherry peppers,
 centers removed and peppers
 thinly slivered
⅛ teaspoon ground thyme
5 parsley sprigs

1. Marinate shallots in lime juice 30 minutes, or until they turn pink.
2. Put shallots into a saucepan, add water and bacon drippings, and bring to the boiling point. Set aside.
3. In a mortar, pound together to a paste the garlic, pepper, thyme, and parsley.
4. Add seasoning paste to shallots in saucepan and bring to a boil, stirring to blend.
5. Serve in a sauceboat to accompany fried foods.

130 *Four Thieves Sauce (Sauce des Quatre Voleurs)*

2 tablespoons butter
2 tablespoons flour
1½ cups chicken broth
 Salt and freshly ground pepper
 to taste
1 egg yolk
● 3 tablespoons Four Thieves
 Vinegar
1 egg white, beaten stiff but not dry

1. Melt butter in a saucepan over medium heat. Add flour and, stirring constantly with a whisk, make a lightly browned roux. Continue to stir rapidly with a whisk while gradually adding broth. When all the broth is added, boil 4 minutes to reduce the liquid. Season with salt and pepper.
2. Remove from heat and beat a small amount of hot sauce into egg yolk; return mixture to saucepan. Cool thoroughly.
3. Blend sauce into vinegar. Just before serving, fold in beaten egg white.
4. Serve sauce with cold fish or poultry.

131 *Dilled Avocado Sauce for Fish*

1 large firm avocado, peeled and
 cubed
¼ cup olive oil
3 tablespoons lime juice, strained
 Salt, pepper, and cayenne or red
 pepper to taste
½ teaspoon dried dill or
 4 fresh dill sprigs

Put all ingredients into container of an electric blender; process until puréed.

132 *Creole Barbecue Sauce*

1 can (28 ounces) Italian plum
    tomatoes, drained
1 medium onion, finely chopped
⅔ cup olive oil
2 garlic cloves, crushed in a
    garlic press
¼ cup lime juice
1 teaspoon salt
⅛ teaspoon dried basil
    Dash pepper
    Bouquet garni
5 drops Tabasco

1. Chop tomatoes; put tomato and onion into a saucepan and cook uncovered over medium heat for 15 minutes.
2. Force tomato mixture through a fine sieve into another saucepan. Discard remaining solids.
3. Add remaining ingredients to saucepan. Stir until blended. Simmer uncovered about 1 hour, stirring occasionally.
4. Brush sauce over meat for barbecuing.

About 3½ cups

133 *Beef Stock*

2 pounds beef pot roast or brisket
    or beef for stew
2 pounds beef short ribs
1 marrow bone
4 quarts water
1 large onion, chopped
1 stalk celery, sliced
2 carrots, pared and sliced
1 cup canned tomatoes
1 clove garlic, minced
2 teaspoons salt
¼ teaspoon pepper
1 bay leaf (optional)

1. Put meats and bone into a large kettle. Cover with the water. Bring to boiling. Add all remaining ingredients. Cover kettle, reduce heat, and simmer until meat is tender (3 to 4 hours).
2. Skim fat from broth. Cool, remove meat, and use in recipes such as Picadillo (●). Strain broth and refrigerate until ready to use. (Or the broth, with or without vegetables, may be used as a simple soup.)

About 3 quarts stock

134 *French Dressing Antillaise for Salads*

½ cup olive oil
1 teaspoon salt
½ teaspoon freshly ground pepper
2 garlic cloves
    Tarragon, dill, or oregano to taste
5 parsley sprigs
2 scallions or green onions,
    finely chopped
1 tablespoon wine vinegar

1. Pour oil into a salad bowl; add remaining ingredients. With a pestle or wooden spoon, rub herbs against the side of the bowl and mix with oil.
2. For salad, marinate your choice of **celery pieces**, **chickpeas**, **onion slices**, **cherry tomatoes**, **sliced mushrooms**, **sliced cooked beets**, or **beans** (never more than two) in dressing for at least 1 hour before serving.
3. To serve, toss chilled **salad greens** with marinated vegetables.

135 *Tomato Sauce Creole*

⅓ cup peanut oil
2 medium onions, thinly sliced
6 Italian plum tomatoes, peeled, seeded, and finely chopped
½ cup beef stock
   Salt and freshly ground pepper to taste
3 drops Tabasco
1 garlic clove, crushed in a garlic press

1. Heat oil in a saucepan, add onion, and cook over low heat until translucent but not browned. Add tomato, stock, and seasonings; stir with a wooden spoon until tomato pulp is cooked to a fine purée.
2. Serve with rice or grilled meats.

136 *Mayonnaise*

2 egg yolks
½ teaspoon salt
¼ teaspoon white pepper
1 teaspoon prepared mustard
1 cup olive oil
1½ teaspoons vinegar*

Rinse a soup plate with hot water and dry well. Put egg yolks and seasoning into plate. Pour a few drops of oil over these ingredients and, with a fork or wooden spoon, stir in a slow circular motion until all the ingredients have been blended together. Continue the dripping of oil and the slow, even motion until ¼ cup oil has been blended in, then add ½ teaspoon vinegar, still stirring, then begin to pour the oil in a thin stream, never changing the pace of the beating. If the emulsion gets too thick and forms a ball, add a little more vinegar. To do it right takes about 20 minutes. The result is much richer than with the electric beater used at medium speed. When all the oil is blended in, finish with 1 teaspoon vinegar.

*The quality of the vinegar is important. Herb-flavored vinegar should be used to enhance certain dishes and salads.

137 *Watercress Mayonnaise*

   Handful watercress, finely chopped
● ¾ cup Mayonnaise
4 drops Tabasco

Blend all ingredients and serve with cold fish or shellfish.

Note: Dill, capers, chervil, or horseradish may be substituted for the watercress.

138 *Herbal Mayonnaise Odette Mennesson*

3 parsley sprigs
3 basil sprigs
2 fennel or dill sprigs
6 watercress sprigs
3 leaves Boston or Bibb lettuce
2 scallions or green onions
2 hard-cooked eggs
● 1 cup Mayonnaise

Stem herbs, watercress, and lettuce. Chop very finely along with scallions and eggs. Blend in Mayonnaise.

2 cups

139 *Bean Sauce*

3 scallions or green onions, chopped
2 parsley sprigs
2 shallots
1 green hot pepper or
    6 dried Italian pepper pods
2 tablespoons peanut oil
2 cups dried red beans, rinsed
    Bouquet garni
2 quarts water (see Note)
1 small ham hock
1 cup cubed ham
    Salt and pepper to taste

1. In a mortar, pound to a paste the scallions, parsley, shallots, and hot pepper.
2. Heat oil in a Dutch oven over medium heat, add seasoning paste, beans, and bouquet garni. Stir until beans are lightly coated with oil.
3. Add water, ham hock, and cubed ham and bring to boiling. Cover and simmer 2 hours, or until beans are tender.
4. Remove ham hock. Process beans and juice in an electric blender or force through a food mill.
5. Return sauce to Dutch oven and bring to boiling. Season with salt and pepper. Serve warm over Caribbean Rice ● or meats.

1½ quarts

Note: If using fresh beans, add only 1 quart water.

140 *Four Thieves Vinegar*

The "four thieves" are, like the bouquet garni, a standard combination of narrow-leaved basil, rosemary, sage, and marjoram commonly used in eighteenth-century French cuisine.

Several sprigs each of
    narrow-leaved basil, rosemary,
    sage, and majoram
10 cloves
1 cinnamon stick
10 peppercorns, cracked
2 garlic cloves
1 bay leaf
    Thyme sprig
2 tablespoons salt
8 dried Italian pepper pods
3½ cups wine vinegar
2 garlic cloves

1. Stem the basil, rosemary, sage, and majoram and put into a 1-quart jar along with the spices, 2 garlic cloves, bay leaf, thyme, salt, and pepper pods. Pour vinegar into jar; cover. Allow to stand 1 month in a sunny window, then strain through wet cheesecloth.
2. Put a garlic clove into each of 2 decorative 1-pint bottles; cover tightly.
3. Use for sauces and to make Condiments ●

141 *Condiments*

Some people like their food very spicy, so on every table in the islands sits a bottle of pickled mixture of hot peppers and vegetables. A great deal of pride is taken in the coloring and general aspect of the condiment, as well as in the container which, in certain families, is of the most precious antique crystal.

1 medium head cabbage, very finely shredded
2 small heads cauliflower (tips of flowerets only)
1 cup frenched green beans
1 cup green onions (white part only)
1 cup thinly sliced small carrots
1 cucumber, diced
1 cup julienned red and green sweet pepper
Snow peas (fresh or frozen), halved
Small shallots
Lime juice
6 peppercorns, cracked
2 cloves
2 bay leaves
2 cherry peppers (fresh or pickled)
4 small green hot peppers (fresh or pickled)
2 fresh cayenne pepper pods (if available)

1. Combine the vegetables.
2. Marinate desired number of shallots in lime juice 30 minutes, or until a deep purple color.
3. Drain vegetables and shallots well on paper towels. Arrange mixture decoratively in jars, then add spices and pepper to each so they can be seen from the outside.

142 *Orange Rum Sauce*

1½ cups orange juice
½ cup amber rum
Sugar to taste
1 tablespoon butter
1 tablespoon cornstarch
½ teaspoon grated orange peel

1. Combine orange juice, rum, and sugar in a small saucepan. Bring to a boil.
2. Mix butter and cornstarch and add to sauce. Cook until thickened. Remove from heat. Mix in orange peel.
3. Cool before serving.

About 2 cups

Salads

143 *Cucumber Salad* (Tsatziki)

2 cups plain yogurt
1 scallion, chopped
1 teaspoon mint
½ teaspoon salt
Freshly ground pepper
Pinch dill
1 garlic clove, crushed in a garlic
    press
4 cucumbers, pared and thinly
    sliced

Mix yogurt with scallion, mint, salt, pepper, dill, and garlic. Add cucumber and toss to coat with dressing. Refrigerate 1 hour.

6 servings

144 *Potato Salad* (Patatosalata)

½ cup olive oil
3 tablespoons wine vinegar
1 teaspoon oregano, crushed
2 tablespoons chopped parsley
1 medium onion, finely sliced
5 large red potatoes
Salt and pepper to taste

1. Combine olive oil, vinegar, oregano, parsley, and onion. Mix well. Set aside to marinate.
2. Scrub potatoes. Boil them in salted water in their jackets. When just tender (about 40 minutes), remove and plunge into cold water so they can be handled at once. Peel while hot and cut into even slices.
3. Pour the dressing over the potatoes; toss lightly. Add salt and pepper.

6 servings

145 *Anchovy Potato Salad*

Dressing:
1 cup olive oil
½ cup wine vinegar
¼ teaspoon sugar
1 teaspoon dill
1 teaspoon marjoram
Pepper to taste

Salad:
● 8 Anchovy Fillets or 1
    can (2 ounces) anchovies
    preserved in olive oil,
    drained
1 bunch escarole, torn in
    bite-size pieces
2 potatoes, boiled and diced
1 small jar pickled beets, drained
    and diced
2 green peppers, cleaned and
    thinly sliced
4 scallions, minced
3 hard-cooked eggs, sliced, for
    garnish
1 teaspoon capers for garnish
Salt and pepper to taste

1. For dressing, combine all ingredients in a jar. Shake well. Refrigerate 1 or 2 hours before serving.
2. For salad, combine anchovies with remaining ingredients, except eggs, capers, salt, and pepper. Add the salad dressing and toss to coat. Garnish with eggs and capers. Season with salt and pepper.

4 to 6 servings

146 *Cucumber and Tomato Salad* (*Angourodomatosalata*)

3 firm-ripe homegrown tomatoes,
    cut in wedges
3 pickle cucumbers (as straight
    as possible), pared and sliced
    ¼ inch thick
4 scallions, finely chopped
¼ pound feta cheese, crumbled
    Kalamata olives (about 8)
    Oregano and freshly dried dill,
    a generous pinch of each
    Salt and pepper to taste
3 tablespoons wine vinegar
⅓ cup olive oil

1. In a salad bowl, combine tomatoes, cucumbers, scallions, cheese, and olives. Season with oregano, dill, salt, and pepper.
2. Combine vinegar and olive oil in a small jar; shake well. Add to salad and toss.

6 to 8 servings

147 *Lobster Salad* (*Astakos Mayoneza*)

6 cups diced fresh lobster meat,
    chilled
3 hard-cooked eggs, mashed
    through a sieve
1 large scallion, minced
1 small leek, finely chopped
2 teaspoons tarragon
½ teaspoon thyme
2 garlic cloves, crushed in a
    garlic press
2 cups Mayonnaise
1 tablespoon capers
    Juice of 1 lemon
    Cucumber, sliced paper thin
    Tomato wedges for garnish

1. Combine all ingredients except cucumber and tomato. Adjust seasoning.
2. Spoon into heated **pastry shells**, a **lobster** cavity, or on a bed of **lettuce.** Garnish with cucumber slices and tomato wedges.

About 12 servings

148 *Russian Salad* (*Salata Roseiki*)

⅓ cup olive oil
3 tablespoons vinegar
1 cup diced cooked carrots
1 cup diced cooked beets
2 potatoes, cooked and diced
1 cup french-cut green beans,
    cooked and diced
1 cup cooked peas
¼ cup minced parsley
● Mayonnaise
    Salt and pepper to taste
2 teaspoons capers

1. Mix olive oil and vinegar and pour over vegetables; allow to marinate 1 to 2 hours. Drain. Discard dressing.
2. Mix vegetables and parsley with enough Mayonnaise to bind together (about 1 cup). Season with salt and pepper. Garnish with capers to serve.

6 servings

Note: Russian Salad makes an excellent appetizer. Serve in small dishes with heated **Sourdough Greek Bread** ●

149 *Warsaw Salad (Sałatka Warszawska)*

1 cup mayonnaise
⅓ cup dairy sour cream
1 tablespoon prepared mustard
2 cups julienne beets, cooked or canned
1½ cups kidney beans, cooked or canned
1½ cups cooked or canned peas
1 cup diced dill pickles
6 ounces (about 1¼ cups) cooked crab meat
3 scallions, chopped
1 hard-cooked egg, sliced
Carrot curls and radish roses to garnish

1. Combine mayonnaise, sour cream, and mustard in a large bowl.
2. Add remaining ingredients, except egg, carrots, and radishes; toss gently to mix.
3. Garnish with egg slices, carrot curls, and radish roses.

8 to 12 servings

150 *Sauerkraut Salad with Carrots and Apples (Surówka z Kiszonej Kapusty)*

¼ cup salad or olive oil
1½ teaspoons sugar
1 teaspoon caraway seed
½ teaspoon salt
1 teaspoon vinegar
1 pound sauerkraut, drained
2 medium tart apples, peeled, cored, and diced
¾ cup grated carrot

1. Combine oil, sugar, caraway seed, salt, and vinegar.
2. Rinse and drain sauerkraut well; chop. Stir into oil mixture.
3. Add apples and carrot; toss to mix.

About 6 servings

151 *Potato Salad with Wine (Sałatka Kartoflana z Winem)*

2 pounds potatoes
2 teaspoons salt
Boiling water
1 cup white wine
1 stalk celery
⅓ cup olive oil
¼ cup chopped fresh dill
¼ cup chopped parsley
3 tablespoons lemon juice
2 tablespoons chopped chives
¼ teaspoon pepper

1. Cook potatoes with salt in enough boiling water to cover until tender, about 30 minutes. Peel and slice; put into a bowl.
2. Pour wine over potatoes; let stand 30 minutes.
3. Cook celery in a small amount of boiling water until soft. Press celery through a sieve. Combine 2 tablespoons cooking liquid with puréed celery, oil, dill, parsley, lemon juice, chives, and pepper.
4. Add celery mixture to potatoes; mix.

6 servings

152 *Rose Salad*

10 small potatoes (about 2½ pounds), cooked
¼ cup olive oil
3 tablespoons lemon juice or vinegar
1 tablespoon water
1 tablespoon sugar
1 teaspoon salt
¼ teaspoon pepper
2 cups shell beans, cooked or canned
¼ pound sauerkraut, drained
4 stalks celery, sliced lengthwise
6 cups shredded red cabbage
Boiling water
3 tablespoons tarragon vinegar
4 cooked or canned beets, sliced

1. Slice potatoes. Mix olive oil, lemon juice, 1 tablespoon water, sugar, salt, and pepper. Pour over potatoes. Add beans, sauerkraut, and celery.
2. Add red cabbage to boiling water. Let stand 2 minutes. Drain well. Stir in tarragon vinegar; mix until cabbage is pink.
3. Mound red cabbage in center of a large platter. Arrange beet slices in cabbage to form a rose.
4. Place potatoes and other vegetables around edges. Use **celery** for rose stem. Garnish with **lettuce leaves.**

8 to 12 servings

153 *Green Bean and Onion Salad*

1 pound small boiling onions
1½ pounds fresh green beans
● Chicken Stock
● ½ cup Mock Crème Fraîche
¼ cup low-fat cottage cheese
2 tablespoons snipped fresh chives
1 teaspoon snipped fresh or ½ teaspoon dried thyme leaves
1 teaspoon snipped fresh or ½ teaspoon dried marjoram leaves
Salt
Freshly ground pepper
Juice of ½ lemon

1. Simmer onions and beans in 1 inch of stock in a covered saucepan until tender (15 to 18 minutes). Drain; refrigerate covered until chilled (about 2 hours).
2. Mix remaining ingredients except salt, pepper, and lemon juice; refrigerate covered until chilled.
3. Arrange vegetables on a platter; sprinkle lightly with salt and pepper. Squeeze lemon juice over. Spoon sauce over or pass sauce separately.

6 servings

154 *Beet Mousse*

Both elegant and unusual, this salad is worth the effort to make. Try as a first course, too.

8 medium beets
1 tablespoon vinegar
1½ teaspoons unflavored gelatin
¼ cup orange juice
½ cup instant nonfat dry-milk solids
2 to 3 ice cubes
1½ teaspoons prepared horseradish
Salad greens

1. Cut greens from beets; discard. Simmer beets in 2 inches water and vinegar until tender (about 30 minutes). Slip off skins. Cut thin slice from bottoms of beets; hollow out centers with melon-baller, leaving ½-inch shells; reserve centers. Refrigerate beets until chilled.
2. Sprinkle gelatin over orange juice in a small saucepan; let stand 5 minutes. Set over low heat, stirring occasionally, until gelatin is dissolved (about 3 minutes). Pour gelatin mixture into a food processor or blender; add beet centers and dry-milk solids. Process, adding ice cubes one at a time, until mixture is the consistency of thick whipped cream. Stir in horseradish. Fill beets with mixture; refrigerate until serving time. Serve on salad greens.

4 servings

155 *Red Cabbage-Apple Salad*

In this cross between coleslaw and Waldorf salad, you will enjoy crisp textures and tart flavors.

3 cups shredded red cabbage
1 red apple, cut in 1½x¼-inch strips
1 sweet red pepper, cut in 1½x¼-inch strips
2 tablespoons cider vinegar
¼ cup apple juice
¼ teaspoon caraway seed
⅛ teaspoon salt
⅛ teaspoon freshly ground pepper
Salad greens

Mix all ingredients except salad greens in a medium bowl. Refrigerate covered 2 hours. Serve on salad greens on individual plates.

4 servings

156 *Raw Broccoli Salad*

If you have never eaten broccoli raw, you have a treat in store.

3 cups raw bite-size pieces broccoli spears
● ½ cup Low-Fat Yogurt
½ teaspoon salt
¼ teaspoon freshly ground pepper
2 ounces Cheddar cheese, shredded
1 large carrot, cut in thin slices

Mix broccoli with yogurt, salt, and pepper. Spoon mixture on 4 salad plates. Sprinkle tops of salads with cheese; arrange carrot slices around salads.

4 servings

Note: See recipe for Garden Vegetables in Sweet Seasoned Vinegar (●) to use broccoli stalks.

157 *Fresh Spinach Salad*

This is an example of a composed salad, where ingredients have been carefully arranged for eye and appetite appeal.

4 cups bite-size pieces spinach
1 cup ½-inch pieces yellow
    squash
1 can (7¾ ounces) water
    chestnuts, drained and sliced
2 hard-cooked eggs, chopped
½ cup sliced green onions
    Salt
    Freshly ground pepper
● ½ cup Mustard Sauce
● ½ cup Low-Fat Yogurt

Arrange spinach, squash, water chestnuts, eggs, and onion attractively in rows on a medium platter; sprinkle lightly with salt and pepper. Mix Mustard Sauce and yogurt; drizzle over salad.

6 servings

Note: This recipe will make 4 luncheon servings with the addition of **2 cups flaked tuna.**

158 *Greek Salad in Peppers*

The natural juice from the tomato and the lemon juice are the "salad dressing" for this salad. Add a dollop of yogurt, if desired.

1 large tomato, chopped
1 green onion, sliced
⅛ teaspoon salt
1 teaspoon snipped fresh or ½
    teaspoon dried basil leaves
1 tablespoon fresh lemon juice
4 small green peppers, cored
½ cup crumbled feta cheese
8 anchovies, drained and rinsed
8 lemon wedges

1. Mix tomato, onion, salt, basil, and lemon juice; refrigerate covered 1 hour.
2. Spoon half the tomato mixture into green peppers; layer cheese over tomatoes. Spoon remaining tomato mixture over cheese. Arrange 2 anchovies over top of each pepper. Serve with lemon wedges.

4 servings

159 *Cucumbers with Buttermilk Dressing*

1 medium cucumber, pared,
    seeded, and finely chopped
1 teaspoon salt
1 tablespoon fresh lemon juice
● 1 tablespoon Mock Crème
    Fraîche
¾ cup buttermilk
1 tablespoon snipped fresh or 1
    teaspoon dried dill weed
½ teaspoon salt
⅛ teaspoon freshly ground
    pepper
1 cucumber, sliced
2 large tomatoes, sliced

1. Sprinkle chopped cucumber with 1 teaspoon salt; let stand 10 minutes. Rinse cucumber; pat dry and place in a mixing bowl. Mix lemon juice, crème fraîche, buttermilk, dill, ½ teaspoon salt, and the pepper; pour over cucumber and refrigerate covered 1 hour.
2. Arrange sliced cucumber and tomatoes on individual plates; spoon buttermilk mixture over.

4 servings

Note: This recipe can be increased and served as a first-course soup; stir in skim milk if thinner consistency is desired.

160 *Fruited Carrot Salad*

Tart apple pieces would be an interesting addition to this salad.

4 carrots
1 cup unsweetened pineapple
   juice
2½ cups orange juice
   Lettuce cups
   Snipped mint

1. Pare carrots into strips with a vegetable peeler. Place in a shallow glass dish; pour fruit juices over. Refrigerate covered 6 hours or overnight, stirring occasionally.
2. Drain carrots, spoon into lettuce cups, and garnish with mint.

4 servings

161 *Oriental Cucumber Salad*

10 baby cucumbers (about 3
   inches long), sliced in very
   thin rounds
1 bunch green onions, tops only,
   finely chopped
2 teaspoons honey or sugar
2 teaspoons toasted sesame seed
½ cup distilled white vinegar
½ teaspoon sesame oil
5 tablespoons light soy sauce
   Salad greens

1. Arrange cucumber and onion in a shallow glass dish. Shake remaining ingredients except salad greens in a covered jar; pour over the vegetables. Refrigerate for 2 hours, stirring occasionally.
2. Drain cucumber and onion; marinade can be strained and refrigerated for use again. Serve salad on lettuce or other salad greens.

4 servings

162 *Garden Vegetables in Sweet Seasoned Vinegar*

1½ cups very thinly sliced baby
   cucumbers
2 cups very thinly sliced broccoli
   stalks
½ cup cider vinegar
½ teaspoon salt
¼ teaspoon freshly ground
   pepper
1½ teaspoons sugar
   Salad greens

1. Arrange vegetable slices in a shallow glass dish. Shake remaining ingredients except salad greens in a covered jar; pour over vegetables. Refrigerate covered 30 minutes; stir occasionally. Drain; marinade can be strained and refrigerated for use again.
2. Serve vegetables on salad greens.

4 servings

163 *Vegetable Salad with Yogurt Dressing*

Vivid colors dominate this unusual salad combination.

- ● ¾ cup Low-Fat Yogurt
  - 2 tablespoons snipped parsley
  - ½ cup finely chopped dill pickle
  - ½ cup chopped tomato
  - 1 teaspoon salt
  - 1 cup sliced radishes
  - 1 medium zucchini, shredded
  - 2 medium carrots, shredded
  - 1 large beet, shredded

1. Mix yogurt, parsley, pickle, chopped tomato, and salt; refrigerate covered 1 hour.
2. Arrange radish slices around edge of a serving plate. Arrange zucchini, carrots, and beet decoratively in center of plate. Serve yogurt mixture with salad.

4 servings

164 *Vegetable Platter Vinaigrette*

Use any fresh vegetables that you want in this recipe—let your imagination be your guide.

- 1 pound fresh green beans
- 1 small head cauliflower
- ● Chicken Stock
- ● 1 cup Vinaigrette Dressing
- 1 pint cherry tomatoes, halved
  Salt
  Freshly ground pepper
- 1 medium red onion, thinly
  sliced

1. Steam green beans and whole cauliflower in separate covered saucepans in 1 inch of stock until tender (about 15 minutes). Drain. Mix beans with ½ cup dressing and refrigerate covered 3 hours, stirring occasionally. Refrigerate cauliflower. Mix cherry tomatoes with ½ cup dressing; refrigerate covered 3 hours, stirring occasionally.
2. Drain beans and tomatoes; reserve dressing. Place cauliflower in center of a platter; arrange beans and tomatoes around cauliflower. Sprinkle vegetables lightly with salt and pepper. Arrange onion slices over beans and tomatoes. Cut cauliflower into wedges to serve. Pass reserved dressing.

8 to 10 servings

165 *Red Vegetable Salad*

- 1 pint cherry tomatoes, stems
    removed, cut in half
- 20 radishes, sliced
- 1 small red onion, sliced
- 3 tablespoons wine vinegar
- 2 teaspoons salad oil
- 1 teaspoon salt
- 2 teaspoons snipped fresh mint
- ⅛ teaspoon freshly ground white
    pepper
  Lettuce leaves

1. Combine all ingredients except lettuce leaves in a medium bowl; refrigerate covered 2 hours, stirring occasionally.
2. Serve vegetables on lettuce.

4 to 6 servings

166 *Pineapple-Mint Salad*

1 can (20 ounces) unsweetened
    pineapple chunks, drained
2 cups low-fat cottage cheese
½ bunch mint, snipped
    Bibb lettuce
1 cup sliced celery
    Mint sprigs
8 orange slices

1. Dice 1 cup of the pineapple; mix with cottage cheese and snipped mint.
2. Arrange lettuce leaves on a platter or individual plates; mound pineapple mixture on lettuce. Arrange remaining pineapple and the celery around mounds of pineapple mixture. Garnish with mint sprigs and orange slices.

4 to 6 servings

167 *California Fruit Plate*

Fresh fruits are a must for this recipe. If figs and raspberries are not available, substitute other ingredients such as strawberries and melon.

2 cups low-fat cottage cheese
8 fresh figs, cut in quarters
2 cups fresh raspberries
2 tablespoons honey
4 lemon wedges

Place ½ cup cottage cheese on each of 4 salad plates. Surround cottage cheese with 8 quarters of fig; sprinkle raspberries over figs. Drizzle honey over fruit and cottage cheese. Squeeze lemon over all.

4 servings

168 *Broccoli Salad (Insalata di Broccoli)*

1 pound broccoli
3 tablespoons olive oil
3 tablespoons lemon juice
1 medium clove garlic
¼ teaspoon salt
⅛ teaspoon pepper

1. Trim off leaves and bottoms of broccoli stalks, and split thick stems lengthwise. Cook, covered, in a small amount of salted water until just tender. Drain and chill.
2. Combine olive oil, lemon juice, garlic, salt, and pepper. Drizzle over thoroughly chilled broccoli and serve.

About 3 servings

Cauliflower Salad: Follow recipe for Broccoli Salad. Substitute **1 medium head cauliflower** for broccoli. Separate into flowerets and cook as for broccoli. Peel and dice **1 boiled potato**; combine with cauliflower and chill. Substitute **wine vinegar** for the lemon juice and add ¼ **teaspoon oregano.**

Green Bean Salad: Follow recipe for Broccoli Salad. Clean and cook ½ **pound green beans** and substitute for broccoli. Use wine vinegar instead of lemon juice.

Asparagus Salad: Follow recipe for Broccoli Salad. Clean and cook **1 pound asparagus** and substitute for the broccoli.

169 *Pickled Pepper Salad (Insalata di Peperoni)*

2 cups sliced pickled red peppers
¾ cup chopped celery
½ cup sliced ripe olives
8 anchovy fillets, chopped
2 tablespoons olive oil
2 tablespoons wine vinegar
¼ teaspoon oregano
⅛ teaspoon salt
¼ teaspoon pepper

1. Gently combine the red peppers, celery, olives, and anchovy fillets. Mix oil, vinegar, oregano, salt, and pepper; pour over the red pepper mixture. Toss gently.
2. Serve very cold.

6 to 8 servings

170 *Red Kidney Bean Salad (Insalata di Fagioli)*

1 can (16 ounces) kidney beans
¼ cup wine vinegar
3 tablespoons olive oil
¼ teaspoon oregano
¼ teaspoon salt
⅛ teaspoon pepper
¼ cup sliced celery
2 tablespoons chopped onion
Lettuce cups

1. Thoroughly rinse and drain kidney beans.
2. Combine vinegar, oil, oregano, salt, and pepper; mix with beans. Blend in celery and onion; chill.
3. Serve in crisp lettuce cups.

About 4 servings

171 *Italian Potato Salad (Insalata di Patate)*

2 medium potatoes, boiled, peeled, and diced
⅓ cup chopped celery
½ cup diced pared cucumber
½ cup chopped ripe olives
2 tablespoons minced onion
● ¾ cup Italian Dressing
¼ teaspoon oregano

1. Lightly toss together the potatoes, celery, cucumber, olives, and onion. With a fork, thoroughly but carefully blend in the dressing mixed with oregano.
2. Cover the salad. Chill about 1 hour before serving.

About 4 servings

172 *Green Salad (Insalata Verde)*

1 large head lettuce, or an equal
amount of another salad green
(curly endive, romaine,
escarole, chicory, or dandelion
greens)
1 clove garlic
Italian Dressing

1. Wash lettuce in cold water, removing core, separating leaves, and removing any bruised leaves. Drain; dry thoroughly and carefully. Tear lettuce into bite-size pieces, put into a plastic bag, and chill 1 hour.
2. Just before serving, cut garlic in half and rub a wooden bowl. Put greens in bowl and pour on desired amount of dressing. Turn and toss the greens until well coated with dressing and no dressing remains in the bottom of the bowl.

About 6 servings

Green Salad with Anchovy Dressing: Follow recipe for Green Salad. Add **2 tomatoes,** cut in wedges, **¼ cup diced celery,** and **½ cup chopped ripe olives** to lettuce in bowl. Toss with **Anchovy Dressing.**

Mixed Salad: Follow recipe for Green Salad. Add **¼ cup chopped cucumber, ¼ cup chopped celery, ¼ cup sliced radishes,** and **¼ cup chopped ripe olives** to lettuce before tossing with dressing.

173 *Fresh Bean Sprout Salad*

A crisp, colorful, light salad.

1 pound fresh bean sprouts,
rinsed (see Note)
2 medium carrots, shredded
1 tablespoon toasted sesame seed
2 teaspoons vegetable oil
⅓ cup distilled white vinegar
2 teaspoons sugar

1. Mix bean sprouts and carrots in a shallow glass dish.
2. Shake remaining ingredients in a covered jar; pour over vegetables.
3. Refrigerate covered 1½ hours; stir occasionally. Serve in shallow bowls.

4 to 6 servings

Note: If fresh bean sprouts are not available, you can substitute **1 large pared, seeded, shredded cucumber.**

174 *Guacamole I*

2 very ripe avocados
1 medium fresh tomato
1 small onion, chopped (about ⅓ cup)
2 tablespoons lemon juice
1 teaspoon salt
1 to 2 teaspoons chili powder

1. Peel avocados and mash pulp, leaving a few small lumps throughout.
2. Peel and chop tomato and add to mashed avocado. Add onion, lemon juice, salt, and chili powder to taste. If not serving immediately, refrigerate in covered bowl, with avocado pits immersed in guacamole; this is said to help keep avocado from darkening on standing.
3. Serve on lettuce as a salad, as a ''dip'' with tostada chips, or as a condiment to top taco fillings.

About 2 cups guacamole

Note: If you prefer a smoother guacamole, ingredients may be blended to desired consistency.

175 *Guacamole II*

2 large ripe avocados
3 tablespoons lemon juice
1 medium tomato
1 slice onion
1 small green chili
1 small clove garlic, minced
⅛ teaspoon coriander
Salt

1. Halve avocados, peel, remove pits, and cut avocado into pieces. Put into an electric blender with lemon juice.
2. Peel, halve, and seed tomato. Add to blender along with onion, chili, garlic, coriander, and salt to taste. Blend.
3. Serve as a dip with **corn chips, cauliflowerets,** and **carrot and celery sticks.**

About 3 cups dip

176 *Christmas Eve Salad* (*Ensalada de Noche Buena*)

This salad is customarily served at the traditional Mexican midnight supper on Christmas Eve. It usually precedes a turkey entrée. You might enjoy it in a similar menu. Or, it could provide an interestingly different light luncheon main dish.

1 cup diced cooked beets
1 cup diced tart apple, not peeled
1 cup orange sections
1 cup sliced bananas
1 cup diced pineapple (fresh or canned)
  Juice of 1 lime
  Oil and Vinegar Dressing (see below)
  Shredded lettuce
½ cup chopped peanuts
  Seeds from 1 pomegranate

1. Drain beets well. Combine beets, apple, oranges, bananas, and pineapple. Refrigerate until ready to serve.
2. Add lime juice to beet-fruit mixture. Add desired amount of dressing and toss until evenly mixed and coated with dressing.
3. To serve, make a bed of shredded lettuce in salad bowl. Mound salad on top. Sprinkle with peanuts and pomegranate seeds.

8 to 10 servings

Oil and Vinegar Dressing: Mix **2 tablespoons white wine vinegar, 1½ teaspoons sugar,** and **¼ teaspoon salt.** Add **⅓ cup salad oil;** mix well.

177 *Rooster's Bill* (Pico de Gallo)

1 medium jícama*
1 large orange
¼ cup chopped onion
Juice of 1 lemon
1 teaspoon salt
1 teaspoon chili powder
½ teaspoon oregano, crumbled

*3 large tart crisp apples may be substituted for jícama.

1. Wash, pare, and chop jícama into ½-inch chunks.
2. Pare and section orange, reserving juice, and add to jícama; pour orange juice over fruit chunks. Add onion, lemon juice, and salt and stir until evenly mixed. Let stand at least 1 hour in refrigerator before serving.
3. When ready to serve, sprinkle with chili powder and oregano.

4 to 6 servings

178 *Coliflor Acapulco*

1 large head cauliflower
Marinade (see below)
1 can (15 ounces) garbanzos, drained
1 cup pimento-stuffed olives
Pimentos, drained and cut lengthwise in strips
Lettuce
1 jar (16 ounces) sliced pickled beets, drained and chilled
1 large cucumber, thinly sliced and chilled
Parsley sprigs
Radish roses
● Guacamole I

1. Bring 1 inch of salted water to boiling in a large saucepan. Add cauliflower, cover, and cook about 20 minutes, or until just tender; drain.
2. Place cauliflower, head down, in a deep bowl and pour marinade over it. Chill several hours or overnight; occasionally spoon marinade over all.
3. Shortly before serving, thread garbanzos, olives, and pimento strips onto wooden picks for decorative kabobs. Set aside while arranging salad.
4. Drain cauliflower. Line a chilled serving plate with lettuce and place cauliflower, head up, in the center. Arrange pickled beet and cucumber slices around the base, tucking in parsley sprigs and radish roses.
5. Spoon and spread guacamole over cauliflower. Decorate with kabobs. Serve cold.

6 to 8 servings

Marinade: Combine 1½ cups vegetable oil, ½ cup lemon juice, 1½ teaspoons salt, and 1 teaspoon chili powder. Shake marinade well before using.

179 *Avocados Stuffed with Cauliflower Salad*

2 cups very small, crisp raw
   cauliflowerets
1 cup cooked green peas
½ cup sliced ripe olives
¼ cup chopped pimento
¼ cup chopped onion
● Oil and Vinegar Dressing
   Salt to taste
6 small lettuce leaves
3 large ripe avocados
   Lemon wedges

1. Combine all ingredients, except lettuce, avocados, and lemon wedges; stir gently until evenly mixed and coated with dressing.
2. Refrigerate at least 1 hour before serving.
3. When ready to serve, peel, halve, and remove pits from avocados. Place a lettuce leaf on each serving plate; top with avocado half filled with a mound of cauliflower salad. Serve with lemon wedges.

6 servings

180 *Garbanzo Salad*

1 can (15 ounces) garbanzos,
   drained
¼ cup chopped parsley
1 can or jar (4 ounces) pimentos,
   drained and chopped
3 green onions, chopped
¼ cup wine vinegar
2 tablespoons olive or salad oil
1 teaspoon salt
½ teaspoon sugar
¼ teaspoon pepper

Combine all ingredients in a bowl; cover and refrigerate until chilled.

About 6 servings

181 *Shrimp Salad*

1½ cups cooked shrimp, sliced in
   half lengthwise
½ cup diced cooked potatoes
2 hard-cooked eggs, sliced
½ cup chopped celery
¼ cup chopped green onions
½ cup mayonnaise or salad
   dressing
½ cup dairy sour cream
½ teaspoon chili powder
   Salt to taste
   Lettuce leaves
   Lemon wedges

1. Combine all ingredients, except lettuce and lemon wedges, and stir gently until evenly mixed and coated with dressing.
2. Refrigerate at least 1 hour before serving.
3. When ready to serve, place on lettuce leaves. Serve with lemon wedges.

6 servings

Note: Shrimp salad also makes a delicious avocado filling.

182 *Cucumber Mousse*

1 package (3 ounces) lime-flavored gelatin
¾ cup boiling water
1 cup cottage cheese
1 cup mayonnaise or salad dressing
2 tablespoons grated onion
¾ cup grated cucumber
1 cup slivered almonds

1. Dissolve gelatin in boiling water. Stir in cottage cheese, mayonnaise, and onion until well blended. Fold in cucumber and almonds.
2. Pour mixture into a 1-quart mold. Refrigerate until set.

4 to 6 servings

Soups

183 *Beef Stock*

6 to 8 pounds beef soup bones
Salt to taste
2 large onions, peeled and left whole
10 peppercorns
2 whole allspice
2 carrots, scraped
4 parsley sprigs
2 bay leaves
2 celery stalks
Water to cover bones

1. Combine all ingredients in a 12-quart saucepot. Bring to boiling, lower heat, and simmer 10 to 12 hours, skimming off foam from top.
2. Strain. Discard solids. Cool. Skim off fat. Taste for salt.

7 to 8 quarts

184 *Creamed Avgolemono Soup* (Soupa Xerokosta Avgolemono)

1 cup butter, softened
6 tablespoons flour
2 cups milk, scalded
2 cups cream, scalded
1½ quarts homemade chicken stock, strained
2 cups cooked rice
4 egg yolks
Juice of 3 lemons
1 lemon, thinly sliced for garnish

1. Beat butter in a small bowl. Beating constantly, slowly add flour.
2. Combine butter mixture with scalded milk and cream in a soup pot. Cook over medium heat, stirring frequently, until boiling. Reduce heat at once.
3. Pour in stock and add rice. Simmer 30 minutes, skimming off fat.
4. Beat egg yolks in a large bowl until fluffy. Pour in lemon juice a little at a time, while beating. Add 2 cups hot stock, a tablespoon at a time, while beating.
5. Pour stock mixture into soup. Heat, but do not boil. Garnish with sliced lemon.

6 servings

185 *Egg and Lemon Soup* (Avgolemono Soupa)

1½ quarts chicken stock
(homemade or canned)
1½ cups uncooked parboiled rice
1 whole egg
3 egg yolks
Juice of 2 lemons
Salt and pepper to taste

1. Heat stock in a saucepan. Add rice and simmer, covered, until tender (about 20 minutes).
2. Beat egg and yolks until light. Beating constantly, slowly add lemon juice.
3. Measure 2 cups hot chicken stock and add, tablespoon by tablespoon, to egg mixture, beating constantly to prevent curdling. Add this mixture to the remaining hot chicken stock with rice. Season with salt and pepper.
4. Serve at once.

6 servings

186 *Egg and Lemon Soup with Sour-Dough Noodles* (Trahana Avgolemono)

1½ quarts chicken broth
1 cup trahana (see Note)
Salt and pepper to taste
2 eggs, separated
Juice of 2 lemons

1. Bring broth to boiling; boil 6 minutes. Add trahana, salt, and pepper. Simmer covered 10 minutes.
2. In a small bowl, using a wire whisk, beat egg whites until frothy. In another bowl, beat egg yolks. Combine. Slowly beat in lemon juice, then 1 cup hot broth. Add to soup. Serve immediately.

About 2½ cups

Note: There are three varieties of trahana dough—sour, sweet, sweet-sour. It may be made at home (see recipe for Sweet-Sour Trahana and variations) or purchased at a Greek grocery store.

187 *Sweet-Sour Trahana*

2 eggs, slightly beaten
½ cup plain yogurt
½ cup milk
1 teaspoon salt
1½ cups all-purpose flour
Semolina (about 1½ cups)

1. Blend eggs, yogurt, milk, and salt. Add flour and semolina, a little at a time, to form a stiff dough.
2. Knead for about 5 minutes (dough will be very sticky). Divide into small portions. Roll with hands into balls. Place on a clean cloth.
3. Flatten each piece as thin as possible. Let dry undisturbed on trivets at least 12 hours.
4. Cut into small pieces. Turn pieces over and continue drying for another 12 hours or more.
5. When completely dry, mash into crumbs with rolling pin. Spread on a baking sheet.
6. Bake at 200°F for 2 hours.

Note: The weather affects the drying of the trahana. When it is humid, allow more time for drying. Homemade trahana is far superior to the commercially made product. Store in an airtight jar indefinitely.

Sweet Trahana: Follow recipe for Sweet-Sour Trahana; omit yogurt and increase milk to 1 cup.

Sour Trahana: Follow recipe for Sweet-Sour Trahana; omit milk and increase yogurt to 1 cup.

188 *Bean Soup* (Fassoulatha)

1 cup large dried white beans
2 quarts water
1 cup sliced celery (½-inch
 pieces)
2 cups chopped onion
4 medium carrots, cut in ½-inch
 slices
½ cup chopped parsley
1 tablespoon tomato paste
1 cup olive oil
1 tablespoon oregano, crushed
3 tablespoons wine vinegar

Bring beans to a boil in the water. Reduce heat and simmer 1 hour. Add remaining ingredients. Simmer 2 hours more. Add **salt** and **pepper** to taste. Serve with **toasted bread.**

6 to 8 servings

189 *Lentil Soup* (Faki)

1 package (16 ounces) dried
 lentils
2 quarts water
½ cup olive oil
1 cup chopped celery
½ cup grated carrot
1 onion, quartered
1 tablespoon tomato paste
3 garlic cloves, peeled
2 bay leaves
 Salt and pepper to taste
 Vinegar

1. Rinse lentils several times. Drain.
2. In a kettle, put lentils, water, olive oil, celery, carrot, onion, tomato paste, garlic, bay leaves, salt, and pepper. Bring to a boil. Reduce heat and simmer covered 2 hours. Adjust salt and pepper.
3. Serve with a cruet of vinegar.

6 to 8 servings

190 *Soupa Aravanaiko*

This soup is a delicious main course with homemade bread on a cold night.

3 quarts beef stock
3 pounds lean beef, cut in
 2½-inch squares
2 cans (15 ounces each) tomato
 sauce or 4 cups Tomato
 Sauce
4 medium ripe tomatoes, peeled,
 seeded, and diced (optional)
1 pound macaroni, cooked
 according to directions on
 package
1 cup freshly grated kefalotyri
 cheese, or more to taste

1. Heat stock to boiling. Add meat and tomato sauce. Simmer until meat is tender (about 2 hours).
2. Add tomato pieces. Simmer 20 minutes. Add cooked macaroni. Heat thoroughly.
3. Top with grated cheese before serving.

8 servings

191 *Fish Soup* (Psarosoupa)

2 small cleaned fish or 2 heads
and bones from large fish
such as red snapper or
mackerel (tied together in
cheesecloth)
1 bay leaf
2 quarts water or enough to
cover
8 or 10 small onions, peeled and
left whole
8 or 10 small new potatoes,
pared and left whole
3 or 4 carrots, pared and sliced in
1-inch pieces
1 stalk celery, sliced in 1-inch
pieces
3 tomatoes, peeled, seeded, and
chopped
2 garlic cloves, crushed in a
garlic press
2 pounds mackerel fillets
1 pound red snapper fillets
1 pound codfish fillets
Parsley sprigs
Juice of 1 large lemon
½ cup olive oil

1. Put fish heads and bones into a stock pot with bay leaf and water. Bring to a boil and cook 20 minutes, removing scum as it forms. Strain broth; return to pot. Discard heads and bones. Add onions, potatoes, carrots, celery, tomatoes, and garlic. Place mackerel and snapper on top of vegetables. Add water if necessary to cover. Bring to a boil quickly. Boil 10 minutes. Add codfish. Boil another 10 minutes. Remove fish and place in a heated serving dish. Garnish with parsley.
2. Blend lemon juice and olive oil. Drizzle half over fish and add the rest to the stock. Pour soup and vegetables into a tureen. Serve the fish and soup in separate dishes.

8 servings

192 *Tripe Soup*

4 pounds prepared tripe
1½ quarts water
Salt and pepper to taste
5 tablespoons butter
2½ tablespoons flour
3 eggs
Juice of 2 lemons
1 teaspoon paprika
Pinch red pepper seeds
Croutons

1. Rinse tripe thoroughly. Place in a large saucepan. Add water, cover, and simmer for 3 hours, adding more water as the water in the pan boils away.
2. Remove tripe from the stock. Put through a meat grinder. Return to the stock. Season with salt and pepper. Cook over medium heat for 2 hours.
3. Meanwhile, melt 3 tablespoons butter in a saucepan, add flour and cook over low heat, stirring constantly, for 3 minutes. Add 1 cup stock in a thick stream to the butter and flour, stirring constantly with a whisk to prevent lumps. Pour this mixture into the soup. Simmer 15 minutes.
4. Beat eggs until frothy. Slowly add lemon juice while beating. Add 2 cups of stock in a thin stream, stirring constantly. Season with paprika and red pepper.
5. Add remaining butter just before serving. Serve with croutons and a cruet of **garlic-flavored vinegar.**

6 to 8 servings

193 *Traditional Greek Easter Soup* (Mayeritsa Avgolemono)

1 small bunch green onions,
    trimmed
2 cups diced celery root
4 parsley sprigs
1 dill sprig
2½ quarts water
    Salt and freshly ground pepper
    to taste
½ cup lamb's intestines
½ pound lamb's liver
½ pound lamb's heart
    Cold water
½ cup finely chopped parsley
2 tablespoons finely chopped dill
6 egg yolks
    Juice of 1 lemon

1. Tie green onions, celery root, parsley, and dill in cheese-cloth and place in a kettle. Add the 2½ quarts water, salt, and pepper; bring to a boil.
2. Meanwhile, clean lamb's intestines. Rinse them well, then turn them inside out. To do this, use a small stick about the size of a pencil. Tie one end of one length of intestine. Fit this onto the tip of the stick, then reverse the intestine down the stick much as you would a stocking, pushing the inside out with the fingers. Rinse well and add the intestines to the kettle. Bring to a boil and cook about 1 hour.
3. Place liver and heart in a saucepan and add cold water to cover. Add salt and pepper and simmer until tender (20 minutes or longer).
4. Remove the intestines from the stock. Discard the cheese-cloth bag. Chop the intestines. Dice the heart and liver. Add all this to the stock, then add parsley and dill. Heat thoroughly. Strain, reserving stock.
5. Heat small bowl of an electric mixer. Add egg yolks to the bowl and beat well. Add lemon juice, a little at a time, beating rapidly. Beat in 2 cups strained hot stock, tablespoon by tablespoon, beating rapidly. Beat in the remaining stock, strained, and serve immediately.

8 to 10 servings

194 *Bread Kvas*

1 quart hot water
1 pound beets, pared and sliced
1 rye bread crust

1. Pour hot water over beets in a casserole. Add bread. Cover with a cloth. Let stand 3 to 4 days.
2. Drain off clear juice and use as a base for soup.

About 3 cups

195 *Beet Kvas*

5 to 6 cups boiling water
3 cooked beets, sliced
½ cup vinegar

1. Pour boiling water over beets; add vinegar. Let stand at room temperature 2 to 4 days.
2. Drain off juice and use as a base for soup.

About 4 cups

196 *Rye Flour Kvas*

4 cups rye flour
6 to 8 cups lukewarm water

1. Put flour into a crock and gradually mix water into flour until smooth and the consistency of pancake batter. Cover with a cloth.
2. Keep in warm place 48 hours. Mixture will bubble. When brown liquid comes to top and bubbling stops, it is done. Skim off foam.
3. Fill crock with cold water; stir. Flour settles to bottom in a few hours. Pour off clear liquid and refrigerate in jars.

About 6 cups

197 "Nothing" Soup (Zupa Nic)

4 eggs, separated
⅓ cup sugar
1 quart milk
½ teaspoon vanilla extract
¼ teaspoon salt
Dash of cinnamon or nutmeg
(optional)

1. Beat egg yolks with 3 tablespoons of the sugar until very fluffy.
2. With clean beaters, beat the egg whites until frothy. Gradually beat in the remaining sugar. Continue beating until stiff, not dry, peaks form.
3. Heat milk over medium heat in a deep 10-inch skillet or 5- or 6-quart Dutch oven just until a "skin" forms on top, about 3 minutes.
4. Drop beaten egg whites by rounded spoonfuls into hot milk. Cook until the egg white "kisses" are set and firm to the touch, about 5 minutes. Remove kisses with a slotted spoon to waxed or absorbent paper.
5. Stirring constantly, gradually add hot milk to egg yolks. Strain into a heavy saucepan. Add vanilla extract and salt. Cook and stir over medium low heat about 3 minutes, until thickened, and soup coats a spoon.
6. Serve soup with 2 or 3 meringues in each portion. Sprinkle with cinnamon, if desired. Serve hot or cold.

4 servings

198 Pumpkin Soup (Zupa z Dynią)

1 quart milk
1 can (16 ounces) pumpkin
½ teaspoon allspice
¼ teaspoon nutmeg
¼ teaspoon pepper
½ teaspoon salt
1 cup cooked rice
2 tablespoons butter or margarine

1. Beat milk into pumpkin in saucepan. Stir in spices and salt. Bring just to boiling.
2. Stir in rice and butter. Cook and stir 5 to 10 minutes, or until rice is heated through; do not boil.

8 to 10 servings

199 Mushroom Soup (Zupa Grzybowa)

1 carrot
2 sprigs parsley
1 stalk celery
2 small onions, sliced
1 teaspoon salt
2 cups water
½ pound fresh mushrooms, sliced, or 2 cans (4 ounces each) mushrooms
1 cup water or mushroom liquid
1 teaspoon dill weed
1 teaspoon chopped parsley
1 tablespoon flour
¼ cup cold water
½ cup dairy sour cream or whipping cream

1. Cook carrot, parsley, celery, 1 onion, and salt in 2 cups water 20 minutes. Strain; discard vegetables.
2. Cook mushrooms and remaining onion in ½ cup water 8 minutes. Add to the vegetable broth along with ½ cup water, dill, and parsley.
3. Mix flour with ¼ cup cold water. Stir into soup. Bring to boiling. Cook and stir 3 minutes. Remove from heat.
4. Beat in sour cream. Serve hot.

About 4 servings

200 *Duck Soup (Czarnina)*

1 duck (5½ to 6½ pounds), cut up
1 quart duck, goose, or pork blood
1½ pounds pork loin back ribs
2 quarts water
2 teaspoons salt
1 stalk celery
1 sprig parsley
5 whole allspice
2 whole cloves
1 pound dried prunes, pitted
½ cup raisins
1 small tart apple, chopped (optional)
2 tablespoons flour
1 tablespoon sugar
1 cup whipping cream or dairy sour cream
   Salt, pepper, lemon juice, or vinegar

1. Purchase duck and blood from butcher. The blood will contain vinegar. (If preparing your own poultry, put ½ cup vinegar into glass bowl with blood to prevent coagulation. Set aside.)
2. Cover duck and back ribs with water in a large kettle. Add salt. Bring to boiling. Skim off foam.
3. Put celery, parsley, allspice, and cloves into cheesecloth bag and add to soup. Cover and cook over low heat until meat is tender, about 1½ hours.
4. Remove spice bag from kettle. Discard bones, cut up meat. Return meat to soup. Add prunes, raisins, and apple (if desired); mix. Cook 30 minutes.
5. With beater, blend flour and sugar into cream until smooth. Then add blood mixture, a little at a time, continuing to beat.
6. Add about ½ cup hot soup stock to blood mixture, blending thoroughly. Pour mixture slowly into the soup, stirring constantly until soup comes just to boiling.
7. Season to taste with salt, pepper, and lemon juice or vinegar. Serve with homemade noodles, if desired.

About 2½ quarts

Note: If a thicker soup is desired, increase flour to 3 to 4 tablespoons or add 1 cup puréed prunes.

201 *Dill Pickle Soup (Zupa Ogórkowa)*

4 large dill pickles, diced or thinly sliced
2 tablespoons flour
2 tablespoons butter or margarine
3 cups meat broth, bouillon, or meat stock
⅔ cup liquid from pickles or water
2½ cups cubed boiled potatoes (optional)
1 cup dairy sour cream

1. Coat pickles with flour.
2. Melt butter in a large skillet. Add pickles and stir-fry over medium heat 3 minutes.
3. Stir in beef broth, pickle liquid, and potatoes, if desired. Cook over medium heat 15 minutes, stirring occasionally.
4. To serve, mix in sour cream or spoon dollops of sour cream into each bowl before ladling in soup.

About 6 servings

202 *Kohlrabi Soup (Zupa z Kalarepy)*

5 cups meat broth or bouillon or meat stock
1 pound kohlrabi, peeled and diced
2 tablespoons water
1 tablespoon cornstarch or potato flour
1 teaspoon salt
¼ teaspoon pepper
1 tablespoon butter, melted
2 egg yolks

1. Boil broth and kohlrabi in large saucepan. Cover; reduce heat and simmer 20 to 30 minutes, until kohlrabi is tender.
2. Mash or purée the kohlrabi.
3. Make a smooth paste by stirring water into cornstarch. Add to soup. Season with salt and pepper. Cook soup over medium heat until it boils.
4. Beat melted butter into egg yolks. Then beat in a little of the hot soup.
5. Remove soup from heat. Beat in egg yolk mixture. Serve hot with **croutons.**

About 8 servings

203 *Barley Soup* (Krupnik)

1 cup pearl barley
2 quarts meat stock
¼ cup butter or margarine, cut in pieces
2 carrots, diced
2 potatoes, diced
4 ounces (canned or frozen) mushrooms, sliced
1 stalk celery, chopped
Giblets from 1 chicken or turkey, diced (optional)
1 teaspoon dried parsley flakes
1½ teaspoons salt
½ teaspoon pepper
1 cup dairy sour cream (optional)
Sprigs of fresh dill

1. Combine barley with 1 cup of the meat stock in large saucepan. Bring to boiling; reduce heat and simmer until all stock is absorbed. Add butter piece by piece, stirring.
2. Boil vegetables and, if desired, giblets in the remaining stock until crisp-tender. Then add barley, parsley, salt, and pepper. Cook until barley is tender.
3. Garnish each serving with sour cream, if desired, and dill.

About 2½ quarts

204 *Black Bread Soup* (Zupa Chlebowa)

2 cups stale dark bread pieces (rye or whole wheat)
2 medium onions, quartered
1 carrot, quartered
1 leek, sliced
3 sprigs parsley
½ cup cut fresh or frozen green beans, lima beans, or peas
1 stalk celery, sliced
1 celery root or parsnip, sliced
1½ quarts water or meat broth or bouillon
1½ teaspoons salt
½ teaspoon pepper
Dash nutmeg
1 cup milk or water
3 egg yolks (optional)
Croutons or sliced hard-cooked eggs (optional)

1. Combine bread, all vegetables, and water in a 3-quart saucepan. Simmer 30 or 40 minutes, or until vegetables are tender.
2. Purée vegetables by pressing through a sieve or using an electric blender. Add vegetable purée to broth in pan. Stir in salt, pepper, nutmeg, and milk. Cook until soup simmers; do not boil.
3. If using egg yolks, beat them and then stir in a small amount of hot soup. Immediately beat mixture into soup. Remove from heat.
4. Serve hot with croutons or sliced hard-cooked eggs, if desired.

About 6 servings

205 *Caraway Soup* (Zupa Kminkowa)

5 cups meat broth or bouillon or meat stock
2 tablespoons caraway seed
2 tablespoons browned flour
2 tablespoons melted butter
½ pound diced cooked or smoked kiełbasa (Polish sausage) or salami (optional)
Buttered croutons
Dairy sour cream (optional)

1. Rapidly simmer broth with caraway seed 15 minutes. Strain and discard seed.
2. Blend flour into butter until smooth.
3. Return broth to saucepan. Stir in flour mixture and sausage. Bring just to boiling, stirring.
4. Serve garnished with croutons and, if desired, sour cream.

About 6 servings

206 *Sauerkraut Soup (Kapuśniak)*

2 pounds pork shanks, ham hocks,
    or pigs' feet
1 quart water
1 medium onion, sliced
1 bay leaf
5 peppercorns
1 sprig parsley or ¼ teaspoon dried
    parsley flakes
1 pound sauerkraut
2 cups meat broth, bouillon, or
    meat stock
8 to 12 ounces bacon or smoked
    link sausage, diced (optional)
¼ cup raisins or 2 tablespoons
    sugar (optional)
3 tablespoons lard or margarine (at
    room temperature)
3 tablespoons flour
½ teaspoon salt
¼ teaspoon pepper

1. Cook pork shanks in water in a 5-quart kettle 20 minutes. Skim off foam. Add onion, bay leaf, peppercorns, and parsley. Cook about 45 minutes, or until meat is tender.
2. Remove meat from broth. Strain broth; return to kettle.
3. Remove meat from bones; discard skin and bones. Dice meat.
4. Rinse sauerkraut with cold water; drain.
5. Add diced meat, drained sauerkraut, beef broth, and if desired, bacon and raisins to kettle. Simmer 1 hour.
6. Mix lard and flour to a smooth paste; stir into simmering soup. Cook and stir over medium heat until thickened. Mix in salt and pepper.
7. Serve with plain boiled potatoes or potato dumplings, if desired.

About 10 servings

207 *Fish Broth (Rosół z Ryby)*

1 large onion, quartered
2 tablespoons butter or margarine
½ small head savoy cabbage
2 carrots, cut up
2 celery stalks, cut up
1 parsley root, cut up
3 quarts water
6 peppercorns
1 bay leaf
  Salt
2 pounds fish fillets
1 teaspoon lemon juice
1 teaspoon salt
½ teaspoon nutmeg

1. Brown onion in butter in a small skillet.
2. Meanwhile, simmer the vegetables in water with peppercorns, bay leaf, and salt to taste 15 minutes.
3. Add onion and fish to vegetables; simmer about 10 minutes, or until fish flakes easily.
4. Remove fish and vegetables. Use for another dish, if desired, or discard.
5. Strain broth. Add lemon juice, salt, and nutmeg.
6. Boil broth rapidly 10 minutes. Strain again, if desired. Serve as a clear soup.

About 2 quarts

208 *Chicken Broth (Rosół z Kury)*

1 chicken (3½ pounds)
2 teaspoons salt
7 cups boiling water
2 carrots
¼ small head savoy cabbage
2 stalks celery
1 parsley root (optional)
1 large onion, quartered
5 whole peppercorns
1 tablespoon chopped parsley

1. Simmer chicken with salt in boiling water 30 minutes.
2. Add carrots, cabbage, celery, parsley root (if desired), onion, peppercorns, and parsley.
3. Remove chicken. Strain broth. Quickly chill broth, then skim off fat. Store broth in refrigerator or serve hot with dumplings.
4. Use chicken meat for other dishes. Fat can be used in cooking instead of butter.

About 1½ quarts

209 *Meat Broth* (*Rosół z Mięsa*)

2 pounds beef shank or short ribs,
    or pork neckbones
1 pound marrow bones
3 quarts water
1 large onion, quartered
2 leaves cabbage
2 sprigs fresh parsley or 1
    tablespoon dried parsley flakes
1 carrot, cut up
1 parsnip, cut up
1 stalk celery, cut up
5 peppercorns
1 tablespoon salt

1. Combine beef, bones, and water in a 6-quart kettle. Bring to boiling. Boil 15 minutes, skimming frequently.
2. Add remaining ingredients. Simmer rapidly about 1½ hours, or until meat is tender.
3. Strain off broth. Chill quickly. Skim off fat.
4. Remove meat from bones. Set meat aside for use in other dishes. Discard bones, vegetables, and peppercorns.
5. Return skimmed broth to kettle. Boil rapidly about 15 minutes, or until reduced to about 6 cups. Store in refrigerator until needed.

About 1½ quarts

Meat Stock: Prepare Meat Broth as directed. Chill. Lift off fat. Boil until reduced to 3 cups, about 45 minutes.

210 *Borscht with Meat* (*Barszcz z Mięsa*)

¼ pound salt pork, diced
1 large leek, thinly sliced
1 medium onion, sliced
1 celery or parsley root (about 6
    ounces), peeled and cut in
    thin strips
3 beets (about ½ pound), peeled
    and shredded
½ head cabbage (about ½ pound),
    thinly sliced
2 quarts water
1½ pounds cooked meat such as
    kiełbasa (Polish sausage),
    ham, beef, or pork, diced
1 can (8 ounces) whole tomatoes
● 1 cup Rye Flour Kvas
2 tablespoons butter (at room
    temperature)
2 tablespoons flour
1 teaspoon salt
½ teaspoon pepper
1½ tablespoons lemon juice or
    vinegar
1 cup whipping cream or dairy
    sour cream
Prepared horseradish (optional)

1. Fry salt pork until golden in a 5-quart kettle. Add leek and onion. Fry until onion is transparent.
2. Add celery root, beets, cabbage, water, and meat. Cook until celery root is crisp tender; about 25 minutes.
3. Add tomatoes and kvas; mix. Cook over medium heat 30 minutes.
4. Make a smooth paste of butter and flour; stir into the simmering soup. Cook and stir until soup thickens. Add salt, pepper, and lemon juice; mix.
5. To serve, spoon a small amount of cream and horseradish into each bowl. Ladle hot soup into bowl and stir to blend with the cream and horseradish.

About 2½ quarts

211 *Volhynian Beet Soup (Barszcz Wołński)*

¼ cup dried navy or pea beans
2 cups water
● 2 cups Bread Kvas
2 cups meat broth, bouillon, or meat stock
6 medium beets, cooked and peeled
1 can (16 ounces) tomatoes (undrained)
1 small head cabbage (about 1½ pounds)
1 small sour apple
Salt and pepper
1 tablespoon butter (optional)
Dairy sour cream

1. Bring beans and water just to boiling in a large kettle. Remove from heat. Let stand 1 hour. Then boil for 20 minutes, or until beans are tender. Add kvas and meat broth.
2. Slice beets. Mash tomatoes or make a purée by pressing through a sieve or using an electric blender. Add beets and tomatoes to beans.
3. Cut cabbage into sixths; remove core. Pare apple, if desired; core and dice. Add cabbage and apple to beans.
4. Season to taste with salt and pepper. Stir in butter, if desired. Cook soup over medium heat 30 minutes.
5. To serve, spoon a small amount of sour cream into each bowl. Ladle in hot soup and stir.

About 2½ quarts

212 *Fresh Cabbage Soup*

(Kapuśniak ze Świeżej Kapusty)

5 slices bacon, diced
1 pound cabbage, chopped
2 carrots, sliced
2 potatoes, sliced
1 stalk celery, sliced
1½ quarts water
2 tablespoons flour
2 tablespoons butter or margarine (at room temperature)
Salt and pepper

1. Fry bacon until golden but not crisp in a 3-quart saucepan.
2. Add vegetables and water. Simmer 30 minutes, or until vegetables are tender.
3. Blend flour into butter; stir into soup. Bring soup to boiling, stirring. Season to taste with salt and pepper. If desired, serve with dumplings or pierogi.

6 to 8 servings

213 *Cold Cucumber-Beet Soup (Chłodnik)*

1 small bunch beets with beet greens (about 1 pound)
1½ quarts water or chicken broth
1 teaspoon salt
2 medium cucumbers, pared and diced
6 radishes, sliced
6 green onions with tops, sliced
2 tablespoons fresh lemon juice
2 cups dairy sour cream or buttermilk
1 dill pickle, minced (optional)
3 tablespoons chopped fresh dill or 4 teaspoons dill weed
Salt and pepper
1 lemon, sliced
2 hard-cooked eggs, chopped or sliced
12 large shrimp, cooked, peeled, and deveined (optional)

1. Scrub beets and carefully wash greens. Leave beets whole; do not peel. Put beets and greens into a kettle with water and salt. Bring to boiling. Cover. Reduce heat, and cook slowly until tender, about 30 minutes, depending on size of beets. Drain, reserving liquid in a large bowl.
2. Peel and chop beets, mince the greens.
3. Add beets and greens to reserved liquid along with cucumber, radish, green onion, lemon juice, sour cream, pickle (if desired), and dill. Season with salt and pepper to taste; mix. Chill.
4. Serve garnished with lemon slices and hard-cooked egg and, if desired, whole shrimp.

About 2 quarts soup

214 *Clear Borscht (Barszca Klarowny)*

● 1 cup Beet Kvas
5 cups meat or vegetable broth (or use 3 beef and 3 vegetable bouillon cubes dissolved in 5 cups boiling water)
2 tablespoons brown sugar
Dairy sour cream (optional)

1. Heat kvas and broth to boiling in a saucepan. Skim surface if necessary.
2. Serve hot or chilled with **rye bread** and a large dollop of sour cream, if desired.

About 1½ quarts

215 *Wine Soup (Polewka z Wina)*

1 quart white wine
2 cups water
1 piece cinnamon stick (3 inches)
3 whole cloves
3 whole allspice
5 egg yolks
2 tablespoons sugar

1. Bring wine, water, and spices to boiling. Strain; discard spices.
2. Beat egg yolks with sugar until thick. Slowly add the hot wine mixture, beating constantly until a thick foam forms at the top. Be careful not to curdle the yolks by pouring hot wine too fast. Serve in cups with **wafers.**

8 to 10 servings

216 *Beer Soup (Polewka z Piwa)*

2 cans (12 ounces each) beer
3 egg yolks
4 teaspoons sugar
Croutons or grated cheese

1. Bring beer to boiling.
2. Meanwhile, beat egg yolks with sugar until thick.
3. Stirring constantly, gradually add a small amount of beer to egg yolks. Then carefully stir egg yolk mixture into boiling beer, reduce heat, and stir 1 minute; do not boil.
4. At once remove from heat. Serve with hot croutons.

About 4 servings

217 *Apple Soup (Zupa Jabłkowa)*

6 large apples (see Note)
1 quart water
¾ cup sugar
½ teaspoon cinnamon (optional)
½ cup lemon juice
1 cup whipping cream
⅔ cup white wine (optional)

1. Pare and core 5 apples. Cook in water until soft. Rub through a sieve, or purée in an electric blender to make an applesauce.
2. Combine applesauce, sugar, and cinnamon (if desired) in a large bowl.
3. Shred or mince remaining apple; mix with lemon juice. Stir into applesauce mixture. Chill.
4. To serve, blend cream into applesauce mixture. Stir in wine, if desired.

8 to 10 servings

Note: If desired, substitute 1 can or jar (16 ounces) applesauce and 1 cup water for apples and water.

218 *Prune Soup (Zupa z Suszonych Śliwek)*

1 package (12 ounces) pitted dried
  prunes
3 cups hot water
½ pound rhubarb, cut in pieces
2 cups boiling water
½ teaspoon cinnamon
¼ teaspoon cloves
⅔ cup sugar
1 tablespoon cornstarch or potato
  flour (optional)
¼ cup cold water (optional)
¾ cup dairy sour cream
  Cooked macaroni or croutons

1. Soak prunes in 3 cups hot water 1 hour. Cook in the same water 3 to 5 minutes.
2. Cook rhubarb in 2 cups boiling water 10 minutes.
3. Combine cooked fruits; press through a sieve, or purée in an electric blender.
4. Combine purée in a saucepan with cinnamon, cloves, sugar, and, if desired, a blend of cornstarch and cold water. Bring to boiling, stirring constantly. Remove from heat.
5. Cool slightly; beat in sour cream. Mix in macaroni. Or top with croutons and serve after the meat course.

8 to 10 servings

219 *Plum or Apricot Soup (Zupa ze Śliwek lub Moreli)*

1 pound fresh apricots or plums
1 quart water
1 tablespoon potato flour
⅓ cup sugar or ½ cup apricot or
  plum jam
  Peel and juice of ½ lemon
  (optional)
¼ teaspoon salt
1 pint dairy sour cream
  Buttered croutons

1. Cook fruit in water until tender, 20 to 30 minutes.
2. Discard pits. Purée fruits by pressing through a sieve or using an electric blender. (Fruit may be pitted raw for easier handling, but the taste will be less subtle.)
3. Stir potato flour into liquid in which fruit was cooked. Bring to boiling, stirring until thickened.
4. Pour thickened liquid into fruit purée. Stir in sugar, lemon peel and juice, if desired, and salt. Cook, stirring, 3 minutes.
5. Serve hot or cold. Spoon sour cream on top of each serving of soup. Garnish with croutons.

8 to 10 servings

220 *Berry Soup (Zupa Jagodowa)*

1 quart fresh blueberries,
  blackberries, raspberries, or
  strawberries; or 2 packages (10
  ounces each) frozen berries
1 cup fresh currants (optional)
2 cups water
1 tablespoon cornstarch or potato
  flour
2 tablespoons water
  Peel and juice of ½ lemon
⅔ cup sugar
½ teaspoon cinnamon or ¼
  teaspoon cloves
1 pint whipping cream or dairy
  sour cream

1. Using a potato masher, crush 3 cups of the berries in a large kettle. Reserve 1 cup berries for garnish. Purée fruits by pressing through a sieve, or use an electric blender.
2. Add the 2 cups water; simmer 15 minutes.
3. Mix cornstarch with 2 tablespoons water. Stir in soup. Bring to boiling, stirring until soup thickens.
4. Stir in lemon peel and juice, sugar, and cinnamon. Chill.
5. To serve, beat in cream. Or spoon soup over dollops of sour cream. Garnish with reserved whole berries.

6 to 8 servings

221 Cherry Soup (Zupa Wiśniowa)

3 pints pitted fresh red tart cherries or 3 cans (16 ounces each) pitted red tart cherries, drained
½ teaspoon cinnamon
¼ teaspoon cloves
1 quart water
½ cup sugar
¾ cup dairy sour cream
Cooked noodles or croutons

1. Combine cherries, cinnamon, and cloves with the water in large saucepan. Bring to boiling. Reduce heat and simmer 15 minutes.
2. If desired, purée fruits by pressing through a sieve, or use an electric blender.
3. Add sugar and stir until it dissolves. Cool thoroughly.
4. Beat in sour cream. Serve with noodles or croutons after the meat course.

8 to 10 servings

222 Easter Soup (Żurek Wielkanocny)

2 cups rolled oats
2 cups warm water
Crust of sour rye bread
1½ pounds Polish sausage (kiełbasa)
1½ quarts water
1 tablespoon prepared horseradish
1 teaspoon brown sugar
1 teaspoon salt
¼ teaspoon pepper

1. Mix oats and warm water. Add bread crust. Let stand until mixture sours, at least 24 hours. Strain; reserve liquid.
2. Cook sausage in 1½ quarts water 1 hour. Remove sausage. Skim off fat. Combine skimmed broth and oatmeal liquid.
3. Add horseradish, brown sugar, salt, and pepper. Slice sausage; add to broth. Bring just to boiling.
4. Serve hot with **boiled potatoes** and **hard-cooked eggs.**

About 4 servings

223 Borscht without Meat (Barszcz Postny)

7 medium beets (about 1½ pounds)
2 medium potatoes (about ½ pound) (optional)
½ cup chopped parsley root or 2 tablespoons dried parsley flakes
⅓ cup chopped celery leaves
4 dried mushrooms or 4 fresh mushrooms
1 clove garlic, crushed (optional)
2 quarts water
● 1½ cups Beet Kvas
3 beef bouillon cubes or 1 tablespoon concentrated meat extract
2 teaspoons salt
1 tablespoon sugar
Dairy sour cream (optional)

1. Pare beets and potatoes, then dice them.
2. Combine all ingredients in a 6-quart kettle. Bring to boiling. Reduce heat. Cover and cook over medium heat until vegetables are tender, 30 to 40 minutes.
3. Remove vegetables and force through a sieve or purée in an electric blender. Return purée to kettle. (This is optional and may be omitted.)
4. Various ingredients may be added to soup: prepared horseradish, lemon juice or vinegar, dill, more salt and sugar, pepper, chunks of rye bread, or filled pastries such as pierogi. Sometimes sliced or chopped hard-cooked eggs, beet tops, and baked beans are added. Simmer just long enough to heat thoroughly.
5. Serve in large bowls with dollops of sour cream, if desired.

About 5 quarts

224 *Almond Soup (Zupa Migdałowa)*

5 cups milk
½ pound blanched almonds, ground twice
5 bitter almonds (optional)
1 teaspoon almond extract
2 cups cooked rice
⅓ cup sugar
¼ cup raisins or currants

1. Heat milk just to simmering in a large saucepan.
2. Add all the ingredients; stir until well mixed. Cook over low heat 3 to 5 minutes.
3. Serve hot as is traditional for Christmas, or chill before serving.

About 2 quarts

225 *Jellied Consommé*

2 envelopes unflavored gelatin
½ cup cold water
● 5 cups Beef Stock
1 teaspoon Worcestershire sauce
1 tablespoon dry sherry
2 teaspoons lemon juice
Lemon twists
2 tablespoons chopped ripe olives

1. Pour gelatin over cold water in a medium saucepan; let stand 5 minutes. Set over low heat until gelatin is dissolved (about 3 minutes), stirring occasionally. Stir in remaining ingredients, except lemon twists and olives. Heat thoroughly, then cool slightly.
2. Pour consommé into a mixing bowl; refrigerate covered until set (3 to 4 hours).
3. Beat slightly before serving. Spoon into consommé cups or wine glasses. Garnish with lemon twists and chopped olives.

6 servings (about ¾ cup each)

226 *Fragrant Mushroom Soup*

The flavor of the dried mushrooms is "woodsy" and full-bodied. The combination of fresh and dried mushrooms is unusual.

● 1½ quarts Chicken Stock
1 cup dried mushrooms
1 small onion, chopped
Salt
Freshly ground pepper
10 fresh mushrooms, cleaned and sliced
● Low-Fat Yogurt, if desired

1. Pour 2 cups of the stock over the dried mushrooms in a bowl. Cover with a plate to keep mushrooms submerged. Let stand until mushrooms are soft (about 45 minutes). Drain; reserve liquid. Remove tough center stems with a sharp knife and discard; chop mushrooms.
2. Combine reserved mushroom liquid, remaining chicken stock, dried mushrooms, and onion in a medium saucepan. Simmer covered 30 minutes. Season to taste with salt and pepper. Stir fresh mushrooms into stock; cook 1 minute.
3. Serve immediately in soup cups. Top with dollops of yogurt, if desired.

8 servings (¾ cup each)

227 Egg-Drop Soup

The addition of rice and chicken livers adds heartiness to this Oriental favorite.

- 6 cups Chicken Stock
  2 teaspoons clarified butter
  ¼ cup uncooked long-grain rice
  6 chicken livers, cooked and chopped
  1 egg yolk, beaten
  2 tablespoons snipped parsley
  Salt
  Freshly ground white pepper
  1 tablespoon snipped chives

1. Heat stock to boiling in a medium saucepan.
2. Heat butter in a small skillet until bubbly; stir in rice. Cook and stir rice until lightly browned; stir into boiling stock. Simmer covered until rice is tender (about 25 minutes).
3. Stir liver, egg yolk, and parsley into stock; cook and stir until egg is cooked and liver hot (about 2 minutes). Season to taste with salt and pepper.
4. Spoon into bowls; garnish with chives.

6 servings (1⅓ cups each)

228 Spinach Soup with Onion Petals

- 8 small onions, peeled
  6 cups Chicken Stock
  2 pounds fresh spinach, washed and stems removed
  3 cups water
  Salt
  1 tablespoon finely chopped green onion tops

1. Cut each onion into ¼-inch slices, cutting almost to, but not through, base. Give onion a quarter turn; cut into ¼-inch slices, intersecting previous slices.
2. Simmer onions in stock in a large covered skillet or saucepan until onions are tender (about 20 minutes).
3. Simmer spinach in water in a covered saucepan 10 minutes; drain, adding cooking liquid to stock with onions. Reserve spinach for other use.
4. Taste stock; add salt if necessary. Lift onions from stock and into individual soup bowls with slotted spoon. Ladle stock around onions in each bowl. Sprinkle with green onion tops. Serve with knives, forks, and spoons.

8 servings (1 cup each)

229 Jellied Gazpacho

Colorful Mexican fare that is a traditional crowd pleaser.

- 4 cups chilled tomato juice
  2 envelopes unflavored gelatin
  1 cup Low-Fat Yogurt
  1 garlic clove, minced
  1 pound tomatoes, peeled, seeded, and chopped
  1 small cucumber, pared, seeded, and chopped
  1 medium green pepper, chopped
  ⅓ cup shredded carrot
  2 tablespoons minced red onion
  ½ cup finely chopped celery
  3 tablespoons fresh lemon juice
  1 to 1½ teaspoons salt
  ¼ teaspoon freshly ground pepper
  ⅛ teaspoon chili powder
  2 garlic cloves, minced
  Salad greens

1. Pour ½ cup of the tomato juice into a small saucepan. Sprinkle the gelatin over the juice; let stand 5 minutes. Set over low heat, stirring constantly, until gelatin is dissolved (about 3 minutes).
2. Pour mixture and remaining tomato juice into a large mixing bowl. Refrigerate until slightly thickened, but not set.
3. Mix yogurt and garlic; refrigerate covered.
4. Stir vegetables, lemon juice, salt, pepper, chili powder, and 2 garlic cloves into tomato mixture. Mix well.
5. Spoon tomato mixture into 6 individual soup bowls or a 2-quart bowl. Refrigerate covered until mixture has set (about 4 hours).
6. Unmold on salad greens and serve with the garlic yogurt.

6 servings (about 1 cup each)

Note: Jellied Gazpacho is excellent for lunch served with steamed shrimp.

230 *Yogurt Soup*

Middle Eastern influence has been translated for this rich, filling, but low-calorie soup.

- 1½ quarts Chicken Stock
  2 tablespoons cornstarch
- 1 cup Low-Fat Yogurt
  Juice of ½ lemon, if desired
  2 teaspoons clarified butter
  ¼ teaspoon paprika
  Snipped parsley

1. Heat stock to boiling. Mix cornstarch thoroughly with yogurt; stir into stock. Simmer, stirring rapidly, until stock mixture thickens slightly (about 4 minutes). Taste; add lemon juice if needed for tartness.
2. Melt butter; stir in paprika. Spoon butter mixture onto top of soup. Pour soup into bowls. Sprinkle with parsley.

8 servings (¾ cup each)

231 *Chicken-Mushroom Pudding*

Though soufflélike in texture, this recipe has only half the eggs, flour, and butter of a soufflé.

  1 tablespoon butter
  1 tablespoon flour
  ½ cup nonfat dry-milk solids
  ½ cup cold water
- ½ cup Chicken Stock
  1¼ cups finely chopped cooked
      chicken
  1 cup finely chopped mushrooms
  2 teaspoons snipped parsley
  1 tablespoon finely snipped
      chives or green onion tops
  2 teaspoons Dijon mustard
  ½ teaspoon salt
  ¼ teaspoon freshly ground
      pepper
  2 egg yolks
  3 egg whites
      Shredded carrot or radish roses

1. Melt butter in a medium skillet; mix in flour, stirring constantly until mixture is smooth and bubbly. Remove from heat. Mix milk solids, water, and stock; stir into flour mixture gradually. Return sauce to heat; boil and stir until thickened (about 2 minutes). Stir in remaining ingredients, except eggs and carrot. Cook and stir 3 minutes; let cool to room temperature.
2. Beat egg yolks; stir into chicken mixture. Beat egg whites until stiff but not dry peaks form; fold gently into chicken mixture until blended. Spoon mixture into lightly buttered 1-quart soufflé dish.
3. Bake at 350°F 35 to 40 minutes, or until puffy and light brown. Garnish with carrot. Serve immediately.

6 to 8 servings

Note: Chicken-Mushroom Pudding is also delicious served cold. Let cool 30 minutes after baking, then refrigerate covered until completely chilled (about 4 hours).

232 *Spiced Pumpkin Soup*

The crunchy green pepper garnish adds an interesting texture and flavor contrast to this soup.

  1 small pumpkin (about 3
      pounds), pared and cut in
      2-inch pieces; or 2½ cups
      canned pumpkin
  1 cup chopped onion
  1 teaspoon minced ginger root
- 3 cups Chicken Stock
  ½ teaspoon salt
  ½ teaspoon freshly ground
      pepper
  ½ teaspoon ground cloves
  ½ cup white wine
  1¼ cups chopped green pepper

1. Simmer pumpkin, onion, and ginger root in stock in a covered saucepan until pumpkin is tender (about 20 minutes).
2. Purée mixture in two batches in a food processor or blender. Pour purée back into saucepan; stir in remaining ingredients except green pepper. Simmer uncovered 10 minutes.
3. Serve soup in bowls; garnish with green pepper.

6 servings (about ¾ cup each)

Note: This soup is also excellent served cold. If desired, Low-Fat Yogurt (●) can be used in place of the wine, or as a garnish.

233 *Minestrone*

Derived from the Latin "to hand out," this soup was a staple in the days when the monks kept it always on the fire to be ready for sojourners or travelers. Even today, it is a favorite.

6 cups water
1¼ cups (about ½ pound) dried navy beans, rinsed
¼ pound salt pork
3 tablespoons olive oil
1 small onion, chopped
1 clove garlic, chopped
¼ head cabbage
2 stalks celery, cut in ½-inch slices
2 small carrots, pared and cut in ½-inch slices
1 medium potato, pared and diced
1 tablespoon chopped parsley
½ teaspoon salt
¼ teaspoon pepper
1 quart hot water
¼ cup packaged precooked rice
½ cup frozen green peas
¼ cup tomato paste
Grated Parmesan cheese

1. Bring the 6 cups water to boiling in a large saucepot. Gradually add the beans to the boiling water so the boiling does not stop. Simmer the beans 2 minutes, and remove from heat. Set aside to soak 1 hour.
2. Add salt pork to beans and return to heat. Bring to boiling, reduce heat, and simmer 1 hour, stirring once or twice.
3. While beans are simmering with salt pork, heat the olive oil in a skillet, and brown the onion and garlic lightly. Set aside.
4. Wash the cabbage, discarding coarse outer leaves, and shred finely.
5. After the beans have simmered an hour, add the onion, garlic, celery, carrots, potato, cabbage, parsley, salt, and pepper. Slowly pour in 1 quart hot water and simmer about 1 hour, or until the beans are tender.
6. Meanwhile, cook the rice according to package directions. About 10 minutes before the beans should be done, stir in the rice and peas. When the peas are tender, stir in the tomato paste. Simmer about 5 minutes. Serve sprinkled with cheese.

About 6 servings

234 *"Little Hats" in Broth (Cappelletti in Brodo)*

½ cup (4 ounces) ricotta or cottage cheese
2 tablespoons grated Parmesan cheese
½ cup finely chopped cooked chicken
1 egg, slightly beaten
⅛ teaspoon salt
Few grains nutmeg
Few grains pepper
2 cups sifted all-purpose flour
¼ teaspoon salt
2 eggs
3 tablespoons cold water
2 quarts chicken broth or bouillon

1. Combine cheeses, chicken, 1 egg, ⅛ teaspoon salt, nutmeg, and pepper; set aside.
2. Combine flour and ¼ teaspoon salt in a large bowl. Make a well in the center of the flour. Place 2 eggs, one at a time, in the well, mixing slightly after each one is added. Gradually add the water; mix well to make a stiff dough. Turn dough onto a lightly floured surface and knead until smooth and elastic (5 to 8 minutes).
3. Roll dough out to about ¹⁄₁₆ inch thick. Cut into 2½-inch circles. Place ½ teaspoon of the chicken-cheese mixture in the center of each round. Dampen the edges with water, fold in half, and press together to seal. Bring the two ends together, dampen, and pinch together.
4. Bring the chicken broth to boiling. Add pasta and cook 20 to 25 minutes, or until pasta is tender. Pour broth and pasta into soup bowls, and serve immediately.

8 servings

235 *Zuppa di Pesce: Royal Danieli*

This fish soup recipe is from the Danieli Royal Excelsior, a hotel in Venice.

3 pounds skinned and boned fish
  (haddock, trout, cod, salmon,
  and red snapper)
1 lobster (about 1 pound)
1 pound shrimp with shells
1 quart water
½ cup coarsely cut onion
1 stalk celery with leaves, coarsely
  cut
2 tablespoons cider vinegar
2 teaspoons salt
¼ cup olive oil
2 cloves garlic, minced
1 bay leaf, crumbled
1 teaspoon basil
½ teaspoon thyme
2 tablespoons minced parsley
½ to 1 cup dry white wine
½ cup chopped peeled tomatoes
8 shreds saffron
1 teaspoon salt
½ teaspoon freshly ground black
  pepper
6 slices French bread
¼ cup olive oil

1. Reserve heads and tails of fish. Cut fish into bite-size pieces.
2. In a saucepot or kettle, boil lobster and shrimp 5 minutes in water with onion, celery, vinegar, and 2 teaspoons salt.
3. Remove and shell lobster and shrimp; devein shrimp. Cut lobster into bite-size pieces. Set lobster and shrimp aside.
4. Return shells to the broth and add heads and tails of fish. Simmer 20 minutes.
5. Strain broth, pour into saucepot, and set aside.
6. Sauté all of the fish in ¼ cup oil with garlic, bay leaf, basil, thyme, and parsley 5 minutes, stirring constantly.
7. Add to reserved broth along with wine, tomatoes, saffron, 1 teaspoon salt, and the pepper. Bring to boiling; cover and simmer 10 minutes, stirring occasionally.
8. Serve with slices of bread sautéed in the remaining ¼ cup olive oil.

About 2½ quarts soup

236 *Roman Egg Soup with Noodles*
(Stracciatella con Pasta)

4 cups chicken broth
1½ tablespoons semolina or flour
1½ tablespoons grated Parmesan
  cheese
⅛ teaspoon salt
⅛ teaspoon pepper
4 eggs, well beaten
1 cup cooked noodles
  Snipped parsley

1. Bring chicken broth to boiling.
2. Meanwhile, mix semolina, cheese, salt, and pepper together. Add to beaten eggs and beat until combined.
3. Add noodles to boiling broth, then gradually add egg mixture, stirring constantly. Continue stirring and simmer 5 minutes.
4. Serve topped with parsley.

4 servings

Roman Egg Soup with Spinach: Follow recipe for Roman Egg Soup with Noodles; omit noodles. Add ½ **pound chopped cooked fresh spinach** to broth before adding egg mixture.

237 *Escarole Soup*

3 pounds beef shank cross cuts
1 can (6 ounces) tomato paste
1 tablespoon salt
1 teaspoon basil, crushed
½ teaspoon oregano, crushed
8 cups water
1 pound escarole, chopped
1 medium onion, peeled and diced
1 medium potato, pared and diced
2 stalks celery, diced
  Fresh parsley, snipped
  Freshly ground black pepper

1. Put beef shank into a saucepot or Dutch oven. Add tomato paste, salt, basil, oregano, and water; stir. Cover; bring to boiling, reduce heat, and simmer until meat is tender (about 3 hours).
2. Add escarole, onion, potato, and celery; stir. Bring to boiling; simmer, uncovered, 45 minutes, or until vegetables are tender.
3. Remove meat and bone; cut meat into pieces and transfer to soup plates. Ladle hot soup over meat and garnish each serving with parsley and pepper.

About 3 quarts soup

238 *Vegetable Soup Italienne (Minestrone)*

1 cup thinly sliced carrots
1 cup thinly sliced zucchini
1 cup thinly sliced celery
1 cup finely shredded cabbage
2 tablespoons butter
2 tablespoons cooking oil
2 beef bouillon cubes
8 cups boiling water
2 teaspoons salt
2 medium tomatoes, cut in pieces
½ cup uncooked broken spaghetti
½ teaspoon thyme

1. Add carrots, zucchini, celery, and cabbage to hot butter and oil in a saucepot. Cook, uncovered, about 10 minutes, stirring occasionally.
2. Add bouillon cubes, water, and salt to the vegetables. Bring to boiling; reduce heat and simmer, uncovered, 30 minutes.
3. Stir in tomatoes, spaghetti, and thyme; cook 20 minutes longer.
4. Serve hot from soup tureen with shredded Parmesan cheese sprinkled over the top of each serving.

About 6 servings

239 *Chicken Broth (Brodo di Pollo)*

1 stewing chicken (4 to 5 pounds)
5 cups water
2 teaspoons salt
5 pieces (3 inches each) celery with leaves
3 small carrots, washed and scraped
2 medium onions
1 large tomato, rinsed and quartered

1. Clean chicken, disjoint, cut into pieces, and rinse. Put into a saucepot. Rinse giblets, refrigerate liver, and put remaining giblets into pot. Add water, salt, celery, carrots, onions, and tomato. Cover and bring to boiling. Uncover and skim off foam.
2. Cover tightly. Simmer 2 to 3 hours. When chicken is almost tender, add liver. Cook about 15 minutes.
3. Remove chicken and giblets from broth, cool slightly, and remove skin. Remove meat from bones, and use as needed in recipes.
4. Strain broth and cool slightly. Remove fat that rises to surface. Refrigerate fat; use as needed. Cool broth and refrigerate until needed.

About 1 quart broth

240 *Zuppa Pavese*

● 1 quart Chicken Broth
4 slices bread (½ inch thick), toasted and generously buttered
4 eggs
¼ cup freshly grated Parmesan cheese

1. Heat Chicken Broth.
2. Place slices of buttered toast in individual heat-resistant soup bowls. Break an egg over each toast slice. Carefully pour broth into bowls, taking care not to break the egg yolks.
3. Set bowls in a 350°F oven and cook until egg whites are firm.
4. Before serving, sprinkle generously with grated cheese.

4 servings

Note: Instead of toasting and buttering the bread, the slices may be browned on both sides in butter in a skillet or on a griddle. If desired, use poached eggs and omit oven cooking.

To poach eggs, grease the bottom of a deep skillet. Add enough water to come about 1 inch above eggs. Lightly salt the water; bring to boiling, then reduce heat to simmering. Break the eggs, one at a time, into a small dish and slip each into the water. Cook 3 to 5 minutes, depending on firmness desired. Remove with slotted·spoon.

241 *Miniatures Florentine*

Float these vivid green cutouts on individual servings of hot bouillon or consommé.

1 egg, well beaten
¼ cup finely chopped fresh spinach
1 tablespoon finely chopped unblanched almonds
¼ clove garlic, minced
⅛ teaspoon salt
Few grains black pepper

1. Mix all ingredients thoroughly in a bowl.
2. Meanwhile, heat a griddle or heavy skillet until moderately hot.
3. Lightly butter the griddle. Spoon the batter onto it, spreading to make a round about 7 inches in diameter. Bake until lightly browned, about 3 minutes; turn and brown second side.
4. Using hors d'oeuvre cutters (½ inch in diameter), cut out shapes from the griddlecake. Serve a spoonful in each serving of **soup.**

242 Specialty Soup (Zuppa Specialita)

6 cups canned chicken broth
2 tablespoons minced parsley
2 tablespoons flour
3 eggs, well beaten
3 tablespoons shredded Parmesan
  cheese

1. Heat broth to boiling in a large saucepan.
2. Meanwhile, add parsley and flour to beaten eggs; stir in cheese and blend thoroughly.
3. Gradually add the egg mixture to boiling broth; while stirring with a fork. Cook over low heat several minutes, or until egg mixture is set.

About 6 servings

243 Tortilla Soup

This is a light soup, good for a first course at dinner, and is one use for stale tortillas.

2 quarts chicken or beef stock,
  canned consommé, or water
  plus bouillon cubes
½ cup chopped onion
1 cup canned tomato sauce or
  purée
1 teaspoon salt
¼ teaspoon pepper
6 to 8 stale tortillas
  Oil for frying
1½ cups shredded Monterey Jack or
  mild Cheddar cheese
  (optional)

1. Heat stock with onion to boiling. Reduce heat and simmer about 5 minutes. Stir in tomato sauce, salt, and pepper; simmer about 5 minutes.
2. Meanwhile, cut tortillas into ½-inch strips and fry in hot oil until crisp; drain on absorbent paper.
3. To serve soup, place a handful of crisp tortilla strips in soup bowl and ladle soup on top. Sprinkle with cheese, if desired.

About 2 quarts soup

244 Pozole

This hearty soup comes from Guadalajara, capital of the Mexican state of Jalisco. The everyday variety calls for pork head as the only meat. This richer version uses pork hocks and loin as well as chicken, and obviously is a meal in itself. Pozole is always served with a variety of crisp vegetable garnishes which are sprinkled on top of the hot soup at the diner's discretion.

2 pork hocks, split in two or three
  pieces each
1 large onion, sliced
2 cloves garlic, minced
  Water
1 stewing chicken, cut in serving
  pieces
1 pound pork loin, boneless, cut in
  1-inch chunks
2 cups canned hominy or canned
  garbanzos
1 tablespoon salt
½ teaspoon pepper
1 cup sliced crisp radishes
1 cup shredded cabbage
1 cup shredded lettuce
½ cup chopped green onions
  Lime or lemon wedges

1. Put split pork hocks, onion, and garlic into a kettle, cover with water, and cook until almost tender (about 3 hours).
2. Add chicken and pork loin and cook 45 minutes, or until chicken is almost tender.
3. Add hominy, salt, and pepper. Cook about 15 minutes, or until all meat is tender.
4. Remove pork hocks and chicken from soup. Remove meat from bones and return meat to soup.
5. Serve in large soup bowls. Accompany with a relish tray offering the radishes, cabbage, lettuce, green onions, and lime or lemon wedges as garnishes.

8 to 10 servings

245 *Fish Soup*

1 head and bones from large fish,
    such as red snapper
1 bay leaf
1 onion, coarsely chopped
2 stalks celery
1½ quarts water
2 cups (16-ounce can) tomatoes
    with juice
1 cup sliced carrots
1 cup diced pared potatoes
1 or 2 diced jalapeño chilies
1 cup dry sherry
1 pound diced, boneless fillets of
    white fish, or deveined
    shrimp
½ teaspoon garlic salt
½ teaspoon marjoram
    Salt and pepper

1. Put fish head and bones into a kettle with bay leaf, onion, celery, and water. Boil 15 minutes. Remove from heat and strain liquid, returning it to kettle. Discard solids.
2. Add tomatoes, carrots, potatoes, and chilies to liquid in kettle. Simmer until carrots and potatoes are almost tender (about 15 minutes).
3. Add sherry, diced fish, garlic salt, marjoram, and salt and pepper to taste to kettle. Cook about 5 minutes, or until fish flakes easily with fork.

2½ to 3 quarts soup

246 *Soup Mexicana*

1 chicken breast
1½ quarts chicken broth
2 onions, chopped
1 tablespoon butter or margarine
1½ teaspoons grated onion
2 cups chopped zucchini
1 cup drained canned whole
    kernel corn
⅓ cup tomato purée
2 ounces cream cheese, cut in
    small cubes
2 avocados, sliced

1. Combine chicken breast, broth, and onion in a large saucepan. Cover, bring to boiling, reduce heat, and cook 30 minutes, or until chicken is tender.
2. Remove chicken; dice and set aside. Reserve broth.
3. Heat butter and grated onion in a large saucepan; stir in zucchini and corn. Cook about 5 minutes, stirring occasionally. Mix in broth and tomato purée. Cover and simmer about 20 minutes.
4. Just before serving, mix in diced chicken, cream cheese, and avocado slices.

6 to 8 servings

Note: Any remaining soup may be stored, covered, in refrigerator.

247 *Avocado Soup*

4 fully ripe avocados, peeled and
    pitted
3 cups cold chicken broth
2 teaspoons lime juice
½ teaspoon salt
⅛ teaspoon garlic powder
2 cups chilled cream

1. Put all ingredients except cream into an electric blender container. Cover and blend until smooth. Mix with the cream and chill thoroughly.
2. Serve with **lemon slices** or garnish as desired.

6 servings

248 *Corn Soup I*

½ cup finely chopped onion
2 tablespoons butter
1 quart beef stock or canned beef
   broth
2½ cups cooked whole kernel
   golden corn
3 tomatoes, peeled, halved, and
   seeded
Salt and pepper
1 cup whipping cream
Dairy sour cream

1. Cook onion in butter in a saucepan until onion is soft.
2. Put onion and a small amount of stock into an electric blender. Add 2 cups corn and tomato halves; blend until smooth.
3. Turn purée into saucepan and mix in remaining stock. Season to taste with salt and pepper. Bring to boiling, reduce heat, and cook 5 minutes. Add cream gradually, stirring constantly. Heat thoroughly, but do not boil.
4. Garnish soup with dollops of sour cream and remaining corn.

6 to 8 servings

249 *Corn Soup II*

2 tablespoons butter or margarine
½ cup chopped onion
2 cups (17-ounce can) cream-style
   corn
1 cup canned tomato sauce
3 cups chicken stock, canned
   chicken broth, or 3 cups water
   plus 3 chicken bouillon cubes
1 cup cream
Salt and pepper

1. Melt butter in a large saucepan. Add onion and cook until soft. Add corn, tomato sauce, and stock. Bring to boiling, reduce heat, and simmer about 10 minutes to blend flavors, stirring frequently.
2. Remove from heat and stir in cream. Season to taste with salt and pepper. Serve hot.

6 to 8 servings

250 *Bean Soup*

● 2 cups cooked Basic Mexican Beans
   or canned kidney
   beans with liquid
1 cup beef stock, canned beef
   broth, or 1 cup water plus 1
   beef bouillon cube
1 cup cooked tomatoes with liquid
1 clove garlic, minced
½ teaspoon oregano
½ teaspoon chili powder
Salt and pepper

1. Put beans into a large saucepan. Mash with a potato masher, leaving some large pieces. Add meat stock, tomatoes, garlic, oregano, and chili powder. Bring to boiling, reduce heat, and simmer about 10 minutes, stirring frequently.
2. Add salt and pepper to taste. Serve hot.

About 1 quart soup

251 *Black Bean Soup*

1 pound dried black beans, washed
2 quarts boiling water
2 tablespoons salt
5 cloves garlic
1½ teaspoons cumin (comino)
1½ teaspoons oregano
2 tablespoons white vinegar
10 tablespoons olive oil
½ pound onions, peeled and chopped
½ pound green peppers, trimmed and chopped

1. Put beans into a large, heavy saucepot or Dutch oven and add boiling water; boil rapidly 2 minutes. Cover tightly, remove from heat, and set aside 1 hour. Add salt to beans and liquid; bring to boiling and simmer, covered, until beans are soft, about 2 hours.
2. Put the garlic, cumin, oregano, and vinegar into a mortar and crush to a paste.
3. Heat olive oil in a large skillet. Mix in onion and green pepper and fry until onion is browned, stirring occasionally. Thoroughly blend in the paste, then stir the skillet mixture into the beans. Cook over low heat until ready to serve.
4. Meanwhile, mix a small portion of **cooked rice, minced onion, olive oil,** and **vinegar** in a bowl; set aside to marinate. Add a soup spoon of rice mixture to each serving of soup.

About 2 quarts soup

252 *Gazpacho*

Gazpacho is a refreshing cold soup made with fresh, raw vegetables. It is so filled with vegetable chunks that it seems almost like a salad. Serve it very well chilled, and keep bowls over ice, or place an ice cube in each bowl just as it is served.

1 clove garlic
2 cups chopped peeled fresh tomatoes
1 large cucumber, pared and chopped
½ cup diced green pepper
½ cup chopped onion
1 cup tomato juice
3 tablespoons olive oil
2 tablespoons vinegar
Salt and pepper
Dash Tabasco
½ cup crisp croutons

1. Cut garlic in half and rub onto bottom and sides of a large bowl. Add tomatoes, cucumber, green pepper, onion, tomato juice, olive oil, and vinegar to bowl and stir until evenly mixed. Season to taste with salt, pepper, and Tabasco.
2. Chill in refrigerator at least 1 hour before serving.
3. Serve soup in chilled bowls. Top each serving with a few croutons.

8 to 10 servings

253 *Avocado Yogurt Soup*

Here is another cold soup, very different from Gazpacho, and perfect as a warm-weather meal appetizer.

1 cup avocado pulp (2 to 3 avocados, depending on size)
⅔ cup unsweetened yogurt
⅔ cup beef stock, or bouillon made with ⅔ cup water and 1 bouillon cube, then chilled
1 tablespoon lemon juice
1 teaspoon onion juice or grated onion
½ teaspoon salt
Dash Tabasco

1. Put avocado pulp and yogurt into an electric blender and blend until evenly mixed. Adding gradually, blend in beef stock, lemon juice, onion juice, salt, and Tabasco. Chill well.
2. Serve soup in chilled bowls.

4 to 6 servings

Fruit Bread, Milan Style, page 112

254 Cream-Style Gazpacho with Avocado

4 hard-cooked eggs
¼ cup oil
1 tablespoon prepared mustard
1 tablespoon Worcestershire sauce
¼ cup lemon juice
1 teaspoon garlic salt
¼ teaspoon pepper
5 fresh medium tomatoes
1 large cucumber
1 medium onion
1 ripe avocado
1 cup dairy sour cream

1. Peel eggs; slice in half and remove yolks; set whites aside. Put egg yolks into a small bowl and mash with fork; blend in oil until of paste consistency. Blend in mustard, Worcestershire sauce, lemon juice, garlic salt, and pepper. Set aside.
2. Peel tomatoes; set aside one for garnish; coarsely chop remaining 4 and put into an electric blender. Pare and seed cucumber. Set aside ¼ as garnish; chop remaining ¾ and place in blender with tomatoes. Peel, coarsely chop, and add onion to blender. Peel avocado and place half in blender with vegetables. Reserve remaining half for garnish. Blend contents of blender until smooth. Add egg yolk mixture and blend until thoroughly mixed. Add sour cream gradually, blending well.
3. Pour soup into container with cover.
4. Chop remaining tomato, cucumber, and hard-cooked egg whites and add to soup. Slice remaining avocado half thinly and add to soup. Stir in lightly. Cover and refrigerate until well chilled.

About 6 servings

255 Breadfruit Soup Guadeloupe

1 breadfruit (about 1½ pounds)*
2 bacon slices, fried and crumbled
● 4 cups Coconut Milk
2 tablespoons soft butter (optional)

1. Bake breadfruit at 350°F 45 minutes. Open it and remove the center; peel and dice the meat. Put breadfruit, bacon, and Coconut Milk in a bowl. Purée a little at a time in an electric blender or in a food mill, adding butter if necessary. Heat.
2. Serve in bouillon cups and garnish with **toasted grated coconut.**

*Breadfruit can now be found in many supermarkets and most Puerto Rican markets.

256 Chili con Carne

Chili con Carne is not, strictly speaking, an authentic Mexican soup. However, it is so associated with Mexican food in the minds of most North Americans, and besides, is so delicious, that a recipe is included here.

1½ pounds ground beef
1 large onion, chopped
1 clove garlic, minced
4 cups (two 16-ounce cans) cooked tomatoes
2 cups (one 15-ounce can) red kidney beans
1 tablespoon chili powder
2 teaspoons salt
¼ teaspoon pepper

1. Cook ground beef in a large skillet, stirring until crumbled into small pieces and well browned.
2. Add onion and garlic to meat; cook about 5 minutes, stirring frequently.
3. Add tomatoes to skillet and chop into bite-size chunks. Stir in kidney beans, chili powder, salt, and pepper. Reduce heat to simmering and cook, stirring occasionally, about 30 minutes.

6 to 8 servings

Island Bread, page 107
Yogurt, page 36
Drop Doughnuts, page 106

257 Quick Tomato-Fish Stew

3 tablespoons oil
½ cup chopped onion
1 clove garlic, minced
2 cups canned tomatoes with juice
 (16-ounce can)
2 cups cooked garbanzos, drained
 (16-ounce can)
½ pound boned white fish, flaked
 Salt and pepper

1. Heat oil in a kettle. Add onion and garlic and cook until soft (about 5 minutes). Add tomatoes and garbanzos and bring to boiling. Add flaked fish, reduce heat, and cook about 15 minutes longer. Season to taste with salt and pepper.
2. Serve with **pickled hot chilies.**

6 to 8 servings

258 Spinach-Ball Soup

Here is another example of the Mexican way with unusual soups. The little deep-fried spinach-wrapped balls give the soup its name. They're so delicious by themselves that you might like to serve them as a hot appetizer.

Spinach Balls:
2 pounds fresh spinach
½ cup cooked cubed ham
½ cup cubed Cheddar cheese
3 eggs, separated
1 tablespoon flour
 Dash salt
 Oil for deep frying
Soup:
2 tablespoons oil
½ cup chopped onion
1 clove garlic, minced
1 can (6 ounces) tomato paste
3 cups chicken or meat stock or
 canned bouillon
 Salt and pepper

1. For spinach balls, wash spinach well and remove hard stalks. Steam until tender, in a small amount of boiling salted water in a large saucepot. Drain. Cool slightly and form into balls about 1¼ inches in diameter. Push a piece of ham or cheese into center of each ball.
2. Beat egg whites until stiff; gradually beat in yolks, flour, and salt. Coat spinach balls with egg batter and fry one layer of balls at a time in hot oil until lightly browned.
3. Meanwhile, prepare soup. Heat 2 tablespoons oil in a large kettle. Add onion and garlic and cook until soft (about 5 minutes). Stir in tomato paste and stock. Heat to boiling, reduce heat, and simmer gently about 15 minutes. Season to taste with salt and pepper.
4. Serve the spinach balls in the soup.

4 to 6 servings

259 Green Rice

1 cup (1 small can) salsa verde
 mexicana (Mexican green
 tomato sauce)
1 cup (lightly packed) fresh parsley
1 clove garlic
2 tablespoons vegetable oil
2 cups beef or chicken stock, or 2
 cups water plus 2 bouillon
 cubes
 Salt and pepper
1 cup uncooked rice

1. Put salsa verde, parsley, and garlic in an electric blender and blend until liquefied.
2. Heat oil in a large saucepan. Add blended sauce and mix well; cook about 5 minutes.
3. Add stock to saucepan and bring to boiling, stirring to blend ingredients. Season to taste with salt and pepper. Add rice, stir, cover tightly, and cook until all liquid is absorbed (about 25 minutes).

6 servings

260 *Tortilla-Ball Soup*

8 large stale tortillas
1 cup milk
1 small onion, coarsely chopped
1 clove garlic, minced
¼ cup grated Parmesan cheese
1 whole egg plus 1 egg yolk,
  beaten
½ teaspoon salt
⅛ teaspoon pepper
  Lard or oil for frying
● 2 quarts meat stock, or
  2 quarts canned
    beef broth (3 cans condensed
    beef broth plus equal amount
    water)
1 cup canned tomato sauce

1. Tear tortillas into pieces and soak in milk until soft. Place in an electric blender with onion and garlic and blend until puréed. Turn purée into a bowl. Beat in cheese, whole egg and egg yolk, salt, and pepper. Shape into small balls.
2. Fry in hot lard until lightly browned.
3. Meanwhile, heat meat stock and tomato sauce together in a large kettle. When bubbling, add tortilla balls. Serve at once.

6 to 8 servings

261 *Baked Noodles with Chorizo*

¼ pound chorizo sausage (see
● Chorizo Filling, or
  use bulk pork sausage
2 to 4 tablespoons lard or oil
1 package (7 ounces) fine noodles
¼ cup chopped onion
2 cups beef or chicken stock, or
  water plus bouillon cubes
1 cup cottage cheese
1 cup dairy sour cream
  Dash Tabasco (if bulk pork
    sausage used)
  Salt and pepper
  Grated Parmesan cheese

1. Fry chorizo in a large skillet with heat-resistant handle until cooked through, crumbling and stirring as it cooks.
2. Remove meat from skillet and set aside. Add lard or oil to skillet to make about 1¼-inch layer in bottom. Stir in uncooked noodles and onion and fry until noodles are lightly browned and onion is soft, stirring often to prevent burning.
3. Return cooked chorizo to skillet. Stir in stock.
4. Bake at 350°F about 15 minutes, or until all liquid is absorbed by noodles.
5. Remove skillet from oven. Stir in cottage cheese and sour cream. Season to taste with Tabasco, if using, and salt and pepper to taste. Sprinkle with Parmesan cheese. Return to oven and bake about 10 minutes, or until bubbling hot.

6 servings

262 Dry Soup of Tortillas with Tomatoes and Cheese

½ cup oil
1 cup chopped onion
1 clove garlic, minced
2 cups (16-ounce can) cooked
    tomatoes with juice, slightly
    chopped
1 teaspoon salt
¼ teaspoon pepper
½ teaspoon oregano
10 to 12 stale tortillas, cut in
    ½-inch strips
1 cup whipping cream
1 cup (about ¼ pound) grated
    Parmesan cheese
    Paprika

1. Heat 2 tablespoons oil in a heavy saucepan. Cook onion and garlic in hot oil until onion is soft (about 5 minutes). Add tomatoes, salt, pepper, and oregano and stir until blended. Heat to simmering and cook about 10 minutes to blend flavors.
2. Meanwhile, heat remaining oil in a heavy skillet. Fry tortilla strips in hot oil until limp, not crisp; drain on paper towels.
3. In an ovenproof casserole arrange layers as follows: a little tomato sauce, a handful of tortilla strips, some cream, then cheese. Repeat until all ingredients are used, ending with cheese. Sprinkle with paprika.
4. Bake at 350°F about 20 minutes, or until bubbling hot.

6 servings

263 Bouillon Cocq

This soup is traditionally served on Christmas Eve when the family and guests return from midnight mass.

1 meaty smoked ham hock
1 capon (7 to 8 pounds)
½ lime
½ orange
2 tablespoons bacon drippings
1 tablespoon butter
1 tablespoon peanut oil
3 quarts water
    Bouquet garni
1 pound cabbage, cut in chunks
4 small potatoes, pared and
    cut in chunks
2 carrots, pared and cut in chunks
2 white turnips, pared and
    cut in chunks
2 onions studded with
    8 whole cloves
2 celery stalks, cut in pieces
2 leeks, washed and cut in chunks
    Salt, pepper, and cayenne or red
    pepper to taste
● Caribbean Rice

1. Soak ham hock in cold water to remove excess salt. Drain.
2. Truss capon as for roasting. Rub skin with cut side of lime half, then cut side of orange half. Let stand to drain.
3. Heat bacon drippings, butter, and peanut oil in a deep soup kettle. Brown capon. Add ham hock, water, and bouquet garni; bring to a boil, reduce heat, and simmer 30 minutes, skimming twice.
4. Add vegetables and seasonings, bring to a boil, skim, then cook over low heat 30 minutes, or until vegetables and meats are tender.
5. Put the capon on a large platter and surround with drained vegetables and rice. Drink the broth from cups.

264 *Consommé with Oxtails*

3 tablespoons olive oil
1 medium oxtail (about 4 pounds)
8 large tomatoes, peeled and seeded
2 medium onions
2 quarts beef broth
    Freshly ground pepper
    Coarse salt
1 large garlic clove, crushed in a
    garlic press
    Sprig fresh basil or ⅛ teaspoon
    dried basil
1 cup sliced carrot
1 cup fresh peas
4 plantains, boiled

1. Heat oil in a soup kettle. Add oxtail and cook until well browned.
2. Mince tomatoes and onions together. Add to meat in kettle, reduce heat, and simmer 3 minutes. Add broth and seasonings. Cook uncovered 1½ hours, then add carrot and peas; continue to cook until meat easily comes from the bones.
3. Serve consommé with a piece of meat and a plantain half in each soup plate.

8 servings

265 *Congo Soup* *(Gros Bouillon Habitant)*

3 tablespoons lard
3 pounds beef shin bones
1 pound lean beef for soup
    Marrow bone
3 quarts water
2 tablespoons coarse salt
1 teaspoon ground pepper
8 dried Italian pepper pods or
    1 green hot pepper, pricked
3 carrots, pared and cubed
3 leeks, washed and cubed
3 parsnips, pared and cubed
3 plantains, peeled and cubed
12 shallots, halved
4 cups cubed pumpkin
1 pound cabbage, cut in chunks
1 pound malanga root or rutabaga,
    peeled and cubed
    Handful spinach or sorrel leaves
2 tablespoons tomato purée
¾ cup cooked rice

1. Heat lard in a large soup kettle. Add shin bones, soup beef, and marrow bone and brown to a rich golden color. Add water and bring to a boil. Add salt, ground pepper, and pepper pods. Simmer covered 45 minutes, skimming soup twice.
2. Add remaining ingredients except spinach, tomato purée, and rice; simmer covered 40 minutes, or until vegetables are tender.
3. Remove bones and meat. Slice marrow and cube the meat; reserve.
4. Press vegetables against side of kettle with the back of a large wooden spoon. Add spinach and cook 5 minutes, then stir in tomato purée.
5. Spoon 1 tablespoon cooked rice in center of each soup plate and pour in soup.

12 servings

266 *Pumpkin Bread Soup* *(Panade of Pumpkin)*

4 garlic cloves
1 green hot pepper or
    6 dried Italian pepper pods
4 cups beef broth
4 slices white bread
2 tablespoons peanut oil
1¼ cups minced onion
1 can (16 ounces) pumpkin or
    1 pound pared and cubed
    fresh pumpkin (see Note)
¼ pound spinach leaves

1. Put garlic and hot pepper into a mortar and pound to a paste. Set aside.
2. Pour beef broth over bread; set aside.
3. Heat peanut oil in a large saucepan; sauté onion. Add bread with beef broth, pumpkin, and seasoning paste; mix well. Simmer 10 minutes.
4. Add spinach; bring to boiling, reduce heat, and cook 5 minutes.

About 1½ quarts

Note: If fresh pumpkin is used, process the soup in an electric blender before adding the spinach.

267 *Purée of Malanga Soup*

3 tablespoons peanut oil
1 bunch scallions or green onions, minced
3 pounds malanga root, peeled and diced
2 quarts rich stock
Salt, black pepper, and cayenne or red pepper to taste
⅛ teaspoon nutmeg
1 garlic clove, crushed in a garlic press
Bouquet garni
Few celery leaves
Fresh basil sprig

1. Heat peanut oil in a soup kettle. Add minced scallions and cook until translucent but not brown. Add malanga root, stock, and seasonings and cook until malanga root is tender.
2. Purée through a food mill or in an electric blender.
3. Serve with **toasted white bread**.

About 12 servings

268 *Creamy Fresh Tomato Soup*

2 shallots
1 tablespoon coarse salt
1 large garlic clove
8 peppercorns
8 large tomatoes, peeled, seeded, and quartered
2 quarts beef broth or rich stock
1 small beet, pared
1 cup uncooked rice
1 cup whipping cream
½ cup chopped mixed parsley and chives

1. In a mortar, pound shallots, salt, garlic, and peppercorns to a paste.
2. Put tomato quarters into a soup kettle and add broth, seasoning paste, and beet. Cook 12 minutes, then add rice, bring to a boil, reduce heat, and cook 30 minutes.
3. Purée tomato-rice mixture in an electric blender or force through a food mill. Return to kettle, bring to a boil, and stir in cream.
4. Serve in soup cups and sprinkle with parsley and chive mixture.

269 *Cream of Turnip Soup*

¼ cup peanut oil
½ cup minced onion
6 medium white turnips, pared and quartered
1½ quarts chicken broth
Marrow bone
Bouquet garni
Salt and pepper to taste
3 dried Italian pepper pods or 1 whole pink hot pepper
1 cup whipping cream

1. Heat oil in a soup kettle. Add onion and cook over low heat until translucent but not brown, stirring constantly. Add turnips, broth, marrow bone, and seasonings; bring to a boil, reduce heat, and cook 30 minutes. Remove marrow bone and pepper pods. Slice bone marrow thinly and set aside.
2. Purée turnip mixture in an electric blender or force through a food mill. Return to kettle, add cream, and stir to blend. Bring to boiling point.
3. Serve garnished with **avocado cubes**, **red sweet pepper strips**, and reserved bone-marrow slices.

Note: This soup can also be served iced, but then omit the bone marrow which will congeal and be unappetizing.

270 Head Soup

1 veal, pork, or lamb head
2 limes, halved
¼ pound salt pork
6 dried Italian pepper pods or
    1 green hot pepper
2 garlic cloves
5 parsley sprigs
1½ to 2 quarts chicken broth or stock
4 tomatoes, peeled, seeded, and
    quartered
3 carrots, pared and cut in chunks
2 onions, cut in chunks
2 leeks, washed and cut in chunks
2 plantains or green bananas, peeled
    and cut in chunks
2 purple yams, pared and cut
    in chunks
1 parsnip, pared and cut in chunks
2 cups cubed pared pumpkin
½ cup corn kernels
½ pound lima beans
¼ pound cabbage, cut in chunks
    Bouquet garni
    Pepper to taste
● Caribbean Rice

1. Have your meat man trim the head and prepare it with the tongue separated. Rub the head with cut sides of lime halves, squeezing gently and going into all cavities.
2. Render the salt pork in a small skillet over low heat.
3. Meanwhile, in a mortar pound the pepper pods, garlic, and parsley to a paste.
4. Pour the fat from the salt pork into a large soup kettle, add the head, tongue, and seasoning paste (no salt is needed). Pour in enough broth to cover, bring to a boil, skim twice, reduce heat, and simmer 1 hour.
5. Add vegetables and seasonings; bring to a boil and simmer until vegetables are tender and meat comes from the bones. Remove the bones and meat. Cut meat into pieces.
6. Crush the vegetables against side of kettle with a spatula, potato masher, or large wooden spoon.
7. Serve in soup plates with a generous portion of meat and a small mound of rice in each.

271 Velouté Martinique

1 cup crab meat from boiled crab
1 cup fish broth from a fish head or
    boiled crab
2 chicken breasts
2 tablespoons olive oil
1 cup water
    Bouquet garni
3 dried Italian pepper pods
● 1 cup Coconut Milk

1. Have crab meat and broth ready.
2. Sauté chicken breasts in oil until golden. Add water, bouquet garni, and pepper pods; cover and simmer until chicken is tender. Remove chicken and reserve liquid.
3. Cut the chicken into small pieces; add crab meat, reserved liquid, fish broth, and Coconut Milk. Purée, a little at a time, in an electric blender.
4. Serve hot in soup cups and garnish with **grated coconut**.

272 Pickled Oyster Stew

1 cup milk
1 jar pickled oysters, drained
¼ cup peanut oil
½ pound onions, minced
    Salt and freshly ground pepper
    to taste
1½ quarts stock
2 egg yolks
1 cup whipping cream

1. Pour milk over oysters and let stand 2 hours.
2. Meanwhile, heat oil in a soup kettle. Add onion and cook slowly until translucent but not brown. Season with salt and pepper and add stock; cook 30 minutes.
3. Beat egg yolks with cream and set aside.
4. Drain oysters, rinse with water, and pat dry on absorbent paper. Add to the stock and bring to a boil. Immediately stir in cream-egg mixture and remove from heat.
5. Serve from a tureen and sprinkle each serving with **freshly ground pepper** and **cayenne** or **ground red pepper**.

273 *Fisherman's Soup* *(Bouillon Pecheur)*

1 pound each halibut, whiting, sea
    trout, and red snapper
Juice of 1 lime (reserve halves)
Juice of 1 orange
Salt and pepper to taste
1 pound shrimp
8 small crabs
1 small lobster
1 pound conches removed from
    shells
Meat tenderizer
4 garlic cloves
5 parsley sprigs
5 scallions or green onions,
    cut in pieces
8 dried Italian pepper pods or
    1 pink hot pepper
1 tablespoon coarse salt
¼ cup peanut oil
12 shallots
8 small potatoes, pared and cut
    in chunks
4 onions, sliced
3 carrots, pared and cut in chunks
3 plantains, peeled and cut in chunks
1 chayote, cut in chunks
1 leek, washed and cut in chunks
1 parsnip, pared and cut in chunks
1 yam, pared and cut in chunks
1 pound pumpkin meat, cut
    in chunks
½ pound malanga root, peeled and
    cut in chunks (optional)
3 quarts water
1 cup amber rum
12 slices white bread with crusts
    removed, fried

1. Cut fish into serving pieces and put into a shallow dish. Season with lime juice, orange juice, salt, and pepper; let stand 30 minutes.
2. Shell and devein shrimp; rub crabs and lobster with pieces of lime. Set aside.
3. Rinse shelled conches in many waters. Sprinkle them with meat tenderizer and beat them with a meat hammer to make them soft. Cut into strips. Set aside.
4. In a mortar, pound to a paste the garlic, parsley, scallions, pepper pods, and salt.
5. Heat oil in a large soup kettle. Sauté onion, adding the seasoning paste, until mixture is golden but not brown. Add conch strips, vegetables, water, and rum; bring to a boil, then reduce heat and simmer 30 minutes. Add lobster and crabs; cook 10 minutes. Add fish and cook 10 minutes, then add shrimp and cook 5 minutes.
6. With a wooden spoon or potato masher, press some of the vegetables against side of kettle. Remove lobster and cut into serving pieces.
7. Put fried bread into deep soup plates and add the soup.

12 servings

274 *Snapper Chowder à l'Ancienne*

4 pounds red snapper fillets
Juice of 1 lime
Salt, freshly ground pepper, and
    cayenne or red pepper to taste
8 tomatoes, peeled and seeded
5 scallions or green onions
2 tablespoons soybean or peanut oil
● Court Bouillon for Fish and
    Shellfish
2 cups potato balls
1 cup diced carrot
1 cup diced turnip
8 bread slices, fried

1. Drizzle fish with lime juice and season with salt and peppers. Set aside.
2. Chop tomatoes and scallions together finely.
3. Heat oil in a large saucepan, add tomato-scallion mixture, and cook slowly until mixture is like a liquid paste. Add bouillon and bring to a boil. Add vegetables and cook 20 minutes.
4. Cut fish into small portions, add to saucepan mixture, and simmer 7 minutes, or until fish flakes.
5. To serve, spoon chowder over fried bread in soup plates.

8 servings

Breads

275 *Greek Easter Bread* (Lambropsomo)

2 packages active dry yeast
½ cup warm water
½ cup milk, scalded and cooled
1 cup unsalted butter, melted
    and cooled to lukewarm
4 eggs, slightly beaten
1 egg yolk
¾ cup sugar
1 tablespoon anise seed, crushed
1 teaspoon salt
7 cups all-purpose flour
1 egg white, slightly beaten
¼ cup sesame seed

1. Blend yeast with warm water in a large bowl and stir until dissolved. Add milk, butter, eggs, egg yolk, sugar, anise seed, and salt; blend thoroughly. Add flour gradually, beating until smooth.
2. Turn dough onto a lightly floured board and knead for 10 minutes, or until dough is smooth and elastic.
3. Place dough in a lightly oiled large bowl, turning dough to coat surface. Cover and let rise in a warm place for about 2 hours, or until double in bulk. Test by inserting a finger about ½ inch into dough. If indentation remains, the dough is ready to shape.
4. Punch dough down. Knead on unfloured board to make a smooth ball. Cut off four pieces, each the size of a large egg. Place remaining dough in a greased round pan, 10 inches in diameter and 2 inches high. Shape small pieces into twists about 4½ inches long. Arrange the twists from the center of the dough so they radiate out to the edge. Brush the loaf lightly with beaten egg white. Sprinkle with sesame seed. Cover loaf lightly and set in a warm place until double in bulk (about 1½ hours).
5. Bake at 375°F for 30 minutes, or until a wooden pick inserted in center of loaf comes out clean. Transfer to wire rack to cool.

1 large loaf

Note: For Easter, place a red egg in center of the dough in pan. Shape small pieces of dough into loops and place a red egg in the center of each.

New Year's Day Bread (Vasilopita): Follow recipe for Greek Easter Bread; substitute **grated peel of 1 large orange** for the anise seed. Wrap a coin in foil and knead into the dough. Proceed as directed.

276 *Drop Doughnuts* (Svingi)

4 eggs
1 cup buttermilk
2 teaspoons vanilla extract
1 teaspoon grated lemon or
    orange peel (optional)
3 cups all-purpose flour
1½ teaspoons baking powder
Cooking oil for deep frying
Honey
Cinnamon

1. Beat eggs; stir in buttermilk, vanilla extract, and grated peel. Combine flour and baking powder. Stir into the egg mixture. Cover with a cloth. Let stand at room temperature for 1 hour.
2. In a deep fryer, heat oil to 375°F. Drop batter by the tablespoon. Cook 4 minutes, or until doughnuts are golden brown. Drain on paper towels. Drizzle with honey and sprinkle with cinnamon. Serve hot.

About 30 doughnuts

Note: Batter keeps well in the refrigerator. Bring to room temperature before cooking.

277 *Christmas Bread* (*Christopsomo*)

2 envelopes active dry yeast
2 cups scalded milk, cooled to 105° to 115°F
1 cup sugar
1 teaspoon salt
4 eggs (or 8 yolks), well beaten
½ cup unsalted butter, melted
7½ to 8 cups all-purpose flour
1½ teaspoons cardamom, pounded, or 1 teaspoon mastic
½ cup dried golden currants
¾ cup chopped walnuts
2 egg whites, beaten
3 to 4 tablespoons sugar

1. Sprinkle yeast over 1 cup warm milk in a small bowl; stir until dissolved. Set aside.
2. Reserve 2 teaspoons sugar for pounding with mastic, if using. Put sugar into a bowl and add salt, eggs, remaining 1 cup milk, and butter; mix well.
3. Put 7 cups flour into a large bowl. Stir in cardamom, or pound mastic with 2 teaspoons sugar (so it will not become gummy) and add. Make a well and add dissolved yeast, egg mixture, currants, and nuts; mix well.
4. Knead dough on a floured board, adding the remaining 1 cup flour as required. Knead dough until smooth (5 to 6 minutes).
5. Place dough in a greased bowl. Turn until surface is completely greased. Cover. Set in a warm place until double in bulk.
6. Punch dough down. Form into two round loaves and place in buttered 10-inch pans.
7. Cover and let rise again in a warm place until double in bulk.
8. Bake at 375°F 15 minutes. Remove from oven and brush with beaten egg whites, then sprinkle with sugar. Return to oven. Turn oven control to 325°F and bake about 35 to 40 minutes, or until bread is done.

2 loaves

278 *Island Bread*

2 packages active dry yeast
1½ cups warm water (105° to 115°F)
¼ cup packed dark brown sugar
2 tablespoons honey
3 cups whole wheat flour
¼ cup olive oil
2 tablespoons grated orange peel
1 tablespoon grated lemon peel
2½ teaspoons salt
1 teaspoon anise seed, crushed
2 cups all-purpose flour

1. Dissolve yeast in warm water; stir in brown sugar, honey, and whole wheat flour. Beat with a wooden spoon until smooth. Cover and let rise in a warm place until almost double in bulk (about 2 hours).
2. Stir in oil, orange and lemon peels, salt, and anise seed. Gradually add 1¾ cups all-purpose flour, beating vigorously. Cover for 10 minutes.
3. Sprinkle remaining ¼ cup flour on a board and work it in. Put dough on board, cover, and let rise until double in bulk. Shape into a round loaf; put onto a well-greased cookie sheet.
4. Let rise until dough is double in bulk.
5. Bake at 375°F 45 minutes. Turn out of pan immediately and cool on a rack.

1 loaf

279 *Sourdough Greek Bread*

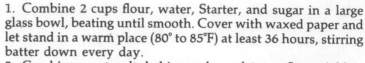

5 to 5½ cups all-purpose flour
2 cups warm water (105° to 115°F)
½ cup Starter
3 tablespoons sugar
1 package active dry yeast
2 teaspoons salt
1½ teaspoons baking soda

1. Combine 2 cups flour, water, Starter, and sugar in a large glass bowl, beating until smooth. Cover with waxed paper and let stand in a warm place (80° to 85°F) at least 36 hours, stirring batter down every day.
2. Combine yeast, salt, baking soda, and 1 cup flour. Add to starter mixture and stir until well blended. Stir in the remaining flour, using enough to make a moderately stiff dough. Turn onto lightly floured surface and knead until smooth and satiny (10 to 15 minutes).
3. Put into a large deep bowl and cover with plastic wrap or aluminum foil. Let rise in a warm place until double in bulk (about 2 hours).
4. Divide dough in half, shape into balls, and place in 2 greased 2-quart round baking dishes. Make a crisscross with a sharp knife on the top of each ball of dough. Cover and let rise in a warm place until double in bulk.
5. Brush loaves with water and place a shallow pan of boiling water on bottom rack of the oven.
6. Bake at 400°F 45 minutes, or until loaves test done. Brush loaves with water twice during baking. Remove from baking dishes immediately; cool.

2 round loaves

280 *Starter*

1 package active dry yeast
2 cups warm water
2 cups all-purpose flour

1. Combine yeast, water, and flour in a large glass bowl, mixing until well blended. Let stand uncovered in a warm place for 48 hours, stirring occasionally. Stir well before use.
2. Measure out required amount and replenish remaining starter by mixing in equal parts of flour and water. If ½ cup starter is removed, mix in ¼ cup water and ¼ cup flour to replace. Let starter stand until it bubbles again before covering loosely and refrigerating. Use and replenish every two weeks.

281 *Corn Bread* (Bobota)

2 eggs
2 cups buttermilk
3 tablespoons shortening, melted
1½ teaspoons salt
2½ cups cornmeal
1 teaspoon baking powder
½ teaspoon baking soda

1. Beat eggs until light. Add buttermilk and melted shortening; mix well.
2. Mix dry ingredients together. Add to egg mixture; beat until smooth. Pour into a greased 9-inch square baking pan.
3. Bake at 425°F about 25 minutes. Serve hot.

About 16 pieces

282 *Whole Wheat Bread*

¼ cup warm water (105°F for dry yeast, 95°F for compressed yeast)
1 package yeast, active dry or compressed
1½ cups scalded milk, cooled to 105° or 95°F
½ cup honey
2 tablespoons olive oil
2 tablespoons salt
6 to 6½ cups whole wheat flour

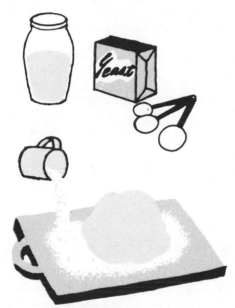

1. Pour water into a bowl; add yeast and stir until dissolved. Add milk, honey, olive oil, and salt. Stir with a wooden spoon until well blended.
2. Stir in 4 cups of flour, 1 cup at a time. Beat until dough is smooth and elastic. Mix in another cup of flour. The dough will be very stiff.
3. Measure another cup of flour; sprinkle half of it on a board. Turn dough onto the board. Knead dough, adding flour to board until the dough no longer sticks. Continue kneading until dough is not sticky (about 8 minutes).
4. Put dough into a greased bowl about three times the size of the dough. Turn dough to grease surface lightly. Cover bowl with a towel and let rise in a warm place for about 2 hours, or until double in bulk. Test by inserting a finger about ½ inch into dough. If indentation remains, the dough is ready to shape.
5. Punch dough down; squeeze out air bubbles and shape into a smooth ball. Let rise again in warm place for about 30 minutes.
6. Divide into equal portions for 2 loaves. Form each into a smooth oval loaf. Let stand covered for 15 minutes.
7. Place the loaves seam side down in 2 greased 9x5x3-inch loaf pans. Cover with a towel and let rise in warm place until almost double in bulk (about 1 hour).
8. Bake at 375°F about 30 minutes, or until crust is medium brown.
9. Turn out of pans at once. Cool on wire racks.

2 loaves

283 *Oregano and Kefalotyri Cheese Bread*
(Psomi me Rigani ke Kefalotyri)

3 to 3½ cups all-purpose flour
2 tablespoons sugar
1½ teaspoons salt
2 packages active dry yeast
¾ cup milk
¼ cup water
¼ cup shortening
1 egg
3 tablespoons oregano
¼ teaspoon garlic powder
½ cup grated kefalotyri cheese
1 teaspoon mint
2 tablespoons basil
¼ cup instant minced onion
1 tablespoon sesame seed

1. Combine 1 cup flour, sugar, salt, and dry yeast in a large bowl.
2. Heat milk, water, and shortening in a saucepan until warm. (Shortening will not melt completely.) Add milk mixture and egg to flour mixture. Beat until smooth.
3. Mix oregano, garlic powder, cheese, mint, basil, onion, and sesame seed. Stir into dough. Gradually add more flour to form a stiff dough.
4. Turn into a greased loaf pan. Cover with a towel. Let rise in a warm place until double in bulk (about 1 hour).
5. Bake at 350°F about 40 minutes, or until golden brown.

1 loaf

284 *Church Bread* (Prosphoron)

1 package active dry yeast
2½ cups warm water (105° to
    115°F)
6 cups all-purpose flour
1 teaspoon salt
    Prosphoron seal

1. Sprinkle yeast over ¼ cup warm water; stir until dissolved.
2. Combine 5½ cups of flour and salt in a large bowl and make a well in the center. Pour in yeast and remaining warm water. Mix with a wooden spoon.
3. Sprinkle remaining flour over a board. Knead 10 minutes, adding as little flour as possible to the board. Dough will be sticky.
4. Put dough into a large bowl, cover with a cloth, and let rise in a warm place until double in bulk.
5. Sprinkle board with a little flour, punch dough down, and knead 15 minutes. (Dough should be firm and smooth.)
6. Form into a large round loaf and place in a heavily floured 12-inch round pan. Lightly flour the top of the loaf. Flour the prosphoron seal. Press seal down firmly in the center to make a sharp impression and leave on the dough.
7. Cover and allow to rise in a warm place until double in bulk. Remove seal.
8. Bake at 350°F for 1 hour. Remove from pan to cool.

285 *Dark Rye Bread*

2 cups milk, scalded
2 tablespoons butter
2 tablespoons sugar
1 teaspoon salt
1 package active dry yeast
½ cup lukewarm water
4 cups rye flour
2½ cups whole-wheat flour
2 tablespoons caraway seed

1. Pour scalded milk over butter, sugar, and salt in a large bowl; stir. Cool.
2. Dissolve yeast in lukewarm water.
3. Add softened yeast and 3 cups rye flour to milk mixture. Beat thoroughly, then beat in remaining rye flour.
4. Cover and let rise in warm place until doubled in bulk. Turn onto well-floured surface. Knead in whole-wheat flour and caraway seed. Knead until dough is smooth.
5. Divide dough in half and shape into 2 round or oblong loaves. Place round loaves in greased round pans; oblong loaves in greased loaf pans. Cover and let rise in warm place until doubled in bulk.
6. Bake at 450°F 15 minutes; reduce heat to 350°F and bake 35 to 40 minutes longer. Brush with melted butter 5 minutes before done if a more tender crust is desired.

2 large loaves

286 *Croutons for Fruit Soups*

4 stale dinner rolls or slices baba
    or bread
½ cup whipping cream
2 tablespoons butter or margarine
¼ cup confectioners' sugar

1. Cut rolls into 1-inch cubes.
2. Dip cubes in cream; quickly sauté in butter.
3. Dust with confectioners' sugar.

About 14 to 18

287 *Croutons (Grzanki)*

2 slices stale bread
2 tablespoons butter or margarine

1. Trim crusts from bread. Cut bread into ½-inch cubes. Spread cubes on bottom of a shallow pan or baking sheet.
2. Bake at 350°F until golden but not browned.
3. Melt butter in a large skillet. Add toasted bread cubes. Stir-fry until all cubes are coated with butter. Cool and drain croutons on paper towels.

About ¾ cup

Cheese Croutons: Prepare croutons as directed. Mix **4 teaspoons grated Parmesan or Romano cheese and ½ teaspoon paprika.** Toss hot croutons with cheese mixture.

288 *Poppy Seed Rolls (Strucle z Makiem)*

Dough:
  2 packages active dry yeast
  ½ cup warm water
4½ cups all-purpose flour
  ¾ cup sugar
  ½ teaspoon salt
  ½ cup butter or margarine
  2 eggs
  2 egg yolks
  ½ cup dairy sour cream
  1 teaspoon vanilla extract

Filling:
  2 tablespoons butter
10 ounces poppy seed, ground twice (may be purchased already ground in gourmet shops)
  2 tablespoons honey
  2 teaspoons lemon juice or vanilla extract
  ¼ cup raisins, steamed
  2 egg whites
  ½ cup sugar
  ¼ cup finely chopped candied orange peel
  2 teaspoons grated lemon peel

Icing:
  1 cup confectioners' sugar
  2 tablespoons lemon juice

1. For dough, soften yeast in warm water in a bowl.
2. Mix flour with sugar and salt. Cut in butter with a pastry blender or two knives until mixture has a fine, even crumb.
3. Beat eggs and egg yolks; mix with yeast, then stir into flour mixture. Add sour cream and vanilla extract; mix well.
4. Knead dough on floured surface for 5 minutes. Divide in half. Roll each half of dough into a 12-inch square. Cover.
5. For filling, melt butter in a large saucepan. Add poppy seed. Stir-fry 3 minutes.
6. Add honey, lemon juice, and raisins to poppy seed. Cover and remove from heat; let stand 10 minutes.
7. Beat egg whites with sugar until stiff, not dry, peaks form. Fold in orange and lemon peels. Gently fold in poppy seed mixture.
8. Spread half of filling over each square of dough. Roll up, jelly-roll fashion. Seal edges. Place on greased baking sheets. Cover. Let rise until doubled in bulk, about 1½ hours.
9. Bake at 350°F about 45 minutes. Cool.
10. For icing, blend sugar and lemon juice until smooth. Spread over rolls.

2 poppy seed rolls

289 *Christmas Bread (Placek Świąteczny)*

5 eggs
2 cups confectioners' sugar
2¼ cups all-purpose flour
¾ cup finely chopped walnuts
⅔ cup raisins
4 ounces candied orange peel, finely chopped
2 teaspoons baking powder
½ teaspoon salt
1 cup butter or margarine (at room temperature)
1 tablespoon grated lemon peel
1 teaspoon vanilla extract
3 tablespoons vodka or brandy

1. Beat eggs with sugar 5 minutes at high speed of electric mixer.
2. Mix nuts, raisins, and orange peel with 2 tablespoons flour. Mix remaining flour with baking powder and salt.
3. Cream butter, lemon peel, and vanilla extract until fluffy. Beat in vodka. Add egg mixture gradually, beating constantly. Add flour mixture and beat 5 minutes. Fold fruit-nut mixture into the batter. Turn into a generously greased and floured 9×5×3-inch loaf pan or 1½-quart ring mold.
4. Bake at 350°F 1 hour.
5. Cool cake in pan on wire rack 10 minutes. Turn cake out onto rack; cool completely.
6. Wrap in plastic wrap. Store 1 or 2 days to mellow. Sprinkle with confectioners' sugar, if desired, or ice with Lemon Icing (page 70).

1 loaf

290 *Fruit Bread, Milan Style (Panettone)*

The traditional Christmas bread of Italy.

2 packages active dry yeast
¼ cup warm water
1 cup butter, melted
1 cup sugar
1 teaspoon salt
2 cups sifted all-purpose flour
½ cup milk, scalded and cooled to lukewarm
2 eggs
4 egg yolks
3½ cups all-purpose flour
1 cup dark seedless raisins
¾ cup chopped citron
½ cup all-purpose flour
1 egg, slightly beaten
1 tablespoon water

1. Dissolve yeast in the warm water.
2. Pour melted butter into large bowl of electric mixer. Add the sugar and salt gradually, beating constantly.
3. Beating thoroughly after each addition, alternately add the 2 cups flour in thirds and lukewarm milk in halves to the butter mixture. Add yeast and beat well.
4. Combine eggs and egg yolks and beat until thick and piled softly. Add the beaten eggs all at one time to yeast mixture and beat well. Beating thoroughly after each addition, gradually add the 3½ cups flour. Stir in raisins and citron.
5. Sift half of the remaining ½ cup flour over a pastry canvas or board. Turn dough onto floured surface; cover and let rest 10 minutes.
6. Sift remaining flour over dough. Pull dough from edges toward center until flour is worked in. (It will be sticky.) Put dough into a greased deep bowl and grease top of dough. Cover; let rise in a warm place (about 80°F) about 2½ hours.
7. Punch down dough and pull edges of dough in to center. Let rise again about 1 hour.
8. Divide dough into halves and shape each into a round loaf. Put each loaf into a well-greased 8-inch layer cake pan. Brush surfaces generously with a mixture of slightly beaten egg and water. Cover; let rise again about 1 hour.
9. Bake at 350°F 40 to 45 minutes, or until golden brown. Remove to wire racks to cool.

2 panettoni

291 *Italian Bread (Pane)*

1 package active dry yeast
2 cups warm water
1 tablespoon salt
5 to 5½ cups sifted all-purpose flour

1. Soften yeast in ¼ cup warm water. Set aside.
2. Combine remaining 1¾ cups warm water and salt in a large bowl. Blend in 3 cups flour. Stir softened yeast and add to flour mixture, mixing well.
3. Add about half the remaining flour to the yeast mixture and beat until very smooth. Mix in enough remaining flour to make a soft dough. Turn dough onto lightly floured surface. Allow to rest 5 to 10 minutes. Knead 5 to 8 minutes, until dough is smooth and elastic.
4. Shape dough into a smooth ball and place in a greased bowl, just large enough to allow dough to double. Turn dough to bring greased surface to the top. Cover bowl with waxed paper and a towel. Let stand in warm place (about 80°F) until dough is doubled (1½ to 2 hours).
5. When dough has doubled in bulk, punch down with fist. Knead on a lightly floured surface about 2 minutes. Divide into 2 equal balls. Cover with towel and let stand 10 minutes.
6. Roll each ball into a 14×8-inch rectangle. Roll up lightly from wide side into a long, slender loaf. Pinch ends to seal. Place loaves on a lightly greased 15×10-inch baking sheet. Cover loaves loosely with a towel and set aside in a warm place until doubled.
7. Bake at 425°F 10 minutes. Turn oven control to 350°F and bake 1 hour, or until golden brown.

2 loaves

Note: To increase crustiness, place shallow pan on the bottom of the oven and fill with boiling water at the beginning of the baking time.

292 *Corn Bread*

1 cup all-purpose flour
1 cup yellow cornmeal
2 teaspoons baking powder
½ teaspoon baking soda
1 teaspoon salt
1 cup milk
2½ teaspoons lime juice
1 egg, beaten
2 tablespoons lard, melted

1. Combine flour, cornmeal, baking powder, baking soda, and salt in a bowl.
2. Mix milk and lime juice; add to dry ingredients along with egg and lard. Mix well, but do not beat. Pour into a greased 11x7x1½-inch baking pan.
3. Bake at 450°F 15 to 20 minutes, or until it is brown and tests done. Cool slightly and cut into squares.

About 8 servings

293 *Tomato-Cheese Pizza*
(Pizza al Formaggio e Pomodoro)

½ package active dry yeast
1 cup plus 2 tablespoons warm water
4 cups sifted all-purpose flour
1 teaspoon salt
3 cups drained canned tomatoes
8 ounces mozzarella cheese, thinly sliced
½ cup olive oil
¼ cup grated Parmesan cheese
1 teaspoon salt
½ teaspoon pepper
2 teaspoons oregano

1. Soften yeast in 2 tablespoons warm water. Set aside.
2. Pour remaining cup of warm water into a large bowl. Blend in 2 cups flour and 1 teaspoon salt. Stir softened yeast and add to flour-water mixture, mixing well.
3. Add about 1 cup flour to yeast mixture and beat until very smooth. Mix in enough remaining flour to make a soft dough. Turn dough onto a lightly floured surface and allow to rest 5 to 10 minutes. Knead 5 to 8 minutes, until dough is smooth and elastic.
4. Shape dough into a smooth ball and place in a greased bowl just large enough to allow dough to double. Turn dough to bring greased surface to top. Cover with waxed paper and let stand in warm place (about 80°F) until dough is doubled (about 1½ to 2 hours).
5. Punch down with fist. Fold edge towards center and turn dough over. Divide dough into two equal balls. Grease another bowl and place one of the balls in it. Turn dough in both bowls so greased side is on top. Cover and let rise again until almost doubled (about 45 minutes).
6. Roll each ball of dough into a 14×10-inch rectangle, ⅛ inch thick. Place on two lightly greased 15½×12-inch baking sheets. Shape edges by pressing dough between thumb and forefinger to make a ridge. If desired, dough may be rolled into rounds, ⅛ inch thick.
7. Force tomatoes through a sieve or food mill and spread 1½ cups on each pizza. Arrange 4 ounces of mozzarella cheese on each pizza. Sprinkle over each pizza, in the order given, ¼ cup olive oil, 2 tablespoons grated Parmesan cheese, ½ teaspoon salt, ¼ teaspoon pepper, and 1 teaspoon oregano.
8. Bake at 400°F 25 to 30 minutes, or until crust is browned. Cut into wedges to serve.

6 to 8 servings

Mushroom Pizza: Follow Tomato-Cheese Pizza recipe. Before baking, place on each pizza 1 cup (8-ounce can) drained **button mushrooms.**

Sausage Pizza: Follow Tomato-Cheese Pizza recipe. Before baking, place on each pizza 1 pound **hot Italian sausage** (with casing removed), cut in ¼-inch pieces.

Anchovy Pizza: Follow Tomato-Cheese Pizza recipe. Omit mozzarella and Parmesan cheeses, decrease amount of oregano to ¼ teaspoon, and top each pizza with 8 **anchovy fillets,** cut in ¼-inch pieces.

Miniature Pizza: Follow Tomato-Cheese Pizza recipe. After rolling dough, cut dough into 3½-inch rounds. Shape edge of rounds as in Tomato-Cheese Pizza recipe. Using half the amount of ingredients in that recipe, spread each pizza with 2 tablespoons sieved canned tomatoes. Top with a slice of mozzarella cheese. Sprinkle cheese with ½ teaspoon olive oil, ½ teaspoon grated Parmesan cheese, and a few grains salt and pepper. Bake at 400°F 15 to 20 minutes, or until crust is browned.

About 24 miniature pizzas

English Muffin Pizza: Split 12 **English muffins** and spread cut sides with **butter or margarine.** Toast under the broiler until lightly browned. Top each half as for Miniature Pizza. Bake at 400°F 5 to 8 minutes, or until tomato mixture is bubbling hot.

294 *Easter Egg Bread (Pane di Pasqua all' Uovo)*

2 packages active dry yeast
½ cup warm water
1 cup all-purpose flour
⅓ cup water
¾ cup butter or margarine ,
1 tablespoon grated lemon peel
1½ tablespoons lemon juice
¾ cup sugar
1 teaspoon salt
2 eggs, well beaten
3¾ to 4¼ cups all-purpose flour
6 colored eggs (uncooked)

1. Soften yeast in the warm water in a bowl. Mix in the 1 cup flour, then the ⅓ cup water. Beat until smooth. Cover; let rise in a warm place until doubled (about 1 hour).
2. Cream butter with lemon peel and juice. Add beaten eggs in halves, beating thoroughly after each addition.
3. Add yeast mixture and beat until blended. Add about half of the remaining flour and beat thoroughly. Beat in enough flour to make a soft dough.
4. Knead on floured surface until smooth. Put into a greased deep bowl; turn dough to bring greased surface to top, Cover; let rise in a warm place until doubled.
5. Punch down dough; divide into thirds. Cover; let rest about 10 minutes.
6. With hands, roll and stretch each piece into a roll about 26 inches long and ¾ inch thick. Loosely braid rolls together. On a lightly greased baking sheet or jelly-roll pan shape into a ring, pressing ends together. At even intervals, gently spread dough apart and tuck in a colored egg. Cover; let rise again until doubled.
7. Bake at 375°F about 30 minutes. During baking check bread for browning, and when sufficiently browned, cover loosely with aluminum foil.
8. Transfer coffee cake to a wire rack. If desired, spread a confectioners' sugar icing over top of warm bread.

1 large wreath

295 *Biscuits Port-au-Prince*

2 cups sifted all-purpose flour
2 teaspoons baking powder
1 teaspoon salt
5 tablespoons vegetable shortening
¾ cup milk

1. Combine flour, baking powder, and salt in a bowl. Cut in shortening with pastry blender or two knives until mixture resembles small peas.
2. Make a well in center of mixture and add milk. Stir with fork until dough holds together.
3. Knead on a lightly floured board 30 seconds. Roll dough to ½-inch thickness. Cut with a floured 1½-inch cutter.
4. Place on greased baking sheets about 1 inch apart.
5. Bake at 425°F 15 to 20 minutes, or until golden brown.

About 2 dozen biscuits

296 *Kings' Bread Ring* (Rosca de Reyes)

2 packages active dry yeast or 2 cakes compressed yeast
½ cup water water (hot for dry yeast, lukewarm for compressed)
½ cup milk, scalded
⅓ cup sugar
⅓ cup shortening
2 teaspoons salt
4 cups all-purpose flour (about)
3 eggs, well beaten
2 cups chopped candied fruits (citron, cherries, and orange peel)
Melted butter or margarine
Confectioners' Sugar Icing

1. Soften yeast in water.
2. Pour hot milk over sugar, shortening, and salt in large bowl, stirring until sugar is dissolved and shortening melted. Cool to lukewarm. Beat in 1 cup of the flour, then eggs and softened yeast. Add enough more flour to make a stiff dough. Stir in 1½ cups candied fruits, reserving remainder to decorate baked ring.
3. Turn dough onto a floured surface and knead until smooth and satiny. Roll dough under hands into a long rope; shape into a ring, sealing ends together. Transfer to a greased cookie sheet. Push a tiny china doll into dough so it is completely covered. Brush with melted butter.
4. Cover with a towel and let rise in a warm place until double in bulk (about 1½ hours).
5. Bake at 375°F 25 to 30 minutes, or until golden brown.
6. Cool on wire rack. Frost with Confectioners' Sugar Icing and decorate with reserved candied fruit.

1 large bread ring

Confectioners' Sugar Icing: Blend 1⅓ cups confectioners' sugar, 4 teaspoons water, and ½ teaspoon vanilla extract.

297 *Sweet Rolls* (Molletes)

2 packages active dry yeast
½ cup warm water
½ cup sugar
½ teaspoon salt
1 tablespoon anise seed
½ cup butter or margarine, melted
3 eggs, at room temperature
3¾ to 4¾ cups all-purpose flour
1 egg yolk
2 tablespoons light corn syrup

1. Sprinkle yeast over water in a large warm bowl. Stir until yeast is dissolved. Add sugar, salt, anise seed, melted butter, eggs, and 2 cups of flour; beat until smooth. Stir in enough additional flour to make a soft dough.
2. Turn dough onto a lightly floured surface; knead until smooth and elastic (8 to 10 minutes).
3. Put dough into a greased bowl; turn to grease top. Cover; let rise in a warm place until double in bulk (about 1 hour).
4. Punch dough down and turn onto lightly floured surface; roll into a 12-inch square. Cut into fourths and cut each square into 4 triangles.
5. Allowing space for rising, place triangles on greased cookie sheets. Cover; let rise in warm place until double in bulk (about 1 hour).
6. Beat egg yolk and corn syrup together until blended. Generously brush over triangles.
7. Bake at 350°F 10 to 15 minutes. Serve warm.

16 large rolls

Pastas

298 *Pasta with Fresh Tomatoes and Artichoke Hearts*

For each serving:

1 medium ripe tomato, peeled, seeded, and diced
2 cooked artichoke hearts, cut in half
1 teaspoon oregano
½ teaspoon basil
1 garlic clove, crushed in a garlic press
Salt and pepper to taste
1 tablespoon wine vinegar
3 tablespoons olive oil
½ cup macaroni, cooked according to package directions
Mizithra cheese, cut in slices, for garnish
Kalamata olives for garnish

1. Combine all ingredients except macaroni and garnishes in a bowl. Cover and marinate several hours.
2. Turn macaroni onto a plate. Cover with marinated mixture. Garnish with cheese and olives. Serve cool.

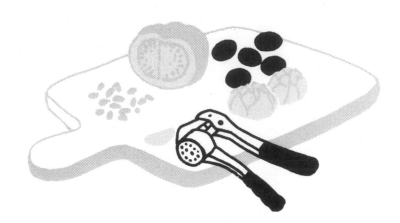

299 *Spaghetti Timbale*

2 tablespoons oil
1 medium onion, minced
2 tomatoes, peeled and coarsely chopped, or ½ cup drained canned Italian-style tomatoes
Salt and pepper to taste
2 tablespoons chopped fresh parsley
1 package (16 ounces) spaghetti
2 tablespoons oil
4 eggs, lightly beaten with a fork
¾ cup freshly grated mizithra cheese
3 tablespoons butter
1 cup cubed salami or Pork
● Sausage with Orange Peel

1. Heat 2 tablespoons oil in a heavy saucepan. Cook onion over low heat until translucent. Add tomatoes, salt, and pepper, stirring often, until mixture thickens. Stir in parsley.
2. Cook spaghetti according to package directions; add 2 tablespoons oil to water.
3. Toss cooked spaghetti with eggs, cheese, salt, and pepper until thoroughly mixed.
4. Butter a baking dish with some of the butter. Add a layer of half the spaghetti and a layer of salami; spoon the tomato sauce over. Cover with spaghetti and dot with remaining butter.
5. Bake at 300°F 20 minutes.

6 servings

300 *Cracked Wheat Pilafi* (Pligouri)

3 tablespoons butter
1¼ cups cracked wheat
3 cups stock, heated
Salt and pepper to taste

Melt butter in a large saucepan, add wheat, and cook over low heat, tossing lightly with a fork until lightly browned. Add stock, cover, and simmer about 30 minutes until wheat is done. Season with salt and pepper.

4 servings

301 *Macaroni with Sausage* (Makaronatha me Loukanika)

- 2 pounds Pork Sausage with Orange Peel
  1 garlic clove, sliced
  1 large onion, minced
  1 can (24 ounces) tomato sauce or 3 cups Tomato Sauce, heated
  Salt and pepper to taste
  1 teaspoon oregano
  1 tablespoon chopped parsley
  ½ cup water
  1 package (16 ounces) macaroni
  ½ to ¾ cup grated kefalotyri cheese

1. Pull off sausage casings.
2. Brown meat in a large skillet. Add garlic and onion, cook until lightly browned. Discard fat. Add tomato sauce, salt, pepper, oregano, parsley, and water; cover. Simmer over low heat 30 minutes.
3. Boil macaroni according to directions on the package; drain. Put macaroni into a serving dish and cover with sauce. Sprinkle with cheese. Serve hot.

6 to 8 servings

302 *Macaroni in Browned Butter with Grated Cheese* (Makaronatha me Voutero ke Kefalotyri)

1 pound macaroni
1 cup butter
½ cup freshly grated kefalotyri or Parmesan cheese (or more to taste)

1. Cook macaroni according to directions on the package, adding **¼ cup cooking oil** and **1 tablespoon salt.** Drain. Rinse under hot water.
2. Brown butter in a saucepan, stirring constantly.
3. Return the macaroni to the pot in which it was cooked, or place it in a warm serving dish. Drizzle the browned butter over it. With two spoons lift the macaroni to coat all the strands evenly. Cover with freshly grated kefalotyri. Serve at once.

4 to 6 servings

303 *Homemade Noodles* (Hilopites)

3 cups semolina
3 eggs
3 tablespoons olive oil (do not substitute)
1½ teaspoons salt
1½ teaspoons warm water

1. Combine all ingredients in a mixing bowl and work with fingers until dough holds together and can be shaped into a ball. A few drops of water may be added, if necessary, but do not let dough get sticky.
2. Knead dough on a board until smooth and shiny. Cover and let rest 15 minutes. Divide dough into 4 portions. Roll out each portion into a paper-thin sheet.
3. Lay sheets on a linen cloth and allow to dry for 1 to 2 hours.
4. Loosely fold sheets over jelly-roll fashion. Cut strips no more than ¼ inch wide. Holding in place, cut again at right angles, the same width, to make square noodles. Hilopites may be cooked right away or dried.
5. To dry, transfer to a large tray, and spread on a linen surface for about 3 days, turning occasionally.
6. To cook, bring a large quantity of water, with **salt** and **2 tablespoons oil** added, to a rolling boil. Add noodles and boil until they have doubled in size (about 5 minutes).
7. Serve hot with **browned butter** or **tomato sauce.** Sprinkle with **grated kefalotyri cheese.**

About 2 pounds noodles

304 *Spanakopeta*

10 pounds fresh spinach or 8
   packages (10 ounces each)
   frozen leaf spinach
1½ cups olive oil
2 large onions, chopped
1 bunch scallions, chopped
1 bunch parsley, chopped
½ cup freshly dried dill leaves
¼ cup freshly dried mint leaves
¼ cup oregano, crushed
   Salt and pepper to taste
1½ pounds feta cheese, crumbled
2 cups milk
4 eggs, lightly beaten
   Olive oil (about 1 cup) or ½
      olive oil and ½ vegetable oil
2 packages filo

1. Prepare the fresh spinach by removing the coarse stems and washing it well in cool water. Set aside for 10 minutes. Pat all the leaves dry with paper towels. If frozen spinach is used, thaw it completely and squeeze out all the moisture with the hands or with a heavy weight.
2. In a large skillet, heat 1½ cups olive oil. Add onion, scallion, parsley, dill, mint, oregano, salt, and pepper. Cook 5 minutes over low heat, stirring constantly.
3. In a bowl, crumble cheese. Mix in milk and eggs. Pour over the spinach. Add the cooked herbs and mix well. Adjust the seasoning.
4. Oil an 18x12-inch baking pan. Line the bottom of the pan with 10 layers of filo, brushing each layer with oil before adding the next. After the last layer of filo has been oiled, spread the spinach mixture evenly over the surface.
5. Cover with the remaining filo, oiling each layer. With a sharp knife or a single-edge razor blade, using a ruler as a guide, cut into the topmost layers, tracing square shapes.
6. Bake at 350°F 30 minutes. Turn oven control to 275°F and bake an additional 30 minutes. Cool. Cut through to separate each piece.
7. Serve as a main course, an appetizer, or vegetable dish. Freeze, if desired.

20 to 50 pieces depending on size

305 *Feta Cheese Triangles* (*Tyropites*)

1 pound feta cheese, crumbled
2 egg yolks
1 whole egg
3 tablespoons chopped parsley
   Dash finely ground pepper
¾ pound butter, melted and kept
   warm
1 pound filo

1. Mash feta cheese with a fork. Add egg yolks, egg, parsley, and pepper.
2. Melt butter in a saucepan. Keep warm, but do not allow to brown.
3. Lay a sheet of filo on a large cutting board. Brush with melted butter. Cut into strips about 1½ to 2 inches wide. See pages 80-81 for how to handle filo. Place ½ teaspoon of the cheese mixture on each strip about 1 inch from base. Fold to form a triangle. Continue until all cheese mixture and filo have been used.
4. Place triangles, side by side, in a shallow roasting pan or baking sheet.*
5. Bake at 350°F about 20 minutes, or until golden brown. Serve at once.

About 100 pieces

Note: Tyropites freeze well. Before serving, remove from freezer and let stand 15 to 20 minutes. Bake at 325°F until golden brown.

*Pan must have four joined sides; otherwise butter will fall to bottom of the oven and burn.

306 *Meat Pasties (Trigonopitakia me Kima)*

3 tablespoons butter, melted
1 pound lean ground beef
1 medium onion, finely chopped
2 tablespoons tomato sauce
½ cup dry white wine
   Salt and pepper to taste
1 tablespoon minced parsley
1 tablespoon mint
1 cup crumbled feta cheese
1 egg, beaten
2 teaspoons cracker meal
1 package filo
   Butter for filo

1. Melt butter in a skillet. Add beef, onion, tomato sauce, wine, salt, pepper, parsley, and mint. Cook over low heat, stirring frequently until all liquid evaporates. Cool.
2. Add cheese, egg, and cracker meal to meat mixture; stir to mix.
3. See pages 80-81 for how to handle filo.
4. Arrange the pasties in a shallow baking pan.
5. Bake at 350°F about 15 minutes, or until golden brown. Serve hot.

50 to 100 pieces depending on size

307 *Meat Pie Ioannina (Kreatopita Yianniotiki)*

½ cup butter, melted
2 pounds ground lean lamb
1 large onion, chopped
2 scallions, chopped
2 tablespoons tomato paste
   mixed with 1 cup wine
   Salt and pepper to taste
½ teaspoon cinnamon or more to
   taste
¼ cup chopped parsley
2 cups fresh bread crumbs
½ cups milk
1½ cups stock
7 eggs, separated
¾ cup grated kefalotyri cheese
1 package filo or 2 double recipes
   of pie crust
   Butter, melted and kept warm,
   or equal parts olive oil and
   vegetable oil

1. Melt butter in a large skillet. Add meat, onion, and scallions, and cook until browned, stirring occasionally. Add tomato paste with wine, salt, pepper, cinnamon, and parsley; mix well. Cover. Simmer 20 minutes.
2. Toss bread crumbs with milk and stock. Stir into meat mixture.
3. Beat egg whites in a bowl to form soft peaks. Beat yolks in another bowl until thick. Fold yolks into whites. Mix in cheese. Set aside.
4. Line bottom and sides of a 12x9-inch baking pan with 4 filo leaves. (See pages 80-81 for how to handle filo.) Spread with the meat filling. Cover with egg and cheese mixture. Top with remaining filo sheets. Score the top 2 or 3 filo sheets in squares, using a sharp knife. If using pie crust, prick with a fork.
5. Bake at 350°F 40 minutes. Let stand 15 minutes before cutting.

10 to 12 servings

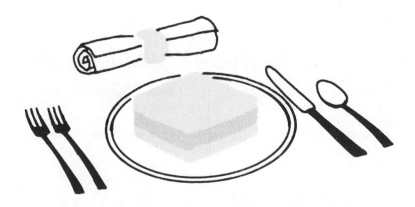

308 *Kefalonian Meat Pie* *(Kreatopita Kefalonias)*

¼ cup butter
2 pounds lean lamb, cut in
  1-inch cubes
2 cups lamb stock or water
½ pound feta cheese, crumbled
1 large onion, chopped
4 medium potatoes, parboiled,
  peeled, and diced
1 tablespoon olive oil
¼ cup chopped parsley
1 teaspoon grated orange peel
1 garlic clove, crushed in a garlic
  press
2 teaspoons dill
½ teaspoon cinnamon
  Salt and pepper
4 hard-cooked eggs, sliced
1 package filo
  Butter, melted and kept warm
  without browning

1. Melt butter in a skillet, add meat, and brown lightly on all sides. Pour in lamb stock and simmer covered about 20 minutes, or until meat is just tender. Remove from heat. Cool. Add cheese, onion, potatoes, oil, parsley, orange peel, garlic, dill, cinnamon, salt, and pepper; mix well. Set aside.

2. Place 1 sheet of filo in a 12x9-inch baking dish, allowing the filo to hang over the dish a little on all sides. Lightly butter filo. (See pages 80-81 for how to handle filo.) Repeat 4 times. Pour filling evenly in the pan. Arrange sliced eggs over the filling. Adjust salt and pepper. Flip the edges of filo onto the filling. Cover with remaining filo. Score the top·2 or 3 filo sheets in squares with a sharp knife.

3. Bake at 325°F about 1 hour, or until filo is golden brown.

10 to 12 servings

Note: Pie crust can be substituted for filo. Use a double recipe. Prick top crust with a fork.

309 *Chiffon Noodles* *(Kluski z Piany)*

2 eggs, separated
2 tablespoons flour
¼ teaspoon salt

1. Beat egg whites and salt until stiff, not dry, peaks form.
2. Beat yolks separately just until frothy. Fold into whites. Fold in flour.
3. Gently spoon onto **boiling soup or broth.** Cover; cook 2 minutes. Turn; cook a few seconds longer.
4. To serve, break into separate portions with a spoon.

About 4 servings

310 *Beaten Noodles* *(Kluski Rozcierane)*

1 tablespoon butter or margarine
  (at room temperature)
2 whole eggs
2 egg yolks
3 tablespoons flour
¼ teaspoon salt

1. Beat butter until fluffy. Beat in whole eggs and egg yolks, one at a time. Mix in flour and salt.
2. Spoon into **boiling soup or bouillon.** Cover; cook 2 minutes. Turn. Cover and cook a few seconds longer.
3. To serve, break noodles into separate portions with a spoon.

About 6 servings

311 *Rice Noodles* (Kluski z Ryżu)

1½ cups cooked rice
2 eggs
1 tablespoon butter or margarine
¼ teaspoon salt

1. Combine all ingredients. Beat until well mixed.
2. Drop by small spoonfuls into **boiling soup or broth.** Cook until noodles float, about 3 minutes.

About 2 cups

312 *Egg Barley* (Zacierki)

1 egg
3 tablespoons grated Parmesan
   cheese (optional)
Dash salt
1 cup all-purpose flour (about)

1. Beat egg with cheese (if desired) and salt, then add flour until a thick dough forms.
2. On a floured surface, knead in more flour until a stiff, dry dough forms.
3. Grate dough onto waxed paper. Let dry 1 to 2 hours.
4. Cook in **boiling soup** about 5 minutes, or until egg barley floats.

About 1 cup dry; about 1¾ cups cooked

313 *Egg Noodles* (Makaron)

1 cup all-purpose flour
1 large egg
¼ teaspoon salt
½ eggshell of water (about 1
   tablespoon)

1. Mound flour on a board. Make a well in center; drop in egg and salt. Beat in water with a fork.
2. Knead from center to outer edges until dough is smooth.
3. Roll out very thin on a floured surface. Place sheet of dough on a cloth; let dry until not sticky but not too brittle to handle.
4. Sprinkle the sheet of noodle dough with flour. Roll up tightly and slice into thin threads. Toss the threads lightly to separate. Let dry 2 hours.
5. To cook, boil in **salted water** until the noodles rise to the top. Drain. Rinse in cold water. Drain again. Toss in **hot melted butter.**

About 2 cups uncooked

314 *Egg Drops* (Kluski Lane)

2 eggs, beaten
¼ teaspoon salt
1 tablespoon water
⅓ cup all-purpose flour

1. Combine all ingredients and stir until smooth.
2. Hold spoonfuls of batter about 12 inches from **boiling soup;** pour slowly from end of spoon. Let boil 2 to 3 minutes, until egg drops float.

About 4 servings

String Dumplings: Prepare Egg Drops batter. Pour almost continuously from a cup or spoon into boiling soup to form long "strings." Break apart after cooking.

315 *Potato Dumplings (Kartoflane Kluski)*

2 cups hot mashed potatoes
⅓ cup fine dry bread crumbs
2 egg yolks
¾ teaspoon salt
¼ teaspoon pepper
⅓ cup all-purpose flour
2 egg whites, beaten until stiff, but not dry

1. Mix ingredients in a large bowl in the order given.
2. Place on floured board and roll to pencil thickness. Cut into 2- or 3-inch strips.
3. Drop into **boiling salted water.** Cook until dumplings float to top.

Croquettes: Sauté ½ cup chopped onion in **2 table-spoons butter.** Proceed as in recipe for Potato Dumplings; add onion to potatoes. Roll strips in **fine dry bread crumbs.** Pan-fry in **butter** until golden brown.

316 *Suet or Marrow Balls (Pulpety z Łoju lub Szpiku)*

½ pound white beef suet from kidneys, or marrow
2 eggs, slightly beaten
½ teaspoon salt
¼ teaspoon pepper
½ cup fine dry bread crumbs or cracker meal
2 teaspoons chopped fresh dill or parsley
Flour
Broth or desired soup

1. Remove membrane from suet or marrow. Chop fine and put into a bowl.
2. Add eggs, salt, pepper, bread crumbs, and dill to suet; mix thoroughly but lightly. Form into small round balls.
3. Roll in flour and drop into gently boiling broth or soup. Cook 10 minutes, or until balls float.

About 2½ dozen balls

317 *Egg Balls (Kluski z Żółtek)*

4 hard-cooked egg yolks
4 raw egg yolks
¼ teaspoon salt
⅛ teaspoon nutmeg
⅛ teaspoon pepper

1. Mash the cooked egg yolks or press through a sieve. Add raw yolks and seasonings. Mix until a smooth thick paste forms.
2. Drop by spoonfuls into **boiling soup or broth.** Cook a few seconds until egg balls float. Serve immediately.

4 to 6 servings

318 *Fish Dumplings (Pulpety z Ryby)*

1 onion, minced
1 tablespoon butter or margarine
1 pound cooked fish or 2 cups flaked cooked fish
1 slice white bread, soaked in water and squeezed
2 eggs
¾ teaspoon salt
2 tablespoons fine dry bread crumbs
1 teaspoon dill weed
1 teaspoon chopped parsley
2 tablespoons flour

1. Fry onion in butter until golden.
2. Flake or chop fish very fine. Or, grind fish with the onion.
3. Mix fish with bread and eggs. Season with salt and pepper. Stir in bread crumbs, dill, and parsley.
4. Form balls about 1½ inches in diameter. Roll in flour.
5. Cook in **boiling water** until dumplings float, about 4 minutes.

4 to 6 servings

319 *Liver Mounds* (*Babki z Wątróbek*)

¾ pound chicken, turkey, or capon
    livers
1 cup milk
1 tablespoon butter or margarine
⅓ cup minced onion
⅓ cup fine dry bread crumbs
3 eggs, separated
½ teaspoon salt

1. Soak livers in milk in a glass or pottery bowl 3 hours in refrigerator. Drain livers, discarding milk. Mince livers.
2. Melt butter in a skillet. Add onion and stir-fry until golden. Remove from heat.
3. Combine minced liver, onion with butter, bread crumbs, and egg yolks. Mix until thoroughly combined.
4. Beat egg whites with salt until stiff, not dry, peaks are formed. Fold into liver mixture.
5. Spoon liver mixture into well-greased muffin-pan wells. Grease a piece of brown paper or waxed paper on one side. Place paper, greased side down, on top of muffin pan.
6. Bake at 350°F 25 to 35 minutes. Remove at once from pan. Serve hot with **a piquant sauce** or in **chicken broth.**

About 6 servings

320 *Raw Potato Dumplings* (*Kartoflane Kluski*)

2 cups grated raw potatoes
2 eggs
1 teaspoon salt
½ cup fine dry bread crumbs
1½ cups all-purpose flour (about)
    Boiling salted water

1. Rinse potatoes in cold water; drain well.
2. Combine potatoes in a large bowl with eggs, salt, crumbs, and enough flour to make a stiff dough.
3. Using a wet spoon, drop tablespoonfuls of dough into boiling salted water.
4. Cook until dumplings float to the top. Dumplings should be about 1½ × ½ inches when done.

About 6 servings

321 *Yeast Pierogi* (*Pierożki*)

4 eggs
1 tablespoon melted butter
1 teaspoon salt
1 package active dry yeast
¼ cup warm water
1 cup dairy sour cream
1 tablespoon sugar
1½ teaspoons grated lemon peel
    (optional)
4 cups all-purpose flour (about)
● Filling

1. Beat eggs with melted butter and salt until thick and fluffy.
2. Dissolve yeast in warm water in a large bowl. Let stand 10 minutes.
3. Add egg mixture to yeast. Beat in sour cream, sugar, and, if desired, lemon peel. Stir in flour, 1 cup at a time, until dough is firm but not stiff.
4. Turn dough on floured surface; knead 3 minutes. Place dough in a greased bowl. Cover with plastic wrap. Let rise in a warm place until doubled, about 1 hour.
5. Roll out dough to ⅜-inch thickness on floured surface. Cut into 3-inch rounds.
6. Place a spoonful of filling a little to one side of each round. Moisten edges. Fold over and seal. Place on greased baking sheet.
7. Bake at 350°F about 20 to 35 minutes, or until golden brown.

About 3 dozen

322 Pierogi

2 cups all-purpose flour
2 eggs
½ teaspoon salt
⅓ cup water
● Filling

1. Mound flour on a bread board and make a well in the center.
2. Drop eggs and salt into well. Add water; working from the center to outside of flour mound, mix flour into liquid in center with one hand and keep flour mounded with other hand. Knead until dough is firm and well mixed.
3. Cover dough with a warm bowl; let rest 10 minutes.
4. Divide dough into halves. On floured surface, using half of dough at a time, roll dough as thin as possible.
5. Cut out 3-inch rounds with large biscuit cutter.
6. Place a small spoonful of filling a little to one side on each round of dough. Moisten edge with water, fold over and press edges together firmly. Be sure they are well sealed to prevent the filling from leaking out.
7. Drop pierogi into **boiling salted water.** Cook gently 3 to 5 minutes, or until pierogi float. Lift out of water with perforated spoon.

1½ to 2 dozen

Note: The dough will have a tendency to dry. A dry dough will not seal completely. Work with half the dough at a time, rolling out a large circle of dough and placing small mounds of filling far enough apart to allow for cutting. Then cut with biscuit cutter and seal firmly.

Never put too many pierogi in cooking water. The uncooked will stick together and the cooked get lumpy and tough.

323 Little Ears (Uszka)

2 cups all-purpose flour
½ cup water
1 egg
⅛ teaspoon salt
● Filling

1. Mound flour on a bread board and make a well in the center. Place remaining ingredients in the well. Mix flour into liquid in center until a dough is formed. Knead thoroughly.
2. Roll dough very thinly on a floured surface. Cut into 2-inch squares.
3. Put a spoonful of filling in center of each square. Fold so that the corners meet in the middle. Press together with fingers to seal. Fold in half diagonally, so the square becomes a triangle. Seal edges. Then bring the 2 long ends of triangle together; press firmly to seal.
4. Drop into **boiling soup.** Cook until the uszka float.

About 3 dozen

324 Thin Pancakes (Naleśniki)

½ cup all-purpose flour
1 egg
1 egg yolk
½ cup milk
1 teaspoon sugar
⅛ teaspoon salt

1. Combine flour, egg, and egg yolk in a small bowl of electric mixer. Beat just to mix. Add milk, sugar, and salt; beat at low speed 2 minutes.
2. Heat a small, heavy skillet. Brush bottom with oil.
3. Pour about 2 tablespoons batter into skillet; at once tilt skillet to spread batter evenly over bottom of skillet. When

Salad oil
● Filling

edges are dry, turn pancake and cook other side.
4. Repeat until all batter is used, reserve some batter for coating stuffed pancakes, if desired.
5. For stuffed pancakes, place 1 heaping tablespoonful of filling in center of pancake. Fold sides toward center, over filling, and roll up pancakes.
6. Dip in **egg** beaten with **water** or in reserved batter. Coat with **fine dry bread crumbs.**
7. Quickly fry coated pancakes in a small amount of hot oil. Turn and cook until golden on all sides.

12 pancakes

325 *Thick Pancakes (Naleśniki)*

1 cup milk
1 egg
1 cup all-purpose flour
⅓ cup water
¼ teaspoon salt
Salad oil or melted butter
● Filling

1. Beat milk and egg until frothy. Add flour and beat rapidly 1 minute. Add water and salt. Beat rapidly 1 minute longer.
2. Heat a small, heavy skillet. Brush bottom with oil or wipe with cloth dipped in oil. (Do not use too much oil.)
3. Pour about 2 tablespoons batter onto bottom of skillet; at once tilt skillet so batter spreads evenly. When edge of pancake begins to dry, turn and cook other side.
4. Repeat until all the batter is used.

12 pancakes

326 *Yeast Fingers (Drożdżowe Paluszki)*

2 cups all-purpose flour
1 package active dry yeast
1 teaspoon sugar
½ teaspoon salt
½ cup butter or margarine
1 egg
2 egg yolks
2 tablespoons dairy sour cream
1 egg white
2 tablespoons caraway seed or poppy seed

1. Combine flour, yeast, sugar, and salt in a bowl. Cut in butter with a pastry blender or two knives until well mixed. Stir in egg, egg yolks, and sour cream.
2. Knead the dough in the bowl a few minutes until it forms a smooth ball.
3. Break off small bits of dough, about 1 tablespoonful each; roll between palms of hands to form long, thin rolls.
4. Place on a greased baking sheet. Let rise in a warm place until doubled in bulk.
5. Brush with egg white, then sprinkle with caraway seed.
6. Bake at 375°F 15 minutes, or until golden. Remove immediately from the baking sheet.

About 40 fingers

Stuffed Yeast Fingers: Two ways are typical, either a long roll which is sliced after baking, or individual fingers.

For long roll, roll out the dough on a floured surface to form a rectangle about 18×6 inches. Spoon filling lengthwise down center of dough. Fold over both long sides and seal the top seam and ends. Carefully place, seam-side down, on a greased baking sheet. Cover with plastic wrap. Let rise in a warm place 30 minutes. Brush top with slightly beaten **egg white.** Cut ½-inch deep slashes across top, about 1 inch apart. Bake at 375°F 1 hour. Cool 15 minutes before slicing.

For individual fingers, roll out dough as directed. Cut into 48 pieces and roll each piece into a rectangle. Place 1 tablespoon filling on each rectangle. Fold dough lengthwise over filling and pinch to seal all seams. Place on greased baking sheet. Cover; let rise, and brush with egg white as directed. Do not slash. Bake at 375°F about 20 to 35 minutes, or until golden brown.

327 *Beef Filling*

1 large onion, halved and sliced
2 tablespoons margarine or
   shortening
1¾ cups ground cooked beef
¾ cup cooked rice
2 teaspoons instant bouillon or
   meat extract
3 tablespoons hot water
1 tablespoon chopped fresh
   parsley
   Salt and pepper

1. Stir-fry onion in margarine in a large skillet until golden. Stir in meat and rice.
2. Dissolve bouillon in hot water. Add to meat mixture with parsley and salt and pepper to taste.

About 2½ cups

328 *Cooked Meat Filling*

2 onions, minced
2 tablespoons butter or margarine
1 cup ground cooked meat
2 slices stale white bread
   Milk or water
½ teaspoon salt
¼ teaspoon pepper

1. Stir-fry onion in butter in a heavy skillet 5 minutes. Add ground meat. Remove from heat.
2. Soak bread in just enough milk to cover. When thoroughly soaked, about 10 minutes, squeeze out excess milk.
3. Stir bread, salt, and pepper into onion mixture until well combined.

2 to 3 cups

329 *Meat Filling*

¼ pound suet, chopped
2 cups grated onion
½ pound ground lean beef
½ pound ground lean lamb
½ pound ground lean veal
1 teaspoon salt
¾ teaspoon marjoram
¾ teaspoon sweet basil
¼ teaspoon pepper
⅓ cup fine dry bread crumbs
   Meat stock

1. Fry suet and onion just until onion is tender. Add meat; fry until meat changes color.
2. Stir in all seasonings and bread crumbs. Add just enough meat stock to make a paste.

About 3½ cups

330 *Sausage Filling*

10 ounces Polish sausage (kiełbasa),
   skinned and chopped
½ cup grated cheese or chopped
   mushrooms
¼ cup fine dry bread crumbs
1 egg

Combine all ingredients thoroughly.

About 2 cups

Red Vegetable Salad, page 63
Brussels Sprouts and Grapes, page 175
Herbed Stuffed Mushrooms, page 172

331 Brains Filling

1 pair fresh veal or pork brains
    (about 12 ounces)
Water
1 teaspoon salt
5 peppercorns
1 bay leaf
1 tablespoon vinegar
⅓ cup finely chopped onion
3 tablespoons butter
1 egg yolk
Salt and pepper

1. Rinse brains under running cold water.
2. Put brains into a saucepan with water to cover, 1 teaspoon salt, peppercorns, bay leaf, and vinegar. Bring to boiling and cook 3 minutes.
3. Drain brains; remove and discard white tough membrane. Chop brains coarsely.
4. Sauté onion in butter until golden. Add the brains and stir to mix well. Cook 2 minutes. Add egg yolk to mixture and blend well. Season to taste with salt and pepper.

About 1 cup

332 Mushroom Filling

1½ cups chopped mushrooms
½ cup chopped onion
2 tablespoons butter or margarine
¼ teaspoon salt
⅛ teaspoon pepper
2 egg yolks or 1 egg, beaten

1. Stir-fry mushrooms and onion in butter until onion is soft. Remove from heat.
2. Stir in remaining ingredients.

About 1 cup

333 Cabbage and Mushroom Filling with Egg

1 small head cabbage (about 1 pound) shredded
⅓ cup water
1 large onion, halved and sliced
1 can (4 ounces) mushroom stems and pieces
2 tablespoons butter or margarine
1 teaspoon salt
¼ teaspoon pepper
2 hard-cooked eggs, chopped

1. Combine the cabbage, water, onion, mushrooms, and butter in a large saucepan. Cook, covered, over low heat until tender, about 30 minutes.
2. Add salt, pepper, and chopped eggs; mix well.

About 3½ cups

334 Sauerkraut Filling

⅓ cup chopped onion
1 tablespoon butter or margarine
1½ cups finely chopped sauerkraut
2 tablespoons dairy sour cream

1. Stir-fry onion in butter in a saucepan 3 minutes.
2. Rinse and drain sauerkraut. Add to onion and cook 2 minutes.
3. Remove from heat. Stir in sour cream.

About 1½ cups

335 Potato Filling

½ cup chopped onion
2 tablespoons butter
½ teaspoon salt
¼ teaspoon white pepper
2 cups mashed potatoes

1. Sauté onion in butter 5 minutes. Stir in salt and pepper.
2. Combine potatoes and onion mixture. Blend well.

About 2 cups

Fish Stew, page 305
Sole with Shrimp Pate in Champagne, page 302

336 *Sauerkraut and Mushroom Filling*

2½ cups sauerkraut
Boiling water
2 tablespoons fat
½ cup chopped onion
4 ounces mushrooms, sliced
¼ teaspoon salt
¼ teaspoon pepper
1 hard-cooked egg, chopped
2 tablespoons dairy sour cream

1. Rinse sauerkraut and drain. Put into a saucepan. Cover with a small amount of boiling water. Cook 20 minutes; drain.
2. Heat fat in a skillet. Add onion and fry until golden. Add mushrooms and fry 3 minutes. Stir in sauerkraut, salt, and pepper. Fry until the sauerkraut becomes golden, about 20 minutes.
3. Remove from heat. Add chopped egg and sour cream; mix well.

About 2 cups

337 *Savory Cheese Filling*

1½ cups pot cheese or farmer cheese
1 teaspoon lemon juice
1 teaspoon sugar
1 egg
1 egg yolk
¼ teaspoon salt

Press cheese through a sieve into a bowl. Add remaining ingredients; mix well.

About 1½ cups

338 *Sweet Cheese Filling*

1½ cups pot cheese, farmer cheese, or ricotta
1 egg, beaten
3 tablespoons sugar
¼ cup raisins or currants
½ teaspoon vanilla extract
¼ teaspoon cinnamon

Press cheese through a sieve into a bowl. Add remaining ingredients; mix well.

About 1¾ cups

339 *Cooked Fruit Filling*

2 cups pitted cherries, apples, or blueberries
¾ cup water
⅓ cup sugar (optional)
½ teaspoon cinnamon or cardamom (optional)
1 teaspoon lemon juice (optional)
2 to 4 tablespoons fine dry bread crumbs

1. Combine fruit, water, and sugar in a saucepan. Bring to boiling; cook and stir until fruit is tender and water is almost gone. Remove from heat.
2. Mash fruit slightly with potato masher. Add cinnamon and lemon juice. Cook and stir over low heat just until fruit mixture is thick.
3. Stir in enough bread crumbs to make filling very thick.

About 1½ cups

340 *Prune Filling*

2 cups dried prunes
1 tablespoon lemon juice
1 tablespoon brown sugar

1. Cover prunes with **water.** Bring just to boiling. Cover. Remove from heat and let stand 20 minutes. Remove and discard pits.
2. Add lemon juice and sugar. Cook until almost all liquid is gone.

About 1½ cups

341 Egg Noodles with Poppy Seed
(Kluski z Makiem)

1½ quarts boiling water
1 teaspoon salt
3 cups egg noodles
½ cup milk
½ cup poppy seed, ground
3 tablespoons sugar or 2 tablespoons honey

1. Combine boiling water and salt in a large saucepan. Add noodles and cook until tender. Drain.
2. Meanwhile, scald milk; mix in poppy seed and sugar. Cook 5 minutes.
3. Combine poppy seed mixture with the noodles. Serve hot.

4 to 6 servings

342 Noodles with Poppy Seed and Raisins
(Kluski z Makiem i Rodzynkami)

2 cups cooked egg noodles
2 tablespoons butter, melted
1 can (12 ounces) poppy seed cake and pastry filling
1 teaspoon vanilla extract
1 teaspoon lemon juice
1½ teaspoons grated lemon peel
⅓ cup raisins

1. Toss noodles with butter in a saucepan.
2. Combine poppy seed filling with vanilla extract, lemon juice and peel, and raisins. Add to noodles and mix well. Cook just until heated through.

About 6 servings.

343 Lasagne with Green Garlic Sauce
(Lasagne al Pesto)

1 pound lasagne noodles
● Green Garlic Sauce
1 cup grated Parmesan cheese

1. Cook lasagne noodles according to package directions. Drain. Alternate layers of lasagne, sauce, and cheese in a 2-quart baking dish.
2. Bake at 425°F 15 to 20 minutes, or until hot.

8 to 10 servings

344 Spaghetti Genoese (Spaghetti alla Genovese)

1 pound long spaghetti
¼ cup olive oil
½ cup butter
2 cloves garlic, finely minced
6 tablespoons chopped parsley
1 pint half-and-half
½ cup grated Parmesan cheese

1. Cook spaghetti according to package directions. Drain.
2. In a large skillet, heat oil and butter over low heat. Add garlic, but do not brown. Stir in parsley and half-and-half; heat slightly, but do not boil.
3. Add spaghetti to cream sauce in skillet; mix well. Blend in cheese, a little at a time, coating all the spaghetti well. Serve on hot plates.

6 to 8 servings

345 *Soup Dumplings (Canederli)*

1 slice bacon, diced
1 teaspoon butter
½ cup minced onion
½ cup peeled fresh Italian sausage, cut in small pieces
2½ cups coarsely crumbled dry bread
1 cup milk
3 eggs
1 tablespoon minced parsley
2 tablespoons grated Parmesan cheese
Dash nutmeg
½ teaspoon salt
Dash pepper
2 cups all-purpose flour
2 quarts chicken consommé or broth, boiling

1. Place bacon, butter, onion, and sausage in saucepan. Cook until onion is soft. Mix in bread and cook 1 or 2 minutes.
2. Remove mixture from heat and stir in milk. Set aside for at least 1 hour.
3. Add eggs, one at a time, mixing well after each is added. Stir in parsley, cheese, nutmeg, salt, and pepper. Add the flour, stirring until mixture holds together.
4. Form mixture into balls no larger than a walnut, and drop, one at a time, into the boiling consommé in a large pot. Reduce heat and allow dumplings to cook 20 to 25 minutes.
5. Serve broth and dumplings, sprinkled with grated Parmesan cheese.

6 to 8 servings

Note: If desired, dumplings may be cooked in boiling salted water, drained, and served with melted butter or a meat sauce.

346 *Polenta*

3 cups water
2 chicken bouillon cubes
1 cup yellow cornmeal
2 tablespoons butter or margarine

1. Bring water to boiling. Stir in bouillon cubes to dissolve. Slowly stir in cornmeal. Reduce heat and cook, stirring, until very thick (about 7 minutes).
2. Remove from heat and stir in butter until melted.
3. Spoon onto plates and top each serving with 1 tablespoon butter or 2 tablespoons shredded mozzarella, Monterey Jack, or Cheddar cheese. Serve as a meat accompaniment.

4 servings

347 *Polenta with Sausage (Polenta con Salsiccia)*

1 pound Italian sausage
2 tablespoons olive oil
1 pound mushrooms, cleaned and sliced
2½ cups canned tomatoes
1 teaspoon salt
¼ teaspoon pepper
3 cups water
1½ teaspoons salt
1 cup yellow cornmeal
1 cup cold water
Grated Parmesan or Romano cheese

1. Cut sausage casing, remove sausage, and crumble into small pieces with a fork.
2. Heat olive oil in large skillet. Add sausage and mushrooms to skillet. Cook slowly, stirring occasionally, until the mushrooms and sausage are lightly browned.
3. Slowly stir in the tomatoes, 1 teaspoon salt, and pepper. Simmer 20 to 30 minutes.
4. While the tomato and sausage mixture is simmering, bring 3 cups water with 1½ teaspoons salt to boiling. Gradually stir in the cornmeal and 1 cup cold water. Continue boiling, stirring constantly, until the mixture is thickened.
5. Cover, lower the heat, and cook slowly 10 minutes or longer, if necessary. Transfer the cooked cornmeal to warm platter, and top with the tomato mixture.
6. Sprinkle with cheese and serve immediately.

6 to 8 servings

348 Baked Green Lasagne Bolognese
(Lasagne Verdi al Forno Bolognese)

6 quarts water
1 teaspoon salt
● ¾ pound Green Lasagne
● 2½ cups Bolognese Meat Sauce
2 cups Cream Sauce
¾ cup grated Parmesan cheese

1. Bring water to boiling in a large saucepot. Add salt and cook lasagne strips a few at a time for 3 minutes. Remove from boiling water with a strainer, and drop into cold water. Drain again and spread on damp towels.
2. Cover the bottom of a buttered 2-quart baking dish with meat sauce, a small amount of Cream Sauce, and a sprinkling of cheese. Next form a layer of noodles with the ends turning part way up at the sides of the dish. Repeat layering with meat sauce, Cream Sauce, cheese, and lasagne, forming about 6 layers. Finish top with meat sauce, Cream Sauce, and a generous amount of cheese.
3. Bake at 375°F 20 to 25 minutes, or until hot and bubbly.

6 servings

Cream Sauce: Melt **2 tablespoons butter** in a saucepan and blend with **2 tablespoons flour**. Gradually stir in **1 cup milk** and **1 cup half-and-half**. Season with **½ teaspoon salt** and a **dash nutmeg**. Cook, stirring constantly, until sauce boils and thickens. Cover with a sheet of waxed paper on surface and keep warm until ready to use.

2 cups sauce

349 Green Lasagne (Lasagne Verdi)

½ pound spinach
4 cups all-purpose flour
1 teaspoon salt
2 large eggs, beaten

1. Wash spinach and place in heavy saucepan. Do not add water; cook only in moisture remaining on leaves from washing. Partially cover and cook 5 minutes, stirring occasionally with a fork.
2. Drain spinach, press out the water, chop it, and force it through a sieve; or drain, press out water, and purée in an electric blender. It should retain its fresh green color and become a smooth purée. If the purée is very wet, heat it in the saucepan, about a minute, over very high heat to evaporate some of the moisture. Allow it to cool.
3. Sift the flour and salt into a large mixing bowl. Make a well in the center of the flour and put the beaten eggs and puréed spinach in it. Mix gradually with one hand, or with a fork, until the paste is well blended. If the mixture is too dry, add some water until it forms a ball. If the dough is too sticky, add more flour.
4. Knead the dough at least 12 minutes, until it is smooth and elastic. Divide dough in 4 pieces and roll out to ⅟₁₆-inch thick. Cut the sheets of dough into 4×2-inch rectangles, or longer, if desired. The dough may also be cut in squares. Let cut pieces of dough dry on towels for an hour. If not using immediately, store at room temperature.

About 1¼ pounds pasta

Green Noodles: Follow recipe for Green Lasagne. Roll the sheets of dough up and cut in ¼-inch-wide strips. Unroll and place on towels for half an hour to dry. Place in **boiling salted water** and cook 5 minutes; drain. Serve tossed with **butter** and **grated cheese,** or any sauce desired.

350 *Stuffed Pasta Rings in Cream*
(Tortellini alla Bolognese)

½ turkey breast (about 2½ pounds), boned
4 slices prosciutto
1 medium-size veal sweetbread, blanched and cleaned
¼ pound lean pork
¼ pound lean beef
7 tablespoons butter
¼ pound Parmesan cheese, grated
2 egg yolks, beaten
Pinch grated nutmeg
Pinch ground cinnamon
Salt and pepper
Pasta Dough for Tortellini
4 quarts chicken broth
1 cup whipping cream

1. Cut turkey breast, prosciutto, sweetbread, pork, and beef into pieces.
2. Melt 4 tablespoons of the butter in a large skillet. Sauté meats until sweetbread pieces are cooked. Remove from heat and cool.
3. Put meat mixture through a meat grinder twice, so it is very finely ground. Place the ground meat in a large bowl and stir in half the cheese, the egg yolks, nutmeg, cinnamon, and salt and pepper to taste. Blend well.
4. Prepare Pasta Dough for Tortellini, using turkey mixture for filling. Set aside on a cloth, cover with another cloth, and allow to dry 30 minutes.
5. Bring the chicken broth to a gentle simmer, not a violent boil or the pasta will break apart. Melt the remaining 3 tablespoons butter in a large saucepot over low heat.
6. Carefully drop filled tortellini, a few at a time, into the gently simmering broth. Simmer until cooked through, but still a little firm (about 10 minutes). Remove, using a slotted spoon, and place in melted butter in saucepot. When all the tortellini are cooked and in the saucepot, pour in the whipping cream and sprinkle remaining cheese over tortellini. Stir gently with a wooden spoon until sauce is smooth.
7. Serve immediately in heated soup bowls. Accompany with additional grated Parmesan cheese.

About 8 servings

Note: A 2-pound frozen boneless turkey roast (thawed) may be substituted for the turkey breast.

351 *Pasta Dough for Tortellini*

3½ cups all-purpose flour
1 teaspoon salt
2 eggs, beaten
1 tablespoon olive oil
Warm water (about ½ cup)

1. Put flour on a board and sprinkle with salt. Make a well and add eggs and oil. Mix well until a soft smooth dough is formed. Add warm water gradually, if necessary, to soften dough. Knead 5 to 10 minutes until dough is smooth and elastic. Cover with a bowl for 30 minutes.
2. Divide dough in quarters. Roll each quarter into a round as thin as possible. Cut into 2-inch rounds.
3. For each tortellini, place ¼ to ½ teaspoon filling in center of round. Moisten edges with water. Fold in half; seal edges. Shape into rings by stretching the tips of half circle slightly and wrapping the ring around your index finger. Gently press tips together.
4. Cook as directed.

About 12 dozen tortellini

352 *Manicotti Tuscan Style (Manicotti alla Toscana)*

- ● **Egg Pasta Dough for Manicotti**
- ● **Tomato Sauce**
- 3 **tablespoons butter**
- 1 **tablespoon olive oil**
- 1 **clove garlic, minced**
- 6 **mushrooms, minced**
- 1 **pound ground beef round**
- 1 **teaspoon salt**
- ¼ **teaspoon pepper**
- ½ **pound ricotta**
- ¼ **pound Parmesan cheese, grated**

1. Prepare pasta dough and Tomato Sauce.
2. Heat butter and oil in a skillet. Add garlic; sauté until soft. Stir in mushrooms, beef, salt, and pepper. Cook until meat is brown, stirring often. Add ricotta and half the Parmesan cheese, blending well.
3. When dough squares are dry, spread ½ tablespoon of the beef mixture on each square and roll up tightly. Press edges together to seal, moistening edges with water if necessary. Filling must be sealed in completely, or it will fall out during the cooking in boiling water.
4. Cook manicotti in gently boiling salted water until just tender. Remove with a slotted spoon and drain. Arrange a layer of manicotti (about 30) in a buttered 3-quart casserole. Cover with Tomato Sauce and sprinkle with half of remaining Parmesan cheese. Arrange remaining manicotti crosswise in another layer, cover with Tomato Sauce, and sprinkle with remaining Parmesan cheese.
5. Bake at 350°F 25 minutes, or until cheese browns and sauce bubbles.

About 60 manicotti

353 *Egg Pasta Dough for Manicotti*

- 4 **cups all-purpose flour**
- 4 **eggs, beaten**
- 1½ **teaspoons salt**
- 2 **teaspoons olive oil**
  Warm water (about ½ cup)

1. Put flour onto a board, make a well in center, and add eggs, salt, and olive oil. Mix until a soft dough is formed, adding warm water as needed.
2. Knead about 10 minutes until dough is smooth and elastic. Add more flour if dough is too soft.
3. Divide dough in quarters. Roll each quarter into as thin a sheet as possible. Cut the sheets into 3-inch squares. Dry on cloth or cloth-covered board for 1 hour before using.

About 1¾ pounds dough

354 *Fettuccine Alfredo*

- 1 **pound green noodles**
  Boiling salted water
- 2 **tablespoons olive oil**
- 1 **teaspoon chopped fresh basil**
- 1 **clove garlic, minced**
  Grated Parmesan cheese
  Butter

1. Cook noodles in boiling salted water until just tender; drain.
2. In a chafing dish, heat olive oil, basil, and garlic. Toss the noodles in hot oil with a fork until they are very hot.
3. Sprinkle generously with Parmesan cheese, adding a generous piece of butter, and toss again a moment before serving.

About 8 servings

Fettuccine al Burro Alfredo: Cook egg noodles in boiling salted water until barely tender, *al dente;* drain thoroughly. Bring quickly to the table in a heated serving bowl and rapidly toss and twirl with a generous amount of unsalted butter and finely grated Parmesan or Romano cheese so that the butter and cheese melt so quickly that the fettuccine can be served piping hot.

355 *Meat-Stuffed Manicotti*

2 tablespoons olive oil
½ pound fresh spinach, washed, dried, and finely chopped
2 tablespoons chopped onion
½ teaspoon salt
½ teaspoon oregano
½ pound ground beef
2 tablespoons fine dry bread crumbs
1 egg, slightly beaten
1 can (6 ounces) tomato paste
8 manicotti shells (two thirds of a 5½-ounce package), cooked and drained
1½ tablespoons butter, softened (optional)
1 to 2 tablespoons grated Parmesan or Romano cheese (optional)
Mozzarella cheese, shredded

1. Heat olive oil in a skillet. Add spinach, onion, salt, oregano, and meat. Mix well, separating meat into small pieces. Cook, stirring frequently, until meat is no longer pink.
2. Set aside to cool slightly. Add bread crumbs, egg, and 2 tablespoons tomato paste; mix well. Stuff manicotti with mixture. Put side by side in a greased 2-quart baking dish. If desired, spread butter over stuffed manicotti and sprinkle with the grated cheese.
3. Spoon remaining tomato paste on top of the manicotti down the center of the dish. Sprinkle mozzarella cheese on top of tomato paste. Cover baking dish.
4. Bake at 425°F 12 to 15 minutes, or until mozzarella melts.

4 servings

356 *Gnocchi*

● **Tomato Meat Sauce**
3 medium (about 1 pound) potatoes, pared and quartered
1¾ cups sifted all-purpose flour
Grated Parmesan cheese

1. Prepare sauce, allowing 4½ hours for cooking.
2. While sauce is cooking, place the potatoes in enough boiling salted water to cover. Cook, covered, about 20 minutes, or until tender when pierced with a fork. Drain. Dry potatoes by shaking in pan over low heat.
3. Mash or rice the potatoes with a potato masher, food mill, or ricer that has been scalded with boiling water. Keep the potatoes hot.
4. Place the flour in a bowl, make a well in the center, and add the mashed potatoes. Mix well to make a soft dough. Turn dough onto lightly floured surface and knead 5 to 8 minutes until it is smooth and elastic.
5. Break off small pieces of dough and, using palms of hands, roll to pencil thickness. Cut into ¾-inch pieces. Curl each piece by pressing lightly with the index finger and pulling the finger along the dough toward you. Gnocchi may also be shaped by pressing each piece with a lightly floured fork.
6. Gradually add the gnocchi to 3 quarts boiling water, cooking about half at a time. Boil rapidly, uncovered, 8 to 10 minutes, or until gnocchi are tender and float to the surface.
7. Drain gnocchi in a colander or large sieve, and mix with 2 cups Tomato Meat Sauce, top with remaining sauce, and sprinkle generously with cheese. Serve immediately.

About 6 servings

357 *Lasagne I*

● **Tomato Sauce with Meat**
3 tablespoons olive oil
1 pound ground beef
1 pound lasagne noodles, cooked and drained
¾ pound mozzarella cheese, thinly sliced
2 hard-cooked eggs, sliced
¼ cup grated Parmesan cheese
½ teaspoon pepper
1 cup ricotta

1. Prepare sauce, allowing 4½ hours for cooking.
2. Heat olive oil in a skillet. Add ground beef and cook until browned, separating into small pieces.
3. Spread ½ cup sauce in a 2-quart baking dish. Top with a layer of noodles and half the mozzarella cheese. Spread half the ground beef and half the egg slices on top. Sprinkle on half the Parmesan cheese and ¼ teaspoon pepper. Top with ½ cup ricotta.
4. Beginning with sauce, repeat layering, ending with ricotta. Top ricotta with ½ cup sauce. Arrange over this the remaining lasagne noodles. Top with more sauce.
5. Bake at 350°F about 30 minutes, or until mixture is bubbling. Let stand 5 to 10 minutes to set the layers. Cut in squares and serve topped with remaining sauce.

6 to 8 servings

358 *Egg Noodles Abruzzi (Maccheroni alla Chitarra)*

1 tablespoon butter
¼ cup olive oil
1 pound ground lamb
2 green peppers, chopped
1 teaspoon salt
¼ teaspoon pepper
½ cup dry white wine
2 large tomatoes, peeled and coarsely chopped
1 pound egg noodles

1. Heat butter and oil in a large skillet. Stir in lamb and green peppers; season with salt and pepper. Brown the meat slightly, stirring occasionally.
2. Add wine and simmer until liquid is almost evaporated. Stir in tomatoes and simmer mixture 30 minutes, or until sauce is thick.
3. Cook noodles according to package directions; drain. Place noodles on a hot platter, pour sauce over noodles, and serve.

4 to 6 servings

359 *Stuffed Pancakes (Scrippelle Imbusse)*

4 eggs
1 cup all-purpose flour
½ teaspoon salt
¾ cup water
Cooking oil
½ cup freshly grated Parmesan or Romano cheese
1 cup minced prosciutto
1 cup chicken broth

1. Beat eggs well in a medium-size mixing bowl. Gradually add flour and salt; mix well. When the mixture is smooth and creamy, add water, more if needed to make a thin batter.
2. Heat a 5-inch skillet and brush with oil. Pour in 2 tablespoons batter, spreading over bottom of skillet to form a thin pancake. As soon as bubbles appear on the top, turn and brown other side.
3. Continue making pancakes, greasing the skillet between each one. Combine cheese with prosciutto; sprinkle each pancake with about 1½ tablespoons of the mixture. Roll up pancakes tightly and place side by side in a shallow baking dish.
4. Bring chicken broth to boiling and pour over rolled pancakes. Cover the dish and set in a hot place (a heated oven with the heat turned off) for a few minutes, so the broth will be partially absorbed. Serve immediately.

16 filled pancakes

360 *Pasta with Potatoes (Lumachine con Patate)*

2 white onions, chopped
2 tablespoons olive oil
2 tablespoons butter
1 pound potatoes, pared and diced
2 pounds very ripe tomatoes, peeled and coarsely chopped
1½ teaspoons salt
½ teaspoon freshly ground pepper
1 tablespoon minced Italian parsley
1 pound lumachine
6 tablespoons grated Romano cheese

1. Sauté onions in oil and butter until soft. Stir in potatoes and simmer, covered, 15 minutes.
2. Stir in tomatoes, salt, pepper, and parsley. Simmer, covered, 25 minutes, then uncovered 10 minutes, stirring often.
3. Cook lumachine according to package directions; drain. Add to tomatoes and potatoes; mix well. Blend in 4 tablespoons cheese.
4. Serve immediately in hot soup bowls with remaining cheese sprinkled on top.

6 to 8 servings

361 *Basic Noodle Dough (Pasta)*

4 cups sifted all-purpose flour
½ teaspoon salt
4 eggs
6 tablespoons cold water

1. Mix flour and salt in a bowl; make a well in center. Add eggs, one at a time, mixing slightly after each addition. Add water gradually, mixing to make a stiff dough.
2. Turn dough onto a lightly floured surface and knead until smooth.
3. Proceed as directed in recipes.

362 *Pasta with Beans Sorrento Style*
(Conchigliette con Fagioli alla Sorrento)

2 cups dried Great Northern beans
5 cups water
1 teaspoon salt
1 cup chopped celery
1 cup chopped onion
3 tablespoons olive oil
1 teaspoon salt
6 ripe tomatoes, peeled and diced
1 tablespoon chopped Italian parsley
4 fresh basil leaves, chopped, or 1 teaspoon dried basil
½ pound conchigliette

1. Rinse beans and put into a heavy saucepot or kettle. Add water and bring rapidly to boiling; boil 2 minutes and remove from heat. Cover; set aside 1 hour.
2. Stir 1 teaspoon salt into beans, cover, and bring to boiling. Cook until beans are nearly done, but still firm (about 2 hours). Drain and set aside.
3. Sauté the celery and onion in olive oil until soft. Sprinkle in 1 teaspoon salt, then stir in tomatoes, parsley, and basil.
4. Simmer 15 minutes, uncovered. Add the beans to tomato mixture; stir well. Cook the conchigliette according to package directions, drain, and stir into bean mixture. Serve in hot soup bowls.

4 to 6 servings

363 *Spaghetti Sicilian Style (Spaghetti alla Siciliana)*

½ cup olive oil
2 cloves garlic, peeled and quartered
½ medium-size eggplant, pared and diced
6 large ripe tomatoes, peeled and coarsely chopped
2 green peppers
1 tablespoon chopped fresh basil or ½ teaspoon dried sweet basil
1 tablespoon capers
4 anchovy fillets, cut in small pieces
12 ripe olives, pitted and halved
1 teaspoon salt
¼ teaspoon pepper
1 pound spaghetti

1. Heat olive oil in a skillet; stir in garlic. Remove garlic from oil when brown. Stir eggplant and tomatoes into skillet; simmer 30 minutes.
2. Cut peppers vertically in half; remove membrane and seeds. Place peppers under broiler, skin side up, to loosen skins. Peel off skin, slice peppers, and add to tomato mixture.
3. Stir basil, capers, anchovies, olives, salt, and pepper into tomato mixture. Cover the skillet and simmer 10 minutes, or until sauce is well blended and is thickened.
4. Cook spaghetti according to package directions and drain. Immediately pour sauce over spaghetti and serve.

About 6 servings

364 *Lasagnette*

● Tomato Meat Sauce (half recipe)
Basic Noodle Dough
8 quarts water
¼ cup salt
1 tablespoon olive oil
1 cup (8 ounces) ricotta
2 tablespoons grated Parmesan cheese
¼ teaspoon salt
⅛ teaspoon pepper

1. Prepare Tomato Meat Sauce.
2. Prepare noodle dough. Roll lightly ⅛ inch thick to form a rectangle about 12 inches long. Cut dough lengthwise with pastry cutter into strips ½ to ¾ inch wide.
3. Bring water to boiling in a large saucepot. Add ¼ cup salt, then noodles. Boil rapidly, uncovered, about 15 minutes, or until tender. Drain by pouring into a colander or large sieve; keep warm.
4. Put ½ cup meat sauce into a saucepan. Mix in ricotta, Parmesan cheese, ¼ teaspoon salt, and pepper. Cook over low heat until thoroughly heated.
5. Put noodles on a warm serving platter and pour cheese sauce over them. Cover with meat sauce. Serve immediately.

About 8 servings

365 *Lasagne II*

● Tomato Sauce with Meat
1 pound lasagne noodles, cooked, drained, and rinsed
2 pounds ricotta
1 pound mozzarella or scamorze cheese, shredded
1 cup shredded Parmesan cheese

1. Prepare Tomato Sauce with Meat.
2. Spread about 1 cup tomato sauce in a buttered 13×9×2-inch baking dish. Using a fourth of each, add a layer of noodles and then one of tomato sauce. Using a third of each, top evenly with 3 cheeses. Repeat layering and end with sauce.
3. Heat in a 375°F oven about 30 minutes, or until bubbly. Allow to stand 10 to 15 minutes to set layers before serving. Cut into squares.

12 to 15 servings

366 *Shells with Clam Sauce*
(Conchiglie con Salsa alle Vongole)

4 quarts water
1 tablespoon salt
2 cups (8-ounce package) macaroni
    shells
● White Clam Sauce
1 tablespoon minced parsley

1. Bring water to boiling in a large saucepan or saucepot. Add salt, then macaroni. Boil rapidly, uncovered, 10 to 12 minutes, or until tender.
2. Meanwhile, prepare clam sauce.
3. Drain macaroni and put into a warm serving bowl. Pour clam sauce over macaroni and sprinkle with parsley.

4 to 6 servings

367 *Macaroni Muffs (Manicotti)*

● Tomato Meat Sauce
2 tablespoons olive oil
½ pound ground beef
2 cups (about 1 pound) ricotta
¼ pound mozzarella cheese, diced
2 teaspoons grated Parmesan
    cheese
2 eggs, well beaten
¾ teaspoon salt
¼ teaspoon pepper
● Basic Noodle Dough (one-half
    recipe)
5 quarts water
1 tablespoon salt

1. Prepare Tomato Meat Sauce.
2. While sauce is cooking, heat oil in a skillet. Add ground beef and cook until no pink color remains.
3. Combine cheeses, eggs, ¾ teaspoon salt, and pepper. Mix in meat. Set aside.
4. Prepare noodle dough. Divide dough into halves. Lightly roll each half ⅛ inch thick to form a rectangle. Cut dough lengthwise with pastry cutter into strips 5 inches wide. Cut strips every 6 inches to form noodles 5×6 inches.
5. Bring water to boiling in a large saucepot. Add 1 table-spoon salt, then noodles. Boil rapidly, uncovered, 10 to 12 minutes, or until noodles are tender. Drain.
6. Lay noodles out flat on a working surface. About ½ inch from the lengthwise edge of the noodle, put 4 tablespoons filling. Spread filling from narrow edge to narrow edge so filling is in a ½-inch-wide mound. Roll the ½-inch edge of the dough over filling and continue to roll. Press edges to seal. Put 4 to 6 manicotti into each of two 11×7×1½-inch baking dishes in a single layer. Cover with sauce.
7. Bake at 400°F 15 to 20 minutes, or until tomato sauce is bubbly hot. Serve with remaining sauce.

8 to 12 manicotti

368 *Mostaccioli and Cheese (Mostaccioli al Formaggio)*

● Tomato Meat Sauce
4 quarts water
1 tablespoon salt
2 cups (8-ounce package)
    mostaccioli
1 cup chopped mozzarella cheese
2 tablespoons grated Parmesan
    cheese
¼ teaspoon pepper
    Grated Parmesan or Romano
    cheese

1. Prepare Tomato Meat Sauce.
2. Heat water to boiling in a large saucepan. Add salt, then mostaccioli. Boil rapidly, uncovered, 12 to 15 minutes, or until tender. Drain.
3. Returned drained mostaccioli to saucepan and mix in 2 tablespoons meat sauce. Turn half of mostaccioli into an 8-inch square baking dish. Add cheeses and pepper in layers, then the remaining mostaccioli. Cover with additional meat sauce.
4. Bake at 350°F 15 to 20 minutes, or until sauce is bubbling.
5. Serve with remaining meat sauce. Sprinkle with grated cheese.

4 to 6 servings

369 *Green Noodles in Pastry* (*Tagliatelle Verdi Pasticciate*)

1 unbaked deep 9-inch pie shell
6 large mushrooms, cleaned and sliced
2 tablespoons butter
12 ounces green noodles
1 tablespoon butter
¼ cup grated Parmesan cheese
● 1 cup Bolognese Meat Sauce
● 1½ cups Cream Sauce
1 mushroom cap
6 to 8 mushroom halves
1 tablespoon butter, melted
Grated Parmesan cheese

1. Thoroughly prick bottom and sides of pie shell. Bake at 450°F about 7 minutes, or until lightly browned; set aside.
2. Sauté mushrooms in 2 tablespoons butter 3 minutes. Cook noodles according to package directions and drain.
3. Combine noodles, mushrooms, 1 tablespoon butter, ¼ cup cheese, meat sauce, and 1 cup Cream Sauce. Turn mixture into pie shell. Spread remaining ½ cup Cream Sauce over top. Put mushroom cap in center and surround with mushroom halves. Drizzle melted butter over all and sprinkle with additional cheese.
4. Bake at 400°F about 8 minutes, or until heated through and top is slightly browned.

About 6 servings

370 *Green Noodles* (*Pasta Verde*)

¼ pound spinach
3 cups sifted all-purpose flour
½ teaspoon salt
3 eggs
6 quarts water
1 tablespoon salt
¾ cup grated Parmesan cheese
½ teaspoon salt
¼ cup butter

1. Wash spinach and put into a heavy saucepan. Do not add water; cook only in moisture remaining on leaves from washing. Partially cover and cook 5 minutes, stirring occasionally with a fork.
2. Drain spinach, pressing out water, and chop finely.
3. Mix flour and ½ teaspoon salt in a bowl; make a well in center. Add eggs, one at a time, mixing slightly after each addition. Add the chopped spinach and mix well.
4. Turn dough onto a lightly floured surface and knead until smooth, adding flour if needed for a stiff dough.
5. Divide dough in half. Lightly roll each half into a rectangle, about ⅛ inch thick. Cover; let stand 1 hour. Beginning with a narrow end, gently fold over about 2 inches of dough and continue folding over so final width is about 3 inches. (Dough must be dry enough so layers do not stick together.) Beginning at a narrow edge, cut dough into strips ¼ inch wide. Unroll strips and arrange on waxed paper on a flat surface. Let stand until noodles are dry (2 to 3 hours).
6. Bring water to boiling in a large saucepot. Add 1 tablespoon salt. Add noodles gradually. Boil rapidly, uncovered, 8 to 10 minutes, or until tender.
7. Drain noodles and put a third of them into a greased 2-quart casserole. Top with a third each of the cheese and remaining salt. Dot with a third of butter. Repeat layering twice.
8. Bake at 350°F 15 to 20 minutes, or until cheese is melted.

About 8 servings

371 *Ravioli*

- Tomato Meat Sauce
- 3 cups (about 1½ pounds) ricotta
- 1½ tablespoons chopped parsley
- 2 eggs, well beaten
- 1 tablespoon grated Parmesan cheese
- ¾ teaspoon salt
- ¼ teaspoon pepper
- ● Basic Noodle Dough
- 7 quarts water
- 2 tablespoons salt
  Grated Parmesan or Romano cheese

1. Prepare Tomato Meat Sauce.
2. Mix ricotta, parsley, eggs, 1 tablespoon grated Parmesan, ¾ teaspoon salt, and pepper.
3. Prepare noodle dough. Divide dough in fourths. Lightly roll each fourth ⅛ inch thick to form a rectangle. Cut dough lengthwise with pastry cutter into strips 5 inches wide. Put 2 teaspoons filling 1½ inches from narrow end in center of each strip. Continuing along strip, put 2 teaspoons filling at 3½-inch intervals.
4. Fold each strip in half lengthwise, covering mounds of filling. To seal, press the edges together with the tines of a fork. Press gently between mounds to form rectangles about 3½ inches long. Cut apart with a pastry cutter and press cut edges of rectangles with tines of fork to seal.
5. Bring water to boiling in a large saucepot. Add 2 tablespoons salt. Add ravioli gradually; cook about half of ravioli at one time. Boil, uncovered, about 20 minutes, or until tender. Remove with slotted spoon and drain. Put on a warm platter and top with Tomato Meat Sauce. Sprinkle with grated cheese.

About 3 dozen ravioli

Ravioli with Meat Filling: Follow recipe for Ravioli. Prepare sauce. Omit ricotta and parsley. Heat **2 tablespoons olive oil** in a skillet. Add **¾ pound ground beef** and cook until no pink color remains. Cook **½ pound spinach** until tender (see step 1 of Green Noodles, page 61); drain. Mix spinach and ground beef with egg mixture. Proceed as directed.

372 *Seafood-Sauced Green Noodles*

- 1½ pounds medium-size fresh shrimp
- 3 tablespoons olive oil
- 2 tablespoons lemon juice
- 1 clove garlic, minced
- 2 tablespoons butter
- ● Clam Sauce
- 8 ounces green noodles (packaged or homemade), cooked and drained

1. Shell and devein shrimp; rinse under running cold water and drain.
2. Mix olive oil, lemon juice, and garlic in a bowl. Add shrimp; cover and marinate about 2 hours, tossing occasionally. Remove shrimp; set marinade aside.
3. Add shrimp to hot butter in a skillet; cook, turning frequently, until pink and tender, about 10 minutes.
4. Remove shrimp with a slotted spoon. Cut about two thirds of shrimp into pieces; reserve remainder. Blend pieces into Clam Sauce; keep warm.
5. Add reserved marinade to skillet; heat. Toss cooked noodles with hot marinade; turn into a heated serving dish. Pour sauce over noodles, sprinkle with **grated Romano cheese**, and garnish with whole shrimp.

About 6 servings

373 *Macaroni alla Savonarola*

½ pound ground veal
¾ cup fine dry bread crumbs
1 egg, beaten
2 tablespoons shredded Parmesan cheese
¼ teaspoon ground nutmeg
¼ teaspoon salt
1 cup uncooked green peas, fresh or frozen
2 tablespoons butter
⅓ cup finely chopped onion
1 cup finely chopped cooked ham
3 tablespoons butter
3 hard-cooked eggs, cut in ¼-inch cubes
2 cups whipping cream
1 pound maccaroncini (big spaghetti with a hole), cooked and drained
½ cup shredded Parmesan cheese

1. Mix half of the ground veal with bread crumbs, egg, 2 tablespoons cheese, nutmeg, and salt to make a smooth mixture. Form into small balls.
2. In a large ovenware skillet, cook peas in 2 tablespoons hot butter until lightly browned. Add the meatballs to the skillet. Set in a 375°F oven for 20 minutes.
3. Lightly brown onion, ham, and remaining veal in 3 tablespoons butter in a saucepan.
4. Add the ham-veal mixture, hard-cooked eggs, and cream to the skillet; mix well. Bring to boiling; simmer about 15 minutes.
5. Turn maccaroncini onto a platter, pour sauce over it, and sprinkle remaining Parmesan cheese over all.

6 to 8 servings

374 *Spaghetti with Meatballs (Spaghetti con Polpette)*

● Tomato Meat Sauce
½ pound ground beef
½ pound ground pork
1 cup soft bread crumbs
1 tablespoon grated Parmesan cheese
1 tablespoon minced parsley
1 egg, well beaten
1 teaspoon salt
¼ teaspoon pepper
2 tablespoons olive oil
1 clove garlic, minced
4 quarts water
1 tablespoon salt
8 ounces long spaghetti
Grated Parmesan or Romano cheese

1. Prepare Tomato Meat Sauce.
2. While sauce is cooking, lightly mix ground meat with bread crumbs, 1 tablespoon Parmesan cheese, parsley, egg, 1 teaspoon salt, and pepper. Shape mixture into balls about 1 inch in diameter.
3. Heat oil and garlic in a skillet. Add meatballs and brown on all sides. Add meatballs to sauce about 20 minutes before sauce is cooked.
4. Heat water to boiling in a saucepot. Add 1 tablespoon salt. Add spaghetti and stir with a fork. Boil rapidly; uncovered, 10 to 12 minutes, or until tender. Drain.
5. Put spaghetti on a warm platter and top with sauce. Sprinkle with grated cheese.

4 to 6 servings

Spaghetti with Wine Tomato Sauce: Follow recipe for Spaghetti with Meatballs. About 30 minutes before sauce is done, add ½ cup dry red wine.

Spaghetti with Tomato Sauce: Follow recipe for Spaghetti with Meatballs. Omit meatballs. Top spaghetti with Tomato Meat Sauce or a variation.

375 *Pasta with Broccoli (Pasta e Broccoli)*

4 quarts water
2 teaspoons salt
4 cups (1-pound package) ditalini
1 pound broccoli, washed and trimmed
¼ cup olive oil
2 cloves garlic, sliced
⅛ teaspoon pepper
Grated Parmesan or Romano cheese

1. Heat water to boiling in a large saucepan. Add salt, then ditalini. Boil rapidly, uncovered, about 12 minutes, or until tender. Drain, reserving 3 cups liquid. Set aside.
2. Put broccoli into a small amount of boiling salted water. Cook uncovered 5 minutes, then cover and cook 10 to 15 minutes, or until just tender. Drain if necessary and keep warm.
3. Heat oil and garlic in a large saucepan until garlic is lightly browned.
4. Add broccoli and ditalini with the reserved cooking liquid. Season with pepper. Simmer about 10 minutes.
5. Top with grated cheese and serve immediately.

About 6 servings

376 *Pasta with Peas (Pasta e Piselli)*

2 quarts water
1 teaspoon salt
2 cups (8-ounce package) ditalini
¼ cup olive oil
¼ cup chopped onion
½ cup canned tomatoes, sieved
¾ teaspoon salt
⅛ teaspoon pepper
⅛ teaspoon oregano
2 cans (16 ounces each) green peas, drained
Grated Parmesan or Romano cheese

1. Heat water to boiling in a large saucepan. Add 1 teaspoon salt, then ditalini. Boil rapidly, uncovered, about 12 minutes, or until tender. Drain, reserving 2 cups liquid.
2. Heat oil in a large saucepan. Add onion and cook until lightly browned. Add tomatoes, ¾ teaspoon salt, pepper, and oregano; mix well. Simmer about 10 minutes.
3. Add cooked ditalini, reserved cooking liquid, and drained peas. Simmer about 10 minutes.
4. Top with grated cheese and serve immediately.

4 to 6 servings

377 *Pasta with Beans (Pasta e Fagioli)*

3 cups water
1¼ cups (about ½ pound) dried navy beans, rinsed
½ teaspoon salt
2 quarts water
1 teaspoon salt

1. Heat 3 cups water to boiling in a large saucepan. Add beans gradually to water. Boil 2 minutes. Remove from heat and cover, and set aside 1 hour.
2. Add ½ teaspoon salt to soaked beans. Bring to boiling, reduce heat, and simmer, covered, 2 hours, or until beans are tender; stir once or twice.

2 cups (8-ounce package) ditalini
¼ cup canned tomatoes, sieved
1 tablespoon olive oil
¼ teaspoon pepper
¼ teaspoon oregano
  Grated Parmesan cheese

3. Meanwhile, heat 2 quarts water to boiling in a large saucepan. Add 1 teaspoon salt, then ditalini. Boil rapidly, uncovered, about 12 minutes, or until ditalini is tender. Drain, reserving 1 cup liquid.
4. When beans are tender, add the drained ditalini, the 1 cup reserved liquid, tomatoes, oil, pepper, and oregano. Simmer 10 to 15 minutes.
5. Sprinkle with grated cheese and serve immediately.

About 6 servings

378 *Gnocchi alla Semolino*

1 quart milk
1 teaspoon salt
⅛ teaspoon freshly ground nutmeg
1 cup uncooked farina or semolina
¼ cup butter
3 eggs, well beaten
½ cup freshly shredded Parmesan
  cheese
  Butter
  Freshly shredded Parmesan
  cheese

1. Put milk, salt, and nutmeg into a heavy saucepan and bring to boiling. Add farina gradually, stirring constantly to prevent lumping. Cook and stir over low heat 10 minutes, or until very thick.
2. Remove from heat and beat in ¼ cup butter, eggs, and ½ cup cheese. Spread mixture about ½ inch thick on a greased baking sheet with sides. Chill thoroughly.
3. When ready to bake, top with bits of butter and a generous sprinkling of Parmesan cheese.
4. Heat in a 425°F oven until top is browned.
5. To serve, cut into squares.

About 8 servings

379 *Corn Tortillas*

1 teaspoon salt
2 cups dehydrated masa flour
   (masa harina)
1⅓ cups hot water

1. Stir salt into masa flour. Add water and stir until all flour is moistened and dough sticks together. Add a little more water if necessary; dough should be soft, but not sticky.
2. Break off pieces of dough about the size of a large egg, form into balls, and flatten slightly. Press with a tortilla press (or roll with rolling pin) between two sheets of waxed paper to 6-inch rounds.
3. Bake on a preheated ungreased griddle, about 2 minutes per side; tortillas are ready to be turned when edges begin to curl. Stack hot baked tortillas in a towel-lined bowl. Serve hot.

12 tortillas

Note: Unused tortillas may be wrapped in moisture-proof wrap and stored in the refrigerator. To reheat, simply dampen slightly and warm on a medium-hot griddle, turning several times. Immediately wrap in towel to retain heat until served. Do not let them dry out.

380 *Wheat Flour Tortillas*

2 cups all-purpose flour
1 teaspoon salt
1 teaspoon baking powder
¼ cup lard or shortening
½ to ¾ cup cold water

1. Stir flour with salt and baking powder in bowl. Cut in lard until pieces are the size of small peas. Sprinkle water on top and mix lightly until all dry ingredients are moistened, adding only enough water to make a soft dough.
2. Turn out on a lightly floured surface or pastry canvas and knead gently, about 30 seconds. Divide into 12 equal balls; cover with a towel or waxed paper and let stand about 15 minutes. Roll each ball to a 7-inch round.
3. Bake on an ungreased griddle until lightly browned, turning once; use 2 to 3 minutes total baking time.

12 tortillas

381 *Ground Beef Filling*

This filling may be used alone, but is particularly good sprinkled with shredded mild Cheddar cheese.

1½ pounds ground beef
¼ cup chopped onion
1 clove garlic, minced
1 teaspoon salt
¼ teaspoon pepper
1 teaspoon chili powder
½ teaspoon cumin (optional)
1 cup canned tomato sauce

1. Crumble beef into skillet and brown well; if beef is very fat, pour off excess fat.
2. Add onion and garlic and cook about 5 minutes until onion is soft, stirring frequently.
3. Stir in dry seasonings, then tomato sauce. Continue cooking about 15 minutes longer.

About 3 cups filling

382 *Beef-Onion Filling*

3 tablespoons lard
1 cup finely chopped onion
1 clove garlic, minced
1 pound ground beef
1 teaspoon salt
2 teaspoons chili powder
Pinch ground cumin (comino)

Heat lard in a large, heavy skillet. Add onion and garlic and cook until tender. Add beef and seasonings; mix well. Cook until meat is lightly browned.

About 2½ cups filling

383 *Chicken Filling*

2 cups diced cooked chicken
● 1 cup Guacamole I , or 1
   fresh avocado
1 large fresh tomato, peeled, cored, and chopped

1. Combine chicken with guacamole; or, if using fresh avocado, peel and slice avocado into thin strips.
2. To assemble tacos, spoon chicken onto soft tortillas (top with avocado slices, if using fresh avocado). Spoon on a little chopped tomato and close tacos.

384 *Picadillo I*

1½ pounds beef (chuck or pot roast may be used)
Water
¾ cup chopped onion
1 clove garlic, minced
¼ cup cooking oil
1 cup chili sauce
1 cup cooked peas and diced carrots
½ cup beef broth (from cooked meat)
1 teaspoon salt
¼ teaspoon pepper
¼ teaspoon ginger
1 bay leaf, crumbled
1 or more chopped canned jalapeño chilies

1. Cook meat in water to cover until tender (1 to 3 hours, depending upon cut of meat chosen); add more water during cooking if necessary to prevent drying out. Pour off and reserve beef broth.
2. Shred the meat by pulling it apart into small strips.
3. Sauté the onion and garlic in hot oil until onion is soft; add to the meat. Add remaining ingredients and stir until evenly mixed.

About 3 cups filling

385 *Picadillo II*

1 pound coarsely chopped beef
1 pound coarsely chopped pork
1 cup chopped onion
1 clove garlic, minced
1 cup chopped raw apple
1½ cups chopped tomatoes (fresh peeled tomatoes or canned tomatoes, drained, may be used)
½ cup raisins
1 or more chopped canned jalapeño chilies
1½ teaspoons salt
¼ teaspoon pepper
⅛ teaspoon cinnamon
⅛ teaspoon cloves
½ cup chopped almonds

1. Cook beef and pork together in large skillet until well browned. Add onion and garlic and cook until onion is soft. Add remaining ingredients, except almonds, and simmer 15 to 20 minutes longer until flavors are well blended and filling is slightly thickened.
2. Stir in almonds.

About 4½ cups filling

386 *Grilled Meat Filling*

1½ pounds thinly sliced beef steak (cubed steaks may be used if no more than ¼ inch thick)
Salt and pepper
Oil for frying

1. Sprinkle meat with salt and pepper and rub in slightly.
2. Pour oil into heavy skillet to just cover bottom; heat until sizzling. Quickly fry steaks, turning once; allow about 5 minutes total cooking time.
3. Remove steaks to a heated platter or cutting board and immediately slice into ½-inch squares. Serve at once with **hot soft tortillas** and Fresh Tomato Sauce (●).

387 *Chorizo Filling*

Chorizo is spicy Mexican sausage which is frequently used as filling for tacos, topping for tostadas, in combination with eggs, or in various soups and casserole dishes. It is popular as a taco filling combined with cubed cooked potatoes. You may be able to purchase chorizo in a Mexican specialty store. If not, here is a simple recipe for making your own.

1 pound ground lean pork
½ cup chopped onion
1 clove garlic, minced
2 tablespoons chili powder
1 teaspoon salt
1 teaspoon oregano
½ teaspoon cumin (comino)
¼ cup vinegar

1. Combine all ingredients and let stand several hours, or overnight, in refrigerator.
2. To use as a filling, fry in skillet until well browned, stirring until crumbled.
3. Serve in tacos, combined with cubed cooked potatoes, refried beans, and/or guacamole.

About 2½ cups filling

Note: Chorizo is also delicious formed into patties and fried. The cooked patties make a good breakfast dish.

388 *Flautas*

Flautas are another form of taco, formed with two overlapping tortillas, filled, rolled, and fried until crisp.

Soft tortillas
● Meat filling
Oil for frying

1. To prepare each flauta, arrange 2 soft tortillas on a flat surface, overlapping one about halfway over the other. Spoon desired amount of meat filling down center length. Roll up, starting with one long side and rolling toward other. Pin closed with wooden picks or small skewers, or hold closed with tongs.
2. Fry in oil in a skillet until crisp. Drain. Eat while hot.

389 *Enrollados*

Still another type of taco—batter dipped and then deep fried—is named Enrollados. Use one of the fillings on page 17, or try this version, which is a kind of pork picadillo containing potatoes.

Filling:
- ½ **pound boneless pork loin (lomo)**
- ½ **pound potatoes, pared**
- 2 **tablespoons oil or lard**
- 1 **cup chopped onion**
- 1 **cup tomato purée**
  Salt and pepper
- 12 **soft tortillas**
- ¼ **cup flour**
- 3 **eggs, beaten**
- ¾ **cup oil for frying**

Garnish:
- ¼ **cup shredded Monterey Jack**
- 1½ **cups canned enchilada sauce**
  Avocado slices

1. Prepare filling by cooking pork in a small amount of salted water until tender; shred.
2. Chop potatoes.
3. Heat oil; cook onion in oil until soft (about 5 minutes). Add shredded pork and potatoes. Stir in tomato purée. Season to taste with salt and pepper. Simmer until thick, stirring frequently.
4. Spoon a scoop of this mixture on center of each tortilla. Roll up tortilla; dip in flour and then in beaten eggs.
5. Fry in hot fat until crisp on all sides.
6. Serve hot, sprinkled with shredded cheese, topped with sauce, and garnished with avocado slices.

12 enrollados

390 *Swiss Enchiladas*

- 2 **cans (6 ounces each) tomato paste**
- ¼ **cup coarsely chopped onion**
- 1 **clove garlic**
- 1 **teaspoon salt**
- ⅛ **teaspoon pepper**
- 2 **cups water**
- 1 **chicken bouillon cube**
  Oil for frying
- 12 **soft corn tortillas**
- 1½ **cups finely diced cooked chicken**
- 1½ **cups shredded cheese (Monterey Jack, Chihuahua, or process Swiss)**
- ½ **cup whipping cream**

1. Combine tomato paste, onion, garlic, salt, pepper, and 1 cup of the water in an electric blender. Blend until liquefied.
2. Pour into a medium-size skillet; stir in remaining water and bouillon cube. Bring to boiling and simmer until bouillon cube is dissolved, stirring frequently. Continue to simmer over low heat until smooth and slightly thickened. Remove from heat.
3. Pour about ¼ inch oil into a small skillet and heat to sizzling.
4. To prepare enchiladas, first dip each tortilla into hot sauce, turning to coat both sides; then fry coated tortilla in hot oil, about 30 seconds per side. Remove from oil; drain slightly.
5. Put about 2 tablespoons chicken at one side of tortilla and roll up. Place in a shallow casserole with open flap on bottom. Repeat until all tortillas are filled. Sprinkle with shredded cheese and drizzle with cream. Pour remaining sauce over all.
6. Bake at 350°F about 30 minutes, or until bubbling hot.

About 6 servings

391 *Quesadillas*

1½ cups shredded Monterey Jack or
    mild Cheddar cheese
2 ancho chilies, peeled, seeded,
    stemmed, and chopped; or 2
    or 3 chopped canned jalapeño
    chilies
12 soft corn tortillas
    Oil for frying

1. Combine cheese and chopped chilies.
2. Use as a filling for folded crisp-fried tacos, spooning about 1 heaping tablespoon of filling onto center of each soft tortilla before folding and frying. As taco is fried, cheese will melt and help hold tortilla in folded position.

12 quesadillas

392 *Burritos*

Burritos are a type of taco made with wheat flour tortillas. The filling may be refried beans alone, or combined with meat as in the following recipe.

12 wheat flour tortillas
1½ cups hot refried beans (use
    canned beans or ●
● 1½ cups hot Ground Beef Filling
    Oil for frying (optional)

1. Spread each tortilla with about 1 tablespoon refried beans, spreading only to about ½ inch of edge. Spoon a heaping tablespoon of ground beef filling along one side. Fold in ends about 1 inch to cover filling, then roll up tortilla starting with side on which meat has been placed. Serve at once.
2. Or, fry in hot oil until crisp, placing each burrito in skillet with open flap on bottom to start, then turning to fry top and sides. Drain on absorbent paper. Serve hot.

12 burritos

393 *Totopos*

1 small onion, finely chopped
1 tablespoon butter
1 can (15 ounces) kidney beans
    (undrained)
    Salt and pepper
6 tortillas
    Oil for frying
    Shredded lettuce
2 ripe avocados, peeled, pitted, and
    sliced
2 cups slivered cooked chicken
3 jalapeño chilies, seeded and
    thinly sliced, or 3 pickles,
    thinly sliced
● Oil and Vinegar Dressing
1 fresh tomato, sliced
¾ cup shredded Monterey Jack or
    mild Cheddar cheese

1. Sauté onion in butter in a skillet. Add kidney beans with liquid and cook until liquid is reduced by half.
2. Remove beans from skillet to a bowl. Mash beans and season to taste with salt and pepper.
3. Fry tortillas, one at a time, in oil in a skillet. Drain and cool. Spread tortillas with mashed beans and put on individual plates.
4. Toss lettuce, avocado slices, chicken, and chilies with a small amount of dressing.
5. Pile salad mixture on mashed beans, top with tomato slices, and sprinkle with cheese.

6 servings

394 *Chicken Enchiladas*

3 cups shredded cooked chicken
   white meat
● Green Chili Sauce (double
   recipe)
12 tortillas
   Dairy sour cream

1. Lightly toss chicken with ¾ cup sauce.
2. Dip each tortilla in hot sauce, spoon ¼ cup of chicken down center, and roll up. Place enchiladas, open edge down, in a baking dish, then spoon hot sauce over them; cover dish.
3. Set in a 400°F oven about 10 minutes, or until thoroughly heated.
4. Serve with sour cream.

6 servings

395 *Cheese Enchiladas with Chili Sauce*

6 dried ancho chilies
¼ cup water
¼ teaspoon garlic salt
   Oil for frying
24 soft corn tortillas
1½ pounds shredded Monterey Jack
½ cup chopped onion
1 teaspoon oregano
1 cup whipping cream

1. Put chilies into a saucepan with small amount of water; cook until softened. Drain; remove seeds and pith.
2. Put into an electric blender with ¼ cup water. Blend until puréed. Pour into saucepan, add garlic salt, and heat to bubbling.
3. In another saucepan, pour in oil to about ½-inch depth; heat to boiling.
4. Pass tortillas through oil, one at a time, then through warm sauce. Spoon cheese on tortilla and sprinkle with onion and oregano. Roll up and arrange filled tortillas in a single layer in the bottom of a baking dish. Pour a third of the cream over all and sprinkle with a little cheese. Repeat for two more layers.
5. Bake at 350°F about 15 minutes, or until heated through and cheese is melted.

8 to 10 servings

396 *Ranch-Style Enchiladas*

Sauce:
- 5 ancho chilies
- 1 clove garlic
- ⅛ teaspoon salt
- 1 cup chicken stock or bouillon or 1¼ cups canned enchilada sauce

Enchiladas:
- Oil for frying
- 12 corn tortillas (6- or 7-inch size)
- 2 cups diced cooked chicken or pork
- ½ cup chopped onion
- Shredded lettuce

1. To make sauce, toast and peel chilies; remove stems and seeds.   Put into an electric blender with garlic, salt, and chicken broth. Blend until liquefied. Pour into a medium-size skillet and cook about 5 minutes.

2. Pour about ¼ inch oil into a small skillet and heat to sizzling.

3. To prepare enchiladas, first dip each tortilla in hot sauce, turning to coat both sides; they fry coated tortilla in hot oil, about 30 seconds per side. Remove from oil; drain slightly.

4. Put about 2 tablespoons chicken or pork along one side; sprinkle with onion. Roll up and place in a shallow casserole with open flap on bottom. Repeat until all tortillas are filled.

5. When ready to serve, heat in a 350°F oven about 20 minutes.

6. Serve topped with shredded lettuce.

About 6 servings

397 *Pastel de Tortilla*

- 2 large ancho chilies
- 2 cups canned salsa verde mexicana (Mexican green tomato sauce)
- 1 cup chicken stock or bouillon
- 20 tortillas
- Oil for frying
- 1 pound diced cooked pork
- 1 cup cream
- 1 cup shredded Monterey Jack or mild Cheddar cheese

1. Toast and peel chilies; remove stems and seeds and cut into thin strips.

2. Combine chilies with salsa verde and chicken stock.

3. Meanwhile, slice tortillas into strips and fry in hot oil until crisp; drain on absorbent paper.

4. Layer ingredients in a 2-quart casserole as follows: first ⅓ of fried tortilla strips, next ⅓ of diced pork, then ⅓ of salsa verde mixture. Repeat twice more. Pour cream over all. Sprinkle cheese over top.

5. Heat in a 350°F oven about 30 minutes, or until heated through.

8 servings

398 *Chicken Chalupa*

12 corn tortillas
1¼ cups chicken stock or bouillon
1 cup dairy sour cream
¼ cup chopped onion
1 clove garlic, minced
1 to 3 canned jalapeño chilies, finely chopped
1 teaspoon salt
2 cups diced cooked chicken
2 cups shredded Monterey Jack or mild Cheddar cheese
Paprika

1. Soak tortillas in 1 cup of the chicken stock.
2. Combine remaining ¼ cup chicken stock, sour cream, onion, garlic, chilies, and salt and stir until well mixed.
3. Layer ingredients in a casserole as follows: single layer of soaked tortillas, chicken, sauce, and then cheese; repeat until all ingredients are used, ending with cheese on top. Sprinkle with paprika.
4. Let stand overnight (or about 8 hours) in refrigerator before baking.
5. Bake at 350°F 1 hour.

6 to 8 servings

399 *Meat or Poultry Tamales*

3½ dozen large dry corn husks
1 cup lard
4 cups dehydrated masa flour (masa harina)
2½ to 3 cups warm meat or poultry stock (or water)
2 teaspoons salt
3½ cups meat or poultry filling of
● your choice (Picadillo,
● Ground Beef Filling,
● or Chicken or Turkey Mole Poblano)

1. Wash corn husks in warm water, put into a saucepan, and cover with boiling water. Let soak at least 30 minutes before using.
2. Beat lard until light and fluffy, using spoon or electric mixer. Gradually beat in masa flour and stock until dough sticks together and has a pastelike consistency. Taste dough before adding salt; if stock is salty you will not need all 2 teaspoons of salt.
3. Shake excess water from each softened corn husk and pat dry on paper towels. Spread about 2 tablespoons, tamale dough on center portion of husk, leaving at least a 2-inch margin at both ends and about ½-inch margin at right side. Spoon about 1½ tablespoons filling onto dough. Wrap tamale, overlapping left side first, then right side slightly over left. Fold bottom up and top down.
4. Lay tamales in top section of steamer with open flaps on bottom. (If husks are too short to stay closed, they may be tied with string or thin strips of corn husk.) Tamales may completely fill top section of steamer but should be placed so there are spaces between them for circulation of steam.
5. Steam over simmering water about 1 hour, or until corn husk can be peeled from dough easily.

3½ dozen tamales

400 *Chicken Tamale Pie*

Filling:
- ¼ cup lard or cooking oil
- 1 cup chopped onion
- 1 clove garlic, minced
- 2 cups (16-ounce can) cooked tomatoes
- 1½ teaspoons salt
- 1 tablespoon chili powder
- ½ teaspoon cumin (comino)
- 3 cups diced cooked chicken

Tamale Dough:
- ½ cup lard
- 3 cups dehydrated masa flour (masa harina)
- 1 teaspoon baking powder
- ½ teaspoon salt
- 1 cup chicken stock (or 1 cup water plus 1 chicken bouillon cube)

1. For filling, heat lard in a large skillet. Add onion and garlic and cook until onion is soft, about 5 minutes. Add tomatoes and seasonings and bring to boiling, stirring until evenly mixed. Reduce heat and simmer about 10 minutes. Stir in chicken and simmer about 5 minutes.
2. For the tamale dough, beat lard until light and fluffy, using spoon or electric mixer. Combine masa flour, baking powder, and salt. Gradually beat flour mixture and chicken stock into lard until dough sticks together and has a pastelike consistency.
3. Grease a 2-quart casserole. Press tamale dough onto bottom and sides of casserole in a layer about ½ inch thick, reserving enough dough to cover top. Pour in prepared filling. Cover filling with remaining dough patted into a layer of same thickness as lining.
4. Bake at 350°F about 1 hour.

6 to 8 servings

401 *Pork Tamale Pie*

Filling:
- 1½ pounds ground lean pork
- ½ cup chopped onion
- 2 cups cooked tomatoes (19-ounce can)
- 1 clove garlic
- 1 tablespoon chili powder
- 1½ teaspoons salt
- ½ teaspoon oregano
- ¼ teaspoon pepper

Cornmeal Topping:
- 1 cup yellow or white cornmeal
- 2 tablespoons flour
- 1 tablespoon sugar
- 2 teaspoons baking powder
- ½ teaspoon salt
- 1 egg
- ½ cup milk
- 1 tablespoon melted shortening, bacon drippings, or oil

1. For the filling, brown pork in a large skillet, crumbling and stirring until all meat is browned.
2. Put onion, some of the tomatoes, garlic, and chili powder into an electric blender; blend to a thick purée. Gradually add remaining tomatoes and continue blending until puréed.
3. Pour tomato purée into skillet with meat. Bring to boiling; reduce heat to simmering. Stir in salt, oregano, and pepper. Cover and simmer 30 minutes.
4. Meanwhile, for cornmeal topping, mix cornmeal with flour, sugar, baking powder, and salt in a bowl.
5. Beat egg slightly; beat in milk and shortening. Add liquid ingredients to dry ingredients all at once and stir lightly, just until all dry ingredients are moistened. Do not beat.
6. Spoon batter over simmering filling.
7. Bake at 425°F 20 to 25 minutes, or until topping is golden brown.

About 6 servings

402 *Dessert Tamales*

3½ dozen large dry corn husks
1 cup lard (or ½ cup lard and ½ cup butter or margarine)
4 cups dehydrated masa flour (masa harina)
1 cup sugar
1 teaspoon salt
2½ to 3 cups warm water or fruit
Date-Pecan Filling (or other fruit or nut filling of your choice)

1. Wash corn husks in warm water, put into a saucepan, and cover with boiling water. Let soak at least 30 minutes before using.
2. Beat lard until light and fluffy, using spoon or electric mixer.
3. Combine masa flour, sugar, and salt. Gradually beat in this mixture and water until dough sticks together and has a pastelike consistency.
4. Shake excess water from each softened corn husk and pat dry on paper towels. Spread about 2 tablespoons tamale dough on center portion of husk, leaving at least a 2-inch margin at both ends and about ½-inch margin at right side. Spoon about 1½ tablespoons filling onto dough. Wrap tamale, overlapping left side first, then right side slightly over left. Fold bottom up and top down.
5. Lay tamales in top section of steamer with open flaps on bottom. (If husks are too short to stay closed, they may be tied with string or thin strips of corn husk.) Tamales may completely fill top section of steamer but should be placed so there are spaces between them for circulation of steam.
6. Steam over simmering water about 1 hour, or until corn husks can be peeled from dough easily.

3½ dozen tamales

Date-Pecan Filling: Blend **1 cup brown sugar**, **¼ cup butter or margarine**, and **½ teaspoon cinnamon** until smooth. Add **1 cup chopped pitted dates** and **1 cup chopped pecans**; toss until evenly mixed.

Vegetables

403 *Artichokes in White Wine* *(Angynares Krasata)*

12 whole small onions, peeled
1 cup wine
1 cup water
¾ cup olive oil
   Salt and pepper to taste
1 teaspoon sugar
1 teaspoon marjoram
1 bay leaf
4 parsley sprigs, minced
   Juice of 1 lemon
8 artichokes, cleaned and cut in
   quarters

1. Combine all ingredients in a deep saucepan. Simmer covered until artichokes are tender.
2. Serve either hot or cold.

4 servings

404 *Beans Plaki*

3 cups dried white beans
½ cup olive oil
2 medium onions, chopped
2 garlic cloves, crushed in a
   garlic press
1 can (8 ounces) tomato sauce or
● 1 cup Tomato Sauce
2 celery stalks, diced
1 carrot, diced
1 bay leaf
1 teaspoon oregano
1 teaspoon sugar
   Salt and pepper to taste
   Wine vinegar

1. Place beans in a pot and cover with water. Bring to a boil. Simmer covered 2 to 3 hours, until just tender. Drain.
2. Heat oil in a saucepan, add onion, and cook until translucent. Add garlic, tomato sauce, celery, carrot, bay leaf, oregano, sugar, salt, and pepper. Simmer 5 minutes. (If sauce is too thick, add a little water.)
3. Add beans to sauce and simmer covered about 20 minutes, or until tender.
4. Serve hot or cold with a cruet of wine vinegar.

About 12 servings

405 *Green Beans with Tomatoes* (*Fasolakia me Domates*)

2 pounds green beans or 3
    packages (9 ounces each)
    frozen green beans
1 teaspoon salt
½ cup olive oil
1 can (20 ounces) tomatoes
    (undrained)
1 medium onion, chopped
    Juice of 1 lemon
1 teaspoon oregano, crushed
    Salt and pepper

1. Wash green beans, cut off ends, and cut in half lengthwise. Bring a small amount of water to a boil. Add ½ teaspoon salt and the beans. Cover and cook about 20 minutes. Drain. If frozen beans are used, cook according to directions on the package.
2. Heat olive oil in a skillet. Add tomatoes, onion, lemon juice, oregano, and salt and pepper to taste. Simmer covered 10 minutes. Pour over beans. Simmer together an additional 10 minutes.

8 servings

406 *Green Beans with Onion Rings*

1 cup water
1 onion, thinly sliced
2 pounds green beans, ends
    snipped off and beans sliced
½ cup butter
    Salt and pepper to taste
    Lemon juice to taste

Bring water to boiling. Separate onion slices into rings and add. Add green beans, butter, salt, pepper, and lemon juice. Boil until beans are tender (about 20 minutes).

6 servings

407 *Stewed Cabbage in Tomato Sauce* (*Lahana Brasto me Domata*)

1 head cabbage
    Boiling salted water
½ cup olive oil
1 medium onion, chopped
1 can (16 ounces) tomatoes
    (undrained)
1 celery stalk, diced
1 carrot, diced
1 bay leaf
1 teaspoon sugar
    Salt and pepper to taste

1. Remove outer leaves from cabbage and trim off part of the core. Drop into boiling salted water to cover. Cook until just tender (about 8 minutes). Drain.
2. Meanwhile, heat olive oil in a saucepan and add onion; cook until translucent. Add tomatoes, celery, carrot, bay leaf, and sugar. Simmer 15 minutes.
3. Pour sauce over cabbage. Season with salt and pepper.

4 servings

408 *Baked Carrot Ring*

¾ cup butter
2 eggs, separated
½ cup packed brown sugar
1 teaspoon cinnamon
½ teaspoon nutmeg
½ teaspoon mint
Juice of ½ lemon
2 teaspoons water
1½ cups grated carrots
1 cup dried black currants
1 cup pine nuts
1 cup all-purpose flour
1 teaspoon baking powder
½ teaspoon baking soda
½ teaspoon salt
½ cup cracker meal

1. Using an electric mixer, cream butter, egg yolks, brown sugar, cinnamon, nutmeg, and mint until fluffy. Add lemon juice, water, carrots, currants, and pine nuts; blend thoroughly.
2. Mix flour, baking powder, baking soda, and salt. Add to carrot mixture.
3. Beat egg whites until fluffy. Fold into batter.
4. Grease a 9-inch ring mold or a square cake pan. Sprinkle with cracker meal. Pour in the batter.
5. Bake at 350°F 50 to 55 minutes.
6. Cool on wire rack. Place a serving dish over the top of carrot ring. Invert to unmold.

8 servings

409 *Dilled Carrots* (Karota me Anitho)

1 cup water
¼ cup white wine vinegar
1 medium onion, quartered
½ teaspoon salt
1 tablespoon dill
6 large carrots, pared and cut in thick slices

1. Bring water and vinegar to boiling. Put in onion, salt, dill, and carrots. Reduce heat and simmer 10 minutes. Cool.
2. Refrigerate in liquid until chilled.
3. Drain and serve cold.

4 to 6 servings

410 *Cauliflower in Béchamel Sauce* (Kounoupidi me Béchamel Saltsa)

1 head cauliflower
Boiling water
Juice of 1 small lemon
● 2 cups Béchamel Sauce
½ cup grated mizithra cheese
¼ cup fresh bread crumbs
¼ teaspoon ground allspice
Salt and pepper to taste

1. Remove leaves from the cauliflower and cut off tough end. Soak in cold salted water for 15 minutes. Rinse and drain. Keep whole or break into flowerets.
2. Boil enough water to cover cauliflower. Add lemon juice and the cauliflower. Cook until stalks are just tender (10 to 20 minutes). Drain.
3. Place cauliflower in a baking dish. Cover with Béchamel Sauce, sprinkle with cheese, bread crumbs, allspice, salt, and pepper.
4. Bake at 375°F 20 minutes.

4 to 6 servings

Vegetable (Cauliflower) Polonaise, page 167

411 *Stewed Cauliflower* (Kounoupidi Sigovrasmeno)

1 head cauliflower
½ cup olive oil
1 medium onion, chopped
1 garlic clove
1 bay leaf
1 tablespoon wine vinegar
¼ cup chopped parsley

1. Remove leaves from cauliflower and cut off tough end. Soak in cold salted water for 15 minutes. Rinse and drain. Keep whole or break into flowerets.
2. Heat olive oil in a saucepan. Add onion and cook until translucent. Add garlic, bay leaf, wine vinegar, parsley, cauliflower, and enough water to cover. Cover. Simmer, turning several times until tender (10 to 20 minutes).
3. Serve hot or cooled.

4 servings

412 *Fried Eggplant* (Melitzanes Tyganites)

2 medium eggplants
Salt
¾ cup olive oil
¾ cup vegetable oil
2 cups all-purpose flour
Salt and pepper to taste

1. Slice eggplants horizontally 1/3 inch thick. Sprinkle both sides generously with salt. Arrange in a single layer in baking dish. Allow to stand 1 hour.
2. Squeeze each eggplant slice firmly between palms of hands or use a heavy weight wrapped in aluminum foil to press out excess liquid.
3. Heat oils together to smoking.
4. Meanwhile, season flour with salt and pepper. Dip each slice in the flour. Fry the eggplant slices until golden brown, turning once. Remove. Serve immediately.

About 6 servings

413 *Stuffed Eggplant* (Melitzanes Yemistes)

¼ cup olive oil
2 large onions, minced
1 cup minced celery
1 carrot, thinly sliced
1 tablespoon long-grain rice
1 garlic clove, crushed in a garlic press
⅓ cup chopped parsley
1 teaspoon mint
½ teaspoon oregano
½ teaspoon thyme
1 can (8 ounces) whole tomatoes, drained
Salt and pepper to taste
1 firm ripe eggplant

1. Heat oil in a large skillet, add onion, and sauté. Remove from heat. Add celery, carrot, rice, garlic, parsley, mint, oregano, thyme, tomatoes, salt, and pepper. Cover. Simmer 10 to 15 minutes.
2. Cut off the stem end of the eggplant. Scoop out the center pulp. Sprinkle inside with salt. Set shell aside. Mash pulp and add to vegetables. Simmer, stirring occasionally, for 10 minutes.
3. Rinse inside of eggplant with a little water. Spoon in vegetable mixture. Replace top and secure with wooden picks.
4. Pour ½ cup water into a baking pan. Place eggplant on a trivet in pan.
5. Bake at 350°F 1 hour.
6. To serve, slice eggplant in half from top to bottom. Lay portions flat. Slice each lengthwise again.

4 servings

Chicken Vesuvio, page 279

414 *Boiled Endive with Lemon Juice and Olive Oil*
(Vrasta Antithia)

2 bunches young curly endive
3 cups water
1 teaspoon salt
1 lemon, cut in wedges, or use
    wine vinegar
    Olive oil

1. Slice endive in half lengthwise. Rinse several times to remove all traces of dirt. Cut stem 1 inch from bottom and discard.
2. Boil the endive in water with salt added in a covered pot until tender (about 20 to 25 minutes).
3. Serve with lemon juice and olive oil.

4 servings

415 *Braised Leeks* (Prassa Vrasta)

¼ cup lemon juice
6 tablespoons olive oil
1½ cups chicken stock
1 teaspoon fennel seed, crushed
1 teaspoon coriander seed,
    crushed
½ teaspoon thyme
1 bay leaf
1 garlic clove, sliced
    Salt and pepper to taste
9 medium leeks, white part only,
    split and cleaned, attached at
    the root

1. Combine lemon juice, olive oil, chicken stock, fennel seed, coriander seed, thyme, bay leaf, garlic, salt, and pepper in a skillet and bring to boiling. Simmer covered 15 minutes.
2. Arrange the prepared leeks in skillet in one layer. Simmer covered 20 to 30 minutes, or until tender.
3. Remove leeks carefully, arrange on serving platter, and pour liquid over.

3 servings

416 *Okra with Tomatoes* (Bamies Giahni me Lathi)

2 pounds fresh okra
½ cup olive oil
1 large onion, minced
5 tomatoes, peeled, seeded, and
    coarsely chopped
3 garlic cloves, halved
1 teaspoon sugar
    Salt and pepper to taste
    Juice of 1 lemon

1. Wash okra and cut off any hard stems. Blanch in salted water for 3 minutes.
2. Heat olive oil. Add onion and cook until translucent. Add okra and cook until it begins to soften. Add tomatoes, garlic, sugar, salt, and pepper. Cook 2 to 3 minutes. Pour in enough water to cover. Cover and simmer about 1 hour, or until okra is tender. Stir in lemon juice. Serve hot.

8 servings

417 *Simmered Zucchini*

6 zucchini (5 inches long), cut in
    thick slices
1 cup water
½ cup olive oil
¼ cup wine vinegar
1 parsley sprig
1 garlic clove
    Salt and pepper to taste

Combine all ingredients in a saucepan. Bring to a boil and reduce heat. Simmer covered about 8 minutes, or until just tender. Let cool in the liquid. Serve hot or chilled.

6 servings

418 *Potato Cakes* (Patates Keftethes)

2 pounds potatoes
3 tablespoons grated kefalotyri
    cheese
2 tablespoons chopped parsley
    Salt and pepper to taste
6 eggs, beaten
1 garlic clove, crushed in a garlic
    press
    Flour for coating
    Oil for frying

1. Boil potatoes in skins until tender. Peel and mash thoroughly. Mix in cheese, parsley, salt, pepper, eggs, and garlic. Shape into flat cakes. Coat with flour.
2. Heat oil in a skillet and add cakes, a few at a time. Fry until golden brown, turning once.

6 servings

419 *Spinach Casserole*

4 packages (10 ounces each)
    frozen spinach, defrosted
7 slices day-old whole wheat
    bread with crusts removed
    Water
¼ cup olive oil
3 garlic cloves, crushed in a
    garlic press
2 bunches scallions, minced
1 leek, minced
½ pound mushrooms
    Salt and pepper to taste
2 tablespoons dill weed
1 tablespoon oregano
½ teaspoon cinnamon
1 tablespoon mint
6 eggs, beaten
¾ cup grated kefalotyri cheese
1½ cups water or chicken broth
1 cup freshly toasted coarse
    bread crumbs
    Olive oil

1. Squeeze excess liquid from spinach. Sprinkle bread slices with water. Squeeze water out.
2. Heat olive oil in a large skillet. Sauté garlic, scallions, leek, and mushrooms for 3 minutes. Remove from heat. Add salt, pepper, dill, oregano, cinnamon, mint, and spinach. Sauté the mixture for 3 minutes. Add bread, eggs, cheese, and water; mix well.
3. Oil a 3½-quart baking dish and sprinkle bottom with bread crumbs. Pour in the spinach mixture.
4. Bake at 350°F 40 to 50 minutes, or until mixture is firm.

8 to 12 servings

420 *Spinach with Rice* (Spanakorizo)

1 medium onion, finely chopped
3 tablespoons olive oil
1 pound fresh spinach, washed
    well and drained, or 2
    packages (10 ounces each)
    frozen leaf spinach, partially
    thawed
1 tablespoon tomato paste
¼ cup water
2 tablespoons long-grain rice
    Salt and pepper to taste

In a saucepan, cook onion in olive oil until translucent. Add the spinach. Mix tomato paste with the water and add along with rice; cover. Simmer until rice is tender (about 20 minutes). Season with salt and pepper.

4 servings

421 *Stuffed Tomatoes with Rice and Pine Nuts*
(Domates Yemistes Neptisima)

8 large firm tomatoes with tops
    sliced off and reserved
  Salt, pepper, and sugar to taste
¾ cup olive oil
4 onions, minced
1 cup long-grain rice
½ cup water
½ cup chopped parsley
½ cup dried currants
½ cup pine nuts
1 teaspoon mint
  Juice of 1 lemon
2 cups water

1. Scoop out pulp from tomatoes and reserve. Sprinkle insides of tomatoes with salt, pepper, and sugar. Arrange in a baking dish.
2. Heat ¼ cup oil in a large skillet. Add onion, pulp, rice, water, parsley, currants, pine nuts, mint, and lemon juice. Simmer, covered, stirring occasionally, until liquid is absorbed. Cool slightly. Adjust seasonings.
3. Fill tomatoes with rice mixture. Replace tops and put into baking dish. Drizzle remaining olive oil between tomatoes. Add water.
4. Bake at 350°F about 40 minutes, or until rice is cooked; baste occasionally. If necessary, add a little water. Serve hot or chilled.

6 servings

422 *Grilled Tomatoes with Rosemary and Dill*

6 large ripe red tomatoes, cored
    and sliced in half
    horizontally
¼ cup olive oil
3 teaspoons rosemary
2 teaspoons dill
12 teaspoons grated kefalotyri
    cheese
  Salt and pepper to taste

1. Arrange tomatoes, cut side up, in a baking dish. Pour olive oil onto tomatoes, letting some fall into the dish.
2. Sprinkle with rosemary, dill, and cheese. Season with salt and pepper.
3. Broil until topping begins to brown (about 5 minutes).

6 servings

423 *Steamed Yellow Squash* *(Kolokithia Vrasta)*

1 can (10 ounces) plum tomatoes
1 large onion, minced
1 tablespoon minced parsley
1 teaspoon mint
1 teaspoon oregano
  Salt and pepper to taste
1 cup chicken stock
3 tablespoons butter
2 pounds small yellow squash,
    sliced in half lengthwise

Combine all ingredients except squash. Bring to a boil. Add squash. Reduce heat and simmer about 15 minutes, or until squash is tender.

6 servings

424 *Mixed Baked Vegetables* (Tourlou Tava)

1 pound fresh green beans, ends snipped off and beans sliced vertically
2 large potatoes, pared and quartered
2 medium zucchini, pared and cut in ½-inch slices
4 celery stalks, cut in ½-inch slices
1 can (20 ounces) whole tomatoes, quartered, or 4 fresh tomatoes, peeled and cut in wedges
2 large onions, peeled and sliced
3 tablespoons olive oil
2 garlic cloves, crushed in a garlic press
½ cup chopped parsley
½ cup chopped dill
Salt and pepper to taste
Warm water

1. Oil a 2½-quart casserole. Arrange green beans, potatoes, zucchini, celery, tomatoes, and onions in layers, drizzling with oil and seasoning layers with garlic, parsley, dill, salt, and pepper. Add enough water to reach three fourths the depth of vegetables. Cover casserole.
2. Bake at 400°F about 15 minutes, or until liquid begins to simmer. Turn oven control to 325°F and bake 20 minutes longer. Remove cover and bake another 10 minutes. Adjust seasoning.

6 servings

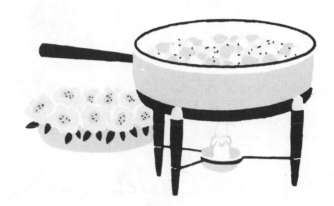

425 *Cooked Vegetables with Garlic Mayonnaise*

1 cup french-cut green beans, cooked
1 cup green peas, cooked
4 artichoke hearts, cooked
1 cup broccoli pieces, cooked
1 cup cauliflowerets, cooked
Paprika
Garlic Mayonnaise
Parsley sprigs for garnish

Arrange vegetables in separate mounds in a serving dish, leaving a space in the center. Sprinkle with paprika. Mound Garlic Mayonnaise in the center. Garnish with parsley.

6 to 8 servings

426 *Rice with Pine Nuts* (Pilafi me Koukounaria)

¼ cup butter
1 small onion, minced
4 cups rice, cooked in chicken broth
¼ cup pine nuts
Juice of 1 lemon
1 teaspoon dill
½ teaspoon mint
Salt and pepper to taste

Melt butter in a saucepan. Add onion and sauté until translucent. Add cooked rice, pine nuts, lemon juice, dill, mint, salt, and pepper. Heat thoroughly.

6 servings

427 *Rice in Tomato Sauce* *(Pilafi me Domata)*

½ cup canned tomato sauce
1½ cups water
¼ cup butter
1 small onion, minced
Juice of 1 lemon
1 cup long-grain rice
Salt and pepper to taste

In a saucepan, combine tomato sauce, water, butter, onion, and lemon juice. Simmer covered until butter is melted. Add rice. Continue simmering until the liquid is absorbed (about 20 minutes). Season with salt and pepper.

4 to 6 servings

428 *Mushroom Cutlets* *(Kotlety z Grzybów)*

1 pound fresh mushrooms or 2
    cups drained canned
    mushrooms
1 cup chopped onion
2 tablespoons butter
2 cups stale bread cubes
½ cup milk or water
3 eggs, beaten
1 tablespoon chopped parsley
½ teaspoon salt
¼ teaspoon pepper
Fine dry bread crumbs

1. Chop mushrooms. Sauté with onion in butter.
2. Soak bread cubes in milk 10 minutes. Add to mushrooms. Stir in eggs, parsley, salt, and pepper.
3. Shape into patties, using about 3 tablespoons for each. Coat with bread crumbs.
4. Fry in **butter** in a skillet until golden brown on both sides.

About 12 to 14 cutlets

Baked Mushroom Mounds: Prepare Mushroom Cutlets as directed; add **¼ teaspoon mace** along with salt. Spoon mushroom mixture into well-greased muffin pans. Dot tops with small pieces of **butter**. Bake at 350°F 15 to 20 minutes, or until set.

429 *Beets* *(Buraki)*

6 cooked beets, peeled
2 tablespoons butter
1 tablespoon flour
1 tablespoon vinegar
½ teaspoon salt
1 tablespoon sugar
¼ teaspoon caraway seed
½ cup dairy sour cream

1. Grate the beets.
2. Melt butter in a saucepan; add flour and blend. Stir in vinegar, salt, sugar, and caraway seed.
3. Add beets. Cook over high heat 2 or 3 minutes. Stir in sour cream. Serve at once.

4 servings

430 Cucumbers in Sour Cream (Mizeria ze Śmietaną)

3 cups sliced cucumbers
Salt
¼ cup chopped fresh dill or 2 tablespoons dill weed
1 cup dairy sour cream or yogurt

1. Sprinkle cucumbers with salt. Let stand 30 minutes. Pat dry with paper towels.
2. Stir dill into sour cream. Add cucumbers; mix well.

4 to 6 servings

Radishes with Sour Cream: Follow directions for Cucumbers in Sour Cream; substitute **radishes** for cucumbers and omit step 1.

431 Vegetables Polonaise (Jarzyny po Polsku)

1½ pounds vegetables (Brussels sprouts or savoy cabbage or carrots or cauliflower or green .beans or leeks)
1 cup boiling water
1 teaspoon salt
½ teaspoon sugar (optional)
2 tablespoons butter
¼ teaspoon salt
⅛ teaspoon pepper
1 tablespoon lemon juice (optional)
2 tablespoons fine dry bread crumbs

1. Choose one vegetable to prepare at a time. Trim and pare as necessary. (Leave Brussels sprouts and green beans whole. Cut cabbage into six wedges. Leave cauliflower whole or break into flowerets. Slice leeks.)
2. Cook vegetable, covered, in boiling water with 1 teaspoon salt and the sugar, if desired, until tender. Drain off water.
3. Melt butter. Stir in ¼ teaspoon salt, pepper, and lemon juice. Add bread crumbs. Sauté until golden. Spoon over top of vegetable.

About 4 servings

432 Sauerkraut (Kapusta Kiszona)

1 pound sauerkraut, drained
5 slices bacon, diced
1½ cups water
1 tablespoon flour
½ cup dairy sour cream (optional)

1. Rinse sauerkraut if mild favor is desired. Drain well.
2. Fry bacon in a skillet until golden. Drain off 1 tablespoon fat; set aside.
3. Add sauerkraut to skillet. Fry 3 minutes, stirring often.
4. Add water. Cover and cook 45 minutes over medium heat.
5. Blend flour into reserved bacon fat. Stir into sauerkraut. Cook and stir over high heat 2 minutes. Stir in sour cream, if desired. Remove from heat.

About 4 servings

433 Stuffed Tomatoes (Pomidory Faszerowane)

4 medium tomatoes
⅓ cup chopped onion
2 tablespoons butter or margarine
½ pound ground beef or pork (optional)
1 cup cooked rice
1 tablespoon chopped fresh dill or 1 teaspoon dill weed
½ teaspoon salt
¼ teaspoon pepper
⅓ cup dairy sour cream
Fine dry bread crumbs

1. Remove cores and seeds from tomatoes.
2. Sauté onion in butter. Add meat; cook until browned. Add rice, dill, salt, pepper, and sour cream; mix well.
3. Stuff tomatoes with rice mixture. Sprinkle bread crumbs on top. Place in a shallow casserole or baking dish. Cover.
4. Bake at 375°F 20 minutes. Remove cover. Continue baking until tender.

4 servings

Note: Green peppers may be substituted for tomatoes, if desired.

434 *Smothered Green Peas or Salad Greens* (Groszek Zielony lub Sałata Duszona)

2 packages (10 ounces each) frozen peas or 1¼ pounds escarole or endive, trimmed
1 teaspoon salt
2 cups boiling water
½ cup dairy sour cream
1 teaspoon dill weed
2 tablespoons melted butter or bacon drippings
2 tablespoons flour
¼ teaspoon pepper
1 tablespoon chopped parsley

1. Add peas and salt to boiling water. Cover; remove from heat. Let stand 10 minutes. Drain.
2. Combine sour cream, dill weed, butter, flour, pepper, and parsley; mix well. Add to vegetables. Cover. Cook over medium-low heat 10 to 15 minutes, or until tender; stirring occasionally. Garnish with croutons, if desired.

4 to 6 servings

435 *Stuffed Vegetables* (Jarzyny Faszerowane)

6 turnips, kohlrabi, cucumbers, or celery roots (about 1½ pounds)
2 cups boiling water or chicken broth
1½ teaspoons salt
½ teaspoon sugar (optional)
¼ pound ground beef or pork
¼ cup sliced mushrooms
¼ cup chopped onion
1 tablespoon grated Parmesan cheese (optional)
¼ teaspoon salt
⅛ teaspoon pepper
1 egg, beaten
2 tablespoons fine dry bread crumbs

1. Trim and pare vegetables. Cook in boiling water with 1½ teaspoons salt and sugar, if desired, until tender.
2. Scoop out centers of vegetables until a thick, hollow shell is left.
3. Fry ground beef with mushrooms and onion in a skillet until onion is golden. Add cheese, salt, and pepper; mix well. Remove from heat. Blend in egg.
4. Mash scooped-out portion of vegetables. Combine with meat mixture.
5. Fill vegetable shells with stuffing. Sprinkle bread crumbs on top.
6. Place stuffed vegetables in a shallow casserole or baking dish.
7. Bake at 400°F 10 to 15 minutes, or until lightly browned on top.

6 servings

436 *Smothered Vegetables* (Jarzyny Duszone)

1½ pounds potatoes, carrots, turnips, or celery roots
1 cup boiling water
1 teaspoon salt
4 teaspoons butter
4 teaspoons flour
¼ teaspoon pepper
1 tablespoon lemon juice (optional)
1 cup bouillon

1. Choose one vegetable to prepare at a time. Pare and slice or dice. Cook in boiling water with 1 teaspoon salt about 10 minutes, until crisp-tender. Drain.
2. Melt butter in a saucepan. Stir in flour, pepper, and, if desired, lemon juice. Gradually stir in bouillon. Add vegetable; stir to coat with sauce.
3. Cook, covered, 15 minutes, or until vegetable is tender. Garnish with Croutons if desired.

About 4 servings

Note: For extra flavor, dice **2 slices bacon.** Stir-fry until golden but not crisp. Substitute for butter.

437 Stuffed Artichokes or Tomatoes
(Karczochy lub Pomidory Faszerowane)

4 cooked artichokes or 4 small
    tomatoes
¾ cup chopped onion
1 clove garlic, crushed
2 tablespoons butter
⅓ cup fine dry bread crumbs
1 tablespoon chopped fresh parsley
½ teaspoon dried basil leaves
½ teaspoon salt
¼ teaspoon pepper
1 tablespoon grated Parmesan
    cheese (optional)
4 teaspoons butter or margarine

1. Remove center leaves of artichokes; remove chokes. (Remove core from tomatoes and scoop out seeds; sprinkle inside with sugar and salt.)
2. Sauté onion and garlic in 2 tablespoons butter. Stir in bread crumbs, parsley, basil, salt, and pepper.
3. Fill vegetables with onion mixture. Sprinkle cheese on top. Set in a shallow casserole or baking dish. Place 1 teaspoon butter on top of each stuffed vegetable.
4. Bake at 375°F about 20 minutes, or until tender and browned on top.

4 servings

438 Red Beets with Horseradish (Ćwikła)

3 cups cooked or canned red beets,
    drained and coarsely chopped
6 ounces prepared cream-style
    horseradish
1 tablespoon brown sugar
1 teaspoon vinegar
¼ teaspoon salt

1. Combine all ingredients. Cover; refrigerate 3 days.
2. Serve with cold meats.

About 3 cups

439 Sauerkraut with Dried Peas (for Christmas Eve) (Kapustą z Grochem)

1 cup dried split green or yellow
    peas, rinsed
2⅔ cups boiling water
1 quart sauerkraut, rinsed and
    drained
½ cup chopped mushrooms
3 cups water
    Salt and pepper
1 can (2 ounces) anchovies,
    drained

1. Combine peas and 2⅔ cups boiling water in a saucepan. Bring to boiling and boil 2 minutes. Remove from heat. Cover and let soak 30 minutes. Bring to boiling; simmer 20 minutes.
2. Cover sauerkraut and mushrooms with 3 cups water in a saucepan; cover and cook 1 hour.
3. Add cooked peas to sauerkraut mixture. Season to taste with salt and pepper; mix well. Turn into a buttered baking dish. Top with anchovies. Cover.
4. Bake at 325°F 30 minutes.

4 to 6 servings

Sauerkraut with Dried Peas (for nonfast days): Prepare Sauerkraut with Dried Peas; omit anchovies and baking. Fry **1 onion, chopped,** with **½ pound salt pork or bacon,** chopped, until lightly browned. Blend in **2 tablespoons flour** and add **1 cup sauerkraut cooking liquid.** Cook and stir until smooth. Mix with sauerkraut and peas; heat thoroughly.

440 Mushrooms with Sour Cream
(Grzybki z Kwaśną Śmietaną)

1 large onion, minced
2 tablespoons butter
1 pound fresh mushrooms, diced
1 tablespoon flour
½ teaspoon salt
¼ teaspoon pepper
½ cup whipping cream
½ cup dairy sour cream
¼ cup grated cheese (Parmesan, Swiss, or Cheddar)
2 tablespoons butter, melted

1. Sauté onion in 2 tablespoons butter in a skillet 5 minutes. Add mushrooms; sauté 5 minutes longer.
2. Blend flour, salt, and pepper with skillet mixture. Add whipping cream and sour cream gradually; mixing thoroughly. Turn into 1-quart casserole. Top with cheese. Drizzle melted butter over top.
3. Bake at 350°F about 20 minutes, or until thoroughly heated.

4 to 6 servings

441 Stewed Sauerkraut with Mushrooms
(Kapusta Kiszona z Grzybami)

1 ounce dried mushrooms or ¼ pound fresh mushrooms
½ cup warm water
1 large onion, diced
2½ tablespoons butter or shortening
1½ pounds sauerkraut, rinsed and drained
⅓ cup water
2 tablespoons flour
Salt and pepper

1. Soak the dried mushrooms in ½ cup warm water 1 hour.
2. Sauté mushrooms and onion in butter in a skillet 3 minutes.
3. Add sauerkraut to mushrooms; cook and stir 10 minutes.
4. Blend ⅓ cup water into flour. Mix with sauerkraut and simmer 15 minutes. Season to taste with salt and pepper. Serve with **fish**.

About 6 servings

442 Pickled Beets (Ćwikła)

3 cups sliced cooked or canned beets
1 tablespoon grated fresh horseradish or 4 teaspoons prepared horseradish
8 whole cloves or ½ teaspoon caraway seed
2 cups vinegar
1 tablespoon brown sugar
2 teaspoons salt

1. Layer beets in a glass or earthenware bowl, sprinkling layers with horseradish and cloves.
2. Boil vinegar with sugar and salt 2 minutes. Pour over the beets. Cover; refrigerate 24 hours.

About 3 cups

443 *Asparagus Extraordinaire*

1½ **pounds fresh asparagus**
1 **medium sweet red pepper, cut in ¼-inch strips**
● **Chicken Stock**
  Salt
  Freshly ground pepper
¼ **pound prosciutto or boiled ham, cut in 1x⅛-inch strips**
● ½ **cup Mock Hollandaise Sauce**

1. Break off and discard tough parts of asparagus stalks. Pare stalks. Simmer asparagus and pepper strips in 1 inch of stock in a covered skillet until tender (about 7 minutes); drain.
2. Arrange asparagus spears on a serving platter; arrange pepper strips over center of asparagus. Sprinkle lightly with salt and pepper. Arrange ham along sides of asparagus. Spoon hollandaise over all.

4 servings

Note: For a special luncheon entrée, increase amount of asparagus to 2 pounds and the ham to ½ pound. Arrange on individual plates; top each with a **poached egg.**

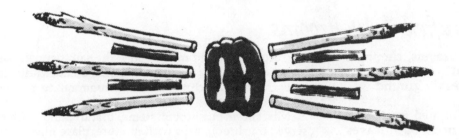

444 *Herbed Cabbage*

3 **cups shredded cabbage**
1 **large onion, sliced**
½ **teaspoon snipped fresh or ¼ teaspoon dried tarragon leaves**
½ **teaspoon snipped fresh or ¼ teaspoon dried basil leaves**
2 **teaspoons snipped fresh or 1 teaspoon dried marjoram leaves**
¼ **teaspoon freshly ground pepper**
● **Chicken Stock**
2 **teaspoons clarified butter**
½ **pound mushrooms, sliced**
1 **teaspoon salt**
  Snipped parsley

1. Place cabbage and onion in a medium saucepan: sprinkle with tarragon, basil, marjoram, and pepper. Pour in 1 inch of stock; simmer covered until cabbage is tender (about 10 minutes). Drain.
2. Heat butter in a medium skillet until bubbly; add mushrooms and cook 4 minutes, stirring occasionally. Stir mushrooms and salt into cabbage mixture. Sprinkle with snipped parsley. Serve with Mock Crème Fraîche (●) or yogurt, if desired.

4 to 6 servings

445 *Vegetable Kabobs*

Colorful vegetables, threaded on a skewer and covered with Cauliflower Sauce, make an elegant presentation.

24 Brussels sprouts
2 small zucchini, each cut in 6 pieces
● Chicken Stock
12 cherry tomatoes
12 mushrooms
  Salt
● 1⅓ cups Cauliflower Sauce

1. Simmer Brussels sprouts and zucchini in 1 inch of stock in a covered saucepan 5 minutes. Drain vegetables; cool.
2. Thread vegetables alternately on skewers. Sprinkle lightly with salt. Arrange kabobs in a shallow baking dish.
3. Bake at 400°F about 10 to 15 minutes, or until vegetables are tender; baste occasionally with stock. Serve hot sauce over kabobs.

6 servings

446 *Herbed Stuffed Mushrooms*

*¾ pound mushrooms, chopped
¼ teaspoon salt
⅛ teaspoon freshly ground pepper
1½ teaspoons snipped fresh or ½ teaspoon dried basil leaves
1 tablespoon snipped parsley
½ cup chopped onion
8 large mushrooms, stems removed and sliced into rounds; reserve caps
2 tablespoons brandy
1 tablespoon clarified butter
  Parsley for garnish (optional)

1. Process ¾ pound mushrooms, the salt, pepper, basil, parsley, and onion in a food processor or blender until thick and smooth. Layer ½ cup of the mushroom mixture in bottom of a baking dish.
2. Mix sliced mushroom stems, brandy, and butter. Fill reserved mushroom caps with mixture; place filled caps in baking dish. Spoon remaining mushroom mixture around mushrooms.
3. Bake at 400°F 20 minutes. Garnish with parsley.

4 servings

Note: This recipe is also excellent for a first course.

*If desired, chop mushrooms in food processor or blender, following manufacturer's directions.

447 *French-Style Peas*

2 cups shelled peas (see Note)
8 small boiling onions, cut in half
1 cup shredded lettuce
1 teaspoon sugar
2 teaspoons snipped parsley
2 teaspoons clarified butter
½ teaspoon salt
¼ teaspoon freshly ground pepper
¾ cup water

Combine all ingredients except water; let stand 1 hour, stirring occasionally. Transfer mixture to a saucepan; add water. Simmer covered until peas and onions are tender (about 15 minutes). Serve hot.

4 servings

Note: Two packages (10 ounces each) frozen peas can be substituted in this recipe; do not mix with other ingredients. Add to saucepan during last 5 minutes of cooking.

448 *Whipped Carrots with Dill*

1 pound carrots, sliced
● Chicken Stock
● ½ cup Mock Crème Fraîche
2 tablespoons snipped fresh or 1 tablespoon dried dill weed
1 teaspoon salt

1. Simmer carrots in 1 inch of stock in a covered saucepan until tender (about 15 minutes); drain.
2. Purée in a food processor or blender with remaining ingredients. Return to saucepan; heat thoroughly.

4 servings

449 *Whipped Carrots and Pears*

Vegetables no longer need to be dull or monotonous; this unexpected combination proves how exciting they can be.

1 pound carrots, sliced
Chicken Stock (page 25)
2 medium pears, pared, cored, and chopped
½ cup Citrus Mayonnaise
¼ teaspoon salt
1 teaspoon toasted sesame seed

1. Simmer carrots in 1 inch of stock in a covered saucepan until tender (about 10 minutes); drain.
2. Purée in a food processor or blender with pears, mayonnaise, and salt. Return to saucepan; heat thoroughly. Sprinkle with sesame seed.

6 servings

450 *Stewed Okra and Tomatoes*

1 pound okra, cut in 1-inch pieces
4 medium onions, chopped
4 large tomatoes, cored and chopped (see Note)
● ½ cup Beef Stock
2 tablespoons fresh lemon juice
½ teaspoon coriander seed, crushed
1 teaspoon salt
¼ teaspoon freshly ground pepper
Lemon wedges

Combine all ingredients except lemon wedges in a medium saucepan. Simmer covered over low heat 45 minutes. Serve hot, or refrigerate and serve cold. Accompany with lemon wedges.

6 to 8 servings

Note: If fully ripe fresh tomatoes are not available, use drained tomatoes from a 29-ounce can.

451 *Squash and Tomatoes Parmesan*

2 large yellow squash, pared and
cut in thirds lengthwise
● Chicken Stock
¾ teaspoon salt
¼ teaspoon freshly ground
pepper
1½ teaspoons snipped fresh or ¾
teaspoon dried basil leaves
1½ teaspoons snipped fresh or ¾
teaspoon dried oregano
leaves
¼ teaspoon garlic powder
3 medium tomatoes, cut in thin
slices
3 tablespoons freshly grated
Parmesan cheese

1. Simmer squash in a large covered skillet in 1 inch stock until tender (about 8 minutes).
2. Remove squash to broiler pan. Sprinkle with half the salt, pepper, basil, oregano, and garlic. Top squash with tomato slices; sprinkle with remaining spices and cheese.
3. Broil 3 inches from heat until cheese browns (3 to 5 minutes).

6 servings

452 *Broiled Tomatoes with Piquant Sauce*

Serve this versatile recipe as a first course, too.

6 medium tomatoes, cut in half
Salt
Freshly ground pepper
1 hard-cooked egg, minced
1 egg, slightly beaten
1 tablespoon wine vinegar
1 tablespoon Worcestershire
sauce
1 teaspoon curry powder
½ teaspoon sugar
½ teaspoon dry mustard
3 tablespoons low-fat ricotta
cheese
½ teaspoon salt
¼ cup water

1. Arrange tomatoes cut side up on a broiler pan. Season with salt and pepper. Broil 5 inches from heat 8 minutes.
2. Mix remaining ingredients except water in top of a double boiler. Cook and stir over simmering water 2 minutes; add ¼ cup water. Stir until sauce has thickened (about 3 minutes). Spoon sauce over tomatoes.

6 servings

Note: The sauce in this recipe can be served over any cooked vegetables. It is also delicious over steaks or roast beef.

453 *Cauliflower with Seasoned Dark Green Sauce*

1 medium head cauliflower
● Chicken Stock
Juice of ½ lemon
Fresh spinach leaves
●1 cup Seasoned Dark Green
Sauce

1. Remove leaves and tough parts of stalks from cauliflower. Place whole cauliflower in a deep saucepan. Pour in 2 inches of stock and the lemon juice. Simmer covered until cauliflower is tender (20 to 25 minutes). Drain and remove cauliflower to a platter.
2. Arrange spinach leaves on platter. Pour sauce over cauliflower. Cut into wedges to serve.

6 servings

454 *Brussels Sprouts and Grapes*

1½ pounds fresh Brussels sprouts, cut in half
1½ cups beer
2 teaspoons clarified butter
¼ teaspoon salt
⅛ teaspoon freshly ground white pepper
1 cup seedless white grapes
Snipped parsley

1. Simmer Brussels sprouts in beer in covered saucepan until tender (about 8 minutes); drain.
2. Drizzle butter over sprouts; sprinkle with salt and pepper. Add grapes; heat thoroughly. Sprinkle with parsley.

4 to 6 servings

455 *Green Onions with Mock Hollandaise*

4 bunches green onions, cleaned and trimmed
● 1¼ cups Chicken Stock
Salt
● ⅔ cup Mock Hollandaise Sauce
¼ teaspoon freshly grated nutmeg
Orange wedges

1. Arrange green onions in a large skillet; pour stock over. Simmer until onions are tender (about 10 minutes). Drain; arrange onions on a platter; sprinkle lightly with salt.
2. Blend hollandaise and nutmeg. Serve over onions. Garnish platter with orange wedges.

4 to 6 servings

456 *Baked Cheddar Onions*

6 medium onions
3 cups chopped carrots
1½ cups (6 ounces) shredded Cheddar cheese
1 teaspoon thyme
½ teaspoon salt
● Chicken Stock

1. Cut a thin slice off both ends of each onion; peel. Carefully scoop out inside of onions with a sharp knife or melon-baller, leaving a shell 2 or 3 rings thick. Chop onion centers; mix with carrots, cheese, thyme, and salt. Fill onions with mixture; place in a shallow baking pan. Pour ½ inch stock around onions.
2. Bake at 400°F 1 to 1¼ hours, or until onions are tender.

6 servings

Note: This recipe is also excellent served as a first course.

457 *Zucchini Squares*

Mint and zucchini are an interesting and refreshing combination. Cut into smaller squares, the mixture can be served as a first course.

1 pound zucchini, shredded
2 teaspoons salt
4 ounces feta cheese, crumbled
2 eggs, beaten
2 teaspoons flour
2 teaspoons snipped fresh or 1 teaspoon crumbled dried mint leaves
¼ cup finely chopped green onion tops
¼ teaspoon freshly ground pepper
● 1 cup Low-Fat Yogurt
1 teaspoon snipped fresh or ½ teaspoon crumbled dried mint leaves

1. Mix zucchini with 2 teaspoons salt. Let stand 10 minutes; rinse and drain well between paper toweling. Mix zucchini with remaining ingredients except yogurt and 1 teaspoon mint. Beat mixture well with a fork. Pour mixture into a lightly oiled 8-inch square baking pan.
2. Bake at 375°F 45 minutes. If further browning is desired, place under broiler 1 minute. Cut into squares to serve.
3. Mix yogurt and 1 teaspoon snipped mint. Serve over zucchini squares.

6 to 8 servings

Note: **Dill weed** can be substituted for the mint in this recipe, using the same amounts.

458 *Gingered Turnips*

Oriental seasonings give this often neglected vegetable new flavor appeal.

2 pounds yellow turnips, pared and cubed
1 tablespoon minced onion
● 1¼ cups Beef Stock
½ teaspoon ground ginger
½ teaspoon sugar
2 teaspoons soy sauce

Combine all ingredients in a saucepan; simmer covered until turnips are tender (about 15 minutes). Drain; mash turnips with potato masher or electric mixer until fluffy, adding cooking liquid as needed for desired consistency.

6 servings

459 *Composed Vegetable Platter*

Eye appeal promotes appetite appeal—add other fresh vegetables if desired.

1 large sweet red pepper, cut in 1-inch pieces
3 large green peppers, sliced
3 medium kohlrabi, pared, cut in half lengthwise, and sliced
6 carrots, sliced
● Chicken Stock
● Herbed Mock Mayonnaise

1. Simmer vegetables in a covered saucepan in 1 inch of stock just until tender (about 10 minutes). Drain.
2. Arrange red pepper pieces in center of a large round platter. Arrange remaining vegetables in circles around the red pepper. Pass the mayonnaise or spoon over vegetables.
3. The vegetable platter can be refrigerated and served cold as a salad.

8 servings

Note: You may desire to serve 2 or 3 sauces with the vegetable platter; Cucumber Sauce, Seasoned Dark Green Sauce, and Green Onion Sauce (●   ) would be excellent.

460 *Vegetable-Stuffed Grapevine Leaves*

For a Greek accent, serve this tasty vegetable combination with a lamb entrée.

1 small eggplant, pared and cut
  in ¼-inch cubes
  Water
⅔ cup chopped onion
⅔ cup chopped celery
⅔ cup chopped carrot
1¼ teaspoons salt
¼ teaspoon freshly ground
  pepper
½ teaspoon poultry seasoning
½ teaspoon cinnamon
2 tablespoons snipped parsley
2 teaspoons snipped fresh or 1
  teaspoon dried mint leaves
*1 jar (8 ounces) grapevine leaves
  preserved in brine
  Cold water
1 cup water
2 tablespoons fresh lemon juice
● ¾ cup Mock Hollandaise Sauce

1. Simmer eggplant in 1 inch of salted water in a covered saucepan until tender (about 10 minutes); drain.
2. Process onion, celery, and carrot in a food processor or blender until finely ground; transfer mixture to mixing bowl. Mix in eggplant, salt, pepper, poultry seasoning, cinnamon, parsley, and mint. Spoon vegetable mixture into a 1-quart casserole.
3. Bake at 325°F 40 minutes; cool slightly.
4. Soak grapevine leaves in cold water 20 minutes; pat dry. Cover bottom of large skillet with four leaves. Place a rounded tablespoon of vegetable mixture on stem end of each leaf; roll up leaf, tucking in sides. Place filled leaf seam side down in skillet. Repeat with remaining leaves and vegetable mixture.
5. Pour 1 cup water and the lemon juice over rolls. Simmer covered 30 to 35 minutes. Serve hot, or refrigerate and serve cold. Pass hollandaise. This recipe can also be served as a first course.

8 servings (4 rolls each)

*Grapevine leaves can be purchased in a gourmet shop or in the specialty department of a supermarket.

461 *Soy Pilaf with Fresh Vegetables*

A Middle Eastern influence is found in the ingredients of this unusual recipe.

1½ cups chopped onion
½ cup soy grits or granules (see
  Note)
1 small eggplant, pared and cut
  in ½-inch cubes
● 1½ cups Chicken Stock
½ teaspoon curry powder
¼ teaspoon salt
½ teaspoon paprika
½ teaspoon cumin
¼ teaspoon chili powder
⅛ teaspoon garlic powder
¼ teaspoon salt
2 medium tomatoes, chopped
1 green onion, chopped
1½ tablespoons lemon juice
¼ teaspoon salt
⅛ teaspoon freshly ground
  pepper
1 tablespoon snipped parsley

1. Spread onion in a 9x5x2-inch baking dish; sprinkle with soy. Layer eggplant over top. Mix stock with curry, salt, paprika, cumin, chili powder, and garlic; pour over eggplant.
2. Bake covered at 350°F 1 hour. Mound mixture on a serving platter; sprinkle with ¼ teaspoon salt.
3. While eggplant mixture is baking, mix tomatoes and remaining ingredients in a small bowl. Refrigerate covered. Spoon around pilaf on platter.

4 to 6 servings

Note: Soy grits can be purchased in specialty or health food stores. They have a flavor similar to cracked wheat.

Cracked wheat can be used in this recipe. You will need **2 cups cooked cracked wheat;** cook according to package directions.

462 *Vegetable Mélange*

In our version of scalloped tomatoes, eggplant replaces the bread cubes.

- 1 **medium eggplant, pared and cut in ¾-inch pieces**
- 1 **can (16 ounces) tomatoes, cut in thirds; use juice**
- 4 **stalks celery, cut in ¾-inch pieces**
- ½ **cup snipped parsley**
- ½ **cup dry vermouth**
- 1½ **teaspoons salt**
- ¼ **teaspoon freshly ground pepper**
- 2 **tablespoons snipped fresh or 1½ teaspoons dried fennel leaves**
- 1 **cup coarsely chopped onion**
- 1½ **cups coarsely chopped green pepper**

Combine all ingredients except onion and green pepper in a Dutch oven; simmer covered 30 minutes. Add onion and green pepper; simmer uncovered 20 minutes, stirring occasionally. Serve in small bowls.

6 to 8 servings

Note: Try different herb combinations in place of the fennel: **2 teaspoons snipped fresh basil** and **1 teaspoon snipped fresh oregano**, or **2 teaspoons curry powder** and **1 teaspoon cumin**.

463 *Vegetable Casserole Niçoise*

- ½ **head iceberg lettuce, cut in 2-inch pieces**
- 3 **tomatoes, cut in quarters**
- 4 **heads Belgian endive, cut in ½-inch slices**
- ½ **cup ripe olives, sliced**
- 4 **slices prosciutto or 2 slices boiled ham, cut in 2x⅛x⅛-inch strips**
- 4 **anchovies, minced**
- ½ **teaspoon salt**
- ¼ **teaspoon freshly ground pepper**
- ● ¾ **cup Beef Stock**
- ¼ **cup dry white wine or Beef Stock**
- ¼ **cup grated Gruyère cheese**

1. Arrange lettuce, tomatoes, and endive in a 9x5x2-inch casserole. Sprinkle with olives, prosciutto, anchovies, salt, and pepper. Pour stock and wine over all.
2. Bake at 350°F 25 minutes. Sprinkle with cheese and bake until cheese is melted (about 5 minutes).

6 to 8 servings

464 *Cheese-Spinach Gnocchi (Gnocchi Verdi)*

1½ cups milk
1 tablespoon butter
¼ teaspoon salt
Few grains ground nutmeg
¼ cup uncooked farina
½ cup well-drained cooked
    chopped spinach
1 egg, well beaten
1 tablespoon chopped onion,
    lightly browned in 1 teaspoon
    butter
1½ cups shredded Swiss cheese
2 eggs, well beaten
¾ cup milk
1 tablespoon flour
1 teaspoon salt
Few grains ground nutmeg

1. Bring milk, butter, salt, and nutmeg to boiling in a saucepan. Add farina gradually, stirring constantly over low heat until mixture thickens.
2. Stir in spinach, egg, onion, and 1 cup shredded cheese; mix well. Remove from heat and set aside to cool slightly.
3. Drop mixture by tablespoonfuls close together in a well-greased 9-inch shallow baking pan or casserole. Sprinkle mounds with remaining cheese.
4. Combine remaining ingredients and pour over spinach mounds.
5. Bake at 350°F 35 to 40 minutes, or until topping is golden brown.

About 6 servings

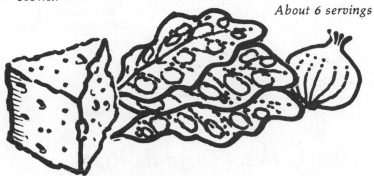

465 *Venetian Rice and Peas (Risi e Bisi)*

3 tablespoons olive oil
3 tablespoons unsalted butter
2 slices prosciutto, cut in pieces
1 small onion, minced
3 tablespoons chopped parsley
1 package (10 ounces) frozen green
    peas (or 1 pound fresh)
Water
1 cup uncooked rice, long or short
    grain
1 quart chicken broth
Grated Parmesan cheese

1. Put oil and butter into a large saucepan over medium heat. Add prosciutto, onion, and parsley. Sauté until onion is translucent. Add peas and enough water to cover (about ½ inch), and cook 5 minutes.
2. Stir in rice and chicken broth; bring to a boil. Reduce heat and simmer about 15 minutes, stirring frequently, or until the rice is tender.
3. Serve with Parmesan cheese.

6 to 8 servings

466 *Braised Rice with Saffron (Risotto alla Milanese)*

¼ cup butter
¼ cup finely chopped onion
1 cup uncooked rice
3 cups chicken broth
½ cup Marsala
1 teaspoon salt
¼ teaspoon saffron
2 tablespoons hot water
¼ cup grated Parmesan cheese

1. Melt butter in a heavy 1½-quart saucepan with a tight-fitting cover. Add onion and cook until lightly browned. Stir in uncooked rice. Cook slowly until rice is lightly browned, stirring occasionally with a fork.
2. Slowly stir in broth, wine, and salt. Place over high heat and stir with a fork until mixture boils. Cover pan, reduce heat, and allow rice to simmer without stirring 18 minutes.
3. Turn off heat, leave pan in place, and keep on cover to allow rice to steam. While rice is steaming, dissolve saffron in hot water.
4. After 30 minutes, the rice should absorb all the liquid and be tender, fluffy, and dry. Add saffron mixture to rice and mix well, using a fork to lift and turn the rice.
5. Serve rice warm, topped with cheese.

4 or 5 servings

467 *Rice Cake (Torta de Riso)*

3 cups milk
¼ cup uncooked long grain white rice
½ cup sugar
¼ teaspoon salt
2 tablespoons butter
1 cup all-purpose flour
2 tablespoons sugar
6 tablespoons firm butter
1 egg yolk, beaten
½ cup chopped blanched almonds
3 eggs, beaten
¼ teaspoon almond extract

1. Combine milk, rice, ½ cup sugar, salt, and 2 tablespoons butter in the top of a double boiler. Set over simmering water, cover, and cook 2¼ to 2½ hours, or until rice is soft; stir occasionally.
2. While the rice is cooking, prepare the pastry. Combine flour, 2 tablespoons sugar, and 6 tablespoons butter. Rub mixture between fingers until butter is the size of rolled oats. Stir in egg yolk and work dough until it forms a ball. Press dough onto bottom and sides of a 9-inch layer cake pan with removable bottom.
3. Bake pastry at 325°F 30 minutes, or until lightly browned. Cool on a wire rack. Place almonds in a shallow pan. Bake at 325°F 15 minutes, or until golden; stir occasionally.
4. Stir some of the hot cooked rice mixture into the beaten eggs. Immediately stir back into mixture in double boiler. Stir in almonds and almond extract, and pour filling into baked pastry crust.
5. Bake at 400°F 20 minutes, or until center is set. Remove pan sides, leaving cake on pan bottom. Serve warm or cool, cut in wedges.

About 8 servings

468 *Cauliflower à la Romagna*
(Cavolfiore alla Romagna)

1 head cauliflower, washed and
   trimmed
⅔ cup fine dry bread crumbs
1 teaspoon grated Parmesan cheese
½ teaspoon salt
¼ teaspoon pepper
2 eggs, slightly beaten
¼ cup milk
   Fat for deep frying heated to
   365°F

1. Put whole cauliflower into a saucepan containing a 1-inch depth of boiling salted water. Cook, uncovered, 5 minutes. Cover and cook 15 to 20 minutes, or until cauliflower is tender. Drain, separate into flowerets, and set aside to cool.
2. Combine crumbs, cheese, salt, and pepper. Mix eggs and milk in a small bowl. Coat flowerets with egg mixture, then with crumbs.
3. Put only as many flowerets into fat at one time as will float uncrowded. Fry 2 to 4 minutes, or until golden brown; turn occasionally during frying.
4. Drain and serve hot.

About 4 servings

469 *Artichoke Pie (Tortino di Carciofi alla Fiorentina)*

1 package (9 ounces) frozen
   artichoke hearts
   Lemon juice
2 tablespoons olive oil
1½ tablespoons butter
   Flour
4 eggs
½ teaspoon salt
   Pinch pepper
2 tablespoons milk or water

1. Thinly slice the artichoke hearts vertically and spread out on paper towels. Pat dry when thawed, and drizzle with lemon juice.
2. Heat olive oil and butter in a 10-inch skillet with an ovenproof handle. Coat artichoke heart slices with flour and brown on both sides in hot fat.
3. Beat eggs slightly. Mix in salt, pepper, and milk. Pour over artichoke slices in skillet.
4. Bake at 350°F 5 to 10 minutes, or until egg mixture is set.

4 servings

470 *Broccoli Florentine (Broccoli alla Fiorentina)*

1 pound broccoli, washed and
   trimmed
2 tablespoons olive oil
2 cloves garlic, sliced thin
¼ teaspoon salt
¼ teaspoon pepper

1. Split the heavy broccoli stalks (over ½ inch thick) lengthwise through stalks up to flowerets. Put into a small amount of boiling salted water. Cook, uncovered, 5 minutes, then cover and cook 10 to 15 minutes, or until broccoli is just tender.
2. Meanwhile, heat oil and garlic in a large skillet until garlic is lightly browned.
3. Drain broccoli and add to skillet; turn to coat with oil. Cook about 10 minutes, stirring occasionally. Season with salt and pepper. Serve hot.

4 servings

Broccoli Roman Style: Follow recipe for Broccoli Florentine. Omit cooking broccoli in boiling water. Cook broccoli in oil only 5 minutes. Add **1½ cups dry red wine** to skillet. Cook, covered, over low heat about 20 minutes, or until broccoli is tender; stir occasionally.

Spinach Sautéed in Oil: Follow recipe for Broccoli Florentine; substitute **2 cups chopped cooked spinach** for broccoli. Add spinach, **1 tablespoon chopped pinenuts or almonds,** and **1 tablespoon raisins** to oil mixture.

471 *Florentine Spinach (Spinaci alla Fiorentina)*

2 pounds spinach
● 2 cups Medium White Sauce
3 eggs, slightly beaten
3 tablespoons minced onion
½ teaspoon salt
½ teaspoon pepper

1. Wash spinach. Put into a large saucepan with only the water clinging to the leaves; cover. Cook rapidly about 5 minutes, or until tender. Drain well.
2. Prepare white sauce. Pour hot sauce into beaten eggs, stirring vigorously to blend. Set aside to cool to lukewarm.
3. Finely chop spinach. Combine spinach, sauce mixture, onion, salt, and pepper. Turn into a thoroughly greased 9-inch ring mold.
4. Set filled mold in a pan and pour hot water into pan to a depth of 1 inch.
5. Bake at 350°F 45 to 55 minutes, or until set.
6. Remove from oven; remove mold from water and let stand 5 minutes. Loosen spinach from mold and unmold onto a warm serving plate.

6 servings

472 *Eggplant Pugliese Style (Melanzane alla Pugliese)*

3 medium-size eggplants (about ½ pound each)
2 tablespoons olive oil
1 tablespoon chopped parsley
1 medium onion, chopped
1 clove garlic, peeled and chopped
1½ cups chopped cooked meat (see Note)
½ cup fine dry bread crumbs
1 tablespoon chopped pinenuts or almonds
Salt and pepper
3 or 4 tablespoons olive oil
1 can (8 ounces) tomato sauce

1. Wash and dry eggplants; remove stems. Cut eggplants in half crosswise, and scoop out most of the pulp; reserve pulp.
2. Heat 2 tablespoons olive oil in a skillet. Sauté pulp, parsley, onion, and garlic. Add meat, bread crumbs, and pinenuts. Season with salt and pepper; set aside.
3. Heat 3 or 4 tablespoons olive oil in another skillet. Cook eggplant shells in hot oil until the skins start to brown. Fill each half with the meat mixture. Pour tomato sauce over each half and cover skillet.
4. Cook eggplant slowly 20 to 30 minutes, or until tender.
5. If desired, place eggplant in a serving dish, add more tomato sauce, and keep in warm oven until ready to serve.

4 to 6 servings

Note: If desired, ¾ pound uncooked chopped beef, lamb, or pork may be used. Sauté with pulp, parsley, onion, and garlic until browned before combining with other ingredients.

473 *Artichokes in Lemon (Carciofi con Limone)*

1 can (14 ounces) artichoke hearts
3 tablespoons lemon juice
2 tablespoons olive oil
1 clove garlic, peeled and finely chopped
¼ teaspoon salt
⅛ teaspoon pepper

1. Drain artichoke hearts and place in refrigerator to chill. Combine remaining ingredients and chill.
2. When ready to serve, stir lemon-olive oil mixture and pour over artichoke hearts.

6 appetizer servings

474 *Stuffed Eggplant (Melanzane Ripiene)*

3 medium eggplants (about 3 pounds)
1½ teaspoons salt
1 cup boiling water
¼ cup butter
1 cup chopped onion
2 cups coarsely chopped peeled tomatoes
1 to 2 teaspoons salt
¼ teaspoon pepper
1 teaspoon dried basil
½ teaspoon oregano
2 cups chopped cooked ham
1 cup fine dry bread crumbs
¼ teaspoon oregano
¼ cup butter, melted
6 slices mozzarella cheese, halved
12 anchovy fillets
2 tablespoons chopped parsley

1. Cut the eggplants in half lengthwise. Make several cuts into the pulp, being careful not to pierce skin. Sprinkle cut sides with 1½ teaspoons salt. Let stand 30 minutes.
2. Pat eggplant halves dry with paper towels. Place flat-side down in a baking pan. Add boiling water.
3. Bake at 375°F, uncovered, 15 minutes, or until just tender. Cool on wire rack. Scoop out pulp, leaving ¼-inch-thick shell walls. Chop pulp coarsely and drain. Set pulp and shells aside.
4. Melt ¼ cup butter in a large skillet. Add the onion and sauté about 5 minutes, or until golden. Stir in tomatoes, 1 to 2 teaspoons salt, pepper, basil, ½ teaspoon oregano, ham, ½ cup of the bread crumbs, and the eggplant pulp. Simmer, covered, 5 minutes.
5. Fill eggplant shells with mixture, mounding slightly. Place in a shallow baking pan. Combine remaining ½ cup bread crumbs, ¼ teaspoon oregano, and melted butter; sprinkle over each eggplant.
6. Place 2 pieces cheese on top of each eggplant half. Lay 2 anchovy fillets on each half.
7. Bake at 375°F about 15 minutes, or until cheese melts and filling is heated through. Sprinkle each half with 1 teaspoon chopped parsley.

6 servings

475 *Vegetable Omelet (Frittata)*

3 tablespoons olive oil
½ cup chopped onion
½ cup sliced mushrooms
½ cup sliced zucchini
10 frozen artichoke heart halves, thawed
1 teaspoon salt
¼ teaspoon freshly ground black pepper
6 eggs
¼ cup canned tomato sauce

1. Heat oil in a 9-inch skillet with an oven-proof handle. Sauté onion 5 minutes. Add mushrooms, zucchini, and artichoke heart halves; cook 10 minutes over low heat. Sprinkle ½ teaspoon salt and ⅛ teaspoon pepper over vegetables.
2. Beat eggs with remaining ½ teaspoon salt and ⅛ teaspoon pepper; pour over vegetables. Spoon tomato sauce over the top.
3. Bake at 350°F 15 minutes, or until eggs are set. Cut in wedges and serve immediately.

4 to 6 servings

476 *Artichokes Basilicata Style (Carciofi alla Basilicata)*

1 package (9 ounces) frozen
    artichoke hearts
1 tablespoon lemon juice
½ cup fine dry bread crumbs
1 tablespoon grated Parmesan or
    Romano cheese
1 teaspoon chopped fresh basil
    leaves or ½ teaspoon dried
    basil
1 egg
½ teaspoon salt
⅛ teaspoon pepper
½ cup olive oil

1. Slice artichoke hearts vertically into thin slices. Spread out on paper towels to thaw. Sprinkle with lemon juice and let stand 30 minutes.
2. Combine bread crumbs, cheese, and basil. Beat egg with salt and pepper. Dip artichoke heart slices in egg, then roll in bread-crumb mixture.
3. Heat olive oil in skillet. Add artichoke heart slices and cook over low heat until browned. Serve while crisp.

3 or 4 servings

477 *Green Beans Basilicata Style (Fagiolini alla Basilicata)*

1½ pounds fresh green beans
1 teaspoon salt
2 quarts boiling water
¼ cup chopped onion
2 tablespoons olive oil
½ teaspoon salt
⅛ teaspoon pepper
2 tablespoons chopped fresh mint
    or basil leaves
3 tablespoons wine vinegar

1. Wash beans and break off ends. Leave whole or cut as desired.
2. Add 1 teaspoon salt to boiling water, stir in beans, cover, and bring to boiling. Cook 10 minutes, or until crisp-tender.
3. While beans are cooking, sauté onion in olive oil until transparent (about 8 minutes). When beans are done cooking, drain and add to onion. Season with ½ teaspoon salt and the pepper. Add mint leaves and vinegar; toss gently. Serve while hot.

4 to 6 servings

478 *Buttered Carrots (Carote al Burro)*

1½ pounds carrots
1 teaspoon sugar
½ teaspoon salt
⅛ teaspoon pepper
3 tablespoons butter
¾ cup water
1 tablespoon chopped parsley

1. Pare carrots and cut into julienne strips. Place in a large, heavy saucepan with sugar, salt, pepper, butter, and water. Cover.
2. Bring to boiling, then simmer 10 to 15 minutes, or until carrots are tender and moisture is evaporated. Remove cover to evaporate moisture, if necessary.
3. Turn carrots into a serving bowl and sprinkle with parsley.

6 servings

479 *Baked Rice Balls (Arancine)*

1½ pounds ground beef
1 small onion, chopped
1 can (6 ounces) tomato paste
¾ cup water
1 teaspoon salt
⅛ teaspoon pepper
1 tablespoon chopped parsley
6 cups cooked rice, hot
½ cup grated Romano cheese
¼ cup butter
1 cup all-purpose flour
2 eggs, slightly beaten
All-purpose flour (1 to 1½ cups)
3 eggs, slightly beaten
2 cups fine dry bread crumbs
1 can (8 ounces) tomato sauce

1. Brown ground beef with onion in a skillet. Add tomato paste, stir, and cook 5 minutes. Add water, salt, pepper, and parsley. Mix well and cool about 15 minutes.
2. Combine rice, cheese, butter, 1 cup flour, and 2 eggs. Mix until butter is melted and ingredients are well blended.
3. With well-floured hands, shape some rice into a small ball. Flatten slightly and top with 1 tablespoon of the meat mixture. Top with more rice to cover meat, and make into a ball the size of a small orange.
4. Hold the ball over a shallow pan filled with about 1 cup flour; add more flour when needed. Sprinkle rice ball with flour while gently packing and turning in palm of hand.
5. Carefully dip ball in beaten eggs, then roll gently in bread crumbs to coat. Repeat with remaining rice. Place finished rice balls in a jelly-roll pan or baking sheet lined with aluminum foil.
6. Bake at 350°F 30 minutes. While rice balls are baking, stir tomato sauce into meat sauce and heat. Serve sauce over baked rice balls.

7 or 8 servings

480 *Stuffed Artichokes Sicilian (Carciofi Imbottiti alla Siciliana)*

4 medium artichokes
1 teaspoon salt
⅔ cup fine dry bread crumbs
1 clove garlic, peeled and thinly sliced
1 teaspoon grated Parmesan cheese
1 teaspoon chopped parsley
1 teaspoon salt
¾ teaspoon pepper
2 cloves garlic, peeled and thinly sliced
1 tablespoon chopped parsley
2 cups boiling water
2 tablespoons olive oil

1. Cut off 1 inch from the top and base of each artichoke. Remove lower outer leaves. If desired, snip off tips of remaining leaves. Cover with cold water and add 1 teaspoon salt. Let stand 5 to 10 minutes. Drain upside down.
2. Mix together bread crumbs, 1 clove garlic, thinly sliced, cheese, 1 teaspoon chopped parsley, 1 teaspoon salt, and pepper. Set aside.
3. Spread leaves of drained artichokes open slightly. Place 3 slices garlic in each artichoke. Sprinkle bread crumb mixture between leaves and over top of artichokes. Sprinkle with chopped parsley.
4. Place artichokes close together in a 10-inch skillet so they will remain upright during cooking. Pour the boiling water in the skillet and sprinkle the artichokes with olive oil.
5. Cook, covered, about 30 minutes, or until artichoke leaves are tender.

4 servings

481 *Lemon Rice with Egg (Riso all' Uovo e Limone)*

1¾ cups chicken broth
¾ cup uncooked long grain rice
1 egg
1 tablespoon lemon juice
¼ cup grated Parmesan cheese

1. Bring broth to boiling in a saucepan. Stir in rice; cover tightly. Cook 15 to 20 minutes, or until rice is tender and liquid is absorbed.
2. Place egg, lemon juice, and cheese in a bowl; beat until foamy. Stir into rice over low heat. Serve immediately.

About 4 servings

482 *Asparagus Parmesan (Asparagi alla Parmigiana)*

1½ pounds asparagus
½ cup butter, melted
½ cup grated Parmesan or Romano cheese
1 teaspoon salt
½ teaspoon pepper

1. Wash asparagus. Put into a small amount of boiling salted water in a skillet. Bring to boiling, reduce heat, and cook 5 minutes, uncovered; cover and cook 10 minutes, or until just tender.
2. Pour melted butter into a greased 1½-quart casserole. Put cooked asparagus into casserole and sprinkle with mixture of grated cheese, salt, and pepper.
3. Bake at 450°F 5 to 10 minutes, or until cheese is melted.

About 6 servings

483 *Green Beans with Onions (Fagiolini con Cipolla)*

8 to 12 small whole onions, peeled
1 pound green beans
¼ teaspoon salt
2 tablespoons olive oil
1 clove garlic, chopped
½ teaspoon salt
⅛ teaspoon pepper

1. Put onions into a small amount of boiling salted water in a saucepan. Cover and cook 15 to 20 minutes, or until onions are tender.
2. Meanwhile, wash beans, break off ends, and cut beans lengthwise into fine strips. Bring a small amount of water to boiling in a saucepan, add ¼ teaspoon salt and beans. Cover and cook 10 to 15 minutes, or until beans are tender. Drain.
3. Heat oil and garlic in a skillet until garlic is lightly browned. Add green beans and onions, season with salt and pepper, and cook 5 to 10 minutes, or until thoroughly heated, stirring occasionally.

About 4 servings

484 *Green Beans in Sauce (Fagiolini al Sugo)*

2 tablespoons olive oil
1 clove garlic, chopped
2½ cups canned tomatoes, sieved
1 cup boiling water
½ teaspoon salt
⅛ teaspoon pepper
⅛ teaspoon oregano
2 teaspoons chopped parsley
1 pound green beans
¼ teaspoon salt

1. Heat olive oil and garlic in a skillet until garlic is lightly browned. Add tomatoes and water slowly. Stir in ½ teaspoon salt, pepper, oregano, and parsley. Bring to boiling, cover, and simmer 20 minutes, stirring occasionally.
2. Meanwhile, wash beans, break off ends, and cut crosswise into pieces. Bring a small amount of water to boiling in a saucepan. Add ¼ teaspoon salt and beans. Cover and cook about 15 minutes, or until beans are tender. Drain.
3. Turn beans into a warm serving bowl and pour sauce over them. Serve immediately.

About 4 servings

485 *Broccoli, Southern Style*

1 medium onion, thinly sliced
1 clove garlic, thinly sliced
2 tablespoons olive oil
1½ tablespoons flour
½ teaspoon salt
⅛ teaspoon pepper
1 cup chicken broth
4 anchovy fillets, chopped
½ cup sliced ripe olives
2 cups shredded process Cheddar
   cheese
2 pounds broccoli, cooked and
   drained

1. Cook onion and garlic in hot olive oil in a saucepan until onion is soft. Blend in a mixture of flour, salt, and pepper. Heat until bubbly.
2. Add chicken broth, stirring constantly. Bring to boiling and cook 1 or 2 minutes, or until sauce thickens.
3. Blend in anchovies, olives, and cheese. Pour sauce over hot broccoli.

About 6 servings

486 *Italian Cauliflower (Cavolfiore Italiana)*

1 large head cauliflower, washed
   and trimmed
2 tablespoons butter
½ clove garlic, minced
2 teaspoons flour
1 teaspoon salt
2 cups canned tomatoes
1 small green pepper, coarsely
   chopped
¼ teaspoon oregano

1. Separate cauliflower into flowerets. Put into a saucepan containing a small amount of boiling salted water. Cook, uncovered, 5 minutes. Cover and cook 8 to 10 minutes, or until cauliflower is tender. Drain if necessary and keep hot.
2. Heat butter with garlic; stir in flour and salt and cook until bubbly.
3. Add tomatoes and bring to boiling, stirring constantly; cook 1 to 2 minutes. Mix in green pepper and oregano.
4. Pour sauce over hot cauliflower.

About 6 servings

487 *Baked Eggplant (Melanzane alla Sardegna)*

4 eggplants (about ¾ pound each)
½ cup olive oil
2 teaspoons salt
1 teaspoon pepper

1. Wash and dry eggplants; remove stems. Leave eggplant whole and unpeeled. Make a slit the length of each eggplant only to the center, not completely through to the other side.
2. In each slit, drizzle 1 tablespoon olive oil and season with ½ teaspoon salt and ¼ teaspoon pepper. Gently press eggplant together and rub completely with olive oil. Rub an 11×7-inch baking dish with olive oil. Place eggplants in dish.
3. Bake at 375°F about 30 minutes, or until eggplants are tender.

6 to 8 servings

488 *Eggplant Parmesan (Melanzane alla Parmigiana)*

- ● **Tomato Meat Sauce**
- **4 quarts water**
- **1 tablespoon salt**
- **3 cups (about 8 ounces) noodles**
- **1 eggplant (about 1 pound)**
- **2 eggs, slightly beaten**
- **¼ cup cream**
- **3 tablespoons olive oil**
- **⅔ cup fine dry bread crumbs**
- **1 cup grated Parmesan cheese**
- **6 slices (3 ounces) mozzarella cheese**

1. Prepare Tomato Meat Sauce.
2. Heat water in a large saucepan. Add salt, then noodles; stir with a fork. Boil rapidly. uncovered, 10 to 15 minutes, or until noodles are tender. Drain. Set aside.
3. Wash eggplant, pare, and cut into ½-inch-thick slices.
4. Combine eggs and cream.
5. Heat oil in a skillet. Dip eggplant into egg mixture, then into bread crumbs. Put eggplant slices into skillet and brown slowly on both sides.
6. Put a third of the drained noodles into a greased 2-quart casserole. Layer with a third of eggplant slices. Add 1 cup meat sauce. Sprinkle with a third of grated cheese. Repeat layers, ending with eggplant slices. Top with cheese slices. Cover casserole.
7. Bake at 350°F about 20 minutes. Remove cover and bake 10 to 15 minutes, or until cheese is lightly browned. Serve with remaining meat sauce.

About 6 servings

489 *Mushrooms Parmesan (Funghi alla Parmigiana)*

- **1 pound mushrooms with 1- to 2-inch caps**
- **2 tablespoons olive oil**
- **¼ cup chopped onion**
- **½ clove garlic, finely chopped**
- **⅓ cup fine dry bread crumbs**
- **3 tablespoons grated Parmesan cheese**
- **1 tablespoon chopped parsley**
- **½ teaspoon salt**
- **⅛ teaspoon oregano**
- **2 tablespoons olive oil**

1. Clean mushrooms and remove stems. Place caps open-end up in a shallow greased 1½-quart baking dish; set aside. Finely chop mushroom stems.
2. Heat 2 tablespoons olive oil in a skillet. Add mushroom stems, onion, and garlic. Cook slowly until onion and garlic are slightly browned.
3. Combine bread crumbs, cheese, parsley, salt, and oregano. Mix in the onion, garlic, and mushroom stems. Lightly fill mushroom caps with mixture. Pour 2 tablespoons olive oil into the baking dish.
4. Bake at 400°F 15 to 20 minutes, or until mushrooms are tender and tops are browned.

6 to 8 servings

Anchovy-Stuffed Mushrooms: Follow recipe for Mushrooms Parmesan. Omit cheese. Mix in **4 anchovy fillets,** finely chopped.

490 *Stuffed Onions (Cipolle Imbottite)*

6 large onions
2 tablespoons butter
1 cup soft bread crumbs
2 tablespoons olive oil
¼ pound ground beef
2 cups soft bread crumbs
1 egg yolk
2 teaspoons chopped parsley
1 teaspoon salt
¼ teaspoon pepper
¼ teaspoon marjoram
2 tablespoons olive oil
1 tablespoon chopped parsley

1. Cut off root ends of onions; peel, rinse, and cut off a ½-inch slice from top of each.
2. Put onions in boiling salted water to cover in a large saucepan. Cook 10 to 15 minutes, or until onions are slightly tender. Drain well and cool.
3. Meanwhile, heat butter in a skillet. Stir in 1 cup bread crumbs. Turn into a small bowl and set aside.
4. With a sharp knife, cut down around onions, about ¼ inch from edge, leaving about 3 outside layers. With a spoon, scoop out centers and chop them.
5. Heat 2 tablespoons oil in skillet. Add chopped onion and ground beef to heated oil; cook until beef is browned.
6. Combine beef mixture with 2 cups bread crumbs, egg yolk, 2 teaspoons parsley, salt, pepper, and marjoram. Lightly fill onions with mixture.
7. Put filled onions into a greased 2½-quart casserole. Spoon buttered crumbs on top and sprinkle with remaining oil and parsley.
8. Bake at 350°F about 1 hour.

6 servings

491 *Stuffed Peppers (Peperoni Imbottiti)*

4 green peppers
¼ cup olive oil
1 pound ground beef
1⅓ cups cooked rice
2 tablespoons minced onion
1 tablespoon minced parsley
½ teaspoon salt
¼ teaspoon pepper
1½ cups canned tomatoes, sieved
¼ cup water
¼ cup minced celery
1 tablespoon olive oil
½ teaspoon salt
¼ teaspoon pepper
Mozzarella cheese, cut in strips

1. Rinse peppers and cut a thin slice from stem end of each. Remove white fiber and seeds; rinse. Drop peppers into boiling salted water to cover and simmer 5 minutes. Remove peppers from water; invert and set aside to drain.
2. Heat ¼ cup oil in a skillet. Add ground beef and cook until browned. Stir in cooked rice, onion, parsley, ½ teaspoon salt, and ¼ teaspoon pepper. Lightly fill peppers with rice-meat mixture, heaping slightly. Set in a 2-quart baking dish.
3. Mix tomatoes, water, celery, and remaining oil, salt, and pepper; pour around peppers. Put strips of cheese on each pepper.
4. Bake at 350°F about 15 minutes.

4 servings

492 *Baked Tomatoes, Genoa Style*
(Pomodori alla Genovese)

4 firm ripe tomatoes, cut in halves
    and seeded
  Sugar
¼ cup olive oil
2 cloves garlic, minced
1½ teaspoons salt
½ teaspoon pepper
1½ teaspoons marjoram, crushed
¼ cup finely snipped parsley
½ cup shredded Parmesan cheese

1. Put tomato halves, cut side up, in a shallow baking dish. Sprinkle lightly with sugar.
2. Mix olive oil, garlic, salt, pepper, and marjoram. Spoon an equal amount onto each tomato half. Sprinkle with parsley and cheese.
3. Bake at 350°F about 20 minutes, or until lightly browned.

4 servings

493 *Deep-Fried Potatoes*

Fat for deep frying heated to
  360°F
2 pounds potatoes (about 6
  medium)
  Salt

1. Start heating fat for deep frying.
2. Wash and pare potatoes. Trim off sides and ends to form large blocks. Cut lengthwise into sticks about ⅜ inch wide. Pat dry with absorbent paper.
3. Fry about 1 cup of potatoes at a time in hot fat until potatoes are tender and golden brown. Drain over fat, then put on paper toweling. Sprinkle with salt.
4. Serve hot.

About 4 servings

494 *Zucchini Parmesan (Zucchini alla Parmigiana)*

8 to 10 small zucchini squash
  (about 2½ pounds)
3 tablespoons olive oil
⅔ cup coarsely chopped onion
¼ pound mushrooms, cleaned and
  sliced
⅔ cup grated Parmesan cheese
2 cans (6 ounces each) tomato
  paste
1 clove garlic, minced
1 teaspoon salt
⅛ teaspoon pepper

1. Wash and trim off ends of zucchini; cut crosswise into ⅛-inch-thick slices.
2. Heat olive oil in a large saucepan; add zucchini, onion, and mushrooms. Cover saucepan and cook vegetables over low heat 10 to 15 minutes, or until tender, stirring occasionally.
3. Remove vegetable mixture from heat; stir in about half the cheese. Combine tomato paste, garlic, salt, and pepper; pour into vegetable mixture, blending lightly but thoroughly. Turn mixture into a 2-quart casserole. Sprinkle with remaining cheese.
4. Bake at 350°F 20 to 30 minutes.

About 8 servings

495 *Zucchini in Salsa Verde*

Fat for deep frying
¼ cup olive oil
2 tablespoons wine vinegar
2 tablespoons minced parsley
1 clove garlic, crushed in a garlic press or minced
2 anchovy fillets, finely chopped
Few grains black pepper
4 zucchini squash, washed and thinly sliced
Flour
Salt

1. Start heating the fat to 365°F.
2. Meanwhile, blend oil, vinegar, parsley, garlic, anchovies, and pepper in a small bowl and set mixture aside.
3. Coat zucchini slices slightly with flour. Fry in hot fat, turning frequently, until lightly browned (2 to 3 minutes). Remove from fat and drain. Sprinkle lightly with salt.
4. Put zucchini into a bowl; pour the sauce over it and toss lightly to coat well. Cover and set aside at least an hour before serving.

4 servings

496 *Zucchini Romano*

8 small zucchini (about 1½ pounds)
1 egg, fork beaten
½ cup shredded mozzarella cheese
3 tablespoons bottled Italian salad dressing
1/16 teaspoon black pepper
2 tablespoons melted butter or margarine
½ pound ground ham or veal
● ½ cup Quick Italian Tomato Sauce

1. Wash zucchini and trim ends. Slice off a narrow lengthwise strip. Using an apple corer, remove seeds to make a hollow about ¾ inch deep in each zucchini. Cover with boiling water, simmer about 5 minutes, and drain well.
2. Meanwhile, combine egg, cheese, dressing, pepper, and butter in a bowl. (If using veal, add ¼ teaspoon salt.) Lightly mix in meat. Fill zucchini with meat mixture, using about 3 tablespoons in each hollow.
3. Arrange zucchini, stuffed side up, in a single layer in an oiled shallow 1½-quart baking dish; spread tops with sauce. (Or omit sauce and brush tops with olive oil.)
4. Bake at 375°F about 15 minutes, or until meat is cooked. Serve hot.

8 servings

497 *Basic Mexican Beans*

1 pound dried pinto, pink, black, or red kidney beans
1 cup chopped onion
Water
Salt to taste

1. Wash beans well and put into a large saucepan. Add onion, then add enough water to cover beans completely. Cover, bring water to boiling, reduce heat, and simmer until beans are tender, about 3 hours. Add more water if needed, but add it gradually so water continues to boil.
2. When beans are tender, add salt to taste.
3. Use in recipes calling for cooked beans.

About 5 to 6 cups cooked beans

Soupy Beans: Beans prepared as above are sometimes served in soup bowls without further preparation, or with a sprinkling of grated cheese and chopped green onion.

498 *Refried Beans* (*Frijoles Refritos*)

● 2 to 3 cups cooked beans (see Basic
   Mexican Beans ; or
   use canned kidney beans)
½ cup lard or bacon drippings
1 cup chopped onion
1 clove garlic, minced
½ cup cooked tomatoes or tomato
   sauce
1 teaspoon chili powder
   Salt and pepper

1. Mash beans with a potato masher with half of the lard or bacon drippings (drippings make the best-flavored beans).
2. Heat remaining lard or drippings in skillet. Add onion and garlic and cook until onion is soft, about 5 minutes. Add mashed beans and continue cooking until all fat is absorbed by beans, stirring constantly to prevent sticking. Stir in tomatoes, chili powder, and salt and pepper to taste.

3 to 4 cups beans

499 *Hot Bean Dip*

¼ cup lard or bacon drippings
1 to 3 canned jalapeño chilies,
   chopped
1 cup refried beans (see above; or
   use canned)
½ cup tomato sauce

1. Heat lard in a small skillet or saucepan. Add chopped chilies and fry in hot fat about 5 minutes. Add beans and tomato sauce and stir until well blended.
2. Transfer dip to a small chafing-dish-type server and keep hot during serving. Serve with **tostada chip "dippers."**

About 1½ cups dip

500 *Chili con Queso*

2 tablespoons butter or margarine
½ cup finely chopped onion
1 cup chopped peeled fresh
   tomatoes
1 cup chopped peeled fresh green
   California chilies or canned
   peeled green chilies
1 package (8 ounces) cream cheese
¾ cup whipping cream
   Salt and pepper
   Crisp tortilla chips

1. Melt butter in a large skillet. Add onion and cook about 5 minutes, or until soft. Add tomatoes and chilies and cook about 10 minutes, stirring occasionally.
2. Cut cheese into chunks and stir into skillet mixture. When cheese melts, stir in cream. Add salt and pepper to taste.
3. Serve hot over toasted tortilla chips, or keep warm in chafing dish and serve as a dip with tortilla chips.

About 2½ cups dip

Variation: Substitute 1 or 2 chopped jalapeño chilies for the California green chilies and 8 ounces shredded sharp Cheddar cheese for the cream cheese.

501 *Red Chili Sauce*

4 fresh or dried ancho chilies
1 cup canned tomatoes with juice
1 cup chopped onion
1 clove garlic
1 teaspoon oregano
¼ teaspoon cumin (comino)
¼ cup olive oil
   Salt and pepper
1 tablespoon vinegar
   Few drops Tabasco

1. Prepare the chilies (see this page). Put prepared chilies, tomatoes, onion, garlic, oregano, and cumin into an electric blender and blend to a purée.
2. Heat oil in a skillet. Add puréed sauce and cook about 10 minutes. Stir in salt and pepper to taste, then vinegar and Tabasco to taste. Cool before serving.

About 2 cups sauce

502 *Green Chili Sauce*

1 cup chopped canned peeled green
    chilies
1 cup canned Mexican green
    tomatoes (tomatillos)
¼ cup chopped fresh parsley
¼ cup chopped onion
1 clove garlic
1 canned jalapeño chili, chopped
    Salt and pepper
¼ cup olive oil

1. Put green chilies, green tomatoes, parsley, onion, garlic, and jalapeño chili into an electric blender. Blend to a purée. Add salt and pepper to taste.
2. Heat oil in skillet. Add puréed sauce and cook about 5 minutes, stirring constantly. Cool before serving.

About 2 cups sauce

503 *Chilies Rellenos*

6 fresh or canned California green
    chilies (see Note) or 6 green
    bell peppers
● 2 cups Picadillo or ½
    pound Monterey Jack or mild
    Cheddar cheese
2 eggs, separated
    Flour
    Oil for frying
Sauce:
1 cup chopped onion
1 clove garlic, minced
2 cups canned tomato sauce
1 tablespoon oil
1 cup chicken stock, or water plus
    1 chicken bouillon cube
    Salt and pepper

1. Make a slit in the side of each chili and with a spoon carefully remove seeds and pith, leaving stems intact. (If using peppers, cut around stem with a sharp knife, leaving attached at one side, if possible; slit side. Remove seeds and pith.)
2. Fill chilies with desired filling.
3. Beat egg whites until stiff, not dry, peaks form; beat egg yolks until thick and lemon colored. Fold whites into yolks. Dust chilies with flour, then dip into beaten egg to coat on all sides.
4. Heat oil (about 1-inch depth) in a heavy skillet or large heavy saucepan to about 350°F. Fry stuffed chilies in hot oil, turning to brown on all sides. Stems may be used as "handles" to help turn the chilies.
5. Drain on absorbent paper and set aside while preparing sauce.
6. For sauce, put onion, garlic, and tomato sauce into an electric blender. Blend until liquefied.
7. Heat 1 tablespoon oil in skillet. Cook sauce in oil about 5 minutes. Stir in chicken stock. Season to taste with salt and pepper.
8. Place fried stuffed chilies in sauce and cook a few minutes until they reach serving temperature.

6 servings

Note: If chilies are very hot, they may be soaked in a solution of 1 quart water, 1 tablespoon salt, and 1 tablespoon vinegar for an hour before using.

504 Stuffed Peppers with Nogada Sauce
(Chilies Rellenos en Nogada)

6 medium green peppers
3 tablespoons lard
2 cloves garlic, minced
¼ cup chopped onion
1 pound lean ground pork
½ pound ham with fat, ground
2 cups chopped ripe tomatoes
2 tablespoons snipped parsley
3 tablespoons cider vinegar
½ teaspoon vanilla extract
2 tablespoons sugar
4 whole cloves, crushed
5 peppercorns, crushed
¼ teaspoon nutmeg
⅛ teaspoon powdered saffron
¼ cup finely chopped almonds
¼ cup dark seedless raisins
1 teaspoon chopped capers
2 tablespoons chopped candied
    lemon peel
¼ cup pitted chopped green olives
Nogada Sauce (see below)
Flour
2 eggs, beaten
Lard for deep frying, heated to
    365°F (see Note)
Pomegranate seeds

1. Cut out stems of peppers; remove seeds and membrane. Place peppers in a large saucepan; cover with boiling water, bring to boiling, and cook about 2 minutes. Drain and invert peppers on absorbent paper.
2. Heat 3 tablespoons lard in a heavy skillet; add garlic, onion, and meat. Cook until meat is browned, stirring occasionally.
3. Meanwhile, mix tomatoes, parsley, vinegar, vanilla extract, sugar, and spices.
4. Add tomato mixture to meat along with almonds, raisins, capers, lemon peel, and olives; stir. Cook over low heat, stirring frequently, until mixture is almost dry (30 to 40 minutes).
5. Meanwhile, prepare Nogada Sauce.
6. Spoon filling into peppers, packing lightly so mixture will remain in cavities during frying.
7. Roll peppers in flour, coating entire surface. Dip in beaten eggs.
8. Fry peppers in hot deep fat until coating is golden. Remove peppers with a slotted spoon and drain on absorbent paper.
9. Arrange stuffed peppers on a serving plate and top with Nogada Sauce. Sprinkle with pomegranate seeds.

6 servings

Note: If desired, use 2 inches of fat in a deep skillet, heat to 365°F, and fry peppers, turning to brown evenly.

505 Nogada Sauce

1 cup walnuts, ground
½ clove garlic, ground
5 peppercorns, crushed
¼ cup fine dry bread crumbs
2 tablespoons sugar
½ teaspoon salt
2 tablespoons cider vinegar
6 to 8 tablespoons water

Mix walnuts, garlic, peppercorns, crumbs, sugar, and salt. Add to vinegar, then stir in enough water to make a very thick sauce. Let stand 30 minutes.

506 Garbanzos with Condiments

¼ pound bulk pork sausage
½ cup chopped onion
1 clove garlic, minced
1 teaspoon chili powder
2 cups (16-ounce can) cooked
    garbanzos, drained and rinsed
1 can (4 ounces) pimentos, drained
    and cut in strips
  Salt
¼ teaspoon oregano
⅛ teaspoon pepper

1. Brown sausage in skillet, crumbling and stirring as it cooks. Add onion, garlic, and chili powder and cook until onion is soft. Add garbanzos and pimentos and stir to mix well. Bring to simmering. Season to taste with salt; add oregano and pepper.
2. Serve as an accompaniment to meat.

4 to 6 servings

507 Cauliflower Tortas

1 head cauliflower
2 eggs, separated
2 tablespoons flour
1 teaspoon salt
  Dash pepper
  Oil or shortening for deep frying
    heated to 375°F

1. Rinse cauliflower, remove outer leaves, and separate into cauliflowerets. Cook in boiling salted water until almost tender (about 8 to 10 minutes). Drain.
2. Beat egg whites until they form rounded peaks. Beat egg yolks until smooth. Pour yolks into whites gradually, beating lightly with fork to combine.
3. In separate small bowl combine flour, salt, and pepper. Roll cooked cauliflowerets, a few at a time, in flour, then dip in eggs, coating well.
4. Fry in heated fat until golden brown, turning to brown on all sides. Serve very hot.

8 to 10 servings

508 Lima Beans Mexicana

2 packages (10 ounces each) frozen
    green lima beans
2 tablespoons butter or margarine
½ cup chopped onion
1 clove garlic, minced
1 cup canned tomatoes
1 jalapeño chili, chopped
  Salt and pepper
1 hard-cooked egg, chopped

1. Cook beans until tender, following package directions.
2. Meanwhile, heat butter in a small skillet. Add onion and garlic and cook about 5 minutes, until onion is soft. Stir in tomatoes and chili. Season to taste with salt and pepper.
3. Drain beans. Pour tomato sauce over beans and stir gently until evenly mixed. Turn into a serving dish and garnish with chopped hard-cooked egg.

6 servings

509 Corn-Chili Casserole

1 can (17 ounces) cream style corn
1 can (4 ounces) chopped green
    chilies (undrained)
2 eggs, beaten
2 tablespoons flour
1 teaspoon sugar
½ teaspoon salt
⅛ teaspoon oregano
1 tablespoon butter

1. Mix corn, chilies, and eggs. Blend flour, sugar, salt, and oregano; stir into corn mixture. Turn into a greased 1-quart casserole. Dot with butter.
2. Bake at 350°F 55 to 60 minutes, or until set.

About 6 servings

510 *Chili-Hominy Casserole*

2 cans (15 ounces each) whole
   hominy, drained and rinsed
1 can (4 ounces) green chilies,
   drained (discard seeds) and
   finely chopped
1 tablespoon butter
1½ cups dairy sour cream
   Salt and pepper
1 cup shredded Monterey Jack or
   mild Cheddar cheese

1. Layer half of hominy and the chopped chilies in a well-buttered 1½-quart baking dish. Dot with butter and spread with half of sour cream. Add a layer of remaining hominy, cover with remaining sour cream, and sprinkle with salt and pepper to taste. Top with cheese.
2. Bake at 350°F about 25 minutes, or just until thoroughly heated.

About 6 servings

511 *Hominy and Bacon*

½ pound sliced bacon
1 green pepper, chopped
1 small onion, chopped
1 can (16 ounces) tomatoes
   (undrained)
1 tablespoon sugar
1 teaspoon salt
2 cans (15 ounces each) whole
   hominy, drained

1. Fry bacon in a skillet until lightly browned; drain. Reserve 2 tablespoons drippings in skillet. Mix in green pepper and onion; cook until tender. Add tomatoes with liquid, sugar, and salt; simmer 10 minutes.
2. Turn hominy into a greased shallow baking dish; crumble bacon over top and mix with hominy. Pour tomato mixture over all.
3. Bake at 325°F about 45 minutes.

6 to 8 servings

512 *Hominy in Tomato Sauce*

1 can (15 ounces) whole hominy,
   drained
1 can (16 ounces) tomatoes
1 tablespoon chili powder
½ teaspoon salt
1 medium onion, chopped
8 ounces sharp Cheddar cheese,
   shredded

1. Combine hominy and tomatoes in a saucepan. Cook, stirring occasionally, until thickened (about 15 minutes). Stir in chili powder, salt, and onion.
2. Layer hominy and cheese in a shallow 1½-quart baking dish, ending with cheese.
3. Bake at 350°F about 20 minutes.

About 6 servings

513 *Green Chili Cornbread I*

1 cup yellow cornmeal
2 teaspoons baking powder
½ teaspoon salt
2 eggs
¼ cup vegetable oil
1 can (4 ounces) green chilies,
   drained, seeded, and finely
   chopped
1 can (8 ounces) cream style corn
½ cup dairy sour cream
2 cups shredded mild Cheddar
   cheese

1. Mix cornmeal, baking powder, and salt; set aside.
2. Beat eggs with oil until blended. Add chilies, corn, sour cream, cornmeal mixture, and 1½ cups cheese; mix well.
3. Turn into a greased 9-inch round pan. Sprinkle with remaining cheese.
4. Bake at 350°F 45 minutes, or until lightly browned.
5. Serve warm with butter, if desired.

6 to 8 servings

514 *Green Chili Cornbread II*

1½ cups cornmeal
1½ tablespoons flour
1 tablespoon salt
½ teaspoon baking soda
1 cup buttermilk
⅔ cup vegetable oil
2 eggs, beaten
1 can (8 ounces) cream style corn
1 can (about 4 ounces) chopped green chilies, drained
4 green onions, chopped
1½ cups shredded Monterey Jack

1. Mix cornmeal, flour, salt, and baking soda in a bowl. Add buttermilk, oil, eggs, and corn; mix well. Stir in chilies and onions.
2. Grease a 13×9-inch baking dish with **bacon fat;** heat in oven.
3. Pour half of batter into heated pan and sprinkle with half of cheese; repeat, using remaining batter and cheese.
4. Bake at 375°F about 35 minutes.
5. Cut into squares and serve warm.

8 to 12 servings

515 *Cornbread Pie*

1 cup soft butter or margarine
1 cup sugar
4 eggs
2 cups (17-ounce can) cream style corn
1 cup shredded Monterey Jack
1 can (4 ounces) green chilies, drained, seeded, and chopped
1 cup yellow or white cornmeal
1 cup sifted all-purpose flour
4 teaspoons baking powder
½ teaspoon salt

1. Cream butter and sugar until light and fluffy. Beat in eggs, one at a time. Stir in corn, cheese, chilies, and cornmeal.
2. Sift flour, baking powder, and salt together and stir into batter.
3. Pour into greased 13×9-inch baking pan or two 9-inch pie pans.
4. Bake at 300°F 60 to 70 minutes, or until a wooden pick inserted in center comes out clean.
5. To serve, cut while still hot into squares or wedges. Serve with butter, if desired.

6 to 8 servings

516 *Mexican Eggplant*

1 eggplant (¾ to 1 pound)
2 cloves garlic
1 large green pepper
1 can (4 ounces) hot green chilies, drained and seeded
2 tablespoons olive oil
1 can (6 ounces) tomato paste
⅔ cup water
1 teaspoon salt
⅛ teaspoon pepper
2 eggs
¼ cup olive oil
1 cup shredded Monterey Jack or mild Cheddar cheese

1. Pare eggplant and cut into ¼-inch slices; set aside.
2. Finely chop garlic, pepper, and chilies. Sauté in olive oil until soft. Add tomato paste, water, and salt and pepper to taste. Simmer, stirring occasionally, until sauce is thickened.
3. Beat eggs and coat eggplant slices with egg.
4. Heat olive oil in a large skillet, add eggplant, and quickly brown on both sides.
5. Put browned eggplant into a shallow baking dish, cover with sauce, and sprinkle with cheese.
6. Bake at 350°F about 30 minutes, or until eggplant is tender and cheese is lightly browned.

About 6 servings

517 *Greens with Chilies*

3 fresh or dried ancho chilies
1½ pounds fresh greens (spinach, kale, collard greens, mustard greens, Swiss chard, etc.)
2 tablespoons butter or margarine
½ cup chopped onion
1 clove garlic, minced
Salt and pepper

1. Prepare chilies and chop them.
2. Wash greens well. Cook in small amount of boiling salted water until tender. Drain and chop. Return to saucepan.
3. Melt butter in a small skillet. Add chilies, onion, and garlic and cook until onion is soft, about 5 minutes. Stir chili mixture into chopped greens. Season to taste with salt and pepper. Heat thoroughly.

6 servings

518 *Peas with Condiments*

2 packages (10 ounces each) frozen green peas
2 tablespoons butter or margarine
½ cup chopped onion
3 canned pimentos, cut in 1-inch strips
Salt and pepper

1. Cook peas until tender, following package directions.
2. Meanwhile, heat butter in a small skillet. Add onion and cook about 5 minutes, or until onion is soft. Stir in pimento.
3. Drain peas. Stir onion and pimento into peas. Season to taste with salt and pepper.

6 servings

519 *Aztec Patties*

This unique use for leftover mashed potatoes is a well-known Mexican side dish. If you live in an area where fresh masa is available, use that in place of the dehydrated masa flour and water.

1 cup dehydrated masa flour (masa harina)
¾ cup warm water
1½ cups mashed potatoes
Salt (about 1 teaspoon)
½ cup shredded Monterey Jack
1 egg, beaten
Lard or oil

1. Mix masa flour with warm water until dough can be formed into a soft ball. Combine with mashed potatoes and mix well. Stir in salt to taste, then add cheese and beaten egg. Form into patties about ¾ inch thick.
2. Fry patties in hot lard in a skillet.
3. Serve as an accompaniment to meat.

6 to 8 servings

520 *Squash and Corn Dish*

2 tablespoons oil
⅓ cup chopped onion
1 small clove garlic, minced
2 pounds summer squash, pared and cubed
1 cup whole kernel corn, drained
1 large fresh tomato, peeled and cubed
1 jalapeño chili, finely chopped
1 teaspoon salt
¼ teaspoon pepper
½ cup milk
Grated Parmesan cheese

1. Heat oil in a skillet that can be transferred to oven. Add onion and garlic and cook until soft (about 5 minutes). Add squash, corn, tomato, chili, salt, and pepper and cook over low heat about 10 minutes, stirring occasionally. If skillet cannot be put into oven, transfer mixture to an ovenproof dish; pour milk over top.
2. Bake at 350°F about 30 minutes.
3. Remove from oven and sprinkle with Parmesan cheese.

About 8 servings

521 *Spinach with Tomato*

2 packages (10 ounces each) fresh
   spinach
3 slices bacon
2 tablespoons bacon fat
½ cup chopped onion
1 cup chopped fresh tomato
¾ teaspoon salt
⅛ teaspoon pepper

1. Wash spinach thoroughly. Put spinach with water that clings to leaves into a large saucepan. Cook rapidly about 5 minutes, or until tender. Drain.
2. Meanwhile, fry bacon until crisp in a large skillet. Drain bacon, crumble, and set aside. Add onion to 2 tablespoons bacon fat in skillet and cook until soft. Add tomato, spinach, salt, and pepper. Heat thoroughly.
3. Garnish with sliced hard-cooked egg, if desired.

About 6 servings

522 *Green Tomatoes and Zucchini*

2 tablespoons butter
1 large onion, chopped
¾ cup chopped canned Mexican
   green tomatoes (tomatillos)
3 medium zucchini, thinly sliced
½ teaspoon oregano
½ teaspoon salt
1 tablespoon water
¼ cup grated Parmesan cheese

1. Heat butter in a large skillet. Add onion and cook until soft. Add green tomatoes, zucchini, oregano, salt, and water; stir. Cover; bring to boiling, reduce heat, and cook until zucchini is crisp-tender (5 to 7 minutes).
2. Stir in cheese just before serving.

6 to 8 servings

523 *Baked Zucchini*

2 pounds zucchini
1 cup shredded mild Cheddar
   cheese
½ cup cottage cheese
4 eggs, beaten
¾ cup dry bread crumbs
3 tablespoons chopped parsley
1½ teaspoons salt
½ teaspoon pepper
3 tablespoons butter

1. Wash zucchini and slice crosswise into ¼-inch slices. (It is not necessary to peel zucchini, unless skin seems very tough.)
2. Combine cheeses, eggs, bread crumbs, parsley, salt, and pepper until evenly mixed. Layer into baking dish, alternating zucchini with sauce. Dot top with butter.
3. Bake at 375°F about 45 minutes, or until slightly set.

6 to 8 servings

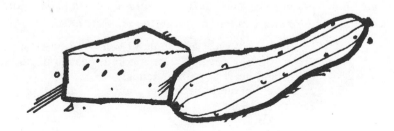

524 *Artichokes à la Four Thieves*

8 artichokes
Boiling salted water
● Four Thieves Sauce

1. Wash artichokes under running water. Let them stand 10 minutes in cold salted water; drain.
2. With a sharp kitchen knife, remove stem and bottom leaves from each artichoke, and with kitchen shears snip ¼ inch off the top of each leaf.
3. Cook the artichokes uncovered in a pot of boiling salted water 30 minutes; drain and cool.
4. To serve, gently spread artichoke leaves to the sides and, with a grapefruit knife, remove the very small purplish leaves and the choke that covers the bottom, scraping it clean. Accompany with hot Four Thieves Sauce.

8 servings

525 *Braised Lettuce*

8 small heads Boston lettuce or
  16 heads Bibb lettuce
1 cup chicken broth
  Juice of 1 lime
6 tablespoons butter
  Salt and freshly ground pepper
    to taste

1. Rinse lettuce under running cold water; tie each head firmly with string.
2. Put lettuce into a skillet with broth, lime juice, butter, salt, and pepper. Bring to a boil, then cover, reduce heat, and simmer 15 minutes.
3. Remove cover, increase heat, and boil rapidly until no liquid remains and edges of lettuce are golden. Remove the string. Serve with roasts.

526 *Barbecued Sweet Peppers*

4 red sweet peppers
4 green sweet peppers
  Peanut oil
  French dressing

1. Core the peppers and cut each into three strips.
2. Coat both sides of pepper strips with oil; let them stand 40 minutes.
3. Brush pepper strips lightly with oil and place in a hinged grill. Barbecue 2 inches from ash-covered coals, allowing peppers to blister.
4. Chill and serve with French dressing as an antipasto or with other marinated vegetables.

527 *Cooked Hearts of Palm*

To obtain this vegetable a full-grown palm tree has to be felled. It is, therefore, understandable that heart of palm is expensive. It looks like a chunk of ivory and is rarely found in the market stalls.

½ cup cubed salt pork
2 cups cubed heart of palm
1 cup chicken broth

1. Render salt pork in a Dutch oven. Add heart of palm and broth; simmer covered over medium heat until no liquid remains and heart of palm is tender.
2. Serve hot with Béchamel Sauce (●) or cold with **French dressing.**

528 *Raw Heart of Palm Salad*

1 pound heart of palm
Mayonnaise or French dressing

1. Slice the heart of palm paper thin. Soak it 1 hour in cold water. Drain well on absorbent paper.
2. Serve heart of palm with mayonnaise or in a tossed green salad with French dressing.

529 *Smothered Cabbage (Chou Touffe)*

2 small heads cabbage
2 tablespoons peanut oil
1 onion, minced
1 garlic clove, crushed in a
   garlic press
8 bacon slices
½ cup stock
Freshly ground pepper to taste
3 drops Tabasco
1 tablespoon butter
1 tablespoon cornstarch
1 teaspoon tomato paste
1 teaspoon lime juice
Lime wedges

1. Remove wilted leaves from cabbage. Quarter and core cabbage.
2. Heat oil in a top-of-range casserole, add onion and garlic and sauté until golden. Add cabbage pieces and lay a bacon slice on each. Add stock, pepper, and Tabasco. Bring to a boil, reduce heat, and simmer covered 15 minutes; cabbage will still be a little crisp.
3. Meanwhile, mix butter and cornstarch.
4. Transfer cabbage to a heated platter. Mix tomato paste and lime juice into cooking liquid and bring rapidly to a boil, then add butter-cornstarch mixture and stir until liquid is slightly thicker.
5. To serve, pour sauce over cabbage. Accompany with lime wedges.

8 servings

530 *Fried Okra Pods*

2 pounds large okra pods, washed
   and stems trimmed
Salt, pepper, and cayenne or
   red pepper to taste
1 egg yolk
1 tablespoon olive oil
1 cup dried bread crumbs
Oil for deep frying,
   heated to 365°F
Watercress and wedges of avocado
   and tomato for garnish

1. Cook okra in lightly salted boiling water 7 minutes. Drain and season.
2. Roll them in egg yolk beaten with oil, then in bread crumbs.
3. Fry the pods in heated oil until golden and drain on absorbent paper.
4. Serve surrounded with watercress, avocado, and tomato.

531 *Sweet Potato Soufflé*

2 cups hot mashed sweet potatoes
⅓ cup hot milk
⅓ cup amber rum
¼ cup butter
⅛ teaspoon nutmeg
Dash Tabasco
1 teaspoon grated lime peel
4 egg yolks, beaten
5 egg whites, stiffly beaten

1. Beat sweet potatoes, milk, rum, and butter together until smooth. Add nutmeg, Tabasco, lime peel, and beaten egg yolk; beat well. Fold in beaten egg white.
2. Pour into a well-greased 1½-quart soufflé dish. Set in pan of hot water.
3. Bake at 425°F 25 to 30 minutes. Serve at once.

532 *Ratatouille of Pumpkin*

1 cup diced salt pork
4 slices ham or Canadian bacon
3 scallions or green onions including green tops, cut in pieces
3 garlic cloves
5 parsley sprigs
6 dried Italian pepper pods or ½ green hot pepper
2½ pounds pumpkin meat, pared and cubed
2 cups stock or chicken broth
3 tablespoons butter
¼ cup chopped parsley

1. Sauté salt pork and ham in a Dutch oven until brown.
2. In a mortar, pound together to a paste the scallions, garlic, parsley, and pepper pods.
3. Add pumpkin, seasoning paste, and stock to Dutch oven. Cover and simmer until pumpkin is tender enough to mash with a fork.
4. Remove cover and, stirring constantly, cook off most of the liquid, being careful that pumpkin does not stick. Add butter and stir until melted.
5. Serve sprinkled with parsley.

533 *Smothered Mixed Vegetables (Touffé)*

8 small carrots, sliced
8 small potatoes
4 medium white turnips, pared and sliced
4 medium tomatoes, peeled, seeded, and quartered
2 small chayote or zucchini, sliced
1 green and 1 red sweet pepper, cut in strips
1 small eggplant (unpeeled), diced
Cauliflower chunks
½ cup green peas
½ cup lima beans
2 tablespoons peanut oil
1 large Spanish onion, sliced
1 cup stock or beef broth
¼ cup peanut oil
1 tablespoon salt
Freshly ground pepper
1 garlic clove, crushed in a garlic press
4 dried Italian pepper pods or 1 pink hot pepper
1 tablespoon tomato paste

1. Arrange in a top-of-range casserole with lid the sliced carrot, potatoes, turnip slices, tomato quarters, sliced chayote, pepper strips, diced eggplant, cauliflower chunks, peas, and beans.
2. Heat 2 tablespoons oil in a skillet over medium heat. Add onion and sauté until golden. Add stock, ¼ cup oil, salt, pepper, and garlic; pour over vegetables in casserole. Lay pepper pods over vegetables; cover and cook covered over low heat 45 minutes.
3. Remove cover, increase heat, and cook off most of the liquid. Remove peppers and stir tomato paste into vegetable mixture. Serve with **pepper steak** or well-browned **spareribs** or **pork chops.**

534 *Yams and Sweet Potatoes*

Yams or sweet potatoes
Salt
Butter (optional)

Boil yams and serve plain sprinkled with salt and, if desired, topped with butter. Or barbecue yams on a grill 4 inches from ash-covered coals, turning frequently, until soft. Or bake yams until tender.

535 *Stuffed Sweet Peppers*

4 red or green sweet peppers,
  halved lengthwise
Stock
1 cup cooked rice
2 cups cooked ground beef, ham,
  or poultry
Shredded cheese
● Tomato Sauce Creole

1. Parboil pepper halves in stock to cover. Drain peppers and reserve stock.
2. Mix rice and meat; stuff peppers. Sprinkle tops with cheese. Arrange peppers in a baking dish; add reserved stock to dish.
3. Bake at 350°F 30 minutes, or until well browned. Serve in the baking dish and accompany with the sauce.

4 servings

536 *Cornmeal*

1 cup ground cornmeal
3 cups water
4 dried Italian pepper pods or
  1 piece hot pepper
3 garlic cloves
1 parsley sprig
1 tablespoon coarse salt
¼ cup peanut oil
1 medium onion, chopped
¼ cup unsalted butter
● Bean Sauce

1. Stir cornmeal into water and let stand 5 minutes.
2. Meanwhile, in a mortar, pound together to a paste the pepper pods, garlic, parsley, and salt.
3. Heat oil in a Dutch oven over medium heat, add onion, and sauté until translucent but not brown. Add the seasoning paste and the cornmeal with water; mix well. Bring to a boil, reduce heat, and simmer covered 30 minutes. Remove cover, add butter, and fluff the cornmeal. Serve with Bean Sauce.

Cornmeal with Beans: Drain **1 large can Puerto Rican red or black beans**, reserving liquid. Add enough **stock** to liquid to make 3 cups. Follow recipe for Cornmeal, substituting bean liquid for water. Add the beans when you fluff the cornmeal.

Cornmeal with Kippers: Follow recipe for Cornmeal. Add desired amount of **flaked canned fillet of kippered herring** when you fluff the cornmeal.

Fried Cornmeal: Follow recipe for Cornmeal or Cornmeal with Beans. Spread 4 cups cornmeal mixture in a rectangular dish; refrigerate overnight. Cut chilled mixture into finger-size strips. Heat **3 tablespoons butter** and **3 tablespoons peanut oil** in a skillet and fry cornmeal over medium heat until golden and crisp.

537 *French-Fried Breadfruit*

1 large heavy breadfruit
Oil for deep frying,
  heated to 365°F
Salt to taste

1. Cut the breadfruit into wedges about 1½ inches thick; discard the center. Soak the wedges in lightly salted water 30 minutes. Dry with absorbent paper.
2. Fry breadfruit wedges, a few at a time, in heated oil until golden (about 8 minutes). Drain on absorbent paper. Salt lightly and serve very hot where you would serve French-fried potatoes.

Rice and Beans

2 quarts water
2 cups dried red beans, rinsed
1 can (13¾ ounces) beef broth
Water
1 tablespoon salt
8 parsley sprigs
3 scallions or green onions, chopped
3 garlic cloves
¼ teaspoon dried rosemary
3 tablespoons peanut oil
2 cups rice

1. Bring water to boiling. Add red beans and cook covered for 1½ hours.
2. Drain beans, reserving liquid, and set aside. Add beef broth and enough water to bean liquid to equal 4¾ cups liquid. Set aside.
3. In a mortar, pound together to form a paste the salt, parsley, scallions, garlic, and rosemary.
4. Heat oil and seasoning paste in a Dutch oven over medium heat. Put rice in Dutch oven and stir until well coated with oil. Add reserved liquid and bring to a boil, stirring. Add beans and again bring to a boil. Reduce heat, cover, and cook undisturbed for 20 minutes.
5. Remove cover, stir, and cook about 5 minutes longer, or until no liquid remains.

8 to 10 servings

Caribbean Rice

4 parsley sprigs
3 peppercorns
2 garlic cloves
2 scallions or green onions,
    cut in pieces
1½ teaspoons salt
½ teaspoon thyme
2 tablespoons peanut oil
2 cups rice
4½ cups chicken broth
1 bay leaf
1 green hot pepper or
    ½ teaspoon cayenne or
    red pepper

1. In a mortar, pound parsley, peppercorns, garlic, scallions, salt, and thyme to a paste. Set aside.
2. Heat oil in a large, heavy saucepan; add rice. Stir until all the rice is coated with oil and turns chalky.
3. Add seasoning paste and chicken broth; bring to a boil. Reduce heat and add bay leaf and pepper. Cover saucepan and cook undisturbed for 20 minutes.
4. Remove the cover; continue to cook over low heat for 5 minutes, or until no liquid remains.
5. Discard bay leaf and whole pepper. Fluff rice and serve.

8 servings

Rice and Avocado: Follow recipe for Caribbean Rice. Place **cubed avocado** on top of the rice for the last 5 minutes of cooking. Mix in avocado when rice is fluffed. Serve with Bean Sauce (page 65).

Coconut and Rice: Follow recipe for Caribbean Rice, using **brown rice** and an additional **½ cup chicken broth**. Add **1 cup freshly grated coconut** along with bay leaf and pepper. Proceed as directed.

Saffron Rice: Steep **½ teaspoon Spanish saffron** in **2¼ cups boiling water** until it turns bright orange. Strain. Follow recipe for Caribbean Rice, using saffron water in place of some of the chicken broth to cook the rice.

Meat

538 *Roast Beef with Wine* (Roz Bif)

1 beef rolled rump roast (5
    pounds or more)
Salt and pepper
2 garlic cloves, crushed in a
    garlic press
1 tablespoon oregano
2 tablespoons grated kefalotyri
    cheese
Chicken stock (about ¾ cup)
1 medium onion, quartered
½ cup red wine
1 package macaroni, cooked
    according to directions on
    package
1 cup grated kefalotyri cheese

1. Sprinkle beef roast with salt and generously cover with pepper. Slit the meat with a small sharp knife in several places on a diagonal slant about 1 inch deep.
2. Mix garlic, oregano, and 2 tablespoons cheese. Fill each incision with some of this mixture. Pinch to close incision.
3. Place beef on a trivet in a roasting pan. Pour enough stock into the pan to barely reach top of trivet. Add the quartered onion.
4. Roast at 325°F until done to taste. (A meat thermometer will register 140°F for rare, 160°F for medium, and 170°F for well-done meat.)
5. During the last 15 minutes of roasting, pour in wine.
6. Remove meat to a platter. Keep warm. Remove fat from pan juices. Toss in cooked pasta. Sprinkle with remaining cheese. Serve hot.

About 8 servings

539 *Meatballs with Lemon Sauce* (Youverlakia Avgolemono)

2 pounds lean beef, ground
1 large onion, minced
3 tablespoons minced parsley
2 tablespoons mint leaves
½ cup long-grain rice
Salt and pepper to taste
1 garlic clove, crushed in a garlic
    press
½ cup flour
2 cups water
Salt to taste
2 tablespoons butter
Juice of 1 or 2 lemons
2 eggs, separated

1. Mix thoroughly meat, onion, parsley, mint, rice, salt, pepper, and garlic. Dip hands in flour. Shape meat into round balls about 1 inch in diameter.
2. Bring water and salt to boiling in a large Dutch oven. Add butter and meatballs in a single layer. Simmer covered 40 minutes.
3. Pour stock into a small bowl and add lemon juice. Beat egg yolks until frothy. In another bowl, beat whites until peaks form. Fold in yolks. In a thin stream, pour stock into eggs. Pour over meatballs. Serve hot.

6 servings

540 *Tournedos*

6 slices beef loin tenderloin steak
    (1½ inches thick)
Salt and pepper to taste
½ cup butter
¼ cup flour
¾ cup dry white wine
½ cup chopped parsley
Juice of 1 lemon

1. Season meat with salt and pepper on both sides.
2. Melt butter in a heavy skillet. Add meat and brown quickly on each side. Remove to a dish.
3. Using a whisk, stir flour into pan juices. Cook, stirring constantly, over low heat for 2 minutes.
4. Stir in wine and cover. Simmer 5 minutes.
5. Add meat, parsley, and lemon juice. Simmer 5 minutes.

6 servings

541 *Braised Beef Corfu Style* (*Soffrito*)

3 cups all-purpose flour
Salt and pepper to taste
1 teaspoon paprika
Olive oil for frying
4 pounds beef round top round, cut in slices ¼ inch thick or less
4 garlic cloves, crushed in a garlic press
1 cup red wine vinegar
1½ cups water
1 teaspoon sugar
1 bay leaf
¼ cup chopped parsley

1. Season flour with salt, pepper, and paprika.
2. Heat olive oil in a skillet. Lightly dip meat slices in flour. Shake off excess. Brown meat on each side in the olive oil. Arrange in a casserole.
3. Combine garlic, vinegar, water, sugar, bay leaf, and parsley in a small saucepan; heat to boiling. Pour over the meat.
4. Bake at 325°F 1 hour, or until the meat is tender and almost all the liquid is absorbed.
5. Serve with **mashed potatoes.**

About 8 servings

542 *Beef Stew with Lentils or Lima Beans*

5 pounds beef chuck roast
¼ cup olive oil
2 large onions, thinly sliced
4 celery stalks, chopped
2 large carrots, chopped
1½ pounds fresh tomatoes, peeled and diced
2 parsley sprigs, minced
1 pound dried lentils (or lima beans)
Salt and pepper to taste
3 garlic cloves, crushed in a garlic press
1 cup dry red wine
3 cups beef stock (or more if necessary)

1. Trim excess fat from beef roast. Cut meat into large cubes.
2. Heat oil in a large Dutch oven. Brown meat on all sides and remove to platter.
3. Put onions into the Dutch oven and cook until translucent. Pour off excess fat.
4. Return meat to the Dutch oven. Arrange vegetables, parsley, and lentils around the meat. Season with salt and pepper.
5. Combine garlic, wine, and stock in a saucepan. Bring to boiling. Pour over meat and vegetables. Cover. Simmer until meat is tender. (Meat should be covered with liquid throughout cooking.)

8 to 10 servings

Note: This dish is tastier when made early and allowed to rest several hours or overnight, then reheated.

543 *Beef with Baby Onions* (Stifatho)

¼ cup olive oil
4 pounds beef shoulder, cut in large pieces
   Salt and pepper to taste
1 can (16 ounces) tomatoes (undrained)
1 tablespoon tomato paste mixed with ½ cup water
5 garlic cloves, crushed in a garlic press
1 cup red wine
1 teaspoon sugar
1 tablespoon lemon juice
1 bay leaf
   Pinch cinnamon
1 teaspoon oregano
¼ cup chopped parsley
3 tablespoons pickling spice (put in a tea infuser or wrapped and securely tied in cheesecloth)
3 pounds whole fresh baby onions, peeled

1. Heat oil in a large Dutch oven. Brown meat well on all sides. Season with salt and pepper.
2. Add tomatoes and diluted tomato paste. Cover and simmer 10 minutes.
3. Add remaining ingredients, except onions. Cover. Bring to a boil. Reduce heat. Simmer 2 to 3 hours until meat is tender.
4. Meanwhile, cut a small cross at the base of each onion. During the last ½ hour of cooking, add onions. Adjust salt and pepper.
5. Serve with **rice** or **pasta**.

8 servings

544 *Moussaka*

Fried Eggplant:
3 medium eggplants
   Salt
2 cups flour (about)
   Olive oil combined with vegetable oil for frying

Meat Filling:
¼ cup butter
2 pounds lean beef or lamb, ground
1 large onion, minced
¼ cup minced parsley
1½ teaspoons tomato paste mixed with ½ cup water
½ cup dry white wine
   Salt and pepper to taste
3 egg whites, beaten until stiff
6 tablespoons fine bread crumbs

Béchamel Sauce with Egg Yolks:
7 tablespoons butter
7 tablespoons flour
1½ quarts milk, scalded
3 egg yolks, beaten
1 cup grated kefalotyri cheese

1. Slice eggplants ¼ inch thick, and place on a large platter in a single layer. Sprinkle with salt on both sides. Let stand at least 30 minutes, or until liquid beads form on surfaces. Take each slice, squeeze well between both hands or press down with a heavy weight, being sure all liquid is squeezed out.
2. Dip each slice lightly in flour. Shake off excess. Heat oil in a large skillet. Fry eggplant, turning once, until golden brown. Drain on paper towels. Set aside.
3. For Meat Filling, melt butter in a large skillet; add meat and onion, and cook until browned. Add parsley, tomato paste and water, wine, salt, and pepper. Cook until all liquid has evaporated (about 30 minutes). Cool.
4. Beat egg whites until they form soft mounds. Fold in half the bread crumbs. Fold egg-white mixture into meat mixture.
5. For Béchamel Sauce, heat butter until melted. Stir in flour. Cook 4 minutes over low heat, stirring constantly; do not brown. Pour in warm milk slowly. Cook over low heat until sauce thickens. Cool. Stir in yolks with a whisk.
6. To assemble, oil an 18x12-inch baking pan. Dust with remaining bread crumbs. Line bottom of pan with 1 layer of eggplant. Cover with meat. Layer remaining eggplant on top. Sprinkle with cheese. Pour Béchamel Sauce over.
7. Bake at 350°F about 40 minutes, or until golden brown. Cool. Cut into squares and serve.

About 10 servings

545 *Pastichio*

3 tablespoons olive oil
2 pounds ground beef or lamb
1 large onion, grated
Few parsley sprigs, chopped
1 tablespoon tomato paste mixed with ½ cup water
1 pound elbow macaroni, cooked according to directions on package and drained
1 pound fresh kefalotyri cheese, grated

Béchamel Sauce:
½ cup butter, melted
7 tablespoons flour
1½ quarts milk, heated to lukewarm
10 eggs, separated

1. Heat oil in a large skillet. Add meat and onion and cook until meat is brown. Add chopped parsley and diluted tomato paste. Cover and simmer for 30 minutes. If any liquid remains, cook meat uncovered until liquid has evaporated.
2. Spread half the cooked macaroni in an 18x12-inch baking dish and cover with all the meat mixture. Sprinkle top with three fourths of the cheese. Form a layer with remaining macaroni.
3. Meanwhile, to make sauce, melt butter in a large saucepan. Add flour and mix with a whisk for several minutes. Gradually add milk while stirring; simmer until sauce thickens, stirring frequently.
4. Separate eggs. Beat whites in a bowl until they pile softly. Beat yolks in another bowl. Fold yolks and whites together, then fold in sauce. Spoon over meat and macaroni. Sprinkle with remaining cheese.
5. Bake at 325°F about 45 minutes, or until golden brown. Cool slightly before serving.

8 servings

Note: Pastichio may be prepared and baked in advance. To reheat, cover tightly with foil and heat in a 200°F oven.

546 *Meatballs with Tomato Sauce (Giouverlakia me Domata)*

1 pound beef, freshly ground
1 large onion, minced
3 tablespoons long-grain rice
1 garlic clove
½ cup minced parsley
1 tablespoon basil
Salt and pepper to taste
1 cup flour for rolling
Olive oil for frying
2 tablespoons tomato paste mixed with 1 cup water or beef stock

1. In a large bowl, combine meat, onion, rice, garlic, parsley, basil, salt, and pepper. Dip hands in flour. Shape meat mixture into round balls about 1½ inches in diameter.
2. Heat oil in a skillet. Sauté the meatballs, turning to brown on all sides. Remove to a baking dish.
3. Pour tomato paste liquid into the skillet. Simmer 3 minutes, stirring and scraping constantly. Strain the juices over the meatballs and add as much water or beef stock as needed to half cover them. Loosely cover with foil.
4. Bake at 350°F about 40 minutes. Once or twice during the cooking, turn meatballs with a wooden spoon. Serve hot with **pilafi** or **mashed potatoes.**

About 6 servings

547 *Sautéed Sweetbreads (Glykathia Tyganita)*

4 pairs sweetbreads from milk-fed calves
Ice water
2 teaspoons salt
1 tablespoon lemon juice
5 tablespoons butter or olive oil for frying
Flour seasoned with salt and pepper

1. Soak sweetbreads in ice water mixed with salt for 1 hour. Drain.
2. Place sweetbreads in boiling water to cover. Add lemon juice and simmer 10 minutes. Drain. Plunge at once into ice water. Remove membranes and connective tissue, and split into 2 pieces.
3. Melt butter or heat olive oil in a skillet. Dip sweetbreads into flour. Fry until golden brown on all sides.

2 servings

548 *Stuffed Grapevine Leaves with Egg and Lemon Sauce*

(Dolmathes Avgolemono)

1 jar (32 ounces) grapevine leaves
1 quart water
¼ cup butter
2 medium onions, minced
1 pound ground lean beef or lamb or a combination of the two
Salt and pepper to taste
2 tablespoons mint
2 tablespoons minced parsley
½ cup long-grain rice
2½ cups lukewarm water or more to barely cover dolmathes
4 egg yolks
½ cup lemon juice

1. Rinse grapevine leaves thoroughly in cold running water to remove brine. Bring 1 quart water to boiling. Add the leaves and parboil 3 minutes. Strain. Select 4 to 6 coarse, large leaves and line the bottom of a Dutch oven with them.
2. For filling, melt butter in a skillet. Add onion and cook until translucent. Remove from heat. Add meat, salt, pepper, mint, parsley, and rice. Toss lightly with 2 forks.
3. To fill, place a leaf, glossy side down, with the stem pointing toward you. (If a leaf is too small, use 2, overlapping 1 over the other by ¾ inch.) Place 2 teaspoons filling just above where the stem begins. Tuck base up and over. To seal, loosely fold one side, then the other, over toward the middle. Roll up to form oblong rolls, leaving room for the rice to expand while cooking.
4. To cook, arrange the dolmathes side by side in Dutch oven, layer upon layer. Place a ceramic plate on the last layer to keep dolmathes from floating to the surface during cooking. Pour water into pan to cover dolmathes. Cover pot and simmer 50 to 60 minutes. Check occasionally to see if too much water has evaporated. Add a little at a time, if necessary.
5. To make sauce, beat egg yolks until frothy. While continuing to beat, add lemon juice, a tablespoon at a time. Drain 1 cup broth from the cooked dolmathes and add slowly to the egg mixture, beating constantly.
6. Remove plate from dolmathes. Pour egg and lemon sauce over. Set over low heat until hot; do not boil. Serve immediately.

20 to 30 dolmathes

549 *Tomatoes Stuffed with Meat and Rice*

(Domates Yemistes me Kimake Rizi)

12 large firm tomatoes
1 teaspoon sugar
½ teaspoon salt
¾ cup olive oil
2 onions, minced
1 garlic clove, crushed in a garlic press
1 pound lean ground beef or lamb
¼ cup long-grain rice
¼ cup chopped parsley
1 teaspoon mint
½ teaspoon cinnamon
Salt and pepper to taste
½ cup water

1. Slice tops from tomatoes and save. Remove pulp and save. Sprinkle insides of tomatoes with sugar and salt.
2. Heat ¼ cup oil in a large skillet. Add onion and garlic and sauté until onion is translucent. Add meat and cook until no longer red. Add rice, seasonings, and tomato pulp. Simmer 10 minutes. Cool slightly.
3. Fill tomatoes two thirds full, leaving room for rice to expand. (If too much filling is added, tomatoes may break open.) Place in a baking dish. Put tops on tomatoes. Drizzle remaining olive oil between tomatoes. Add ½ cup water.
4. Bake at 350°F about 40 minutes, or until rice is tender, basting occasionally. (Add more liquid to dish, if necessary.)

12 servings

Stuffed Peppers: Follow recipe for Tomatoes Stuffed with Meat and Rice, substituting **green peppers** for tomatoes. Remove seeds from peppers and discard. Proceed as directed.

550 *Roast Leg of Lamb with Orzo (Ghiouvetsi)*

1 lamb leg (6½ to 7 pounds)
4 large garlic cloves, peeled and
    cut in half lengthwise
¼ cup oregano, crushed
1 tablespoon salt
2 tablespoons freshly ground
    pepper
  Juice of 2 lemons
1 pound orzo (a pasta)
¼ cup cooking oil
1 tablespoon salt
1 cup boiling water
2 medium onions, quartered
¾ cup shredded or grated
    kefalotyri cheese

1. First prepare the lamb by placing it on a large sheet of aluminum foil. With a small, sharp knife, make eight 1-inch-deep diagonal incisions on the top and bottom the lamb. Into each incision, insert half a garlic clove. Press meat back to cover incisions.
2. Combine oregano, 1 tablespoon salt, and the pepper. Rub this all over the lamb. Fold the four sides of foil up to form a cuff. Pour on lemon juice. Seal the foil and refrigerate at least 6 hours, or preferably overnight.
3. Place leg of lamb on a rack in a roasting pan.
4. Roast in a 450°F oven 20 minutes. Turn oven control to 350°F. Roast until meat is cooked as desired; a meat thermometer inserted in the leg will register 160°F for medium and 170°F to 180°F for well-done meat.
5. Remove from roasting pan to a carving board. Keep warm. When ready to serve, slice meat on the diagonal. Save the pan drippings to use for making gravy.
6. Prepare orzo by boiling it according to directions on the package, adding cooking oil and 1 tablespoon salt. Drain. Rinse under hot water.
7. To make gravy for the orzo, remove the fat from the pan drippings. Add boiling water while stirring with a spoon to loosen drippings on bottom of the pan. Add onions.
8. Bake at 350°F 15 minutes.
9. Pour the gravy with onions into a blender and purée. Return to the roasting pan. Combine the orzo with the gravy. Toss quickly. Serve with shredded kefalotyri as an accompaniment to the lamb.

6 to 8 servings

551 *Saddle of Lamb with Artichoke Purée*

1 (5 pounds) saddle of lamb
    (lamb loin roast)
2 tablespoons olive oil
  Salt and pepper
2 teaspoons oregano
4 garlic cloves, crushed in a
    garlic press
8 to 10 thick grapevine leaves
8 artichoke bottoms, cooked
1 pound mushrooms, cooked
2 tablespoons butter
½ cup red wine
½ cup water

1. Rub lamb with olive oil. Combine salt, pepper, oregano, and garlic. Rub over lamb. Cover with grapevine leaves. Seal with foil. Refrigerate overnight.
2. Purée artichoke bottoms and mushrooms. Combine with butter and heat.
3. Set roast in a roasting pan. Remove grapevine leaves and season with salt and pepper.
4. Roast in a 325°F oven 50 minutes. Remove from oven. Reserve juices in the pan. Separate each loin from the saddle in one piece. Cut the meat into slices. Spread each slice with some of the purée. Reassemble the loins and tie securely in place. Return the meat to the roasting pan and add wine and water. Continue roasting, basting frequently, for 15 minutes.
5. Remove to a serving platter and discard strings. Skim fat from the pan juices and strain juices over the meat.

About 10 servings

552 *Lamb Shank in Parchment Paper*

1 lamb shank per serving
For each serving:
   1 garlic clove, peeled and
      slivered
   1 slice hard mizithra cheese
   1 small onion, sliced
   1 small tomato, peeled and diced
   1 teaspoon minced parsley
   ¼ teaspoon dill
   ¼ teaspoon mint flakes
   ½ teaspoon oregano
   Juice of ½ lemon
   Salt and pepper to taste
   1 teaspoon olive oil
   Parchment paper
   Cotton string

1. Make several incisions in the meat, top and bottom. Insert sliver of garlic in each incision.
2. Place meat on a piece of parchment paper ample enough to seal meat and vegetables securely. Put cheese on meat, then arrange onion and tomato on top. Sprinkle with herbs, lemon juice, salt, and pepper. Drizzle with olive oil.
3. Wrap securely in parchment paper. Tie with string. Set in a roasting pan.
4. Bake at 350°F about 1½ hours, or until meat is done. Serve package unopened.

Note: Oiled brown paper may be substituted for the parchment paper.

553 *Braised Lamb Shanks*

   3 tablespoons olive oil
   6 lamb shanks
   Salt and pepper to taste
   1 can (16 ounces) tomatoes
      (undrained)
   2 cups red wine
   ¼ cup dried oregano
   2 bay leaves
   ¼ cup minced parsley
   2 garlic cloves, minced
   2 onions, quartered

1. Heat olive oil until it begins to smoke. Brown lamb shanks on all sides. Season with salt and pepper. Add tomatoes, wine, oregano, bay leaves, parsley, garlic, and onion. Cover. Simmer 2 to 2½ hours, or until meat is fork tender.
2. Remove from heat. Cool. Skim off fat. Reheat and serve hot.

6 servings

554 *Lamb with Endive Avgolemono (Arni me Antithia Avgolemono)*

   3 large bunches curly endive
   1 quart water
   3 tablespoons olive oil
   5 pounds lamb shoulder with
      bone, cut in large pieces
   1 medium onion, minced
   2 tablespoons flour
   2 cups water
   Salt and pepper to taste
   3 eggs
   Juice of 2 lemons

1. Wash endive thoroughly under running cold water to remove grit. Cut off coarse stems. Bring 1 quart water to boiling in a large saucepot. Remove from heat and add endive. Let stand 3 minutes. Drain.
2. Heat olive oil in a large Dutch oven. Add meat and brown on all sides. Add onion. Cover and simmer, stirring occasionally.
3. Combine flour with 2 cups water in a bowl; stir well. Pour into meat. Season with salt and pepper. Add endive, cover, and continue cooking 1½ to 2 hours, or until meat is tender. (There should be enough stock for avgolemono sauce.)
4. To prepare sauce, beat eggs in a bowl and, beating constantly with a whisk, add lemon juice in a steady stream. Take 1 cup stock from meat and add, a tablespoon at a time, beating constantly.
5. Pour sauce over meat and endive. Heat; do not boil.

6 servings

555 *Lamb Shish Kebob* (*Arni Souvlakia*)

¾ cup dry red wine
¼ cup lemon juice
3 tablespoons olive oil
1 teaspoon salt
Freshly ground pepper to taste
2 garlic cloves, crushed in a
garlic press
1 onion, minced
Bay leaf
2 tablespoons oregano, crushed
3 pounds leg of lamb, boneless,
cut in 1½-inch cubes
Green peppers, cored and cut
in squares
Baby onions, peeled and left
whole
Large mushroom caps
Tomato wedges

1. Make a marinade of wine, lemon juice, olive oil, salt, pepper, garlic, onion, bay leaf, and oregano in a large bowl and add lamb cubes. Cover securely and refrigerate at least 6 hours. Turn lamb several times while marinating.
2. Remove meat from marinade and place on skewers with green pepper squares, onions, mushroom caps, and tomato wedges.
3. Barbecue over hot coals or broil about 20 minutes, or until done; baste with marinade during cooking.

8 to 10 servings

556 *Lamb Stew with Eggplant* (*Arni me Melitzana*)

2 pounds lean lamb shoulder, cut
in large pieces
1 cup flour seasoned with salt
and pepper
2 tablespoons olive oil
1 large onion, minced
3 large tomatoes, peeled and
diced
¾ cup water
1 bay leaf
Salt and pepper to taste
3 cups water
2 medium eggplants, cut in large
cubes
2 garlic cloves, crushed in a
garlic press
1 tablespoon tomato paste

1. Dip lamb lightly in flour.
2. Heat oil in a large skillet. Add meat and brown on all sides. Remove meat with a slotted spoon.
3. Put onion in the oil and sauté until translucent.
4. Return meat to skillet. Add tomatoes, water, and bay leaf. Season with salt and pepper. Bring to boiling. Reduce heat and simmer, covered, for 1½ hours.
5. Meanwhile, bring water to a boil in a saucepan. Add eggplant and simmer 5 minutes (to remove bitter taste). Pour off water.
6. Add eggplant, garlic, and tomato paste to meat. Stir to blend. Cover. Simmer about 40 minutes, or until meat is tender.

4 to 6 servings

557 *Lamb Chops with Oregano* (*Kotolettes Arniou me Rigani*)

2 lamb chops (rib or loin) per
serving

For each serving:
1 tablespoon oregano
Salt to taste
1 lemon, cut in half
1 tablespoon olive oil (optional)
Pepper to taste

1. An hour before cooking, sprinkle lamb chops with oregano. Season with salt. Set aside.
2. Place lamb chops on a broiler rack and broil 7 minutes on each side.
3. Remove from broiler and squeeze lemon juice over the chops. Drizzle with oil. Season with pepper.

558 *Lamb-Stuffed Zucchini with Avgolemono Sauce*

8 medium straight zucchini
1 pound ground beef round or
    lamb
½ cup long-grain rice
1 small onion, minced
2 tablespoons chopped parsley
1 teaspoon chopped mint
    Salt and pepper
    Water (about 2 cups)

Sauce:
2 egg yolks
    Juice of 2 lemons
½ cup broth

1. Remove the ends and scrape the skins of the zucchini. With a corer, scoop out the zucchini centers and discard. Soak the zucchini in cold water.
2. Meanwhile, mix meat with rice, onion, parsley, mint, salt, and pepper. Drain zucchini and stuff with meat mixture.
3. Arrange stuffed zucchini in a single layer in a Dutch oven. Add enough water to half cover the zucchini. Bring the water to a boil, reduce heat, and simmer, covered, about 35 minutes.
4. Before serving, beat egg yolks until frothy. Slowly add lemon juice, beating constantly. Add broth, tablespoon by tablespoon, beating constantly. Heat thoroughly, but do not boil. Pour over zucchini. Serve immediately.

4 servings

559 *Roast Baby Lamb's Head* (*Arni Kefalaki Psito*)

1 head per serving, split in half
    and tied with a string to
    keep brains intact
    Juice of 1 lemon
2 tablespoons olive oil
1 tablespoon oregano or more to
    taste
    Salt and pepper to taste

1. Soak head in cold salted water for 1 hour. Drain. Pat dry. Cut string and place halves in a shallow pan, brains up.
2. Combine lemon juice, olive oil, oregano, salt, and pepper. Drizzle over head.
3. Roast in a 350°F oven for about 20 minutes, basting frequently until brains are tender. Remove brains with a spoon and keep warm. Continue roasting about 45 minutes more, or until other parts are tender.

560 *Lamb Kidneys in Wine Sauce* (*Nefra Krasata*)

4 lamb kidneys
    Water
1 tablespoon wine vinegar
3 tablespoons flour
¼ cup butter
1½ cups white wine
1 bay leaf
1 garlic clove
2 tablespoons minced parsley
2 teaspoons oregano
½ teaspoon cumin
    Salt and pepper to taste

1. Soak kidneys in cold water and vinegar for 15 minutes. Drain. Remove opaque skin and cut out the core. Slice kidneys thinly.
2. Dip slices in flour.
3. Melt butter in a skillet. Sauté the kidneys until browned on both sides. Add wine, bay leaf, garlic, parsley, oregano, cumin, salt, and pepper. Cover and simmer 20 minutes.

4 servings

561 *Shepherdess' Pie (Pita tys Voskopoulas)*

1½ cups Béchamel Sauce
1 medium onion, minced
1 egg, beaten
¼ cup fresh cracker crumbs
¼ cup chopped parsley
1 teaspoon salt
1 teaspoon thyme
¼ teaspoon ground red pepper
1 teaspoon vinegar
1 pound coarsely ground lamb or lean beef
4 cups mashed potatoes
½ cup grated kefalotyri cheese
1 teaspoon paprika

1. Combine ¾ cup of Béchamel Sauce, onion, egg, cracker crumbs, parsley, salt, thyme, red pepper, and vinegar.
2. Combine sauce with meat, tossing with 2 forks to mix lightly. Spoon mixture into a baking dish. Level top lightly with the back of the spoon. Make an indentation in the center.
3. Bake at 350°F 30 minutes, removing fat as it collects in the indentation.
4. Combine potatoes with remaining sauce.
5. Remove meat from oven when done. Sprinkle with cheese. Cover with potatoes. Sprinkle with paprika. Bake 20 minutes.

4 servings

Béchamel Sauce: Melt ¼ **cup butter.** Whisk in **3 tablespoons flour.** Cook, stirring constantly, for 1 minute. Slowly pour in **1½ cups milk,** scalded. Cook, stirring constantly, until mixture coats a wooden spoon.

562 *Charcoal-Roasted Pig (Gourounipoulo tys Skaras)*

3 garlic cloves, crushed in a garlic press
2 cups dry white wine
Juice of 2 lemons
1 tablespoon salt
¼ cup oregano
2 tablespoons crushed peppercorns
1 piglet (12 to 15 pounds), with eyes, tongue, and feet removed
½ cup olive oil
1 tablespoon paprika

1. Make a marinade by combining garlic, wine, lemon juice, salt, oregano, and peppercorns. Refrigerate 1 hour.
2. Score pig several places with a knife. Rub interior cavity and exterior surface with marinade. Allow to marinate 12 hours in refrigerator.
3. Crush aluminum foil into a firm, thick ball and put in mouth to keep open. Cover ears with foil so they will not burn. Pull front feet forward and tie together. Pull hind feet backwards and tie together. Cover feet loosely with foil.
4. Attach pig to revolving spit and roast, basting frequently with a mixture of oil and paprika, until skin is brown and crisp and meat is tender (about 5 hours). In the last hour, remove foil so ears and feet can brown.
5. Remove pig from spit. Set on a platter. Put an apple or other piece of fruit in its mouth. Pour off fat from pan juices and serve.

8 to 10 servings

563 *Pork Chops with Vegetables*

3 tablespoons vegetable oil
8 lean pork chops
1 can (15 ounces) stewed tomatoes
1¾ cups water
1 cup minced celery
1 large green pepper, minced
1 medium onion, minced
1 bay leaf
1 thyme sprig
¼ teaspoon paprika
Salt and pepper to taste

1. Heat oil in a large deep skillet. Add chops and brown on both sides.
2. Turn stewed tomatoes into a bowl. Add water, celery, green pepper, onion, bay leaf, thyme, paprika, salt, and pepper; mix well.
3. Remove excess fat from skillet; add tomato mixture. Cover.
4. Bake at 325°F about 2 hours, or until tender. Serve pork chops with **pilafi** or **potatoes.** Pass gravy separately.

8 servings

564 *Pork Braised with Celery in Egg and Lemon Sauce*
(Hoirino Selin Avgolemono)

¼ cup butter
4 pounds lean pork, cut in 2-inch cubes
1 large onion, minced
2 cups water
2 bunches celery (stalks only), cut in 1-inch pieces

Avgolemono Sauce:
¼ cup butter
3 tablespoons flour
2 cups pork stock
Juice of 2 lemons
3 eggs, separated
Salt and pepper to taste

1. Melt butter in a Dutch oven and sauté pork until golden brown. Add onion and cook until translucent. Add water. Cover and simmer 1 to 1½ hours, or until meat is just tender. Add celery and simmer about 15 minutes, or until tender. Drain off 2 cups stock and strain. Keep meat warm.
2. To make sauce, melt butter in a saucepan; add flour and cook about 1 minute, stirring constantly; do not brown. Add pork stock and lemon juice. Simmer, stirring constantly, until sauce thickens.
3. Separate eggs. Beat whites until soft peaks form. Beat yolks until thick. Fold yolks into whites. Using a wire whisk, slowly add sauce to eggs. Pour over pork mixture. Heat and serve at once.

8 servings

565 *Pork Sausage with Orange Peel* (Loukanika)

2 pounds pork shoulder, ground
½ pound pork fat back, ground
Grated peel of 1 navel orange
2 garlic cloves, crushed in a garlic press
1 tablespoon minced parsley
1 tablespoon oregano
2 teaspoons salt
2 teaspoons anise seed
2 teaspoons coriander, ground
1½ teaspoons allspice, ground
1 teaspoon pepper
1 long casing, cut in 7- to 8-inch pieces

1. Combine pork shoulder, fat back, and remaining ingredients, except casings, in a bowl and mix thoroughly. Cover and refrigerate several hours.
2. Rinse casings thoroughly in lukewarm water. Tie one end of a casing and stuff by pushing meat through a funnel inserted in the untied end; tie other end. Continue until all the meat and casings have been used.
3. Poach sausages in boiling water for 1 hour. Cool. Cut into slices and fry in a skillet until browned.

Note: If desired, omit casing, form sausage into patties, and fry until cooked.

566 *Roast Veal*

3 pounds veal rump roast, boned, rolled, and tied
1 garlic clove
1 tablespoon dill
1 teaspoon oregano
Salt and pepper to taste
3 tablespoons butter
¼ cup water
¼ cup white wine
1 teaspoon rosemary

1. Rub roast with garlic, dill, and oregano. Season with salt and pepper.
2. Melt butter in a roasting pan. Brown veal well on all sides.
3. Place a rack under veal. Pour water and wine into bottom of pan. Add rosemary. Cover pan.
4. Roast in a 350°F oven 2 hours.
5. Serve with pan juices.

6 to 8 servings

567 *Sautéed Veal Brains in Browned Butter (Myala Tyganita)*

4 veal brains
Juice of 2 lemons
1 teaspoon salt
½ cup flour seasoned with salt
    and pepper
½ cup butter
2 tablespoons chopped fresh dill
1 lemon, cut in wedges

1. Rinse brains thoroughly. Soak in water with ice cubes for 15 minutes. Drain; remove membranes.
2. Pour enough water into a saucepot to cover brains. Add lemon juice and salt; bring to boiling. Reduce heat and drop in brains. Simmer 15 minutes. Drain. Plunge into ice water to cool quickly.
3. Dip brains into seasoned flour.
4. Put butter into a skillet and heat until deep brown. Add brains and sauté briefly. Remove to a warm platter. Sprinkle with dill. Serve with lemon wedges.

4 servings

568 *Braised Veal with Lemon and Anchovies*

6 thick slices veal shin, sawed
    through so marrow shows
½ cup flour
½ cup butter
1 cup dry white wine
¼ cup chicken or veal stock
1 can (16 ounces) tomatoes
    (undrained)
2 teaspoons salt
1 teaspoon ground pepper
1 teaspoon thyme
2 garlic cloves, crushed in a garlic
    press
1 teaspoon grated lemon peel
½ cup minced parsley
2 anchovies, minced

1. Roll veal shin slices lightly in flour.
2. Melt butter in a Dutch oven and add veal, browning on all sides. Add wine, stock, tomatoes, salt, pepper, thyme, and garlic. Cover. Simmer about 2 hours, or until meat is tender, adding a little liquid when necessary.
3. Sprinkle with lemon peel, parsley, and anchovies before serving.

3 servings

569 *Cypriote Sausages*

1 pound coarsely ground beef
1 pound coarsely ground pork
1 cup fresh bread crumbs
3 garlic cloves, crushed in a
    garlic press
2 teaspoons salt
2 teaspoons coriander
1 teaspoon cumin
1 teaspoon thyme
½ teaspoon paprika
¼ teaspoon ground red pepper
1 bay leaf, ground
1 egg
½ cup minced parsley
1 large onion, minced
2 tablespoons tomato paste
    mixed with ½ cup water
Flour for rolling
Oil for frying

1. Combine meats in a large bowl, tossing with 2 forks.
2. Combine remaining ingredients except flour and oil in a separate bowl. Toss with meat mixture.
3. Break off enough meat to form a 2-inch-long sausage. Lightly flour palms of hands. Roll meat into sausage shapes.
4. Heat oil to smoking in a skillet. Fry sausages until deep brown on all sides. Serve hot or cold.

20 to 30 sausages

570 *Veal Stew with Onions* (Moskari Stifatho)

Flour seasoned with salt,
  pepper, and paprika
6 veal shanks, cut in pieces
3 tablespoons olive oil
3 tomatoes, peeled, seeded, and
  cubed
2 tablespoons chopped parsley
1 cup water
1 tablespoon wine vinegar
2 garlic cloves, minced
1 teaspoon sugar
1 bay leaf
2 whole cloves
2 whole allspice
  Pinch red pepper seed
2 pounds whole baby onions
  Water

1. Put seasoned flour into a bag. Add shank pieces and shake to coat evenly.
2. Heat oil in a Dutch oven and brown meat on all sides. Add tomatoes, parsley, 1 cup water, wine vinegar, garlic, and sugar. Tie bay leaf, cloves, allspice, and red pepper seed in cheesecloth. Add to meat mixture. Cover and simmer 1 hour.
3. Meanwhile, peel onions. Cut a small cross on the bottom of each. Add to stew and pour in enough water to cover. Simmer until onions are tender (about 25 minutes). Discard spices. Serve hot with **rice** or **cracked wheat pilafi.**

3 or 4 servings

571 *Rabbit Stew* (Kounelli Stifatho)

2 rabbits, skinned, cleaned, and
  cut in four pieces each
1½ cups mild vinegar
1 cup water
1 large onion, quartered
2 teaspoons salt
1 teaspoon pepper
2 bay leaves
2 pounds whole baby onions
3 tablespoons olive oil
2 tablespoons tomato paste
  mixed with 1 cup water
1 cup red wine
1 garlic clove, crushed in a garlic
  press
1 bay leaf
⅛ teaspoon cinnamon
  Salt and pepper to taste
  Water to cover

1. Put rabbit pieces into a large bowl. Add vinegar, water, onion, salt, pepper, and bay leaves. Cover. Refrigerate 24 hours, turning occasionally. Pat dry.
2. Peel onions. Cut a small cross at the base of each (to keep onions whole during cooking).
3. Heat olive oil in a large Dutch oven and sear rabbit on all sides until reddened. Add all ingredients including onions and water to barely cover. Bring to a boil. Cover.
4. Bake at 250°F about 2 hours, or until rabbit is tender.

8 servings

Note: If a thick sauce is desired, pour the sauce into a saucepan and simmer uncovered for ½ hour. Pour over rabbit.

572 *Beef Pot Roast (Pieczeń Wołowa Duszona)*

1 beef round rump or chuck roast,
    boneless (3½ pounds)
3 tablespoons salad oil or ¼
    pound salt pork, diced
    Bouillon or meat broth (about 1½
    cups)
1 bay leaf
2 onions, quartered
2 carrots, cut in pieces
½ teaspoon salt
½ teaspoon coarse pepper
    Flour
    Salt and pepper

1. Brown the beef in oil. Add ¼ cup bouillon, bay leaf, onions, carrots, salt, and pepper; cover and simmer 2½ hours, basting with additional bouillon to prevent burning.
2. Sprinkle flour over meat and turn it over. Sprinkle with more flour. If necessary, add more bouillon for the sauce. Cook uncovered 30 minutes. Serve the pot roast with **noodles** or **potatoes** and any kind of vegetables.

8 to 10 servings

Pot Roast with Sour Cream: Prepare Beef Pot Roast as directed. Add **1½ cups dairy sour cream** instead of bouillon after flouring the meat. Finish cooking as directed.

Pot Roast with Sour Cream and Pickles or Mushrooms: Prepare Beef Pot Roast as directed. Add **1½ cups dairy sour cream** instead of bouillon after flouring the meat. Then stir in **⅔ cup chopped dill pickles** or **1 cup sliced mushrooms**. Finish cooking as directed.

573 *Beef Slices with Sour Cream and Mushrooms (Zrazy z Grzybami i ze Śmietaną)*

½ cup all-purpose flour
1 teaspoon salt
½ teaspoon pepper
2 pounds beef eye round, top
    round, or sirloin (cut in thin
    steaks)
3 tablespoons butter or fat
1 can (4 ounces) mushrooms with
    liquid
1 cup water
6 medium potatoes, cooked; or 3
    cups sauerkraut, drained
1 tablespoon flour
1 cup dairy sour cream

1. Mix flour with salt and pepper. Coat meat with seasoned flour.
2. Melt butter in a large skillet or Dutch oven. Brown meat quickly on both sides.
3. Add mushrooms with liquid and water. Cover. Simmer 1 hour, basting occasionally with sauce.
4. Add potatoes to meat; cook 10 minutes, or until meat and potatoes are tender.
5. Blend flour into sour cream. Blend into sauce. Bring to boiling, then simmer 5 minutes.

6 servings

574 *Steamed Beef (Sztuka Mięsa w Parze)*

3 to 4 pounds beef round rump or
    eye round steak
    Salt and pepper
2 onions, sliced
1 cup each diced carrot, parsley
    root, and parsnips
1 cup green peas
½ cup sliced celery
½ cup asparagus stems (optional)
1 cauliflower or cabbage core, diced
    (optional)
2 tablespoons butter

1. Pound the meat. Sprinkle with salt and pepper. Let stand 30 minutes. Pound again.
2. In a steamer top, combine meat and vegetables. Add butter. Cook over gently boiling water about 3 hours, or until meat is tender.
3. Slice meat. Serve with the steamed vegetables.

6 to 8 servings

575 *Roast Leg of Lamb (Pieczeń Baraniha z Pieca)*

Vinegar
1 lamb leg, whole
Garlic cloves, slivered
Salt and pepper

1. Soak a towel with vinegar; wrap around the leg of lamb. Let stand overnight.
2. Remove towel. Trim off fell, if necessary, and excess fat. Make small slits in fat cover on meat. Push a sliver of garlic into each slit.
3. Place lamb, fat side up, on rack in a roasting pan. Sprinkle with salt and pepper.
4. Roast in a 325°F oven until done as desired. Allow 30 minutes per pound for medium; 35 minutes per pound for well-done.

About 8 to 12 servings

576 *Roast Loin of Pork (Schab Pieczony)*

2 tablespoons flour
1½ teaspoons salt
1 teaspoon dry mustard or
     caraway seed
½ teaspoon sugar
¼ teaspoon black pepper
¼ teaspoon ground sage
1 pork loin roast (4 to 5 pounds)
Topping:
1½ cups applesauce
½ cup brown sugar
¼ teaspoon cinnamon or allspice
¼ teaspoon mace
¼ teaspoon salt

1. Mix flour, salt, mustard, sugar, pepper and sage. Rub over surface of meat. Set meat fat side up in a roasting pan.
2. Roast at 325°F 1½ hours.
3. For topping, mix applesauce with brown sugar, cinnamon, mace, and salt. Spread on top of meat.
4. Roast about 45 minutes longer, or until done.

8 to 10 servings

577 *Sauerkraut with Pork (Kapusta z Wieprzowiną)*

2 pounds pig's feet or ham hocks
2 pounds neck bones or spareribs
3 tablespoons lard or margarine
1 large onion
1 clove garlic, crushed
1½ quarts boiling water
1 green pepper, diced
4 whole allspice
1 bay leaf
½ teaspoon celery seed
1 quart (about 2 pounds)
     sauerkraut
¼ cup barley
1 small apple, chopped
½ teaspoon caraway seed
2 teaspoons salt
½ teaspoon pepper

1. Brown all meat in lard in a large kettle.
2. Add onion and garlic. Fry 1 minute.
3. Add boiling water, green pepper, allspice, bay leaf, and celery seed. Cover; cook 1 hour or until meat is tender.
4. Remove meat; cool. Boil until broth is reduced to 3 cups.
5. Discard bones and gristle from meat. Drain and rinse sauerkraut.
6. Cook barley in the broth 15 minutes. Add meat, sauerkraut, apple, caraway seed, salt, and pepper. Cook 45 minutes longer.
7. Serve with potato dumplings, if desired.

About 6 servings

578 *Pork Pot Roast (Pieczeń Wieprzowa Duszona)*

1 pork shoulder arm picnic or pork loin roast, boneless (3 pounds)
2 tablespoons butter or lard
2 tomatoes, peeled and cored
1 celery root
1 parsley root
1 onion, sliced
2 sprigs parsley
2 tablespoons spices to taste:
allspice, caraway seed, whole cloves, juniper berries, dried marjoram leaves, peppercorns (tie in cheesecloth)
¼ cup water
½ cup bouillon or meat broth
½ cup Madeira, Marsala, or sherry

1. Rub meat with salt and pepper. Let stand 1 hour.
2. Brown meat in butter in a large, heavy skillet. Add vegetables, parsley, spice bag, and water. Cover tightly. Cook over medium heat 1½ hours; stirring as necessary and turning meat occasionally.
3. Sprinkle a small amount of flour over top of meat. Pour bouillon and wine over meat. Simmer 15 minutes.
4. Slice and arrange meat on a warm platter. Strain sauce and pour over meat.

6 to 8 servings

579 *Boiled Tongue (Ozór Szpikowany w Potrawie)*

1 beef tongue (about 3 pounds); fresh, smoked, or corned tongue may be used
Boiling water
¼ pound salt pork, diced
2 onions, quartered
2 bay leaves
1 celery root or 3 stalks celery
2 carrots
2 parsnips or turnips
1 fresh horseradish root (optional)
1 parsley root
2 sprigs fresh parsley
1 tablespoon salt
6 whole peppercorns
Sauce:
1 cup white wine
1 bouillon cube
1 tablespoon flour
2 tablespoons butter (at room temperature)
2 tablespoons prepared cream-style horseradish

1. Rinse tongue under cold, running water. Cook in enough boiling water to cover 1 hour.
2. Add salt pork, 1 onion, and 1 bay leaf. Cover; cook 1 to 2 hours, or until tongue is tender. Remove skin, fat, and gristle. Strain liquid.
3. Combine tongue, strained liquid, remaining onion, and bay leaf with vegetables, parsley, salt, and peppercorns. Cover; simmer until vegetables are tender, 30 to 45 minutes.
4. For sauce, purée vegetables in an electric blender or press through a sieve.
5. Combine 1½ cups cooking liquid, wine, and bouillon cube. Bring to boiling. Blend flour into butter; stir into boiling broth. Add vegetable purée and prepared horseradish. Cook and stir until sauce is smooth.
6. Slice tongue. Simmer in sauce 10 minutes.

About 8 servings

580 *Liver à la Nelson*

1½ pounds sliced calf's liver
Milk
8 medium potatoes, pared
1 onion, sliced
½ cup sliced mushrooms
¼ cup butter
½ cup all-purpose flour
½ teaspoon salt
¼ teaspoon pepper
1 cup bouillon or meat broth
½ cup sweet red wine or Madeira

1. Soak liver 45 minutes in enough milk to cover.
2. Cook potatoes in boiling water until tender; cut in thick slices.
3. Sauté onion and mushrooms in butter in a large skillet until tender, about 5 minutes.
4. Mix flour with salt and pepper. Drain liver; pat dry with paper towels. Coat liver with seasoned flour.
5. Quickly brown liver in skillet with onion and mushrooms. Add sliced potatoes, bouillon, and wine. Cover. Simmer just until liver is tender, about 10 to 15 minutes.

6 servings

581 *Tripe and Vegetables Warsaw Style*
(Flaki z Jarzynami po Warszawsku)

2 pounds fresh tripe
1 pound beef or veal soup bones
Water
Salt
4 carrots, sliced
1 celery root, chopped, or 3 stalks celery, sliced
1 bunch green onions, sliced
1 tablespoon chopped fresh parsley
3 cups bouillon or meat broth
2 tablespoons butter or margarine
2 tablespoons flour
½ teaspoon salt
¼ teaspoon ginger
¼ teaspoon mace
¼ teaspoon marjoram
¼ teaspoon pepper
1 cup light cream or vegetable broth

1. Clean tripe well and rinse thoroughly under running cold water.
2. Combine tripe and soup bones with enough water to cover in a large kettle. Season with ½ teaspoon salt for each cup of water added. Cover. Bring to boiling; reduce heat and simmer 3 to 5 hours, or until tripe is tender.
3. Drain tripe; discard bones and cooking liquid. Cut tripe into very thin strips.
4. Cook tripe with vegetables and parsley in bouillon until vegetables are tender.
5. Melt butter in a saucepan. Stir in flour to make a smooth paste. Cook and stir until golden. Blend in a small amount of cooking liquid. Add ½ teaspoon salt and spices. Add cream gradually, stirring until smooth.
6. Drain vegetables and tripe. Stir into sauce. Simmer 5 minutes.

4 to 6 servings

582 *Polish Sausage with Red Cabbage*
(Kiełbasa z Czerwoną Kapustą)

1 head red cabbage, sliced (about 2
   pounds)
  Boiling water
2 tablespoons butter
⅓ cup lemon juice
½ cup red wine or beef broth
½ teaspoon salt
¼ teaspoon pepper
¾ pound Polish sausage, diced
2 teaspoons brown sugar
1 tablespoon cornstarch or potato
  flour

1. Place cabbage in a colander. Pour boiling water over cabbage. Drain well.
2. Melt butter in a Dutch oven or large heavy skillet. Add cabbage. Stir in lemon juice. Cook and stir about 5 minutes, or until cabbage is pink. Add wine, salt, and pepper. Cover. Simmer over medium-low heat 45 minutes.
3. Mix sugar and cornstarch. Stir into simmering liquid. Bring to boiling, stirring constantly. Reduce heat; add sausage. Cover; cook 30 minutes.

About 4 servings

583 *Sausage in Polish Sauce*
(Kiełbasa w Polskim Sosie)

2 onions, sliced
3 tablespoons butter or margarine
  Ring Polish sausage (about 1½
  pounds)
1½ cups bouillon or meat broth
12 ounces beer
2 tablespoons flour
1 tablespoon vinegar
2 teaspoons brown sugar
¾ teaspoon salt
¼ teaspoon pepper
4 to 6 boiled potatoes

1. Sauté onion in 2 tablespoons butter until golden. Add sausage, bouillon, and beer. Simmer 20 minutes.
2. Blend flour into remaining 1 tablespoon butter. Stir into broth. Add vinegar, brown sugar, salt, and pepper.
3. Add potatoes. Cook over medium heat 10 to 15 minutes.
4. Slice sausage into 2-inch chunks to serve.

4 to 6 servings

584 *Bacon Fry (Grzybek ze Słoninką)*

1 pound sliced bacon, diced
4 eggs
1 cup milk
2 cups all-purpose flour
1 tablespoon sugar
2½ teaspoons baking powder
1½ teaspoons salt

1. Fry bacon just until golden in a 10-inch skillet. Remove ⅔ cup bacon and drippings.
2. Beat eggs with milk. Add 1 cup flour, sugar, baking powder, and salt. Beat until smooth. Beat in remaining flour.
3. Pour half of batter just in center of skillet over bacon and drippings. Tilt skillet slightly to spread batter. Cook until browned on bottom and set on top. Turn.
4. Sprinkle half the reserved bacon and 1 tablespoon drippings over top. Pour on half the remaining batter. Turn when bottom is browned.
5. Sprinkle remaining bacon and 2 tablespoons drippings on top. Pour on remaining batter. Turn when bottom is browned. Cook just until browned.
6. Cut into wedges for serving.

About 4 servings

585 *Cabbage Rolls (Gołąbki)*

1 whole head cabbage (about 3
    pounds)
  Boiling water
1 pound ground beef
½ pound ground veal
¾ cup chopped onion
½ cup packaged precooked rice
1 egg, beaten
1 teaspoon salt
¼ teaspoon pepper
5 slices bacon
1 can (16 ounces) tomatoes or
    sauerkraut
⅓ cup bouillon or meat broth
½ teaspoon sugar
¼ teaspoon salt
¼ teaspoon pepper

1. Remove core from cabbage. Place whole head in a large kettle filled with boiling water. Cover; cook 3 minutes. Remove softened outer leaves. Repeat until all large leaves have been removed (about 20 leaves). Cut thick center stem from each slice.
2. Sauté meat with onion 5 minutes. Remove from heat. Stir in rice, egg, 1 teaspoon salt, and ¼ teaspoon pepper.
3. Place 3 tablespoons meat mixture on each cabbage leaf. Roll each leaf, tucking ends in toward center. Fasten securely with wooden picks. Place each roll seam side down in a large skillet or Dutch oven.
4. Lay bacon slices over top of cabbage rolls.
5. Mix tomatoes, bouillon, sugar, ¼ teaspoon salt, and ¼ teaspoon pepper. Pour over cabbage rolls.
6. Cover; simmer about 1 hour, turning occasionally.

About 10 servings

586 *Cabbage Rolls with Mushroom Sauce*
(Gołąbki w Grzybowym Sosie)

1 onion, chopped
1 clove garlic, crushed (optional)
2 tablespoons butter
¾ cup uncooked raw rice
½ pound ground beef or veal
½ pound ground pork
1 teaspoon salt
¼ teaspoon pepper
1 whole head cabbage (about 3
    pounds)
  Boiling water
2 cups beef broth or stock
1 can (about 10 ounces) condensed
    cream of mushroom soup

1. Sauté onion and garlic in butter in a large skillet, about 5 minutes. Add rice, meat, salt, and pepper. Stir-fry just to mix well. Remove from heat.
2. Remove core from cabbage. Place whole head in a large kettle filled with boiling water. Cover; cook 3 minutes. Remove softened outer leaves. Repeat until all leaves are softened and have been removed. Cut thick stem from each leaf.
3. Taking one large cabbage leaf at a time, spoon about 1 rounded tablespoonful of meat mixture in center of leaf. Cover with a small leaf. Tuck ends up and just over edge of filling; place one end of leaf over filling and roll up loosely. If desired, secure with a wooden pick. Repeat until all filling and leaves are used. Place cabbage rolls in a large casserole; do not make more than 2 layers.
4. Combine beef broth and mushroom soup; pour over cabbage rolls.
5. Bake at 350°F about 1½ hours.

8 to 12 servings

Easy Hunter's Stew, page 223

587 Stuffed Cabbage Rolls (Gołąbki)

1 whole head cabbage (about 4 pounds)
Boiling salted water
1 onion, chopped
2 tablespoons oil
1½ pounds ground beef
½ pound ground fresh pork
1½ cups cooked rice
1 teaspoon salt
¼ teaspoon pepper
2 cans (about 10 ounces each) condensed tomato soup
2½ cups water

1. Remove core from cabbage. Place whole head in a large kettle filled with boiling salted water. Cover; cook 3 minutes, or until softened enough to pull off individual leaves. Repeat to remove all large leaves (about 30). Cut thick center stem from each leaf. Chop remaining cabbage.
2. Sauté onion in oil. Add meat, rice, salt, and pepper. Mix thoroughly. Place a heaping tablespoonful of meat mixture on each cabbage leaf. Tuck sides over filling while rolling leaf around filling. Secure with wooden picks.
3. Place half the chopped cabbage on bottom of a large Dutch oven. Fill with layers of the cabbage rolls. Cover with remaining chopped cabbage.
4. Combine tomato soup with water; mix until smooth. Pour over cabbage rolls. Cover and bring to boiling. Reduce heat and simmer 1½ hours.
5. Serve cabbage rolls with the sauce.

About 15 servings

588 Ham in Rye Crust

Dough:
1 package active dry yeast
½ cup warm water
⅓ cup caraway seed
¾ cup water
2 tablespoons molasses
3 cups rye flour (about)

Topping for ham:
½ cup firmly packed brown sugar
1 teaspoon dry mustard
¼ teaspoon cloves

1 canned fully cooked ham (5 pounds)

1. For dough, dissolve yeast in ½ cup warm water and add caraway seed; let stand 10 minutes.
2. Stir in ¾ cup water, molasses, and half of the flour.
3. Turn out dough onto floured surface. Knead in remaining flour to make a stiff dough. Cover with plastic wrap. Let rest 20 minutes.
4. Mix brown sugar with mustard and cloves.
5. Remove gelatin and wipe ham with paper towels.
6. Roll out dough on a floured surface to form a 28×10-inch rectangle.
7. Sprinkle about 1 tablespoon brown sugar mixture in center of dough. Place ham on sugar mixture. Sprinkle remaining sugar mixture over top of ham.
8. Fold dough over top of ham, cutting out corners to fit with only one layer of dough. Pinch edges to seal.
9. Set dough-wrapped ham on rack in pan lined with foil.
10. Roast at 350°F 1½ to 1¾ hours, or until meat thermometer reaches 140°F. Remove from oven; let rest 10 minutes.
11. To serve, remove crust and discard. Slice ham.

12 to 15 servings

589 Polish Sausage (Kiełbasa)

1½ pounds lean boneless pork
½ pound boneless veal
1 teaspoon salt
¼ teaspoon pepper
1 clove garlic, crushed
1 tablespoon mustard seed
¼ cup crushed ice
Casing

1. Cut meat into small chunks. Grind meat with seasonings and ice; mix well.
2. Stuff meat mixture into casing.
3. Smoke in a smoker, following manufacturer's directions. Or, place sausage in a casserole; cover with water. Bake at 350°F until water is absorbed, about 1½ hours. Roast 10 minutes.

About 2 pounds

Pastichio, page 209
Braised Beef, Corfu Style, page 207
Lamb Shish Kebob, page 213

590 *Roasted Veal (Pieczeń Cielęca)*

1 veal leg round roast or shoulder
   arm roast (4 to 5 pounds)
  Boiling water
3 tablespoons lemon juice
1 tablespoon salt
1 teaspoon pepper
½ cup butter, melted
  Flour for dusting

1. Dip meat quickly in boiling water; drain well.
2. Mix lemon juice, salt, and pepper. Spread over surface of meat.
3. Place meat on a spit or rack in a roasting pan.
4. Roast at 400°F 20 minutes. Reduce heat to 325°F. Roast 55 minutes.
5. Baste with melted butter. Sprinkle flour over top. Roast 10 minutes longer, or until done as desired.

6 to 8 servings

591 *Roast Suckling Pig (Prosię Pieczone)*

1 suckling pig, about 25 to 30
   pounds
  Salt and pepper
1½ pounds stale bread, diced
1½ cups milk
2 eggs
2 apples, sliced
2 onions, diced
⅓ cup chopped parsley
1 potato
  Melted lard or salad oil
1 small whole apple
  Parsley sprigs or small fruits
   and leaves

1. Wipe pig, inside and out, with a clean damp cloth. Sprinkle entire cavity with salt and pepper. If necessary to make pig fit into pan (and oven) cut crosswise in half just behind shoulders.
2. Put bread into a large mixing bowl. Add milk and let soak 20 minutes. Add eggs, sliced apples, onion, and parsley; mix well.
3. Spoon stuffing into cavity of pig. (There will not be enough stuffing to entirely fill cavity.)
4. Use metal skewers to hold cavity closed and lace with string.
5. Set pig belly side down in roasting pan. Tuck feet under body. Cover tail, snout, and ears with foil. Place whole potato in mouth.
6. Roast at 375°F 8 to 10 hours. Baste frequently with melted lard. When pig is done, juices run golden and skin is a crackling, translucent, golden-chocolate brown.
7. Set pig on platter. Remove potato from mouth; replace with apple. Make a wreath of parsley sprigs for neck or to cover joint behind shoulders.

About 25 servings

592 *Rabbit (Zając Pieczony)*

1 rabbit (2 to 3 pounds), cut in
   pieces
  Salt and pepper
  Flour
¼ cup butter
1 cup chopped mushrooms
1 onion, sliced
1 clove garlic, sliced
1 cup meat stock

1. Sprinkle rabbit pieces with salt and pepper. Coat with flour.
2. Melt butter in a Dutch oven or flame-proof casserole. Add mushrooms, onion, and garlic. Add rabbit pieces and brown quickly. Remove garlic.
3. Mix stock with wine, thyme, and bay leaves. Add to rabbit.
4. Bake at 350°F or simmer about 1½ hours, or until rabbit is very tender.

⅔ cup dry white wine*
½ teaspoon ground thyme
2 bay leaves
Sauce:
  1 cup dairy sour cream
  1 teaspoon dried parsley flakes
  ¼ teaspoon nutmeg

  * Or substitute ½ cup water and 1
    tablespoon lemon juice

5. Remove rabbit and place on heated platter. Stir sauce ingredients into broth in pan. Cook and stir just until sauce begins to simmer. Spoon over rabbit.

4 to 6 servings

593 *Leg of Venison (Sarna Duszona)*

Marinade:
  1 bottle (4/5 quart) dry white wine
  3 cups vinegar
  2 cups olive oil or salad oil
  1 cup sliced carrots
  1 cup sliced onions
  2 stalks celery, cut in pieces
  2 cloves garlic, crushed
  3 sprigs parsley
  1 bay leaf
  6 whole cloves
  6 peppercorns
Venison and Sauce:
  1 leg of venison (5 to 6 pounds)
  ¼ cup oil
  2 tablespoons butter
  1 onion, diced
  1 cup red wine
  3 tablespoons sugar
  6 whole cloves
  1 cup dairy sour cream
  ½ cup all-purpose flour
    Salt and pepper

1. Combine all ingredients for marinade in a large crock. Soak the venison 2 or 3 days in the marinade. Remove and wipe dry with a cloth.
2. Heat oil and butter in a heavy skillet. Add venison; brown evenly on all sides. Fry onion in the same butter.
3. Strain 1 cup marinade. Add to skillet.
4. Place venison in a Dutch oven or roaster. Add liquid and onion from skillet. Add wine, sugar, and cloves.
5. Cover; simmer or bake at 350°F about 2½ hours, or until meat is tender.
6. Remove venison to carving board.
7. Make sauce by combining sour cream and flour. Gradually stir in 1 cup strained cooking broth. Return to Dutch oven; cook, stirring, until smooth and thick. Season to taste with salt and pepper.
8. To serve, carve venison; place slices on a warmed platter. Pour sauce over top.

8 to 12 servings

594 *Veal à la Nelson (Zrazy po Nelsońsku)*

3 ounces dried mushrooms
    (optional)
2 cups warm milk
3 slices bacon
1 pound fresh mushrooms, sliced
4 large onions, chopped
8 veal cutlets (about 3 pounds)
3 bouillon cubes
3 tablespoons flour
¼ cup butter or margarine, melted
1 cup dairy sour cream
    Salt and pepper
8 medium potatoes, cooked

1. Soak dried mushrooms in warm milk 2 hours.
2. Fry bacon in a large skillet. Add mushrooms and onion. Sauté until onion is soft. Add fried bacon, mushrooms, and onion to milk.
3. Sauté veal in drippings. Add oil, if needed.
4. Add milk mixture and bouillon cubes. Cover; simmer 1 hour.
5. Stir flour into melted butter. Blend in a small amount of cooking liquid. Stir into remainder of liquid in skillet. Cook and stir until sauce is smooth and thick. Then blend in sour cream. Season to taste with salt and pepper.
6. Add potatoes. Cook 10 to 15 minutes, or until potatoes are hot.

8 servings

595 *Braised Lamb with Savoy Cabbage*
(Baranina Duszona z Włoską Kapustą)

3 pounds lamb breast
1 teaspoon salt
2 cloves garlic, crushed
2 carrots
2 stalks celery with leaves
1 large onion
1 large celery root, pared
1 leek
½ parsley root
3 tablespoons butter or margarine
   Water
1 head (about 2 pounds) savoy
   cabbage, cut in quarters
1 bay leaf
½ teaspoon salt
¼ teaspoon pepper
1 tablespoon flour

1. Rub meat with 1 teaspoon salt and garlic. Let stand 1 hour.
2. Cut meat into 2-rib pieces. Dice vegetables, except for cabbage.
3. Melt 2 tablespoons butter in a large kettle. Add meat and brown. Drain off fat. Add vegetables with just enough water to cover. Simmer covered about 1 hour, or until meat is tender. Remove vegetables; discard or reserve for other use. Reduce broth to 2 cups.
4. Add cabbage and bay leaf to meat. Season with ½ teaspoon salt and pepper. Continue simmering, tightly covered, until meat and cabbage are done.
5. Blend flour into remaining 1 tablespoon butter. Stir into simmering broth. Simmer until sauce thickens, about 15 minutes.

6 servings

Braised Lamb with Caraway Seed: Prepare Braised Lamb with Savoy Cabbage, substituting **2 tablespoons caraway seed** for carrots, celery, celery root, leek, and bay leaf.

596 *Hunter's Stew (Bigos)*

6 **pounds diced cooked meat (use at
   least ½ pound of each of the
   following: beef, ham, lamb,
   sausage, veal, pork, venison or
   rabbit, wild duck, wild goose,
   or pheasant)***
5 **ounces salt pork, diced**
1 **onion, minced**
2 **leeks, minced**
2 **tablespoons flour**
1 **pound fresh mushrooms, sliced,
   or 3 cans (4 ounces each) sliced
   mushrooms (undrained)**
1 **to 2 cups water or bouillon**
6 **pounds sauerkraut**
2 **teaspoons salt**
1 **teaspoon pepper**
2 **teaspoons sugar**
1 **cup Madeira**

1. Fry salt pork until golden but not crisp in an 8-quart kettle. Add onion and leeks. Stir-fry 3 minutes. Stir in flour.
2. Add mushrooms with liquid and water to kettle; simmer 5 minutes.
3. Drain and rinse sauerkraut. Add to kettle along with cooked meat, salt, pepper, and sugar. Cover; cook over medium-low heat 1½ hours.
4. Stir in wine. Add more salt, pepper, and sugar to taste. Simmer 15 minutes; do not boil.

12 to 16 servings

*If meat must be prepared especially for this stew, each piece should be braised separately. Put meat, poultry, or game into a Dutch oven with 1 carrot, 1 stalk celery, 1 onion, 1 parsnip, 1 clove garlic or 1 sprig parsley, 5 peppercorns, 1 cup water, and 1 cup wine. Simmer, covered, until meat is tender.

Note: When wine is added, chopped apples, heavy cream, and/or cooked small potatoes may also be added.

597 *Cold Roast Beef Vinaigrette*

Use freshly cooked or leftover beef for this superb entrée. Stock replaces oil in the marinade. Your own selection of vegetables can be used for color and texture contrast.

1½ pounds cooked medium-rare roast beef, sliced ¼ inch thick and cut in 2-inch-wide strips
3 stalks celery, cut in ¼-inch pieces
1 medium tomato, chopped
2 sweet red or green peppers, chopped in ¼-inch pieces
1 tablespoon finely chopped red onion
1 tablespoon olive oil
2 tablespoons wine vinegar
● ¼ cup Beef Stock
2 teaspoons snipped fresh or 1 teaspoon dried basil leaves
1 teaspoon snipped fresh or ½ teaspoon dried coriander leaves (cilantro)
1 tablespoon snipped parsley
1 teaspoon salt
*¼ teaspoon freshly ground Szechuan or black pepper
1 teaspoon snipped fresh or ½ teaspoon dried oregano leaves
2 garlic cloves, finely minced
2 teaspoons Dijon mustard

1. Arrange beef in a shallow glass dish. Mix remaining ingredients and pour over meat. Refrigerate covered 8 hours or overnight.
2. Taste meat and marinade; adjust seasoning, if desired. Let stand at room temperature 45 minutes before serving. Serve beef slices topped with marinade.

4 to 6 servings

*Lightly roast Szechuan pepper over medium heat in a skillet before grinding.

598 *Beef-on-Tomato Medallions*

Oriental stir-frying is a perfect technique for use in New French Cooking as little oil is used and the foods are cooked quickly to retain natural color, flavor, and texture.

3 large ripe tomatoes
Salt
Freshly ground pepper
1 tablespoon vegetable oil
½ teaspoon sesame or walnut oil
2½ pounds lean beef sirloin steak, boneless, cut in paper-thin slices
2 bunches green onions, cut in ¾-inch pieces
1 tablespoon light soy sauce
2 tablespoons dry white wine
¼ teaspoon sugar
½ teaspoon salt

1. Slice each tomato into 4 slices horizontally. Sprinkle with salt and pepper. Bake on a cookie sheet at 325°F until hot (about 15 minutes).
2. Heat vegetable and sesame oils in a wok or skillet until hot but not smoking. Add meat, stirring to coat pieces. Cook 1 minute. Add green onions. Cook and stir 1 minute. Mix soy sauce, wine, sugar, and ½ teaspoon salt; pour over meat. Cook and stir until meat is done (about 3 minutes).
3. Overlap 2 tomato slices at the side of each serving plate. Arrange meat mixture on plates, partially covering tomatoes.

6 servings

Note: Sesame and walnut oils can be purchased in specialty or gourmet shops. These oils have a delicate but distinct flavor which provides an interesting accent in this recipe. The oil can be omitted, or vegetable oil substituted.

599 *Meat-Stuffed Cabbage*

A whole cabbage encases a flavorful and moist meat-and-vegetable combination.

1 large head cabbage (about 4 pounds)
Water
1 tablespoon salt
Cheesecloth
2 pounds lean ground beef
2 bunches green onions, cut in ¼-inch pieces
1 garlic clove, minced
1 medium zucchini, finely chopped (reserve 8 thin slices for garnish)
1 large green pepper, chopped
1 egg, slightly beaten
1 cup fine soft bread crumbs made from whole-grain bread
1½ teaspoons snipped fresh or ¾ teaspoon dried basil leaves
2 teaspoons snipped fresh or 1 teaspoon dried thyme leaves
2 teaspoons snipped fresh or 1 teaspoon dried rosemary leaves
2 teaspoons salt
½ teaspoon freshly ground pepper
1 can (16 ounces) plum tomatoes (reserve liquid)
4 fresh mushrooms, cut in half, for garnish
Water

1. Place cabbage in a Dutch oven. Cover with boiling water; add 1 tablespoon salt. Simmer covered until outer leaves are softened but still firm (about 10 minutes). Drain cabbage; rinse with cold water. Have cheesecloth ready for wrapping stuffed cabbage.
2. Mix remaining ingredients, except the reserved zucchini slices and the mushrooms, until well blended.
3. Core cabbage and pull outside leaves back. Remove inside of cabbage carefully, leaving outside layer 5 or 6 leaves thick. Lay outer leaves on a double thickness of cheesecloth; fill leaves with meat mixture. Wrap stuffed cabbage tightly in cheesecloth; invert on another piece of cheesecloth so that the opening of the cabbage is on the bottom. Wrap cabbage securely, tying the cheesecloth into a handle at the top. Lift wrapped cabbage into Dutch oven. Pour reserved tomato liquid around cabbage. Cover.
4. Bake at 350°F to an internal temperature of 165°F (about 1½ hours). Check temperature by inserting a meat thermometer through leaves and into center of meat. Lift cabbage out of Dutch oven; let stand 10 minutes.
5. While cabbage is standing, place zucchini slices and mushrooms in a medium saucepan. Simmer in a small amount of water until barely tender (about 3 minutes); drain.
6. Remove outside layer of cheesecloth from cabbage; place a pie plate on cabbage and invert. Remove remaining cheesecloth; place serving platter on cabbage and invert. Gently shape cabbage with hands if necessary. Garnish top of cabbage with zucchini slices and mushrooms. Cut into wedges and serve.

8 to 10 servings

600 *Hearty Beef-Cabbage Soup*

2 cups tomato juice
● 4 cups Beef Stock
2 cups shredded red cabbage
1 medium onion, thinly sliced
1 carrot, thinly sliced
3 cups cooked beef cubes
2 tablespoons dark raisins
1 teaspoon caraway seed
1 teaspoon paprika
1 teaspoon salt
1 tablespoon cider vinegar
● Low-Fat Yogurt, if desired, for garnish

Simmer all ingredients in a Dutch oven 20 minutes, stirring occasionally. Serve in bowls. Garnish with dollops of yogurt.

6 servings (2 cups each)

Note: This recipe can be made without the meat and served as a first course.

601 *Steak Tartare with Vegetables*

2 pounds beef sirloin steak, boneless
⅓ cup finely chopped leek or green onion
1½ teaspoons Worcestershire sauce
¼ teaspoon Tabasco
1 teaspoon Dijon mustard
½ teaspoon salt
Freshly ground Szechuan or black pepper
1 egg yolk, if desired
1 teaspoon drained capers
2 bunches parsley, stems removed
1 green pepper, cut in 1-inch pieces
1 sweet red pepper, cut in 1-inch pieces
1 large zucchini, cut in ¼-inch slices
1 medium cucumber, cut in ¼-inch slices
12 medium mushrooms, cut in half lengthwise
1 large carrot, cut in ¼-inch slices
12 large red or white radishes, cut in half

1. Chop meat coarsely in a food processor (or have butcher grind meat coarsely 2 times). Place beef, leek, Worcestershire sauce, Tabasco, mustard, salt, and pepper in a mixing bowl; mix quickly and lightly with 2 forks. Taste; adjust seasonings.
2. Mound beef on a medium serving platter. Make an indentation in top of mound; slip egg yolk into indentation. Sprinkle beef with capers. Surround beef with a thick rim of parsley. Arrange vegetables on parsley. Serve immediately with knives for spreading beef mixture on vegetables.

8 servings

Note: For a party, this recipe would make about 48 appetizer servings.

602 *Elegant Leg of Lamb*

A coating of Dijon mustard, spices, coffee, and wine lends pleasing flavor to the lamb.

1 lamb leg, whole (about 6 pounds)
2 garlic cloves, each sliced in 3 pieces
1 tablespoon Dijon mustard
1 tablespoon strong coffee
2 teaspoons ground ginger
1 cup strong black coffee
¼ cup white port wine
● 1 cup Chicken Stock
4 teaspoons arrowroot
Cold water
2 teaspoons butter, if desired

1. Trim excess fat from roast. Cut 6 small slits in the roast and insert garlic slices. Rub mixture of mustard, 1 tablespoon coffee, and ginger over entire surface of roast.
2. Place in a shallow roasting pan. Insert meat thermometer so that tip is in center of meat, away from bone and fat.
3. Roast in a 325°F oven to an internal temperature of 175°F (about 3 hours). Mix 1 cup coffee and wine; baste roast with mixture several times during last hour of roasting time.
4. Remove roast to meat platter. Cover loosely with a tent of aluminum foil.
5. Carefully spoon fat from roasting pan. Add remaining basting mixture and stock to roasting pan. Heat to boiling, stirring to incorporate meat particles from pan. Mix arrowroot with a little cold water. Stir into stock mixture. Simmer, stirring constantly, until mixture thickens. Stir butter into gravy just before serving.

6 to 8 servings

603 Fruited Lamb Roast

A boned leg of lamb is filled with marinated dried fruits and roasted. The fruit is then puréed for an elegant sauce.

½ pound dried pears or apples
½ pound dried apricots
½ cup golden raisins
1 teaspoon finely minced ginger root or ½ teaspoon ground ginger
1 tablespoon grated orange peel
Juice of 1 orange
½ cup bourbon
Apple cider (about 3 cups)
1 lamb leg, boneless (about 4 pounds)
½ cup bourbon
Apple cider
Salt
2 tablespoons bourbon
Apple cider

1. Place pears, apricots, raisins, ginger root, orange peel, orange juice, and ½ cup bourbon in a medium saucepan. Pour in enough apple cider to cover fruits. Simmer uncovered 20 minutes; cool.
2. Trim roast of excess fat. Lay roast flat in a shallow glass casserole. Drain fruit. Add ½ cup bourbon to drained juice; add enough apple cider to measure 2 cups. Pour juice mixture over roast. Refrigerate roast covered 8 hours or overnight. Refrigerate fruits covered.
3. Remove roast from marinade; salt lightly on both sides. Arrange one third of the fruit on surface of meat; roll up and tie with string at intervals.
4. Place roast on rack in a roasting pan. Insert meat thermometer so tip is in center of roast.
5. Roast uncovered in a 325°F oven to an internal temperature of 175°F (about 2 hours). Add remaining fruit to roasting pan during last half hour of cooking.
6. Place roast and half the fruit on a serving platter. Cover lightly with aluminum foil. Let stand 20 minutes before carving.
7. Purée remaining fruit in a blender or food processor with 2 tablespoons bourbon and enough apple cider to make a sauce consistency. Heat thoroughly; serve with the roast.

8 to 10 servings

604 Lamb and Pork in Cognac

The flavors of these two meats blend uniquely while cooking. Choose your favorite fresh vegetable to add to this recipe.

⅓ cup cognac
1⅔ cups dry white wine
½ teaspoon ground mace
¼ teaspoon ground cinnamon
½ teaspoon salt
1½ pounds lean lamb stew cubes
1½ pounds lean pork stew cubes
3 stalks celery, finely chopped
3 carrots, finely chopped
1 medium yellow onion, finely chopped
2 teaspoons salt
½ pound baby carrots
½ pound fresh broccoli
½ pound baby white onions
● Chicken Stock
Salt
Freshly ground pepper

1. Mix cognac, wine, mace, cinnamon, and ½ teaspoon salt; pour over meat cubes in a shallow glass bowl. Refrigerate covered 6 hours or overnight; stir occasionally. Drain meat, reserving ¾ cup marinade.
2. Mix chopped vegetables and layer them in bottom of a Dutch oven; pour reserved marinade over and simmer on top of range 5 minutes. Layer meat cubes over vegetables and sprinkle with 2 teaspoons salt. Cover Dutch oven.
3. Bake at 350°F 1½ to 2 hours, or until meat is tender.
4. Simmer vegetables in 1 inch of stock until just tender (about 15 minutes). Season with salt and pepper.
5. Remove meat from Dutch oven with a slotted spoon to a shallow serving dish; arrange attractively with vegetables.

6 servings

605 *Lamb Ratatouille*

In this main-dish version of ratatouille, the vegetables remain crisp and flavorful.

- 1 quart Savory Tomato Sauce
- 1 tablespoon snipped fresh or 1½ teaspoons dried coriander leaves
- 2 pounds lean lamb stew cubes
- 2 teaspoons salt
  Freshly ground pepper
- 2 tablespoons fresh lemon juice
- ¼ cup dry vermouth or dry white wine
- 1 small eggplant, pared and cut in 1-inch cubes
  Salted water
- 2 green peppers, cut in 1-inch squares
- 2 medium zucchini, cut in ½-inch slices
- 2 medium yellow onions, cut in ¼-inch slices
- Chicken Stock
  Salt
  Freshly ground pepper
- 1 tablespoon olive oil
  Snipped coriander

1. Spoon tomato sauce into bottom of a Dutch oven; sprinkle with 1 tablespoon coriander. Place lamb cubes in sauce; sprinkle with 2 teaspoons salt, pepper, and lemon juice. Pour vermouth over meat. Simmer covered until lamb is tender (about 2 hours).
2. Soak eggplant in salted water to cover for 1 hour; drain and pat dry.
3. Cook vegetables during last half hour lamb is cooking. Simmer eggplant, green peppers, zucchini, and onions in ½ inch of stock in a large skillet until barely tender, so vegetables retain their shape and texture.
4. Arrange cooked vegetables attractively on a heatproof platter; keep warm in oven. Season vegetables with salt and pepper; drizzle with olive oil. Arrange lamb and tomato mixture over vegetables; sprinkle with coriander.

6 servings

606 *Pork Chops Piquant*

Green pepper and onion stay crisp in this braised pork chop dish. Capers add a hint of pungency.

- 4 pork loin chops, 1 inch thick
- ¼ cup water
- ¼ teaspoon bottled brown bouquet sauce
- ½ teaspoon salt
  Freshly ground pepper
- ½ cup Chicken Stock
- ¼ cup dry white wine
- 1 green pepper, chopped
- 1 medium yellow onion, chopped
- 2 tablespoons capers, drained
  Watercress or parsley sprigs

1. Trim excess fat from chops. Brush chops lightly with a mixture of water and brown bouquet sauce. Brown chops lightly on both sides in a nonstick skillet over medium heat. Sprinkle with salt and pepper.
2. Add stock and wine. Simmer covered 30 minutes. Skim fat from liquid. Stir in green pepper, onion, and capers. Simmer uncovered 10 to 15 minutes until vegetables are just tender. Taste vegetables and sauce; adjust seasoning.
3. Serve vegetables and sauce over chops; garnish with watercress.

4 servings

607 *Savory Veal Stew*

The meat in this stew is unbelievably tender. Caraway and fennel provide a flavorful accent to garden vegetables.

3 pounds veal stew cubes
1½ teaspoons salt
½ teaspoon freshly ground
    pepper
2 garlic cloves
1 teaspoon caraway seed, lightly
    crushed
1 teaspoon fennel seed, lightly
    crushed
2 bay leaves
½ cup dry white wine
● 1 cup Beef Stock
1 small head cabbage, cut in 8
    wedges
3 leeks, cut in 3-inch pieces
¾ teaspoon salt
½ teaspoon freshly ground
    pepper
1 tablespoon arrowroot
    Cold water
½ pound mushrooms, sliced
● ½ cup Mock Crème Fraîche
    if desired

1. Place veal in a 6-quart Dutch oven; sprinkle with 1½ teaspoons salt and ½ teaspoon pepper. Mix garlic, caraway, fennel, bay leaves, wine, and stock. Pour over veal. Simmer covered over low heat 2 hours.
2. Add cabbage and leeks to Dutch oven; sprinkle with ¾ teaspoon salt and ½ teaspoon pepper. Simmer covered until vegetables and veal are just tender (about 15 minutes). Remove veal and vegetables to a shallow serving dish; keep warm.
3. Skim fat from cooking liquid in Dutch oven. Discard bay leaves. Mix arrowroot with a little cold water. Stir into cooking liquid; simmer until thickened (about 3 minutes). Stir in mushrooms and Mock Crème Fraîche; simmer 1 minute. Pour thickened mixture over veal and vegetables. Sprinkle with parsley.

8 servings

608 *Veal Scallops in Lemon Sauce*

This adaptation of Veal Piccata uses stock rather than butter in the sauce. Szechuan pepper adds a flavor accent to the tart sauce; fresh snipped parsley adds color.

12 veal scallops (about 2 pounds)
¼ cup water
¼ teaspoon bottled brown
    bouquet sauce
2 teaspoons clarified butter
    Salt
¾ cup dry white wine
● ¾ cup Chicken Stock
⅓ cup finely chopped onion
1 garlic clove, minced
½ cup fresh lemon juice
¼ teaspoon freshly ground white
    pepper
½ teaspoon salt
1 tablespoon arrowroot
    Cold water
1 tablespoon snipped parsley

1. Pound veal scallops with a mallet until thin and even in thickness. Brush both sides lightly with a mixture of water and brown bouquet sauce. Cook a few pieces of veal in hot butter in a skillet just until done (about 1 minute on each side). Sprinkle lightly with salt. Keep warm in oven while cooking remaining veal.
2. While veal is cooking, mix wine, stock, onion, and garlic in a small saucepan. Simmer until onion is tender (about 3 minutes). Stir in lemon juice, pepper, and salt.
3. Mix arrowroot with a little cold water. Stir into simmering stock mixture. Simmer, stirring constantly, until mixture thickens.
4. Arrange veal on warm plates. Pour sauce over. Sprinkle with parsley.

6 servings

609 *Ham Steak with Parsley Sauce*

2 bunches parsley, washed and
    stems removed
¼ cup dry white wine
1 center-cut smoked ham steak,
    ¾ inch thick (about 1½
    pounds)
● ⅔ cup Mock Hollandaise Sauce
    Salt
    Freshly ground white pepper

1. Line bottom of a shallow baking dish with half the parsley; drizzle with half the wine. Lay ham steak on parsley. Cover ham with remaining parsley; drizzle with remaining wine. Lightly cover baking dish.
2. Bake at 325°F about 30 minutes, or until ham is thoroughly heated.
3. Make Mock Hollandaise Sauce while ham is baking; keep warm.
4. Place ham on platter; cover lightly with aluminum foil. Purée cooked parsley in a blender or food processor; stir mixture into Mock Hollandaise Sauce. Season sauce with salt and pepper. Heat sauce thoroughly; serve with ham.

3 or 4 servings

610 *Ham Mousse on Medallions*

6 slices boiled ham, cut ⅓ inch
    thick (about 1½ pounds)
2 teaspoons unflavored gelatin
1 cup cold water
2 cups low-fat ricotta cheese
3 tablespoons snipped parsley
1½ tablespoons snipped fresh or 2
    teaspoons crumbled dried
    tarragon leaves
2 teaspoons Dijon mustard
⅛ teaspoon salt
    Dash freshly ground pepper
    Parsley sprigs
    Radish roses

1. Cut two 2½-inch circles from each slice ham; refrigerate covered. Mince remaining ham pieces; refrigerate covered.
2. Sprinkle gelatin over cold water in a saucepan; let stand 5 minutes. Set over low heat until dissolved (about 3 minutes), stirring occasionally.
3. Pour gelatin into a food processor or blender; add ricotta cheese, snipped parsley, tarragon, mustard, salt, and pepper. Process until mixture is smooth; transfer mixture to a medium mixing bowl. Stir in minced ham; refrigerate covered until mixture has set (about 1 hour).
4. Place 2 ham circles on each of 6 individual plates. Mound mousse by heaping tablespoonfuls on circles. Garnish with parsley and radish roses.

6 servings

Note: This recipe will make 12 first-course servings.

611 *Rack of Veal with Peppercorn Sauce*

Very easy to prepare, very elegant to serve. Green peppercorns add zest to a low-calorie version of Béarnaise Sauce.

1 veal rib roast (about 5 pounds)
1 teaspoon salt
    Freshly ground white pepper
    White wine
● 1⅓ cups Mock Béarnaise Sauce
    (double recipe)
2 tablespoons drained green
    peppercorns

1. Rub roast with salt and pepper; place in a roasting pan. Insert meat thermometer so tip is in center of meat, away from bone.
2. Roast uncovered in a 325°F oven to an internal temperature of 165°F (about 3 hours). Baste several times with white wine during last hour of roasting. Remove to a platter and cover loosely with aluminum foil; let stand 20 minutes before carving.
3. While roast is standing, make the sauce, adding peppercorns before heating. Pass sauce.

10 servings

Note: A boneless veal roast can also be used in this recipe. Roast as directed above, allowing about 35 minutes per pound.

612 *Stuffed Veal Breast*

Spinach and ricotta cheese are in the filling for this tempting dish with an Italian influence.

2½ pounds boneless breast of veal
  Salt
  Freshly ground pepper
1 large onion, chopped
● 2 tablespoons Chicken Stock
*½ pound fresh spinach, washed
    and stems removed
¾ cup low-fat ricotta cheese
¼ cup grated Jarlsberg or
    Parmesan cheese
2 garlic cloves, minced
1 teaspoon snipped fresh or ½
    teaspoon dried thyme leaves
1½ teaspoons snipped fresh or ¾
    teaspoon dried basil leaves
½ teaspoon snipped fresh or ¼
    teaspoon dried oregano
    leaves
2 tablespoons snipped parsley
1 teaspoon salt
¼ teaspoon pepper
½ cup dry white wine or Chicken
    Stock

1. Trim excess fat from meat. Sprinkle meat lightly on both sides with salt and pepper.
2. Simmer onion in stock just until tender (about 5 minutes).
3. Place spinach with water clinging to leaves in a large saucepan; cook covered over medium heat just until wilted (about 3 minutes).
4. Drain onion and spinach well in a strainer, pressing moisture out with a wooden spoon. Mix onion, spinach, cheeses, garlic, thyme, basil, oregano, parsley, 1 teaspoon salt, and ¼ teaspoon pepper. Spoon mixture on surface of meat; roll up and tie with string at intervals. Place meat in a roasting pan. Pour wine over roast. Cover.
5. Roast in a 325°F oven about 1½ hours, or until tender.
6. Remove roast to a serving platter. Cover lightly with aluminum foil. Let stand 15 minutes before carving.

6 servings

*1 package (10 ounces) frozen spinach can be substituted for the fresh. Thaw and drain thoroughly in strainer.

613 *Calf's Liver with Curried Onions*

The addition of curry and raisins gives this recipe an interesting Indian accent.

1 large yellow onion, sliced
¼ cup sherry
½ teaspoon curry powder
½ teaspoon salt
  Freshly ground pepper
¼ cup golden raisins
2 teaspoons clarified butter
1 pound calf's liver
  Clarified butter

1. Simmer onion slices in wine in a medium skillet until onion is tender and wine is absorbed (about 10 minutes). Stir in curry powder, salt, pepper, raisins, and 2 teaspoons butter.
2. While onion is cooking, brush liver slices very lightly with clarified butter.
3. Broil 4 inches from heat until lightly browned (about 3 minutes on each side). Serve with onion.

4 servings

614 *Pot Roast Jardinière*

A country-style stew with garden vegetables is hearty fare.

1 beef chuck pot roast (4 pounds)
¼ cup prepared horseradish
1 tablespoon salt
1 medium tomato, chopped
● 1 cup Beef Stock
3 medium kohlrabi or turnips, pared and cut in ½-inch cubes
3 medium carrots, cut in ½-inch slices
*1 pound fresh Brussels sprouts, cleaned
1 teaspoon snipped fresh or ½ teaspoon dried thyme leaves
1 teaspoon snipped fresh or ½ teaspoon dried marjoram leaves
1 teaspoon salt
½ teaspoon pepper
2 leeks, cut in 1-inch pieces
2 teaspoons arrowroot
Cold water

1. Rub meat on both sides with a mixture of horseradish and 1 tablespoon salt; place meat in a Dutch oven. Add tomato and stock to Dutch oven. Cover.
2. Cook in a 325°F oven about 3 hours, or until meat is tender.
3. Add vegetables, thyme, marjoram, 1 teaspoon salt, and ½ teaspoon pepper to Dutch oven during last 15 minutes of cooking time; cook just until vegetables are tender.
4. Remove meat and vegetables to platter. Skim fat from cooking liquid. If thicker sauce is desired, mix arrowroot with a little cold water and stir into liquid. Simmer, stirring constantly, until sauce is thickened. Pass sauce.

6 servings

*1 package (10 ounces) frozen Brussels sprouts can be substituted for the fresh. Add to Dutch oven for length of cooking time indicated on package.

615 *Oriental One-Pot Meal*

This recipe has been borrowed from Japanese sukiyaki. The technique is perfect for New French Cooking, as foods are cooked quickly in stock to retain natural color, flavor, and texture.

● 6 cups Beef Stock
¼ cup light soy sauce
⅓ cup beer
2 teaspoons sugar
†¼ teaspoon freshly ground Szechuan or black pepper
½ teaspoon salt
2 cups sliced fresh mushrooms
2 bunches green onions, cut in ½-inch pieces
1 cup sliced bamboo shoots
**1 cup sliced Chinese cabbage or bok choy
1½ pounds lean beef sirloin or rib eye steak, cut in paper-thin slices

1. Mix stock, soy sauce, beer, sugar, pepper, and salt in a 3-quart saucepan. Boil 3 minutes. Simmer vegetables in stock mixture until vegetables are just tender (about 5 minutes). Divide vegetables among 6 shallow bowls; keep warm in oven.
2. Cook half the beef slices in the simmering stock mixture until rare to medium done (2 to 4 minutes). Divide meat among bowls. Cook remaining meat; divide among bowls. Serve hot stock mixture over meat and vegetables or in individual bowls for dipping.

6 servings

*Lightly roast Szechuan pepper over medium heat in a skillet before grinding.
**Chinese cabbage can be purchased in Oriental or specialty shops.

616 *Herbed Skirt Steak*

Mock Crème Fraîche and fresh dill enhance this creative combination.

1½ pounds lean beef skirt steak
2 teaspoons clarified butter
1 large yellow onion, finely
 sliced
● ½ cup Beef Stock
1 garlic clove, minced
¼ teaspoon freshly ground
 pepper
1½ teaspoons salt
● ½ cup Mock Crème Fraîche
¼ cup snipped fresh dill or 2
 tablespoons dried dill weed

1. Slice steak in half lengthwise; cut pieces across the grain into paper-thin slices. Heat butter over high heat in a 12-inch skillet. Add meat slices, stirring quickly to coat meat with butter. Add onion; cook and stir 2 minutes. Add Beef Stock, garlic, pepper, and salt; simmer covered until onion is tender (about 3 minutes).
2. Stir ¼ cup pan juices into Mock Crème Fraîche. Stir mixture back into pan; stir in dill. Serve immediately.

4 to 6 servings

617 *Steak with Mushroom Stuffing*

The texture of fresh mushrooms and the flavor of nutmeg are memorable additions to a perfectly cooked steak.

1 small onion, finely chopped
2 shallots, finely chopped
● 2 tablespoons Beef Stock
½ pound mushrooms, cleaned
 and chopped
1 tablespoon brandy
3 grinds fresh or ¼ teaspoon
 ground nutmeg
¾ teaspoon salt
¼ teaspoon freshly ground
 pepper
2½ pounds lean beef sirloin steak,
 boneless
 Snipped parsley

1. Simmer onion and shallots in stock until tender (about 5 minutes). Mix onion, shallots, mushrooms, brandy, nutmeg, salt, and pepper.
2. Trim excess fat from steak. Cut pocket in steak, cutting to, but not through opposite side and leaving 1 inch intact on each end. Fill pocket loosely with onion mixture; skewer opening with wooden picks.
3. Broil steak 3 inches from heat, 8 minutes on each side for medium rare, 10 minutes on each side for medium. Remove wooden picks. Sprinkle steak with parsley. Slice and serve.

8 servings

618 *Veal Cutlets Valle d'Aosta (Costolette alla Valdostana)*

6 veal chops, boneless, 1 inch thick
6 thin slices fully cooked ham
6 slices fontina or mozzarella
 cheese
1 cup all-purpose flour
1 teaspoon salt
¼ teaspoon pepper
1 egg, beaten with 1 tablespoon
 water
 Fine bread crumbs
¼ cup butter, more if needed

1. Butterfly chops by slicing through the chop almost all the way, and laying chop open so it is ½ inch thick; pound flat.
2. Place a slice of ham, then a slice of cheese, in the center of each chop. Moisten edges of chop and press together.
3. Dip each folded chop first in flour mixed with salt and pepper, then in beaten egg, and finally in the bread crumbs.
4. Heat the butter in a large skillet. Brown the chops slowly, about 5 minutes on each side or until done.

6 servings

619 *Meatballs (Polpette)*

Peel of 1 lemon, grated
1 sprig parsley
2 cloves garlic, peeled
1 pound ground beef
1 teaspoon salt
¼ teaspoon pepper
Pinch grated nutmeg
1 slice bread, crumbled
Milk
1 egg, beaten
2 to 3 tablespoons olive oil or
  other cooking oil

1. Mince together grated lemon peel, parsley, and garlic.
2. Mix ground beef with salt, pepper, nutmeg, and lemon-peel mixture.
3. Soak bread in a small amount of milk, squeeze dry, and add with egg to meat mixture. Blend well.
4. On a lightly floured surface, form mixture into patties about ½ inch thick and 1½ inches wide.
5. Place the patties in hot oil in a skillet. Brown about 2 minutes on each side. Drain and serve hot.

4 to 6 servings

620 *Bollito Misto*

1 fresh beef tongue (3 to 4 pounds)
1 calf's head, prepared for cooking,
  or 2 pounds veal neck
2 pounds beef (neck, rump, or
  chuck roast)
2 pig's feet or 1 pound cotechino or
  other uncooked pork sausage
1 stewing chicken (3 to 4 pounds)
4 medium carrots, pared and cut in
  3-inch pieces
2 large stalks celery, cut in pieces
3 onions, peeled and quartered
4 turnips or parsnips, pared and
  quartered
2 tablespoons chopped parsley
1 teaspoon tarragon
1 teaspoon thyme
Water
Salt
Salsa Verde

1. Combine meats, chicken, vegetables, parsley, tarragon, and thyme in a large sauce pot. Pour in enough water to cover meat, and salt to taste.
2. Cover pot, bring to boiling, and simmer 3 to 4 hours, or until tongue is tender.
3. Remove skin from tongue. Slice meat, cut chicken in serving pieces, and arrange with vegetables on a large platter.
4. Serve with **boiled potatoes, cooked cabbage, beets, pickles,** and Salsa Verde.

10 to 12 servings

Note: A pressure cooker may be used. Follow manufacturer's directions for use of cooker and length of cooking time.

Salsa Verde: Finely chop **3 hard-cooked eggs;** set aside. Combine **½ cup salad oil** and **3 tablespoons wine vinegar.** Add **sugar, salt,** and **pepper** to taste. Mix well and combine with the chopped eggs. Blend in **6 tablespoons chopped herbs** such as **dill, tarragon, chervil, parsley, sorrel,** and **chives.** Refrigerate several hours to allow flavors to blend.

621 *Ossobuco*

4 to 5 pounds veal shank crosscuts
Flour
⅓ cup olive oil
Salt and pepper
½ cup beef broth or bouillon
1 onion, chopped
1 clove garlic, crushed in a garlic press
1 medium carrot, sliced
1 leek, sliced
1 slice celery root
2 whole cloves
1 bay leaf
Pinch each of sage, thyme, and rosemary
½ cup white wine
1 can (28 ounces) whole tomatoes
1 tablespoon grated lemon peel

1. Dredge crosscuts with flour. Heat several tablespoons olive oil in a skillet. Brown the veal well, season with salt and pepper, and transfer to a heatproof casserole or Dutch oven. Handle gently so the marrow remains in the bones. Pour the broth into the casserole.
2. Add more oil to skillet, if needed. In hot oil, sauté onion, garlic, carrot, leek, and celery root over medium heat about 5 minutes.
3. Stir in the cloves, bay leaf, sage, thyme, and rosemary. Pour in the wine and continue cooking until wine is almost evaporated. Stir in tomatoes and grated lemon peel. Cook over medium heat several minutes.
4. Pour tomato mixture over meat in casserole. Cover tightly and simmer about 1½ hours, or until meat is tender. Remove veal to serving dish and keep hot.
5. Force vegetables and juice in casserole through a sieve or food mill. If the resulting sauce is thin, cook over high heat to reduce liquid. Season sauce, if necessary. Pour sauce over meat or serve separately.
6. Serve with **rice** or **spaghetti** tossed with **melted butter** and topped with **grated Parmesan** or **Romano cheese**.

4 or 5 servings

622 *Mixed Fry (Fritto Misto)*

½ pound calf's brains
2 cups water
1½ teaspoons vinegar or lemon juice
½ teaspoon salt
¼ cup flour
½ teaspoon salt
Pinch pepper
½ pound liver (beef, lamb, veal, or calf), sliced ¼ to ½ inch thick
2 cups all-purpose flour
1 teaspoon salt
¼ teaspoon pepper
1½ cups milk
3 eggs, well beaten
2 tablespoons melted shortening
Oil for frying
6 artichoke hearts (canned in water), drained
2 zucchini, washed and cut crosswise in 1-inch slices
3 stalks celery, cut in 3-inch pieces

1. Wash brains in cold water. Combine with 2 cups water, vinegar, and ½ teaspoon salt in a saucepan. Bring to boiling, reduce heat, and simmer gently 20 minutes.
2. Drain the brains and drop into cold water. Drain again and remove membranes. Separate into small pieces and set aside.
3. Combine ¼ cup flour, ½ teaspoon salt, and pinch pepper. Coat the liver with the flour mixture, cut into serving-size pieces, and set aside.
4. Combine 2 cups flour with 1 teaspoon salt and ¼ teaspoon pepper; set aside. Combine milk, eggs, and shortening. Gradually add the flour mixture to the liquid, beating until smooth.
5. Fill a deep saucepan one-half to two-thirds full with oil. Heat slowly to 360°F. Dip pieces of meat and the vegetables in the batter and fry in hot oil, being careful not to crowd the pieces. Fry about 5 minutes, or until golden brown, turning occasionally.
6. Hold cooked pieces over the hot oil to drain before placing on paper towels. Place on a warm platter and serve immediately.

6 servings

623 *Pork Roast Stuffed with Liver (Porchetta)*

1 teaspoon fennel seed
2 cloves garlic, peeled
1 teaspoon salt
½ teaspoon sugar
½ teaspoon coarsely ground pepper
¾ teaspoon rubbed sage
　Boneless pork loin or loin end
　　roast (about 3 pounds)
½ pound pork, lamb, or beef liver,
　　cut in slices ⅓ inch thick
1 tablespoon cornstarch
1 cup cool beef broth

1. Using a mortar and pestle, crush the fennel seed. Add the garlic, salt, sugar, pepper, and sage. Crush until mixture becomes a rough paste.
2. Open pork roast and lay flat side down; cut the meat if necessary to make it lie flat. Rub surface of the roast with about half the garlic paste. Lay liver strips lengthwise over meat.
3. Roll the roast tightly lengthwise with seasoned surface inside. Tie with heavy string at 2-inch intervals. Rub remaining garlic paste on outside of roast. Place roast on a rack in a shallow baking pan.
4. Cook, uncovered, at 375°F until meat thermometer inserted in thickest part of the roast registers 170°F (about 1½ hours). Transfer roast to a serving platter and keep warm.
5. Remove rack from roasting pan and place pan over direct heat. Stir together the cornstarch and broth until blended. Stir into drippings in roasting pan. Cook over medium heat, stirring constantly, until sauce boils and thickens. Pour sauce into a serving bowl.
6. To serve, cut and remove strings from roast, and cut meat into thin slices.

About 8 servings

624 *Veal Peasant Style (Vitello alla Paesano)*

2 tablespoons butter
1 tablespoon olive oil
1 cup finely chopped onion
⅓ cup finely chopped celery
1½ to 2 pounds veal, cubed
1 teaspoon salt
¼ teaspoon pepper
4 tomatoes, peeled and coarsely
　　chopped
　Several basil leaves or ¼
　　teaspoon dried basil leaves
¾ cup beef broth
2 tablespoons butter
1 pound fresh green peas, shelled,
　　or 1 package (10 ounces)
　　frozen green peas
3 carrots, diced
½ teaspoon salt
¾ cup hot water
1 tablespoon minced parsley

1. Heat 2 tablespoons butter and the olive oil in a Dutch oven or large saucepot. Add onion and celery; sauté 3 or 4 minutes.
2. Add meat and brown on all sides. Season with 1 teaspoon salt and the pepper. Stir in tomatoes and basil. Cover Dutch oven.
3. Cook at 275°F about 1¼ hours, or until meat is almost tender. Add broth, a little at a time, during cooking.
4. Heat 2 tablespoons butter in a saucepan. Stir in peas, carrots, ½ teaspoon salt, and water. Cook, covered, until vegetables are tender (about 15 minutes).
5. Skim off fat from meat. Stir in the cooked vegetables and parsley. Continue cooking in oven until meat is tender.
6. Serve meat surrounded with the vegetables and **small sautéed potatoes** on a heated platter. Pour sauce over all.

6 to 8 servings

625 *Perugia Ham and Cheese Pie (Pizzetta alla Perugina)*

2 cups all-purpose flour
½ teaspoon salt
¼ cup butter or margarine
2 eggs
3 tablespoons milk
1½ cups minced cooked ham
½ cup shredded Swiss cheese
½ cup diced Bel Paese cheese
1 egg yolk, slightly beaten

1. Combine flour and salt in a bowl. Cut in butter with pastry blender or two knives until pieces are small. Add eggs and stir in milk to form a soft dough. Knead dough lightly; divide in two equal portions.
2. Roll cut one portion on a lightly floured surface into a rectangle large enough to line the bottom and sides of an 11×7-inch baking pan. Place dough in pan and cover with ham and cheese.
3. Bring dough on sides of pan down over the meat and cheese. Roll out the remaining dough to form an 11×7-inch rectangle and place on top of filling. Press edges of top crust with a fork to seal to bottom crust. Prick top with fork in several places, and brush with egg yolk.
4. Bake at 425°F 10 minutes. Turn oven control to 350°F and bake 10 minutes. Cut into rectangles and serve warm.

6 to 8 servings

626 *Saltimbocca (Sliced Ham and Veal with Wine)*

4 large, thinly sliced veal cutlets
Salt and pepper
4 large, very thin slices ham or prosciutto
Dried sage leaves
Olive oil
¼ cup (2 ounces) Marsala

1. Place veal slices on a cutting board and pound with a mallet until very thin. Divide each slice into 2 or 3 pieces.
2. Season veal with salt and pepper.
3. Cut ham into pieces the same size as veal.
4. Place a sage leaf on each piece of veal and top with a slice of ham. Secure with a wooden pick.
5. Heat several tablespoons olive oil in a skillet; add the meat and cook slowly until golden brown on both sides. Remove meat to heated platter and keep warm.
6. Scrape residue from bottom of pan; add the Marsala and simmer over low heat several minutes. Pour over meat and serve.

4 servings

627 *Veal and Peppers Basilicata Style (Vitello e Pepe alla Basilicata)*

2 tablespoons butter
1 tablespoon lard
1½ pounds boneless veal leg, rump, or shoulder roast, cut in 1-inch pieces
1 teaspoon salt
⅛ teaspoon pepper
1 medium-size onion, sliced
4 large ripe tomatoes
1 tablespoon chopped basil leaves or 1 teaspoon dried sweet basil
4 large firm green or red peppers
3 tablespoons olive oil

1. Heat butter and lard in skillet over medium heat. Add meat and brown on all sides. Stir in salt, pepper, and onion; cook 5 minutes.
2. Cut tomatoes in half, squeeze out seeds, chop pulp, and add with basil to meat. Cover and simmer 20 minutes.
3. Cut out stems, remove seeds, and clean peppers. Cut in quarters, lengthwise. Fry peppers in hot olive oil about 10 minutes, or until softened. Add to meat, cover, and simmer 30 minutes, or until meat is tender. Serve hot.

4 servings

628 *Veal Rollettes (Rosolini di Vitella)*

2 cloves garlic, minced
1 tablespoon grated Parmesan
    cheese
2 teaspoons chopped parsley
½ teaspoon salt
¼ teaspoon pepper
1½ pounds veal round steak, cut
    about ½ inch thick
    Mozzarella cheese, sliced
3 tablespoons olive oil
½ cup butter, melted
¼ cup water

1. Mix garlic, Parmesan cheese, parsley, salt, and pepper. Set aside.
2. Cut veal into 4×3-inch pieces. Put 1 slice mozzarella cheese on each piece of meat. Top each with 1 teaspoon garlic-cheese mixture. Roll each piece of meat to enclose mixture; tie with string, or fasten meat roll with wooden picks or small skewers.
3. Heat oil in a skillet. Add meat rolls and brown slowly on all sides. Put meat into a greased 2-quart casserole. Mix butter and water; pour over meat. Cover casserole.
4. Bake at 300°F about 1 hour, or until meat is tender. Remove string, wooden picks, or skewers.

About 4 servings

629 *Liver and Onions, Italian Style (Fegato con Cipolla)*

1½ pounds beef liver, sliced about
    ¼ to ½ inch thick
½ cup flour
1 teaspoon salt
⅛ teaspoon pepper
2 onions, thinly sliced
⅓ cup olive oil
½ cup Marsala

1. If necessary, remove tubes and membrane from liver; cut liver into serving-size pieces.
2. Coat liver with a mixture of flour, salt, and pepper; set aside.
3. Cook onions until tender in hot oil in a large skillet. Remove onions and add liver. Brown on both sides over medium heat.
4. Return onions to skillet; add the wine. Bring to boiling and cook 1 minute. Serve at once.

4 or 5 servings

Liver and Onions with Mushrooms: Follow recipe for Liver and Onions, Italian Style. Add **1 cup drained canned whole mushrooms** with the Marsala.

630 *Neapolitan Pork Chops (Costatelle di Maiale alla Napoletana)*

2 tablespoons olive oil
1 clove garlic, minced
6 pork rib or loin chops, cut about
    ¾ to 1 inch thick
1 teaspoon salt
¼ teaspoon pepper
1 pound mushrooms, cleaned and
    sliced
2 green peppers, cleaned and
    chopped
½ cup canned tomatoes, sieved
3 tablespoons dry white wine

1. Heat oil in a large, heavy skillet. Add garlic and cook until lightly browned.
2. Season chops with salt and pepper. Put chops in skillet and brown on both sides.
3. Add mushrooms, green pepper, sieved tomato, and wine. Cover and cook over low heat about 1 hour, or until tender.

6 servings

631 *Hunter-Style Lamb with Fettuccine*
(Agnello Cacciatore con Fettuccine)

2 pounds lamb (leg, loin, or
    shoulder), trimmed and cut in
    1½-inch cubes
¾ to 1 teaspoon salt
¼ to ½ teaspoon pepper
2 tablespoons butter
2 tablespoons olive oil
4 anchovies, chopped
1 clove garlic, minced
1 medium green pepper, cleaned
    and cut in pieces
    Olive oil
1 teaspoon rosemary, crushed
1 teaspoon basil, crushed
¼ teaspoon sage, crushed
½ cup red wine vinegar
    Chicken broth
2 teaspoons flour
8 ounces fettuccine noodles,
    cooked and drained
    Grated Parmesan cheese
    Minced parsley

1. Season lamb with salt and pepper.
2. Heat butter and 2 tablespoons oil in a large, heavy skillet; add meat and brown on all sides.
3. Meanwhile, cook anchovies, garlic, and green pepper in a small amount of oil in a small saucepan about 5 minutes. Add rosemary, basil, sage, and vinegar; mix well. Cook and stir until boiling.
4. Remove lamb from skillet with a slotted spoon; set aside. Add enough chicken broth to drippings in skillet to make ¾ cup liquid. Add herb-vinegar mixture and bring to boiling, stirring to blend. Return lamb to skillet, cover tightly, and simmer over low heat about 40 minutes, or until tender.
5. Combine flour with a small amount of water to make a smooth paste. Add to liquid in skillet; cook and stir until mixture comes to boiling; cook 1 to 2 minutes.
6. Serve on a heated serving platter surrounded with fettuccine tossed with grated Parmesan cheese. Sprinkle with parsley.

About 6 servings

632 *Roast Leg of Lamb, Italian Style*
(Cosciotto d'Agnello alla Italiano)

1 lamb leg (5 to 6 pounds); do not
    remove fell
    Garlic cloves, cut in slivers
⅓ cup olive oil
1 tablespoon grated lemon peel
1½ teaspoons salt
¼ teaspoon pepper
1 teaspoon rosemary

1. Cut several small slits in surface of meat and insert a sliver of garlic in each.
2. Place lamb, skin side down, on rack in a roasting pan. Brush meat with olive oil. Sprinkle with lemon peel and a mixture of salt, pepper, and rosemary. Insert meat thermometer so tip is slightly beyond center of thickest part of meat; be sure that it does not rest in fat or on bone.
3. Roast, uncovered, at 325°F 2 to 3¼ hours, allowing 25 to 35 minutes per pound. Meat is medium done when thermometer registers 160°F and is well done at 170°F-180°F.
4. Remove meat to a warm serving platter. Garnish with parsley sprigs, if desired.

8 to 10 servings

633 *Veal Chops Pizzaiola (Scaloppine alla Pizzaiola)*

¼ cup olive oil
6 veal rib or loin chops, cut about ½ inch thick
1 can (28 ounces) tomatoes, sieved
2 cloves garlic, sliced
1 teaspoon oregano
1 teaspoon salt
½ teaspoon pepper
½ teaspoon chopped parsley

1. Heat oil in a large, heavy skillet. Add chops and brown on both sides.
2. Meanwhile, combine tomatoes, garlic, oregano, salt, pepper, and parsley. Slowly add tomato mixture to browned veal. Cover and cook over low heat 45 minutes, or until meat is tender.

6 servings

Beefsteak Pizzaiola: Follow recipe for Veal Chops Pizzaiola. Substitute **2 pounds beef round steak, cut about ¾ inch thick,** for veal chops. Cook about 1½ hours.

634 *Veal Scaloppine with Mushrooms and Capers (Scaloppine di Vitella con Funghi e Capperi)*

1 pound veal round steak, cut about ½ inch thick
½ cup flour
½ teaspoon salt
⅛ teaspoon pepper
¼ cup olive oil
½ clove garlic, minced
¼ cup butter
½ pound mushrooms, cleaned and sliced lengthwise
1 medium onion, thinly sliced
1¾ cups sieved canned tomatoes
¼ cup capers
1 teaspoon salt
⅛ teaspoon pepper
¼ teaspoon minced parsley
¼ teaspoon oregano

1. Put meat on a flat working surface and pound on both sides with a meat hammer. Cut into 1-inch pieces. Coat evenly with a mixture of flour, ½ teaspoon salt, and ⅛ teaspoon pepper.
2. Heat oil with garlic in a large skillet. Add veal and slowly brown on both sides.
3. Meanwhile, heat butter in a skillet. Add mushrooms and onion; cook until mushrooms are lightly browned.
4. Add mushrooms to veal along with tomatoes, capers, 1 teaspoon salt, ⅛ teaspoon pepper, parsley, and oregano; mix well.
5. Cover skillet and simmer about 25 minutes, or until veal is tender; stir occasionally.

About 4 servings

635 *Veal Marsala (Scaloppine di Vitella al Marsala)*

1½ to 2 pounds veal round steak,
    cut about ½ inch thick
¼ cup flour
1 teaspoon salt
⅛ teaspoon pepper
1 clove garlic, thinly sliced
¼ cup olive oil
¼ cup Marsala
¼ cup water
¼ teaspoon chopped parsley
⅛ teaspoon salt
⅛ teaspoon pepper

1. Place meat on a flat working surface and pound with a meat hammer on both sides. Cut into 6 pieces.
2. Coat veal with a mixture of flour, 1 teaspoon salt, and ⅛ teaspoon pepper.
3. Heat garlic and oil in a large, heavy skillet until garlic is slightly browned. Add meat to oil and garlic in skillet; brown slowly on both sides.
4. Meanwhile, combine Marsala, water, parsley, ⅛ teaspoon salt, and ⅛ teaspoon pepper. Slowly add Marsala mixture to browned veal. Cover and cook over low heat 20 minutes, or until veal is tender.

6 servings

636 *Veal Cannelloni*

¼ cup finely chopped onion
¼ cup finely chopped celery
2 tablespoons finely chopped carrot
1 tablespoon minced parsley
2 tablespoons olive oil
2 cups ground cooked veal
¼ teaspoon salt
⅛ teaspoon white pepper
¼ teaspoon oregano, crushed
¼ teaspoon basil, crushed
½ cup strong chicken broth (1
    chicken bouillon cube
    dissolved in ½ cup boiling
    water)
⅛ teaspoon nutmeg
● 2 cups Medium White Sauce
    Pasta for Cannelloni
¼ cup tomato sauce
¼ cup cream
1 cup grated Parmesan cheese

1. Cook onion, celery, carrot, and parsley in hot oil in a skillet about 3 minutes. Stir in veal, salt, pepper, oregano, basil, and chicken broth. Cook about 15 minutes.
2. Stir ½ cup white sauce into veal mixture.
3. Prepare pasta.
4. Spoon veal filling equally on the pasta squares and roll up. Arrange on an oven-proof platter.
5. Blend tomato sauce and cream into remaining white sauce; pour over cannelloni. Sprinkle top with cheese.
6. Set in a 425°F oven 10 minutes, or until top is browned.

4 servings

637 *Pasta for Cannelloni*

2 cups all-purpose flour
¼ teaspoon salt
1 egg, beaten
2 egg yolks, beaten
7 tablespoons water
4 quarts water
1 tablespoon salt

1. Blend flour and ¼ teaspoon salt in a bowl. Using a fork, stir in egg and egg yolks. Gradually add 7 tablespoons water, stirring constantly to make a stiff dough.
2. Turn dough onto a lightly floured surface and knead until smooth. Divide dough into halves and roll each into a rectangle 1/16 inch thick. Cut into eight 6×4-inch rectangles. Dry 1 hour. (Any leftover dough may be cut into strips, dried, and used as noodles.)
3. Bring 4 quarts water to boiling in a large saucepan. Add 1 tablespoon salt, then cannelloni squares. Boil, uncovered, about 8 minutes, or until just tender. Drain, rinse with cold water, and drain again.

8 cannelloni squares

638 Meat-and-Spinach-Filled Pancake Rolls
(Cannelloni alla Piemontese "Maison")

6 thin 10-inch pancakes*
⅓ cup finely chopped onion
3 tablespoons olive oil
½ pound ground veal, cooked (or other cooked meat)
1 package (10 ounces) frozen chopped spinach, cooked and drained
1 egg
⅓ cup grated Parmesan cheese
¼ teaspoon salt
Pinch pepper
Pinch nutmeg
● 1½ cups Béchamel Sauce

1. Prepare pancakes and cut into 2½-inch squares; keep warm.
2. Cook onion in heated olive oil in a skillet about 3 minutes. Add ground meat and cook until lightly browned. Mix spinach with meat mixture; force mixture through medium blade of food chopper.
3. Mix egg, cheese, salt, pepper, and nutmeg with meat mixture until thoroughly blended. Place about 1 tablespoon meat mixture on each pancake square and roll each into a sausage shape.
4. Arrange the filled cannelloni in a shallow buttered baking dish; cover with Béchamel Sauce.
5. Heat in a 375°F oven until golden brown. Serve very hot.

4 to 6 servings

*Prepare pancakes using batter in recipe for Stuffed Pancakes ●

639 Scamorze-Crowned Veal with Mushrooms

2 pounds veal cutlets, cut about ½ inch thick
¼ cup lemon juice
½ teaspoon salt
1/16 teaspoon black pepper
¼ cup butter
½ cup flour
1 egg, beaten
½ cup fine dry bread crumbs
¼ pound mushrooms, cleaned and sliced
6 thin slices cooked ham
6 ounces scamorze cheese, cut in 6 slices
6 mushroom caps, browned in butter

1. Cut meat into 6 serving-size pieces; place on a flat working surface and pound both sides with a meat hammer. Put into a large, shallow dish.
2. Mix lemon juice, salt, and pepper together and spoon over veal. Cover and refrigerate 2 hours.
3. Heat butter in a large, heavy skillet. Coat veal pieces with flour, dip in egg, then in bread crumbs. Add to hot butter in skillet and fry about 5 minutes on one side, or until lightly browned.
4. Turn meat and arrange on each piece a layer of mushroom slices, a slice of ham, a slice of cheese, and a mushroom cap. Continue cooking about 5 minutes, or until second side is browned and cheese is melted.
5. Remove to a warm serving platter and serve immediately.

6 servings

640 *Veal Parmesan (Scaloppine di Vitella alla Parmigiana)*

● 2 cups Tomato Meat Sauce
1½ to 2 pounds veal round steak,
 cut about ½ inch thick
1⅓ cups fine dry bread crumbs
 ⅓ cup grated Parmesan cheese
 3 eggs, beaten
 1 teaspoon salt
 ¼ teaspoon pepper
 ⅓ cup olive oil
 6 slices (3 ounces) mozzarella
  cheese

1. Prepare Tomato Meat Sauce.
2. Put meat on a flat working surface and repeatedly pound on one side with meat hammer. Turn meat over and repeat process. Cut into 6 pieces.
3. Mix bread crumbs and grated cheese; set aside.
4. Mix eggs, salt, and pepper; set aside.
5. Heat oil in a large skillet. Coat meat pieces first with egg, then with crumb mixture. Add to oil in skillet and brown on both sides.
6. Put browned meat into an 11×7×1½-inch baking dish. Pour sauce over meat. Top with slices of mozzarella cheese.
7. Bake at 350°F 15 to 20 minutes, or until cheese is melted and lightly browned.

6 servings

641 *Ham-and-Asparagus-Stuffed Veal Rolls (Manicaretti alla Lucrezia Borgia)*

 6 slices (1½ pounds) veal cutlet,
  boneless
 1 teaspoon salt
 ¼ teaspoon black pepper
 6 slices prosciutto
 6 slices Emmenthaler cheese
 6 white asparagus spears, 4 inches
  long
 ¼ cup butter
 ½ cup port wine
 2 tablespoons butter
 ⅓ cup finely chopped parsley
 2 cloves garlic, crushed
3½ ounces dried mushrooms,
  hydrated (soaked in water)
 ¼ cup beef gravy
 3 cups cream
 1 teaspoon salt

1. Pound veal cutlets until thin. Season with salt and pepper.
2. Place a slice of prosciutto, then a slice of cheese and an asparagus spear, over each veal slice. Roll into fingers; skewer or secure with twine.
3. Melt the ¼ cup butter in a large, heavy skillet. Add veal rolls; brown on all sides. Add port wine; cover and simmer about 10 minutes.
4. Meanwhile, melt the 2 tablespoons butter in a saucepan. Add and lightly brown the parsley and garlic. Mix in the mushrooms, beef gravy, and cream; simmer 5 minutes. Pour sauce over veal rolls; correct seasoning, using the remaining 1 teaspoon salt. Cover and simmer until meat is tender.

6 servings

642 *Beef Stew* (Caldillo)

3 tablespoons lard or vegetable oil
3 pounds lean beef, cut in ½-inch cubes
1 large onion, finely chopped
1 clove garlic, minced
3 fresh ripe tomatoes, peeled, seeded, and chopped
2 cans (4 ounces each) mild red chilies, drained and puréed
2 cups beef broth
2 teaspoons salt
⅛ teaspoon pepper
½ teaspoon oregano

1. Heat lard in a large skillet. Brown meat quickly on all sides. Remove beef from fat and set aside.
2. Add onion and garlic to fat in skillet; cook until onion is soft. Remove from fat and add to beef.
3. Cook tomato in fat in skillet, adding more fat if necessary. Return meat and onion to skillet. Add chili purée, beef broth, and seasonings; stir. Cover; bring to boiling, reduce heat, and cook over low heat about 2 hours, or until meat is tender.

6 to 8 servings

643 *Mexican Beef Stew*

2 pounds beef for stew, cut in 2-inch chunks
1 large onion, chopped
1 clove garlic, minced
1 green pepper, cut in strips
1 cup canned tomato sauce
1 canned chipotle chili, finely chopped
1 tablespoon vinegar
1½ teaspoons salt
1 teaspoon oregano
3 cups cubed pared potatoes
4 or 5 carrots, pared and cut in strips
Beef stock, or water plus beef bouillon cube
2 tablespoons flour

1. Put meat into a Dutch oven or large kettle. Add onion, garlic, green pepper, tomato sauce, chili, vinegar, salt, and oregano. Cover and bring to boiling; reduce heat and simmer 2½ hours, stirring occasionally.
2. Add potatoes and carrots to meat mixture. If more liquid seems needed, add up to 1 cup beef stock. Cover and cook about 30 minutes, or until meat and vegetables are tender.
3. Sprinkle flour over stew and stir in; continue to cook until sauce is thickened.

About 8 servings

644 *Beefsteak à la Mexicana*

2 pounds very thinly sliced tender beef (cubed steaks may be used)
Salt, pepper, and garlic salt
Fat
1 pound fresh tomatoes, peeled, cored, and chopped
1 cup chopped onion
4 jalapeño chilies, seeded and chopped

1. Sprinkle beef with salt, pepper, and garlic salt on both sides.
2. Pan-fry meat quickly in a small amount of hot fat in a skillet (about 2 minutes per side). Smother with chopped tomatoes, onion, and chilies. Cover skillet and cook over low heat about 15 minutes. Serve at once.

4 to 6 servings

645 *Mexican Meatballs* (Albóndigas)

Mexican meatballs often are centered with a chunk of hard-cooked egg as suggested in this recipe. Serve as a meat entrée, or prepare small-size meatballs as a party hors d'oeuvre.

Sauce:
- ½ cup chopped onion
- 1 clove garlic, minced
- ¼ cup oil or lard
- 1 cup tomato sauce
- 2 cups beef broth, or 2 cups water plus 2 beef bouillon cubes
- 1 teaspoon salt
- ½ teaspoon oregano
- ½ teaspoon cumin (comino)
- 2 chipotle chilies, chopped

Meatballs:
- 1 pound ground beef
- ½ pound ground pork
- ¼ pound ground cooked ham
- ½ cup chopped onion
- 2 slices dry bread
- ¼ cup milk
- 1 egg
- 1½ teaspoons salt
- ¼ teaspoon pepper
- 2 canned chipotle chilies, chopped
- 2 hard-cooked eggs, coarsely diced (optional)

1. For sauce, cook onion and garlic in hot oil in a large skillet until onion is soft. Add remaining sauce ingredients and heat to boiling, stirring constantly. Reduce heat and let simmer while preparing meatballs.
2. For meatballs, combine beef, pork, ham, and onion.
3. Tear bread into chunks and soak in milk.
4. Beat egg slightly and add salt, pepper, and chopped chilies. Add egg mixture and bread-milk mixture to meat; mix well.
5. Form into balls about 1½ inches in diameter. If desired, press a chunk of hard-cooked egg into center of each meatball.
6. Put meatballs into simmering sauce; cover and simmer 1 hour.

25 to 30 large meatballs (or about 75 small appetizer-size meatballs)

646 *Mexican Meat Loaf*

- 1 pound ground beef
- ½ pound ground pork
- ½ cup chopped onion
- ⅔ cup uncooked oats
- 1 egg, beaten
- 1 teaspoon salt
- ¼ teaspoon pepper
- ● 1 cup Red Chili Sauce
    or canned enchilada or taco sauce
- 2 hard-cooked eggs, cut in half lengthwise
- ¼ cup sliced pimento-stuffed green olives

1. Combine ground beef, ground pork, onion, oats, beaten egg, salt, pepper, and ½ cup of the sauce, mixing until evenly blended.
2. Pack half of the meat mixture into an 8×4×2-inch loaf pan. Arrange hard-cooked eggs in a row down center of loaf. Arrange olive slices on either side of eggs; press eggs and olives slightly into meat mixture. Cover with remaining half of meat mixture. Pour remaining ½ cup sauce over top.
3. Bake at 350°F 1 hour.

6 servings

647 *Green Chili Meat Loaf*

1½ pounds ground beef
1 cup soft bread crumbs
1 cup canned undrained tomatoes
1 can (4 ounces) green chilies,
    drained, seeded, and chopped
3 tablespoons dried onion flakes
1¼ teaspoons salt
¼ teaspoon garlic salt

1. Combine all ingredients thoroughly. Turn into a 9×5×3-inch loaf dish and press lightly.
2. Bake at 375°F 1 hour.

About 6 servings

648 *Chili con Carne with Beans*

1 pound boneless beef, cut in
    1-inch cubes
1 pound boneless pork, cut in
    1-inch cubes
3 tablespoons lard
1 cup beef broth
1 teaspoon salt
1 to 2 tablespoons chili powder
2 cloves garlic, minced
2 tablespoons lard
1 large onion, coarsely chopped
3 fresh tomatoes, peeled, seeded,
    and cut in pieces
1 can (16 ounces) white beans,
    drained
1 can (15 ounces) red kidney beans,
    drained

1. Brown meat in 3 tablespoons lard in a large skillet. Add broth; cover and cook 30 minutes.
2. Add salt, chili powder, and garlic; mix. Cook covered until meat is tender (about 1 hour).
3. Meanwhile, heat 2 tablespoons lard in a skillet. Add onion and tomato; mix well. Cover and cook until vegetables are soft. Purée vegetables.
4. Add purée and beans to meat; mix well. Heat thoroughly.

6 to 8 servings

649 *Taco Skillet Casserole*

1½ pounds ground beef
½ cup chopped onion
1 clove garlic, minced
1 teaspoon salt
¼ teaspoon pepper
1 teaspoon chili powder (see
    Note)
2 cups canned tomato sauce (see
    Note)
8 tortillas, cut into ½-inch strips
    Oil for frying
½ cup shredded Monterey Jack or
    mild Cheddar cheese
    Shredded lettuce

1. Crumble ground beef into a large skillet and brown well. If beef is very fat, pour off excess fat. Add onion and garlic and cook about 5 minutes, until onion is soft, stirring frequently. Stir in salt, pepper, chili powder, and tomato sauce and continue cooking over low heat about 15 minutes longer.
2. Meanwhile, in a separate skillet, fry tortilla strips in hot oil a few minutes until slightly crisped. Drain on absorbent paper. Stir tortilla strips into meat mixture and cook about 5 minutes longer, stirring frequently to prevent sticking. Sprinkle with cheese. As soon as cheese melts, remove from heat and serve. Top each serving with shredded lettuce.

6 servings

Note: **2 cups canned taco** or **enchilada sauce** may be substituted for chili powder and tomato sauce, if preferred.

650 *Cheese Ball Casserole*

1 pound ground lean pork
½ pound smoked ham, ground
1 green pepper, finely chopped
1 small onion, finely chopped
3 cloves garlic, minced
2 tablespoons snipped parsley
1 can (16 ounces) tomatoes, well drained
2 tablespoons tomato juice
2 teaspoons sugar
½ teaspoon salt
¼ teaspoon pepper
½ cup dark seedless raisins
¼ cup chopped green olives
1 tablespoon capers
2 cups shredded tortillas
½ pound sharp Cheddar cheese, thinly sliced
1 egg, beaten
Tortillas

1. Cook pork in a skillet until no longer pink. Mix in remaining ingredients, except cheese, egg, and whole tortillas. Heat for about 20 minutes, stirring occasionally.
2. Meanwhile, cover bottom and sides of a 1½-quart casserole with overlapping cheese slices.
3. When meat mixture is heated, quickly stir in egg and spoon into lined casserole. Around edge of dish overlap small pieces (quarters) of tortillas and remaining cheese slices.
4. Set in a 325°F oven 15 minutes, or until cheese is bubbly.
5. If desired, garnish center with green pepper strips and parsley arranged to form a flower. Serve with warm tortillas.

8 servings

651 *Empanadas*

Picadillo:
½ pound coarsely chopped beef
½ pound coarsely chopped pork
½ cup chopped onion
1 small clove garlic, minced
½ cup chopped raw apple
¾ cup chopped canned tomatoes
¼ cup raisins
¾ teaspoon salt
⅛ teaspoon pepper
Dash ground cinnamon
Dash ground cloves
¼ cup chopped almonds
Pastry:
4 cups all-purpose flour
1¼ teaspoons salt
1⅓ cups lard or shortening
⅔ cup icy cold water (about)

1. For picadillo, cook beef and pork together in large skillet until well browned. Add onion and garlic and cook until onion is soft. Add remaining ingredients, except almonds, and simmer 15 to 20 minutes longer until flavors are well blended.
2. Stir in almonds. Cool.
3. For pastry, mix flour and salt in a bowl. Cut in lard until mixture resembles coarse crumbs. Sprinkle water over flour mixture, stirring lightly with a fork until all dry ingredients hold together. Divide dough in four portions.
4. On a lightly floured surface, roll one portion of dough at a time to ⅛-inch thickness.
5. Using a 5-inch cardboard circle as a pattern, cut rounds of pastry with a knife. Place a rounded spoonful of filling in center of each round. Fold one side over filling to meet opposite side. Seal by dampening inside edges of pastry and pressing together with tines of fork.
6. Place empanadas on a baking sheet. Bake at 400°F 15 to 20 minutes, or until lightly browned. Or fry in **fat for deep frying** heated to 365°F until browned (about 3 minutes); turn once.

24 to 30 empanadas

652 *Lamb Mayan Style*

The sauce for this dish contains two ingredients typical of Mayan dishes from Yucatan: pepitas (pumpkin seeds), generally available in the United States in the roasted, salted form prepared as a cocktail snack, and annatto seeds (also called achiote). The latter would be available in Mexican specialty sections of large supermarkets and in Mexican grocery stores.

2 pounds boneless lamb for stew, cut in 2-inch chunks
½ cup chopped onion
1 clove garlic, minced
1 cup canned tomatoes, chopped
1 teaspoon salt
¼ teaspoon pepper
   Water
1 cup pepitas
1 tablespoon annatto seeds
2 tablespoons oil
1 tablespoon lemon juice

1. Put lamb, onion, garlic, tomatoes, salt, and pepper into a Dutch oven or heavy saucepot; mix well. Add water to cover. Bring to boiling, reduce heat, cover, and simmer until meat is tender (about 2 hours).
2. Meanwhile, combine pepitas and annatto seeds in an electric blender and blend until pulverized.
3. Fry mixture in a small amount of hot oil in a small skillet 2 or 3 minutes, stirring constantly. Stir into the sauce with meat. Stir in lemon juice. Serve with **cooked rice**.

6 servings

653 *Lomo of Pork with Pineapple*

1 tablespoon lard or oil
3 pounds pork loin, boneless, cut in 2-inch chunks
1 cup chopped onion
2 cups pineapple chunks (a 15¼-ounce can) with juice
1 cup beef stock, or 1 cup water plus 1 beef bouillon cube
¼ cup dry sherry
⅓ cup sliced pimento
1 fresh tomato, peeled and chopped
½ teaspoon chili powder
   Salt and pepper
2 tablespoons flour

1. Heat lard in a large, heavy skillet. Add meat and brown well on all sides. Add onion and cook about 5 minutes, or until soft.
2. Add pineapple with juice, beef stock, sherry, pimento, tomato, and chili powder to the skillet; stir until well mixed. Bring to boiling, reduce heat to simmering, and add salt and pepper to taste. Cover and simmer until meat is tender, about 1½ hours; stir occasionally to prevent sticking.
3. Just before serving, sprinkle flour over simmering sauce and stir in; cook and stir until sauce is thickened. Serve over hot rice.

6 to 8 servings

654 *Whole Lomo of Pork in Tomato Sauce*

1 pork loin roast, boneless (3 to 4 pounds)
1 can (6 ounces) tomato paste
¼ cup chopped onion
1 canned chipotle chili, very finely chopped; or 2 teaspoons chili powder
1 clove garlic, minced
1 teaspoon salt
¼ teaspoon pepper
1½ cups chicken stock, or 1½ cups hot water plus 2 chicken bouillon cubes
1 cup dairy sour cream

1. Put pork loin into a shallow baking pan; if necessary, cut in half so meat will fit into pan.
2. Combine tomato paste, onion, chili, garlic, salt, and pepper in a saucepan. Stir in chicken stock. Cook about 5 minutes.
3. Pour liquid over meat in pan.
4. Bake at 325°F about 1¼ hours. Occasionally spoon sauce over meat during baking, and check to see if additional water is needed to prevent drying.
5. When meat is tender, remove to serving platter.
6. Stir sour cream into sauce remaining in pan; warm slightly but do not boil. Pour over meat on platter.
7. To serve, slice meat about ¾ inch thick.

10 to 12 servings

655 *Lomo of Pork in Red Adobo*

3 pounds pork loin, boneless
1 onion, stuck with 1 clove
1 bay leaf
1 teaspoon salt
Water

Adobo Sauce:
6 fresh or dried ancho chilies
1 cup coarsely chopped onion
1 clove garlic
1 cup canned tomatoes
½ teaspoon oregano
½ teaspoon cumin (comino)
2 tablespoons lard or oil
1½ cups pork stock
Salt and pepper
1 avocado (optional)

1. Put pork, onion stuck with clove, bay leaf, and salt into large kettle or Dutch oven; cover with water. Cover kettle and cook until pork is tender, about 1½ hours.
2. Remove pork from stock; strain stock and save, discarding onion and bay leaf. Slice pork into 1-inch slices and return to kettle.
3. For adobo sauce, first prepare chilies (●). Put prepared chilies, onion, garlic, tomatoes, oregano, and cumin into an electric blender. Blend to a thick purée.
4. Heat lard in skillet. Add purée and cook about 5 minutes, stirring constantly. Stir in pork stock. Season to taste with salt and pepper.
5. Pour sauce over sliced pork in kettle. Cook, uncovered, over low heat for about 30 minutes, or until sauce thickens and coats the meat.
6. Peel and slice avocado. Arrange sliced meat on platter. Garnish with avocado slices, if desired.

6 to 8 servings

656 *Chili with Pork*

2 pounds lean pork, cut in 1-inch cubes
2 tablespoons flour
1 tablespoon chili powder
1½ teaspoons salt
½ teaspoon pepper
1 teaspoon sugar
½ teaspoon cumin (comino) seed
1 clove garlic, minced
2 cans (10 ounces each) mild enchilada sauce
2 cups water

1. Brown pork in a heavy skillet. Stir in flour and chili powder. Add remaining seasonings, sauce, and water. Bring to boiling; cover and simmer about 2 hours.
2. Serve with cooked rice and Mexican Beans (page 27), if desired.

About 8 servings

657 *Pork Slices in Mole Verde*

½ cup finely chopped onion
¼ cup finely chopped blanched almonds
2 tablespoons vegetable oil
2 cans (10 ounces each) Mexican green tomatoes (tomatillos)
1 tablespoon minced fresh coriander (cilantro) or 1 teaspoon dried coriander
1 to 3 tablespoons minced canned green chilies

1. Combine onion, almonds, and oil in a saucepan. Cook over medium heat until onion is soft.
2. Turn contents of cans of green tomatoes into an electric blender and blend until smooth (or force green tomatoes through a sieve).
3. Add purée to onion mixture and stir in coriander, chilies (to taste), and stock. Bring to boiling, reduce heat, and simmer, uncovered, until reduced to 2½ cups; stir occasionally.
4. Arrange meat in a large skillet, sprinkle with salt to taste, and pour sauce over meat. Cover, bring slowly to boiling,

2 cups chicken stock, or 2 cups
    water plus 2 chicken bouillon
    cubes
6 to 8 slices cooked pork loin roast
Salt
Small lettuce leaves
Whole pickled mild chilies
Dairy sour cream

reduce heat, and simmer about 10 minutes, or until thoroughly heated.

5. Arrange sauced meat on a platter. Garnish with lettuce and chilies. Accompany with sour cream.

6 to 8 servings

658 *Dried Lima Casserole*

More Mexican-style beans—limas, this time. This dish makes a delectable luncheon or supper main dish, quite out of the ordinary.

1 pound dried lima beans
1 large onion, sliced
¼ cup lard or oil
¼ pound chorizo or Italian-style
    sausage meat
¼ pound diced ham
1 cup canned enchilada sauce
½ cup shredded Monterey Jack

1. Soak lima beans in water to cover for 1 hour. Bring to boiling, reduce heat, and cook until tender; add more water if necessary.

2. Meanwhile, cook onion in lard until soft (about 5 minutes). If using sausage in casing, remove from casing and add to onion, crumbling slightly. Cook and stir until well browned. Add ham and enchilada sauce; cover and cook about 30 minutes.

3. Skim off excess fat. Add cooked beans and continue cooking about 15 minutes longer to blend flavors. Sprinkle with cheese just before serving.

6 to 8 servings

Note: This skillet-type casserole dish can be transferred to a baking dish before the cheese is sprinkled on top. It may then be refrigerated for later serving. Heat in a 350°F oven 20 to 30 minutes, or until bubbling.

659 *Pork and Beans Mexican Style*

This Mexican-style pork-and-beans dish offers more pork than the North American variety. Therefore it's definitely an entrée.

¼ pound sliced bacon
¼ pound boneless pork loin
    (lomo) or pork tenderloin,
    cubed
¼ pound ham, cubed
1 large onion, sliced
1½ cups fresh or canned, peeled,
    diced tomatoes
1 teaspoon chili powder
½ teaspoon cumin (comino)
½ teaspoon oregano
● 2 cups cooked pinto or kidney
    beans (canned or prepared as
    directed)
12 ounces beer

1. Cook bacon until crisp; drain and crumble. In bacon fat brown pork and ham. Add onion; cover and cook until soft (about 5 minutes).

2. Add tomatoes, chili powder, cumin, oregano, and the crumbled bacon. Add cooked beans; bring to boiling. Gradually stir in beer. Continue to simmer over low heat about 1 hour, or until pork is well done and mixture is consistency of rich stew, stirring occasionally.

3. Serve in bowls as a stew, or with hot, soft tortillas to make tacos.

4 to 6 servings

660 *Pork and Green Tomato Stew*

2½ pounds lean pork, cut in 1-inch cubes
1 tablespoon vegetable oil
1 onion, chopped
2 cloves garlic, minced
1 can (12 ounces) Mexican green tomatoes (tomatillos), drained and chopped
2 cans (4 ounces each) green chilies, drained, seeded, and chopped
1 tablespoon dried cilantro leaves
1 teaspoon marjoram
1 teaspoon salt
½ cup water
Cooked rice
Dairy sour cream

1. Brown meat in oil in a large skillet. Push meat to sides of skillet; add onion and garlic and cook until onion is soft. Add green tomatoes, chilies, cilantro, marjoram, salt, and water; mix well. Cover; bring to boiling, reduce heat, and cook until meat is tender (about 2 hours).
2. Serve with rice and top with dollops of sour cream.

6 to 8 servings

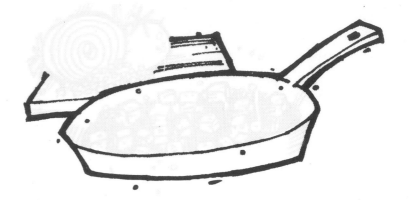

661 *Tongue in Almond Sauce*

2 veal tongues (about 2½ pounds each)
1 medium onion, stuck with 2 or 3 cloves
1 stalk celery with leaves
1 bay leaf
6 peppercorns
2 teaspoons salt
Water
Almond Sauce:
2 fresh or dried ancho chilies
½ cup canned tomatoes with juice
½ cup whole blanched almonds
½ cup raisins
1 slice bread, torn in pieces
2 tablespoons lard or oil
2 cups tongue stock
Salt and pepper
¼ cup blanched slivered almonds

1. Put tongues, onion stuck with cloves, celery, bay leaf, peppercorns, and salt into a Dutch oven or kettle. Cover with water. Cover Dutch oven, bring to boiling, and cook until meat is tender, about 2 hours. Allow to cool in liquid.
2. Remove skin from cooled tongues, trim off roots, and slice meat into ½-inch slices. Strain stock in which meat was cooked and save, discarding onion, celery, and bay leaf. Return sliced meat to kettle.
3. For almond sauce, first prepare chilies (see page 30). Put chilies, tomatoes, the whole almonds, ¼ cup of the raisins, and the bread into an electric blender. Blend to a thick purée.
4. Heat lard in a skillet. Add the puréed mixture and cook about 5 minutes. Stir in tongue stock and remaining ¼ cup raisins. Cook about 5 minutes, stirring constantly. Season to taste with salt and pepper.
5. Pour sauce over sliced meat in Dutch oven and simmer until meat is heated through.
6. Transfer meat and sauce to platter and garnish with slivered almonds.

8 to 10 servings

Baked Rice Balls, page 184

662 *Pan-Fried Steak*

⅓ cup prepared mustard
1 beef boneless sirloin steak
    (4 pounds)
¼ cup lard
1 onion, minced
2 cups beef stock
½ teaspoon beef extract or
    1 beef bouillon cube
1 teaspoon tomato paste
2 tablespoons butter
2 tablespoons cornstarch
    Salt and pepper to taste

1. Spread mustard on all sides of meat.
2. Melt lard in a large, heavy skillet and sauté onion. Add meat and brown well on all sides. Reduce heat and continue to cook until the meat is done. Transfer to a warm platter and keep hot.
3. Remove fat from skillet. Pour in stock to deglaze; add beef extract and tomato paste.
4. Mix butter and cornstarch and put into skillet juices. Stir constantly over medium heat until sauce is slightly thicker. Add salt and pepper.
5. Pour a little sauce over the meat. Serve remaining sauce in a
● sauceboat. Garnish meat with Smothered Mixed Vegetables

663 *Pepper Steak Port-au-Prince*
(Steak au Poivre Port-au-Prince)

2 tablespoons peppercorns
8 beef sirloin steaks (4 pounds),
    about 2 inches thick
2 tablespoons peanut oil
2 tablespoons butter
1 onion, minced
    Salt to taste
½ cup dry white wine
¼ cup beef stock
3 tablespoons butter
2 tablespoons chopped parsley
¼ cup amber rum

1. In a mortar, pound the peppercorns until coarsely crushed. With the heel of the hand, press peppercorns into the meat.
2. Heat oil, 2 tablespoons butter, and onion over high heat in a large skillet. Sauté steaks in the fat until meat is as done as desired. Season with salt. Transfer meat to a warm platter and keep hot.
3. Pour wine and stock into the skillet over high heat to deglaze. Add the remaining butter and parsley. Pour mixture over the meat.
4. Warm rum, ignite it, and pour it, still flaming, over the steak.
● 5. Serve immediately with Smothered Mixed Vegetables

8 servings

664 *Broiled Beef with Barbecue Sauce*

1 beef boneless sirloin steak,
    1 inch thick (about 4 pounds)
½ cup prepared mustard
    Pepper to taste
● Creole Barbecue Sauce
5 tablespoons butter
2 tablespoons chopped parsley
2 tablespoons chopped chives
    Salt to taste

1. Lay beef on a broiler rack and spread mustard over surface. Score meat deeply in a diamond pattern. Season with pepper. Brush Creole Barbecue Sauce over meat.
2. Broil 4 inches from heat 6 to 8 minutes on each side, or until as done as desired. When meat is turned, brush with the barbecue sauce.
3. While meat cooks, combine butter, parsley, and chives. Set aside.
4. Place meat on a hot platter and season with salt. Spread butter mixture over meat. This will melt and mix with meat juice. Serve with French-Fried Breadfruit (●) and Caribbean Rice with Bean Sauce (●).

8 to 10 servings

Red Snapper Veracruz Style, page 311

665 *Tournedos Caribbean*

8	beef tenderloin steaks (about 4 pounds)
½	cup prepared mustard
	Freshly ground pepper to taste
2	tablespoons butter
8	goose liver slices (¼ inch thick)
	Flour
½	cup beef stock
1½	teaspoons beef extract or 3 beef bouillon cubes
⅓	cup amber rum
2	tablespoons butter
2	tablespoons cornstarch

1. Pound steaks until about 1 inch thick. Spread mustard on one side of each steak. Roll up steaks with mustard side in and secure with string. Season with pepper.
2. Melt butter over medium heat in a heavy skillet. Coat liver with flour and sauté until golden brown on both sides. Transfer liver to a warm dish and keep hot.
3. Place steak rolls in skillet and cook until as done as desired. Add more butter if necessary.
4. Arrange the steak rolls on a warm platter and place a sautéed liver slice on each one.
5. Pour the stock and beef extract into skillet to deglaze. Warm the rum, ignite it, and pour it, still flaming, into the skillet.
6. Mix butter and cornstarch and add to liquid in skillet. Bring to a boil, stirring constantly; remove from heat and pour over steak rolls.
7. Serve immediately with French-Fried Breadfruit (●).

8 servings

666 *Beef Stew*

¼	cup peanut oil
1	large onion, thinly sliced
3	to 4 pounds beef boneless chuck or rump, cubed
2	cups beef stock
1	can (10½ ounces) tomato purée
	Bouquet garni
1	green hot pepper or 6 drops Tabasco
	Salt and pepper to taste
3	cups diced potato
3	cups cubed white turnip
3	cups sliced carrot
	Water
2	tablespoons butter
2	tablespoons flour
1	tablespoon chopped parsley

1. Heat oil in a Dutch oven; sauté onion until golden brown, stirring constantly. Add meat and brown on all sides.
2. Add beef stock, tomato purée, bouquet garni, hot pepper, salt, and pepper; stir to blend. Cover and simmer over low heat 2 hours, or until meat is tender.
3. Add potato, turnip, and carrot. If more liquid is needed, add water. Bring to a boil and simmer 20 minutes, or until vegetables are tender.
4. Discard the bouquet garni and hot pepper. Transfer meat and vegetables to a warm platter.
5. Combine butter and flour to make a paste; add to pan juices and boil until thickened. Add parsley, and, if desired, salt and pepper.
6. Pour gravy over meat and vegetables. Serve with Coconut and Rice and Smothered Cabbage (●).

8 to 10 servings

Note: Lamb or kid may be substituted for the beef.

667 *Scallop of Kid or Veal (Escalopes de Cabrit ou de Veau)*

16	small kid or veal scallops, (about 3 pounds)
2	eggs, beaten
2	tablespoons vegetable oil
1	teaspoon lime juice
	Salt and pepper to taste
	Dry bread crumbs
2	tablespoons butter
2	tablespoons vegetable oil

1. Cut meat into pieces the size of a silver dollar, then pound between 2 sheets of waxed paper until very thin.
2. Mix eggs, 2 tablespoons oil, lime juice, salt, and pepper. Dip each piece of meat into the egg mixture, then in the bread crumbs.
3. Heat remaining butter and oil in a skillet over medium heat. Sauté the meat until golden brown on each side. Add more butter and oil to skillet if necessary.
4. Serve with Rice and Avocado (●).

8 servings

668 *Braised Shanks*

8 lamb shanks
1 cup cubed salt pork
½ cup each peas, coarsely chopped onion, sliced green beans, cubed white turnip, and sliced carrot
1 cup boiling water
½ cup dry white wine
7 peppercorns
3 parsley sprigs
1 thyme sprig
1 garlic clove
1 teaspoon salt
½ cup red wine
¾ cup beef broth
1 tablespoon butter
1 tablespoon cornstarch
1 tablespoon chopped parsley

1. Thoroughly wash shanks in cold water; drain. (If necessary, pull off the parchmentlike covering.)
2. In a Dutch oven render the salt pork, and in this fat sauté the shanks over high heat until brown on all sides.
3. Remove Dutch oven from heat; add vegetables, water, and white wine.
4. In a mortar, pound to a paste the peppercorns, parsley, thyme, garlic, and salt. Add to the shanks. Bring to a boil over high heat.
5. Remove Dutch oven from heat and add red wine and ½ cup beef broth.
6. Cook covered in a 375°F oven 2 hours.
7. Mix butter and cornstarch. Set aside.
8. Transfer shanks to a large serving platter; arrange vegetables around shanks.
9. Pour ¼ cup beef broth into Dutch oven to deglaze and place over high heat. Add butter mixture and stir constantly until thickened. Pour into a serving dish and sprinkle with parsley.
10. Serve with Caribbean Rice and Bean Sauce (●   ).

About 4 servings

Note: Beef, veal, or kid shanks may be substituted for lamb shanks.

669 *Veal Roulades*

6 veal cutlets (1½ pounds)
½ cup peanut oil
2 large onions, chopped
½ cup fresh bread crumbs
¼ cup chopped parsley
½ teaspoon salt
½ teaspoon freshly ground pepper
1 egg yolk, beaten
¼ cup butter
1 cup stock
12 small onions
12 small carrots
1 green hot pepper or 5 dried Italian pepper pods
1 tablespoon butter
1 tablespoon cornstarch

1. Pound the meat until flattened. Set aside.
2. Heat oil in a small skillet and sauté the chopped onion. Add bread crumbs, parsley, salt, and pepper; stir to blend. Remove from heat and stir in egg yolk. Cool.
3. Spread some of the mixture on each piece of meat. Roll up the slices of meat and secure with string.
4. Melt ¼ cup butter in a large skillet and brown the roulades. Add stock.
5. Simmer covered over low heat or cook in a 375°F oven about 2 hours, or until tender; add onions, carrots, and pepper halfway through cooking.
6. Transfer meat and vegetables to a warm platter and keep hot. Discard pepper.
7. Mix butter and cornstarch and put into skillet juices. Stir constantly over medium heat until sauce is slightly thicker. Pour sauce over roulades.
8. Serve with Caribbean Rice (●).

6 servings

670 Ham Rolls Guadeloupe

¼ cup amber rum
● 2 cups Béchamel Sauce
  use beef broth)
8 ham slices
  (about ¼ inch thick)
1½ cups Creamed Spinach

1. Add rum to Béchamel Sauce. Pour sauce into a skillet and add ham slices; heat thoroughly.
2. Transfer ham, a slice at a time, to a baking dish, place 3 tablespoons Creamed Spinach on each slice and roll up. Secure with picks, if necessary. Pour sauce in skillet over ham slices.
3. Broil 4 inches from heat about 5 minutes, or until warmed and glazed.
4. Serve with Bananas à l'Antillaise (●).

8 servings

Creamed Spinach: Chop 1½ **cups cooked spinach** very fine. Season with **salt and pepper** to taste. Melt **1 tablespoon butter** and stir in **1 teaspoon flour**. Add ½ **cup milk** and cook 3 minutes, stirring constantly. Add chopped spinach and heat thoroughly.

671 Calf's Liver with Basil

1½ pounds calf's liver, cut in strips
½ cup flour
  Salt and pepper to taste
½ cup butter
2 garlic cloves
1 tablespoon minced onion
½ cup beef stock
1 teaspoon dried basil
2 tablespoons butter
1 tablespoon cornstarch

1. Coat liver strips in a mixture of flour, salt, and pepper.
2. Melt butter in a skillet over medium heat. Add garlic, onion, and liver strips. Sauté meat 3 minutes on each side. Transfer the meat to a warm platter and keep hot.
3. Deglaze the skillet with the stock; add basil. Mix butter and cornstarch and add to the stock. Cook and stir mixture until slightly thickened. Pour over liver.
4. Serve liver with Sweet Potato Soufflé (●).

4 to 6 servings

672 Ragout of Brains

2 pounds calf's brains
6 peppercorns
5 shallots, halved
4 parsley sprigs
1 small carrot, cut in pieces
1 teaspoon salt
¼ teaspoon thyme
¼ cup butter
2 tablespoons soybean oil
¼ cup beef stock
1 tablespoon tomato paste
2 tablespoons butter
1 tablespoon lime juice

1. Remove membrane and blood from brains, then soak brains in cold water for 30 minutes. Simmer for 15 minutes in water. Drain and drop into cold water.
2. In a mortar, pound to a paste the peppercorns, shallots, parsley, carrot, salt, and thyme.
3. Melt ¼ cup butter with oil in a medium skillet. Add the brains and seasoning paste. Sauté, gently stirring, until the meat is golden.
4. Add stock and tomato paste; cook 5 minutes longer, then add the remaining butter and lime juice.
5. Serve immediately with Deep-Fried Plantain (●).

About 8 servings

673 *Beef Liver à la Beauharnais*

½ cup flour
1 tablespoon paprika
½ teaspoon salt
⅛ teaspoon freshly ground pepper
⅛ teaspoon cayenne or red pepper
1½ pounds beef liver, thinly sliced
1 cup minced onion
3 tablespoons peanut oil
2 tablespoons butter
1 tablespoon chopped parsley
1 tablespoon lime juice

1. Combine flour, paprika, salt, and peppers. Coat liver slices with flour mixture. Set aside.
2. Sauté onion in oil over medium heat. When onion is translucent, add butter and liver slices. Cook liver about 5 minutes; do not overcook.
3. Arrange liver on a heated platter and sprinkle with parsley and lime juice. Garnish with **watercress**.

6 servings

674 *Beef Tongue King Christophe*

1 fresh beef tongue (about 4 pounds)
Water
1 carrot
1 onion stuck with 4 cloves
½ cup lime juice
Bouquet garni

1. Wash tongue and put into a large saucepan. Add water to cover and remaining ingredients. Cover and simmer about 2 hours, or until tongue is tender.
2. Cool tongue, then remove skin; cut away roots and gristle.
3. Slice the tongue diagonally and against the grain. Arrange slices on a platter. Garnish with sliced **hard-cooked eggs**, **pickles**, **avocado wedges**, and **sliced tomatoes**.

About 12 servings

675 *Tripe à la Creole*

2 pounds tripe
1 lime, halved
Water
1 tablespoon coarse sea salt
1 tablespoon wine vinegar
4 garlic cloves
1 green hot pepper or
  3 dried Italian pepper pods
½ cup olive oil
2 large Spanish onions, sliced
1 cup cubed cooked ham
5 large tomatoes, peeled, seeded,
  and chopped
¼ cup amber rum
2 thyme sprigs
2 bay leaves

1. Wash tripe thoroughly in cold water; drain. Rub the cut surface of lime over entire tripe. Put into a large kettle, cover with water, and add salt and vinegar. Bring to a boil; simmer 5 hours, adding more water if necessary. (This step is generally done the day before tripe is served; tripe is left to cool in its water.)
2. Cut the tripe into 2-inch slices; set aside.
3. In a mortar, pound to a paste the garlic and green hot pepper; set aside.
4. Heat oil in a top-of-range casserole. Sauté onion, then add tripe, ham, tomato, rum, seasoning paste, thyme, and bay leaves. Simmer 20 minutes. Serve immediately.

6 to 8 servings

676 *Vegetable-Smothered Steak (Filet Touffé)*

8 beef loin tenderloin or boneless
   sirloin steaks (about 4 pounds),
   cut thin
3 garlic cloves
2 parsley sprigs
1 thyme sprig
1 teaspoon coarse salt
2 tablespoons prepared mustard
1 tablespoon orange juice
1 cup sliced carrot
1 cup shredded cabbage
4 medium onions, sliced and
   separated in rings
3 large truffles, sliced
¼ pound ham, cubed
¼ pound salt pork, cubed
   Madeira or port wine
   (about 1 cup)
¾ cup amber rum
   Beef stock
2 tablespoons butter
2 tablespoons cornstarch
   Salt and pepper to taste

1. Pound steaks until flattened.
2. In a mortar, pound to a paste the garlic, parsley, thyme, and salt. Add mustard and orange juice to the seasoning paste.
3. Combine carrot, cabbage, onion, truffles, ham, and the mustard mixture. Set aside.
4. Render salt pork in a skillet. Remove the cracklings and add to the vegetable mixture. Brown the steaks in the fat over medium heat.
5. Alternate layers of the steak and vegetable mixture in a large casserole with a tight-fitting cover. Pour wine into the casserole dish to fill it one third full.
6. Warm the rum, ignite it, and pour it, still flaming, over the meat. Cover casserole tightly.
7. Bake at 450°F 20 minutes, then turn oven control to 325°F and continue to cook 4 hours.
8. Transfer steaks and vegetables to a warm platter and keep hot.
9. Measure liquid in casserole and add enough beef stock to equal 2 cups. Pour liquid into a saucepan and set over medium heat.
10. Mix butter and cornstarch and add to liquid in saucepan. Stir constantly until thickened. Add salt and pepper.
11. Pour sauce over meat or serve in a sauceboat. Accompany with Purée of Breadfruit (●).

Poultry

677 *Chicken with Tomatoes and Onions* (Kotopoulo Riganati)

2 broiler-fryer chickens
3 tablespoons olive oil
Juice of 1 lemon
2 teaspoons salt
½ cup butter
1 can (20 ounces) tomatoes
   (undrained)
1 teaspoon pepper
1 tablespoon oregano
Salt

1. Rinse chickens well and pat dry with paper towels. Rub inside and out with a mixture of olive oil, lemon juice, and 2 teaspoons salt. Place in a large roasting pan.
2. Bake at 375°F 1 hour.
3. Melt butter in a saucepan. Add tomatoes, pepper, and oregano. Simmer 5 minutes.
4. Pour sauce over the chickens. Turn oven heat to 325°F and bake chickens an additional 45 minutes; baste frequently. Salt to taste.

4 servings

Note: Kotopoulo Riganati freezes very well.

678 *Chicken and Grapes*

6 tablespoons butter
2 broiler-fryer chickens, cut in
   pieces
Salt and pepper to taste
3 scallions, chopped
1 cup dry white wine
Clusters of seedless white
   grapes
½ teaspoon paprika

1. Melt butter in a skillet. Add chicken and brown. Season with salt and pepper. Transfer chicken to a casserole.
2. Add scallions to the skillet and cook until browned. Add wine and heat. Pour over the chicken. Cover.
3. Bake at 350°F 30 minutes. Remove cover. Add grapes and bake an additional 5 minutes. Sprinkle with paprika.

4 to 6 servings

679 *Braised Chicken with Tomatoes and Cheese*
(Kotopoulo Vorthonia)

1 chicken (3 pounds), cut in
   small pieces
¼ cup olive oil
Salt and pepper to taste
1 can (16 ounces) tomatoes
   (undrained)
1 medium onion, minced
1 garlic clove, crushed in a garlic
   press
2 tablespoons oregano
¼ teaspoon cinnamon
2 tablespoons whiskey
1 pound orzo (a pasta)
¼ cup vegetable oil
1 cup grated hard mizithra
   cheese

1. Rinse chicken and pat dry with paper towels.
2. Heat olive oil in a large skillet. Add chicken pieces. Season with salt and pepper. Brown on all sides.
3. Mash tomatoes and add to skillet. Add onion, garlic, oregano, cinnamon, and whiskey. Cover and simmer about 30 minutes, or until done. Remove chicken pieces and keep hot.
4. Cook orzo according to directions on the package, adding vegetable oil to the water. Drain thoroughly and put into a deep serving dish. Add the sauce and toss lightly until orzo is coated completely. Adjust seasoning. Add the chicken. Toss again to combine.
5. Serve with grated cheese.

6 to 8 servings

680 *Broiled Chicken in Lemon Juice and Oregano*
(Kotopoulo me Lemoni ke Rigani)

2 broiler-fryer chickens, cut up
½ cup olive oil
  Juice of 2 lemons
¼ cup oregano, crushed
  Salt and pepper to taste

1. Rinse chicken pieces and pat dry.
2. In a bowl, make a marinade by combining olive oil with lemon juice and oregano. Dip each piece of chicken into the marinade. Season with salt and pepper. Marinate for several hours, or overnight if possible.
3. In a preheated broiler, place the chicken fleshy side down. Broil about 6 inches from heat about 15 minutes, or until brown, basting frequently. Turn once. Broil until done.

4 servings

Note: The marinade may be served as a gravy with cooked rice or noodles.

681 *Roast Chicken with Potatoes*
(Kotopoulo tou Fournou me Patates)

1 chicken (about 4 pounds)
  Salt and pepper to taste
  Juice of 1 lemon
¼ cup butter
¼ teaspoon paprika
1 cup water
5 medium potatoes, pared

1. Season chicken, inside and out, with salt, pepper, lemon juice, butter, and paprika. Place chicken on a rack in a baking dish.
2. Bake at 350°F about 1¼ hours, or until chicken is tender, basting occasionally. After the first 30 minutes of cooking, pour in water; add potatoes and baste with drippings.
3. Turn oven control to 400°F. Remove chicken to a platter and keep warm. Turn potatoes over in dish. Bake an additional 5 to 10 minutes.

5 servings

682 *Rock Cornish Hens with Oranges and Almonds*

1 Rock Cornish hen per serving

For each serving:
2 tablespoons butter, melted
2 tablespoons orange juice
  Salt and pepper to taste
¼ teaspoon marjoram
¼ teaspoon thyme
½ garlic clove, crushed in a garlic press
½ navel orange with peel, cut in thin slices
2 tablespoons honey (about)
5 almonds, blanched, slivered, and toasted

1. Rinse hen well. Drain and pat dry. Place in a shallow baking dish. Drizzle inside and out with butter.
2. Combine orange juice, salt, pepper, marjoram, thyme, and garlic in a small bowl. Pour over and into the bird. Marinate 2 hours; turn occasionally.
3. Set bird on a broiler rack and put under broiler about 6 inches from heat. Broil 12 minutes on each side, or until tender, basting frequently with the marinade. During the last few minutes of broiling, arrange orange slices around the bird and drizzle with honey.
4. Garnish with almonds and serve at once.

683 *Chicken Breasts with Yogurt Sauce*
(Kotopoulo me Saltsa Yaourti)

½ cup butter
6 chicken breasts, boned
Salt and pepper to taste
½ teaspoon paprika
6 fresh scallions, chopped
¼ cup minced parsley
2 cups chicken stock
Juice of 1 lemon
1 pound mushrooms, sliced
2 cups plain yogurt
1 cup coarsely ground walnuts

1. Melt butter in a large skillet. Add chicken and season with salt, pepper, and paprika. Brown on both sides.
2. Add scallions, parsley, chicken stock, and lemon juice; bring to a boil. Reduce heat and simmer covered about 20 minutes, or until chicken is tender.
3. Remove chicken and arrange on a serving platter.
4. Add mushrooms to the stock. Simmer uncovered 3 minutes. Blend in yogurt and walnuts. (If sauce is too thick, dilute with a little stock or water.) Heat just to warm yogurt; do not boil.
5. Pour sauce over chicken.

6 servings

684 *Chicken in Filo* *(Kotopita)*

1 stewing chicken, cut in pieces
½ cup unsalted butter
1 medium onion, minced
½ cup finely chopped leek
1 celery stalk, minced
1 garlic clove, crushed in a garlic press
2 tablespoons finely chopped parsley
2 tablespoons pine nuts
3 tablespoons flour
2½ cups chicken stock
½ cup cream
4 eggs, beaten until frothy
¼ teaspoon nutmeg
½ teaspoon dill
2 tablespoons white wine
Salt and pepper
1 package filo
Additional butter for filo

1. Rinse chicken pieces. In a large heavy Dutch oven, add ¼ cup butter. When hot, add the chicken. Cover. Cook, turning, without browning, for about 15 minutes.
2. Remove the chicken pieces and cool slightly. Remove bones and skin from chicken and discard. Chop chicken meat. Set aside.
3. Melt 2 tablespoons butter in a skillet. Add onion, leek, celery, garlic, parsley, and pine nuts. Sauté until vegetables are limp.
4. Melt remaining butter in a saucepan and blend in flour. Cook 2 minutes. Stir in stock. Simmer until sauce boils. Cool. Stir in cream, eggs, nutmeg, dill, chicken, vegetables, and wine, if sauce seems too thick. Season with salt and pepper.
5. Butter a 12x9x3-inch baking pan. Line it with 6 sheets of filo, brushing each with butter
6. Spread chicken filling evenly over filo. Top with filo according to directions.
7. Bake at 350°F about 50 minutes, or until golden in color. Let stand 15 minutes before cutting into squares. Serve warm.

8 to 10 servings

685 *Chicken with Cheese* *(Kotopoulo me Tyri)*

¼ cup butter
1 chicken (3 pounds), cut in pieces
1 medium onion, minced
Salt and pepper to taste
½ teaspoon rosemary
¼ teaspoon paprika
1 garlic clove, crushed in a garlic press
1½ cups chicken broth
⅓ pound kasseri cheese, cut in thin slices

1. Melt butter in a large skillet. Brown chicken on all sides. Add onion. Season with salt and pepper. Add rosemary, paprika, garlic, and chicken broth. Simmer, covered, about 40 minutes, or until chicken is tender.
2. Lay cheese slices on top of chicken. Simmer, covered, 5 minutes more. Serve at once.

2 to 4 servings

686 *Stuffing for a Small Turkey (Yemisi yra Galopoulo)*

½ cup butter
1 onion, minced
1 medium cooking apple, pared, cored, and diced
1 pound mushrooms, sliced
2 medium potatoes, boiled, peeled, and diced
½ cup pine nuts
½ cup dried black currants
1 cup blanched almonds, sliced
2 pounds chestnuts, boiled and cleaned
4 cups prepared bread stuffing
2 cups or more chicken stock to make a moist stuffing
1 can (4½ ounces) pâté de foie gras
Salt and pepper to taste

1. Melt butter in a large deep skillet. Add onion, apple, and mushrooms; cook until tender.
2. Add potatoes, pine nuts, currants, almonds, chestnuts, stuffing, and stock. Heat thoroughly over low heat, adding more liquid if necessary.
3. Stir in pâté. Season with salt and pepper.
4. Cool completely. Stuff bird.

Stuffing for a small turkey or 2 capons

687 *Royal Chicken*

⅓ cup butter
2 medium onions, chopped
1 cup sliced mushrooms
1 chicken or capon, cut in pieces
1 cup hot water
1 teaspoon salt
¼ teaspoon pepper
1 tablespoon flour
1 teaspoon paprika (optional)
1 cup dairy sour cream or white wine

1. Melt butter in a large skillet. Add onion, mushrooms, and chicken pieces. Stir-fry until golden.
2. Add water, salt, and pepper.
3. Cover; cook over medium heat about 35 minutes, or until chicken is tender.
4. Blend flour, paprika (if desired), and sour cream. Stir into liquid in skillet. Bring just to boiling. Simmer 3 minutes.

About 6 servings

688 *Chicken Livers in Madeira Sauce (Wątróbki z Kur w Sosie Maderowym)*

1 pound chicken livers
Milk
1 medium onion, minced
2 tablespoons chicken fat or butter
⅔ cup all-purpose flour
¾ teaspoon salt
⅔ cup chicken broth
½ cup Madeira

1. Cover chicken livers with milk; soak 2 hours. Drain; discard milk.
2. Sauté onion in fat.
3. Mix flour with salt. Coat livers with seasoned flour.
4. Add livers to onions. Stir-fry just until golden, about 5 minutes.
5. Stir in broth and wine. Cover. Simmer 5 to 10 minutes, or just until livers are tender.

4 servings

689 Smothered Stuffed Chicken
(Nadziewane Kurczątko Duszone)

1 chicken (about 3 pounds)
½ teaspoon salt
⅛ teaspoon pepper
2 tablespoons butter
1¼ cups dry bread cubes or pieces
¼ cup chopped onion
½ teaspoon dill weed
¼ cup hot milk
⅓ cup butter, melted

1. Sprinkle inside of chicken with salt and pepper. Tuck wing tips underneath wings. Chop liver.
2. Sauté liver in 2 tablespoons butter 2 minutes. Add bread cubes, onion, dill, and milk; mix.
3. Stuff chicken. Close and secure with poultry pins. Place in a ceramic or earthenware casserole.
4. Pour melted butter over chicken. Cover.
5. Bake at 350°F about 1 hour, or until chicken is tender.
6. If desired, remove cover. Baste. Increase temperature to 450°F. Bake 10 minutes to brown.

4 to 6 servings

690 Chicken with Anchovies
(Pularda Pieczona z Sardelami)

1 chicken (3 pounds), split in half
1 can (2 ounces) flat anchovy fillets, cut in half
1 cup chicken broth
1 tablespoon lemon juice
1 slice bacon, chopped
Hot cooked rice
¼ cup dairy sour cream
¼ teaspoon ginger

1. Slit the skin of the chickens, and insert anchovies in slits as in larding meat.
2. Put chicken, broth, lemon juice, and bacon into a flameproof casserole or Dutch oven. Cover; simmer about 1 hour, or until chicken is tender.
3. Spoon hot rice onto platter. Set chicken on rice.
4. Blend sour cream and ginger into liquid in casserole. Heat just until mixture bubbles; do not boil. Serve sauce over chicken.

4 to 6 servings

691 Chicken Polish Style (Kurczęta po Polsku)

1 chicken (2 to 3 pounds)
Salt
Chicken livers
¾ cup dry bread crumbs
1 egg
1 teaspoon dill weed
¼ teaspoon pepper
½ cup milk (about)
⅓ cup melted butter

1. Sprinkle the chicken with salt. Let stand 1 hour.
2. Chop the livers finely. Combine with bread crumbs, egg, salt to taste, dill, pepper, and as much milk as needed for a loose, sour-cream-like consistency.
3. Fill cavity of chicken with crumb mixture; truss. Place chicken in roasting pan.
4. Bake at 400°F about 45 minutes, or until chicken is tender. Baste often with melted butter.

About 4 servings

Chicken with Ham: Prepare Chicken Polish Style as directed. Substitute **6 ounces (1 cup) ground ham, ½ cup sliced mushrooms,** and **2 crushed juniper berries** for the chicken livers. Add **½ cup sherry** to pan drippings for a sauce.

692 Roast Turkey with Anchovies
(Pieczony Indyk z Sardelami)

1 turkey (12 to 15 pounds)
5 slices bacon
1 large onion, minced
¾ pound veal (2 cups ground)
3 slices stale bread, cubed
⅓ cup milk or chicken broth
1 can (2 ounces) flat anchovies
2 tablespoons butter
2 eggs, beaten
Grated peel and juice of 1 lemon
½ teaspoon pepper
⅔ cup melted butter

1. Rinse turkey with running water. Dry with paper towels.
2. Dice bacon. Fry until transparent. Add onion; stir-fry until golden. Stir in veal, bread cubes, and milk. Remove from heat.
3. Finely chop or mash anchovies. Mix in butter, lemon peel and juice, and pepper; beat until well combined. Add to meat mixture and stir until well blended. Stuffing should be of a paste consistency.
4. Spread stuffing in cavity of turkey. Truss.
5. Place turkey in roasting pan. If desired, insert meat thermometer in thickest part of breast.
6. Roast at 425°F about 3½ hours, basting frequently with melted butter and pan drippings. When done, leg of turkey moves easily and meat thermometer registers 180° to 185°F.

12 to 18 servings

693 Smothered Duck in Caper Sauce
(Kaczka Duszona w Sosie Kaparowym)

1 duck (5 to 6 pounds), cut up
1 clove garlic, crushed (optional)
Salt and pepper
3 tablespoons butter or bacon drippings
1 cup chicken or beef bouillon
2 tablespoons water
2 teaspoons cornstarch
⅓ cup capers
2 teaspoons brown or caramelized sugar
1 tablespoon lemon juice

1. Rub duck with garlic. Sprinkle cavity with salt and pepper to taste. Let stand 1 to 2 hours.
2. Melt butter in a heavy skillet or Dutch oven. Add duck and brown quickly on all sides. Drain off fat, if desired.
3. Add bouillon. Cover. Simmer over medium heat about 1 hour, or until duck is tender.
4. Remove duck to a heated platter.
5. Blend water into cornstarch. Stir into hot liquid in Dutch oven. Add capers, cook and stir over high heat until sauce boils. Reduce heat. Add sugar and lemon juice. Stir just until sauce is thickened.

About 4 servings

694 Duck with Red Cabbage
(Kaczka Duszona z Kapustą)

1 head red cabbage, shredded
1 onion, chopped
Salt
6 ounces salt pork, diced
½ cup red wine or chicken broth
1 duck (5 to 6 pounds)

1. Put cabbage and onion into a bowl, sprinkle with salt, and let stand 10 minutes. Squeeze out liquid.
2. Fry salt pork in a skillet until golden. Add cabbage-onion mixture and wine. Cover and simmer 20 minutes.
3. Place duck in a roasting pan.
4. Bake at 425°F 30 minutes. Drain off fat. Spoon cabbage mixture over duck. Reduce oven temperature to 350°F. Bake about 45 minutes, or until duck is tender. Baste frequently.

About 4 servings

695 *Capon in Cream (Kapłon z Kremem z Pieca)*

1 capon or chicken (5 to 6 pounds)
Salt
2 cups chicken stock or broth
4 egg yolks
1 tablespoon melted butter
4 teaspoons flour
2 cups dairy sour cream
1 teaspoon salt
¼ teaspoon pepper

1. Sprinkle cavity of bird with salt. Place in a large kettle.
2. Add stock to kettle. Cover. Simmer until just tender (about 1 hour). Allow to cool.
3. Meanwhile, cream egg yolks and butter; add flour and blend thoroughly. Stir in sour cream. Season with 1 teaspoon salt and pepper. Beat at high speed until stiff. Cook until thickened in top of a double boiler, stirring constantly to keep from curdling or sticking (handle like hollandaise sauce). Cool.
4. Make cuts in capon as for carving, but without cutting through. Place in a shallow baking pan. Fill cuts with sauce, then spread remainder over the whole surface of the bird.
5. Bake at 425°F about 20 minutes, or until sauce is browned.
6. Meanwhile, boil liquid in which chicken was cooked until it is reduced to 1 cup of stock.
7. To serve, pour stock over capon. Carve at the table.

About 6 servings

696 *Potted Pheasant (Bażant Pieczony)*

¾ cup all-purpose flour
½ teaspoon salt
¼ teaspoon pepper
1 pheasant, cut in pieces
½ cup butter
1 onion, quartered
1 stalk celery, cut up
2 cups meat stock or beef broth
3 whole allspice
½ cup whipping cream
2 tablespoons sherry

1. Mix flour with salt and pepper.
2. Coat each piece of pheasant with seasoned flour. Melt butter in a Dutch oven or flameproof casserole. Brown pheasant in butter. Add onion, celery, and 1 cup meat stock. Cover.
3. Bake at 350°F 40 minutes. Add remaining meat stock. Do not cover. Bake about 40 minutes longer, or until pheasant is tender.
4. Remove pheasant to heated platter. Strain broth; combine 1 cup broth with cream and sherry. Serve over the pheasant.

2 to 4 servings

697 *Smothered Pigeons (Potrawka z Gołębi)*

3 tablespoons butter
2 pigeons (about 2 pounds)
3 onions, sliced
1 cup meat stock or broth
2 tart apples, cored and sliced
¼ cup sliced mushrooms
Juice of ½ lemon
⅓ cup Madeira
1 tablespoon butter or margarine
(at room temperature)
1 tablespoon Browned Flour
1 cup dairy sour cream

1. Melt butter in a large skillet. Sauté pigeons in butter 15 minutes. Remove pigeons.
2. Fry onions in the butter left in skillet until tender. Add stock, sliced apples, mushrooms, and lemon juice. Mix well and bring to boiling. Add wine.
3. Mix butter with flour until smooth. Stir into liquid in skillet. Cook and stir until mixture is thickened.
4. Dip pigeons in sour cream; return to skillet. Cook, covered, until tender.

2 servings

Browned Flour: Spread 1½ cups all-purpose flour in a shallow baking pan. Place on lowest position for broiler. Broil and stir about 20 minutes, or until flour is golden brown. Stirring must be almost constant to prevent burning. If flour burns, skim off burned portion and continue browning remainder. Cool. Store in tightly covered container.

About 1⅓ cups

698 *Baked Pigeon (Gołąb Pieczony)*

1 pigeon
Salt and pepper
1 strip bacon, diced
Melted butter

1. Soak the pigeon about 2 hours in cold water. Dry with paper towels.
2. Sprinkle cavity with salt and pepper.
3. Make small slits in skin; insert pieces of bacon. Place in a roasting pan.
4. Bake at 350°F 30 to 40 minutes, or until tender; baste often with butter.

1 serving

699 *Wild Duck, Goose, or Partridge*
(Dzika Kaczka, Gęś, lub Kuropatwy)

2 partridges, 1 duck, or 1 goose
12 peppercorns
1 onion, quartered
Salt
14 to 20 juniper seeds, ground or mashed
2 tablespoons bacon drippings or butter
½ cup water
2 cups sliced red cabbage
1 large onion, sliced
½ cup water
1 tablespoon cornstarch or potato starch
2 tablespoons water
½ teaspoon sugar
1 teaspoon vinegar
¾ cup red wine

1. Place partridges in a plastic bag with peppercorns and quartered onion. Refrigerate 3 days to age.
2. Discard peppercorns and quartered onion. Cut up bird. Sprinkle with salt and juniper. Let stand 1 hour.
3. Heat bacon drippings in a large skillet. Brown bird in the drippings; add ½ cup water. Cover and simmer 1 hour.
4. Add cabbage, sliced onion, and ½ cup water. Cover and simmer 30 minutes. Remove the meat to a warmed platter.
5. Mix the cornstarch with 2 tablespoons water to make a smooth paste. Stir into drippings in pan.
6. Stir in sugar and vinegar; bring to boiling. Cook and stir 2 minutes. Remove from heat. Stir in wine.

4 servings

700 *Cornish Hens with Raisin Stuffing*

Plumped raisins and rice are the base of the stuffing. Grapevine leaves cover the breasts of the Cornish hens to retain moistness.

4 Cornish hens (1 to 1½ pounds each)
Salt
*16 grapevine leaves preserved in brine
⅔ cup dark raisins
⅓ cup brandy
¾ cup cooked long-grain rice
1¼ cups finely chopped carrot
1¼ cups finely chopped celery
½ teaspoon cinnamon
1 tablespoon clarified butter
¼ teaspoon salt
⅛ teaspoon pepper
½ cup brandy

1. Rinse hens and pat dry; sprinkle lightly with salt.
2. Soak grapevine leaves in cold water 20 minutes. Pat dry. Set aside.
3. Simmer raisins in brandy 15 minutes; remove from heat and let stand 15 minutes. Stir in rice, carrot, celery, cinnamon, clarified butter, ¼ teaspoon salt, and the pepper. Spoon stuffing lightly into cavities of hens. Place hens on rack in a roasting pan. Cover breasts with grapevine leaves.
4. Roast in a 325°F oven 1¼ to 1½ hours, or until hens are tender. Baste with brandy during last ½ hour of roasting. Let hens stand 15 minutes before serving. Remove grapevine leaves.

4 servings

*Grapevine leaves can be purchased in a gourmet shop or in the specialty department of a supermarket.

701 *Roast Chicken Tarragon*

Based on the classic French recipe, the sauce is made without whipping cream, flour, and eggs. It is delicately flavored with tarragon and spooned over roasted chicken.

1 broiler-fryer chicken (2½ to 3 pounds)
2 teaspoons clarified butter
2 teaspoons snipped fresh or 1 teaspoon dried tarragon leaves
Salt
2 carrots, cut in 1-inch pieces
1 small onion, cut in quarters
1 stalk celery, cut in 1-inch pieces
2 sprigs parsley
●1¼ cups Chicken Stock
1 tablespoon arrowroot
Cold water
½ teaspoon salt
¼ teaspoon freshly ground white pepper
2 teaspoons snipped fresh or 1 teaspoon dried tarragon leaves
2 tablespoons dry sherry

1. Rinse chicken; pat dry. Place in a roasting pan. Brush chicken with clarified butter, sprinkle with 2 teaspoons tarragon. Sprinkle cavity with salt; fill cavity with carrot, onion, celery, and parsley.
2. Roast in a 325°F oven about 2½ hours, or until chicken is done; meat on drumstick will be very tender. Remove chicken to a platter. Remove vegetables; reserve. Cover loosely with aluminum foil and let stand 20 minutes before carving.
3. Spoon fat from roasting pan. Heat stock to simmering in roasting pan, stirring to incorporate particles from pan. Mix arrowroot with a little cold water; stir into stock with salt, pepper, 2 teaspoons tarragon, and the sherry. Simmer, stirring constantly, until stock is thickened (about 5 minutes).
4. Slice chicken and arrange on platter. Garnish with reserved vegetables. Serve with sauce.

4 servings

702 *Chicken with Poached Garlic*

The garlic, poached without peeling, imparts a delicate flavor to the chicken.

1 broiler-fryer chicken (2½ to 3 pounds)
1 garlic clove, peeled and cut in half
Juice of 1 lime
Salt
Freshly ground white pepper
16 garlic cloves (unpeeled)
● ½ cup Chicken Stock
¼ cup dry vermouth
Chicken Stock
2 teaspoons arrowroot
Cold water
● ¼ cup Mock Crème Fraîche
1 tablespoon snipped parsley
Salt
Freshly ground white pepper

1. Rinse chicken; pat dry. Place in a roasting pan. Rub entire surface of chicken with cut garlic clove. Squeeze lime juice over chicken. Sprinkle cavity and outside of chicken lightly with salt and pepper. Place remaining garlic cloves around chicken; pour in ½ cup stock and ¼ cup dry vermouth.
2. Roast in a 325°F oven about 2½ hours, or until done; meat on drumstick will be very tender. Add stock if necessary to keep garlic covered. Remove chicken to platter. Cover loosely with aluminum foil. Let stand 20 minutes before carving.
3. Spoon fat from roasting pan. Add enough stock to pan to make 1 cup of liquid. Mix arrowroot with a little cold water; stir into stock. Simmer, stirring constantly, until thickened (about 3 minutes). Stir in Mock Crème Fraîche and parsley. Season to taste with salt and pepper. Pass sauce with chicken.

4 servings

Note: To eat garlic cloves, gently press with fingers; the soft cooked interior will slip out. The flavor of the poached garlic is very delicate.

703 *Chicken en Cocotte*

1½ cups sliced leeks, white part only
1 medium zucchini, cut in ¼-inch slices
2 large sweet red or green peppers, cut in ¼-inch strips
1 large green pepper, cut in ¼-inch strips
2 teaspoons snipped fresh or 1 teaspoon finely crushed dried rosemary leaves
2 teaspoons snipped fresh or 1 teaspoon finely crushed dried thyme leaves
1½ teaspoons salt
⅓ cup dry sauterne or other white wine
1 roasting chicken (about 3 pounds)
1 teaspoon clarified butter
Salt
1 small bunch parsley
1 cup 3-inch pieces leek, green part only
1 tablespoon dry sauterne or other white wine

1. Arrange 1½ cups leeks, the zucchini, and peppers in bottom of a Dutch oven. Mix rosemary, thyme, and 1½ teaspoons salt; sprinkle one third of herb mixture over vegetables. Pour ⅓ cup sauterne over vegetables.
2. Rinse chicken and pat dry. Rub chicken with butter and sprinkle with remaining herb mixture. Lightly salt cavity of chicken. Stuff cavity with parsley and green part of leeks; sprinkle with 1 tablespoon sauterne. Place chicken in Dutch oven; cover with lid.
3. Bake at 325°F 2 hours, or until tender. Remove chicken to platter; discard parsley and leek from cavity. Surround chicken with vegetables.

4 servings

704 *Roast Turkey with Pineapple-Stuffed Breast*

A stuffing of pineapple, cooked poultry, and curry is carefully spread beneath the skin of the turkey breast so that the flavors are absorbed while roasting.

1 turkey (10 to 12 pounds)
1½ tablespoons curry powder
2 teaspoons salt
⅓ cup minced onion
4 garlic cloves, minced
1 teaspoon minced ginger root
2 tablespoons vegetable oil
⅔ cup unsweetened pineapple juice
1 can (20 ounces) unsweetened crushed pineapple, drained
1½ cups minced cooked turkey or chicken
Unsweetened pineapple juice

1. Rinse turkey; pat dry. Carefully loosen skin over turkey breast by running fingers under the skin.
2. Mix curry powder, salt, onion, garlic, ginger root, vegetable oil, and ⅔ cup pineapple juice. Mix one quarter of the spice mixture with the drained pineapple and minced turkey. Spread pineapple mixture gently and evenly under skin of turkey breast with fingers. Place turkey in a roasting pan. Insert meat thermometer in thickest part of thigh. Brush remaining spice mixture over turkey breast.
3. Roast in a 325°F oven until thermometer registers 175°F (3½ to 4 hours); baste occasionally with pineapple juice. Remove turkey to serving platter; cover loosely with aluminum foil. Let stand 20 minutes before carving.

About 16 servings

Note: This recipe can be used for a roasting chicken of about 5 pounds. Use half the spice and pineapple mixtures; proceed as directed. Roast at 325°F about 2½ hours, or until chicken is tender; drumstick meat will feel very soft.

705 *Capon Roasted in Salt*

The salt casing leaves the chicken lean, moist, and tender with just a tinge of salt flavor.

1 capon (about 5 pounds)
Salt
1 carrot, cut in 1-inch pieces
1 medium onion, cut in quarters
2 sprigs parsley
6 to 7 pounds coarse kosher salt
Watercress

1. Rinse capon; pat dry. Salt inside of cavity lightly; fill cavity with vegetables.
2. Line a deep Dutch oven (that will fit size of capon, allowing 1½ to 2 inches space on bottom, sides, and top) with heavy-duty aluminum foil, allowing 2 inches of foil to fold down over top edge of pan. Fill bottom of Dutch oven with a 1½-inch layer of salt. Place capon in Dutch oven. Carefully fill Dutch oven with salt, being careful not to get salt inside cavity of capon. Layer salt over top of capon.
3. Roast uncovered in a 400°F oven 2 hours. Remove from oven. Let stand 15 minutes.
4. Lay Dutch oven on its side. Using foil lining, gently pull salt-encased capon from Dutch oven. Break salt from capon, using an ice pick or screwdriver and hammer. Place capon on serving platter; remove vegetables from cavity. Garnish with watercress. Serve immediately.

4 servings

706 *Capon with Vegetable Dressing*

The intriguing combination of vegetables gives the impression of an old-time stuffing.

1 capon (about 5 pounds)
½ can (10½-ounce size)
    condensed onion soup
1 medium eggplant, pared and
    cut in ½-inch cubes
1 cup chopped onion
1 cup chopped celery
1 cup chopped carrot
1½ to 2 teaspoons salt
¼ teaspoon freshly ground
    pepper
2 teaspoons poultry seasoning
¼ cup snipped parsley
2 eggs, beaten

1. Rinse capon; pat dry with paper toweling. Place capon on rack in a roasting pan. Pour onion soup over.
2. Roast in a 325°F oven about 2½ hours, or until capon is done; meat on drumstick will be very tender.
3. Remove capon to a serving platter; let stand 15 minutes before carving.
4. While capon is roasting, simmer eggplant in 1 inch of **salted water** until tender (about 10 minutes); drain.
5. Process onion, celery, and carrot in a food processor or blender until finely ground; transfer mixture to a mixing bowl. Mix in eggplant and remaining ingredients. Spoon vegetable mixture into a lightly oiled 2-quart casserole; do not cover.
6. Bake at 325°F 45 minutes. Remove to serving bowl.

4 servings

Note: Do not bake vegetable dressing in cavity of capon because the correct texture will not be obtained.

This dressing is excellent served with pork.

707 *Chicken Meringue*

Meringue replaces the need for a pastry crust in this colorful chicken pot pie.

10 tiny boiling onions
2 stalks celery, cut in 1-inch pieces
1 large sweet red pepper, cut in ½-inch pieces
2 carrots, cut in ½-inch slices
● 2 cups Chicken Stock
4 cups cubed cooked chicken
½ pound medium mushrooms, cut in half
½ pound fresh pea pods, or 1 package (10 ounces) frozen pea pods, thawed
2 tablespoons cornstarch
Cold water
Salt
Freshly ground pepper
4 egg whites
½ teaspoon salt
¼ teaspoon cream of tartar
1 tablespoon snipped fresh or 1½ teaspoons dried chervil leaves
2 tablespoons instant nonfat dry-milk solids

1. Simmer onions, celery, red pepper, and carrot in stock until just tender (about 8 minutes). Remove vegetables with slotted spoon and mix with chicken, mushrooms, and pea pods in a 2-quart casserole.
2. Mix cornstarch with a little cold water. Stir into stock: simmer, stirring constantly, until mixture thickens (about 4 minutes). Season to taste with salt and pepper. Pour over chicken in casserole.
3. Bake covered at 350°F 15 minutes.
4. Beat egg whites and ½ teaspoon salt until foamy. Add cream of tartar and chervil; continue beating, adding dry-milk solids gradually, until egg whites form stiff but not dry peaks. Spread meringue over casserole mixture, sealing to edges of casserole.
5. Bake at 350°F 12 to 14 minutes, or until meringue is lightly browned. Serve immediately.

4 to 6 servings

708 *Chicken Livers Marsala*

Green pepper, onion, and water chestnuts provide crisp contrast to the smooth texture of the chicken livers.

1 cup diced green pepper
½ cup finely chopped onion
⅔ cup water chestnuts, sliced in half
● 1½ cups Chicken Stock
¼ cup Marsala wine
1½ pounds chicken livers, cut in half (discard membrane)
2 teaspoons arrowroot
Cold water
½ teaspoon bottled brown bouquet sauce
Salt
Freshly ground pepper
Parsley sprigs

1. Simmer green pepper, onion, and water chestnuts in stock and wine until tender (about 5 minutes). Remove from stock with slotted spoon; keep warm. Add chicken livers to stock; simmer until livers are tender (about 8 minutes). Remove livers from stock with slotted spoon; add to vegetables and keep warm.
2. Mix arrowroot with a little cold water. Stir into stock. Simmer, stirring constantly, until it thickens (about 3 minutes). Stir brown bouquet sauce, vegetables. and livers into sauce. Season with salt and pepper to taste. Heat until hot. Spoon into ramekins. Garnish with parsley. Serve at once.

4 servings

709 *Vegetable-Stuffed Chicken Breasts*

Chicken breasts are rolled around a flavorful vegetable mixture and baked with creamy Cauliflower Sauce and Swiss cheese—elegant for entertaining.

3 whole large chicken breasts (about 3 pounds), boned, halved, and skinned
¾ pound cauliflower
¼ pound broccoli
● Chicken Stock
½ cup finely chopped celery
2 shallots, minced
½ teaspoon salt
● Cauliflower Sauce (do not add cheese or parsley)
3 ounces Swiss cheese, shredded
Snipped parsley

1. Rinse chicken breasts; pat dry. Pound with mallet until even in thickness; set aside.
2. Remove leaves and tough stalks from cauliflower and broccoli; separate into flowerets. Simmer covered in 1 inch of stock until tender (about 8 minutes). Coarsely chop the cauliflower and broccoli; mix with the celery, shallots, and salt.
3. Spoon mixture onto chicken breasts; roll up carefully and place seam side down in a lightly oiled shallow baking pan. Spoon Cauliflower Sauce over breasts.
4. Bake covered at 350°F 40 minutes. Uncover and bake 15 minutes. Sprinkle cheese over breasts; bake until cheese is melted (about 5 minutes). Arrange chicken on platter; sprinkle with parsley.

6 servings

710 *Curried Breast of Chicken Salad*

6 cups bite-size pieces cooked chicken
1½ cups sliced celery
1 can (8½ ounces) water chestnuts, drained and cut in thirds
½ teaspoon salt
¼ teaspoon finely ground pepper
● 1 cup Mock Mayonnaise
1 teaspoon curry powder
2 tablespoons dry sherry
Lettuce leaves
Orange slices

1. Combine chicken, celery, water chestnuts, salt, and pepper.
2. Mix Mock Mayonnaise, curry, and sherry; stir gently into chicken mixture. Serve on lettuce-lined plates; garnish with orange slices.

6 servings

711 *Ducklings with Green Peppercorn Sauce*

2 ducklings (about 4½ pounds each)
1½ teaspoons salt
¼ teaspoon freshly ground pepper
1 teaspoon snipped fresh or ½ teaspoon dried crumbled rosemary leaves
● Chicken Stock
● Green Peppercorn Sauce

1. Rinse ducklings; pat dry. Place ducklings breast side up on rack in a roasting pan. Sprinkle with salt, pepper, and rosemary. Pierce breasts of ducklings with a fork several times.
2. Roast in a 350°F oven about 2½ hours, or until ducklings are done; drumstick meat will feel very tender. Baste ducklings occasionally with stock. Remove ducklings to a serving platter; let stand 15 minutes before carving.
3. Serve with the sauce.

6 to 8 servings

712 *Duckling with Fruit Salad*

2 ducklings (about 4½ pounds each)
2 teaspoons salt
½ teaspoon freshly ground pepper
¾ teaspoon allspice
½ cup fruit juice
6 slices fresh or canned pineapple
6 preserved kumquats, thinly sliced
3 oranges, peeled and segments removed
2 apples, sliced
2 papayas, peeled and sliced, if desired
2 bananas, sliced
1 pound white grapes
1 lime, cut in 6 wedges
1 lemon, cut in 6 wedges
● 1½ cups Low-Fat Yogurt
2 tablespoons snipped mint
Mint sprigs

1. Rinse ducklings; pat dry. Place ducklings breast side up on rack in a roasting pan. Sprinkle with salt, pepper, and allspice. Pierce breasts of ducklings with a fork several times.
2. Roast in a 350°F oven about 2½ hours, or until ducklings are done; drumstick meat will feel very soft. Baste ducklings occasionally with fruit juice. Remove ducklings to platter; let cool.
3. While ducklings are roasting, prepare fruits; refrigerate. Mix yogurt and snipped mint; refrigerate.
4. Carefully cut skin and fat from ducklings. Remove meat from carcass carefully, keeping meat in as large pieces as possible. Arrange duckling meat and fruits attractively on individual plates. Garnish with mint. Pass chilled yogurt sauce.

6 servings

713 *Crumb-Crusted Duckling Halves*

The ducklings are covered with grapevine leaves to insure moistness. A delicious crumb coating adds crispness. Serve with a variety of sauces.

*16 grapevine leaves preserved in brine
2 ducklings (about 4½ pounds each), cut in half
2 teaspoons salt
● ½ cup Chicken Stock
Juice of 1 lemon
Clarified butter
⅓ cup seasoned stuffing crumbs, slightly crushed
● Cumberland Sauce or
● Madeira Sauce

1. Soak grapevine leaves in cold water 20 minutes. Pat dry. Set aside.
2. Using fingers and a sharp knife, remove skin and excess fat from ducklings (do not skin wings). Place ducklings breast side up on rack in a roasting pan; sprinkle with salt. Cover surface of ducks with grapevine leaves.
3. Roast in a 325°F oven about 2½ hours, or until ducklings are done; drumstick meat will feel soft. Baste ducklings every half hour with a mixture of stock and lemon juice.
4. Remove grapevine leaves. Brush ducklings very lightly with butter and sprinkle with crumbs. Broil 4 inches from heat until crumbs are browned (about 5 minutes). Remove ducklings to platter; let stand 10 minutes before serving. Serve with desired sauce.

4 servings

*Grapevine leaves can be purchased in a gourmet shop or in the specialty section of a supermarket.

714 *Fried Chicken (Pollo Fritto)*

1 frying chicken (about 3
    pounds), cut in serving pieces
½ cup flour
1½ teaspoons salt
¼ teaspoon pepper
    Olive oil
2 eggs, well beaten
¼ cup milk
1 tablespoon chopped parsley
½ cup grated Parmesan cheese
1 to 2 tablespoons water

1. Rinse chicken and pat dry with paper towels. To coat chicken evenly, shake 2 or 3 pieces at a time in a plastic bag containing the flour, salt, and pepper.
2. Fill a large, heavy skillet ½-inch deep with olive oil; place over medium heat.
3. Combine eggs, milk, and parsley. Dip each chicken piece in the egg mixture and roll in cheese. Starting with meaty pieces, place the chicken, skin-side down, in the hot oil. Turn pieces as necessary to brown evenly on all sides.
4. When chicken is browned, reduce heat, pour in water, and cover pan tightly. Cook chicken slowly 25 to 40 minutes, or until all pieces are tender. For crisp skin, uncover chicken the last 10 minutes of cooking.

3 or 4 servings

715 *Chicken Breasts Regina (Petti di Pollo Regina)*

2 whole chicken breasts, skinned,
    boned, and cut in half
4 thin slices ham
4 thin slices liver sausage or liver
    pâté
    Water
    Flour
1 egg, beaten
    Fine dry bread crumbs
3 tablespoons butter
● Madeira Sauce

1. Split chicken breast halves lengthwise, but not completely through. Open breast halves and pound until very thin.
2. Place a slice of ham, then a slice of liver sausage in center of each breast. Fold in half, enclosing the ham and liver sausage, moisten the edges with water, and press together.
3. Coat chicken breasts with flour, dip in beaten egg, and coat with bread crumbs.
4. Fry in butter in a skillet until golden brown on both sides. Serve with hot Madeira Sauce.

4 servings

716 *Wild Pigeons Perugian (Palombacci alla Perugina)*

3 pigeons or Rock Cornish hens
4 to 6 tablespoons olive oil
1 cup dry red wine
10 green olives
4 fresh sage leaves or ¼ teaspoon
    ground sage
½ teaspoon juniper berries
½ teaspoon salt
    Dash pepper

1. Brown pigeons in 2 tablespoons hot olive oil in a Dutch oven, adding more oil if necessary. Stir in wine, 2 tablespoons olive oil, olives, sage, juniper berries, salt, and pepper.
2. Cook in a 300°F oven 50 to 60 minutes, or until pigeons are tender.

4 servings

717 *Chicken Vesuvio (Pollo alla Vesuviana)*

1 broiler-fryer chicken (2 to 3
    pounds), cut in pieces
½ cup flour
1½ teaspoons salt
¼ teaspoon pepper
½ cup olive oil
2 tablespoons olive oil
1 clove garlic, sliced
2 tablespoons Marsala
½ teaspoon chopped parsley
● Deep-Fried Potatoes

1. Coat chicken pieces with a mixture of flour, salt, and pepper.
2. Heat ½ cup oil in a large skillet. Add chicken pieces and brown on all sides. Put into a large, shallow baking dish.
3. Heat 2 tablespoons oil and garlic until garlic is lightly browned. Add Marsala and parsley; mix well. Pour over chicken in baking dish.
4. Bake at 325°F about 45 minutes, or until chicken is tender; turn once.
5. Prepare potatoes and place around edges of baking dish.

4 servings

718 *Country Style Chicken (Pollo alla Paesana)*

1 frying chicken (about 3
    pounds), cut in serving pieces
2 tablespoons butter
2 tablespoons olive oil
1 medium-size onion, sliced
1 teaspoon salt
⅛ teaspoon pepper
1 pound zucchini
2 large green peppers
1½ tablespoons olive oil
1 teaspoon chopped basil leaves,
    or ¼ teaspoon dried sweet
    basil
½ cup dry white wine

1. In a large skillet, brown the chicken in butter and 2 tablespoons olive oil. Place onion around chicken; sprinkle with salt and pepper. Cover and cook slowly about 15 minutes.
2. While chicken is cooking, wash and cut zucchini in ½-inch-thick slices. Wash peppers; remove stems and seeds. Rinse in cold water and slice lengthwise into 1-inch-wide strips.
3. In another skillet, heat 1½ tablespoons olive oil and sauté zucchini and peppers until soft (about 10 minutes). Sprinkle with basil. Transfer vegetables to skillet with chicken and pour in wine.
4. Simmer, covered, about 15 minutes, or until chicken is very tender and vegetables are cooked.

About 4 servings

719 *Chicken Cacciatore*

Cacciatore, meaning "hunter" in Italian, indicates that the food (usually chicken), is prepared in the "hunter's style," that is, simmering the fowl in a well-seasoned tomato and wine sauce.

¼ cup cooking oil
1 broiler-fryer (2½ pounds), cut up
2 onions, sliced
2 cloves garlic, minced
3 tomatoes, cored and quartered
2 green peppers, sliced
1 small bay leaf
1 teaspoon salt
¼ teaspoon pepper
½ teaspoon celery seed
1 teaspoon crushed oregano or
    basil
1 can (8 ounces) tomato sauce
¼ cup sauterne
8 ounces spaghetti, cooked
    according to package directions

1. Heat oil in a large, heavy skillet; add chicken and brown on all sides. Remove from skillet.
2. Add onion and garlic to oil remaining in skillet and cook until onion is tender, but not brown; stir occasionally.
3. Return chicken to skillet and add the tomatoes, green pepper, and bay leaf.
4. Mix salt, pepper, celery seed, and oregano and blend with tomato sauce; pour over all.
5. Cover and cook over low heat 45 minutes. Blend in wine and cook, uncovered, 20 minutes longer. Discard bay leaf.
6. Put the cooked spaghetti onto a hot serving platter and top with the chicken and sauce.

About 6 servings

720 *Chicken and Mushrooms in Sour Cream Sauce*

2 frying chickens, cut in serving pieces
¼ cup oil
1 pound fresh mushrooms, cleaned and sliced
2 cups canned tomatoes with juice (16-ounce can)
2 canned green chilies, seeded
½ cup chopped onion
1 clove garlic, minced
1 cup chicken stock (or water plus chicken bouillon cube)
1½ teaspoons salt
1 cup dairy sour cream

1. Brown chicken pieces in hot oil in a large skillet. Place chicken in Dutch oven or heavy saucepot.
2. Sauté mushrooms in oil remaining in skillet; spoon mushrooms over chicken.
3. Combine tomatoes, chilies, onion, and garlic in an electric blender and blend to a purée (if amount is too large for blender container, blend in two portions).
4. Pour purée into fat remaining in skillet in which chicken and mushrooms were cooked; bring to boiling and cook about 5 minutes. Stir in chicken stock and salt.
5. Pour sauce over chicken and mushrooms in Dutch oven. Cover and cook over low heat until chicken is tender (about 1 hour).
6. Just before serving, stir in sour cream and heat through, but do not boil.

6 to 8 servings

721 *Chicken Tablecloth Stainer*

Mexicans love to give humorous names to foods, and this particular dish is undoubtedly well-named. The reason becomes obvious when you see the deep red color of the sauce, caused by the dark pasilla chilies called for in the recipe. This same sauce is often used with pork, and occasionally both pork and chicken are combined in the same recipe.

2 frying chickens (about 2½ pounds each), cut in serving pieces
½ pound link sausages
½ cup canned pineapple chunks, drained
1 apple, pared, cored, and sliced
1 large, firm banana, sliced
Sauce:
2 fresh or dried ancho chilies and 2 fresh or dried pasilla chilies, or 1 tablespoon chili powder
1 cup coarsely chopped onion
1 clove garlic
2 cups (16-ounce can) tomatoes with juice
½ cup whole blanched almonds
¼ teaspoon cinnamon
⅛ teaspoon cloves
2 cups chicken stock, or 2 cups water plus 2 chicken bouillon cubes
Salt and pepper

1. Put chicken pieces into a Dutch oven or heavy kettle.
2. Fry sausages in a skillet until browned. Put into Dutch oven with chicken. Arrange pineapple, apple, and banana over chicken.
3. For sauce, first prepare chilies . (If chilies are not available, substitute chili powder.) Combine chilies, onion, garlic, tomatoes, almonds, cinnamon, and cloves in an electric blender. Blend to a smooth purée.
4. Heat the fat remaining in the skillet in which the sausages were cooked. Add the blended sauce and cook about 5 minutes, stirring constantly. Stir in chicken stock. Season to taste with salt and pepper.
5. Pour sauce over chicken in Dutch oven. Cover and simmer over low heat 1 hour, or until chicken is tender.

6 to 8 servings

722 *Chicken with Rice* (Arroz con Pollo)

1 broiler-fryer chicken, (2 to 3 pounds), cut in pieces
¼ cup fat
½ cup chopped onion
1 clove garlic, minced
1 large tomato, chopped
3 cups hot water
1 cup uncooked rice
1 tablespoon minced parsley
2 teaspoons salt
½ teaspoon paprika
¼ teaspoon pepper
¼ teaspoon saffron
1 bay leaf

1. Rinse chicken and pat dry with absorbent paper.
2. Heat fat in a skillet over medium heat. Add onion and garlic; cook until onion is tender. Remove with a slotted spoon; set aside.
3. Put chicken pieces, skin side down, in skillet. Turn to brown pieces on all sides.
4. When chicken is browned, add tomato, onion, water, rice, parsley, and dry seasonings. Cover and cook over low heat about 45 minutes, or until thickest pieces of chicken are tender when pierced with a fork.

6 to 8 servings

723 *Marinated Chicken* (Pollo Escabeche)

2 broiler-fryer chickens, cut in serving pieces
1½ cups oil
1 cup cooked sliced carrots
2 large onions, sliced
2 stalks celery, cut in 2-inch pieces
1 clove garlic, minced
⅛ teaspoon thyme
⅛ teaspoon marjoram
1 small bay leaf
12 peppercorns
1 teaspoon salt
3 cups vinegar
Olives, radishes, pickled chilies

1. Brown chicken pieces in hot oil in a skillet. Place browned chicken in a Dutch oven or heavy kettle. Top with carrots, onions, celery, garlic, thyme, marjoram, bay leaf, peppercorns, and salt. Pour vinegar over all.
2. Simmer over low heat until chicken is tender (about 30 to 45 minutes).
3. Remove from heat and let cool to room temperature. Place in refrigerator and chill for at least 1 hour.
4. Garnish with olives, radishes, and chilies.

8 to 10 servings

724 *Green Chicken* (Pollo Verde)

1 medium onion, coarsely chopped
1 clove garlic, peeled
1 cup (small can) salsa verde mexicana (Mexican green tomato sauce)
¼ cup (lightly filled) fresh parsley
1 teaspoon salt
¼ teaspoon pepper
2 frying chickens, cut in serving pieces

1. Put onion, garlic, salsa verde, and parsley into an electric blender. Blend until liquefied. Stir in salt and pepper.
2. Rinse chicken pieces and pat dry; arrange pieces in a heavy skillet. Pour green sauce over chicken. Cover; bring to boiling. Cook over low heat until chicken is tender, about 1 hour.

6 servings

725 Chicken or Turkey Mole Poblano I (with canned mole sauce)

1 jar (8 ounces) mole poblano paste
1 cup canned tomato sauce
1 cup chicken stock or water
  Sugar and salt
3 cups diced cooked chicken or
  turkey

1. Blend mole paste, tomato sauce, and stock in a large saucepan. Heat to boiling; add sugar and salt to taste. Reduce heat. Stir in chicken. Simmer about 10 to 15 minutes, stirring occasionally, to blend flavors.
2. To use as a tamale filling, the sauce must be fairly thick, so may be simmered until of desired consistency. Then spoon poultry pieces and sauce onto tamale dough spread on corn husk; use leftover sauce to serve over cooked tamales.
3. Or, Chicken or Turkey Mole Poblano may be served over hot rice.

*About 4 cups filling (enough for
3½ dozen tamales)*

726 Chicken or Turkey Mole Poblano II (from basic ingredients)

6 ancho chilies, fresh or dried
2 cups (16-ounce can) cooked
  tomatoes
1 large onion, coarsely chopped
1 clove garlic, peeled
½ cup salted peanuts or ½ cup
  peanut butter
1 tortilla or 1 piece of toast, torn in
  pieces
⅓ cup raisins
2 tablespoons sesame seed
¼ cup oil
1 tablespoon sugar
¼ teaspoon anise
¼ teaspoon cinnamon
¼ teaspoon cloves
¼ teaspoon coriander
¼ teaspoon cumin (comino)
1 cup chicken or turkey stock
1 ounce (1 square) unsweetened
  chocolate
  Salt and pepper
3 cups diced cooked chicken or
  turkey

1. Prepare chilies . Combine with tomatoes, onion, garlic, peanuts, tortilla, raisins, and sesame seed. Put a small amount at a time into an electric blender and blend to make a thick purée.
2. Heat oil in a large skillet. Add the purée and cook, stirring constantly, about 5 minutes. Stir in sugar, anise, cinnamon, cloves, coriander, cumin, and stock. Bring to boiling, reduce heat, and simmer. Add chocolate and continue simmering, stirring constantly, until chocolate is melted and blended into sauce. Add salt and pepper to taste. Stir in chicken pieces and simmer about 10 minutes.
3. To use as a tamale filling, the sauce must be fairly thick, so it may be simmered until desired consistency is reached. Then spoon poultry pieces and a little sauce onto tamale dough spread on a corn husk. Use leftover sauce to serve over cooked tamales.
4. Or, Chicken or Turkey Mole Poblano may be served over hot rice.

*About 4 cups filling (enough for
3½ dozen tamales)*

727 Piquant Chicken

1 frying chicken, cut in serving
  pieces
  Butter or margarine
6 limes or 4 lemons, sliced as
  thinly as possible
  Salt and pepper

1. Brown chicken pieces in butter in a skillet.
2. Place chicken in an ovenproof casserole. Cover completely with lime or lemon slices. Sprinkle with salt and pepper. Cover tightly with foil.
3. Bake at 325°F about 1¼ hours, or until chicken is tender.
4. Serve plain or with Red Chili Sauce (●).

4 servings

728 *Spiced Fruited Chicken*

1½ teaspoons salt
¼ teaspoon pepper
¼ teaspoon cinnamon
¼ teaspoon cloves
2 cloves garlic, minced
2 frying chickens, cut in serving
     pieces
¼ cup oil
½ cup chopped onion
½ cup raisins
½ cup crushed pineapple
2 cups orange juice
½ cup dry sherry

1. Combine salt, pepper, cinnamon, cloves, and garlic. Rub into chicken pieces.
2. Heat oil in a heavy skillet. Brown chicken in hot oil. Place browned chicken in a Dutch oven or heavy saucepot.
3. Cook onion in remaining oil in skillet until soft (about 5 minutes).
4. Add onion to chicken along with raisins, pineapple, and orange juice. Add water, if needed, to just cover chicken. Bring to boiling, reduce heat, cover, and cook until chicken is tender (about 1 hour). Add sherry and cook about 5 minutes longer to blend flavors.

6 to 8 servings

729 *Stuffed Turkey*

1 turkey (12 to 16 pounds)
  Salt and pepper
  Juice of 1 lemon
  Stuffing (see below)
  Melted butter
Gravy:
  Flour
  Chicken broth
  White wine
  Salt and pepper

1. Clean turkey. Sprinkle inside and out with salt and pepper, then drizzle with lemon juice.
2. Spoon desired amount of stuffing into cavities of turkey. Secure openings with skewers and twine.
3. Put turkey, breast side up, on a rack in a shallow roasting pan. Cover bird with a double thickness of cheesecloth soaked in butter.
4. Roast in a 325°F oven 4½ to 5½ hours, or until done (180°F to 185°F on a meat thermometer inserted in inside thigh muscle or thickest part of breast); baste with drippings several times during roasting.
5. For gravy, stir a small amount of flour with pan drippings. Cook until bubbly. Stir in equal parts of broth and wine. Season to taste with salt and pepper.
6. Put turkey on a platter and garnish with **watercress.** Accompany with gravy.

12 to 16 servings

730 *Stuffing*

5 slices bacon, diced
1 onion, chopped
1 clove garlic, minced
3 pounds ground pork loin
½ cup tomato purée
¾ cup blanched almonds, chopped
½ cup ripe olives, coarsely chopped
6 jalapeño chilies, seeded and
     chopped
3 carrots, pared and sliced
3 bananas, peeled and sliced
3 apples, pared, cored, and diced
¾ cup raisins
2 teaspoons sugar
  Salt and pepper
  Cinnamon

1. Fry bacon until brown in a large skillet. Remove bacon from fat; reserve. Brown onion and garlic in fat in skillet, then brown meat. Discard excess fat.
2. Add tomato purée, almonds, olives, chilies, carrots, fruit, sugar, and salt, pepper, and cinnamon to taste; mix well. Cook several minutes. Mix in bacon. Cool before stuffing turkey.

731 *Martinique Stuffed Chicken in Rum*

1 roaster chicken (about 4 pounds)
1 lime, halved
　Salt and pepper
2 white bread slices with crusts
　　trimmed
1 cup milk
1 package (3 ounces) cream cheese
2 tablespoons amber rum
½ cup chopped chicken livers
2 pork sausage links, casing removed
　　and meat chopped finely
1 scallion or green onion, chopped
1 tablespoon chopped parsley
⅛ teaspoon cayenne or red pepper
　Salt and pepper (optional)

1. Rub chicken skin with the cut side of lime. Season with salt and pepper. Remove the fat deposits from the opening of the cavity. Set chicken and fat aside.
2. Soak bread in milk. Set aside.
3. Combine cream cheese, rum, chicken liver, sausage, scallion, parsley, and cayenne.
4. Squeeze bread and add to mixture; discard milk. Add salt and pepper, if desired. Mix well.
5. Stuff cavity of chicken with the mixture, then tie chicken legs and wings to hold close to body.
6. Place chicken, breast side up, on rack in a shallow roasting pan. Lay reserved fat across breast.
7. Roast in a 375°F oven about 2 hours.
8. Garnish with **watercress** and serve with Smothered Mixed Vegetables (●).

4 to 6 servings

732 *Braised Chicken and Onions*
(Maman Poule à la Chaudière)

1 stewing chicken (about 4 pounds)
　Papaya leaves
1 lime, halved
1 orange, halved
　Salt and freshly ground pepper
　　to taste
3 tablespoons soybean, olive, or
　　peanut oil
3 tablespoons bacon drippings
2 tablespoons water
24 small onions
2 cups chicken stock
2 tablespoons butter
2 tablespoons cornstarch
　Chopped parsley
　Chopped scallions or green onions

1. Truss chicken. Wrap in papaya leaves and refrigerate for 12 hours.
2. Rub the chicken with the cut sides of the lime and orange. Season with salt and pepper.
3. Heat oil and bacon drippings in a Dutch oven. Brown chicken. Add water and cover.
4. Cook in a 375°F oven about 2 hours, or until almost tender; turn occasionally and stir the juices. Add stock if more liquid is needed.
5. Add onions and continue cooking until onions are tender and well browned (about 30 minutes).
6. Place chicken and onions on a large serving platter. Carve bird.
7. Pour stock into Dutch oven and set over medium heat to deglaze. Mix butter and cornstarch and add to stock. Stir until sauce is slightly thicker.
8. Pour sauce over meat and sprinkle with chopped parsley and scallions. Serve with Coconut and Rice (●).

6 to 8 servings

733 *Barbecued Chicken, Quail, or Guinea Fowl*

　Chicken, quail, or guinea fowl
● Creole Barbecue Sauce

1. Split the birds in half and remove the backbone and neck.
2. Marinate birds overnight in Creole Barbecue Sauce.
3. Place bird halves on a grill 5 inches from glowing coals. Barbecue 25 minutes, turning several times and basting with the barbecue sauce.
4. Serve with **barbecued yams**

Allow ½ bird per serving

734 *Chicken with Cashews*

In the Caribbean, this dish is traditionally served with preserves made from the cashew fruit, but in the United States, guava jelly is an acceptable substitute.

2 broiler-fryer chickens (about
    2 pounds each), cut in pieces
1 lime, halved
    Salt, freshly ground pepper, and
      cayenne or red pepper
½ cup peanut oil
4 shallots, minced
¾ cup dry white wine
½ cup chicken broth
1 cup split cashews
½ cup amber rum
2 tablespoons butter
2 tablespoons cornstarch

1. Rub chicken with the cut side of lime. Season with salt, pepper, and cayenne.
2. Heat oil in a Dutch oven and sauté the chicken until golden brown. Add shallots and brown. Add wine and chicken broth. Cover. Simmer over low heat 25 minutes. Add cashews and simmer about 10 minutes.
3. Remove chicken and cashews with a slotted spoon and keep warm. Remove excess fat from Dutch oven, leaving drippings. Deglaze with rum.
4. Mix butter and cornstarch and add to drippings. Cook over high heat, stirring constantly, until sauce is slightly thicker.
5. Pour sauce over chicken and nuts. Serve with Bananas à l'Antillaise and Guava Jelly (●).

6 servings

735 *Chicken with Peas (Poulet Pois France)*

3 broiler-fryer chickens
    (3 pounds each), cut in pieces
1 tablespoon lime juice
    Salt and freshly ground pepper
¼ cup soybean oil
1 shallot
1 garlic clove
1 teaspoon dried thyme
1 green hot pepper or
    3 dried Italian pepper pods
2 cups chicken stock
3 pounds fresh green peas, shelled
2 tablespoons butter
2 tablespoons cornstarch

1. Season chicken with lime juice, salt, and pepper.
2. Heat oil in a Dutch oven and sauté the chicken pieces until golden brown on all sides.
3. In a mortar, pound to a paste the shallot and garlic. Add seasoning paste, thyme, green hot pepper, 1 cup stock, and peas to the chicken. Reduce heat and simmer 25 minutes, or until chicken and peas are tender.
4. Remove chicken, peas, and hot pepper to a heated platter and keep hot. Add remaining stock to Dutch oven; bring to a boil. Mix butter and cornstarch and add to stock. Stir until sauce is slightly thicker. Add salt and pepper, if desired.
5. Garnish chicken with **chopped parsley** and serve sauce in a sauceboat.

About 10 servings

Squab with Peas: Follow recipe for Chicken with Peas, allowing ½ **squab per serving.** Carve birds and place meat on slices of **bread fried in butter.** Pour sauce over meat and croutons.

Quail with Peas: Follow recipe for Chicken with Peas, substituting **1 cup red wine** for the cooking stock. Allow **1 quail per serving.** Carve birds and place meat on slices of **bread fried in butter.** Pour sauce over meat and croutons.

736 *Wild Duck Pâté*

2 wild ducks (about 4 pounds each);
   reserve livers
¼ cup olive oil
   Juice of 2 limes
1 garlic clove, halved
   Water
1 carrot
1 leek
1 teaspoon salt
⅛ teaspoon pepper
1 cup port wine
2 bay leaves
1 small onion, minced
1 green hot pepper
⅛ teaspoon thyme
3 tablespoons olive oil
3 tablespoons butter
½ pound beef liver, cubed
¼ cup amber rum
1 egg
   Lard
   Truffles (optional)
   Bay leaves and green hot peppers
     for garnish

1. Marinate the ducks for ½ hour in a mixture of ¼ cup oil and lime juice. Rub ducks with the cut surface of garlic clove.
2. Place birds in a Dutch oven and cover with water; add carrot, leek, salt, and pepper and bring to a boil. Simmer covered over low heat until birds are tender.
3. Remove birds from broth and cool. Reserve ¼ cup broth; store remaining broth for future use. Remove the meat from the carcasses, cutting the breast meat into long, even strips.
4. Mix port wine, bay leaves, onion, pepper, and thyme; marinate the breast meat for ½ hour. Set aside remaining duck meat.
5. Heat 3 tablespoons oil and butter in a medium skillet. Sauté duck livers and beef liver over high heat until golden. Warm the rum, ignite it, and pour it, still flaming, over the livers. Stir in ¼ cup of the reserved broth to deglaze the skillet.
6. Purée in an electric blender the liver mixture, reserved duck meat, and egg.
7. Coat heavily with lard 1 large terrine or loaf dish, or 2 small terrines or loaf dishes. Put in half the puréed mixture, then arrange the marinated strips of duck breast on top with slices of truffles, if desired. Cover with the remaining duck mixture, then with a thick coat of lard.
8. Garnish with bay leaves and green hot peppers. Cover terrine and place in a pan of hot water.
9. Bake at 375°F about 1½ hours.
10. Wipe clean the sides of the terrine. Cool and store covered in refrigerator up to a week.
11. To serve, remove bay leaves and peppers; slice pâté and accompany with salad.

737 *Curried Duck Martinique*
(Colombo de Canard Martiniquaise)

3 cups coarsely chopped
   cooked duck
3 cups sliced mushrooms
6 tablespoons butter, melted
1 cup diced apple
⅓ cup grated onion
1 garlic clove, crushed in a
   garlic press
3 tablespoons flour
1 tablespoon curry powder
½ teaspoon salt
¼ teaspoon freshly ground pepper
1 cup whipping cream
½ cup duck stock
   (made from cooking the carcass)
3 tablespoons Madeira or
   sweet sherry

1. Cook duck and mushrooms in half the melted butter in a skillet over low heat, until the duck is slightly browned and the mushrooms are tender. Remove from heat and cover.
2. Sauté apple, onion, and garlic in remaining butter in a large skillet until soft. Remove skillet from the heat and stir in flour, curry, salt, and pepper.
3. Place skillet over low heat and blend in cream, stock, and Madeira. Stir constantly until the mixture thickens. Stir in the duck and mushroom mixture.
4. Serve with cooked white rice tossed with 1 cup diced banana.

6 servings

738 *Pot-Roasted Wild Duck*

4 wild ducks (about 2 pounds each)
Amber rum
8 limes, peeled
8 peppercorns, cracked
Papaya leaves
Bacon drippings
3 tablespoons soybean oil
12 shallots
⅓ cup amber rum
½ cup stock
1 carrot
1 garlic clove, crushed in a
    garlic press
1 thyme sprig
1 parsley sprig
1 green hot pepper
2 cups hot stock
2 tablespoons butter
2 tablespoons cornstarch
Salt and pepper to taste
8 slices bread, toasted
¼ cup butter

1. Wipe the duck with rum. Place 2 limes and 2 peppercorns in the cavity of each duck. Wrap the birds in papaya leaves to tenderize and refrigerate 12 hours.
2. Brush bacon drippings on each bird. Heat the oil in a Dutch oven and sauté ducks and shallots until the birds are brown on all sides.
3. Heat rum, ignite it, and pour it, while still flaming, over the birds. Add the ½ cup stock, carrot, garlic, thyme, parsley, and hot pepper. Cover Dutch oven.
4. Cook in a 475°F oven 30 minutes.
5. Cut the breasts in one piece and slice off remaining meat; reserve. Discard limes and peppercorns.
6. In a mortar, pound the carcasses until broken up. Pour the hot stock into the Dutch oven; add the broken carcasses and boil 10 minutes. Remove the hot pepper. Strain the stock and return to the Dutch oven.
7. Mix butter and cornstarch. Add to the stock; stir over medium heat until slightly thickened. Add salt and pepper to taste.
8. Fry toasted bread in butter until golden and crisp. Arrange meat on croutons. Pour sauce over all.
9. Garnish with Stuffed Sweet Peppers (●). Serve remaining sauce from a sauceboat.

8 servings

739 *Guinea Stew*

½ teaspoon monosodium glutamate
Salt and freshly ground pepper
1 guinea fowl (2½ to 3 pounds)
1 lime, halved
¼ pound salt pork, cubed
4 parsley sprigs
2 scallions or green onions, chopped
2 garlic cloves
2 cloves
½ teaspoon salt
¼ cup soybean oil
½ cup amber rum
2 cups red wine
1 cup chicken stock
12 shallots
2 carrots, sliced
2 turnips, sliced
1 tablespoon butter
1 tablespoon cornstarch

1. Sprinkle monosodium glutamate, salt, and pepper over bird and refrigerate overnight. The next day, rub the skin with the cut side of the lime. Cut bird into pieces.
2. Render salt pork over medium heat in a Dutch oven. When crisp, remove the cracklings.
3. In a mortar, pound to a paste the parsley, scallions, garlic, cloves, and salt. Add the seasoning paste and oil to the Dutch oven.
4. Sauté the meat until golden brown on all sides.
5. Heat rum, ignite it, and pour it, still flaming, over the meat. Add wine and stock; reduce heat, cover, and simmer 30 mintues.
6. Add shallots, carrots, and turnips. Simmer until meat and vegetables are tender.
7. Place meat and vegetables on a serving platter.
8. Mix butter and cornstarch; add to liquid in Dutch oven and stir over high heat until sauce is slightly thickened. Season with salt and pepper, if necessary. Pour sauce over meat and vegetables.
9. Serve with Caribbean Rice (●).

2 servings

Chicken Stew: Follow recipe for Guinea Stew, substituting **1 broiler-fryer chicken (about 2 pounds)** for guinea fowl.

740 *Barbecued Wild Game Birds*

4 ready-to-cook wild game birds
  such as duckling, snipe, teal, or
  woodcock
Amber rum
6 peppercorns
4 parsley sprigs
3 garlic cloves
1 green hot pepper
1 tablespoon salt
1 tablespoon olive or peanut oil
1 cup red wine
Bacon drippings
Dry bread crumbs
● Creole Barbecue Sauce

1. Brush surface of birds with rum. Split birds in half and pound with a meat hammer.
2. In a mortar, pound to a paste the peppercorns, parsley, garlic, pepper, and salt. Mix seasoning paste with olive oil and wine. Pour marinade over birds and refrigerate 12 hours.
3. Thoroughly drain bird halves. Brush with bacon drippings and coat with bread crumbs.
4. Barbecue bird halves in a hinged grill 4 inches from glowing coals about 10 minutes on each side, basting twice with Creole Barbecue Sauce; time depends on their size. Turn birds once and baste again.
5. Birds should be eaten on the rare side; when birds are pricked with a fork, a droplet of blood should surface slowly.
6. Serve with Purée of Breadfruit (●).

741 *Teal on the Spit*

Teal, a small wild duck, is in season October to February.

4 teals; reserve livers
1 orange, halved
8 chicken livers
1 tablespoon flour
¼ teaspoon garlic powder
Salt and pepper
2 tablespoons olive oil
4 bacon slices
2 tablespoons flour
2 tablespoons butter
1 can (13 ounces) clear consommé
  madrilène
1½ teaspoons lime juice
1½ teaspoons orange juice

1. Rub teals with cut sides of orange halves. Set aside.
2. Coat the teal livers and chicken livers with a mixture of 1 tablespoon flour, garlic powder, salt, and pepper. Heat oil and sauté the livers until golden brown.
3. Put the livers into the bird cavities. Wrap each bird in a slice of bacon, securing with skewers.
4. Spear birds on a spit and broil on the electric broiler about 25 minutes or, if charcoal is used, place the spitted bird 4 inches from the hot coals and turn often.
5. Brown 2 tablespoons flour in butter in a small saucepan over high heat. Add enough consommé madrilène to just moisten the mixture, stirring rapidly with a whisk. While it thickens, slowly pour in the remaining consommé in a thin stream. Boil rapidly, uncovered, stirring constantly for about 4 minutes, or until the sauce is reduced to ½ cup. Remove from heat and add lime juice and orange juice.
6. Serve teal with Tomatoes Stuffed with Rice and Peanuts (●) and the sauce separately.

4 servings

742 *Ortolans on Croutons*

8 ortolans
½ lime
Salt and freshly ground pepper
½ cup cubed salt pork
¼ cup amber rum
½ cup red wine
1 tablespoon butter
1 tablespoon cornstarch
8 white bread slices with crusts
  trimmed
¼ cup butter

1. Truss ortolans. Rub the skin with the cut side of the lime half. Season with salt and pepper.
2. Render the salt pork over high heat in a Dutch oven. Sauté ortolans for 6 minutes, or until well browned.
3. Heat rum, ignite it, and pour it, still flaming, over the birds. Place birds on a serving platter.
4. Pour wine into Dutch oven to deglaze. Mix 1 tablespoon butter and cornstarch and add to wine. Stir until sauce is slightly thicker.
5. Make croutons by frying bread slices in butter until brown on both sides.
6. Serve each ortolan on a crouton, top with a slice of sautéed liver pâté, if desired, and pour sauce over all.

8 servings

Twelve-Fruit Compote, page 344

743 *Roast Turkey*

1 ready-to-cook turkey
   (reserve giblets)
1 lime, halved
1 orange, halved
1 teaspoon monosodium glutamate
   Salt and freshly ground pepper
¼ cup olive oil
1 tablespoon tomato paste
1 garlic clove, crushed in a
   garlic press
1 quart water
1 large onion, sliced
4 parsley sprigs
1 bay leaf
2 teaspoons salt
   Lettuce
   Cherry tomato
   Avocado half
   Green pepper ring
2 tablespoons butter
2 tablespoons cornstarch

1. Rub the skin of the bird with the cut side of the lime and orange. Sprinkle monosodium glutamate, salt, and pepper over surface. Refrigerate 2 hours.
2. Combine oil, tomato paste, and garlic. Brush mixture over bird. Set on a rack in a shallow roasting pan.
3. Roast, uncovered, in a 375°F oven until turkey tests done (the thickest part of the drumstick feels soft when pressed with fingers, or meat thermometer inserted in the thickest part of inner thigh muscle registers 180° to 185°F).
4. Meanwhile, prepare giblet broth. Put turkey neck and giblets (except liver), water, onion, parsley, bay leaf, and salt in a saucepan. Cover and simmer about 2 hours, or until giblets are tender. Add the liver the last 15 minutes of cooking. Strain.
5. Carve turkey and arrange meat on a bed of lettuce. Garnish with tomato, avocado, and green pepper.
6. Remove excess fat from roasting pan. Pour in 2 cups giblet broth to deglaze over medium heat.
7. Mix butter and cornstarch and add to broth. Stir until sauce is slightly thicker.
8. Serve sauce with turkey.

744 *Turkey Croquettes*

2 tablespoons butter
2 tablespoons minced shallot
1½ tablespoons flour
½ cup chicken broth
2 egg yolks, beaten
2 cups ground turkey
1 tablespoon chopped parsley
1 teaspoon salt
¼ teaspoon freshly ground pepper
2 egg yolks
2 teaspoons cooking oil
   Dry bread crumbs
   Fat for deep frying,
   heated to 375°F

1. Melt butter in a skillet. Cook shallot over low heat until translucent. Stir in flour. Gradually add chicken broth, blending until smooth.
2. Remove from heat and beat in 2 egg yolks. Add turkey, parsley, salt, and pepper; mix well.
3. Spread mixture on a platter and cool in refrigerator.
4. Shape mixture into small balls. Coat balls with a mixture of 2 egg yolks and oil and then roll in bread crumbs.
5. Fry in heated fat until golden. Drain on absorbent paper.
6. Serve with Tomato Sauce Creole (●).

Grandmother's Cheese Cake, page 340
Baba, page 336

745 *Duck Bigarade*

A bigarade is a small, bitter orange which grows in profusion in the islands. The sour orange taste can be duplicated by mixing lime and orange juices.

2 limes, halved
1 ready-to-cook duck
   (about 5 pounds)
   Salt, freshly ground pepper, and
   cayenne or red pepper
2 cups firmly packed brown sugar
1 cup water
2 teaspoons vanilla extract
½ cup orange peel strips
4 small oranges, halved and seeded
2 cups chicken broth
¼ cup orange juice
½ cup amber rum
¼ cup butter
¼ cup cornstarch

1. Squeeze lime juice over the entire duck. Season with salt, pepper, and cayenne. Place on a rack in a roasting pan.
2. Roast uncovered in a 425°F oven 25 minutes. Turn oven control to 350°F and continue to roast 30 minutes.
3. Combine brown sugar, water, and vanilla extract in a large, heavy saucepan. Bring to a boil over high heat and boil about 6 minutes. Add orange peel and orange halves and continue boiling 1 minute. Remove from heat and cool. Set ¼ cup syrup aside in a small saucepan.
4. Transfer duck to a warm platter. Remove fat from roasting pan. Stir in chicken broth and orange juice to deglaze. Heat the rum, ignite it, and when flames die down, pour it into the chicken broth.
5. Heat the reserved syrup until it caramelizes. Add to chicken broth mixture and blend well.
6. Mix butter and cornstarch and add to roasting pan. Cook over medium heat, stirring constantly, until the gravy is slightly thicker.
7. Carve the duck. Sprinkle the glazed orange peel strips over the meat. Pour a little gravy over the meat. Serve remaining gravy separately. Arrange glazed orange halves around the duck, alternating with bouquets of **watercress**. Serve with Caribbean Rice (●).

4 servings

Seafood

746 *Baked Halibut in Parchment Paper*

1 tablespoon olive oil
Juice of ½ lemon
Pinch basil
Pinch oregano
1 halibut steak (or any other
    preferred steak)
Salt and pepper
2 thin lemon slices
4 capers

1. Combine oil, lemon juice, basil, and oregano; spoon over both sides of the fish. Season with salt and pepper.
2. Place the fish on a piece of parchment paper. Lay lemon slices and capers on top of fish. Seal paper and tie. Put into a baking dish.
3. Bake at 325°F 30 minutes.
4. Serve hot sealed in parchment.

1 serving

747 *Fried Codfish in Garlic Sauce*
(Bakaliaros Tiganitos me Skorthalia)

4 frozen codfish fillets, thawed
Flour, seasoned with salt and
    pepper
Flour and water to make a
    thick paste (about 1¼ cups
    water to 1 cup flour)
Oil for frying
Garlic and Potato Sauce
Lemon wedges

1. Pat fillets dry. Coat with seasoned flour. Dip in flour and water mixture.
2. Pour oil into a deep skillet and heat to smoking.
3. Put fillets in oil. Fry until golden brown, turning once.
4. Serve with Garlic and Potato Sauce and lemon wedges.

2 to 4 servings

748 *Garlic and Potato Sauce* *(Skorthalia)*

1 pound potatoes, pared and cut
    in small pieces
4 garlic cloves, crushed in a
    garlic press
1 cup olive oil
¼ cup vinegar
Salt and freshly ground pepper

1. Boil potatoes until they can be pierced easily with a fork. Drain in a colander or on paper towels.
2. Mash potatoes in a potato ricer. Add garlic and then olive oil, a tablespoon at a time, beating well after each spoonful. Beat in vinegar. Season with salt and pepper to taste. If sauce is too thick, beat in a little warm water or more olive oil.
3. Serve with **fried** or **broiled seafood,** on **crackers** or **toasted bread,** or as a dip for **fresh vegetables.**

1 quart sauce

749 *Baked Fish à la Spetses*

4 pounds fish fillets (turbot, whitefish, bass, mullet)
4 fresh tomatoes, peeled and sliced
¾ cup olive oil
1 cup white wine
2 tablespoons chopped parsley
1 large garlic clove, crushed in a garlic press
Salt and pepper to taste
1 teaspoon basil (optional)
1 cup fresh bread crumbs
1 slice feta cheese for each portion

1. Put fillets into a baking dish.
2. In a bowl, combine tomatoes, olive oil, wine, parsley, garlic, salt, pepper, and basil. Pour over fillets. Sprinkle with bread crumbs.
3. Bake at 375°F 40 minutes.
4. Top fillets with feta cheese slices. Broil 1 or 2 minutes.

6 to 8 servings

750 *Charcoal-Grilled Fish* (Psari tys Skaras)

Fish for grilling
¼ cup olive oil
Juice of 1 lemon
2 tablespoons oregano, crushed
Salt and pepper to taste

1. Fish suitable for grilling are trout, whitefish, bluefish, snapper, or mackerel. (In Greece, the fish are usually served with their heads and tails intact. You may prefer to remove the heads at least, because some people are revolted by a whole fish on their plate. However you decide to serve the fish, allow 1 pound for each person.)
2. Heat charcoal until white. Arrange grill so that it is about 4 inches from coals. Use a hinged basket grill for easier turning; oil it well to prevent fish from sticking.
3. Combine olive oil, lemon juice, oregano, salt, and pepper. Brush fish generously with mixture. Place in basket grill.
4. Cook on one side about 7 minutes. Turn over and cook an additional 7 minutes.
5. Serve fish with remaining sauce.

751 *Baked Fish with Tomatoes, Onions, and Parsley* (Psari Plaki)

½ cup olive oil
2 large onions, coarsely chopped
1 can (20 ounces) tomatoes (undrained)
½ cup white wine
½ cup chopped parsley
1 garlic clove, crushed in a garlic press
Salt and pepper to taste
3 pounds fish fillets (any firm fish such as turbot, bass, grouper, or red snapper may be used)

1. Heat olive oil in a saucepan. Add onion and cook until translucent. Add tomatoes, wine, parsley, garlic, salt, and pepper. Simmer covered 10 minutes.
2. Place fish in a large baking dish. Cover with sauce.
3. Bake at 350°F about 25 minutes, or until fish flakes easily when tested with a fork.

4 servings

752 *Fish Kebob*

2 pounds swordfish or halibut
    with bones removed, cut in
    large cubes
1 cup olive oil
    Juice of 2 lemons
1 teaspoon oregano
1 teaspoon dill
1 bay leaf
    Salt and pepper to taste
    Small whole onions, peeled
    Whole cherry tomatoes

1. Marinate fish in a mixture of the oil, lemon juice, oregano, dill, bay leaf, salt, and pepper for 2 hours, basting occasionally. Reserve marinade.
2. Alternate fish, onions, and tomatoes on skewers.
3. Broil, turning frequently, until done (about 5 minutes).
4. Heat marinade. Serve with Fish Kebob.

4 servings

753 *Poached Striped Bass*

1 quart water
1 quart dry white wine
    Juice of 3 lemons
2 cups olive oil
2 medium onions, quartered
1 large carrot, pared and left
    whole
2 celery stalks with leaves
2 leeks
    Salt to taste
10 coriander seeds
8 whole peppercorns
1 bay leaf
4 parsley sprigs
1 thyme sprig
3 garlic cloves, peeled and left
    whole
5 pounds bass, cleaned, with
    gills removed and head and
    tail left on

1. Pour water, wine, lemon juice, and olive oil into a saucepot.
2. Wrap remaining ingredients, except fish, in cheesecloth and add. Bring to boiling and simmer covered 15 minutes.
3. Wrap fish in cheesecloth. Place in a fish poacher or a deep greased baking dish.
4. Pour in stock, discarding vegetables; cover and simmer 15 minutes. Remove from heat.
5. Let fish remain in the liquid for another 15 minutes. Lift out of pan and drain; reserve fish stock for other use. Remove cheesecloth and peel off skin.
6. Serve fish at room temperature with Vinegar and Oil Dressing with Tomato, Mayonnaise, or Garlic and Potato Sauce

6 to 8 servings

754 *Poached Tuna Rolls with Garlic Mayonnaise*

1 can (9¼ ounces) solid-pack
    tuna, drained and flaked
3 anchovies, minced
    Salt and pepper to taste
2 eggs, lightly beaten
    Bread crumbs
1 tomato, thinly sliced
1 onion, thinly sliced
1 cucumber, thinly sliced
● Garlic Mayonnaise

1. Combine tuna with anchovies. Add pepper and taste before adding salt. Mix in eggs and enough bread crumbs to make a paste firm enough to shape into four 1½-inch-thick rolls.
2. Wrap rolls tightly in cheesecloth. Tie at both ends.
3. Put into boiling salted water to cover. Reduce heat and simmer 20 minutes. Remove from water.
4. Slice rolls and garnish with tomato, onion, and cucumber. Serve with Garlic Mayonnaise.

4 servings

755 *Fish Casserole Haramogli* (*Psari Haramogli*)

3 pounds whitefish, sole, or any
  other lean fish (head and tail
  removed), cut in 4 portions
5 cups fish stock
● 3 cups Béchamel Sauce
2 tablespoons minced parsley
1 teaspoon basil
1 garlic clove, crushed in a garlic
  press
4 cups cooked rice
½ cup freshly grated kefalotyri
  cheese

1. Wrap fish loosely in cheesecloth. Knot the ends. Heat fish stock until boiling. Add fish and simmer until done (about 10 minutes).
2. Remove fish from liquid and discard cheesecloth.
3. Mix Béchamel Sauce with parsley, basil, and garlic.
4. Turn rice into a casserole. Put fish on top. Top with Béchamel Sauce and cheese. Cover tightly with aluminum foil.
5. Set in a 300°F oven 12 to 15 minutes, or until thoroughly heated.

8 servings

756 *Marinated Fish* (*Psari Marinata*)

2 pounds halibut, sole, or
  grouper fillets or fish with
  heads and tails intact
Salt
Juice of 2 lemons
2 cups flour, seasoned with salt
  and pepper
Olive oil for frying
½ cup olive oil
¼ cup flour
½ cup white wine
½ cup white wine vinegar
● 1 can (8 ounces) tomato sauce or
  1 cup Tomato Sauce
1 teaspoon sugar
1 teaspoon fennel
2 garlic cloves, minced (optional)

1. Season fish with salt and lemon juice. Dip in flour. Heat olive oil in a large skillet; add fish and fry on both sides until medium brown, being careful not to burn the oil.
2. Arrange fish in a baking dish. Discard cooking oil.
3. Combine ½ cup oil and flour in a skillet and, stirring constantly with a wooden spoon, cook until flour browns.
4. Add remaining ingredients and simmer, covered, 15 minutes. Strain over fish. Allow to marinate out of the refrigerator several hours before serving. Adjust salt and pepper. Serve at room temperature or chilled.

6 servings

757 *Vinegar and Oil Dressing with Tomato* (*Ladoxido me Domata*)

1 tablespoon imported mustard
  (Dijon, preferably)
2 tablespoons red wine vinegar,
  or more to taste
½ cup olive oil
1 large tomato, peeled and diced
2 whole scallions, minced
2 tablespoons minced parsley
1 tablespoon chopped capers
1 teaspoon dill

Put mustard and vinegar into a small bowl. Add olive oil while stirring with a whisk. Add remaining ingredients; mix well. Refrigerate several hours before serving.

1 ¾ cups

758 *Trout in Grapevine Leaves*

1 jar (32 ounces) grapevine
    leaves, drained
4 medium trout, cleaned, with
    heads and tails left on
2 tablespoons olive oil
2 tablespoons butter, melted
2 teaspoons oregano
1 teaspoon dill
    Additional oil to brush outside
        of trout
    Salt and pepper to taste
2 lemons, cut in wedges

1. Rinse grapevine leaves thoroughly under cold running water to remove brine.
2. Rinse trout; pat dry.
3. Drizzle 2 tablespoons olive oil and butter in trout cavities. Sprinkle with oregano and dill. Brush oil on outside of fish. Season inside and out with salt and pepper.
4. Wrap each trout in 5 or 6 grapevine leaves. Refrigerate 1 to 2 hours.
5. To charcoal-broil, adjust grill 4 inches from heated coals. Grease a rectangular, long-handled grill on all sides. Place fish in the grill, side by side. Grill one side about 8 minutes, turn, grill until fish flakes easily with a fork (about 8 minutes more).
6. Discard browned outer leaves. Serve trout in remaining leaves. Garnish with lemon wedges.

4 servings

Note: Trout may also be broiled under the broiler. For easy turning, use a long-handled grill.

759 *Sea Chowder*

¼ cup olive oil
3 garlic cloves
1 medium onion, quartered
2 bay leaves
    Water to cover fish
1 cup dry white wine
    Juice of 1 lemon
6 squid, cleaned and cut in
        pieces
    Salt and pepper to taste
2 tomatoes, peeled, seeded, and
        diced
3 pounds fish (several kinds),
        skinned and boned
1 pound shrimp, shelled and
        deveined

1. Heat oil in a deep saucepan. Add garlic, onion, and bay leaves. Cook until onion is translucent.
2. Pour in water, wine, and lemon juice. Add squid. Season with salt and pepper. Cover and simmer 40 minutes.
3. Add tomatoes and fish; simmer 8 minutes. Add shrimp; simmer just until shrimp are cooked. Adjust seasonings. Serve at once.

6 servings

760 *Pickled Octopus* (Oktapodi Tursi)

1 small octopus (about 2 pounds)
½ cup olive oil
¼ cup white wine vinegar
    Juice of ½ lemon
1 tablespoon minced parsley
½ teaspoon marjoram
    Salt and pepper to taste

1. Beat octopus with the flat side of a metal meat hammer 15 to 20 minutes; it will feel soft and excrete a grayish liquid.
2. Wash octopus thoroughly, drain, and cook in skillet without water until it becomes bright pink. Cut into bite-size pieces.
3. Make a salad dressing of the olive oil, vinegar, lemon juice, parsley, marjoram, salt, and pepper. Mix well.
4. Pour over octopus and store in the refrigerator in a covered container for 5 days before serving.
5. Serve cold as an appetizer.

4 to 6 servings

761 *Steamed Mussels in Wine Sauce* (Mithia Krassata)

2 pounds mussels
1 large onion, minced
1 large celery stalk, minced
4 peppercorns
3 cups dry white wine
¼ cup butter (at room
   temperature)
1 tablespoon flour
1 teaspoon vinegar
1 tablespoon chopped parsley
1 garlic clove
   Salt and pepper to taste

1. Scrub mussels well with a vegetable brush and rinse. Put into a kettle with onion, celery, peppercorns, and white wine. Cover and steam until they open, discarding any that are unopened.
2. Put mussels onto a deep platter. Cover and keep warm.
3. Strain liquid and simmer. Mix butter and flour together in a small bowl; stir into hot liquid. Add vinegar, parsley, garlic, salt, and pepper; continue to simmer until liquid is reduced by half.
4. To serve, pour sauce over mussels.

6 servings

762 *Shrimp Giahni with Feta Cheese*

1 medium onion, minced
½ cup olive oil
1 can (28 ounces) tomatoes
   (undrained)
4 ounces white wine
1 small bunch parsley, finely
   chopped
1 celery stalk, finely chopped
   Salt and pepper
1 pound large shrimp, cleaned
   and deveined
¼ pound feta cheese, crumbled

1. Brown onion in oil. Add tomatoes, stirring until mixture reaches boiling. Lower heat and simmer, covered, 5 minutes. Add wine, parsley, celery, and salt and pepper to taste. Simmer 30 minutes.
2. While tomato sauce is simmering, parboil shrimp 2 minutes in **3 quarts boiling water** with **2 teaspoons salt.** Drain immediately.
3. Add shrimp to sauce. Simmer 1 minute. Garnish with feta.

6 servings

763 *Spiced Shrimp with Onions*

4 quarts water
1 tablespoon salt
3 pounds raw shrimp, shelled
   and deveined
¾ cup white wine vinegar
1 cup olive oil
2 cups white wine
1 tablespoon salt
1 teaspoon pepper
2 jars whole baby onions,
   drained
3 garlic cloves
1 bay leaf
1 celery stalk, cut in half
   Juice of 1 lemon

1. Bring water and 1 tablespoon salt to a rolling boil in a saucepot. Add shrimp. Boil 1 minute. Drain.
2. Combine remaining ingredients in a saucepot and bring to boiling. Simmer uncovered 5 minutes. Cool.
3. Pour onion mixture over shrimp. Refrigerate 6 to 8 hours.
4. Drain shrimp and onions and serve chilled.

6 to 8 servings

764 *Stuffed Squid* (Kalamarakia Yemista)

32 squid, cleaned and tentacles
    removed
¾ cup olive oil
1 large onion, chopped
1½ cups water
1 cup long-grain rice
½ cup chopped parsley
1 teaspoon mint
1 teaspoon basil
2 cloves garlic, crushed in a
    garlic press
½ cup pine nuts
¼ cup dried black currants
1 cup dry white wine
    Salt and pepper to taste
    Water
    Juice of 2 lemons

1. Reserve squid. Rinse tentacles in cold water. Drain and mince finely.
2. In a large saucepan, heat 2 tablespoons of the oil, add onion and minced tentacles and cook over low heat until tentacles turn pink. Add water. Heat to boiling. Reduce heat, add rice, parsley, mint, basil, garlic, pine nuts, currants, and ½ cup of the wine.
3. Simmer until liquid is absorbed. Season with salt and pepper. Cool.
4. Using a teaspoon, stuff each squid cavity loosely with the rice mixture. Arrange squid in rows in a large baking dish. Combine the remaining wine and olive oil with enough water to reach half the depth of the squid. Season with additional salt and pepper. Cover.
5. Bake at 325°F about 40 minutes, or until squid is tender. Drizzle with lemon juice just before serving.

8 servings

Note: Stuffing may also be used as a side dish. Stuff 16 squid. Put remaining stuffing in a baking dish. Add a little water, salt, and pepper and cover. Bake at 325°F 30 minutes.

765 *Fish au Gratin* (Ryba Zapiekana)

1 cup chicken or vegetable broth
    or stock
1 tablespoon flour
1 tablespoon butter or margarine
    (at room temperature)
½ teaspoon salt
¼ teaspoon parsley flakes
¼ teaspoon pepper
    Pinch ground thyme
¼ cup whipping cream
1½ pounds sole, trout, pike, or
    other white fish
3 tablespoons grated Parmesan,
    Swiss, or Gruyère cheese
2 tablespoons dry bread crumbs
1 tablespoon melted butter or
    margarine
1 teaspoon lemon juice (optional)

1. Bring broth to boiling in a small saucepan. Blend flour into butter and stir into boiling broth. Cook and stir until thickened. Reduce heat. Stir in salt, parsley flakes, pepper, thyme, and cream.
2. Place fish in a well-buttered pan. Pour sauce over fish.
3. Bake at 375°F 15 minutes.
4. Mix cheese, bread crumbs, melted butter, and lemon juice (if desired). Sprinkle over fish in pan. Bake about 15 minutes longer, or until fish flakes easily.

4 to 6 servings

Fish au Gratin with Tomatoes: Prepare Fish au Gratin as directed, except sprinkle ½ cup chopped tomato over top of fish before covering with sauce.

Fish au Gratin with Mushrooms: Prepare Fish au Gratin as directed, adding ½ cup sliced mushrooms to partially baked fish before topping with crumb mixture.

Fish au Gratin with Horseradish: Prepare Fish au Gratin as directed, adding 4 teaspoons prepared horseradish to sauce along with cream.

766 *Sole with Vegetables* (Sola z Jarzynami)

2 tablespoons butter or margarine
1 large onion, diced
1 cup savoy cabbage, shredded
    (optional)
1 leek, thinly sliced
1 large carrot, thinly sliced
1 stalk celery, thinly sliced

1. Melt butter in a Dutch oven or large skillet. Add vegetables and stir-fry 5 minutes.
2. Sprinkle fish fillets with salt. Place on the vegetables. Add water. Cover; simmer 15 minutes.
3. For sauce, melt butter in a saucepan. Stir in flour. Cook and stir until golden. Then gradually stir in broth. Cook, stirring constantly, until sauce boils.

1 parsley root, thinly sliced
2 pounds sole or any white fish
    fillets
½ teaspoon salt
2 tablespoons water
Sauce:
    2 tablespoons butter or margarine
    2 tablespoons flour
    1 cup chicken broth or fish stock
    ½ teaspoon salt
    ¼ teaspoon pepper
    ¼ cup dairy sour cream

4. Transfer the fish to a warm platter. Stir the sauce into the vegetables. Remove from heat. Season with salt and pepper; stir in sour cream. Pour over the fish.

About 6 servings

767 *Deep-Fried Squid* (Kalamarakia Tyganita)

12 squid, cleaned, with their
    tentacles left on
  Flour seasoned generously with
    salt and pepper
  Vegetable oil for deep frying
3 lemons, cut in wedges

1. Rinse the cleaned squid in cold water and pat dry with paper towels. Dip the squid into the seasoned flour and coat all surfaces evenly.
2. Heat the oil in a deep fryer to 375°F. Drop in the squid, a few at a time. Fry until golden brown (about 5 minutes). Transfer the squid with a slotted spoon to a baking dish lined with paper towels. Keep in a 200°F oven until all the squid are fried.
3. Remove paper; serve squid with lemon.

3 servings

768 *Baked Leftover Fish* (Potrawa Zapiekana)

3 boiled potatoes, sliced
1½ cups diced cooked fish
¾ cup sliced cooked cauliflower or
    mushrooms (optional)
2 hard-cooked eggs, sliced
  Salt and pepper
1 tablespoon flour
1 cup dairy sour cream
¼ cup water
3 tablespoons bread crumbs
2 tablespoons grated Parmesan
    cheese
2 tablespoons butter

1. Arrange layers of half the potatoes, fish, cauliflower, eggs, and remaining potatoes in a greased 1½-quart casserole. Lightly sprinkle salt and pepper over each layer.
2. Blend flour into sour cream; stir in water. Spoon over casserole mixture.
3. Mix bread crumbs, cheese, and butter together. Sprinkle over top of casserole.
4. Bake at 350°F 30 minutes.

About 4 servings

769 *Roulade of Eel* (Rolada z Węgorza)

1 eel (2 pounds)
3 hard-cooked eggs, chopped
2 dill pickles, chopped
4 mushrooms, sliced
1 egg
1 teaspoon salt
¼ teaspoon pepper
1 quart vegetable stock or
    consommé
⅓ cup vinegar

1. Skin eel. Split in half; remove bones. Lay half the eel on a double thickness of cheesecloth.
2. Mix hard-cooked eggs, pickles, mushrooms, raw egg, salt, and pepper. Spread over the eel on cloth. Top with other half of eel. Wrap eel in the cloth. Place in a large kettle.
3. Add stock and vinegar to kettle. Boil gently 30 minutes. Let cool 1½ hours.
4. To serve, remove eel from cloth. Set on platter. Garnish, if desired. Serve with a sauce such as Mustard Sauce (●) or Horseradish Sauce (●).

About 6 servings

770 *Northern Pike Polish Style*
(Szczupak po Polsku)

1 dressed northern pike, perch, or
    other white fish (2 pounds)
1 carrot
1 onion
1 stalk celery
10 peppercorns
1½ teaspoons salt
    Water
Topping:
¼ cup butter
6 hard-cooked eggs, finely
    chopped
¼ cup lemon juice
1 tablespoon chopped fresh dill or
    parsley
¾ teaspoon salt
¼ teaspoon pepper

1. Put fish into a large kettle. Add carrot, onion, celery, peppercorns, and salt. Add enough water to cover. Cover; boil gently about 15 to 20 minutes, or until fish flakes easily.
2. Meanwhile, heat butter in a skillet. Add chopped eggs, lemon juice, dill, salt, and pepper. Cook 5 minutes, stirring frequently.
3. When fish is cooked, set it on a warm platter. Spoon topping over fish. Serve with boiled potatoes, if desired.

4 to 6 servings

771 *Pike or Carp Stuffed with Anchovies*
(Szczupak lub Karp Nadziewany Sardelami)

1 can (2 ounces) flat anchovy fillets
1 pike (3 pounds) with milt and
    liver, or other white fish
¼ cup butter or margarine (at room
    temperature)
2 eggs, separated
½ cup grated fresh bread
¼ cup melted butter for basting
1 cup dairy sour cream

1. Cut half the anchovies in thin strips. Lard the fish with strips of anchovy.
2. Chop or mash remaining anchovies; cream with 2 tablespoons of butter. Divide in half.
3. For stuffing, beat egg yolks. Chop liver. Combine grated bread, egg yolks, milt, and liver. Add half of anchovy butter; mix well. Beat egg whites until stiff peaks are formed; fold into bread mixture.
4. Fill cavity of fish with stuffing. Close cavity with skewers or wooden picks. Place fish in roasting pan. Drizzle with half the melted butter.
5. Bake at 350°F 30 minutes. Baste with remaining melted butter. Bake 10 minutes longer. Spread remaining anchovy butter over fish. Top with sour cream. Continue baking until fish is tender and flakes easily.

6 to 8 servings

772 *Stuffed Baked Fish* (Nadziewana Pieczona Ryba)

1 dressed pike, trout, or carp (4 to
    5 pounds)
    Salt and pepper
⅓ cup butter or margarine
2 onions, chopped
3 stalks celery, chopped
3 apples, cored and chopped

1. Sprinkle cavity of fish with salt and pepper.
2. For stuffing, melt ⅓ cup butter in skillet. Add onion and celery. Stir-fry until onion is transparent. Add apples, parsley, and mushrooms. Stir-fry 2 minutes longer.
3. Mix cooked vegetables with bread cubes, sugar, thyme, lemon juice, eggs, and water. Blend well.
4. Fill fish cavity with the stuffing. Close cavity with skewers

1 tablespoon chopped parsley
1 cup sliced mushrooms
4 cups dry bread cubes
2 teaspoons sugar
½ teaspoon thyme
2 teaspoons lemon juice
3 eggs
1 cup water or wine

or wooden picks. Place fish in a roasting pan and drizzle with **melted butter.**
5. Bake at 350°F about 40 minutes, or until fish flakes easily. Baste occasionally with additional melted butter.

About 8 servings

773 *Fish in Greek Sauce (Ryba po Grecku)*

1 pound carp, white fish, or
  flounder fillets
3 tablespoons olive oil
  Salt
  Fresh parsley sprigs
Greek Sauce:
  2 tablespoons olive oil
  ½ cup sliced celery
  ½ cup coarsely shredded carrots
  ½ cup coarsely shredded parsley root
  ¾ cup diced onion
  ½ cup water
  ½ teaspoon salt
  1 can (6 ounces) tomato paste
  ¼ teaspoon pepper
  ½ teaspoon sugar
  1 tablespoon lemon juice
  ½ teaspoon paprika

1. Cut fish fillets into 2-inch pieces.
2. Fry fish in hot oil in a skillet, then sprinkle with salt. Drain on paper towels. Arrange on a serving platter and keep warm. Garnish with parsley.
3. For sauce, heat oil in a skillet. Stir-fry celery, carrots, and parsley root for 3 minutes. Add onion, water, and salt. Cover; cook over low heat 15 minutes.
4. Add remaining sauce ingredients; stir to mix.
5. Chill sauce or serve hot over fish.

About 4 servings

774 *Fish in Horseradish Sauce*
(Ryba w Sosie Chrzanowym)

2 carrots
2 stalks celery (optional)
1 parsley root
1 onion, quartered
1 bay leaf
5 peppercorns
2 teaspoons salt
1½ quarts water
2 pounds carp, sole, or pike fillets
Horseradish Sauce:
  3 tablespoons butter or margarine
  3 tablespoons flour
  ¾ cup prepared cream-style
    horseradish
  ½ teaspoon sugar
  ¼ teaspoon salt
  ⅔ cup dairy sour cream
  2 hard-cooked eggs, peeled and
    sieved
Garnish:
  Shredded lettuce

1. Combine vegetables, dry seasonings, and water in a saucepot. Bring to boiling; simmer 20 minutes. Strain.
2. Cook fish in the strained vegetable stock 6 to 10 minutes, or until fish flakes easily.
3. Remove fish from stock. Arrange on serving platter and cover with plastic wrap. Chill.
4. Strain fish stock and reserve ¾ cup for horseradish sauce; cool.
5. For horseradish sauce, melt butter in a saucepan; blend in flour until smooth.
6. Add the cooked fish stock gradually, stirring constantly. Cook and stir until the sauce boils and becomes thick and smooth.
7. Remove from heat. Stir in horseradish, sugar, salt, sour cream, and eggs. Cool 15 minutes.
8. Pour the horseradish sauce over chilled fish. Garnish with shredded lettuce.

About 6 servings

775 *Citrus Steamed Salmon and Shrimp*

1½ pounds salmon fillets, cut in
    2x1-inch pieces
¾ pound uncooked shelled
    shrimp
½ cup lemon juice
¼ cup lime juice
¾ teaspoon salt
1 teaspoon paprika
1 teaspoon coriander seed,
    crushed
1 teaspoon cardamom seed,
    crushed (discard shells)
    Parsley sprigs

1. Place salmon and shrimp in a shallow glass dish. Mix remaining ingredients except parsley and pour over fish. Refrigerate covered 30 minutes; stir twice.
2. Transfer fish and marinade to a large skillet. Simmer covered 4 minutes; stir and simmer uncovered 2 minutes. Add shrimp to skillet; simmer covered just until shrimp are done (about 3 minutes). Arrange fish and shrimp on a serving platter. Spoon pan juices over. Garnish with parsley.

6 to 8 servings

776 *Sole with Shrimp Pâté in Champagne*

Fillets are rolled with asparagus and a filling of shrimp, creamy cheese, and anchovy. Poached in champagne and served with our version of hollandaise sauce, this entrée is just right for special occasions.

*1 pound fresh asparagus, spears
    only (2-inch pieces)
● Fish Stock
8 sole fillets (about 3 pounds)
2 cups cooked, shelled shrimp
2 ounces Neufchatel cheese
2 teaspoons anchovy paste
1 cup champagne or Fish Stock
●1 cup Mock Hollandaise Sauce
    Lemon wedges

1. Simmer asparagus spears in 1 inch of stock 4 minutes; drain. Set aside.
2. Lay fillets on a flat surface. Purée shrimp with cheese and anchovy paste in a food processor or blender. Spoon shrimp mixture in center of fillets.
3. Arrange asparagus on shrimp mixture in center of fillets so spears are visible on sides; roll fillets and place seam side down in a large skillet. Pour champagne into skillet; simmer covered until fish is tender and flakes with a fork (about 5 minutes). Remove fish carefully with a slotted spoon to serving platter. Spoon hollandaise sauce over fillets; garnish with lemon wedges.

8 servings

⁺Frozen asparagus spears can be substituted for the fresh. Thaw and drain; do not cook.

777 *Mock Crab Meat Salad*

You will hardly be able to tell that the crab meat is mock, but use fresh fish and cook it carefully.

1¾ pounds halibut steaks
● 1 cup Fish Stock
½ cup dry white wine
1 teaspoon salt
¼ teaspoon freshly ground
    white pepper
2 tablespoons snipped fresh or 2
    teaspoons dried dill weed
● ¾ cup Mock Mayonnaise

1. Simmer halibut in stock and wine in a large skillet until fish is tender and flakes with a fork (about 10 minutes). Remove fish from skillet; let cool to room temperature. Discard skin and bones.
2. Flake two thirds of the fish; cut remaining fish into ½-inch pieces. Stir salt, pepper, and dill into mayonnaise. Mix flaked fish into ½ cup of the mayonnaise; mix fish pieces into remaining mayonnaise.
3. Arrange lettuce leaves on 4 individual salad plates; place melon rings on lettuce. Mound flaked fish mixture inside mel-

Lettuce leaves
4 rings cut from honeydew or
    cantaloupe
½ pound white grapes
1 lime, cut in 4 wedges

on rings; top with mixture of fish pieces. Garnish salads with clusters of grapes and lime wedges.

4 servings

Note: This recipe makes 8 first-course servings. Prepare recipe as directed except substitute melon pieces for the melon rings, increase grapes to ¾ pound, and use 2 limes for wedges.

778 *Steamed Red Snapper Oriental*

Soy sauce and sesame oil lend a distinctive Oriental flavor to this lively dish.

3 red snapper (about 1½ pounds
    each), drawn and scaled
5 garlic cloves, finely sliced
● Fish Stock
1 cup light soy sauce
½ cup dry white wine
3 tablespoons peanut or
    vegetable oil
1 tablespoon sesame oil
1 bunch green onions, tops only,
    cut in 2-inch matchstick-size
    pieces
*½ teaspoon freshly ground
    Szechuan or black pepper
3 zucchini slices
3 thin carrot slices
3 cloves
    Lemon or lime slices
    Watercress

1. Place fish on a piece of cheesecloth which is 18 inches longer than the fish. Using cheesecloth, lower fish onto rack in a fish steamer or large, deep roasting pan with 1½ inches of stock in bottom. Arrange garlic slices on fish. Simmer covered until fish is tender and flakes with a fork (about 40 minutes).
2. Using cheesecloth, lift fish from steamer to a heated platter. Remove cheesecloth from fish, carefully lifting fish with spatula and cutting cheesecloth with scissors if necessary.
3. Mix soy sauce, wine, and peanut and sesame oils in a small saucepan; heat to boiling. Drizzle 3 tablespoons soy mixture over fish; arrange green onion tops decoratively on fish. Sprinkle ground pepper over fish. Place zucchini and carrot slices over eyes of fish and secure with cloves. Arrange lemon slices and watercress around fish. Pass remaining soy mixture to spoon over individual servings.
4. If desired, let fish stand 45 minutes after poaching, then refrigerate until chilled (about 4 hours). Spoon hot soy mixture over fish and garnish as directed. Pass remaining soy mixture.

8 to 10 servings

Note: Whole white fish, lake trout, or other lean fish can be substituted for the red snapper.

*Lightly roast Szechuan pepper over medium heat in skillet before grinding.

779 *Baked Fish with Red Sauce*

The sauce, made with puréed red peppers, is piquant and distinctive.

*2 pounds haddock fillets, cut in
    serving-size pieces
1 teaspoon salt
¼ teaspoon freshly ground white
    pepper
1 lemon, thinly sliced
1 medium red onion, sliced
4 large sweet red peppers, cut in
    quarters
¼ cup dry vermouth
½ teaspoon salt
    Dry vermouth
    Watercress

1. Sprinkle haddock with 1 teaspoon salt and the pepper; place in a lightly oiled baking pan. Arrange lemon, onion, and peppers over fish. Pour ¼ cup vermouth over top.
2. Bake at 350°F about 20 minutes, or until fish is tender and flakes with a fork.
3. Place peppers and onion slices in a food processor or blender container; discard lemon. Arrange fish on serving platter; keep warm.
4. Purée peppers, onion, and salt, adding additional vermouth, if needed, to make a thick sauce. Heat mixture thoroughly; spoon over fish. Garnish with watercress.

6 servings

*Flounder, halibut, or whitefish fillets, or poultry can be used in this recipe.

780 *Chilled Decorated Whitefish*

1 whole whitefish (about 5 pounds), dressed
● Fish Stock
2 cups minced celery
2 cups minced carrot
2 hard-cooked eggs, minced
¾ teaspoon salt
⅛ teaspoon freshly ground white pepper
● 1⅓ cups Mock Mayonnaise
1 cup sliced carrot
1 cup ¼- to ⅛-inch strips red or green pepper
1 green olive slice
2 lemons, thinly sliced
Selection of sauces: Light
● Green Sauce, Seasoned Dark
● Green Sauce, Citrus
● Mayonnaise, Mock
● Hollandaise Sauce

1. Place fish on a piece of cheesecloth which is 18 inches longer than the fish. Using cheesecloth, lower fish onto rack in a fish steamer or a large, deep roasting pan with 1½ inches stock in bottom. Simmer covered until fish is tender and flakes with a fork (about 40 minutes). Using cheesecloth, lift fish from steamer. Let cool to room temperature. Carefully remove skin and transfer fish to a serving platter.

2. Stir celery, minced carrot, salt, eggs, and pepper into mayonnaise. Form the head and tail and fins of the fish, using the vegetable-mayonnaise mixture. Decorate the head and fins with the carrot slices. Decorate the tail and gills with strips of pepper. Place an olive slice in position for the eye. Garnish fish with lemon slices. Refrigerate until chilled (about 2 hours). Serve with 2 or 3 of the sauces.

8 to 10 servings

781 *Crab-Stuffed Trout with Tarragon*

The flavor of onions, mushrooms, crab meat, and tarragon permeates the trout while baking. Use fresh tarragon if it is available.

2 large onions, finely chopped
¼ cup dry white wine
1 cup sliced fresh mushrooms
8 ounces fresh or 1 can (7¾ ounces) chunk crab meat, drained and flaked
1 tablespoon snipped fresh or 1½ teaspoons dried tarragon leaves
¼ cup snipped parsley
½ teaspoon salt
¼ teaspoon freshly ground white pepper
6 dressed trout (1 to 1½ pounds each)
1 tablespoon snipped fresh or 1½ teaspoons dried tarragon leaves
Lemon twists

1. Simmer onion in wine until tender (about 5 minutes). Mix 1½ cups cooked onion with the mushrooms, crab meat, 1 tablespoon tarragon, the parsley, salt, and pepper. Stuff trout with onion mixture.

2. Spread remaining onion in a shallow baking pan; arrange trout over onion.

3. Bake at 400°F about 20 minutes, or until fish is tender and flakes with a fork. Remove fish to serving platter. Sprinkle with 1 tablespoon tarragon and garnish with lemon twists.

6 servings

782 *Sole Véronique in Parchment*

Baked in parchment paper, the fish retains its natural moisture and flavor.

2 pounds sole fillets
¾ teaspoon salt
3 tablespoons snipped parsley
2 teaspoons minced lemon peel
1½ cups seedless white grapes
⅔ cup dry white wine
Lemon wedges

1. Lay each fillet on a piece of parchment paper or aluminum foil, 12x12 inches. Sprinkle fillets with salt, parsley, and lemon peel. Divide grapes over fish; sprinkle with wine. Bring edges of parchment up, crimp edges and seal; place on a jelly-roll pan.
2. Bake at 350°F 20 minutes.
3. Place parchment packets on individual plates; let each person open packet. Serve with lemon wedges.

4 servings

783 *Fish Stew*

French fish stew (bouillabaisse) is traditionally made with a selection of fresh shellfish. Our version uses fish which is more available and less expensive. Add shellfish if you like.

*3 pounds fish fillets, skinned
5 medium tomatoes, peeled and chopped
3 carrots, chopped
1 large onion, thinly sliced
2 teaspoons salt
¼ teaspoon freshly ground pepper
2 garlic cloves, minced
1 teaspoon fennel seed, crushed
1 tablespoon minced orange peel
1 cup dry white wine
● 1 quart Fish Stock

1. Cut fish into 1½-inch pieces. Set aside.
2. Simmer tomatoes, carrots, onion, salt, pepper, garlic, fennel, and orange peel in a mixture of wine and stock 15 minutes. Add fish to stock mixture; simmer covered until fish is tender and flakes with a fork (about 20 minutes).
3. Serve immediately in large shallow soup bowls.

8 servings (2 cups each)

*Flounder, haddock, cod, whitefish, halibut, bass, or other fish can be used in this recipe. For maximum flavor and variety, select at least 3 kinds of fish.

784 *Crab Meat Soup with Sherry*

1 cup 1-inch celery pieces
●1⅓ cups Fish Stock
2 cans (7¾ ounces each) crab meat, drained (reserve 1 cup flaked crab meat)
½ cup instant nonfat dry-milk solids
½ cup water
½ cup whole milk
¼ teaspoon salt
⅛ teaspoon ground mace
4 teaspoons arrowroot
Cold water
2 tablespoons dry sherry
3 tablespoons finely sliced celery for garnish

1. Simmer celery in stock in a covered saucepan 15 minutes. Place celery and stock in a food processor or blender; add 1 cup of flaked crab meat, the milk solids, water, milk, salt, and mace. Purée mixture; pour back into saucepan.
2. Heat crab mixture to simmering. Mix arrowroot with a little cold water; stir into crab mixture. Simmer, stirring constantly, until mixture has thickened. Stir in sherry and remaining crab meat. Heat thoroughly. Garnish with celery slices. Serve immediately.

4 servings (1½ cups each)

785 *Oysters Rockefeller*

No cream, eggs, or bread crumbs in this version of a popular classic.

1 pint oysters
*2 pounds fresh spinach, washed and stems removed
1 cup instant nonfat dry-milk solids
2 tablespoons chopped onion
2 garlic cloves, minced
1 teaspoon salt
¼ teaspoon freshly ground pepper
⅛ teaspoon freshly ground nutmeg
2 egg whites
⅓ cup grated Jarlsberg or Parmesan cheese

1. Drain oysters; reserve liquor. Cook spinach in a covered saucepan with water clinging to leaves until tender (about 7 minutes); drain. Purée spinach with reserved liquor, the milk solids, onion, garlic, salt, pepper, nutmeg, and egg whites in a food processor or blender. Pour mixture into a saucepan; heat thoroughly.
2. Layer half the spinach mixture into large shell dishes or ramekins. Top with oysters; spoon remaining spinach mixture over oysters. Sprinkle with cheese. Set on a cookie sheet.
3. Bake at 400°F about 10 minutes, or until bubbly. Broil 1 to 2 minutes to brown tops. Serve immediately.

4 servings

Note: This recipe will make 8 first-course servings. Prepare recipe as directed; serve in shell-shaped ramekins or custard cups.

*If desired, substitute 2 packages (10 ounces each) frozen chopped spinach for fresh; cook following package directions.

786 *Bay Scallops with Cucumber Rings*

Serve this entrée in a clear bowl so that the layering is visible.

2 pounds bay scallops or sea scallops, cut in thirds
1 tablespoon minced onion
½ cup minced celery
1 cup minced carrot
● 1½ cups Chicken Stock
½ teaspoon salt
2 large cucumbers, pared, sliced lengthwise, seeded, and cut in 1-inch slices
¼ cup dry white wine
1 tablespoon arrowroot
Cold water
Salt

1. Simmer scallops, onion, celery, and carrot in the stock until scallops are tender (about 4 minutes). Strain stock into a medium saucepan. Sprinkle ½ teaspoon salt over scallop mixture; keep warm.
2. Simmer cucumbers in stock until just tender (about 4 minutes). Remove cucumbers with slotted spoon; keep warm.
3. Heat remaining stock and wine to boiling. Mix arrowroot with a little cold water; stir into stock. Simmer, stirring constantly, until thickened (about 3 minutes). Season to taste with salt. Spoon half the cucumbers into a clear glass serving bowl. Arrange scallops on top. Spoon remaining cucumbers over scallops; pour sauce over. Serve immediately.

6 servings

787 *Gingered Scallops*

- 3 cups Fish Stock
- 1 tablespoon minced fresh ginger root
- 2 tablespoons dry sherry
- ½ teaspoon ground ginger
- 1½ pounds bay scallops or sea scallops, cut in ½-inch pieces
- ¾ cup chopped celery
- 2 teaspoons arrowroot
- Cold water
- Salt
- Snipped parsley

1. Combine stock and ginger root in a medium skillet. Simmer until stock is reduced to 1 cup (about 15 minutes). Strain stock and discard ginger root. Return stock to skillet; stir in sherry and ground ginger.
2. Simmer scallops and celery in stock until tender (about 4 minutes). Remove scallops with a slotted spoon to small shell dishes. Mix arrowroot with a little cold water; stir into stock. Simmer, stirring constantly, until sauce is thickened (about 2 minutes). Taste and season with salt. Spoon sauce over scallops; sprinkle with parsley.

4 servings

Note: This recipe will make 6 first-course servings.

788 *Herbed Shrimp in Beer*

Simmer the shrimp in the marinade instead of broiling them, if you desire. Also excellent served as an appetizer with Mock Hollandaise Sauce (●) or Cucumber Sauce (●) for dipping.

- 2 pounds peeled raw shrimp
- 1½ cups beer
- 2 teaspoons lemon juice
- 2 garlic cloves, minced
- 2 tablespoons snipped chives
- 2 tablespoons snipped parsley
- 1½ teaspoons salt
- ½ teaspoon freshly ground pepper
- Shredded lettuce
- 2 green onions, finely chopped

1. Combine all ingredients except lettuce and green onions in a bowl. Refrigerate covered 8 hours or overnight; stir occasionally. Drain; reserve marinade.
2. Broil shrimp 4 inches from heat until cooked and tender (about 2 minutes on each side; less time for small shrimp). Do not overcook or shrimp will become tough. Brush occasionally with marinade. Marinade can be heated and served for dipping, if desired.
3. Serve shrimp on shredded lettuce; sprinkle with chopped green onion.

6 servings

789 *Citrus Seafood Salad*

Seafood and citrus flavors team for a refreshing salad entrée.

- 3 cups shredded iceberg lettuce
- ● ½ cup Citrus Mayonnaise
- 1 teaspoon celery seed
- 1½ pounds cooked crab meat, lobster, flounder, or whitefish, cut in ½-inch pieces
- Salt
- Freshly ground white pepper
- 1 navel orange, sliced

Arrange lettuce on a serving platter or individual plates. Mix Citrus Mayonnaise and celery seed; gently fold fish into mixture. Mound fish mixture on lettuce; sprinkle very lightly with salt and pepper. Arrange orange slices around fish mixture.

4 servings

790 *Baked Shrimp (Scampi al Forno)*

2 pounds large fresh uncooked
    shrimp
⅓ cup butter
1 teaspoon salt
4 cloves garlic, crushed in a garlic
    press
¼ cup chopped parsley
2 teaspoons grated lemon peel
2 tablespoons lemon juice

1. Remove shells from shrimp, leaving shell on tail section. Remove vein down the back, wash under cold running water, and drain on paper towels.
2. Place butter in a 13×9-inch baking dish; heat in oven at 400°F until melted. Stir in salt, garlic, and 1 tablespoon parsley. Place shrimp in a single layer in the baking dish.
3. Bake at 400°F 5 minutes. Turn the shrimp and sprinkle with lemon peel, lemon juice, and remaining parsley. Continue baking about 15 minutes, or until tender.
4. Serve shrimp with sauce over **hot fluffy rice.**

About 6 servings

791 *Shrimp San Giusto (Scampi Imperiali San Giusto)*

1 pound large uncooked shrimp
½ teaspoon salt
⅛ teaspoon pepper
1 bay leaf
3 tablespoons lemon juice
2½ cups water
1 bay leaf
1 thick slice onion
    Pinch each salt, pepper, thyme,
    and oregano
2 tablespoons olive oil
1 tablespoon butter
½ cup finely chopped onion
1 clove garlic, finely chopped
1 teaspoon finely chopped parsley
    Flour
⅓ cup dry white wine
1 large tomato, peeled, seeded,
    and chopped

1. Using scissors, cut the shells of the shrimp down middle of back; remove shells and set aside. Clean and devein shrimp.
2. Place cleaned shrimp in a bowl with salt, pepper, and a bay leaf; drizzle with lemon juice. Set shrimp aside to marinate 1 hour.
3. To make fish stock, place shrimp shells in a saucepan with water, a bay leaf, onion slice, salt, pepper, thyme, and oregano. Cover and simmer 30 minutes; strain.
4. Heat olive oil and butter in a skillet. Add chopped onion, garlic, and parsley; cook until soft. Coat marinated shrimp with flour, add to skillet with vegetables, and cook until lightly browned on both sides.
5. Add wine and simmer until it is almost evaporated. Stir in tomato and ½ cup or more of the strained fish stock. Simmer 15 to 20 minutes, or until the sauce is desired consistency.

3 or 4 servings

792 *Rice with Lobster Sardinian Style (Riso con Aragosta alla Sardegna)*

2 large frozen lobster tails
⅔ cup minced onion
1 large clove garlic, minced
¼ cup olive oil
2 cans (16 ounces each) tomato
    purée
1 tablespoon chopped fresh basil
    leaves, or 1 teaspoon dried
    basil
1 tablespoon mild honey
1 teaspoon salt
⅛ teaspoon pepper
4 cups hot cooked rice

1. Boil lobster tails according to package directions. Cool. Remove meat from shells and cut into chunks; set aside.
2. Sauté onion and garlic in olive oil 5 minutes. Stir in tomato purée, basil, honey, salt, and pepper.
3. Simmer sauce, covered, 45 minutes. If sauce becomes too thick while it is cooking, stir in ½ cup water.
4. Combine lobster with rice, pour hot sauce over rice, and serve.

793 *Baked Fettuccine with Perch Florentine*
(Fettuccine con Persici alla Fiorentina)

White Sauce
12 small perch fillets
1 teaspoon salt
¼ teaspoon pepper
2 cups white wine
3 pounds spinach
1 pound fettuccine noodles, cooked
    according to package
    directions and drained
¼ cup grated Parmesan cheese

1. Prepare sauce, place a piece of waxed paper directly on surface, and keep warm.
2. Wash and dry the fillets; place in a saucepan. Sprinkle with salt and pepper and pour in the wine. Simmer 15 minutes, or less, being sure fish remains intact.
3. Wash spinach. Place in a saucepan only with water that clings to leaves from washing. Cover saucepan and cook rapidly about 5 minutes, or until tender. Drain well and chop.
4. Arrange half the spinach in a 3-quart baking dish. Place half the fettuccine over spinach, and top with 6 fillets. Repeat layering with remaining spinach, fettuccine, and fish. Pour the warm sauce over all and sprinkle cheese on top.
5. Bake at 400°F 20 minutes, or until top is browned. Serve 2 fillets per person on a mound of fettuccine and spinach.

6 servings

White Sauce: Melt **5 tablespoons butter** in a saucepan. Blend in **5 tablespoons flour, 1 teaspoon salt,** and **⅛ teaspoon pepper;** heat until bubbly. Gradually add **2½ cups milk,** stirring until smooth. Bring to boiling and cook, stirring constantly, 1 to 2 minutes. Stir in **pinch nutmeg.**

About 2½ cups sauce

794 *Fried Scampi (Scampi Fritti)*

3 pounds fresh prawns or shrimp
    with shells
Fat for deep frying heated to
    360°F
½ cup olive oil
4 cloves garlic, minced
1 teaspoon salt
½ teaspoon oregano
¼ teaspoon pepper
1 teaspoon chopped parsley

1. Wash prawns in cold water. Remove tiny legs, peel off shells, and devein prawns. Rinse in cold water, then pat dry with absorbent paper.
2. Put only as many prawns in fat as will float uncrowded one layer deep. Fry 3 to 5 minutes, or until golden brown. Drain over fat before removing to absorbent paper. Turn fried prawns onto a warm platter.
3. Heat oil in a skillet. Add garlic, salt, oregano, and pepper and cook until garlic is lightly browned. Pour sauce over prawns and sprinkle with parsley.

About 6 servings

795 *Lobster Fra Diavolo (Aragosta alla Diavola)*

● Marinara Sauce
2 live lobsters (about 1½ pounds
    each)
½ cup red wine
Few grains cayenne pepper

1. Prepare Marinara Sauce.
2. While sauce is cooking, fill a large, deep kettle about two thirds full with water. Bring to boiling and plunge lobsters, one at a time, head first into boiling water. Cover and boil about 8 minutes (Lobsters will turn pink.) Remove lobsters with tongs. With a sharp knife, slit underside lengthwise and remove stomach, lungs, and vein. Keep warm.
3. When sauce is cooked, stir in wine and cayenne, bring to boiling, and pour over lobsters. Serve immediately.

2 servings

796 *Scampi Flamingo*

A recipe from the Danieli Royal Excelsior in Venice.

½ cup butter
1 cup chopped celery
¼ cup chopped carrot
¼ cup chopped onion
¼ teaspoon thyme
2 pounds fresh shrimp with shells
3 tablespoons cognac
2 cups light cream
⅓ cup sherry
½ cup butter
½ teaspoon lemon juice
⅛ teaspoon ground nutmeg
● ¼ cup Béchamel Sauce

1. Heat ½ cup butter in a large skillet. Sauté vegetables with thyme until lightly browned. Add the shrimp and brown carefully.
2. Add cognac and flame it. Add cream, sherry, and sauce; cook 15 minutes.
3. Remove shrimp; shell and devein them; keep warm.
4. Add ½ cup butter, lemon juice, and nutmeg to sauce; cook about 5 minutes. Strain through a fine sieve and pour over the shrimp.
5. Serve sauce and shrimp with hot cooked rice.

About 4 servings

797 *Ancona Fish Stew (Brodetto Anconetana)*

2 pounds assorted fish (mullet, sole, and halibut fillets)
1 large onion, thinly sliced
½ cup olive oil
2 teaspoons salt
½ teaspoon pepper
Pinch saffron
Water (about 2 cups)
Dry white wine (about 2 cups)

1. Cut fish fillets in 2½-inch pieces; set aside.
2. Sauté onion in olive oil until golden. Sprinkle in salt, pepper, and saffron. Add the fish and enough water and wine to cover the fish. Bring to boiling and cook over high heat 10 to 15 minutes.
3. Serve very hot in warmed soup bowls with crusts of fried bread, if desired.

6 servings

798 *Fillet of Sole in White Wine (Filetti di Sogliole al Vino)*

2 pounds sole fillets
½ cup dry white wine
½ cup chopped onion
3 tablespoons butter, melted
2 bay leaves, crushed
1 teaspoon chopped parsley
½ teaspoon salt
¼ teaspoon pepper

1. Put fillets into a greased shallow 2-quart casserole.
2. Mix wine, onion, butter, and dry seasonings. Pour over fish. Cover casserole.
3. Bake at 375°F 25 minutes, or until fish flakes easily when tested with a fork.

6 servings

799 Cod Sailor Style (Baccalà alla Marinara)

2 pounds cod steaks, about 1 inch thick
2 cups canned tomatoes, sieved
¼ cup chopped green olives
2 tablespoons capers
1 tablespoon parsley
1 teaspoon salt
½ teaspoon pepper
½ teaspoon oregano

1. Put cod steaks into a greased 1½-quart casserole.
2. Combine tomatoes, olives, capers, parsley, salt, pepper, and oregano in a saucepan. Bring to boiling and pour over cod.
3. Bake at 350°F 25 to 30 minutes, or until fish flakes easily when tested with a fork.

4 servings

800 Red Snapper Veracruz Style

Red Snapper Veracruz Style is one of Mexico's famous fish entrées. The sauce of tomatoes, onion, olives, and capers is also frequently used with haddock, and is equally delicious with other similar fish.

¼ cup olive oil
1 cup chopped onion
1 clove garlic, minced
2 cups (16-ounce can) tomatoes with liquid
1 teaspoon salt
¼ teaspoon pepper
2 pounds red snapper fillets
¼ cup sliced pimento-stuffed olives
2 tablespoons capers
Lemon wedges

1. Heat oil in a large skillet. Cook onion and garlic in hot oil until onion is soft, about 5 minutes. Add tomatoes, salt, and pepper and cook about 5 minutes to blend flavors; slightly chop tomatoes as they cook.
2. Arrange red snapper fillets in a 3-quart baking dish. Pour sauce over fish. Sprinkle with olives and capers.
3. Bake at 350°F 25 to 30 minutes, or until fish can be flaked easily with a fork. Serve with lemon wedges.

About 6 servings

801 Drunken Fish

A number of traditional Mexican recipes call for "drunken" sauce—another example of the penchant for humorous food names. They may use dry white or red wine, tequila, or pulque (another alcoholic beverage made from the maguey cactus, like tequila). This recipe for Drunken Fish calls for dry red wine in a chili-tomato sauce.

1 whole red snapper or similar fish, or 5 pounds fish fillets
Flour, seasoned with salt and pepper
¼ cup oil
1 cup chopped onion
1 clove garlic, minced
6 fresh or dried ancho chilies
1½ cups canned tomatoes
2 tablespoons dried parsley
⅓ teaspoon oregano
½ teaspoon cumin (comino)
Salt and pepper
2 cups dry red wine
2 tablespoons capers

1. Dredge the fish with seasoned flour. Heat oil in a large skillet and brown fish on both sides. Remove fish from skillet and place in a shallow baking dish.
2. Add onion and garlic to oil remaining in skillet and cook until onion is soft, about 5 minutes.
3. Prepare chilies (see page 30); place in an electric blender and blend to a thick purée. Add to onion and garlic in skillet and cook about 5 minutes. Add tomatoes, parsley, oregano, and cumin. Bring to boiling, stirring constantly. Season to taste with salt and pepper. Stir in red wine and mix well.
4. Pour sauce over fish in baking dish.
5. Bake at 400°F about 30 minutes, or until fish flakes easily. Garnish with capers and serve.

6 to 8 servings

802 *Codfish for Christmas*

1 pound salted codfish (1 piece)
2 small onions, peeled
    Salt and pepper
3 medium (1 pound) tomatoes,
    peeled, seeded, and cut in
    pieces
2 cloves garlic, peeled
3 tablespoons oil
5 pickled chilies, seeded and cut in
    strips
3 canned pimentos, cut in strips
½ cup pimento-stuffed olives
1 tablespoon chopped parsley

1. Soak codfish several hours in cold water; change water several times.
2. Drain codfish and put into a saucepan; add 1 onion and water to cover. Bring to simmering, cover, and cook gently about 15 minutes, or until fish flakes easily when tested with a fork. Drain. Season with salt and pepper.
3. Meanwhile, purée tomatoes, remaining onion (cut in quarters), and garlic in an electric blender.
4. Heat oil in a skillet and add the red sauce. Cook until thicker, stirring occasionally. Mix in chili and pimento strips.
5. To serve, put the codfish on a platter, pour the sauce over it, and garnish with whole olives and parsley. Accompany with **cooked rice.**

About 4 servings

803 *Pickled Tuna (Atún en Escabeche)*

This is an adaptation of a Mexican favorite, Escabeche. The word escabeche means pickled, and usually refers to one of the popular recipes for chilled pickled fish. Normally a mild-flavored white fish is called for, but in this recipe canned tuna is prepared "en escabeche." Serve as an appetizer, as Escabeche is usually served in Mexico, or as a luncheon salad.

2 cans (6½ to 7 ounces each) tuna,
    drained
    Juice of 2 limes or 1 lemon
¼ cup oil
1 medium onion, thinly sliced
    (about ½ cup)
2 canned jalapeño chilies, seeded
    and cut in thin strips
1 clove garlic, minced
½ teaspoon oregano
½ teaspoon cumin (comino)
¾ cup wine or cider vinegar
    Lettuce leaves
    Sliced pimento-stuffed olives

1. Put tuna into a jar or bowl with lid; flake with fork. Pour lime juice over fish and let stand while preparing pickling mixture.
2. Heat oil in skillet. Add onion, chilies, and garlic; cook about 5 minutes, until onion is soft. Stir in oregano and cumin, then stir in vinegar. Bring to boiling.
3. Pour sauce over fish and stir until well coated.
4. Cover and refrigerate several hours. Serve on lettuce garnished with olive slices.

6 servings

804 *Fish Campeche Style*

1 pound fish fillets, fresh or frozen
½ cup orange juice
1 can (6 ounces) tomato paste
1 cup water
¼ cup chopped onion

1. Place fish fillets in a medium-sized skillet and add water to cover. Add ¼ cup of the orange juice. Bring to boiling, reduce heat, and simmer about 10 minutes, or until fish flakes when tested with a fork. Drain and skin, if necessary. Cut fish into finger-sized pieces. Return to skillet.

1 teaspoon chili powder
Salt and pepper

2. Meanwhile, in a small saucepan, combine remaining orange juice, tomato paste, 1 cup of water, onion, and chili powder. Bring to boiling; season with salt and pepper to taste. Pour over fish fingers. Simmer fish in this sauce until well coated and sauce starts to thicken.

4 to 6 servings

805 *Seviche I*

1 pound pompano (or other
    mild-flavored fish fillets)
  Juice of 6 limes (or lemons)
2 medium tomatoes, peeled and
    chopped
2 tablespoons finely chopped onion
1 or 2 canned jalapeño chilies,
    seeded and finely chopped
¼ cup olive oil
1 tablespoon vinegar
¼ teaspoon oregano
  Salt and pepper
  Sliced green olives
  Chopped parsley

1. Wash the fish very well. Cut into small chunks or strips and place in a glass jar or glass bowl with cover. Pour lime juice over fish; cover and refrigerate about 6 hours. (Lime juice will "cook" raw fish until it is white and firm.)
2. At least a half hour before serving, add tomato, onion, chili, olive oil, vinegar, oregano, and salt and pepper to taste; stir gently until evenly mixed.
3. When ready to serve, garnish with sliced olives and parsley.

6 servings

806 *Seviche II*

1 pound fresh firm-fleshed
    boneless white fish
¾ cup lemon juice
1 teaspoon salt
3 canned green chilies, seeded and
    chopped
2 ripe medium tomatoes, peeled,
    seeded, and chopped
2 small onions, thinly sliced
2 teaspoons coriander
⅓ cup olive oil
2 tablespoons vinegar

1. Remove skin from fish; cut into small pieces and put into a deep bowl. Add lemon juice and salt; toss. Cover and refrigerate 1 to 2 hours.
2. Toss gently. Add remaining ingredients; mix thoroughly. Chill.
3. Serve in shells or cocktail glasses and, if desired, garnish with avocado slices.

About 6 servings

807 *Poached Fish with Almonds*

Poached fish garnished with nuts is another seafood entrée. This sauce calls for dry white wine and Mexican green tomato sauce.

1 cup dry white wine
1 small can salsa verde mexicana
   (Mexican green tomato sauce)
½ cup chopped onion
1 clove garlic, minced
   Salt and pepper
2 pounds fish fillets (halibut,
   flounder, sole, or other white
   fish)
½ cup toasted slivered almonds ·
   Lemon wedges

1. Combine wine, salsa verde, onion, and garlic in a large skillet. Season with salt and pepper to taste. Bring to boiling, reduce heat, and simmer about 10 to 15 minutes.
2. Place fish fillets in simmering sauce and cook until fish flakes easily with a fork, about 5 to 10 minutes.
3. Transfer fish to a heated platter, spoon some of the sauce over fish, and sprinkle wtih almonds. Serve with lemon wedges.

About 6 servings

808 *Veracruz Style Crab-Filled Fish Rolls*

6 fish fillets (such as red snapper
   or sole), cut into long, thin
   slices
   Juice of 1 lemon or lime
½ cup milk
2 tablespoons olive oil
½ cup chopped onion
1 clove garlic, minced
1 small tomato, peeled and
   chopped
1 teaspoon minced parsley
1 teaspoon salt
   Dash of pepper
¼ pound crab meat, shredded
¼ pound shredded Monterey Jack
1 cup dairy sour cream
1 egg yolk
¼ pound butter or margarine

1. Rinse fish; rub with lemon or lime juice; soak in milk.
2. Meanwhile, heat olive oil in a small skillet. Sauté onion and garlic in oil; add tomato and cook until no longer juicy. Remove from heat and stir in parsley, salt, and pepper. Add crab meat and ⅓ of the cheese and mix well.
3. Remove fish from milk and pat dry with paper towels. Place a small amount of crab meat filling on one end of fillet and roll up, as for a jelly roll. Place fish rolls in one layer in a greased baking dish.
4. Beat sour cream with egg yolk and pour over fish. Dot with butter. Sprinkle remaining cheese over top.
5. Bake at 350°F until golden brown and cheese is melted (about 20 minutes).

6 servings

809 *Shrimp with Red Rice*

¼ cup oil
½ cup chopped onion
1 clove garlic, minced
1 medium green pepper, seeded
   and sliced in ½-inch strips
1 pound shelled green shrimp
1 can (6 ounces) tomato paste
2½ cups water
1 teaspoon salt
¼ teaspoon pepper
¼ teaspoon marjoram
1 cup uncooked rice

1. Heat oil in a large, heavy saucepan. Add onion and garlic and cook until soft (about 5 minutes). Add green pepper and uncooked shrimp and cook until shrimp turn pink.
2. Stir tomato paste, water, and seasonings into shrimp mixture and bring to boiling. Add rice; mix well. Cover and simmer over very low heat until all liquid is absorbed by rice (about 25 to 30 minutes).

4 to 6 servings

810 *Shrimp with Sesame Seed Sauce*

½ cup plain pumpkin seed
3 tablespoons sesame seed
1 small clove garlic
2 tablespoons vegetable oil
¾ teaspoon chili powder
¼ teaspoon cinnamon
⅛ teaspoon cloves
¾ cup canned chicken broth
½ teaspoon salt
1½ tablespoons lime juice
1½ pounds hot cooked shelled shrimp

1. Combine pumpkin seed, sesame seed, garlic, and oil in a saucepan. Stir and cook over medium heat until sesame seed is light golden brown.
2. Remove from heat and stir in chili powder, cinnamon, and cloves. Turn into an electric blender and grind. Add broth and salt; blend.
3. Turn mixture into a saucepan, mix in lime juice, and heat over low heat, stirring in one direction, until thickened.
4. Arrange hot shrimp on a platter and spoon sauce over it. If desired, garnish with sliced green onion and lime wedges.

4 servings

811 *Paella I*

1 cup sliced carrots
1 small onion, sliced
2 bay leaves
1 tablespoon dried parsley
¼ teaspoon pepper
3 cups water
½ cup oil
2 broiler-fryer chickens, cut in serving pieces
2 cloves garlic, minced
1 green pepper, cut in thin strips
1 teaspoon crumbled saffron
1 can (12 ounces) clams or 8 to 12 fresh clams
1½ cups uncooked rice
1 tablespoon salt
2 large tomatoes, peeled and chopped
1 can (8 ounces) artichoke hearts
1 pound cooked shrimp, shelled and deveined

1. Place carrots, onion, bay leaves, dried parsley, pepper, and water in saucepan; simmer over low heat about 20 minutes, or until carrots are tender.
2. Meanwhile, heat oil in a large Dutch oven or heavy kettle. Brown chicken pieces in oil, a few at a time, removing as they are well browned.
3. In same oil, sauté garlic, pepper strips, and saffron. Return chicken pieces to Dutch oven. Drain liquid from clams and add enough of this liquid to vegetable liquid to make 3 cups. Pour over chicken in Dutch oven. Bring to simmering and gradually stir in rice and salt.
4. Bake at 350°F 1 hour.
5. During last part of baking, prepare clams by cutting in half; chop tomatoes; cut artichoke hearts into quarters vertically. Add clams, tomatoes, shrimp, and artichoke hearts to chicken-rice mixture, and mix in carefully. Return to oven for 10 to 15 minutes more, or until heated through. Serve hot.

8 to 10 servings

812 *Paella II*

1 cup olive oil or vegetable oil
1 broiler-fryer chicken (2 pounds), cut in pieces
½ cup diced boiled ham or smoky sausage
1 tablespoon minced onion
2 cloves garlic, minced
2 ripe tomatoes, peeled and coarsely chopped
1½ teaspoons salt
1½ pounds fresh shrimp, shelled and deveined
12 small clams in shells, scrubbed
2 cups uncooked rice
1 quart hot water
1 cup fresh or frozen green peas
¼ cup coarsely chopped parsley
Few shreds saffron
1 rock lobster tail, cooked and meat cut in pieces
1 can or jar (7 ounces) whole pimentos

1. Heat oil in paellera or large skillet; cook chicken and ham about 10 minutes, turning chicken to brown on all sides. Add onion and garlic and cook 2 minutes. Add tomatoes, salt, shrimp, and clams; cover and cook 5 to 10 minutes, or until clam shells open. Remove clams and keep warm.
2. Add rice, water, peas, parsley, and saffron; mix well. Cover and cook, stirring occasionally, 25 minutes, or until rice is just tender. Mix in lobster, half of pimento, and the reserved clams in shells; heat until very hot. Serve garnished with remaining pimento.

8 to 10 servings

813 *Court Bouillon for Fish and Shellfish*

1 onion
1 leek
1 carrot
3 celery stalks
5 parsley sprigs
1 basil sprig
2 tablespoons olive oil
2 quarts boiling water
Bouquet garni
6 peppercorns, cracked
2 whole cloves
6 dried Italian pepper pods or
    1 whole pink hot pepper
½ cup amber rum

1. Finely chop fresh vegetables and herbs together.
2. Heat oil in a large saucepan, add chopped mixture, and cook until lightly browned. Add boiling water, bouquet garni, peppercorns, cloves, pepper pods, and rum. Cover; boil 30 minutes. Boil uncovered to reduce volume by half.
3. Strain and cool before using.

About 1 quart

814 *Scrambled Eggs with Salt Cod*

5 parsley sprigs
2 green onions, chopped
1 garlic clove, crushed in a garlic press
1 dried Italian pepper pod or
    1 sliver green hot pepper
1½ cups shredded soaked salt cod
3 tablespoons peanut oil
1 cup hot milk
6 eggs

1. In a mortar, pound together to a paste the parsley, onion, garlic, and pepper pod. Mix this seasoning paste with the shredded cod.
2. Heat oil in a skillet, add fish mixture, and brown it, adding hot milk.
3. In another skillet, scramble eggs to a soft consistency while gradually adding the fish mixture.

4 servings

815 *Stuffed Fish Odette Mennesson*

1 large grouper or bluefish
  (4 to 5 pounds)
Court Bouillon for Fish and
● Shellfish
6 hard-cooked eggs
2 cups Herbal Mayonnaise Odette
● Mennesson , chilled
1 cup crab meat
Parsley
Lime wedges and avocado slices
  for garnish

1. Have the fish split and boned without removing the head or tail.
2. Bring court bouillon to boiling in a large roasting pan. Wrap fish in cheesecloth and put into pan, leaving the ends of the cloth out of the pan. Poach 7 to 10 minutes, or until fish is thoroughly cooked.
3. Meanwhile, mash eggs with mayonnaise; mix in crab meat.
4. Gently remove fish from bouillon and transfer from cloth to a platter. Spoon crab mixture between the two halves of fish. Serve warm, or if desired, chill thoroughly.
5. To serve, arrange parsley around fish and garnish with slices of lime and avocado.

816 *Red Snapper Meuniere*

2 red snappers (2 pounds each)
2 limes, halved
Salt and pepper to taste
½ cup flour
Peanut oil (about ¼ cup)
Butter (about 2 tablespoons)
5 drops Tabasco
¼ cup butter
1 tablespoon chopped parsley
1 tablespoon lime juice
Lime wedges for garnish

1. Have the fins and tails trimmed from fish, without removing the heads. Rub the fish with cut side of lime halves, squeezing gently to release the juice. Season with salt and pepper. Superficially slash the skin of the fish in a diamond design.
2. Put flour into a bag large enough to hold fish; put fish into bag and coat them evenly with flour.
3. Heat enough oil and butter to cover the bottom of a skillet large enough to hold both fish. When fat is sizzling, add Tabasco. Sauté fish about 12 minutes on each side, or until done, reducing the heat if necessary so as not to scorch them.
4. Meanwhile, cream ¼ cup butter with parsley.
5. Remove fish to a heated plater and keep warm. Discard all the fat in bottom of the skillet and add butter with parsley and the lime juice; stir until blended. Spoon over fish.
6. Garnish platter with lime wedges.

6 servings

817 *Stuffed Red Snapper*

1 red snapper (about 5 pounds)
Salt and pepper to taste
½ lime
¼ cup flour
1 cup cooked rice
1 cup chopped raw shrimp
½ cup chopped green onion
  (including top)
½ cup very thinly sliced celery
1 tablespoon grated ginger root
2 bacon slices
¼ cup dry white wine

1. Season red snapper inside and out with salt and pepper. Rub with cut side of lime. Sprinkle evenly with flour.
2. Combine rice, shrimp, onion, celery, and ginger root. Spoon into fish; skewer or sew the opening. Lay fish in a very heavily buttered baking pan. Score the top of fish in an attractive design to prevent it from buckling. Lay bacon slices over top.
3. Bake at 350°F 45 minutes, or until fish flakes. Transfer fish to a heated platter.
4. Deglaze baking pan with white wine. Pour liquid over fish.

818 *Red Snapper à l'Orange*

1 red snapper (5½ to 6 pounds)
Salt and cayenne or red pepper
  to taste
Juices of 1 lime and 1 orange
● Court Bouillon for Fish and
  Shellfish
Bouquet garni
16 potato balls
16 small carrots, cut in chunks
6 leeks (white part only), halved
8 unpeeled orange slices
3 tablespoons tomato paste
● Saffron Rice

1. Season red snapper with salt, cayenne, and juices; allow to marinate 30 minutes.
2. Pour court bouillon into a fish steamer. Place the fish in steamer along with bouquet garni, vegetables, and orange slices. Simmer uncovered on top of the range or bake at 450°F 20 minutes.
3. Transfer fish carefully to a heated platter. Arrange the vegetables around it. Garnish with orange slices.
4. Measure 2 cups fish broth and blend with tomato paste; pour over vegetables. Serve with the rice.

819 *Dr. Gagneron's Fish in Pastry*

1 cup cold water
1 teaspoon salt
2 cups all-purpose flour
½ cup butter
1 grouper (about 2½ pounds)
● Court Bouillon for Fish and
  Shellfish
●1 cup Béchamel Sauce ;
  made with strained court
  bouillon
12 raw oysters, shelled
¼ cup capers
½ cup chopped red and green sweet
  peppers
Milk

1. For pastry, chill a bowl and pastry board. Combine water and salt. Put flour into the chilled bowl, make a well, and pour in the salted water; mix without kneading. Refrigerate dough 30 minutes.
2. Roll the dough into a rectangle ¼ inch thick on chilled and floured pastry board. Lightly trace lines dividing the rectangle into 3 even sections.
3. Spread the butter on the middle section, working quickly. Fold the 2 sides over the middle. Roll again to ¼-inch thickness. Fold into thirds and roll again. Fold into thirds and refrigerate overnight.
4. For filling, poach grouper in court bouillon. When the fish flakes at the touch of a knife near the backbone, remove from broth. Cool and shred it, discarding the skin and bones.
5. Combine sauce, the shredded grouper, oysters, capers, and peppers. Set aside.
6. Roll pastry to ¼-inch thickness. Spread the filling on half the pastry; fold the other half over it. Brush the edges with milk and press to seal. Brush the top surface with milk. Put on a baking sheet with sides.
7. Bake at 400°F 30 minutes; turn oven control to 350°F and bake 15 minutes, or until pastry is browned.

820 *Macadam of Cod Martinique*

2 pounds salt cod
¼ cup olive oil
2 large onions, chopped
⅛ teaspoon cayenne or red pepper
   Bouquet garni
1 garlic clove, crushed in a
    garlic press
3 tomatoes, peeled, seeded,
    and cut in chunks
1 tablespoon olive oil
1 teaspoon lime juice
¼ cup chopped parlsey
● Caribbean Rice

1. Soak cod in cold water overnight. The next day, drain, trim edges from fish, and coarsely shred fish.
2. Heat ¼ cup oil in a large skillet. Add onion and cod; cook until lightly browned. Add pepper, bouquet garni, garlic, and tomato; mix well. Cook covered over low heat 15 minutes. Add 1 tablespoon oil and the lime juice; mix well.
3. Transfer cod mixture to a serving platter and sprinkle with parsley. Serve with the rice.

821 *Eggplant and Salt Cod* (Morue e Beregenes)

2 pounds salt cod
1 eggplant (2 pounds),
    pared and sliced
½ cup olive oil
2 garlic cloves, crushed in a
    garlic press
5 drops Tabasco
1 tablespoon tomato paste
   Bouquet garni
   Juice of ½ lime
   Salt and pepper to taste
● French-Fried Breadfruit or
● Deep-Fried Plantain

1. Soak cod in cold water overnight. The next day, place the fish in a sieve and slowly pour 1 quart boiling water over it. Bone fish, trim, and remove any skin, then shred and set aside.
2. Cook eggplant slices in salted water 3 minutes, then drain.
3. Put oil, garlic, Tabasco, and tomato paste into a Dutch oven; mix. Add reserved fish, the eggplant, and bouquet garni. Cook over medium heat until eggplant falls apart. Mix in lime juice, salt, and pepper.
4. Serve hot with breadfruit.

Crab Zoumba: Follow recipe for Eggplant and Salt Cod, substituting **2 pounds crab meat** for cod.

822 *Guadelupean Blaffe*

2 pounds salt cod
3 garlic cloves
⅛ teaspoon cayenne or red pepper
10 parsley sprigs
3 peppercorns
3 scallions or green onions,
    cut in pieces
3 celery leaves
1 fresh dill sprig or
    ⅛ teaspoon dried dill
2 quarts water
   Bouquet garni
● Caribbean Rice

1. Soak cod in cold water overnight. The next day, drain cod and reserve.
2. In a mortar, pound together to a paste the garlic, cayenne, parsley, peppercorns, scallions, celery leaves, and dill.
3. Bring water to boiling in a soup kettle. Add the seasoning paste and bouquet garni; bring to a boil. Add reserved cod and simmer until the cod flakes.
4. Serve in soup plates with the rice.

823 *Crab Meat Omelet Martinique*
(Omelette aux Ouassous)

3 tablespoons butter or margarine
1 package (6 ounces) frozen crab
    meat, thawed, drained,
    and flaked
2 teaspoons finely chopped onion
2 teaspoons chopped parsley
¼ cup dairy sour cream
1 tablespoon dry sherry
4 eggs
2 tablespoons water
    Salt and pepper to taste

1. For filling, melt 1 tablespoon butter in a skillet. Add crab meat, onion, and parsley; heat thoroughly. Stir in sour cream and sherry. Set aside.
2. For omelets, beat eggs in a bowl; add water, salt, and pepper.
3. In a small skillet, melt 1 tablespoon butter over high heat. Add half the beaten eggs. Immediately use a fork or spoon to push the edges of the thickened egg mass towards the center; the liquid will immediately fill the vacant spaces. Repeat this procedure until the eggs are cooked but still soft. Remove from heat.
4. Place half the crab filling in the middle of the omelet. Fold the omelet in thirds to enclose the filling.
5. Repeat procedure for making an omelet, using the remaining beaten eggs and crab meat filling. Serve immediately.

2 omelets

824 *Lobster Canapé*

6 rock lobster tails
    (at least ½ pound each)
● Court Bouillon for Fish and
    Shellfish
9 tablespoons olive oil
6 tablespoons butter
16 white bread slices with crusts
    trimmed
● 2½ cups Béchamel Sauce
2 egg yolks
⅓ cup amber rum, warmed and
    flamed
¾ cup chopped cashews
2 tablespoons chopped parsley
1 tablespoon chopped dill

1. Cook lobster tails in court bouillon until tender; drain, reserving bouillon. Slice lobster into chunks ½ inch thick.
2. Heat 3 tablespoons oil and 2 tablespoons butter in a large skillet. Add a few bread slices and fry until golden, turning once. Repeat frying procedure with more oil, butter, and bread slices. Set croutons aside and keep hot.
3. Prepare Béchamel Sauce with the reserved bouillon; blend in egg yolks and rum. Mix in lobster pieces. Keep warm in a chafing dish.
4. Sauté cashews in 2 tablespoons butter; stir in parsley and dill.
5. To serve, spoon lobster mixture onto croutons and sprinkle with herbed cashews.

825 *Barbecued Eel*

1 eel (about 3 pounds)
2 garlic cloves
1 scallion or green onion,
    cut in pieces
4 dried Italian pepper pods
1 basil sprig
3 parsley sprigs
2 peppercorns
1 tablespoon coarse salt
¼ cup lime juice
1 cup peanut or olive oil
1 cup cornmeal

1. Have eel skinned and cleaned; cut into 3-inch chunks.
2. In a mortar, pound together to a paste the garlic, scallion, pepper pods, basil, parsley, peppercorns, and salt. Blend lime juice and oil into seasoning paste. Pour over eel chunks and marinate overnight.
3. When ready to barbecue, pour cornmeal into a bag, add chunks of eel, and shake to coat. Place eel in a hinged grill and barbecue 5 inches from ash-covered coals, basting frequently with the marinade; turn pieces so they brown on both sides.
4. Serve with Creole Barbecue Sauce (●) or Ti-Malice Sauce (●) and **barbecued yams** (see Yams and Sweet Potatoes, ●

826 Cod Casserole

1 pound salt cod
12 small potatoes
12 small onions, peeled
3 tablespoons olive oil
⅛ teaspoon cayenne or red pepper
Black pepper
½ cup half-and-half

1. Soak cod in cold water overnight. The next day, drain and then rinse under running cold water.
2. Cook cod, potatoes, and onions separately in water, adding no salt. Drain when tender.
3. Remove all bones from cod, trim edges from fish, and cut into 2-inch pieces. Place fish in alternating layers with onions and potatoes in a top-of-range casserole. Drizzle with olive oil, sprinkle with cayenne and black pepper, and pour half-and-half over all. Cover and simmer over low heat 20 minutes.
4. Serve cool, but not cold, with a green salad.

827 Cod Soup (Chaudrée of Cod)

1 pound salt cod
¼ pound salt pork, cubed
1 tablespoon chopped onion
2 sprigs celery leaves
4 parsley sprigs
4 peppercorns, cracked
1 shallot, halved
¼ cup tomato paste
4 drops Tabasco
Bouquet garni
1 cup potato balls
1 quart stock
● Boiled Plantain

1. Soak cod in cold water overnight. The next day, put cod in a sieve and gently pour 1 quart boiling water over it. Flake cod and reserve.
2. Sauté salt pork and onion in a soup kettle until light brown. Set aside.
3. In a mortar, pound together to a paste the celery leaves, parsley, peppercorns, and shallot.
4. Add seasoning paste to kettle along with tomato paste, Tabasco, bouquet garni, potato balls, flaked cod, and stock; stir. Bring to a boil, reduce heat, and simmer gently until vegetables are tender.
5. To serve, put plantain into soup plates and add soup.

828 Barbecued Crabs

8 large hard-shell crabs
½ lime
● Creole Barbecue Sauce
● Caribbean Rice

1. Rinse crabs in water several times. Rub the shells with the cut side of a lime half, squeezing a little to release some of the juice. Cut off the heads just behind the eyes and discard the green sac; lift the belly apron and cut it away, too.
2. Put the crabs in a hinged grill and barbecue 5 inches away from glowing coals for about 5 minutes on each side. Immediately brush with the sauce.
3. Serve crabs with the rice.

8 servings

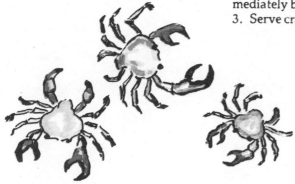

829 *Haitian Rock Lobster Salad*

8 rock lobster tails
● Court Bouillon for Fish and Shellfish
● 4 cups Caribbean Rice
16 cherry tomatoes, washed and stemmed
1 cup cubed pared cucumber
3 celery stalks, diced
1 cup cubed fresh pineapple
1 cup small Greek black olives
¼ cup capers
● 1 cup French Dressing Antillaise for Salads
4 hard-cooked eggs, peeled and quartered
¾ cup amber rum

1. Simmer lobster tails in court bouillon 20 minutes. Belly side down on a board, split the tail lengthwise with a sharp knife and keep warm in the bouillon until serving time (see Note).
2. Toss rice with vegetables, pineapple, olives, and capers. Add dressing and toss again.
3. Mound the rice mixture on a large silver platter, garnish with hard-cooked egg quarters, and edge platter with drained cooked lobster tails.
4. At the table, warm rum, ignite it, and pour it flaming over the lobster.

8 servings

Note: If you have room in the freezer, save the court bouillon to use as a base for Béchamel Sauce for fish or for a chowder.

830 *Crawfish or Jumbo Shrimp au Gratin Guadeloupe*

50 small crawfish in their shells or 50 shelled raw jumbo shrimp
● Court Bouillon for Fish and Shellfish
3 tablespoons butter
1 tablespoon peanut oil
1 pound sliced calf's liver
6 mushrooms, sliced
1 tablespoon chopped parsley
⅛ teaspoon dried marjoram
⅛ teaspoon dried rosemary
Salt, freshly ground pepper, and cayenne or red pepper to taste
3 white bread slices with crusts trimmed
1 egg, beaten
½ cup dried bread crumbs
½ cup finely shredded Swiss cheese
½ cup whipping cream
2 tablespoons amber rum, warmed and flamed

1. Cook crawfish in boiling court bouillon 10 minutes, then cool. Reserve 1 cup bouillon.
2. Heat butter and oil in a skillet; sauté liver and mushrooms until liver is firm on the outside and pink inside. Season with parsley, marjoram, rosemary, salt, and peppers.
3. Soak bread slices in reserved bouillon; stir to break up bread. Process soaked bread with bouillon and liver-mushroom mixture, a little at a time, in an electric blender or force through a food mill. Stir in egg.
4. Spread mixture on bottom of a shallow baking dish. Arrange crawfish decoratively on top. Sprinkle with a mixture of bread crumbs and cheese. Blend cream and rum; pour over all. Broil until lightly browned.

Desserts

831 *Figs with Mavrodaphne Wine* *(Syka me Mavrodaphne Krasi)*

12 ripe figs
2 cups Mavrodaphne wine
2 cups whipping cream, whipped
¼ cup walnuts

1. Peel figs. Prick each 3 or 4 times on sides and bottoms. Arrange figs in a dish and pour wine over them. Refrigerate for 2 hours, turning occasionally.
2. Remove figs to a serving platter. Reserve the wine. Arrange whipping cream around the figs. Garnish with walnuts. Serve wine separately.

4 servings

832 *Whole Wheat Porridge with Currants and Almonds* *(Kourkourti)*

5 cups whole wheat
Water
Salt, sugar, and cinnamon
1 cup coarsely ground blanched almonds
½ cup dried currants (optional)

1. Place whole wheat in a large saucepan. Cover with cold water and let stand overnight.
2. The next day, drain wheat. Cover with fresh cold water. Simmer about 4 hours, or until tender, stirring frequently to prevent scorching and adding water as needed. Stock will become very thick.
3. Drain wheat stock into a saucepan. Add salt, sugar, and cinnamon to taste. Stir in almonds, currants, and 1 cup of the boiled wheat, if desired. Serve hot.

4 servings

833 *Revani*

1 cup unsalted butter
½ cup sugar
1 teaspoon grated lemon or orange peel
5 eggs
2 cups semolina
1 cup flour
1 tablespoon baking powder
Syrup:
3 cups sugar
1 quart water
1 cinnamon stick

1. Cream butter with sugar and grated peel. Beat together 5 minutes. Add eggs, one at a time, beating until well blended after each.
2. Combine semolina, flour, and baking powder. Add to creamed mixture and mix together by hand. Spread in a buttered 9-inch square pan.
3. Bake at 350°F 40 to 45 minutes. Cool 5 minutes.
4. While Revani is baking, prepare the syrup. Combine sugar, water, and cinnamon. Bring to boiling, reduce heat at once, and simmer covered 20 minutes.
5. Pour syrup over cake. Cool, then slice into squares. Serve plain or garnished with **whipped cream** and **toasted almonds** or accompanied with **fresh fruit.**

10 to 12 servings

834 *Butter Horns* *(Rogaliki)*

1 cup sweet unsalted butter or margarine
½ cup sugar
1 egg yolk
1 teaspoon vanilla extract
¼ cup chopped blanched almonds
1⅔ cups all-purpose flour
Confectioners' sugar

1. Beat butter at high speed and add sugar gradually, creaming until light and fluffy. Beat in egg yolk and vanilla extract. Beat in almonds, then flour.
2. With hands, shape 1-inch pieces of dough into crescents. Place on ungreased baking sheets, about 1 inch apart.
3. Bake at 350°F about 20 minutes, or until just golden on edges.
4. While warm, coat crescents with confectioners' sugar.

About 3 dozen

835 *Drop Yeast Doughnuts (Loukoumathes)*

2 packages active dry yeast
2 cups warm water (105° to 115°F)
3 to 4 cups all-purpose flour
1 teaspoon salt
Vegetable oil or olive oil or a combination of the two for deep frying
Honey and cinnamon

1. Dissolve yeast in 1 cup warm water in a small bowl.
2. Add 1½ cups flour to yeast. Beat batter with a wooden spoon until smooth.
3. Cover with a towel and put into a warm place until batter is double in bulk.
4. Pour into a larger bowl, add remaining water, salt, and flour to make a thick but runny batter.
5. Cover with a towel and put into a warm place until batter is double in bulk and begins to bubble.
6. Half fill a deep fryer with oil. Heat just until smoking.
7. Drop batter by tablespoonfuls into oil; occasionally dip spoon in oil before dipping in batter. Cook until golden brown. Remove with a slotted spoon.
8. Drizzle with honey and sprinkle with cinnamon. Serve hot.

About 30

836 *Diples*

2 eggs
1 egg yolk
1 tablespoon butter, melted
Grated peel of 1 orange (optional)
¼ cup orange juice
2 tablespoons lemon juice
Semolina (about 2½ cups)
½ teaspoon baking powder
½ teaspoon salt
Oil for deep frying (4 to 5 inches deep)
Honey
Cinnamon
Chopped walnuts

1. Beat eggs and egg yolk until fluffy. Add melted butter, grated peel, orange juice, and lemon juice.
2. Mix 1 cup semolina with baking powder and salt. Stir into egg mixture. Add another cup semolina and mix well. Add remaining ½ cup semolina as necessary to make a soft dough. It will be a little sticky. Knead on a board until elastic and smooth.
3. Divide dough into 3 portions. Lightly flour a large board and roll dough as thin as for noodles. Using a sharp knife, cut dough into 4-inch-wide strips. Cover dough until ready to fry.
4. Heat oil in a deep saucepan. When oil reaches 350°F, regulate temperature and drop in a piece of dough. Using two forks, turn in one end and roll up quickly to the other. Remove with a slotted spoon as soon as light gold in color. Drain on absorbent towels.
5. To serve, pour warm honey over the Diples and sprinkle with cinnamon and walnuts.

About 4 to 5 dozen

837 *Shredded Wheat Nut Dessert (Kataifi)*

3 cups sugar
1 quart water
Grated peel of 1 lemon
2 whole cloves
4 cups walnuts, coarsely ground
½ cup sugar
2 teaspoons cinnamon
2 pounds kataifi dough
1½ cups unsalted butter, melted
1 tablespoon rosewater

1. Combine 3 cups sugar, water, peel, and cloves in a saucepan. Bring to a boil. Reduce heat, cover, and simmer 20 minutes. Set aside to cool.
2. Combine nuts, ½ cup sugar, and cinnamon in a bowl. Set aside.
3. Take enough kataifi dough to pat into a 4x3-inch flat piece. Put 1 tablespoon of the nut filling in the center, fold dough over, and shape into a roll. Continue until all the filling and dough have been used.
4. Place rolls, 1 inch apart, in a greased large baking pan. Spoon melted butter over each roll.
5. Bake at 325°F about 40 minutes, or until golden brown. Remove from oven and sprinkle with rosewater. Pour cooled syrup over. Cool several hours before serving.

About 30

838 *New Year's Day Cake* (Vasilopita)

3½ cups all-purpose flour
2 teaspoons baking powder
1 cup softened unsalted butter
1 cup sugar
2 eggs (at room temperature)
1 egg yolk
  Grated peel of 1 orange
¼ teaspoon nutmeg (optional)
¼ cup cream
1 tablespoon cognac
1 silver coin, boiled and wrapped
  in foil
  Blanched almonds (about 20)
1 egg white, beaten until frothy

1. Sift flour and baking powder; set aside.
2. Using an electric mixer, beat butter until fluffy. Add sugar gradually, beating 4 minutes. Add eggs and egg yolk, one at a time, beating after each. Add peel and nutmeg. Combine cream and cognac; add gradually while beating.
3. Add dry ingredients, using a wooden spoon to mix in well. Stir in coin.
4. Heavily grease a 10-inch round cake pan. Turn batter into pan. Press edge with fork tines to decorate. Arrange blanched almonds in a decorative pattern on top.
5. Bake at 350°F 15 to 20 minutes, or until cake is set. Pull out from oven, brush with egg white, and return to oven. Continue baking until a wooden pick inserted in the center comes out clean (about 20 minutes). Cool before serving.

8 to 10 servings

839 *Walnut Honey Cake* (Karithopeta)

Syrup:
1 cup sugar
½ cup honey
1 cup water
1 teaspoon lemon juice
1 cinnamon stick

Cake:
¾ cup unsalted butter (at room
  temperature)
½ teaspoon grated orange peel
¾ cup sugar
3 eggs
1 cup all-purpose flour
1½ teaspoons baking powder
½ teaspoon cinnamon
¼ teaspoon salt
¼ cup milk
1 cup chopped walnuts

1. For syrup, bring all ingredients to a boil in a saucepan. Simmer 20 minutes. Set aside to cool.
2. For cake, cream butter, orange peel, and sugar together until fluffy. Beat in eggs, one at a time, beating well after each addition.
3. Mix flour, baking powder, cinnamon, and salt. Fold flour mixture into butter mixture, alternating with milk. Stir in nuts.
4. Pour batter into a greased and floured 8-inch square pan.
5. Bake at 350°F 30 minutes, or until done.
6. Remove cake from oven, cool, and cut into diamonds while in the pan.
7. Pour syrup over cake. Cool. Refrigerate and let soak 24 hours before serving.

2 to 3 dozen

840 *Pasta Flora*

½ cup unsalted butter (at room
  temperature)
2 eggs
1 teaspoon vanilla extract
1 cup sugar
3 cups all-purpose flour
1 tablespoon baking powder
1 pint jam or preserves
1 egg yolk, beaten with ½
  teaspoon water

1. Beat butter 4 minutes, using an electric mixer. Add eggs, vanilla extract, and sugar. Beat until fluffy. Mix flour and baking powder. Slowly work into mixture until well blended.
2. Divide dough into 2 parts; one a ball using three fourths of the total, and one using one fourth of the total.
3. Line the bottom a 13x9-inch baking pan with the larger portion of the dough. Spread the preserves evenly over dough.
4. Roll the remaining quarter of the dough on a lightly floured board to fit the size of the pan. Cut into strips. Form a lattice over the preserves. Brush dough with the egg yolk and water.
5. Bake at 350°F about 45 minutes until pastry is golden brown or a wooden pick comes out clean when inserted. Cool. Cut into squares.

10 servings

841 *Copenhagen Pita* *(Copenhai)*

Syrup:
3 cups sugar
1½ cups honey
5 cups water
½ stick cinnamon

Cake:
1½ cups butter
1 cup confectioners' sugar
5 eggs
1½ cups flour
1 tablespoon baking powder
2 tablespoons cognac

Filling:
5 eggs
2 cups sugar
1 teaspoon cinnamon
3 pieces zwieback, ground
1½ cups almonds, blanched and
    ground

Topping:
1 package filo
1½ cups butter

1. For syrup, combine sugar, honey, water, and cinnamon in a large saucepan. Bring to boiling. Reduce heat and simmer 20 minutes. Set aside to cool.
2. For cake, cream butter and confectioners' sugar. Add eggs, one at a time, beating well after each. Mix flour and baking powder and add to butter mixture. Add cognac and mix well.
3. Spread mixture evenly in a greased 18x12-inch baking pan. Set aside.
4. For filling, separate eggs. Beat yolks slightly, add sugar, and beat until light and fluffy.
5. Beat egg whites in another bowl until stiff, not dry, peaks are formed. Fold whites into yolk mixture. Combine cinnamon, zwieback crumbs, and almonds and fold into egg mixture. Spread evenly over layer in pan.
6. For topping, layer 10 sheets of filo over top, buttering after each layer has been added; see pages 80-81 for how to handle filo. Drizzle a little butter over top layer. Score topmost sheets into diamond shapes.
7. Bake at 350°F about 50 minutes, or until golden in color. Remove from oven and pour cooled syrup over.
8. Let stand several hours before serving.

About 60 pieces

842 *Turkish Delight* *(Loukoumi)*

2 cups granulated sugar
½ cup light corn syrup
½ cup cornstarch plus 3
    tablespoons extra for dusting
3 cups water
1 tablespoon rosewater
⅛ teaspoon ground mastic
2 tablespoons fresh lemon juice
¾ cup unsalted pistachios
Confectioners' sugar for rolling

1. Combine granulated sugar and corn syrup in a saucepan and bring to boiling, stirring constantly. Cook for 30 seconds. Cool.
2. In another saucepan, combine ½ cup cornstarch with water. Simmer mixture until thick. Mix cornstarch into syrup and bring slowly to boiling. Stir to prevent lumps from forming. Reduce heat to very low and cook uncovered, stirring occasionally, until a candy thermometer registers 220°F. Stir in rosewater, mastic, lemon juice, and pistachios.
3. Pour the hot mixture into a square pan lined on bottom and sides with a heavy cotton cloth dusted with cornstarch. Spread mixture and dust top with cornstarch. Cover with a cloth and let it stand 24 hours.
4. Cut the layer into small squares with a sharp knife, roll the pieces in confectioners' sugar, and put into candy paper cups. This confection will keep for weeks.

About 3 dozen pieces

843 *Roast Chestnuts* *(Kastana Karvoudizmena)*

4 pounds chestnuts

1. Cut a cross on the flat side of each chestnut with a small sharp knife, being careful not to damage nutmeat. Spread in a large baking pan.
2. Roast in a 425°F oven about 30 minutes, or until done; shake frequently. Serve hot.

844 *Rusks I* *(Paximathia)*

¼ cup unsalted butter
1 teaspoon vanilla extract
¾ cup sugar
3 eggs (¾ cup)
1 egg yolk
3½ cups sifted cake flour
1 tablespoon baking powder
¼ teaspoon salt
1 egg yolk for glaze

1. Beat butter and vanilla extract, then add sugar gradually, beating thoroughly. Add eggs, one at a time, beating 1 minute after each addition. Combine flour, baking powder, and salt. Add half of flour to creamed mixture and mix with a wooden spoon. Add remaining flour; mix well.
2. Divide dough into four portions. Roll each portion into a long roll about 1½ inches in diameter on a floured pastry cloth. Place rolls 3 inches apart on a well-greased and floured cookie sheet. Flatten dough slightly with hands. Brush tops with egg yolk.
3. Bake at 400°F about 20 to 25 minutes, or until golden and firm to the touch.
4. Remove from oven. Cover with a towel; let stand 2 hours.
5. Cut rolls into ½-inch slices. Place on ungreased cookie sheet, cut sides down.
6. Toast in a 400°F oven 15 to 20 minutes, turning several times until delicately brown.

About 3 dozen

845 *Rusks II* *(Paximathia)*

1 loaf Greek Easter Bread
● (Lambropsomo)
Unsalted butter
Honey

1. Cut bread into thick slices. Place on ungreased cookie sheet.
2. Bake at 225°F 20 minutes on each side.
3. Cool on wire rack. Serve with butter and honey.

846 *Rusks III* *(Paximathia)*

1 cup butter
1 teaspoon vanilla extract
2 cups sugar
2 eggs
1 cup dairy sour cream
5½ cups all-purpose flour
1 teaspoon baking soda
¼ teaspoon salt

1. Cream butter, vanilla extract, and sugar. Add eggs and beat thoroughly. Stir in sour cream.
2. Mix flour, baking soda, and salt. Add to butter mixture and mix until a dough is formed.
3. Divide dough into 3 portions. Shape each portion into a roll 1½ inches in diameter. Place each roll on a cookie sheet.
4. Bake at 350°F 15 minutes. Remove from oven and turn oven control to 425°F. Using a very sharp knife, cut into ¾-inch slices. Arrange slices cut side down on cookie sheets. Bake slices first on one side, then the other, until golden brown and firm (about 6 minutes for each side). Cool on wire racks.

About 3 dozen

847 *Sesame Seed Candy* *(Pasteli)*

½ cup honey
2 cups sugar
½ cup water
3 cups sesame seed, toasted

1. Blend honey, sugar, and water in a heavy skillet. Cook over low heat, stirring frequently. Bring to a firm ball stage, 250°F on a candy thermometer (syrup will be a light gold color). Stir in sesame seed.
2. Spread in a buttered 12x8x1½-inch pan. Break into pieces.

2 to 3 dozen pieces depending on size

848 *Koulourakia I*

1 cup unsalted butter
3 eggs
2 egg yolks
2 tablespoons cognac
2 cups confectioners' sugar
4½ cups sifted cake flour
3½ teaspoons baking powder
Egg white, beaten
Sesame seed, lightly toasted

1. Beat butter until light and fluffy. Add eggs and egg yolks, one at a time, beating well after each. Add cognac, then confectioners' sugar, beating well. Sift flour with baking powder and add to butter mixture; mix well.
2. Knead dough on a floured board until shiny.
3. Break off a small amount of dough and roll on a board to form a strip 5 to 6 inches long. Shape into a ring by joining the ends, or make a snail shape by winding up the strip. Place on a greased cookie sheet. Repeat with remaining dough.
4. Brush tops with beaten egg white. Sprinkle with sesame seed.
5. Bake at 350°F 20 to 25 minutes, or until done.

About 6 dozen

849 *Koulourakia II*

3 cups sifted all-purpose flour
2 teaspoons baking powder
½ teaspoon salt
¾ cup unsalted butter
1 teaspoon anise flavoring
½ cup sugar
1 egg
¼ cup whipping cream
1 egg yolk, beaten, for brushing

1. Sift flour, baking powder, and salt together.
2. Cream butter with anise flavoring until fluffy. Add sugar and beat thoroughly. Add egg and beat well. Pour in whipping cream; mix thoroughly. Stir in flour mixture.
3. Knead dough on a floured board until shiny. Cover and refrigerate 2 hours.
4. Remove from refrigerator 30 minutes before rolling and baking. Break off a small amount of dough and roll on a board to form a strip 5 to 6 inches long. Shape into a ring by joining the ends, or make into a snail shape by winding up the strip. Place on a greased cookie sheet. Brush with egg yolk.
5. Bake at 350°F 20 to 25 minutes, or until done.

3½ dozen

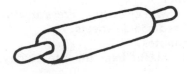

850 *Kourambiethes*

1 cup unsalted butter (at room
   temperature)
2 egg yolks
1 tablespoon granulated sugar
1 cup coarsely chopped blanched
   almonds
2 cups all-purpose flour
1 teaspoon baking powder
Whole cloves
Rosewater
2 pounds confectioners' sugar

1. Beat butter until white in an electric mixer (about 10 minutes). Add egg yolks and sugar; beat well. Add chopped almonds and mix well. Blend flour and baking powder and mix in until blended.
2. Taking a small amount of dough, roll it between palms, shaping it into a ball. Continue until all dough has been used. Or, roll dough into a round log, about 1 inch in diameter; cut diagonally into 1-inch slices. Press a clove into center of each cookie.
3. Bake at 350°F 20 minutes. Remove from oven and sprinkle lightly with rosewater. Immediately sift confectioners' sugar over them, covering the tops and sides. Cool for 1 hour.
4. Using a spatula or fork, lift the cookies, being careful not to disturb the sugar, and place them in medium-size paper cupcake cups. Store cookies at least a day before serving.

About 30 cookies

851 *Polish Pecan Cookies (Ciastka Kurche)*

1 cup butter
3 tablespoons vanilla extract
½ cup confectioners' sugar
1½ tablespoons water
2½ cups sifted all-purpose flour
2 cups pecan halves
  Confectioners' sugar for rolling

1. Cream butter with vanilla extract; add confectioners' sugar gradually, beating until fluffy.
2. Add water and beat thoroughly.
3. Add flour in fourths, mixing until blended after each addition.
4. If necessary, chill the dough until easy to handle.
5. Shape a teaspoonful of dough around each pecan half, covering nut completely. Place on ungreased cookie sheets.
6. Bake at 400°F 10 minutes.
7. Roll in confectioners' sugar while still warm.

About 5 dozen

852 *Honey Cookies (Piernik)*

½ cup honey
½ cup sugar
2 eggs
½ teaspoon vanilla extract
3 cups all-purpose flour
1 teaspoon baking soda
½ teaspoon salt
½ teaspoon cinnamon
½ teaspoon ginger
½ teaspoon nutmeg
¼ teaspoon cloves
1 egg white, beaten
48 blanched almond halves (about)

1. Combine honey and sugar in a bowl; mix well. Beat in eggs and vanilla extract.
2. Blend flour, baking soda, salt, and spices. Stir into honey mixture. Knead to mix thoroughly; dough will be stiff.
3. Shape dough into a ball. Wrap in plastic wrap. Let stand 2 hours.
4. Roll dough on a floured surface to ¼-inch thickness. Cut into 2½-inch rounds or other shapes.
5. Brush top of each cookie with egg white. Press an almond onto center. Place on greased cookie sheets.
6. Bake at 375°F 8 to 10 minutes.
7. Cool on racks. Store in plastic bags for 8 to 10 days to mellow.

About 4 dozen

853 *Kolacky*

1 cup butter or margarine (at room temperature)
1 package (8 ounces) cream cheese (at room temperature)
¼ teaspoon vanilla extract
2¼ cups all-purpose flour
½ teaspoon salt
  Thick jam or canned fruit filling, such as apricot or prune

1. Cream butter and cream cheese until fluffy. Beat in vanilla extract.
2. Combine flour and salt; add in fourths to butter mixture, blending well after each addition. Chill dough until easy to handle.
3. Roll dough to ⅜-inch thickness on a floured surface. Cut out 2-inch circles or other shapes. Place on ungreased baking sheets.
4. Make a "thumbprint" about ¼ inch deep in each cookie. Fill with jam.
5. Bake at 350°F 10 to 15 minutes, or until delicately browned on edges.

About 3½ dozen

854 *Polish Doughnuts (Pączki)*

1 package active dry yeast
¼ cup warm water
⅓ cup butter or margarine (at room temperature)
⅔ cup sugar
1 egg
3 egg yolks
1 teaspoon vanilla extract
1 teaspoon grated orange or lemon peel
¾ teaspoon salt
3½ cups all-purpose flour (about)
Fat for deep frying heated to 375°F
Confectioners' sugar (optional)

1. Dissolve yeast in warm water.
2. Cream butter and sugar until fluffy. Beat in egg, then egg yolks, one at a time. Add vanilla extract, orange peel, dissolved yeast, and salt. Beat until well mixed. Stir in flour gradually, adding enough to make a stiff dough.
3. Turn dough onto a floured surface. Knead until smooth and elastic, about 10 minutes. Place in a greased bowl. Cover. Let rise until doubled in bulk.
4. Turn onto lightly floured surface. Pat or roll to ½-inch thickness. Cut out with doughnut cutter. Cover. Let rise until doubled in bulk.
5. Fry in hot fat 2 to 3 minutes; turn to brown all sides.
6. Drain doughnuts on paper towels and sprinkle with confectioners' sugar, if desired.

About 2 dozen

855 *Wise Men (Mądrzyki)*

1 pound farmer or pot cheese
4 eggs, separated
3 tablespoons sugar
¼ teaspoon salt
¼ cup all-purpose flour
Fat for deep frying heated to 365°F
Dairy sour cream and sugar (optional)

1. Press cheese through a sieve.
2. Combine egg yolks and sugar; beat at high speed until mixture is thick and piles softly, about 7 minutes.
3. Add cheese and salt, then mix in flour, 1 tablespoon at a time. Add just enough flour to form a dough. (Dough will be sticky.)
4. Pat out dough on generously floured surface to ¾-inch thickness.
5. Cut into 2×1-inch rectangles with well-floured knife.
6. Fry the rectangles quickly, turning to brown both sides. (Be sure the temperature of the fat is maintained at 365°F, so the cheese will fry crisply.)
7. Serve at once with dairy sour cream and sugar, if desired.

About 2½ dozen

856 *Favors (Chrust-Faworki)*

4 egg yolks
1 whole egg
½ teaspoon salt
⅓ cup confectioners' sugar
2 tablespoons rum or brandy
1 teaspoon vanilla extract
1¼ cups all-purpose flour
Fat for deep frying heated to 350°F
Confectioners' sugar or honey for topping (optional)

1. Combine egg yolks, whole egg, and salt in small bowl of electric mixer. Beat at highest speed 7 to 10 minutes, until mixture is thick and piles softly. Beat in sugar, a small amount at a time. Then beat in rum and vanilla extract.
2. By hand, fold in flour.
3. Turn onto a generously floured surface. Knead dough until blisters form, about 10 minutes.
4. Divide dough in half. Cover half of dough to prevent drying. Use a towel or plastic wrap.
5. Roll out half of dough as thin as possible. Cut dough into 5×2-inch strips. Make a 2-inch slit from center almost to end of each strip of dough. Then pull opposite end through slit. Repeat with remaining dough.
6. Fry in hot fat until golden brown.
7. Drain on paper towels. If desired, sprinkle with confectioners' sugar or drizzle with honey.

About 2½ dozen

857 *Mazurkas (Mazurek)*

1 cup sweet unsalted butter
¾ cup eggs, beaten
2 cups ground blanched almonds
1¾ cups all-purpose flour
1 cup sugar

1. Cream butter and eggs until fluffy.
2. Mix almonds, flour, and sugar. Add flour mixture, a small amount at a time, to the butter mixture. Beat or knead after each addition.
3. Pat or roll out dough in a greased 15×10×1-inch jelly-roll pan.
4. Bake at 350°F about 20 minutes, or until golden brown.
5. Spread jam over top. Cool for 5 minutes. Cut into 2-inch squares to serve.

About 3 dozen

858 *Royal Mazurkas (Mazurek Królewski)*

1 cup butter or margarine (room temperature)
1½ cups all-purpose flour
1 cup sugar
¼ teaspoon salt
6 egg yolks
¼ cup ground or finely chopped, blanched almonds
1 teaspoon grated orange or lemon peel (optional)

1. Cream butter until fluffy in a large mixing bowl.
2. Mix flour, sugar, and salt.
3. Alternately beat in 1 egg yolk and a sixth of flour mixture. Continue until all ingredients are well combined. Stir in almonds and orange peel. Mix well.
4. Roll or pat dough to fit a greased 15×10×1-inch jelly-roll pan.
5. Bake at 325°F 35 to 40 minutes, or until golden but not browned.
6. Cool in pan on rack 10 minutes. Cut in fourths. Remove from pan. Cool on rack.

About 3 dozen

859 *Almond Mazurkas (Mazurek Migdałowy)*

1 pound blanched almonds, ground (about 4 cups)
2 cups sugar
3 eggs
2 tablespoons lemon juice

1. Combine almonds and sugar; mix well.
2. Beat eggs with lemon juice just until foamy. Stir into almond mixture.
3. Pour batter into a well-greased 15×10×1-inch jelly-roll pan.
4. Bake at 250°F about 1 hour, or until golden.
5. Cut into 2-inch squares while still warm. Remove from pan.

About 3 dozen

860 *Mazurkas with Fruit and Nut Topping*

Mazurkas or Royal Mazurkas or
● Almond Mazurkas

Fruit Filling:
¾ cup raisins or currants
½ cup chopped dried apricots
¾ cup diced dried figs or dates
⅔ cup chopped candied lemon or
   orange peel
¾ cup chopped blanched almonds
½ cup chopped walnuts

Topping:
1 egg
1 egg white
½ cup confectioners' sugar
⅓ cup butter, melted
1 tablespoon lemon juice
1 teaspoon vanilla extract
2 ounces almonds, ground (about
   ¾ cup)
2 tablespoons bread crumbs

1. Prepare and bake mazurkas as directed. Do not cut into squares.
2. For fruit filling, combine apricots and raisins in a saucepan. Add **water.** Bring to boiling. Cover; remove from heat and let stand 10 minutes.
3. Drain raisins and apricots. Combine with other fruits and nuts. Spread evenly over mazurkas.
4. For topping, combine egg and egg white with confectioners' sugar. Beat at high speed until very thick and fluffy, about 7 minutes.
5. Gradually beat in melted butter, lemon juice, and vanilla extract. Fold in ground almonds and bread crumbs.
6. Spread egg mixture over fruit layer.
7. Bake at 350°F about 15 minutes, or until topping is golden but still moist.
8. Cool in pan on rack 5 minutes, then cut into squares.

About 3 dozen

861 *Mazurkas with Chocolate Topping*

Mazurkas or Royal Mazurkas or
● Almond Mazurkas
4 eggs
1 cup sugar
½ teaspoon vanilla extract
1 package (8 ounces) unsweetened
   chocolate, grated
1 tablespoon flour
½ teaspoon salt
1¼ cups chopped blanched almonds

1. Prepare and bake mazurkas as directed. Do not cut into squares.
2. Beat eggs with sugar and vanilla extract until fluffy. Add chocolate; beat until well mixed. Beat in flour, salt, and almonds.
3. Spread chocolate mixture over baked mazurkas.
4. Bake at 250°F 5 to 7 minutes, or until topping is set.
5. Cool. Cut into 2-inch squares.

About 3 dozen

862 *Mazurkas with Apple Topping*

Mazurkas or Royal Mazurkas or
● Almond Mazurkas
1 cup sugar
⅓ cup water
3 pounds apples, pared and thinly
   sliced
2 teaspoons grated lemon or
   orange peel
½ teaspoon salt (optional)
1½ cups finely chopped blanched
   almonds (optional)

1. Prepare and bake mazurkas as directed. Do not cut into squares.
2. Combine sugar and water in a large saucepan. Simmer 5 minutes. Add apples and lemon peel. Cook over medium heat until apples are soft, about 5 to 10 minutes; stir frequently to prevent sticking.
3. If desired, add salt and almonds. Cook and stir until apples are translucent on edges and mixture clings to the spoon. Remove from heat. Cool 15 to 20 minutes.
4. Spread apple filling over warm baked mazurkas. Cool completely. Cut into 2-inch squares.

About 3 dozen

863 *Mazurkas with Lemon Icing*

Mazurkas or Royal Mazurkas or
● Almond Mazurkas
Lemon Icing:
  2 cups confectioners' sugar
  2 to 3 tablespoons lemon juice

1. Prepare and bake mazurkas as directed. Cool on a wire rack.
2. Meanwhile, mix confectioners' sugar with lemon juice until smooth.
3. Spread icing over mazurkas. Cut into 2-inch squares.

About 3 dozen

864 *Black Bread Pudding (Legumina Chlebowa)*

  6 eggs, separated
  ½ cup sugar
  ¼ teaspoon salt
  1 cup fine dry bread crumbs made from black bread (pumpernickel, rye, or whole wheat bread)
  ¾ teaspoon cinnamon
  ¼ teaspoon cloves
  2 tablespoons melted butter
  Fine dry bread crumbs

1. Beat egg yolks at high speed in a small bowl until thick. Gradually beat in sugar. Continue beating at high speed until mixture is very thick and piles softly.
2. Using clean beaters and a large bowl, beat egg whites with salt until stiff, not dry, peaks form.
3. Fold bread crumbs, cinnamon, and cloves into beaten yolks. Then fold in 1 tablespoon melted butter. Fold in egg whites.
4. Brush a 2-quart soufflé dish or deep casserole with remaining 1 tablespoon melted butter. Coat dish with bread crumbs.
5. Gently turn soufflé mixture into prepared dish.
6. Bake at 350°F 25 to 30 minutes, or until set near center.

About 6 servings

865 *Chocolate Torte (Tort Czekoladowy)*

  8 eggs, separated
  1¼ cups sugar
  ¾ cup all-purpose flour
  ¼ cup fine dry bread crumbs
  ¼ teaspoon salt
  2 ounces (2 squares) semisweet chocolate, grated
  1½ teaspoons vanilla extract
  Filling (see below)
  Frosting (see below)

1. Beat egg yolks until very thick and lemon-colored, about 5 minutes. Gradually beat in sugar.
2. Combine flour, bread crumbs, and salt. Add chocolate and mix thoroughly but lightly.
3. Add flour mixture to egg yolks and sugar in 4 portions, folding until well mixed after each addition.
4. With clean beaters, beat egg whites with vanilla extract until stiff, not dry, peaks are formed. Fold into flour mixture.
5. Turn into a well-greased 10-inch springform pan or deep, round layer cake pan.
6. Bake at 325°F 50 to 60 minutes. Remove from pan and cool completely.
7. Split cake in half.
8. Spread filling on bottom half. Replace top. Spread frosting over sides and top. Refrigerate 4 hours or longer for torte to mellow.

One 10-inch torte

Filling: Whip **½ cup whipping cream** until cream piles softly. Fold in **¼ cup ground almonds or walnuts** and **3 tablespoons sugar**.

Frosting: Melt **4 ounces (4 squares) unsweetened chocolate** and **3 tablespoons butter** together in a saucepan. Remove from heat. Stir in **1 tablespoon brandy**. Add **2 to 2½ cups confectioners' sugar** and **2 to 3 tablespoons milk or cream** until frosting is of spreading consistency.

866 *Walnut Torte (Tort Orzechowy)*

12 eggs, separated
1 cup sugar
½ pound finely ground walnuts
⅓ cup all-purpose flour
½ teaspoon salt
Fine dry bread crumbs
2 to 3 tablespoons brandy or rum
Filling
Frosting
Chopped walnuts

1. Beat egg yolks until thick and lemon-colored. Add sugar gradually, beating at high speed until mixture is very thick and piles softly.
2. Fold in ground walnuts and flour; mix thoroughly.
3. Beat egg whites with salt until stiff, but not dry, peaks form. Fold beaten egg whites into egg yolk mixture.
4. Generously grease two 10-inch cake layer pans or one 10-inch springform pan. Line with waxed paper. Grease paper. Coat with bread crumbs.
5. Turn batter into prepared pans.
6. Bake at 350°F about 25 minutes.
7. Remove layers from pans. Cool on racks 15 minutes. (Cut single, high cake, from springform pan, into 2 layers. Layers shrink slightly as they cool.) Sprinkle each layer with brandy. Cool completely.
8. Meanwhile, prepare filling and frosting.
9. Spread filling over 1 layer. Set second layer on top.
10. Spread frosting over top and sides of torte. Frosting is runny and will run down sides. Let stand 30 minutes. Pat chopped walnuts around sides of torte.
11. Refrigerate until ready to serve.

One 10-inch torte

Filling: Whip **1 cup whipping cream** until it is very thick and piles softly. Gradually beat in **¾ cup sugar**, then **½ teaspoon vanilla extract** and, if desired, **2 tablespoons brandy or rum**. Fold in **1 cup finely ground walnuts**, a small amount at a time, until blended.

About 2 cups

Frosting: Beat **1 egg** until thick and foamy. Beat in **2 tablespoons melted butter or margarine, 2 tablespoons brandy or rum, pinch salt**, and about **2½ cups sifted confectioners' sugar**. Add enough confectioners' sugar to make frosting of thin spreading consistency.

867 *Plum Cake (Placek ze Śliwkami)*

2⅓ cups all-purpose flour
2½ teaspoons baking powder
¾ teaspoon salt
1 cup sugar (reserve ¼ cup)
½ cup shortening
¾ cup milk
2 eggs
2 tablespoons fine dry bread crumbs
40 fresh plums (prune, Damson, or greengage), pitted and cut in half; or use 2 cans (30 ounces) whole purple plums, drained and pitted
3 tablespoons butter, cut in pieces
¼ teaspoon cloves

1. Combine flour, baking powder, salt, and ¾ cup sugar in a large mixing bowl. Add shortening, milk, and eggs. Beat at medium speed 4 minutes.
2. Grease bottom and sides of a 13×9×2-inch pan. Coat with bread crumbs.
3. Turn batter into prepared pan. Place plums on top, pushing one edge of each half down ¼ inch into batter. Dot with butter.
4. Combine remaining ¼ cup sugar and cloves; mix well. Sprinkle over plums.
5. Bake at 350°F about 40 minutes.
6. To serve, cut into pieces.

About 32

Apple Cake: Prepare Plum Cake as directed, substituting 4 large apples, pared and thinly sliced, for the plums.

868 *Baba (Babka)*

1 package active dry yeast
½ cup milk, scalded and cooled
½ cup sugar
2 cups all-purpose flour
½ cup butter (at room temperature)
4 eggs
½ teaspoon salt
½ teaspoon cinnamon
¼ teaspoon mace
1 tablespoon grated lemon peel
½ cup raisins, chopped almonds, or
    chopped candied fruits
    (optional)
● Lemon Icing or honey

1. Dissolve yeast in milk 10 minutes. Add 1 tablespoon of the sugar and ½ cup of the flour; mix well. Cover. Let rise until doubled.
2. Cream butter, gradually adding remaining sugar. Beat until fluffy. Beat in 3 whole eggs, 1 at a time. Beat in 1 egg yolk; reserve remaining egg white.
3. Mix remaining flour with salt and spices. Beat into butter mixture. Stir in lemon peel and raisins.
4. Beat yeast mixture into butter mixture. Beat until batter is silky, about 10 to 15 minutes.
5. Turn into a well-greased and floured 10-inch baba or tube pan. Cover. Let rise until tripled in bulk, about 1½ hours.
6. Beat remaining egg white until foamy. Brush over top of baba.
7. Bake at 350°F about 40 minutes, until baba sounds hollow when tapped.
8. Cool on rack 10 minutes. Remove from pan. Drizzle with icing or brush with honey, if desired.

1 baba

Baba au Rhum: Prepare Baba as directed. Set in cake pan or shallow casserole. To prepare Rum Sauce: Boil **⅓ cup water, ⅓ cup sugar,** and **⅓ cup apricot jam** with **1 teaspoon lemon juice** 5 minutes. Add **½ cup rum.** Bring just to simmering. Pour over baba. With wooden pick, poke holes in baba. Continue pouring syrup over baba until all syrup is absorbed.

869 *Filled Baba (Babki Śmietankowe)*

Baba:
2 cups butter or margarine (at
    room temperature)
1 cup sugar
2 eggs
3 egg whites
2½ cups all-purpose flour
Custard:
3 egg yolks
¾ cup whipping cream
¾ cup sugar
¼ teaspoon salt

1. For baba, beat butter at high speed. Gradually add sugar, creaming until fluffy.
2. Beat in whole eggs and 2 egg whites. Stir in flour; mix well.
3. For custard, combine egg yolks, cream, sugar, and salt in the top of a double boiler or in a heavy saucepan. Cook and stir until custard is thickened. Set aside to cool a few minutes.
4. Generously grease muffin-pan wells; coat with fine dry bread crumbs. Line each with 1 tablespoon dough. Spoon in 2 tablespoons custard. Top with more dough.
5. Beat reserved egg white just until foamy. Brush top of each baba.
6. Bake at 350°F 20 to 25 minutes.

About 1½ dozen

870 *Country Cheese Cake (Serowiec)*

Dough:
- 1¾ cups all-purpose flour
- ½ cup confectioners' sugar
- ¾ teaspoon baking powder
- ¼ teaspoon salt
- ¼ cup butter or margarine
- 3 egg yolks
- 3 tablespoons dairy sour cream

Filling:
- 4 eggs
- 1 egg white
- ¾ cup sugar
- 1½ pounds farmer or pot cheese or ricotta
- ½ cup dairy sour cream
- 2 tablespoons grated orange peel
- 1 teaspoon vanilla extract

1. For dough, combine flour, sugar, baking powder, and salt in a bowl. With pastry blender, cut butter into flour mixture until coarse and crumbly.
2. Beat egg yolks into sour cream. Stir into flour mixture. Knead in bowl until dough is well mixed and holds its shape.
3. Refrigerate dough until easy to roll out, at least 1 hour.
4. Roll out dough on a floured surface to fit a 13×9×2-inch pan, about a 15×11-inch rectangle.
5. Line bottom of pan, fitting dough so it comes about ⅔ of the way up sides of pan.
6. For filling, beat eggs and egg white at high speed of electric mixer until thick. Gradually add sugar, beating at high speed until stiff, not dry, peaks form.
7. Press cheese through a sieve. Fold into beaten egg mixture. Add remaining ingredients. Mix gently but thoroughly. Turn filling into dough-lined pan.
8. Bake at 350°F about 40 minutes, or until set.
9. Cool before cutting into squares.

About 16 servings

871 *Apples in Blankets (Jabłuszka w Cieście)*

- 1 pound apples, pared and cored
- 2 eggs
- ⅓ cup sugar
- Dash salt
- 1¼ cups all-purpose flour
- ⅓ cup dairy sour cream
- ¼ cup buttermilk
- Fat for deep frying heated to 365°F
- Confectioners' sugar
- Nutmeg or cinnamon (optional)

1. Slice apples crosswise to make rings about ⅜ inch thick.
2. Beat eggs with sugar until thick and foamy. Add salt. Beat in small amounts of flour alternately with sour cream and buttermilk. Beat until batter is well mixed.
3. Coat apple slices with batter. Fry in hot fat until golden.
4. Drain on paper towels. Sprinkle with confectioners' sugar. Add a dash of nutmeg or cinnamon, if desired.

About 14

872 *Raspberry Syrup (Sok Malinowy)*

- 2 cups sugar
- ½ cup water
- 2 cups fresh or frozen raspberries

1. Combine sugar and water in a saucepan.
2. Bring to boiling; add raspberries. Boil 3 minutes. Remove from heat.
3. Line a strainer or colander with cheesecloth. Set over a bowl. Turn cooked berries into cloth-lined strainer. Let drain 2 hours.
4. Discard seeds and pulp. Return juice to saucepan. Boil about 12 minutes, or until reduced to half the original amount. Skim off foam.
5. Pour into a clean jar. Cover. Store in refrigerator. Serve with fruit compote, fresh fruits, or as a sauce for cake.

About 2 cups

873 *Easter Baba (Babka Wielkanocna)*

1 cup milk
3⅓ cups all-purpose flour
2 packages active dry yeast
¼ cup lukewarm water
⅔ cup sugar
2 teaspoons salt
15 egg yolks
1 teaspoon vanilla extract
¼ teaspoon almond extract
½ cup melted butter
¾ cup mixed chopped candied citron and orange and lemon peel
½ cup chopped almonds
⅓ cup raisins
Blanched almond halves
Fine dry bread crumbs

1. Scald milk; pour into a large bowl. Slowly add ¾ cup flour to hot milk and beat thoroughly. Cool.
2. Dissolve yeast in lukewarm water 5 minutes; add 1 tablespoon of the sugar. Let stand 5 minutes. Add to cooled milk mixture; beat well.
3. Cover; let rise until doubled in bulk.
4. Add salt to egg yolks. Beat until thick and lemon-colored, about 5 minutes. Add remaining sugar and extracts; continue beating. Combine egg mixture with milk mixture, beating thoroughly. Add remaining flour; mix well.
5. Knead 10 minutes in bowl. Add butter and continue kneading 10 more minutes, or until dough leaves the fingers. Add candied peel, almonds, and raisins; knead to mix well.
6. Let rise until doubled in bulk. Punch down and let rise again.
7. Generously grease a 12-inch fluted tube pan or turban mold. Press almond halves around sides and bottom of pan. Coat with bread crumbs.
8. Punch down dough and put into prepared pan. Dough should fill a third of pan. Let rise 1 hour, or until dough fills pan.
9. Bake at 350°F about 50 minutes, or until hollow sounding when tapped on top.

1 large loaf

874 *Baba with Raisins (Babka z Rodzynkami)*

1 cup butter or margarine (at room temperature)
1½ cups confectioners' sugar
4 eggs, separated
¼ cup orange juice
4 teaspoons lemon juice
1 tablespoon grated orange or lemon peel
4 teaspoons baking powder
1½ cups all-purpose flour
1 cup cornstarch
⅓ cup confectioners' sugar
½ teaspoon salt
½ cup raisins
Fine dry bread crumbs
1 tablespoon whipping cream (optional)

1. Cream butter. Gradually add 1½ cups confectioners' sugar, beating at high speed of electric mixer. Beat in egg yolks, one at a time. Beat in orange juice, lemon juice, and orange peel.
2. Mix flour, cornstarch, and ⅓ cup confectioners' sugar.
3. With clean beaters, beat egg whites with salt until stiff, not dry, peaks form.
4. Fold half the flour mixture into the butter mixture. Fold in egg whites.
5. Add raisins to remaining flour mixture; mix well. Fold into batter.
6. Generously grease an 11-cup ring mold or baba pan. Coat with bread crumbs.
7. Turn batter into prepared pan. Brush top with cream.
8. Bake at 350°F about 40 minutes.

1 baba

875 Grandmother's Cheese Cake (Sernik Babci)

Dough:
- 1¼ cups all-purpose flour
- ¾ teaspoon baking powder
- ¼ teaspoon salt
- ¼ cup butter or margarine
- 1 egg
- 3 tablespoons dairy sour cream
- ⅓ cup confectioners' sugar

Filling:
- 6 eggs
- 2 cups confectioners' sugar
- 1½ teaspoons vanilla extract
- 1 pound farmer cheese or ricotta
- ⅔ cup melted butter
- 1½ cups unseasoned mashed potatoes
- 2 teaspoons baking powder
- ½ teaspoon nutmeg
- ½ teaspoon salt
- ¼ cup grated orange or lemon peel

1. For dough, combine flour, baking powder, and salt in a bowl. Cut in butter with a pastry blender.
2. Beat egg into sour cream. Stir into flour mixture. Stir in sugar. Knead dough until well mixed and smooth.
3. Roll dough on a floured surface into a rectangle. Line a 13×9×2-inch pan with dough, and bring dough part way up sides.
4. For filling, separate 1 egg and reserve the white. Beat remaining yolk and whole eggs with the sugar 5 minutes at high speed of electric mixer. Add vanilla extract. Beat at high speed until mixture piles softly.
5. Press cheese through a sieve. Blend cheese with butter; add potatoes, baking powder, nutmeg, and salt. Stir in orange peel. Fold into egg mixture. Turn into prepared crust in pan.
6. Bake at 350°F about 45 minutes, or until set. Cool.
7. Cool well before cutting.

About 32 pieces

876 Lamb Cake

- 2 cups sifted cake flour
- ¾ teaspoon baking powder
- ¼ teaspoon salt
- ¼ teaspoon mace
- 1 cup butter or margarine
- 1 cup plus 2 tablespoons sugar
- 2 teaspoons grated lemon peel
- 1½ teaspoons vanilla extract
- ½ teaspoon almond extract
- 4 eggs
- 1 tablespoon flour
- 2 tablespoons shortening
- Seven-Minute Frosting (see recipe)
- Shredded coconut

1. Sift together cake flour, baking powder, salt, and mace.
2. Cream butter. Gradually add sugar, creaming until fluffy. Add lemon peel and extracts.
3. Alternately beat in eggs and flour mixture.
4. Blend 1 tablespoon flour into shortening. Brush over both inside sections of a lamb mold.
5. Turn batter into face side of mold, filling it level. Spoon a small amount of batter into back side of mold, filling ears. Close and lock mold. Set on baking sheet.
6. Bake at 375°F 50 to 55 minutes.
7. Set mold on wire rack to cool 5 minutes. Remove back side. Cool 5 minutes longer. Turn out on rack to cool completely.
8. Frost with Seven-Minute Frosting. Coat with coconut.

1 lamb cake

877 Seven-Minute Frosting

- 1½ cups sugar
- ⅓ cup water
- 1 tablespoon light corn syrup
- ⅛ teaspoon salt
- 2 egg whites (unbeaten)
- ½ teaspoon vanilla extract

1. Combine sugar, water, corn syrup, salt, and egg whites in the top of a double boiler. Set over boiling water and beat at high speed 7 to 10 minutes, or until stiff peaks form when beater is lifted.
2. Remove from heat. Beat in vanilla extract.

About 5 cups

878 *Pear Compote (Kompot z Gruszek)*

8 pears or 4 cups pitted dark sweet
    cherries
1½ cups wine
⅔ cup sugar
⅓ cup red currant jelly
½ teaspoon vanilla extract or 1
    tablespoon lemon juice
4 whole cloves
1 stick cinnamon

1. Pare pears, leaving whole with stems attached.
2. Combine wine, and remaining ingredients. Bring to boiling.
3. Add pears. Simmer until pears are transparent on the edges, about 45 minutes. (Boil cherries 2 minutes.)
4. Remove fruit to serving dish.
5. Boil syrup until very thick, about 20 minutes. Pour over fruit.
6. Chill. Serve with whipped cream or soft dessert cheese, if desired.

8 servings

879 *Berry Compote (Kompot z Malin lub Truskawek)*

1 pint strawberries or raspberries
1 cup water
½ cup sugar
½ cup white dessert wine

1. Wash and hull berries. Put into a glass bowl.
2. Boil water with sugar 5 minutes. Pour over berries and add wine. Let stand 2 hours before serving. Chill, if desired.

4 servings

880 *Fruit Compote in Spirits (Kompot w Spirytusie)*

2 pounds ripe peaches, pears, or
    apricots
1⅓ cups water
2 cups sugar
¾ cup white rum, vodka, or grain
    alcohol

1. Dip whole fruit, 1 piece at a time, in boiling water for a few seconds to loosen skin. Pull off skin; leave fruit whole.
2. Combine water with sugar in a saucepan. Boil 5 minutes.
3. Add fruits and simmer 3 minutes for small fruit; 5 minutes for large fruit.
4. Remove from heat. Skim off foam. Let stand overnight.
5. Remove fruit from syrup. Boil syrup 1 minute. Skim off foam. Pour syrup over fruit. Let stand overnight.
6. Remove fruits from syrup. Place in sterilized jars. Bring syrup to boiling; skim off foam. Add rum and pour over fruit. Seal.
7. Store in a cool, dry place at least 1 week before using.

6 to 8 servings

881 *Pear and Apple Compote (Kompot z Gruszek i Jabłek)*

2 cups water
⅔ cup sugar
6 pears, pared, cored, quartered
2 apples, pared, cored, quartered
8 whole cloves
½ cup currant or gooseberry jelly

1. Bring water with sugar to boiling in a large saucepan. Boil 5 minutes.
2. Add fruits and cloves. Simmer until fruits are tender, about 7 to 10 minutes.
3. Remove fruits and place in a serving bowl. Discard cloves. Boil syrup until only 1 cup remains.
4. Blend syrup into jelly. Return to saucepan. Bring just to boiling. Pour over fruits. Let stand 1 hour before serving, or chill.

6 to 8 servings

882 *Easter Cheese Cake (Sernik Wielkanocny)*

Dough for Grandmother's
●Cheese Cake or
●Country Cheese Cake

Cheese Filling:
6 eggs
2¼ cups confectioners' sugar
1½ pounds farmer cheese or ricotta
⅔ cup butter or margarine (at room temperature)
½ teaspoon salt
1½ teaspoons vanilla extract
2 teaspoons grated lemon peel
¼ cup finely chopped candied orange peel
⅓ cup raisins

Spread:
¾ cup thick raspberry jam or strawberry preserves

1. Prepare dough for crust; line pan.
2. Beat eggs at high speed until thickened. Slowly beat in sugar, beating until mixture piles softly.
3. Press cheese through a sieve. Beat cheese with butter, salt, vanilla extract, and lemon peel.
4. Fold eggs into cheese mixture. Stir in orange peel and raisins.
5. Spread jam over bottom of prepared crust in pan.
6. Turn cheese mixture into pan.
7. Bake at 325°F 45 minutes to 1 hour or until a knife inserted near center comes out clean.
8. Cool well before cutting.

32 pieces

883 *Cheese Pascha from Lwow (Pascha ze Lwowa)*

1 whole egg
4 egg yolks
2⅔ cups sugar
1 cup whipping cream
1 cup raisins or currants
2 pounds white farmer cheese
½ pound unsalted sweet butter
1 tablespoon vanilla extract
1 cup chopped blanched almonds
2 tablespoons grated orange peel

1. Beat whole egg and egg yolks with sugar until thick and creamy. Add half of cream. Turn into a saucepan. Heat almost to the boiling point, stirring constantly; do not boil. Remove from heat. Add raisins; cover.
2. Combine the rest of the cream, the cheese, butter, and vanilla extract in a large electric blender. Blend until smooth.
3. Turn cheese mixture into a bowl. Fold in the egg mixture. Add almonds and orange peel.
4. Refrigerate 4 hours. Place in a double thickness of cheesecloth. Hang over a bowl in a cold place; let drain 24 hours. Chill. Garnish with **nuts** and **candied fruits** as desired. Serve cold. Cut small slices.

16 to 20 servings

884 *Cross Cake*

1 cup butter or margarine
1½ cups sugar
4 eggs
1 teaspoon vanilla extract
½ teaspoon salt
4 cups sifted cake flour
4 teaspoons baking powder
1⅓ cups milk
Basic Butter Frosting (see recipe)
Butter Cream Decorating Frosting (see recipe)

1. Beat butter until softened. Gradually add sugar, creaming until fluffy. Add eggs, 1 at a time, beating thoroughly after each. Add vanilla extract and salt; beat well.
2. Mix flour with baking powder; alternately add with milk to creamed mixture, beating thoroughly after each addition.
3. Turn into a greased and floured 13×9×2-inch baking pan and spread evenly to edges.
4. Bake at 350°F about 45 minutes, or until top springs back when lightly touched.
5. Cool in pan on rack 5 minutes. Turn out onto rack; cool completely.
6. Cut out 3-inch squares from the two top corners of cake.
7. Cut out 6×2-inch rectangles from the two corners of the lower section of cake, leaving the cake in the form of a cross. Frost and decorate as desired.

1 cross cake

885 *Basic Butter Frosting*

6 tablespoons butter or margarine
1½ teaspoons vanilla extract
3 cups confectioners' sugar
1½ tablespoons milk or cream

1. Cream butter with vanilla extract. Add confectioners' sugar gradually, beating thoroughly after each addition.
2. Stir in milk and beat until frosting is of spreading consistency.

About 2 cups

Lemon Butter Frosting: Follow recipe for Basic Butter Frosting. Substitute **lemon juice** for milk and add **1½ teaspoons grated lemon peel.** If desired, add a few drops yellow food coloring.

Orange Butter Frosting: Follow recipe for Basic Butter Frosting. Substitute **1½ teaspoons grated orange peel** for the vanilla extract and **1½ to 2½ tablespoons orange juice** for the milk. If a deeper orange color is desired, mix 4 drops red food coloring and 3 drops yellow food coloring with orange juice.

886 *Excellent Warsaw Paczki*
(Wyborne Warszawskie Pączki)

12 egg yolks
1 teaspoon salt
2 packages active dry yeast
¼ cup warm water
⅓ cup butter or margarine (at room temperature)
½ cup sugar
4½ cups all-purpose flour
3 tablespoons rum or brandy
1 cup whipping cream, scalded
1½ cups very thick jam or preserves (optional)
   Fat for deep frying heated to 365°F

1. Beat egg yolks with salt in a small mixer bowl at high speed of electric mixer until mixture is thick and piles softly, about 7 minutes.
2. Soften yeast in warm water in a large bowl.
3. Cream butter; add sugar gradually, creaming until fluffy. Beat into softened yeast.
4. Stir one fourth of flour into yeast mixture. Add rum and half the cream. Beat in another one fourth of the flour. Stir in remaining cream. Beat in half the remaining flour. Then beat in egg yolks. Beat 2 minutes. Gradually beat in remaining flour until dough blisters.
5. Cover bowl with plastic wrap. Set in a warm place to rise. When doubled in bulk, punch down. Cover; let dough rise again until doubled. Punch down.
6. Roll dough on a floured surface to about ¾-inch thickness. Cut out 3-inch rounds. Use a regular doughnut cutter for plain. Use a biscuit cutter for filled doughnuts.
7. To fill doughnuts, place 1 teaspoonful of jam in center of half the rounds. Brush edges of rounds with water. Top with remaining rounds. Seal edges.
8. Cover doughnuts on floured surface. Let rise until doubled in bulk, about 20 minutes.
9. Fry doughnuts in hot fat until golden brown on both sides. Drain on absorbent paper. Sprinkle with cinnamon sugar, if desired.

About 3 dozen

887 Butter Cream Decorating Frosting

½ cup all-purpose shortening
¼ cup butter or margarine
1 teaspoon lemon extract
3 cups sifted confectioners' sugar

Beat shortening, margarine, and lemon extract together in an electric mixer bowl. Gradually beat in confectioners' sugar until frosting will hold the shape of a tube design.

About 2 cups

888 Christmas Eve "Kutia" (Kutia Wigilijna)

1 cup cracked wheat or bulgur
2 cups hot water
1 cup honey
2 cups water
1 teaspoon salt

1. Soak wheat in 2 cups hot water 30 minutes. Bring to boiling; cook covered until tender.
2. Cook honey with remaining 2 cups water 20 minutes. Add salt. Cool and serve with wheat.

About 4 servings

889 Christmas Cake

3 cups all-purpose flour
2 cups sugar
2 teaspoons baking soda
1 teaspoon allspice
1 teaspoon cinnamon
1 teaspoon nutmeg
1 teaspoon cloves
1 teaspoon salt
⅔ cup butter or margarine
2 cups buttermilk
1 cup chopped dates, raisins, or
    mixed candied fruits
½ cup chopped almonds or walnuts

1. Combine flour, sugar, baking soda, spices, and salt in a bowl. Cut in butter with pastry blender or two knives until particles resemble rice kernels. Add buttermilk; mix thoroughly. Mix in dates and nuts.
2. Turn batter into a generously greased and floured (bottom only) 9-inch tube pan or into two 8×4×3-inch loaf pans.
3. Bake at 350°F about 1 hour, or until a wooden pick comes out clean.
4. Cool in pan on wire rack 15 minutes. Remove from pan and cool completely on wire rack.

1 tube cake

890 Marzipan (Marcepan)

1 pound blanched almonds
1 pound confectioners' sugar
2 tablespoons orange water or rose
    water
Food coloring
Decorations (colored sugar,
    dragées, or chocolate shot)

1. Grind almonds very fine. Combine in a saucepan with sugar and flavoring. Cook until mixture leaves side of pan.
2. Roll almond mixture on flat surface to ½-inch thickness. Cut out small heart shapes. Or, shape into small fruits or vegetables.
3. Paint with appropriate food coloring or coat as desired, for example, with red sugar for "strawberries" and cocoa for "potatoes." Decorate with dragées or chocolate shot. Place on waxed paper to dry 2 hours.

2 pounds

891 *Light Fruitcake from Warsaw* (*Keks Warszawski*)

5 eggs or 3 whole eggs plus 3 egg
  whites
1¾ cups confectioners' sugar
¾ cup butter
1 teaspoon vanilla extract
¼ cup milk or brandy
½ teaspoon salt
3 cups sifted cake flour
2 teaspoons baking powder
3 ounces candied orange peel,
  finely chopped (about ¾ cup)
⅔ cup currants or raisins
⅔ cup finely chopped walnuts
½ cup sliced dried figs
½ cup diced pitted dried prunes
½ tablespoon cornstarch

1. Beat eggs with sugar at high speed of electric mixer 7 minutes.
2. Cream butter with vanilla extract until fluffy. Beat in milk and salt.
3. Mix half of flour with baking powder. Add to creamed mixture and mix thoroughly. Fold in beaten eggs, then remaining flour.
4. Mix fruits and nuts with cornstarch. Fold in to batter.
5. Butter an 11×7×3-inch loaf pan and sprinkle with bread crumbs. Turn batter into pan.
6. Bake at 350°F 50 minutes, or until a wooden pick comes out clean.
7. Cool before slicing.

1 fruitcake

892 *Baked Apples with Red Wine* (*Jabłka na Winie Czerwonym*)

8 apples, cored
  Cherry or strawberry preserves
½ cup sugar
½ teaspoon mace or nutmeg
1 cup red wine
½ teaspoon vanilla extract

1. Place apples in a buttered casserole or baking dish. Fill each with preserves.
2. Blend sugar and mace; stir in wine and vanilla extract. Pour over apples. Cover.
3. Bake at 350°F 1 hour.
4. Chill 2 to 4 hours before serving.

8 servings

893 *Twelve-Fruit Compote*

3 cups water
1 pound mixed dried fruits
  including pears, figs, apricots,
  and peaches
1 cup pitted prunes
½ cup raisins or currants
1 cup pitted sweet cherries
2 apples, peeled and sliced or 6
  ounces dried apple slices
½ cup cranberries
1 cup sugar
1 lemon, sliced
6 whole cloves
2 cinnamon sticks (3 inches each)
1 orange
½ cup grapes, pomegranate seeds,
  or pitted plums
½ cup fruit-flavored brandy

1. Combine water, mixed dried fruits, prunes, and raisins in a 6-quart kettle. Bring to boiling. Cover; simmer about 20 minutes, or until fruits are plump and tender.
2. Add cherries, apples, and cranberries. Stir in sugar, lemon, and spices. Cover; simmer 5 minutes.
3. Grate peel of orange; reserve. Peel and section orange, removing all skin and white membrane. Add to fruits in kettle.
4. Stir in grapes and brandy. Bring just to boiling. Remove from heat. Stir in orange peel. Cover; let stand 15 minutes.

About 12 servings

894 *Dessert Puff with Fruit*

A fancy "show-off" dessert to impress family and friends.

4 eggs, slightly beaten
¾ cup skim milk
¾ cup flour
2 teaspoons sugar
¼ teaspoon salt
2 teaspoons clarified butter
4 cups assorted sliced fruits
● 1 cup Low-Fat Yogurt
   Freshly ground nutmeg

1. Combine eggs, milk, flour, sugar, and salt; beat with a fork until blended but still slightly lumpy. Heat butter in a 10-inch skillet until bubbly and sides of skillet are hot; pour batter into skillet.
2. Bake at 425°F 20 minutes. Turn oven control to 350°F; bake until golden (10 to 15 minutes). (Do not open oven door during baking. Sides of puff will rise very high; the center will rise only slightly.) Remove from oven and cut into 8 wedges; place on individual plates.
3. Spoon ½ cup fresh fruit on each wedge. Dollop fruit with yogurt; sprinkle with nutmeg. Serve immediately.

8 servings

895 *Squash and Apple Confection*

Apple and squash slices form a decorative pattern in this molded dessert. Try it also as a meat accompaniment.

3 large Golden Delicious apples
1 cup prune juice
1 cup water
¾ teaspoon ground ginger
3 eggs, beaten
1½ pounds acorn squash or
   pumpkin, pared and sliced
● Chicken Stock
3 tablespoons currants or dark
   raisins
● 1¼ cups Custard Sauce

1. Cut each apple into 12 slices; layer slices in a medium skillet. Pour prune juice, water, and ginger over. Simmer covered 5 minutes. Drain, pouring liquid into a small mixing bowl. Stir eggs into liquid.
2. Cook squash in 1 inch of stock in a covered saucepan until tender (about 5 minutes); drain.
3. Alternate half the apple and squash slices in rows in bottom of a lightly oiled 9x5x3-inch loaf pan. Sprinkle with currants; layer remaining apple and squash slices on top. Pour egg mixture over top. Place pan in larger baking pan; fill with 1 inch boiling water.
4. Bake at 375°F about 45 minutes, or until set. Cool to room temperature. Refrigerate covered 2 hours. Run knife around edge of plate; unmold on a platter. Slice; serve sauce over slices.

8 servings

896 *Banana-Sweet Potato Bake*

1 cup mashed cooked sweet
   potato or squash
2 medium bananas
1 cup water
½ cup instant nonfat dry-milk
   solids
2 egg yolks
2 tablespoons honey or sugar
½ teaspoon ground ginger
2 tablespoons dark rum, if
   desired
4 egg whites
● 1 cup Custard Sauce

1. Purée sweet potato, bananas, water, milk solids, egg yolks, honey, ginger, and rum in a food processor or blender. Pour into a mixing bowl.
2. Beat 4 egg whites until stiff but not dry peaks form. Fold into sweet potato mixture. Spoon into a lightly oiled 9x5x2-inch baking dish.
3. Bake at 325°F 45 minutes. Serve at room temperature, or refrigerate and serve cold. Cut into slices. Serve with Custard Sauce.

6 servings

897 *Molded Cheese Dessert*

A not-too-sweet dessert with the unusual flavor of bay leaf.

2 envelopes unflavored gelatin
1 cup cold water
1 cup double-strength coffee
1 pound pot cheese or low-fat cottage cheese
1 teaspoon vanilla extract
¼ cup sugar
2 bay leaves, broken in half
Mint leaves or watercress

1. Sprinkle gelatin over cold water in a small skillet; let stand 5 minutes. Heat, stirring occasionally, over low heat until dissolved (about 3 minutes). Pour gelatin mixture into a food processor or blender; add remaining ingredients except bay leaves and mint. Purée mixture.
2. Spoon mixture into a 1-quart mold. Push bay leaf pieces into mixture. Refrigerate covered 4 to 6 hours; unmold. Garnish with mint.

4 servings

898 *Carrot-Apricot Tart*

1 cup fresh or canned apricot halves, drained and cut into ¼-inch slices
1 pound baby carrots, cut in half lengthwise
½ teaspoon cinnamon
¾ cup carrot juice
2 eggs
½ cup instant nonfat dry-milk solids
¼ cup water
1 tablespoon brandy
¼ teaspoon nutmeg

1. Cover bottom of a 9-inch pie plate with apricots; arrange carrots in spoke design over apricots.
2. Mix remaining ingredients in a food processor or blender; pour over carrots.
3. Bake at 325°F about 45 minutes, or until set. Cool slightly. Cut into wedges to serve.

6 servings

899 *Cheese-Stuffed Strawberries*

A traditional French dessert, served in an elegant manner. If berries are small, slice them and serve the cheese mixture as a sauce.

½ cup low-fat ricotta cheese
1 teaspoon grated lemon peel
1 teaspoon fresh lemon juice
1 teaspoon honey or sugar
48 large strawberries
Mint sprigs (optional)

1. Mix cheese, lemon peel, lemon juice, and honey in a food processor or blender until fluffy; refrigerate until chilled (about 1 hour).
2. Gently scoop centers from strawberries with melon-baller or fruit knife. Fill with cheese mixture.
3. Arrange filled strawberries on small individual plates. Garnish with mint.

4 servings

900 *Pineapple-Berry Dessert*

Puréed strawberries are the sauce for this fruit dessert.

    1 large pineapple
½ cup light rum or orange juice
    1 quart strawberries

1. Cut stem and end off pineapple; cut into quarters lengthwise. Remove core and pare; cut into ½-inch slices and place in a shallow glass dish. Pour rum over pineapple; refrigerate covered 4 hours, turning slices several times.
2. Arrange pineapple slices in overlapping pattern on a large platter.
3. Halve some of the strawberries and arrange on pineapple. Purée remaining strawberries in a food processor or blender and pour into a bowl. Serve with knife and fork.

901 *Fresh Fruit with Brandy Cream*

● ½ cup Mock Crème Fraîche
¼ cup low-fat ricotta cheese
    2 teaspoons brandy or orange juice
¼ teaspoon ground ginger
    2 teaspoons honey or sugar
    3 cups assorted fresh fruit
    2 teaspoons toasted sesame seed (optional)

1. Mix crème fraîche, ricotta, brandy, ginger, and honey in a food processor or blender until fluffy. Refrigerate until chilled (about 1 hour).
2. Arrange fruit on individual plates. Spoon sauce over; sprinkle with sesame seed.

6 servings

902 *Peaches and Cream*

Rice is the secret of this fanciful dessert served in pretty parfait glasses for an elegant effect.

    3 large ripe peaches, peeled
1½ teaspoons fresh lemon juice
½ cup long-grain rice
    1 cup water
½ cup instant nonfat dry-milk solids
½ cup 2% milk
    2 to 3 tablespoons honey or sugar
¼ teaspoon almond extract
    Mint sprigs

1. Purée 2 of the peaches in a food processor or blender; stir in lemon juice. Coarsely chop remaining peach.
2. Cook rice according to package instructions. Purée rice with remaining ingredients except almond extract and mint in a food processor or blender. Simmer rice mixture in a saucepan over medium heat 8 minutes; stir constantly. Remove from heat; stir in almond extract.
3. Spoon rice mixture and peach purée alternately into stemmed parfait glasses. Top with chopped peaches. Garnish with mint. Serve warm, or refrigerate until chilled.

6 servings

Note: Substitute pears, strawberries, or other fresh fruit if peaches are not available.

903 *Baked Banana and Orange Compote*

2 large navel oranges, peeled
½ teaspoon cinnamon
4 large bananas, peeled and cut
    in 1½-inch pieces
½ cup orange juice
    Cherries with stems

1. Cut oranges into ¼-inch slices; cut slices in half. Arrange orange slices in bottom of a shallow casserole; sprinkle with cinnamon.
2. Dip bananas in orange juice; arrange over oranges. Spoon remaining orange juice over fruit.
3. Bake at 400°F 15 minutes. Serve warm in compote dishes; garnish with cherries.

6 servings

904 *Baked Sherried Bananas*

6 medium bananas, cut in half
    lengthwise and crosswise
    Pineapple juice
¼ cup sherry or pineapple juice
1 tablespoon honey
¼ teaspoon ground ginger
1 tablespoon toasted sesame seed

1. Dip bananas in pineapple juice; arrange in a shallow casserole. Spoon sherry and honey over bananas; sprinkle with ginger.
2. Bake at 400°F 15 minutes. Serve in shallow bowls; sprinkle with sesame seed.

6 servings

905 *Broiled Oranges*

3 large navel oranges
3 tablespoons sweet vermouth
36 black cherries with stems

1. Cut oranges in half; cut around sections with fruit knife. Drizzle vermouth over oranges.
2. Broil 3 inches from heat until oranges are hot through (about 5 minutes).
3. Place one cherry in center of each orange half. Arrange remaining cherries around oranges on plates.

6 servings

906 *White Port Granite*

Serve this light, delicate dessert as a summer refresher.

1 tray ice cubes (about 14)
¼ cup white port wine
    Juice of 1 lemon
1½ to 2 tablespoons sugar
    Lemon slices

1. Drop ice cubes, one at a time, into a food processor or blender, following manufacturer's directions. When ice is finely ground, add wine, lemon juice, and sugar. Process until ice is in small crystals.
2. Immediately spoon into stemmed glasses, garnish with lemon slices, and serve.

4 servings (about ⅔ cup each)

Note: This recipe is excellent served as a first course.

907 *Meringue Cakes with Fruit and Custard Sauce*

4 egg whites (room temperature)
¼ teaspoon cream of tartar
¼ teaspoon salt
1½ tablespoons sugar
1½ tablespoons instant nonfat
    dry-milk solids
1 large pear, cut in ¼-inch cubes
¾ cup sliced strawberries
● 1 cup Custard Sauce
6 strawberries

1. Beat egg whites until foamy. Add cream of tartar and salt; beat until stiff, but not dry, peaks are formed, adding sugar and dry-milk solids gradually.
2. Drop meringue by large rounded tablespoonfuls onto cookie sheet lined with brown paper.
3. Place in a 500°F oven; turn oven control to 300°F and bake 15 to 20 minutes, or until light brown. Remove from oven and let cool. Remove from cookie sheet.
4. Slice meringues crosswise in half. Stir pear cubes and sliced strawberries into sauce; spoon mixture into hollow bottom halves of meringues; place tops on meringues. Garnish with strawberries.

6 servings (12 small meringues)

908 *Sliced Poached Pears in Wine*

● ½ cup Mock Crème Fraîche
¾ cup puréed cherries
⅛ teaspoon ground cloves
4 large firm-ripe pears
3 cups water
2 tablespoons lemon juice
2 large sticks cinnamon, broken
    in 1-inch pieces
1½ cups white or pink Chablis
    wine
¼ teaspoon ground cloves

1. Mix crème fraîche, cherries, and ⅛ teaspoon ground cloves. Refrigerate covered 1 hour.
2. Cut pears in half lengthwise; remove cores. Cut halves carefully into thin slices, keeping halves together. Dip pear halves into a mixture of water and lemon juice; place halves close together in a medium saucepan. Tuck cinnamon sticks around pears; pour wine over. Sprinkle pears with ¼ teaspoon ground cloves.
3. Simmer covered until pears are just tender (12 to 15 minutes). Cool slightly. Arrange pears in shallow dishes, fanning slices out slightly. Serve warm, or refrigerate and serve cold. Pass crème fraîche or spoon over pears.

8 servings

● *Note:* This recipe is also excellent served with Custard Sauce

909 *Hot Apple-Raisin Compote*

6 large apples, pared, cored, and
    cut in 1-inch pieces
½ cup golden raisins
1 stick cinnamon, broken in 3
    pieces
⅔ cup water
1 tablespoon lemon juice
2 tablespoons bourbon
1 tablespoon chopped walnuts

1. Put apples, raisins, cinnamon stick, water, and lemon juice into a saucepan. Cook covered until apples are tender (about 10 minutes). Drain; discard cinnamon stick.
2. Add bourbon to saucepan; simmer until liquid is reduced by half. Purée 1 cup of the apples and raisins with liquid in a food processor or blender; pour mixture over remaining fruit and sprinkle with walnuts.

8 servings

910 *Basic Mousse with Variations*

Low in calories, yet superb in flavor, this adaptable recipe can be used to create your own variations.

1 envelope unflavored gelatin
½ cup cold water
1 cup instant nonfat dry-milk solids
¼ cup sugar or honey
1 teaspoon vanilla extract
10 to 12 ice cubes
   Mint sprigs or strawberries for garnish

1. Sprinkle gelatin over cold water in a saucepan; let stand 5 minutes. Set over low heat, stirring constantly until gelatin is dissolved (about 3 minutes).
2. Pour gelatin mixture into a food processor or blender container; add remaining ingredients except ice cubes. Process 10 seconds. Add ice cubes one at a time until mixture has consistency of heavy whipped cream.
3. Pour mixture into a serving bowl or individual stemmed glasses. Refrigerate until set (about ½ hour). Garnish with mint or strawberries.

6 servings

Note: Mousse can be unmolded, if desired. Run knife around side of bowl; dip briefly in hot water. Invert on serving plate.

Mocha Mousse: Follow recipe for Basic Mousse, adding **1 tablespoon instant coffee crystals** and **¼ teaspoon ground cinnamon** to ingredients.

Rum-Pineapple Mousse: Follow recipe for Basic Mousse, adding **1 tablespoon dark rum** to ingredients. When mousse is almost consistency of heavy whipped cream, add **1 cup crushed pineapple.** Continue adding ice cubes until desired consistency is achieved.

Ricotta Mousse: Prepare half the Basic Mousse recipe. When desired consistency is reached, add **1 tablespoon apple concentrate, 1 cup low-fat ricotta cheese, and ¼ teaspoon cinnamon.** Turn food processor on and off 2 times so ingredients are just blended.

Fruit Mousse: Follow recipe for Basic Mousse, adding **1 cup sliced fruit or berries** to ingredients.

Fruit Concentrate Mousse: Follow recipe for Basic Mousse; omit sugar and add **3 tablespoons natural fruit concentrate** to ingredients. Garnish with slices of fresh fruit or **1 to 2 cups of prepared fruit.**

Note: Natural fruit concentrates can be purchased in specialty sections of the supermarket or in gourmet food shops. Many flavors, such as peach, apple, blackberry, and strawberry, are available.

911 *Viennese Fried Cakes (Faschingskrapfen)*

½ envelope active dry yeast
⅓ cup warm water
¼ teaspoon salt
1½ teaspoons sugar
1 cup half-and-half (at room temperature)
3½ tablespoons melted butter
3 egg yolks, lightly beaten
3 cups all-purpose flour
Maraschino cherries or apricot jam
Milk
Clarified butter or butter and lard
Confectioners' sugar

1. Dissolve yeast in warm water. Stir in salt, sugar, half-and-half, melted butter, and egg yolks. Stir in 2 cups flour, and add enough additional flour to form a soft but manageable dough.
2. Knead the dough briefly, place in a floured bowl, and cover with a cloth. Let rise in a warm place until doubled in bulk (about 1 hour).
3. Knead dough down lightly and turn onto a floured board. Pull or roll the dough gently until it is ¼ inch thick. Cut dough into 2-inch rounds, using a biscuit cutter.
4. In the centers of half the rounds, place a maraschino cherry or 1 teaspoon apricot jam. Brush these rounds with milk and cover with remaining rounds, pressing the edges together very lightly.
5. Place the filled rounds on a floured baking sheet or towel and let stand for 30 minutes in a warm place.
6. Fry them a few at a time in hot butter 2 inches deep in a saucepan. Do not crowd. After placing in hot butter, cover the pan for a minute or two; then turn the cakes. When they are golden, remove from butter, and drain on paper towels.
7. Sprinkle generously with confectioners' sugar and serve.

20 cakes

912 *Widows' Kisses (Witwe Küsse)*

4 egg whites
½ cup plus 2 tablespoons granulated sugar
1 cup chopped nuts (almonds or walnuts)
¼ cup finely diced citron

1. In the top of a double boiler set over simmering water, beat egg whites with the sugar. Use a rotary beater and beat the mixture until it is fairly stiff.
2. Remove the top of double boiler from hot water and stir in nuts and citron. Drop by level tablespoons about 1 inch apart onto greased baking sheets.
3. Bake at 300°F 25 to 30 minutes. Cookies should be just lightly browned. Leave on baking sheet 1 to 2 minutes before removing to cooling rack.

About 3½ dozen cookies

913 *Tiny Turnovers (Cuscinetti di Teramo)*

2 cups all-purpose flour
2 teaspoons sugar
½ teaspoon salt
3 tablespoons cooking oil
½ to ¾ cup white wine
¾ cup marmalade or jam
Slivered almonds
Oil for frying heated to 370°F

1. Combine flour, sugar, salt, oil, and wine, mixing just enough to make a tender dough. Knead briefly and roll very thin (⅛ inch or less). Cut into 3¼-inch rounds.
2. Place 1 teaspoon marmalade mixed with a few slivered almonds on each round. Moisten edges of rounds, fold in half, and press together to seal. Spread on a tray or cutting board and let stand several hours to dry a little.
3. Fry in hot oil until golden. Remove, using slotted spoon, and drain on paper towels. Serve warm.

36 turnovers

914 Cream Rolls (Cannoli)

Filling:
2 cartons (15 ounces each) ricotta
2 teaspoons vanilla extract
½ cup confectioners' sugar
½ cup finely chopped candied citron
½ cup semisweet chocolate pieces

Shells:
3 cups all-purpose flour
¼ cup sugar
1 teaspoon cinnamon
¼ teaspoon salt
3 tablespoons shortening
2 eggs, well beaten
2 tablespoons white vinegar
2 tablespoons cold water
Oil or shortening for deep frying
1 egg white, slightly beaten
¼ to ½ cup finely chopped blanched pistachio nuts
Sifted confectioners' sugar

1. To make filling, beat cheese with vanilla extract. Add ½ cup confectioners' sugar and beat until smooth. Fold in candied citron and semisweet chocolate pieces. Chill thoroughly.
2. To make the shells, combine flour, sugar, cinnamon, and salt. Using a pastry blender, cut in shortening until pieces are the size of small peas. Stir in eggs; blend in vinegar and cold water.
3. Turn dough onto a lightly floured surface and knead until smooth and elastic (5 to 10 minutes). Wrap in waxed paper and chill 30 minutes.
4. Fill a deep saucepan a little over half full with oil. Slowly heat oil to 360°F.
5. Roll out chilled dough to ⅛ inch thick. Using a 6×4½-inch oval pattern cut from cardboard, cut ovals from dough with a pastry cutter or sharp knife.
6. Wrap dough loosely around cannoli tubes (see Note), just lapping over opposite edge. Brush overlapping edges with egg white and press together to seal.
7. Fry shells in hot oil about 8 minutes, or until golden brown, turning occasionally. Fry only a few at a time, being careful not to crowd them. Using a slotted spoon or tongs, remove from oil, and drain over pan before removing to paper towels. Cool slightly and remove tubes. Cool completely.
8. When ready to serve, fill shells with ricotta filling. Sprinkle ends of filled shells with pistachio nuts and dust shells generously with confectioners' sugar.

About 16 filled rolls

Note: Aluminum cannoli tubes or clean, unpainted wooden sticks, 6 inches long and ¾ inch in diameter, may be used.

915 Honey-Almond Cakes (Sospiri)

2½ cups all-purpose flour
2 tablespoons baking powder
¼ teaspoon baking soda
½ teaspoon salt
½ cup butter or lard
½ cup sugar
1 egg, beaten
½ cup buckwheat honey or other strong honey
½ cup chopped almonds
Cinnamon sugar (optional)

1. Combine flour, baking powder, baking soda, and salt. Cream together butter, sugar, egg, and honey. Combine with flour mixture and mix well.
2. Add almonds, knead 1 minute, and form into two 7-inch-long rolls. Wrap each roll in waxed paper and chill 2 hours. Remove dough from waxed paper, cut into ¼-inch-thick slices, and place on greased cookie sheets.
3. Bake at 350°F 10 minutes, or until lightly browned. If desired, sprinkle with cinnamon-sugar.

About 4 dozen cookies

King's Bread Ring, page 115

916 *Biscuit Tortoni*

⅓ cup confectioners' sugar
1 tablespoon sherry
½ cup plus 2 tablespoons fine dry macaroon crumbs
1 cup whipping cream, whipped
1 egg white

1. Fold sugar, sherry, and ½ cup macaroon crumbs into whipped cream until well blended.
2. Beat egg white until stiff, not dry, peaks are formed. Fold into whipped cream mixture.
3. Divide mixture equally into ten 2-inch heavy paper baking cups and sprinkle with the remaining crumbs. Freeze until firm.

10 servings

917 *Italian Fried Twists (Cenci)*

¼ cup butter
4 cups cake flour
⅓ cup sugar
4 eggs
2 tablespoons brandy
Oil or shortening for deep frying
Confectioners' sugar

1. In a large bowl, cut butter into flour with a pastry blender until the mixture resembles coarse crumbs. Stir in sugar.
2. In a small bowl, lightly beat the eggs with brandy. Add to flour mixture, stirring until all the flour is moistened. On a lightly floured surface, knead dough until smooth (about 5 minutes). Cover and let rest 10 minutes.
3. Fill a heavy saucepan with oil 4 inches deep; slowly heat to 400°F. Cut off a sixth of the dough at a time, and roll paper thin. Using a pastry cutter or sharp knife, cut into 8 × ¾-inch strips. Leave in strips or tie in knots. If desired, dough may also be cut in 2-inch-long diamonds.
4. Gently drop into hot oil, a few at a time, and cook 1 minute, or until lightly browned. Using a slotted spoon or tongs, lift out of oil and drain on paper towels. Cool slightly.
5. Sprinkle generously with confectioners' sugar and store, loosely covered, in a dry place.

About 8 dozen twists

918 *Italian Butter Cookies (Canestrelli)*

4 cups sifted all-purpose flour
1 cup sugar
2½ teaspoons grated lemon peel
1 tablespoon rum
4 egg yolks, beaten
1 cup firm unsalted butter, cut in pieces
1 egg white, slightly beaten

1. Combine flour, sugar, and lemon peel in a large bowl; mix thoroughly. Add rum and then egg yolks in fourths, mixing thoroughly after each addition.
2. Cut butter into flour mixture with pastry blender until particles are fine. Work with fingertips until a dough is formed.
3. Roll one half of dough at a time about ¼ inch thick on a lightly floured surface. Cut into desired shapes. Brush tops with egg white. Transfer to lightly greased cookie sheets.
4. Bake at 350°F about 15 minutes.

About 6 dozen cookies

Chocolate Torte, page 334
Walnut Torte, page 335

919 *Zuppa Inglese*

Zuppa Inglese, which means English soup, probably has more variations and stories about its origin than any other Italian food. That a rum-soaked cake should be called English soup has given much cause for comment on the origin of this wrongly named delicacy. Perhaps the most logical explanation has been that the name was given to tease the English about their love of rum, and the first Zuppa was so rum-soaked that it had to be eaten with a soup spoon.

Italian Sponge Cake
½ cup rum
2 tablespoons cold water
● Pineapple Cream Filling
● Chocolate Cream Filling chilled
● Whipped Cream Candied cherries

1. Trim corners of each of the sponge cake layers to form ovals. Save all pieces trimmed from cake. Place one layer on a platter; set other two aside.
2. Combine rum and water. Sprinkle a third of rum mixture over first cake layer and spread with desired amount of Pineapple Cream Filling. Top with second layer, sprinkle with half the remaining rum mixture, and spread with desired amount of Chocolate Cream Filling.
3. Place third layer on cake and sprinkle with remaining rum mixture. Cover cake with waxed paper and chill several hours.
4. Make a square, diamond, or heart shape from leftover pieces of cake. Place on top of cake and frost cake with Whipped Cream. If desired, decorate with Whipped Cream using a No. 27 star decorating tip. Garnish with candied cherries.
5. Store dessert in refrigerator until ready to serve.

16 to 20 servings

Note: If desired, **Seven-Minute Frosting (●)** or **Butter Frosting (●)** may be used to frost and decorate the dessert.

920 *Italian Sponge Cake (Pan di Spagna)*

5 egg yolks
½ cup sugar
2 tablespoons lemon juice
1 teaspoon grated lemon peel
1 teaspoon vanilla extract
½ teaspoon salt
5 egg whites
½ cup sugar
1 cup sifted cake flour

1. Combine egg yolks, ½ cup sugar, lemon juice, lemon peel, and vanilla extract. Beat 3 to 4 minutes with an electric mixer on medium-high speed; set aside.
2. Add salt to egg whites and beat until frothy. Gradually add ½ cup sugar, beating constantly until stiff peaks are formed.
3. Gently fold egg yolk mixture into beaten egg whites. Sift flour over the egg mixture, ¼ cup at a time, gently folding until just blended after each addition. Turn batter into a 9-inch tube pan (see Note).
4. Bake at 325°F 60 to 65 minutes, or until cake springs back when lightly touched or when a cake tester or wooden pick inserted comes out clean.
5. Invert and leave cake in pan until completely cooled.

One 9-inch tube cake

Note: For Zuppa Inglese, pour batter into three 11×7×1½-inch baking pans. Bake at 325°F 30 to 35 minutes.

921 *Pineapple Cream Filling (Crema d'Ananasso)*

½ cup sugar
2 tablespoons cornstarch
⅛ teaspoon salt
½ cup cold milk
1½ cups milk, scalded
3 eggs, slightly beaten
1 can (20 ounces) crushed
   pineapple, drained
1 teaspoon vanilla extract

1. Combine sugar, cornstarch, and salt in a saucepan. Gradually add cold milk, stirring well. Slowly stir in the scalded milk.
2. Stirring gently and constantly, rapidly bring mixture to boiling over direct heat and cook 3 minutes. Pour into top of double boiler and place over simmering water. Cover and cook about 12 minutes, stirring three or four times.
3. Vigorously stir about 3 tablespoons hot mixture into the eggs. Immediately blend into mixture in double boiler. Cook over simmering water 3 to 5 minutes. Stir slowly so mixture cooks evenly. Remove from heat and cool.
4. Stir in pineapple and vanilla extract. Chill.

About 4 cups filling

Chocolate Cream Filling: Follow recipe for Pineapple Cream Filling. Add **1½ ounces (1½ squares) unsweetened chocolate** to milk before scalding. Beat smooth with a rotary beater. Increase sugar to ⅔ cup and omit the pineapple.

About 2½ cups filling

922 *Butter Frosting (Ghiacciata di Burro)*

⅔ cup butter, softened
1½ teaspoons rum
1½ teaspoons vanilla extract
6 cups confectioners' sugar
1 egg white, slightly beaten
3 to 6 tablespoons half-and-half

1. Cream butter, rum, and vanilla extract. Gradually add confectioners' sugar, creaming until fluffy after each addition.
2. Stir in egg white and blend in half-and-half, a tablespoon at a time, until frosting is desired consistency.

Enough to frost and decorate a Zuppa Inglese

923 *Whipped Cream (Panna Montata)*

2 cups chilled whipping cream
6 tablespoons confectioners' sugar
2 teaspoons vanilla extract

1. Beat whipping cream, 1 cup at a time, in a chilled 1-quart bowl using chilled beaters. Beat until cream stands in peaks.
2. Put whipped cream into a large chilled bowl. Fold or beat confectioners' sugar and vanilla extract into whipped cream until blended.

4 cups whipped cream

924 *Stuffed Peaches (Pesche Ripiene)*

½ cup blanched almonds, finely
    chopped
½ cup macaroon crumbs (see Note)
¼ cup sugar
1 tablespoon chopped candied
    orange peel
6 large firm peaches
⅓ cup sherry or Marsala

1. Combine almonds, macaroon crumbs, 2 tablespoons sugar, and orange peel; set aside.
2. Peel peaches, cut in half, and remove pits. Lightly fill peach halves with almond mixture. Put two halves together and secure with wooden picks. Place in a 10×6-inch baking dish, pour sherry over peaches, and sprinkle with remaining sugar.
3. Bake at 350°F 15 minutes. Serve either hot or cold.

6 servings

Note: To make macaroon crumbs, grind enough Macaroons (below) in electric blender to make ½ cup crumbs.

925 *Queen's Biscuits (Biscotti di Regina)*

4 cups sifted all-purpose flour
1 cup sugar
1 tablespoon baking powder
¼ teaspoon salt
1 cup shortening
2 eggs, slightly beaten
½ cup milk
⅔ to ¾ cup sesame seed

1. Combine flour, sugar, baking powder, and salt in a mixing bowl. Cut in shortening with a pastry blender or two knives until pieces are the size of small peas.
2. Stir in eggs and milk, one tablespoon at a time. Mix together thoroughly to make a soft dough.
3. Break off small pieces of dough, and roll between palms of hands to form rolls about 1½ inches long. Flatten slightly and roll in sesame seed. Place about ¾ inch apart on lightly greased cookie sheets.
4. Bake at 375°F 12 to 15 minutes, or until cookies are lightly browned.

About 6 dozen cookies

926 *Macaroons (Amaretti)*

¾ cup whole blanched almonds
2 egg whites
¼ teaspoon salt
1 cup sugar
½ teaspoon almond extract

1. Using an electric blender or nut grinder, finely grind almonds; set aside.
2. Beat egg whites with salt until frothy. Beat in sugar, 1 tablespoon at a time, beating thoroughly after each addition. Continue beating until stiff peaks are formed.
3. Fold in ground almonds with almond extract. Drop by teaspoonfuls about 1 inch apart on unglazed paper (baking parchment or brown) on a cookie sheet.
4. Bake at 350°F about 20 minutes, or until very lightly browned.

About 3 dozen macaroons

927 *Apple Tart (Torta di Mele)*

½ cup butter
1 teaspoon grated lemon peel
1 teaspoon lemon juice
½ cup sugar
4 egg yolks, well beaten
2 cups all-purpose flour
¼ teaspoon salt
⅛ teaspoon baking soda
4 egg whites
½ teaspoon vanilla extract
⅔ cup sugar
¾ cup walnuts, finely chopped
2 large apples, coarsely shredded

1. Cream butter with lemon peel and juice. Gradually add ½ cup sugar, creaming well. Add egg yolks in halves, beating well after each addition.

2. Blend flour, salt, and baking soda. Add in thirds to creamed mixture, beating until blended after each addition. Chill thoroughly.

3. Beat egg whites with vanilla extract until frothy. Gradually add the ⅔ cup sugar, beating well; continue beating until stiff peaks are formed. Fold in nuts and apples.

4. Roll out two thirds of the dough and line bottom of a 13×9-inch baking pan. Turn nut-apple mixture into pan and spread evenly into corners.

5. Roll pieces of remaining dough into pencil-thin strips and arrange lattice-fashion over top. Press strips slightly into filling.

6. Bake at 325°F 35 to 40 minutes, or until lightly browned. Set aside on rack to cool completely. Cut into squares and, if desired, serve topped with small scoops of vanilla ice cream.

One 13×9-inch tart

928 *St. Joseph's Day Cream Puffs (Zeppole di San Giuseppe)*

1 cup hot water
½ cup butter
1 tablespoon sugar
½ teaspoon salt
1 cup sifted all-purpose flour
4 eggs
1 teaspoon grated orange peel
1 teaspoon grated lemon peel
● Ricotta filling; use
  one-half recipe)

1. Combine water, butter, sugar, and salt in a saucepan; bring to boiling. Add flour, all at once, and beat vigorously with a wooden spoon until mixture leaves the sides of pan and forms a smooth ball (about 3 minutes). Remove from heat.

2. Quickly beat in eggs one at a time, beating until smooth after each one is added. Continue beating until mixture is smooth and glossy. Add orange and lemon peel; mix thoroughly. Drop by tablespoonfuls 2 inches apart on a lightly greased baking sheet.

3. Bake at 450°F 15 minutes. Turn oven control to 350°F and bake 15 to 20 minutes, or until golden. Cool on wire racks.

4. To serve, cut a slit in side of each puff and fill with ricotta filling.

About 18 puffs

Note: If desired, puffs may be filled with Whipped Cream (●) or Pineapple Cream Filling (●).

929 *Spumone*

½ cup sugar
⅛ teaspoon salt
1 cup milk, scalded
3 egg yolks, beaten
1 cup whipping cream
½ ounce (½ square) unsweetened chocolate, melted
2 teaspoons rum extract
1 tablespoon sugar
⅛ teaspoon pistachio extract
2 drops green food coloring
½ cup whipping cream, whipped
1 maraschino cherry
1 tablespoon sugar
6 unblanched almonds, finely chopped
¼ teaspoon almond extract
½ cup whipping cream, whipped

1. Stir ½ cup sugar and salt into scalded milk in the top of a double boiler. Stir until sugar is dissolved.
2. Stir about 3 tablespoons of the hot milk into the egg yolks. Immediately return to double boiler top. Cook over boiling water, stirring constantly, about 5 minutes, or until mixture coats a spoon. Remove from heat and cool.
3. Stir in 1 cup whipping cream and divide mixture equally into two bowls.
4. Add melted chocolate to mixture in one bowl and mix thoroughly. Set in refrigerator.
5. Add rum extract to remaining mixture and pour into refrigerator tray. Freeze until mushy.
6. Turn into a chilled bowl and beat until mixture is smooth and creamy. Spoon into a chilled 1-quart mold and freeze until firm.
7. Fold 1 tablespoon sugar, pistachio extract, and food coloring into ½ cup whipping cream, whipped. Spoon over firm rum ice cream; freeze until firm.
8. When pistachio cream becomes firm, place the maraschino cherry in the center and return to freezer.
9. Fold 1 tablespoon sugar, chopped almonds, and almond extract into remaining ½ cup whipping cream, whipped. Spoon over firm pistachio cream. Freeze until firm.
10. When almond cream is firm, pour chocolate ice cream mixture into refrigerator tray and freeze until mushy.
11. Turn into a chilled bowl and beat until mixture is smooth and creamy. Spoon mixture over firm almond cream. Cover mold with aluminum foil or waxed paper. Return to freezer and freeze 6 to 8 hours, or until very firm.
12. To unmold, quickly dip mold into warm water and invert. Cut spumone into wedge-shaped pieces.

6 to 8 servings

930 *Rum Cream* (*Mascarpone in Coppe*)

2 packages (3 ounces each) cream cheese, softened
3 egg yolks
⅓ cup sugar
2 tablespoons rum
Ladyfingers

1. Beat cream cheese until very light and fluffy; set aside.
2. Combine egg yolks and sugar, beating until very thick. Thoroughly blend in rum.
3. Pour egg-yolk mixture over cream cheese and fold in gently.
4. Fill 4 champagne or wine glasses to within ½ inch of rim. Chill 2 hours. Serve with ladyfingers.

4 servings

931 *Marsala Custard (Zabaglione)*

6 egg yolks
½ cup sugar
⅛ teaspoon salt
1 cup Marsala

1. In a bowl, beat egg yolks with sugar and salt until lemon colored. Stir in Marsala.
2. Cook in double boiler over simmering water. Beat constantly with rotary beater until mixture foams up and begins to thicken.
3. Turn into sherbet glasses and chill until serving time.

About 6 servings

932 *Cheese and Fruit (Formaggio e Frutta)*

Although used in many entrées, cheese is the most popular of Italian desserts whether served alone or accompanied by sweet, succulent fruits. An Italian family dinner usually is ended with fruit, cheese, and black coffee. Following are a few Italian dessert cheeses with a short description of each and the typical fruit they would usually accompany.

Bel Paese—a soft, mild cheese of the North and often served with ripe cherries or plums.

Gorgonzola—the most popular of the dessert cheeses, a creamy, tangy cheese veined with green mold; often served with sliced fresh pears, ripe Italian bananas, or quartered apples.

Stracchino—a tangy goat's milk cheese of Milan which may be accompanied by any number of fruits including peaches and grapes.

Provolone—whether the pear-shape Provolone, round Provolette, or sausage-shape Provolone salami, this is a favorite when accompanied by quartered apples and small slices of watermelon.

Caciocavallo—typifying a tapering beet root, this smoked cheese is delicious when served as a dessert with small crackers.

Ricotta—a soft, bland pot cheese often used in baking, this can be served as a dessert when accompanied by berries and figs.

933 *Italian Strawberry Water Ice (Granita di Fragole)*

2 cups sugar
1 cup water
4 pints fresh ripe strawberries, rinsed and hulled
⅓ cup orange juice
¼ cup lemon juice

1. Combine sugar and water in a saucepan; stir and bring to boiling. Boil 5 minutes; let cool.
2. Purée the strawberries in an electric blender or force through a sieve or food mill. Add juices to a mixture of the cooked syrup and strawberries; mix well.
3. Turn into refrigerator trays, cover tightly, and freeze.
4. About 45 minutes before serving time, remove trays from freezer to refrigerator to allow the ice to soften slightly. Spoon into sherbet glasses or other serving dishes.

About 2 quarts water ice

934 *Ricotta Pie (Torta di Ricotta)*

Pastry:
2 cups all-purpose flour
½ teaspoon salt
1 cup shortening
2 egg yolks, slightly beaten
1 to 2 tablespoons cold water

Filling:
1½ pounds ricotta
¼ cup flour
2 tablespoons grated orange peel
2 tablespoons grated lemon peel
1 tablespoon vanilla extract
⅛ teaspoon salt
4 eggs
1 cup sugar
2 tablespoons confectioners' sugar

1. To make pastry, combine flour with salt. Cut in shortening with a pastry blender until it is the size of small peas. Gradually sprinkle egg yolks over mixture; mix until thoroughly combined. Stir in just enough water to hold dough together.
2. Shape pastry into a ball and flatten on a lightly floured surface. Roll out to form a circle about 11 inches in diameter and ⅛ inch thick. Fit dough into a 9-inch round layer cake pan. (Handle dough carefully as it breaks easily.) Trim dough, leaving a ½-inch border around top of pan. Pinch dough between index finger and thumb to make it stand about ¼ inch high around edge; set aside.
3. For filling, combine cheese, flour, orange peel, lemon peel, vanilla extract, and salt; set aside. Beat eggs until foamy. Gradually add sugar, and continue beating until eggs are thick and pile softly. Stir eggs into ricotta mixture until well blended and smooth. Pour filling into pastry.
4. Bake at 350°F about 50 to 60 minutes, or until filling is firm and pastry is golden brown. Cool on wire rack. Sift confectioners' sugar over top before serving.

8 to 10 servings

935 *Bread Pudding (Capirotada)*

2 cups firmly packed dark brown sugar
1 quart water
1 stick cinnamon
1 clove
6 slices toast, cubed
3 apples, pared, cored, and sliced
1 cup raisins
1 cup chopped blanched almonds
½ pound Monterey Jack or similar cheese, cubed

1. Put brown sugar, water, cinnamon, and clove into a saucepan and bring to boiling; reduce heat and simmer until a light syrup is formed. Discard spices and set syrup aside.
2. Meanwhile, arrange a layer of toast cubes in a buttered casserole. Cover with a layer of apples, raisins, almonds, and cheese. Repeat until all ingredients are used. Pour syrup over all.
3. Bake at 350°F about 30 minutes.
4. Serve hot.

6 servings

936 *Coconut Flan*

Flan is a baked custard dessert which Mexico has adopted from Spain. A caramelized layer is prepared in the bottom of the baking dish before the custard is poured in, so when the finished dessert is turned out it has a caramel topping. This version is flavored with coconut.

Caramel Topping:
- ½ cup granulated sugar
- 2 tablespoons water

Custard:
- 2 cups milk
- 4 eggs
- ¼ cup sugar
- ⅛ teaspoon salt
- ½ teaspoon vanilla extract
- ⅓ cup shredded or flaked coconut

1. For caramel topping, heat sugar and water in a small skillet, stirring constantly, until sugar melts and turns golden brown.
2. Pour syrup into a 1-quart baking dish or 6 custard cups, tipping to coat bottom and part way up sides. Set dish aside while preparing custard.
3. For custard, scald milk. Beat eggs; beat in sugar, salt, and vanilla extract. Gradually beat scalded milk into egg mixture. Strain into prepared baking dish or custard cups. Sprinkle top with coconut.
4. Place baking dish in pan containing hot water which comes at least 1 inch up sides of dish.
5. Bake at 325°F about 45 minutes for individual custard cups, or 1 hour for baking dish.

6 servings

937 *Quick Flan*

This is a somewhat simpler recipe for flan, made with sweetened condensed milk and "baked" in a pressure cooker. The flavor's a bit different, too.

- ¼ cup granulated sugar
- 4 eggs
- 1 can (14 ounces) sweetened condensed milk
- ½ can water
- 1 teaspoon vanilla extract

1. Select a pan of at least 1-quart capacity which will fit inside pressure cooker. Spread sugar over bottom of pan. Heat over very low heat, stirring constantly, until sugar melts and turns golden brown. Remove from heat.
2. Beat eggs in a bowl; beat in milk, water, and vanilla extract.
3. Pour milk-egg mixture into sugar-coated pan.
4. Place about 1 inch of water in pressure cooker. Place filled pan inside cooker. Lay a sheet of waxed paper over top of milk-egg mixture. Place cover on cooker and heat following manufacturer's directions; cook 10 minutes.
5. Cool, then chill before serving.

6 servings

938 *Almond Snow*

- 2 cups milk
- ½ cup sugar
- ¼ cup ground blanched almonds
- 4 egg whites
  Pinch salt
- 1 tablespoon kirsch
  Toasted slivered almonds

1. Scald milk. Stir in sugar until dissolved. Add almonds. Cook over very low heat about 15 minutes. Cool.
2. Meanwhile, beat egg whites with salt until stiff, not dry, peaks form. Fold egg whites into milk mixture. Stir in kirsch.
3. Butter top of a double boiler; pour in mixture; cover. Cook over hot (not boiling) water until mixture is firm. Chill.
4. Unmold onto serving plate and stud with slivered almonds.

6 servings

939 *Neapolitan Fondant Roll (Fondante Napoletana)*

1 egg white
3 cups confectioners' sugar
1 teaspoon vanilla extract
4 tablespoons unsalted butter,
    softened
3 drops red food coloring
3 drops green food coloring
½ cup finely chopped toasted
    almonds

1. Beat egg white until it forms soft peaks. Sift confectioners' sugar into egg white and combine thoroughly. Add vanilla extract; mix well. Cream butter until it is fluffy, add to the sugar mixture, and beat mixture until it is as fluffy as possible.
2. Divide creamed mixture into 3 equal parts. Blend red food coloring into one part, green into another, and leave remaining part white. Chill in refrigerator until firm enough to handle (about 1 hour).
3. With a spatula that has been dipped in cold water, shape the green part into a 7×3-inch rectangle on a piece of waxed paper. Spread the white part on the green, and the red on the white, forming a rectangle about ½ inch thick.
4. Using waxed paper, roll up rectangle from wide edge into a roll with the green on the outside. Chill 30 minutes, unwrap, and coat well with nuts. Rewrap in waxed paper, and chill in refrigerator 12 hours.
5. To serve, remove paper and cut in ¼-inch slices.

About 40 slices

940 *Rice with Milk (Arroz con Leche)*

This dessert is similar to rice pudding, but is not as firm. It may be served hot or cold.

1 cup uncooked rice
1 cup sugar
1 cinnamon stick
1 can (14 ounces) sweetened
    condensed milk
1 quart milk
1½ teaspoons vanilla extract

1. Put all ingredients into a saucepan; stir. Bring to boiling, then reduce heat to low. Cover and cook until rice is tender, about 2 minutes; stir occasionally to prevent sticking. Remove cinnamon stick.
2. The dessert will be fairly runny. Serve hot or chilled.

6 to 8 servings

941 *Sherried Almond Torte*

4 eggs, separated
½ cup sugar
1 cup sifted all-purpose flour
1 teaspoon baking powder
¼ teaspoon salt
⅓ cup melted butter or margarine,
    cooled
1 teaspoon vanilla extract
½ teaspoon almond extract
    (optional)
Sauce and Topping:
2 cups sugar
2 cups water
½ cup sherry
¾ cup toasted slivered almonds

1. Beat egg whites until foamy; gradually add 4 tablespoons of the sugar and continue beating until soft peaks form.
2. Beat egg yolks with remaining 4 tablespoons of sugar. Gradually fold beaten yolks into beaten whites.
3. Sift flour, baking powder, and salt together. Sprinkle over egg mixture about ¼ cup at a time and fold in gently. Fold in butter, vanilla extract, and almond extract (if used).
4. Pour into a greased 9-inch square baking pan.
5. Bake at 375°F about 30 minutes, or until golden brown. Remove from oven and pierce all over with a long-handled kitchen fork or ice pick, making holes through to bottom.
6. Meanwhile, prepare sauce. Combine sugar and water in a saucepan and boil over low heat, stirring occasionally, to soft ball stage (234°F). Stir in sherry. Pour hot sauce over hot cake, sprinkling entire top with almonds as last third of sauce is poured over top. Let stand in baking pan until thoroughly cooled. Serve from pan, or remove to a serving plate.

8 to 10 servings

942 *Viceroy's Dessert* (Mexican Trifle)

4 eggs, separated
¾ cup sugar
1 cup milk
1 cup dry sherry
1 teaspoon vanilla extract
Pinch salt
1 cup whipping cream
1 tablespoon confectioners' sugar
2 tablespoons brandy
1 pound sponge cake or ladyfingers
Apricot preserves
Grated semisweet chocolate
Toasted slivered almonds

1. Place egg yolks and sugar in top of a double boiler; beat until evenly mixed, then beat in milk. Place over boiling water and cook until thickened, stirring constantly. Stir in ½ cup of the sherry and vanilla extract. Cool; set aside.
2. Beat egg whites with salt until stiff, not dry, peaks form. Beat cream with confectioners' sugar until stiff; stir in brandy. Fold egg whites into whipped cream mixture. Set aside.
3. Slice sponge cake into ½-inch-thick slices (or split ladyfingers). Spread with apricot preserves.
4. Arrange one layer in 2-quart serving dish (preferably glass, as the finished dessert is pretty). Sprinkle with some of remaining sherry. Spread with a layer of one-third of the custard mixture. Add another layer of cake, sprinkle with sherry, and spread with a third of the cream-egg-white mixture. Repeat layers until all ingredients are used, ending with a layer of cream-egg-white mixture.
5. Sprinkle with chocolate and almonds. Chill in refrigerator several hours.

6 to 8 servings

943 *Royal Eggs*

This unusual dessert is typical of those created by the Spanish nuns, who were responsible for a number of the elegant dishes which combined Indian and European ingredients.

¼ cup raisins
½ cup dry sherry
12 egg yolks
2 cups sugar
1 cup water
1 cinnamon stick
¼ cup slivered almonds

1. Soak raisins in ¼ cup of the sherry.
2. Beat egg yolks until they form a ribbon when poured from the beater.
3. Pour into a buttered shallow pan. Set this pan in another larger pan with about 1 inch of water in it.
4. Bake at 325°F about 20 to 25 minutes, or until set.
5. Remove from oven and cool on a wire rack.
6. Cut cooked, cooled eggs into cubes.
7. Meanwhile, combine sugar, water, and cinnamon stick in a saucepan and bring to boiling. Reduce heat and simmer about 5 minutes, stirring until all sugar is dissolved. Remove cinnamon stick.
8. Carefully place egg cubes in saucepan of sauce. Continue simmering over very low heat until cubes are well-saturated with the syrup. Add soaked raisins and remaining sherry. Sprinkle with slivered almonds.

6 servings

944 *Orange Liqueur Mousse*

1 package (3 ounces) orange-flavored gelatin
1 cup boiling water
¼ cup cold water
¼ cup orange liqueur
1 cup whipping cream
Whipped cream (optional)
Shredded coconut (optional)

1. Dissolve gelatin in boiling water. Add cold water and cool mixture to room temperature. Stir in orange liqueur. Chill in refrigerator until mixture starts to thicken (about 30 minutes).
2. Whip cream until it piles softly. Gradually add gelatin mixture, stirring gently until evenly blended.
3. Pour into a mold. Chill until set.
4. Turn out of mold onto serving plate and top with additional whipped cream and coconut, if desired.

4 to 6 servings

945 *Almendrado*

The colors of the Mexican flag and the Mexican eagle are represented in this red, white, and green layered gelatin dessert served with creamy custard sauce.

1 tablespoon unflavored gelatin
½ cup sugar
1 cup cold water
4 egg whites
½ teaspoon almond extract
   Red and green food coloring
1 cup finely ground almonds
   Custard Sauce with Almonds

1. Mix gelatin and sugar in a saucepan. Stir in water. Set over low heat and stir until gelatin and sugar are dissolved. Chill until slightly thickened.
2. Beat egg whites until stiff, not dry, peaks are formed. Fold into gelatin mixture along with almond extract. Beat until mixture resembles whipped cream. Divide equally into 3 portions. Color one portion red, another green, and leave the last one white.
3. Pour red mixture into an 8-inch square dish or pan. Sprinkle with half of the almonds. Pour in white mixture and sprinkle with remaining almonds. Top with green layer. Chill thoroughly.
4. Cut into portions and serve with custard sauce.

12 servings

Custard Sauce with Almonds: Scald **2 cups milk.** Mix **4 egg yolks** and **¼ cup sugar** in the top of a double boiler. Add scalded milk gradually, stirring constantly. Cook over boiling water, stirring constantly until mixture coats a spoon. Remove from water and stir in **¼ teaspoon almond extract** and **½ cup toasted sliced almonds.** Cool; chill thoroughly.

About 2½ cups

946 *Coffee Liqueur Mold*

1 envelope unflavored gelatin
¼ cup coffee liqueur
1 cup strong hot coffee
¼ cup sugar
1 cup whipping cream
   Whipped cream (optional)
¼ cup chopped pecans (optional)

1. Soften gelatin in coffee liqueur. Dissolve in hot coffee. Add sugar and stir until dissolved. Cool to lukewarm. Stir in cream.
2. Pour into a mold. Chill until set.
3. To serve, turn out of mold onto serving plate. If desired, top with whipped cream and sprinkle with chopped pecans.

4 to 6 servings

947 *Buñuelos*

Buñuelos are often described as Mexican fritters, but because they are so thin and crisp they're more like a deep-fried cookies. And that's how they are usually served, as a snack or finger dessert. Sometimes they are made small, but are more fun when large.

4 cups all-purpose flour
2 tablespoons sugar
1 teaspoon baking powder
1 teaspoon salt
2 eggs, well beaten
¾ to 1 cup milk
¼ cup butter or margarine, melted
   Oil for deep frying heated to
    365°F
   Granulated sugar-cinnamon
    mixture for dusting

1. Mix flour with sugar, baking powder, and salt in a bowl.
2. Combine beaten eggs and ¾ cup of the milk. Stir into dry ingredients to make a stiff dough; add more milk if needed to moisten all dry ingredients. Stir in butter.
3. Turn dough onto a lightly floured surface and knead 1 to 2 minutes until smooth. Divide dough into 24 balls. Roll each ball into a round about 6 inches in diameter.
4. Fry each round in hot deep fat until delicately browned, turning to fry on second side. Drain on absorbent paper. Sprinkle with sugar-cinnamon mixture while still warm.

2 dozen buñuelos

948 *Churros*

Oil for deep frying
1 lime or lemon, cut in half
1 cup water
1 tablespoon sugar
1 teaspoon salt
1½ cups all-purpose flour
1 large egg
Granulated sugar

1. Start heating oil in a deep kettle or saucepan; add lime or lemon halves.
2. Put water, sugar, and salt into a saucepan and heat to boiling.
3. Remove from heat and beat in flour until smooth. Add egg and continue to beat until mixture is smooth and satiny.
4. Remove lime pieces from the oil, which should be between 365° and 375°F. Force batter through pastry tube into hot fat. Fry until golden brown.
5. Remove from fat and drain on absorbent paper. Break into 3-inch lengths. Roll in granulated sugar.

About 1 dozen 3-inch churros

949 *Sopaipillas*

Sopaipillas are little pillow-shaped deep-fried pastries. They may be served plain as a bread, or as suggested here, sprinkled with cinnamon-sugar as a dessert. Sometimes they are topped with syrup.

2 cups sifted all-purpose flour
2 teaspoons baking powder
1 teaspoon salt
2 tablespoons shortening
⅔ to ¾ cup cold water
Oil or shortening for deep frying heated to 365°F
Cinnamon sugar

1. Sift flour, baking powder, and salt together into bowl. Cut in shortening until mixture resembles coarse crumbs. Sprinkle water over top and work in gradually until dough will just hold together (as for pie pastry).
2. Turn out on a lightly floured surface and knead gently about 30 seconds. Roll out as thin as possible. Cut into 2-inch squares.
3. Fry one or two at a time in heated fat, turning until puffed and golden brown on both sides.
4. Drain on absorbent paper. Sprinkle with cinnamon sugar while still hot.

2½ to 3 dozen

950 *Gâteau du Mardi-Gras*

Meringue Circles:
3 egg whites
½ teaspoon almond extract
¼ teaspoon salt
¾ cup firmly packed brown sugar
½ cup chopped cashews
1 teaspoon multicolored nonpareilles or colored sugar

Filling:
1 package (6 ounces) semisweet chocolate pieces
1 package (8 ounces) cream cheese
1 tablespoon milk
1 teaspoon vanilla extract
⅛ teaspoon salt
¾ cup firmly packed brown sugar
½ cup whipping cream, whipped

1. For meringue circles, cut four 8-inch circles of brown or waxed paper.
2. Beat egg whites with almond extract and ¼ teaspoon salt until light and foamy. Add brown sugar gradually while beating until stiff and glossy. Fold in cashews.
3. Spread meringue on paper circles; slide onto cookie sheets. Sprinkle top of 1 circle with nonpareilles.
4. Bake at 300°F 35 minutes. Peel off paper from meringue circles.
5. For filling, melt chocolate pieces over hot, not boiling, water. Cool about 10 minutes.
6. Beat cream cheese until creamy. Blend in milk, vanilla extract, and salt. Add brown sugar gradually, beating until smooth. Add cooled melted chocolate and blend well. Fold in whipped cream.
7. Spread a fourth of the filling on each of the 3 plain meringue circles. Stack circles and top with decorated circle. Cover sides with remaining filling. Chill overnight.

12 to 15 servings

951 *Sherried Raisin-Rice Pudding*

⅔ cup raisins
¼ cup sherry
1 cup uncooked rice
1 teaspoon grated lemon peel
Dash salt
1½ cups water
3 cups milk
1 cup sugar
½ teaspoon cinnamon
1 egg, beaten
Whipped cream (optional)

1. Soak raisins in sherry while preparing rest of pudding.
2. Put rice, lemon peel, salt, and water in a saucepan. Bring to boiling, reduce heat, cover, and cook over very low heat until all water is absorbed (about 10 to 15 minutes).
3. Stir in milk, sugar, and cinnamon and cook over very low heat, stirring frequently, until all milk has been absorbed.
4. Stir in soaked raisins, then beaten egg. Continue to heat 1 or 2 minutes, stirring constantly, until egg has cooked.
5. Turn pudding into a serving dish. Chill in refrigerator.
6. Serve with whipped cream, if desired.

6 to 8 servings

952 *Fresh Pineapple and Almond Pudding*

The term "pudding" is somewhat of a misnomer for this dessert, which resembles the luscious English Trifle, but uses readily available and popular Mexican foods—fresh pineapple, almonds, and the inevitable cinnamon flavor.

2 cups pared diced fresh pineapple
½ cup sugar
½ cup ground blanched almonds
½ cup dry sherry
4 egg yolks, beaten
¼ teaspoon cinnamon
1 dozen ladyfingers, or 12 (4×1-inch) slices sponge or angel food cake
½ cup orange marmalade
½ cup dairy sour cream
1 tablespoon sugar
Toasted slivered almonds

1. Combine pineapple, ½ cup sugar, ground almonds, ¼ cup of the sherry, egg yolks, and cinnamon in a saucepan. Cook over low heat, stirring constantly, until thickened. Cool.
2. Meanwhile, split ladyfingers and spread with marmalade. (If using cake slices, they may be toasted lightly if very soft, but do not split before spreading with marmalade.)
3. Arrange half the spread ladyfingers or cake slices in bottom of a 1½-quart serving dish. Sprinkle with 2 tablespoons sherry. Spoon half the pineapple mixture on top. Repeat layers of ladyfingers, sherry, and pineapple mixture.
4. Set in refrigerator until well chilled (at least 1 hour).
5. Sweeten sour cream with 1 tablespoon sugar. Spread over top of chilled dessert. Decorate with toasted almonds.

6 to 8 servings

953 *Mexican Custard* (Jericalla)

This custard is light and less rich than that in flan. It is typically heavily spiced with cinnamon sticks, which are baked right with the custard.

1 quart milk
1 cup sugar
3 or 4 cinnamon sticks
⅛ teaspoon salt
4 eggs
1 teaspoon vanilla extract

1. Combine milk, sugar, and cinnamon sticks in saucepan. Bring to scalding point, stirring constantly. Remove from heat and cool to lukewarm.
2. Meanwhile, beat eggs in a 1½-quart casserole. Gradually beat in milk-sugar mixture; stir in vanilla extract. Place in a shallow pan of water.
3. Bake at 325°F about 1 hour, or until custard is set.
4. Serve warm or cooled.

About 10 servings

954 *Spiked Watermelon*

1 large ripe watermelon
2 cups amber rum

1. Cut a hole 2½ inches wide and 2 inches deep in the watermelon rind. Pour rum through hole and replace rind.
2. Chill 24 hours. Serve ice-cold slices.

955 *Anise Cookies*

1 package active dry yeast
½ cup warm water
2 teaspoons salt
5 cups all-purpose flour
3 tablespoons sugar
1 cup each butter and vegetable shortening (at room temperature)
4 teaspoons anise extract
1 teaspoon baking powder
Red and green decorating sugar

1. Dissolve yeast in water in a large bowl. Add salt and about 1 cup flour; mix very well. Add all other ingredients except the remaining flour and baking powder; mix thoroughly. Add remaining flour and baking powder; mix well.
2. Make 6 or 8 balls; with the palm of your hand, make long, thin rolls (about the size of the ring finger) and cut them into squares.
3. Place pieces, leaving space between them, on a cookie sheet. Make a cut on top of each.
4. Bake at 350°F about 25 minutes, or until golden brown.
5. Remove from cookie sheet and coat with red and green sugar. Cool on wire racks.

About 10 dozen

956 *Mexican Christmas Cookies (Biscochos)*

1 cup vegetable shortening
2 teaspoons grated orange peel
1¼ cups sugar
1 egg
⅓ cup fresh orange juice
3¾ cups all-purpose flour
¼ teaspoon salt
1 teaspoon cinnamon
½ teaspoon ground cloves
½ cup finely chopped pecans
Very fine sugar

1. Cream shortening, orange peel, and sugar until light. Beat in egg, then orange juice.
2. Blend flour, salt, and spices. Stir into creamed mixture. Mix in pecans.
3. Wrap dough and chill overnight.
4. Next day, roll out a small amount at a time on lightly floured surface to ⅛-inch thickness. Cut in desired shapes with fancy cookie cutter.
5. Put on lightly greased cookie sheets.
6. Bake at 375°F 8 to 10 minutes, or until golden brown.
7. Sprinkle with sugar while still warm.

About 10 dozen

957 *Polvorones*

These buttery rich pecan cookies are sometimes called Mexican Wedding Cakes, Bride's Cakes, or simply Polvorones, which Mexicans translate to mean sugar cookies—not because there is much sugar in the dough, but because the warm baked cookies are rolled in confectioners' sugar. Literally the name polvorones means "dusted ones."

1 cup butter or margarine, softened
1 teaspoon vanilla extract
½ cup confectioners' sugar
2 cups all-purpose flour
¼ teaspoon salt
1 cup finely chopped pecans
Confectioners' sugar

1. Cream butter with vanilla extract until light and fluffy. Add sugar, creaming well. Mix in flour and salt, then pecans.
2. Shape dough into 1-inch balls and flatten slightly. Place on ungreased cookie sheets.
3. Bake at 350°F 25 to 30 minutes, or until lightly browned.
4. Remove from cookie sheets and cool slightly. Roll in confectioners' sugar.

About 4 dozen cookies

958 *Baked Bananas*

6 ripe bananas
¼ cup lime juice
½ cup orange juice
¼ cup packed brown sugar
3 tablespoons amber rum
Cinnamon
Butter
1½ cups grated coconut

1. Peel bananas and coat them with lime juice to keep them from darkening. Cut bananas in half lengthwise and arrange in a well-buttered baking dish. Mix orange juice, brown sugar, and rum. Pour over bananas and sprinkle with cinnamon. Dot with butter and cover with grated coconut.
2. Bake at 400°F 12 to 15 minutes.

959 *Empanadas de Dulce*

Empanadas are Mexican-style turnovers, made with a simple pastry. Actually, they are frequently filled with meat, fish, or poultry. But this version is for Empanadas de Dulce—the sweet kind. The pastry has a bit of sugar added. The filling suggestions given are typical of those served for snacks or desserts.

Pastry:
2 cups all-purpose flour
2 tablespoons sugar
2 teaspoons baking powder
1 teaspoon salt
½ cup lard or shortening
⅓ cup ice water (about)

Fillings:
(1) 1 cup chopped pecans
¼ cup brown sugar
2 tablespoons butter or margarine
½ teaspoon cinnamon

(2) 1 cup drained crushed pineapple
2 tablespoons sugar
¼ cup flaked coconut

1. Mix flour with sugar, baking powder, and salt in bowl. Cut in lard until mixture resembles coarse crumbs. Sprinkle ice water over flour mixture, stirring lightly with a fork until all dry ingredients hold together.
2. Turn dough onto a lightly floured surface and knead gently 30 seconds. Roll out to a rectangle about 16×12 inches.
3. With a floured knife, cut into twelve 4-inch squares. Place a spoonful of filling in center of each square. Fold one corner over filling to meet opposite corner. Seal by dampening inside edges of pastry and pressing together with tines of fork. Place on a baking sheet.
4. Bake at 400°F 15 to 20 minutes. While still hot, sprinkle tops with **granulated sugar**.

12 empanadas

960 *Mexican-Style French Toast* (*Torrejas de Coco*)

1 cup sugar
½ cup water
1 coconut, drained, shelled, pared, and shredded
1 loaf egg bread (1½ pounds), sliced
3 eggs
1 tablespoon flour
1 cup lard
3 cups sugar
1 cinnamon stick
1 cup water
3 tablespoons raisins
¼ cup chopped blanched almonds or pinenuts

1. Dissolve 1 cup sugar in ½ cup water in a saucepan over medium heat. Bring to boiling; boil 3 minutes. Add shredded coconut; let it cook until the moisture is absorbed and coconut is dry (about 15 minutes). Remove from heat and cool slightly.
2. Put the coconut paste between each two slices of egg bread.
3. Beat eggs with flour; dip both sides of sandwiches in egg and fry in lard in a skillet (about 1 minute on each side). Drain them on absorbent paper.
4. Make a syrup by heating 3 cups sugar, cinnamon, and 1 cup water to boiling in a large skillet; boil 5 minutes. Add browned sandwiches and simmer several minutes; turn once.
5. Arrange desserts on a serving dish, garnish with raisins and almonds, and strain the syrup over all.

About 12 servings

961 *Pecan Cake*

¾ cup cake flour
1 teaspoon baking powder
3 eggs, separated
⅔ cup sugar
1 tablespoon lemon juice

1. Blend flour and baking powder.
2. Beat egg yolks until thick and lemon colored in large bowl of electric mixer. Gradually beat in sugar. Beat in lemon juice and grated pecans, then gradually beat in flour mixture. Slowly beat in melted butter.

½ cup finely grated pecans (use
  blender or fine knife of
  vegetable grater to get nuts
  very fine)
½ cup butter or margarine, melted
  Pinch salt
  Orange Glaze
  Pecan halves for decoration

3. Beat egg whites with salt until stiff peaks form. Fold beaten egg whites into batter.
4. Pour batter into a greased and floured 9-inch round cake pan.
5. Bake at 350°F 30 to 35 minutes, or until cake tester inserted in center comes out clean.
6. Let cake cool 10 minutes before removing from pan. Cool completely on a wire rack, right side up.
7. Place cake on a serving plate and cover with hot orange glaze. Decorate with pecan halves.

6 to 8 servings

Orange Glaze: Combine **½ cup orange marmalade** and **¼ cup sugar** in a small saucepan and cook until sugar is dissolved (2 to 3 minutes), stirring constantly. Use while still hot.

962 *Cream-Filled Chestnut Cake*

1 pound chestnuts in the shell; or
  use 1¼ cups pecans, chopped
¾ cup butter
1 cup sugar
½ teaspoon vanilla extract
6 eggs, separated
1¼ cups all-purpose flour
1 teaspoon baking powder
½ cup milk
  Chestnut Cream

1. Prepare chestnuts (see Note).
2. Cream butter with sugar and vanilla extract until fluffy. Mixing well after each addition, add the chestnut purée, then the egg yolks, one at a time.
3. Mix flour with baking powder, and add alternately with milk to the chestnut mixture, mixing well after each addition. Beat egg whites until stiff, but not dry. Fold into batter.
4. Turn mixture into 2 greased and floured 9-inch round layer cake pans.
5. Bake at 350°F about 25 minutes, or until done.
6. Let cool, then put layers together and decorate cake with chestnut cream.

One 9-inch layer cake

Note: To prepare chestnuts, rinse chestnuts and make a slit on two sides of each shell. Put into a saucepan; cover with boiling water and boil about 20 minutes. Remove shells and skins; return chestnuts to saucepan and cover with boiling salted water. Cover and simmer until chestnuts are tender (10 to 20 minutes). Drain and finely chop.

Chestnut Cream: Prepare **¾ pound chestnuts** in the shell (see Note above); or use **1 cup pecans**, chopped. Whip **1 cup whipping cream** until thickened. Mix in **⅔ cup confectioners' sugar** and **½ teaspoon vanilla extract**, then chestnuts.

963 *Nut Cookies*

1 cup butter
¼ cup confectioners' sugar
2 cups all-purpose flour
¾ cup chopped nuts

1. Beat butter until softened. Add sugar and cream well. Add flour and nuts; mix well.
2. Shape into small balls. Place on cookie sheets.
3. Bake at 325°F 15 to 20 minutes.
4. While still warm, coat with **confectioners' sugar**.

About 5½ dozen cookies

964 *Apricot-Filled Pastries* (Pastelitos)

1 cup dried apricots
1 cup water
½ cup sugar
½ teaspoon vanilla extract
2 cups all-purpose flour
¾ teaspoon salt
½ teaspoon baking powder
⅔ cup lard
4 to 6 tablespoons icy cold water
Confectioners' Sugar Glaze

1. Put apricots and water into saucepan. Cover, bring to boiling, and cook 20 minutes.
2. Turn contents of saucepan into an electric blender; cover and blend until smooth.
3. Combine blended apricots and sugar in saucepan; cook until thick (about 5 minutes). Cool slightly; stir in vanilla extract.
4. Mix flour, salt, and baking powder in a bowl. Cut in lard until crumbly. Add cold water, 1 tablespoon at a time, tossing with a fork until dough holds together. Divide in half.
5. Roll each half of dough to a 14×10-inch rectangle on a lightly floured surface.
6. Line a 13×9×2-inch baking pan with one rectangle of dough. Spread apricot mixture evenly over dough. Place remaining dough on top; seal edges. Prick top crust.
7. Bake at 400°F 25 minutes, or until lightly browned around edges.
8. Cool slightly. Frost with confectioners' sugar glaze. Cool; cut in squares.

2 dozen filled pastries

Confectioners' Sugar Glaze: Combine **1 cup confectioners' sugar** and **½ teaspoon vanilla extract**. Blend in **milk or cream** (about 3 tablespoons) until glaze is of spreading consistency.

965 *Flaming Bananas*

2 tablespoons butter or margarine
⅔ cup sugar
6 ripe bananas, peeled
½ cup rum

1. Melt butter in a chafing dish or skillet. Stir in sugar and heat until sugar melts.
2. Slice bananas lengthwise and add to butter-sugar mixture; turn to coat on all sides. Pour in rum and keep over medium heat.
3. Flame sauce by pouring a little rum into a teaspoon and holding it over flame of chafing dish or range until it flames; then use this flaming rum to light rum on top of bananas. Spoon flaming sauce over fruit several times.
4. Serve over **vanilla or chocolate ice cream.**

6 servings

966 *Flaming Mangos*

2 fresh mangos, or 12 slices canned mango, about ½ inch thick
1 cup orange juice
2 tablespoons sugar
1 cup tequila

1. Wash and peel fresh mangos; cut each into 6 slices. Place in chafing dish or skillet. Pour orange juice over fruit and sprinkle with sugar. Heat to simmering, stirring gently to dissolve sugar and coat fruit. After 3 or 4 minutes, pour in tequila; keep over medium heat.
2. Flame sauce by pouring a little tequila into teaspoon and holding it over flame of chafing dish or range until it flames; then use this flaming tequila to light tequila on top of mangos.
3. Serve over **vanilla ice cream.**

6 servings

967 *Pinenut Balls*

1 pound pinenuts
1 cup sweetened condensed milk
3 cups confectioners' sugar
Confectioners' sugar to coat

1. Grind pinenuts and mix with sweetened condensed milk and confectioners' sugar.
2. Shape into 1-inch balls and coat them with sugar. Put onto a waxed paper lined tray. Let stand until set.

About 6 dozen

968 *Mexican Molasses Candy*

1 cup light molasses
1 cup firmly packed brown sugar
2 tablespoons butter or margarine
1 teaspoon cider vinegar
¾ teaspoon almond extract
1½ cups toasted slivered almonds

1. Put molasses, brown sugar, butter, and vinegar into a heavy saucepan. Bring to boiling. Boil hard about 7 to 12 minutes, until mixture reaches 260°F on a candy thermometer (firm ball stage).
2. Remove from heat and add almond extract and almonds; stir.
3. Pour onto a greased baking sheet, spread as thin as possible, and cool. Break into 2-inch pieces.

About 1 pound

969 *Orange Candy*

3 cups sugar
¼ cup water
1 cup undiluted evaporated milk
Pinch salt
2 teaspoons grated orange peel
1 cup chopped walnuts

1. Put 1 cup sugar into a heavy, light-colored skillet and stir over medium heat with a wooden spoon until sugar is melted and caramelized (cooked to a golden brown color). Add water and stir until sugar is completely dissolved.
2. Add remaining sugar, milk, and salt. Cook over low heat, stirring until mixture begins to boil. Cook, stirring frequently, to 230°F on candy thermometer (soft-ball stage).
3. Remove from heat. Cool to lukewarm; do not stir.
4. Meanwhile, lightly butter an 8-inch square pan.
5. Add grated peel and nuts to lukewarm mixture. Beat until candy loses gloss and holds its shape when dropped from a spoon.
6. Press into buttered pan and cool. Cut into small squares.

About 1½ pounds

970 *Tutti-Frutti Barbancourt*

2 quarts strawberries
1 quart honey
4 cinnamon sticks
32 whole cloves
¼ cup grated orange peel
¼ cup grated lime peel
Mangoes, peeled and cut in pieces
Bananas, sliced
Pineapple, cubed
Barbancourt rum or other
amber rum

1. Cook strawberries in honey and enough water to cover over low heat 5 minutes. Skim thoroughly; spoon an equal amount into each of four 2-quart wide-mouthed Mason jars. Put into each jar 1 cinnamon stick, 8 cloves, and 1 tablespoon each orange and lime peel. When cool, fill jars with desired amount of remaining fruit and rum. Stir, cover tightly, and refrigerate 3 months.
2. Serve tutti-frutti over ice cream or plain, with cookies.

8 quarts tutti-frutti

971 *Caramel Candy (Cajeta)*

2 quarts milk
3 cups sugar
¼ teaspoon baking soda
1 cinnamon stick (optional)
1 teaspoon vanilla extract

1. Combine 1 quart of the milk and the sugar in a saucepan. Cook over very low heat until golden in color, stirring occasionally (this may take 2 to 3 hours).
2. Place second quart of milk in separate saucepan; add baking soda and cinnamon stick (if used). Bring to boiling; remove from heat and discard cinnamon stick. Add hot milk to caramelized milk-sugar mixture very gradually, stirring constantly. Cook over very low heat until thick, stirring occasionally (another hour of cooking may be needed).
3. Cool and stir in vanilla extract. Pour into a serving bowl or several individual cups.

About 1 quart candy

972 *Christmas Candy Balls*

2 medium potatoes, scrubbed (do not pare)
1 cup sugar
1 teaspoon vanilla extract
2 cups chopped pecans
1 cup confectioners' sugar
1 teaspoon ground cinnamon
Candied red or green cherries, cut in halves

1. Cook potatoes in their skins, peel, press through ricer or food mill. Mix in sugar, vanilla extract, and nuts. Chill.
2. Form little balls; coat them with confectioners' sugar mixed with cinnamon. Put into small fluted paper cups and garnish with cherry halves.
3. Store in refrigerator until ready to serve.

About 2 dozen balls

973 *Guava Preserves*

5 cups peeled ripe guava slices
Sugar
Limes, halved

1. Put guava slices into a deep pot and cover with water; bring to a boil, reduce heat, and simmer until fruit is tender.
2. Measure fruit and add an equal amount of sugar.
3. For 4 cups of fruit, use 2 limes. Discard center and core from lime halves and squeeze. Add the juice and shells to the fruit and sugar. Cook at a rolling boil 10 minutes. Skim.
4. Pack hot mixture into sterilized jars, seal, and store.

Guava Jelly: Follow recipe for Guava Preserves for cooking guava. Allow to drip through a jelly bag or through a strainer lined with cheesecloth. For a clear jelly, do not squeeze the bag. Measure juice and add an equal amount of sugar and 1 tablespoon lime juice per cup of liquid. Boil at a rolling boil until mixture sheets from side of spoon. Skim and cool. Pack in sterilized jars, seal, and store.

974 *Chestnuts with Coffee Cream*

1 pound chestnuts
3 tablespoons brown sugar
● Coffee Cream

1. Slit shells of chestnuts. Simmer chestnuts, in water to cover, 5 minutes. While the chestnuts are still hot, discard shells and skins. Put nuts into boiling water with brown sugar and cook 30 minutes, or until tender. Drain and chill.
2. To serve, pile chestnuts into sherbet glasses. Spoon Coffee Cream over them.

975 *Pineapple Ablaze*

1 cup packed brown sugar
1 cup water
6 fresh pineapple slices
6 raisin bread slices with
   crusts trimmed
½ cup unsalted butter
6 tablespoons coarsely ground
   cashews
1 teaspoon cinnamon
½ cup amber rum

1. Combine brown sugar and water in a saucepan. Bring to boiling and boil rapidly until reduced to half its volume, Add pineapple and poach for 6 minutes. Remove pineapple and keep syrup warm.
2. Fry bread slices in butter in a skillet until golden.
3. Lay these croutons in a circle in a chafing dish. Top with pineapple slices and sprinkle with cashews and cinnamon. Spoon half the syrup into chafing dish pan. Warm rum, ignite, and pour, still flaming, over all.

6 servings

976 *Pineapple Flan*

3 cups pineapple juice
2 cups sugar
½ cup water
1 cup sugar
6 eggs
2 egg yolks

1. Combine pineapple juice and 2 cups sugar in a saucepan. Bring to a boil, then reduce heat and cook until a thin syrup is formed (about 5 minutes). Remove from heat, cool, and reserve.
2. Combine water and 1 cup sugar in a saucepan. Boil rapidly until it turns the color of maple syrup (5 to 7 minutes). Immediately remove from heat and pour it into a 1-quart mold, tilting mold until it is completely coated with caramel. Set aside to cool.
3. Beat eggs and yolks with the reserved pineapple syrup. Pour into mold. Set mold in a pan of hot water.
4. Bake at 325°F 1½ hours. Cool.
5. Chill thoroughly, then unmold on a serving platter.

About 12 servings

977 *Pineapple Pyramids*

● 2½ cups crushed Coconut Macaroons
3 tablespoons amber rum
3 cups whipping cream
⅓ cup sugar
¾ cup chopped cashews
12 pineapple slices
12 whole cashews

1. Sprinkle crushed macaroons with rum.
2. Whip cream with sugar, one half at a time, until it stands in peaks. Fold crumbs and chopped cashews into the whipped cream.
3. Place 1 pineapple slice on each dessert plate, mound cream mixture in a pyramid, and put a cashew on top of each.

12 servings

978 *Rum Pineapple Snow*

1 small fresh fully ripe pineapple
4 egg whites
½ cup sugar
2 cups whipping cream
1 teaspoon vanilla extract
¾ cup amber rum
● Ladyfingers or leftover Génoise

1. Pare pineapple and grate; keep grated pineapple separate from juice.
2. Beat egg whites until frothy; gradually add sugar while beating until meringue is thick and glossy.
3. Whip cream and blend in vanilla extract; fold into meringue along with as much grated pineapple and pineapple juice as meringue will hold and still pile softly.
4. Pour rum over ladyfingers and use to line sherbet glasses. Spoon in pineapple snow.

979 *Pineapple Boat*

1 small pineapple
2 cups whipping cream
1 cup sugar
1 tablespoon lime juice
½ cup whipped cream mixed with chopped flaked coconut
Chopped cashews

1. Cut pineapple in half lengthwise, a little off center. Remove pulp, keeping larger shell intact, and discard core. Chop pineapple finely or process in an electric blender. Measure 2 cups of pineapple and juice. Add to whipping cream along with sugar and lime juice.
2. Cut the leafy top off the pineapple shell and reserve for decoration. Spoon pineapple mixture into the shell and freeze until firm.
3. To serve, pipe large rosettes of the whipped cream around the shell and sprinkle with cashews. Decorate with leafy top.

980 *Boiled Plantain*

Green plantain
½ lime
Boiling salted water

1. Remove the skin and scrape the threads from plantain. Rub the fruit with the cut side of a lime.
2. Cook in boiling salted water 30 minutes.

981 *Baked Pineapple*

1 large sugarloaf pineapple
1 banana, peeled and thinly sliced
¼ cup packed brown sugar
⅓ cup amber rum

1. Cut top from pineapple and remove pulp from inside the top. Reserve leafy top. With a grapefruit knife, remove the core and pulp from the pineapple, being careful to leave a ¼-inch layer of flesh inside the rind to keep juice in during baking.
2. Dice the pineapple pulp and mix with banana and brown sugar in a bowl. Warm rum, ignite it, and, when the flame subsides, pour over fruit mixture. Fill pineapple shell with fruit; replace top, moisten with water, and wrap in foil. Secure top with a few wooden picks. Set upright in oven in a deep casserole.
3. Bake at 350°F 25 minutes. Remove foil and serve hot.

982 Pineapple Cream

1 pineapple, pared, sliced, and cored
2 tablespoons amber rum
½ cup butter or margarine
6 tablespoons sugar
1 tablespoon flour
6 egg yolks

1. Cube pineapple pulp and put with rum into the top of a double boiler over boiling water.
2. Beat remaining ingredients together about 5 minutes.
3. Pour the cream mixture over the pineapple cubes and mix well. Cook and stir over boiling water about 6 minutes, or until thickened.
4. Pour into small bowls or **pots de crème** cups and chill before serving.

About 3 cups

983 Coconut Milk

1 fresh coconut
2 cups boiling water

1. Open coconut, discarding liquid. With a sharp paring knife, remove the meat in chunks and grate it (see Note). Pour boiling water over grated coconut and let stand 4 hours.
2. Place a sieve over a bowl, turn grated coconut into sieve, and press out the liquid. Reserve grated coconut, if desired, to toast in the oven and use to decorate desserts and salads.

About 2 cups

Note: If you have an electric blender, coarsely chop coconut meat and process with boiling water a small amount at a time.

984 Coconut Chocolate Sauce

4 ounces (4 squares) semisweet chocolate
● 1½ cups Coconut Milk
1 teaspoon vanilla extract

1. Combine chocolate and ¼ cup Coconut Milk in a saucepan. Stir over low heat until chocolate is melted. Gradually add the remaining Coconut Milk, stirring until smooth and blended.
2. Remove from heat and mix in vanilla extract.

About 2 cups

985 Mocha Mousse

8 ounces (8 squares) unsweetened chocolate
● ⅔ cup Coffee Extract
2 cups whipping cream
½ cup sugar
● Coconut Chocolate Sauce

1. Put chocolate and Coffee Extract into a saucepan. Stir over low heat until chocolate is blended with coffee. Cool.
2. Whip cream and gradually add sugar, continuing to beat until cream holds its shape. Fold in cooled chocolate mixture. Pour into a mold and freeze without stirring.
3. Serve mousse with the sauce.

986 Caramel Sauce

1½ cups sugar
1 cup water
¼ cup hot water
1 tablespoon butter

1. Put sugar and 1 cup water into a heavy saucepan and bring to a boil. Boil, stirring constantly, until syrup is golden.
2. Remove from heat and stir in hot water and butter.
3. Serve hot.

About 1½ cups

987 *Banana Compote*

½ cup sugar
½ cup apricot jam
1 cup water
6 ripe bananas
¼ cup unsalted butter

1. Combine sugar, jam, and water in a saucepan. Cook over medium heat until the syrup is heavy. Set aside.
2. Peel bananas and slice into ¼-inch pieces. Melt butter in a heavy skillet over medium heat and put in enough banana slices to cover bottom of skillet. Sauté until edges become golden. Pour reserved syrup over all bananas and boil uncovered over high heat until syrup is slightly thicker. Cool.
3. Pour into a crystal bowl, chill, and serve.

988 *Banana Fan*

4 ripe bananas
1 cup water
½ cup sugar
1 cup maraschino cherries
½ cup amber rum, warmed and flamed
1 cup whipped cream
¼ teaspoon vanilla extract

1. Peel bananas and halve them lengthwise. Arrange halves flat side down in the shape of an open fan on a round silver or glass dish.
2. Boil water and sugar together at a rolling boil 4 minutes. Add cherries, reduce heat, and simmer 2 minutes. Remove some of the cherries with a perforated spoon and arrange in a design on upper portion of fan.
3. Put the remaining fruit with syrup into an electric blender along with flamed rum; process until puréed. Or force mixture through a food mill. Spoon over upper part of fan.
4. Blend whipped cream and vanilla extract. Using a pastry bag and decorating tube, make a thick border around upper portion of fan to simulate lace. Serve well chilled.

989 *Banana Fritters*

1 cup all-purpose flour
1 teaspoon baking powder
⅛ teaspoon salt
1 egg, beaten
⅓ cup milk
1 teaspoon grated orange peel
¼ cup orange juice
4 ripe bananas
Fat for deep frying, heated to 365°F
Confectioners' sugar
● Orange Rum Sauce

1. Sift flour, baking powder, and salt. Combine beaten egg and milk; add to dry ingredients along with orange peel and juice; mix until smooth.
2. Peel and slice bananas; stir into batter.
3. Drop by spoonfuls into heated fat and fry until golden. Drain on absorbent paper. Sprinkle with confectioners' sugar. Serve with the sauce.

990 *Purée of Breadfruit*

1 breadfruit (1½ pounds), peeled and cubed
1 cup whipping cream
Salt, freshly ground pepper, and cayenne or red pepper to taste

1. Cook breadfruit in lightly salted water until tender; drain.
2. Process breadfruit, a small amount at a time, with a small amount of cream, in an electric blender to make a purée. Mix in seasonings.

Note: If desired, force breadfruit through a food mill and beat in cream, slightly whipped, and the seasonings.

991 *Haitian Upside-down Cake* (*Gâteau Pistaches*)

Topping:
6 tablespoons butter, melted
½ cup firmly packed dark brown sugar
¼ cup light corn syrup
1 cup chopped pistachios or peanuts
Cake:
4 ounces (4 squares) unsweetened chocolate
6 tablespoons butter
1¼ cups sugar
2 egg yolks
1 teaspoon vanilla extract
2 cups all-purpose flour
1 tablespoon baking powder
1½ cups milk
2 egg whites, beaten stiff, but not dry

1. For topping, blend butter, brown sugar, and corn syrup, then add nuts and mix well.
2. Spread nut mixture over bottom of a greased 13x9-inch baking pan.
3. For cake, melt chocolate over hot, not boiling, water.
4. Cream butter with sugar thoroughly. Beat in egg yolks, vanilla extract, and melted chocolate.
5. Sift flour with baking powder. Alternately add flour mixture with milk to the chocolate mixture, beating until blended after each addition. Fold in beaten egg white. Turn batter into pan over nut mixture.
6. Bake at 350°F about 45 minutes. Invert on a board or platter. If necessary, spread nut mixture evenly over the cake. Cool; serve cut in squares.

One 13x9-inch cake

992 *Génoise*

This light cake is something quite different from "American cake," and is well worth the effort.

1 cup sugar
6 eggs
2 teaspoons vanilla extract
Grated peel of 1 lime
1 cup all-purpose flour
¼ cup clarified butter

1. Combine sugar, eggs, vanilla extract, and grated peel in the top of a double boiler. Beat with an electric mixer over hot water for 15 minutes, or until light and fluffy. Remove from heat. Continue beating until mixture is cooled and has reached the ribbon stage. (The mixture should flow in ribbons and softly peak.)
2. Sift the flour onto the cooled mixture a fourth at a time; fold in gently after each addition. Fold in clarified butter.
3. Pour the batter into 2 greased and floured 9-inch round layer cake pans.
4. Bake at 325°F about 25 minutes, or until cake tests done.
5. Cool on racks. Frost cooled layers with **Rich Chocolate Frosting** (●) or **Italian Meringue** (●).

One 9-inch layer cake

993 *Coconut Macaroons*

4 egg whites
½ teaspoon vanilla extract
1 cup confectioners' sugar
½ cup all-purpose flour
2 cups freshly grated or chopped flaked coconut

1. Beat egg whites until rounded peaks are formed. Mix in vanilla extract. Add sugar gradually, beating until stiff, not dry, peaks form. Fold in flour and coconut.
2. Drop by tablespoonfuls 1 inch apart on a buttered and floured cookie sheet.
3. Bake at 350°F 10 to 15 minutes, or until lightly browned.

About 2½ dozen

Plantation Macaroons: Follow recipe for Coconut Macaroons. When cool, put 2 macaroons together, like a sandwich, with a filling of Rich Chocolate Frosting (●). Roll in **grated** or **flaked coconut**.

994 Coffee Extract (Essence de Café)

5 cups water
1½ cups ground coffee

1. Prepare very strong coffee using water and ground coffee.
2. Pour brewed coffee into a large saucepan. Bring to a boil; simmer 30 minutes. Cool.
3. Store in a tightly covered container and use to flavor custard, buttercream, and ice cream.

About ½ cup extract

995 Coffee Cream

4 cups milk
● 2 tablespoons Coffee Extract
3 tablespoons cornstarch
6 egg yolks, beaten
¾ cup sugar
1 tablespoon butter or margarine
¼ cup whipping cream

1. Combine ½ cup of the milk, Coffee Extract, and cornstarch. Beat in egg yolks. Set aside.
2. Put the remaining milk, sugar, and butter into the top of a metal double boiler. Bring to a boil over direct heat.
3. Half fill the bottom of the double boiler with water; bring to boiling. Place the top of the double boiler over the bottom pan.
4. Add the reserved milk-and-egg mixture to the top pan while stirring. Cook over medium heat, stirring until the custard thickens and coats the spoon.
5. Cool custard, then add cream. Pour into a large bowl or individual custard cups. Serve chilled.

Rum Cream: Follow recipe for Coffee Cream, omitting Coffee Extract and cream. Heat ¼ **cup amber rum** in a small saucepan. Ignite rum and stir it into the thickened custard. Serve chilled.

996 Orange Cake (Gâteau à l'Orange)

1 cup butter
1 cup sugar
3 egg yolks
2 cups sifted all-purpose flour
1 teaspoon baking powder
1 teaspoon baking soda
1 cup milk
1 teaspoon lime juice
1 tablespoon grated
     orange peel
¾ cup cashews, chopped
3 egg whites
   Pinch salt
½ cup orange juice
½ cup corn syrup
¼ cup rum

1. Cream butter with sugar until light and fluffy. Beat in egg yolks.
2. Sift flour with baking powder and baking soda. Mix milk and lime juice. Add dry ingredients alternately with milk to creamed mixture, beating until blended after each addition. Mix in orange peel and cashews.
3. Beat egg whites and salt to stiff, not dry, peaks. Fold into batter.
4. Turn batter into a buttered and lightly floured 9-inch tube pan.
5. Bake at 350°F 40 minutes.
6. Mix orange juice, corn syrup, and rum. While cake is still hot in the pan, pour orange juice mixture over it.

997 *Haitian Chocolate Rum Sauce*

● 1 cup Coffee Extract
4 ounces dark sweet Swiss chocolate
1 ounce (1 square) unsweetened chocolate
1 cup amber rum

1. Combine Coffee Extract and chocolates in a heavy saucepan. Cook over low heat, stirring constantly, until chocolate is melted.
2. Heat rum, ignite it, and when the flames subside, stir into the chocolate mixture.
3. Serve hot over cake.

About 2 cups

998 *Orange Coconut Filling*

1 cup sugar
½ cup orange juice
3½ tablespoons cornstarch
3 tablespoons lime juice
2 tablespoons butter
2 tablespoons water
Grated peel of 1 orange
1 egg, slightly beaten
¾ cup freshly grated or chopped flaked coconut

1. Combine all the ingredients except the coconut in a saucepan. Cook over low heat, stirring constantly, about 10 minutes or until thick and clear; do not boil.
2. Remove from heat and stir in coconut. Cool before using.

About 1 cup

999 *Orange Rum Sauce*

1½ cups orange juice
½ cup amber rum
Sugar to taste
1 tablespoon butter
1 tablespoon cornstarch
½ teaspoon grated orange peel

1. Combine orange juice, rum, and sugar in a small saucepan. Bring to a boil.
2. Mix butter and cornstarch and add to sauce. Cook until thickened. Remove from heat. Mix in orange peel.
3. Cool before serving.

About 2 cups

1,000 *Pineapple Sauce*

1½ cups cubed pineapple, canned or fresh
½ cup sugar
¼ cup rum, flamed
Pineapple juice
½ cup water
1 tablespoon cornstarch

1. Process pineapple, sugar, and rum in an electric blender until completely smooth. Add pineapple juice if more liquid is needed.
2. Turn pineapple mixture into a small saucepan and bring to a boil.
3. Mix water and cornstarch, stir into mixture in saucepan, and cook until sauce is slightly thickened.

1⅔ cups

1,001 *Rich Chocolate Frosting*

1 package (6 ounces) semisweet chocolate pieces
⅓ cup strong black coffee
½ cup butter or margarine, cut in pieces

1. Put chocolate pieces and coffee in a heavy saucepan. Set over low heat and stir constantly just until chocolate is melted.
2. Pour mixture into a bowl. Add butter, piece by piece, beating until mixture is smooth.
3. Chill until frosting is of spreading consistency.

About 1½ cups frosting

Index